The Gregg Press
Science Fiction Series

Science-Fiction Studies
edited by R. D. Mullen and Darko Suvin

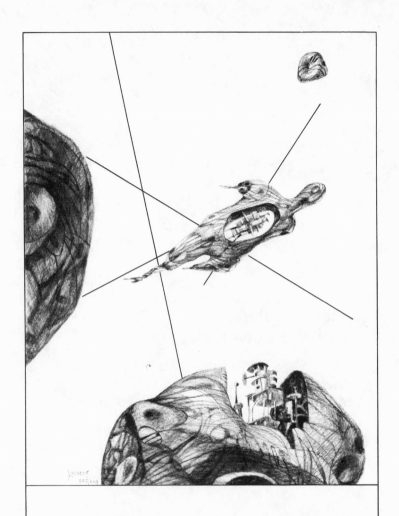

The Gregg Press Science Fiction Series

David G. Hartwell, L. W. Currey, *Editors*
Richard Gid Powers, *Associate Editor*

Science-Fiction Studies

Selected Articles on
Science Fiction 1973-1975

Edited with a New Preface and Notes by
R. D. MULLEN *and* DARKO SUVIN

GREGG PRESS

A DIVISION OF G. K. HALL & CO., BOSTON, 1976

Published in 1976 by Gregg Press, A Division of G. K. Hall & Co.,
70 Lincoln Street, Boston, Massachusetts 02111.

Library of Congress Cataloging in Publication Data

Main entry under title:

Science fiction studies.

  (The Gregg Press science fiction series)
  Reprinted from Science-fiction studies, v. 1,
2, spring 1973-Nov. 1975.
  1. Science fiction — History and criticism
—Addresses, essays, lectures. 2. Dick, Philip K.
—Criticism and interpretation—Addresses, essays,
lectures. 3. Le Guin, Ursula K., 1929-
—Criticism and interpretation—Addresses, essays,
lectures. I. Mullen, Richard D., 1915-
II. Suvin, Darko, 1930-

[PN3448.S45S343]   809.3'876   76-10658
ISBN 0-8398-2338-X

Contents

The Science Fiction of Philip K. Dick

The Science Fiction of Ursula K. Le Guin

Contents

Preface

FOR at least forty years — from "American Fairy-Tales" by Clemence Dane in the Autumn 1936 issue of *The North American Review* to "Science Fiction: The Great Escape" by Peter S. Prescott in the December 22, 1975, issue of *Newsweek* — magazines and newspapers have regularly published articles of the gee-whiz type on science fiction — articles in which the writer informs the presumably incredulous reader that many people actually take a serious interest in science fiction and then goes on to express his own astonishment that among this Buck Rogers stuff there is actually some material of interest even to such normal people as himself and those he writes for. That science fiction has an even longer history of being discovered by people who imagine it to be something new in the world is indicated in the foreword to a book published in 1876, *Caxton's Book* by W. H. Rhodes, where we are told that if the late Mr. Rhodes had in the 1840s persisted in his youthful "fondness for weaving the problems of science with fiction" and had devoted himself to "this *then novel* department of letters" (emphasis added), he would have undoubtedly become a rival to "the great master of scientific fiction, Jules Verne."

Science-Fiction Studies was founded in 1973 to serve students and scholars who already knew that science fiction has been around a long time, who were weary of introductions to the subject, and who wished to see it treated with a critical rigor and depth that had been all too infrequent in the field. We have now published seven issues (Volume 1, 1973 - 1974, consisted of four numbers; Volume 2, 1975, of three); whether or not we have been successful in raising the level of science-fiction criticism, the readers of this collection may judge for themselves.

R. D. Mullen

Notes on Contributors

Recent books by **Brian W. Aldiss,** a member of the *Science-Fiction Studies* Board of Editorial Consultants, include the critical work *Billion Year Spree: The True History of Science Fiction* (1973), the novel *Frankenstein Unbound* (1974), the anthology *Space Opera* (1974), and the picture-book *Science Fiction Art* (1975), the first such work that can be called a critical treatment of science-fiction illustrators. **Edward Balcerzan,** University of Poznan, is an editor of the literary review *Teksty.* **Douglas Barbour,** University of Alberta, has contributed articles on science fiction to *Riverside Quarterly, Foundation,* and *Algol.* **Judah Bierman,** Portland State University, has published articles on utopian literature in *PMLA, Papers on Language and Literature,* and *Studies in the Literary Imagination.*

One of the first authorities in the field to accept appointment to our Board of Editorial Consultants was the late **James Blish** (1921 - 1975), perhaps best known for the SF novels *A Case of Conscience* and *Cities in Flight,* but also the author of critical essays on Joyce, Pound, and Cabell, as well as those on SF collected in *The Issue at Hand* (1964) and *More Issues at Hand* (1970). **Robert H. Canary,** University of Wisconsin-Parkside, co-editor of *Clio: An Interdisciplinary Journal of Literature, History, and the Philosophy of History,* has published at least one other article in our field, "Science Fiction as Fictive History," *Extrapolation* 16 (1974): 81 - 95. **Chandler Davis,** University of Toronto, was represented in both of the 1962 anthologies of science fiction by scientists: in Frederik Pohl's *The Expert Dreamers* by "Adrift on the Policy Level," and in Groff Conklin's *Great Science Fiction by Scientists* by "Last Year's Grave Undug."

The most recent book by **Philip K. Dick** is a realistic novel, *Confessions of a Crap Artist* (1975). **Peter Fitting,** University of

Toronto, one of our editorial consultants, has also written for *SFS* on science fiction and French literary criticism. **H. Bruce Franklin,** Rutgers University, also one of our editorial consultants, is the author of numerous articles and several books in literary criticism, including one of the first important works to emerge from the academic interest in science fiction, *Future Perfect: American Science Fiction of the Nineteenth Century* (1966). **John Huntington,** also of Rutgers University, contributed an article on Arthur C. Clarke to *SFS* #3. **Fredric Jameson,** University of California-San Diego, a member of our board of consultants, is the author of *Marxism and Form* (1972) and *The Prison House of Language* (1973) as well as other books and many articles and reviews. **Damon Knight,** perhaps best known today as an editor of anthologies or as the author of a pioneer critical work, *In Search of Wonder* (1956, rev. ed. 1967), is also the author many SF short stories and several novels. **C. R. La Bossière,** Royal Roads Military College, has written on science fiction for *Riverside Quarterly*.

Ursula K. Le Guin, the subject of a number of articles in this volume, is a contributing editor of *Science-Fiction Studies*. Of the six critical articles that *SFS* has published by its second contributing editor, **Stanislaw Lem,** whose SF novels have been translated into many languages, three were written originally in Polish, one in German, and two in an English that required only minimal editing even though they represented his first efforts to write anything more than letters in our language. **Jeff Levin** operates the Pendragon Press in Portland, Oregon, which has published a chapbook by Ursula K. Le Guin, *From Elfland to Poughkeepsie* (1973).

One of the first to launch a college course in science fiction, **Willis E. McNelly** has written on SF for *The CEA Critic,* edited a CEA chapbook, *Science Fiction: The Academic Awakening,* and co-edited anthologies to serve as textbooks in our field. **R. D. Mullen,** Indiana State University, publisher and co-editor of *Science-Fiction Studies,* is the author of the Afterword to the one-volume edition of James Blish's *Cities in Flight* and of articles on SF in *Extrapolation, Riverside Quarterly,* Thomas D. Clareson's *SF: The Other Side of Realism* (1971), and Darko Suvin's forthcoming *H. G. Wells and Modern Science Fiction.* **Rafail Nudelman,** a critic and theoretician of science fiction (five of his essays are annotated in Darko Suvin's *Russian SF*

Literature and Criticism, Toronto 1971) and co-author with A. Gromova of two Russian SF novels, now lives in Israel.

Aija Ozolins, who earned her doctorate with a dissertation on Mary Shelley, teaches at Luther Rice College. **Carlo Pagetti,** Universita "Gabriele D'Annunzio," is the author of *Il Senso del Futuro* (1970), a study in science fiction. **Robert M. Philmus,** Concordia University, one of our editorial consultants, author of *Into the Unknown: The Evolution of Science Fiction from Francis Godwin to H. G. Wells* (1970) and of articles on SF in *PMLA* and *Extrapolation,* is co-editor with David Y. Hughes of *Early Writings in Science and Science Fiction by H. G. Wells* (1975) and associate editor of Darko Suvin's *H. G. Wells and Modern Science Fiction,* scheduled for 1976. **David L. Porter** teaches at St. Mary's State College.

Mack Reynolds, author of many SF stories and novels, lives in Mexico. **Franz Rottensteiner,** author of *The Science Fiction Book: An Illustrated History* (1975) and editor of the SF critical journal *Quarber Merkur,* is a literary agent in Vienna. **Joanna Russ,** University of Colorado, author of *The Female Man* (1975) and other SF stories and novels, reviews books for *The Magazine of Fantasy and Science Fiction* and has contributed essays on the genre to *College English, Extrapolation,* and other journals. **David N. Samuelson,** California State University-Long Beach, one of our editorial consultants, has contributed articles on SF to *Extrapolation* and other periodicals and is the author of *Visions of Tomorrow: Six Journeys from Outer to Inner Space* and of a forthcoming monograph on Robert A. Heinlein. **Robert Scholes,** Brown University, has published many articles and books in literary criticism, including *The Fabulators* (1967), *Structuralism in Literature* (1974), and *Structural Fabulation: An Essay on Fiction of the Future* (1975).

The co-editor of *Science-Fiction Studies,* **Darko Suvin,** McGill University, who has written a history of SF in, and translated English-language SF into, Serbo-Croatian, is the author of the Afterword to the English-language edition of Lem's *Solaris* and of articles on SF in *Modern Language Review, College English,* and many other journals, and the editor of *Other Worlds, Other Seas: Science-Fiction Stories from Socialist Countries* (1970) and *H. G. Wells and Modern Science Fiction* (scheduled for 1976). **Roy Arthur Swanson,** University of Wisconsin-Milwaukee, is a former editor of *The Minnesota*

Review and *The Classical Journal* and has published, among other books, *Pindar's Odes* (1974) and a translation of Catullus (1959). **Donald F. Theall,** McGill University, one of our editorial consultants, has written extensively on communications, applied linguistics, and literary and cultural theory, including *The Medium is the Rear-View Mirror: Understanding McLuhan* (1971). **Jean-Pierre Vernier,** l'Université de Rouen, is the author of *H. G. Wells et son Temps* (1971). **Ian Watson,** Birmingham Polytechnic (U.K.), is the author of *The Embedding* (1970; U.S., 1975) and other science-fiction stories and of reviews and critical articles in *Foundation*.

Introduction

A, B, and C

The Significant Context of SF:
A Dialogue of Comfort Against Tribulation

(from SFS *1:44 - 50, Spring 1973)*

A [A is an SF fan trying to become an SF writer; he has a B.A. in English literature]. I have just been asked to teach, in a nearby community college, a course in SF, in the "Science and Literature" slot, entitled "SF and Future Shock". So I'm thinking of subscribing to *SFS*, just as to *Extrapolation* or a number of fanzines, because I hope to find in it articles about people like Clarke, Heinlein, Asimov, or Ballard, which I can use in my course.

B [B is a graduate student of literature]. I have lately become somewhat interested in SF because it seems to me some nuggets of social criticism can be found in it, though it feels entirely too comfortable in the Amerikan Empire for my taste. If *SFS* will—as different from the mutual back-scratching and, as far as I can understand, meaningless little feuds in the fanzines--bring out the ideological function of SF as a branch of mass literature to keep the masses quiet and diverted, I might read it in the university library and use it in my freshman course "Literature and Changing the World".

C [C is a university professor in an English department]. I am fascinated by SF as an example of modern urbanized folklore, which is of greatest theoretical interest for anybody interested in poetics and its paradigms. I do not mean that we have to stick to structuralist orthodoxy —indeed, what is so fascinating about SF is how its paradigms evolved out of the oral legend, the *voyage extraordinaire,* the utopia, the Swiftian satire, etc., under the impulse of scientific popularization, sociopolitical changes, etc. I will subscribe to *SFS* on a trial basis hoping it will not be either pragmatic and positivistic, as *A* would like, nor forget that it deals with a genre of literature out of which you cannot pick ideas–critical or otherwise–like raisins out of a cake, as *B* would seem to want.

B. Whatever I seem to you to want, I hope you will agree we do not need one more among the unconscionable overpopulation of academic or quasi-academic journals. If SF is worthy of sustained critical attention. . .

A. Hm. I fear that too much of that will kill it off cleanly.

C. Scholarly and critical attention, I would say.

B. If you wish–I don't see the difference between them. Anyway, we must first of all ask "What are the uses of SF?".

C. Better, "What are and what could be the uses", and furthermore, "What can criticism tell us about them, and which type of criticism can tell us anything significant about them?".

A. SF is the literature of change, more realistic than realism.

B. Ah, but is it? I spent some time yesterday with the *U.N. Statistical Yearbook 1971*, a pastime I recommend to you two gentlemen as quite eye-opening, and culled some figures out of it which I wish to enter into the record of this discussion. I have divided them into two columns, *DC* for Dominant Countries (Europe with USSR, North America, South Africa, Australia, and New Zealand), and *RW* for Rest of the World, and rounded all figures off. So here goes.

	DC	RW
Population	1070	2560 millions
Energy Production (in coal equivalent)	4500 4.3	2500 million tons 1.0 tons per head
Newsprint Consumption	16,900 15.8	4,500 million kilograms 1.8 kilograms per head
Income*	1900	200 $ U.S. per head
Book Production**	370,000 344	90,000 titles 35 titles per million heads

*The ways of UN statistics being inscrutable, the DC statistic here includes Japan but not the USSR and is thus valid for 925 million people; the RW statistic includes only Africa and Asia without the Socialist countries and thus is valid for 1600 million people.

**Without–again the mysterious omission!–the P.R. of China.

To point out the moral: not only each country, but also our old Terra, as *A* might say, is divided–despite our unprecedented technical capacities for making it finally inhabitable in a fashion befitting human potentialities–between the haves and the have-nots. The haves are concentrated in the nations comprising about 30% of mankind, which–as it happens–are also almost exclusively White. The economy and therefore the communication system (including book and periodical dissemination) of the haves differs radically from that of the have-nots. *More than 80% of all book-titles are written by and published in the "have", and therefore politically dominant, countries.*

C. This is a fascinating exercise in literary sociology, to which one should, however, add that, as we know, the number of copies per title is disproportionately higher in North America and Europe than anywhere else, so it's only fair to assume that *over 90% of all books produced and consumed in the world circulate in a closed circuit,* in what you called the politically (and you should have added economically) dominant countries.

B. And of course if we added Japan to those countries, and since the rest of the world quite rightly concentrates on textbooks and similar immediate necessities, we see that "literature" or "fiction" in the sense developed by the European civilization with the rise of mass printing and a bourgeois world view, is in 70% of the world totally unknown... Or if it is known, it is confined to an extremely thin stratum of intellectuals, and it functions as very effective shop-window dressing for the imperialist ideology that more and bigger means better—that, say, the para-military NASA Moon program is the realization of SF dreams. Thus, it conditions and channels in that direction the expectations of people.

C. For better or for worse, it does seem inescapable to conclude that our normative circle of teaching, reading and criticizing "fiction" (a term I'm increasingly dubious about anyway), with all our supporting institutions such as foundations or ministries for culture, prizes and clubs, editors and publishers, kudos and heartbreaks, bestsellers and near-starvations, is a charmed closed circle.

B. Irrelevant to the majority of mankind. And if you see, from some other statistics I will spare you, that even within the 30% of the white bourgeois civilization there are entire social groups that do not consume literature but newspapers, comics, movies or TV, if anything—then that majority becomes quite overwhelming. Then we have to conclude that SF is written for a petty-bourgeois reader, who is indoctrinated by some variant of a late-capitalist, often wildly Individualistic ethos.

C. Well, I would make all kinds of reservations to this big leap of yours, such as saying SF is *here and now* written for such a reader, and that of course there are exceptions, as we know that corporation executives and air-force generals, who are certainly not petty-bourgeois, also read it. And anyway what do you mean by petty-bourgeois—shopkeeper?

B. No, obviously I mean anybody who is not a worker or farmer working with his hands, nor a capitalist employing people to work for him, but in between. The three of us discussing SF are all petty-bourgeois.

A. Now that you have again noticed me, let me ask you one little common-sense question: if SF is all that irrelevant to anybody, except perhaps in the past and to the virtuous socialist society in Russia and China, why bother with it? And with a magazine devoted exclusively to it? Why don't you just go away *(to B)* into the streets or jungles, or *(to C)* into your well-upholstered ivory tower study, and leave us who love SF in peace?

B. First of all, I never said anything about "socialist" societies. In Cuba and China there is, as far as I know, and I tried hard to know, practically no SF; in the Warsaw Pact countries, it has its own troubles which we can save for another discussion. Secondly, even if the circuit within which SF happens comprises only, say, 10% of the world population, it is an extremely important 10% and quite worthy of investigation.

A. But you would investigate them only as petty-bourgeois worms wriggling under your microscope?

C. Well, I don't know what *B* would do, but I would plead for the introduction of another factor into our equation. We have so far talked about the present, or better, synchronic, and thus necessarily sociopolitical context of SF. But it also has a temporal, diachronic context *as a genre*. Now if you'll allow me to go on about this a bit, I have just been going through E.D. Hirsch's *Validity in Interpretation* (1971) for a graduate seminar, and Hirsch—however one may disagree with him on other issues—argues persuasively (as do other people such as R.S. Crane, Claudio Guillen, etc.) that for any utterance, an essential part of its context—by which I mean "the traditions and conventions that the speaker relies on, his attitudes, purposes, kind of vocabulary, relation to his audience," etc. (Hirsch 86-87)—is represented by its genre. A literary genre is a collective system of expectations in the readers' minds, stemming from their past experience with a certain type of writing, so that even its violations—the innovations by which every genre evolves—can be understood only against the backdrop of such a system. The properties of a genre enforce meanings for any given readership. The basic property of all present literary genres is that they are a mode of "leisure activity", made possible by certain existential situations--by normative economic possibilities and political decisions, such as limiting the working time to so many hours per week, putting a certain price upon the reading, etc. As other genres, SF is integrated into the normative system of "literature"—first by opposition to it, then as marginal, now sometimes aspiring to the status of socially approved "high" literature, etc.

A. If I translate what you have been saying into plain English, it says that SF is a recognizable group of works distinct from other groups, which we knew anyway. So why the whole fuss?

C. Ah well, the good old Anglo-Saxon empirical common-sense! But unfortunately, following your logic we would need no science at all, because we all know that a rocket can go to the Moon anyway. Well, perhaps we do, but did we until somebody studied it with a lot of equations and technical jargon? You mean that gravity is self-evident? Or that social gravity—the power-relationships in society, which enmesh culture too—is self-evident? No, what you nicely call "the fuss" is just the sound of specialized science at work. Yes, so far I have used a certain specialized discourse to say that SF is distinct from, but also linked with, other literary genres, which are distinct from, but also linked with, other forms of human behavior within certain normative social expectations. But only such a specialized discourse can eventually provide us with a way of using the sociopolitical insights of friend *B*, without forgetting that we are—as you will agree—dealing with literature. For the most important principle in any genre, as Aristotle suggested some time ago, is its *purpose*, which is to be inferred from the way the genre functions. That purpose channels the genre into determined social forms; it unifies the writers and readers by means of "a notion of the type of meaning to be communicated" (Hirsch 101). Thus, genres are strictly culture-bound, historical and not metaphysical, they are "guiding conceptions that have actually been used by writers" (Hirsch 109); and no criticism of SF has a chance of being relevant if it does not first identify the purposes of the chunk of SF it is considering–a story, the opus of a writer, the works of a period, etc.

A. Why not simply ask the writer?

C. Ah, but common sense is a very limited instrument in scholarship. The writer may be dead, or he may have forgotten, or–most importantly–he may not be right about the purpose of his tale: the creature has a life of its own if it is more than a plug or ad. It communicates something to the readers even if the author is unknown.

A. OK, why not ask the readers? Here this sociology stuff could finally be of some use: just send them forms with questions.

C. Of course, the critical community should try to assemble as much information as possible about the author's overt purpose and about the ways his work was accepted by different categories of readers. But again, what readers–those of the publication date or of today? Opinions about Shakespeare, say, have shifted radically through time, and just imagine how radically they will shift about Arthur Clarke. And why should not all readers of a given time be collectively on the wrong track? The history of Athenian first prizes for tragedy is almost as sad as that of the Hugo Awards. No, I'm afraid that the critic's final evidence is the interaction of his own knowledge and sensibility with the words on the page. In that respect, the formalists were right and we all have to start by applying their insight: when judging literature, one begins by a close reading of it and a discussion of its compositional, characterological, ideational, rhetorical and other inner relationships.

B makes a grimace and a skeptical sound.

A. Well, such things may after all be useful in my teaching, and I hope *SFS* will concentrate on them, and never mind the sweeping theories.

C. No doubt, both *B's* sociological context and your "pragmatic formalism" should have a place under the sun–if done real well. There are too few good SF critiques around for a good review to be able to stick to any scholarly "line". But now we come to my main conclusion which, I think, transcends both your positions. For I maintain that there is no way to understand what one is reading unless one has an approximately full knowledge of the range of the words and the meanings of their juxtapositions. This knowledge forms part of *historical semantics,* that is, it pertains to ever changing social tastes, which differ from period to period, from social class to social class, from language to language. And so, *consistently intelligent formalist criticism leads to consistently intelligent sociological criticism, and vice versa; or better, both must fuse for a criticism that will be able to render justice to any literary genre, and in particular to SF.*

B. This may all be very interesting, but don't you think that we live in a catastrophic world, with genocidal warfare, starvation in half of the world, rising tensions within Amerika itself, ecological collapse, very possibly an economic crisis, and so on, all looming threateningly ahead? And is not therefore the usual SF-as-escape ludicrously irrelevant to us too, not only to the other 90% of the world? And shouldn't it therefore be judged by how much it serves the cause of a liberated mankind?

A. There you go again! Can't you liberate mankind without SF?

C. Well, precisely, I think if you want to liberate mankind–which I am much in favour of–you cannot start by asking for servitude. I think SF cannot be your handmaid, but it could be your ally–and an ally is treated with consideration and met half-way. For SF, as all literature, has always (and I think this is the answer to *A's* objection about why bother) existed in a tension between the sociologically dominant tastes of its readership and its own bent toward the truly, the radically new. This has always been an ideologically subversive genre, and most of its very visible weaknesses today can be traced back to strong existential pressures on its writers and readers.

A. Well, I would admit some of that exists, even in the U.S.A.–just think about the troubles Tom Disch had with *Camp Concentration* and Norman Spinrad with *The Iron Dream*. But this was finally rectified. . . .

B. That's not the most important category. A more sophisticated weapon is financial: hunger has the power to kill, and enforce obedience, more surely than bullets. That is called repressive tolerance, I believe. And I would like to see in *SFS* critics with enough information and guts to take a long cool look at the powerful shapers of taste and enforcers of orthodoxies in SF, such as magazine editors and publishing houses.

C. Serious structural investigations could, and I hope will be undertaken of phenomena such as Campbell's enforcing of his various orthodoxies, or the normative publishing format of 60-80 thousand words for SF novels 1940-1965, and the deep consequences such taboos have had on U.S. SF. And similarly crass taboos should be shown up from other countries and ideological climates. However, the most insidious pressures on SF are neither administrative nor commercial, but psychological. Most of us, readers and writers, have been to some extent brainwashed. . .

A and B [*in chorus*]. Speak for yourself!

C. ... brainwashed, even if with wailing and gnashing of teeth, into the broad individualistic consensus. Many SF writers probably do not feel too unhappy in their little niche within the one-dimensional vision of the world; after all, they have invested great pains into the carving out of that niche. Yet the temptation of being creative somehow, wondrously, pops up here and there even against such terrible pressures–a "mission of gravity", indeed. But creativity has then to pay a high price for emerging: instead of the straight vertical of creative liberation, we get a bent ballistic curve, or, in some exceptionally powerful take-offs, at best a tangent. Yet a tension persists between social institutions–the centres of political, financial and ideological power–and the writer struggling to cut a path through their jungles armed only with a typewriter and some paper. That tension between entropy and energy, between the existential powers-that-be and the creative reaching out toward a vision of the new, is always rekindled and always revolutionary. And it would seem to me the goddam duty of the critic to be always on the side of the writer in his subversions of what exists.

B. Marx called that "a pitiless criticism of all that exists".

C. Quite. Including Marxist orthodoxies. For the demand that we go into the streets or jungles or the rice fields of Honan is, here and now at least–(and that might change)–impractical for most of us, and therefore sectarian. It would, I think, create that very state of emergency, when all specifically humanized pursuits are abolished in favour of direct measures for collective survival, which we are–or at least I am–trying to avoid.

B makes another grimace.

C [somewhat hastily]. This is, of course, not a sneer at working, or if need be fighting, in the streets, jungles or rice fields: it simply acknowledges that the pursuit of life, liberty and happiness-through-reading-SF, or in other words, that the autonomous criteria of all art, including very much SF, will (if we are only consistent enough to hold fast to them without deviating under the pressure of irrational, exploitative and class-bound prejudices) lead us toward a classless humanism. [*Pontificating*]. Thus, all art works against dehumanization in direct proportion to its significance established according to its own autonomous criteria.

A. You mean according to whether there is a poetic theme, a clear plot, consistent characterization, effective composition, and so on?

C. Yes, I mean that too. But beyond those aspects common to all art, I mean that SF has a particular historically determined, scholarly recreatable and critically evaluatable purpose. And I contend that the minimal common denominator of that purpose, the source of its creative pathos and the reason for its existence, is something that I like to call *cognition*–a central and informing concern for conceiving and discussing radically new views and understandings of human relationships and potentialities (even when they are masked as Nautiloids or what not). That is the specific poetry of SF. Therefore, SF which is significant by the most immanent, inner or formalist criteria imaginable, will necessarily clarify hitherto mystified and obscured relationships. It will permit us a better orientation in our common world; it will militate against class, nationalist, sexist or racist obscurantism which prettify the exploitation of man (and nature) by man. I may be too optimistic, but I truly believe that SF at its best does its bit of such a "production of man by man", and does it in a powerful and inimitable way. This is to my mind the answer to "Why SF?", or what are and could be its uses. And if *SFS* can contribute to the understanding of both how and also how come SF does that, then the question of "Why *SFS?*" will also have been answered.

B [not quite persuaded]. Well, let's hope so, but . . .

C [not quite persuaded]. Well, let's wait and see, but . . .

The discussion went on for quite some time, but lack of space in SFS forces us to cut it short here.

Montreal.

Transcribed and edited by Darko Suvin.

Science Fiction and Literary Theory

Stanislaw Lem

On the Structural Analysis of Science Fiction

Translated by Franz Rottensteiner and Bruce R. Gillespie

(from SFS *1:26 - 33, Spring 1973)*

In the early stages of literary development the different branches of literature, the genological types, are distinguished clearly and unmistakably. Only in the more advanced stages do we find hybridization. But since some crossbreedings are always forbidden, there exists a main law of literature that could be called incest prohibition; that is, the taboo of genological incest.

A literary work considered as a game has to be played out to the finish under the same rules with which it was begun. A game can be empty or meaningful. An empty game has only inner semantics, for it derives entirely from the relationships that obtain between the objects with which it is played. On a chessboard, for example, the king has its specific meanings within the rules of the play, but has no reference outside the rules; i.e., it is nothing at all in relation to the world outside the confines of the chessboard. Literary games can never have so great a degree of semantic vacuum, for they are played with "natural language", which always has meanings oriented toward the world of real objects. Only with a language especially constructed to have no outward semantics, such as mathematics, is it possible to play empty games.

In any literary game there are rules of two kinds: those that realize outer semantic functions as the game unfolds and those that make the unfolding possible. "Fantastic" rules of the second kind--those that make the unfolding possible--are not necessarily felt as such even when they imply events that could not possibly occur in the real world. For example, the thoughts of a dying man are often detailed in quite realistic fiction even though it is impossible, therefore fantastic, to read the thoughts of a dying man out of his head and reproduce them in language. In such cases we simply have a convention, a tacit agreement between writer and reader-- in a word, the specific rule of literary games that allows the use of non-realistic means (e.g., thought-reading) for the presentation of realistic happenings.

Literary games are complicated by the fact that the rules that realize outer semantic functions can be oriented in several directions. The main types of literary creation imply different ontologies. But you would be quite mistaken if you believed, for example, that the classical fairy tale has only its autonomous inner meanings and no relationship with the real world. If the real world did not exist, fairy tales would have no meaning. The events that occur in a myth or fairy tale are always semantically connected with what fate has decreed for the inhabitants of the depicted world, which means that the world of a myth or fairy tale is ontologically either *inimical* or *friendly* toward its inhabitants, never *neutral;* it is thus ontologically different from the real world, which may be here defined as consisting of a variety of objects and processes that lack intention, that have no meaning, no message, that wish us neither well nor ill, that are just there. The worlds of myth or fairy tale have been built either as traps or as happiness-giving universes. If a world without intention did not exist; that is, if the real world did not exist, it would be impossible for us to perceive the differentia specifica, the uniqueness, of the myth and fairy-tale worlds.

Literary works can have several semantic relationships at the same time. For fairy tales the inner meaning is derived from the contrast with the ontological properties of the real world, but for anti-fairy tales, such as those by Mark Twain in which the worst children live happily and only the good and well-bred end fatally, the meaning is arrived at by turning the paradigm of the classical fairy tale upside down. In other words, the first referent of a semantic relationship need not be the real world but may instead be the typology of a well-known class of literary games. The rules of the basic game can be inverted, as they are in Mark Twain, and thus is created a new generation, a new set of rules--and a new kind of literary work.

In the 20th century the evolution of mainstream literary rules has both allowed the author new liberties and simultaneously subjected him to new restrictions. This evolution is antinomical, as it were. In earlier times the author was permitted to claim all the attributes of God: nothing that concerned his hero could be hidden from him. But such rules had already lost their validity with Dostoevsky, and god-like omniscience with respect to the world he has created is now forbidden the author. The new restrictions are realistic in that as human beings we act only on the basis of *incomplete* information. The author is now one of us; he is not allowed to play God. At the same time, however, he is allowed to create inner worlds that need not necessarily be similar to the real world, but can instead show different kinds of deviation from it.

These new deviations are very important to the contemporary author. The worlds of myth and fairy tale also deviate from the real world, but individual authors do not invent the ways in which they do so: in writing a fairy tale you must accept certain axioms you haven't invented, or you won't write a fairy tale. In mainstream literature, however, you are now allowed to attribute pseudo-ontological qualities of your personal, private invention to the world you describe. Since all deviations of the described world from the real world necessarily have a *meaning*, the sum of all such deviations is (or should be) a coherent strategy or semantic *intention*.

Therefore we have two kinds of literary fantasy: "final" fantasy as in fairy tales and SF, and "passing" fantasy as in Kafka. In an SF story the presence of intelligent dinosaurs does not usually signal the presence of hidden meaning. The dinosaurs are instead meant to be admired as we would admire a giraffe in a zoological garden; that is, they are intended not as parts of an expressive semantic system but only as parts of the empirical world. In "The Metamorphosis", on the other hand, it is not intended that we should accept the transformation of human being into bug simply as a fantastic marvel but rather that we should pass on to the recognition that Kafka has with objects and their deformations depicted a socio-psychological situation. Only the outer shell of this world is formed by the strange phenomena; the inner core has a solid non-fantastic meaning. Thus a story can depict the world as it is, or interpret the world (attribute values to it, judge it, call it names, laugh at it, etc.), or, in most cases, do both things at the same time.

If the depicted world is oriented positively toward man, it is the world of the classical fairy tale, in which physics is controlled by morality, for in a fairy tale there can be no *physical* accidents that result in anyone's death, no irreparable damage to the positive hero. If it is oriented negatively, it is the world of myth ("Do what you will, you'll still become guilty of killing your father and committing incest."). If it is neutral, it is the real world--the world which realism describes in its contemporary shape and which SF *tries to describe* at other points on the space-time continuum.

For it is the premise of SF that anything shown shall in principle be interpretable empirically and rationally. In SF there can be no inexplicable marvels, no transcendences, no devils or demons--and the pattern of occurrences must be verisimilar.

And now we come near the rub, for what is meant by a verisimilar pattern of occurrences? SF authors try to blackmail us by calling upon the omnipotence of science and the infinity of the cosmos as a continuum. "Anything can happen" and therefore "anything that happens to occur to us" can be presented in SF.

But it is not true, even in a purely mathematical sense, that anything can happen, for there are infinities of quite different powers. But let us leave mathematics alone. SF can be either "real SF" or "pseudo-SF".

When it produces fantasy of the Kafka kind it is only pseudo-SF, for then it concentrates on the content to be signaled. What meaningful and total relationships obtain between the telegram "mother died, funeral monday" and the structure and function of the telegraphic apparatus? None. The apparatus merely enables us to transmit the message, which is also the case with semantically dense objects of a fantastic nature, such as the metamorphosis of man into bug, that nevertheless transmit a realistic communication.

If we were to change railway signals so that they ordered the stopping of trains in moments of danger not by blinking red lights but by pointing with stuffed dragons, we would be using fantastic objects as signals, but those objects would still have a real, non-fantastic function. The fact that there are no dragons has no relationship to the real purpose or method of signaling.

As in life we can solve real problems with the help of images of non-existent beings, so in literature can we signal the existence of real problems with the help of prima-facie impossible occurrences or objects. Even when the happenings it describes are totally impossible, an SF work may still point out meaningful, indeed rational, problems. For example, the social, psychological, political, and economic problems of space travel may be depicted quite realistically in SF even though the *technological* parameters of the spaceships described are quite fantastic in the sense that it will for all eternity be impossible to build a spaceship with such parameters.

But what if everything in an SF work is fantastic? What if not only the objects but also the problems have no chance of ever being realized, as when impossible time-travel machines are used to point out impossible time-travel paradoxes? In such cases SF is playing an empty game.

Since empty games have no hidden meaning, since they represent nothing and predict nothing, they have no relationship at all to the real world and can therefore please us only as logical puzzles, as paradoxes, as intellectual acrobatics. Their value is autonomous, for they lack all semantic reference; therefore they are worthwhile or worthless only as games. But how do we evaluate empty games? Simply by their formal qualities. They must contain a multitude of rules; they must be elegant, strict, witty, precise, and original. They must therefore show at least a minimum of complexity and an inner coherence; that is, it must be forbidden to make during the play any change in the rules that would make the play easier.

Nevertheless, 90 to 98 percent of the empty games in SF are very primitive, very naive one-parameter processes. They are almost always based on only one or two rules, and in most cases it is the rule of inversion that becomes their method of creation. To write such a story you invert the members of a pair of linked concepts. For example, we think the human body quite beautiful, but in the eyes of an extraterrestrial we are all monsters: in Sheckley's "All the Things You Are" the odor of human beings is poisonous for extraterrestrials, and when they touch the skin of humans they get blisters, etc. What appears *normal* to us is *abnormal* to others--about half of Sheckley's stories are built on this principle. The simplest kind of inversion is a chance mistake. Such mistakes are great favorites in SF: something that doesn't belong in our time arrives here accidentally (a wrong time-mailing), etc.

Inversions are interesting only when the change is in a basic property of the world. Time-travel stories originated in that way: time, which is irreversible, acquired a reversible character. On the other hand, any inversion of a local kind is primitive (on Earth humans are the highest biological species, on another planet humans are the cattle of intelligent dinosaurs; we consist of albumen, the aliens of silicon; etc.). Only a non-local inversion can have interesting consequences: we use language as an instrument of communication; any instrument can in principle be used for the good or bad of its inventor. Therefore the idea that language can be used as an instrument of enslavement, as in Delany's *Babel-17*, is interesting as an extension of the hypothesis that world view and conceptual apparatus are interdependent; i.e., because of the ontological character of the inversion.

The pregnancy of a virgo immaculata; the running of 100 meters in 0.1 seconds; the equation 2 x 2 = 7; the pan-psychism of all cosmic phenomena postulated by Stapledon: these are four kinds of fantastic condition.

1. It is in principle possible, even empirically possible, to start embryogenesis in a virgin's egg; although empirically improbable today, this condition may acquire an empirical character in the future.

2. It will always be impossible for a man to run 100 meters in 0.1 seconds. For such a feat a man's body would have to be so totally reconstructed that he would no longer be a man of flesh and blood. Therefore a story based on the premise that a human being as a human being could run so fast would be a work of fantasy, not SF.

3. The product of 2 x 2 can never become 7. To generalize, it is impossible to realize any kind of logical impossibility. For example, it is logically impossible to give a logical proof for the existence or non-existence of a god. It follows that any imaginative literature based on such a postulate is fantasy, not SF.

4. The pan-psychism of Stapledon is an ontological hypothesis. It can never be proved in the scientific sense: any transcendence that can be proved experimentally ceases to be a transcendence, for transcendence is by definition empirically unprovable. God reduced to empirism is no longer God; the frontier between faith and knowledge can therefore never be annulled.

But when any of these conditions, or any condition of the same order, is described not in order to postulate its real existence, but only in order to interpret some content of a semantic character by means of such a condition used as a signal-object, then all such classificatory arguments lose their power.

What therefore is basically wrong in SF is the abolition of differences that have a categorical character: the passing off of myths and fairy tales for quasi-scientific hypotheses or their consequences, and of the wishful dream or horror story as prediction; the postulation of the incommensurable as commensurable; the depiction of the accomplishment of possible tasks with means that have no empirical character; the pretense that insoluble problems (such as those of a logical typus) are soluble.

But why should we deem such procedures wrong when once upon a time myths, fairy tales, sagas, fables were highly valued as keys to all cosmic locks? It is the spirit of the times. When there is no cure for cancer, magic has the same value as chemistry: the two are wholly equal in that both are wholly worthless. But if there arises a realistic expectation of achieving a victory over cancer, at that moment the equality will dissolve, and the possible and workable will be separated from the impossible and unworkable. It is only when the existence of a rational science permits us to rule the phenomena in question that we can differentiate between wishful thinking and reality. When there is no source for such knowledge, all hypotheses, myths, and dreams are equal; but when such knowledge begins to accumulate, it is not interchangeable with anything else, for it involves not just isolated phenomena but the whole structure of reality. When you can only dream of space travel, it makes no difference what you use as technique: sailing ships, balloons, flying carpets or flying saucers. But when space travel becomes fact, you can no longer choose what pleases you rather than real methods.

The emergence of such necessities and restrictions often goes unnoticed in SF. If scientific facts are not simplified to the point where they lose all validity, they are put into worlds categorically, ontologically different from the real world. Since SF portrays the future or the extraterrestrial, the worlds of SF necessarily deviate from the real world, and the ways in which they deviate are the core and meaning of the SF creation. But what we usually find is not what may happen tomorrow but the forever impossible, not the real but the fairy-tale-like. The difference between the real world and the fantastic world arises stochastically, gradually, step by step. It is the same kind of process as that which turns a head full of hair into a bald head: if you lose a hundred, even a thousand hairs, you will not be bald; but when does balding begin--with the loss of 10,000 hairs or 10,950?

Since there are no humans that typify the total ideal average, the paradox of the balding head exists also in realistic fiction, but there at least we have a guide, an apparatus in our head that enables us to separate the likely from the unlikely. We lose this guide when reading portrayals of the future or of galactic empires. SF profits from this paralysis of the reader's critical apparatus, for when it simplifies physical, psychological, social, economic, or anthropological occurrences, the falsifications thus produced are not immediately and unmistakably recognized as such. During the reading one feels instead a general disturbance; one is dissatisfied; but because one doesn't know how it should have been done, is often unable to formulate a clear and pointed criticism.

For if SF is something more than just fairy-tale fiction, it has the right to neglect the fairy-tale world and its rules. It is also not realism, and therefore has the right to neglect the methods of realistic description. Its genological indefiniteness facilitates its existence, for it is supposedly not subject to the whole range of the criteria by which literary works are normally judged. It is not allegorical; but then it says that allegory is not its task: SF and Kafka are two quite different fields of creation. It is not realistic, but then it is not a part of realistic literature. The future? How often have SF authors disclaimed any intention of making predictions! Finally, it is called the Myth of the 21st Century. But the ontological character of myth is anti-empirical, and though a technological civilization may have its myths, it cannot itself embody a myth. For myth is an interpretation, a comparatio, an explication, and first you must have the object that is to be explicated. SF lives in but strives to emerge from this antinomical state of being.

A quite general symptom of the sickness in SF can be found by comparing the spirit in ordinary literary circles to that in SF circles. In the literature of the contemporary scene there is today uncertainty, distrust of all traditional narrative techniques, dissatisfaction with newly created work, general unrest that finds expression in ever new attempts and experiments; in SF, on the other hand, there is general satisfaction, contentedness, pride; and the results of such comparisons must give us some food for thought.

I believe that the existence and continuation of the great and radical changes effected in all fields of life by technological progress will lead SF into a crisis which is perhaps already beginning. It becomes more and more apparent that the narrative structures of SF deviate more and more from all real processes, having been used again and again since they were first introduced and having thus become frozen, fossilized paradigms. SF involves the art of putting hypothetical premises into the very complicated stream of socio-psychological occurrences. Although this art once had its master in H.G. Wells, it has been forgotten and is now lost. But it can be learned again.

The quarrel between the orthodox and heterodox parts of the SF fraternity is regrettably sterile, and it is to be feared that it will remain so, for the readers that could in principle be gained for a new, better, more complex SF, could be won only from the ranks of the readers of mainstream literature, not from the ranks of the fans. For I do not believe that it would be possible to read this hypothetical, non-existent, and phenomenally good SF if you had not first read all the best and most complex works of world literature with joy (that is, without having been forced to read them). The revolutionary improvement of SF is therefore always endangered by the desertion of large masses of readers. And if neither authors nor readers wish such an event, the likelihood of a positive change in the field during the coming years must be considered as very small, as, indeed, almost zero. For it would then be a phenomenon of the kind called in futurology "the changing of a complex trend", and such changes do not occur unless there are powerful factors arising out of the environment rather than out of the will and determination of a few individuals.

POSTSCRIPT. Even the best SF novels tend to show, in the development of the plot, variations in credibility greater than those to be found even in mediocre novels of other kinds. Although events impossible from an *objective-empirical* standpoint (such as a man springing over a wall seven meters high or a woman giving birth in two instead of nine months) do not appear in non-SF novels, events equally impossible from a *speculative* standpoint (such as the totally unnecessary end-game in Disch's *Camp Concentration)* appear frequently in SF. To be sure, separating the unlikely from the likely (finding in the street a diamond the size of your fist as opposed to finding a lost hat) is much simpler when your standard of comparison is everyday things than it is when you are concerned with the consequences of fictive hypotheses. But though separating the likely from the unlikely in SF is difficult, it can be mastered. The art can be learned and taught. But since the lack of selective filters is accompanied by a corresponding lack in reader-evaluations, there are no pressures on authors for such an optimization of SF.

Joanna Russ

Towards an Aesthetic of Science Fiction

(from SFS *2:112 - 119, July 1975)*

Is science fiction literature?
  Yes.
  Can it be judged by the usual literary criteria?
  No.
  Such a statement requires not only justification but considerable elaboration. Written science fiction is, of course, literature, although science fiction in other media (films, drama, perhaps even painting or sculpture) must be judged by standards other than those applied to the written word.[1] Concentrating on science fiction as literature, primarily as prose fiction, this paper will attempt to indicate some of the limitations critics encounter in trying to apply traditional literary criticism to science fiction. To be brief, the access of academic interest in science fiction that has occurred during the last few years has led to considerable difficulty. Not only do academic critics find themselves imprisoned by habitual (and unreflecting) condescension in dealing with this particular genre; quite often their critical tools, however finely honed, are simply not applicable to a body of work that—despite its superficial resemblance to realistic or naturalistic twentieth-century fiction—is fundamentally a drastically different form of literary art.
  Fine beginnings have been made in the typology of science fiction by Darko Suvin[2] of McGill University, who builds on the parameters prescribed for the genre by the Polish writer and critic, Stanislas Lem.[3] Samuel Delany, a science-fiction writer and theorist, has dealt with the same matters in a recent paper concerned largely with problems of definition.[4]
  One very important point which emerges in the work of all three critics is that standards of plausibility—as one may apply them to science fiction—must be derived not only from the observation of life as it is or has been lived, but also, rigorously and systematically, from science. And in this context "science" must include disciplines ranging from mathematics (which is formally empty) through the "hard" sciences (physics, astronomy, chemistry) through the "soft" sciences (ethology, psychology, sociology) all the way to disciplines which as yet exist only in the descriptive or speculative stage (history, for example, or political theory).
  Science fiction is not fantasy, for the standards of plausibility of fantasy derive not from science, but from the observation of life as it is—inner life, perhaps, in this case. Mistakes in scientific possibility do not turn science fiction into fantasy. They are merely mistakes. Nor does the out-dating of scientific theory transform the science fiction of the past into fantasy.[5] Error-free science fiction is an ideal as impossible of achievement as the nineteenth century ideal of an "objective," realistic novel. Not that in either case the

author can be excused for not trying; unreachability is, after all, what ideals are for. But only God can know enough to write either kind of book perfectly.

For the purposes of the aesthetics of science fiction, a remark of Professor Suvin's made casually at the 1968 annual meeting of the Modern Language Association seems to me extremely fruitful. Science fiction, said Suvin, is "quasi-medieval." Professor Suvin has not elaborated on this insight, as he seems at the moment more concerned with the nature of science fiction's cognitive relation to what he calls the "zero world" of "empirically verifiable properties around the author."[6] To me the phrase "quasi-medieval" suggests considerable insight, particularly into the reasons why critical tools developed with an entirely different literature in mind often do not work when applied to science fiction. I should like to propose the following:

That science fiction, like much medieval literature, is *didactic*.

That despite superficial similarities to naturalistic (or other) modern fiction, the protagonists of science fiction are always collective, never individual persons (although individuals often appear as exemplary or representative figures).

That science fiction's emphasis is always on *phenomena*—to the point where reviewers and critics can commonly use such phrases as "the idea as hero."

That science fiction is not only didactic, but very often awed, worshipful, and *religious* in tone. Damon Knight's famous phrase for this is "the sense of wonder."[7] To substantiate this last, one needs only a head-count of Messiahs in recent science fiction novels, the abrupt changes of scale (either spatial or temporal) used to induce cosmic awe in such works as Olaf Stapledon's *Last and First Men*, James Blish's *Surface Tension*, stories like Isaac Asimov's "Nightfall" and "The Last Question," Arthur C. Clarke's "Nine Billion Names of God," and the change of tone at the end of Clarke's *Childhood's End* or Philip José Farmer's story "Sail On! Sail On!" (The film *2001* is another case in point.)

The emphasis on phenomena, often at the complete expense of human character, needs no citation; it is apparent to anyone who has any acquaintance with the field. Even in pulp science fiction populated by grim-jawed heroes, the human protagonist, if not Everyman, is a glamorized version of Supereveryman. That science fiction is didactic hardly needs proof, either. The pleasure science fiction writers take in explaining physics, thirtieth-century jurisprudence, the mechanics of teleportation, patent law, four-dimensional geometry, or whatever happens to be on the tapis, lies open in any book that has not degenerated into outright adventure story with science-fiction frills.[8] Science fiction even has its favorite piece of theology. Just as contemporary psychoanalytic writers cannot seem to write anything without explaining the Oedipus complex at least once, so science fiction writers dwell lovingly on the time dilation consequent to travel at near light-speed. Science is to science fiction (by analogy) what medieval Christianity was to deliberately didactic medieval fiction.

I would like to propose that contemporary literary criticism (not having been developed to handle such material) is not the ideal tool for dealing with fiction that is explicitly, deliberately, and baldly *didactic*. (Modern criticism appears to experience the same difficulty in handling the 18th century *contes philosophiques* Professor Suvin cites as among the ancestors of science fiction.) Certainly if one is to analyze didactic literature, one must first know what system of beliefs or ideas constitutes the substance of the didacticism. A modern critic attempting to understand science fiction without understanding modern science is in the position of a medievalist attempting to read *Piers Plowman* without any but the haziest ideas about medieval Catholicism. (Or, possibly, like a modern critic attempting to understand Bertolt Brecht without any knowledge of Marxist economic analysis beyond a vague and uninformed distrust.)

An eminent critic (who knows better now) once asked me during a discussion of a novel of Kurt Vonnegut's, "But when you get to the science, don't you just make it up?" The answer, of course, is no. Science fiction must not offend against what is known. Only in areas where nothing is known—or knowledge is uncertain—is it permissible to just "Make it up." (Even then what is made up must be systematic, plausible, rigorously logical, and must avoid offending against what is known to be known.)

Of course didactic fiction does not always tell people something new; often it tells them what they already know, and the re-telling becomes a reverent ritual, very gratifying to all concerned. There is some of this in science fiction, although (unlike the situation obtaining in medieval Christianity) this state of affairs is considered neither necessary nor desirable by many readers. There is science fiction that concentrates on the very edges of what is known. There is even science fiction that ignores what is known. The latter is bad science fiction.[9]

How can a criticism developed to treat a post-medieval literature of individual destinies, secular concerns, and the representation of what is (rather than what might be) illuminate science fiction?

Science fiction presents an eerie echo of the attitudes and interests of a pre-industrial, pre-Renaissance, pre-secular, pre-individualistic culture. It has been my experience that medievalists take easily and kindly to science fiction, that they are often attracted to it, that its didacticism presents them with no problems, and that they enjoy this literature much more than do students of later literary periods.[10] So, in fact, do city planners, architects, archaeologists, engineers, rock musicians, anthropologists, and nearly everybody except most English professors.

Without knowledge of or appreciation of the "theology" of science fiction— that is, science—what kind of criticism will be practiced on particular science fiction works?

Often critics may use their knowledge of the recurrent and important themes of Western culture to misperceive what is actually in a science fiction story. For example, recognizable themes or patterns of imagery can be insisted on far beyond their actual importance in the work simply because they are familiar to the critic. Or the symbolic importance of certain material can be mis-read because the significance of the material in the cultural tradition science fiction comes from (which is overwhelmingly that of science, not literature) is simply not known to the critic. Sometimes material may be ignored because it is not part of the critic's cognitive universe.

For example, in H.G. Wells's magnificent novella, *The Time Machine*, a trip into the 8000th century presents us with a world that appears to be directly reminiscent of Eden, a "weedless garden" full of warm sunlight, untended but beautiful flowers, and effortless innocence. Wells even has his Time Traveler call the happy inhabitants of this garden "Eloi" (from the Hebrew "Elohim"). Certainly the derivation of these details is obvious. Nor can one mistake the counter-world the Time Traveler discovers below-ground; a lightless, hellish, urban world populated by bleached monsters. But the critic may make too much of all this. For example, Bernard Bergonzi (I suspect his behavior would be fairly typical) overweights Wells's heavenly/demonic imagery.[11] Certainly *The Time Machine*'s pastoral future does echo a great deal of material important in the Western literary tradition, but it is a mistake to think of these (very obtrusive) clusters of Edenic-pastoral/hellish imagery as the "hidden" meaning of Wells's Social Darwinism. On the contrary, it is the worlds of the Eloi and the Morlocks that are put in the employ of the Social Darwinism, which is itself only an example of mindless evolution, of the cruelty of material determinism, and of the tragic mindlessness of all physical process. The real center of Wells's story is not even in his ironic reversal of the doctrine of the fortunate fall (evolution, in Wells's view in *The Time Machine,* inevitably produces what one might call the unfortunate rise—the very production of intelligence, of mind, is what must, sooner or later, destroy mind). Even the human devolution pictured in the story is only a special case of the iron physical law that constitutes the true center of the book and the true agony of Wells's vision. This vision is easy to overlook not because it is subtle, indirect, or hidden, but because it is so blatantly hammered home in all the Time Traveler's speculations about evolution and—above all—in a chapter explicitly entitled "The Farther Vision." As Eric Bentley once remarked, "clarity is the first requisite of didacticism."[12] Didactic art must, so to speak, wear its meaning on its sleeve. *The Time Machine* is not about a lost Eden; it is—passionately and tragically—about the Three Laws of Thermodynamics, especially the second. The slow cooling of the sun in "The Farther Vision" foreshadows the heat-death of the universe. In fact, the novella is a series of deaths: individual death (as exemplified by Weena's presumed death and the threat to the Time Traveler himself from the Morlocks) is bad enough; the "wilderness of rotting paper" in the Palace of Green Porcelain, an abandoned museum, is perhaps worse; the complete disappearance of mind in humanity's remote descendents (the kangaroo-like animals) is horrible; but the death of absolutely everything, the physical degredation of the entire universe, is a Gotterdämmerung earlier views of the nature of the universe could hardly conceive—*let alone prove.* As the Time Traveler says after leaving "that remote and awful twilight," "I'm sorry to have brought you out here in the cold."

Unless a critic can bring to *The time Machine* not only a knowledge of the science that stands behind it, but the passionate belief that such knowledge is real and that it matters, the critic had better stay away from science fiction. Persons to whom the findings of science seem only bizarre, fanciful, or irrelevant to everyday life, have no business with science fiction—or with science for that matter—although they may deal perfectly well with fiction that ignores both science and the scientific view of reality.

For example, a short story of Ursula K. Le Guin, "The Masters" (in *Fantastic,* Feb. 1963), has as its emotional center the rediscovery of the duodecimal system. To criticize this story properly one must know about three things: the Arabic invention of the zero, the astounding importance of this invention for mathematics (and hence the sciences), and the fact that one may count with any base. In fact, the duodecimal system, with its base of 12, is far superior to our decimal system with its base of 10.

A third example of ways science fiction can be mis-read can be provided by Hal Clement's novel, *Close to Critical.* The story treats of an alien species inhabitating a planet much like Jupiter. Some psychoanalytic critic, whose name I have unfortunately forgotten, once treated material like this (the story was, I think, Milton Rothman's "Heavy Planet") as psychoneurotic, i.e. the projection of repressed infantile fears. And certainly a Jovian or Jovian-like landscape would be extremely bizarre. Clement's invented world, with its atmosphere 3000 times as dense as ours, its gravity three times ours, its total darkness, its pine-cone-shaped inhabitants, its hundred-foot wide "raindrops" that condense at night and evaporate each morning, can easily be perceived by the scientifically ignorant as a series of grotesque morbidities. In such a view *Close to Critical* is merely nightmarish. But to decide this is to ignore the evidence. Clement's gas-giant is neither nightmarish nor grotesque, but merely accurate. In fact, Mr. Clement is the soberest of science fiction writers and his characters are always rational, humane, and highly likeable. The final effect of the novel is exactly the opposite of nightmare; it is affectionate familiarity. The Jovian-like world is a real world. One understands and appreciates it. It is, to its inhabitants, no worse and no better than our own. It is, finally, beautiful—in the same way and for the same reasons that Earth is beautiful. *Close to Critical* evokes Knight's "sense of wonder" because it describes a genuinely possible place, indeed a place that is highly likely according to what we know of the universe. The probability of the setting is what makes the book elegant—in the mathematical sense, that is: aesthetically satisfying. If there is anything grotesque in Clement's work, it is in the strain caused by the split between idea-as-hero (which is superbly handled) and the human protagonists, who are neither interesting, probable, nor necessary, and whose appearance in the book at all is undoubtedly due to the American pulp tradition out of which American science fiction arose after World War I. The book suffers from serious confusion of form.

Science fiction, like medieval painting, addresses itself to the mind, not the eye. We are not presented with a representation of what we know to be true through direct experience; rather we are given what we know to be true through other means—or in the case of science fiction, what we know to be at least possible. Thus the science fiction writer can portray Jupiter as easily as the medieval painter can portray Heaven; neither of them has been there, but that doesn't matter. To turn from other modern fiction to science fiction is oddly like turning from Renaissance painting with all the flesh and foreshortening to the clarity and luminousness of painters who paint ideas. For this reason, science fiction, like much medieval art, can deal with transcendental events. Hence the tendency of science fiction towards wonder, awe, and a religious or quasi-religious attitude towards the universe.

Persons who consider science untrue, or irrelevant to what really matters, or inimical to humane values, can hardly be expected to be interested in science fiction. Nor can one study science fiction as some medievalists (presumably) might study their material—that is, by finding equivalents for a system of beliefs they cannot accept in literal form. To treat medieval Catholicism as irrelevant to medieval literature is bad scholarship; to treat it as somebody else's silly but interesting superstitions is likewise extremely damaging to any consideration of the literature itself. But non-scientific equivalents for the Second Law of Thermodynamics or the intricacies of genetics—or whatever a particular science fiction story is about—will not do, either. Science bears too heavily on all our lives for that. All of us—willy-nilly—must live as if we believed the body of modern science were true. Moreover, science itself contains methods for determining what about it *is* true—not metaphorically true, or metaphysically true, or emotionally true, but simply, plainly, physically, literally true.

If the critic believes that scientific truth is unreal, or irrelevant to his (the critic's) business, then science fiction becomes only a series of very odd metaphors for "the human condition" (which is taken to be different from or unconnected to any scientific truths about the universe). Why should an artist draw metaphors from such a peculiar and totally extra-literary source? Especially when there are so many more intelligent (and intelligible) statements of the human condition which already exist—in our (non-science-fiction) literary tradition? Are writers of science fiction merely kinky? Or perverse? Or stubborn? One can imagine what C.P. Snow would have to say about this split between the two cultures.

One thing he might say is that science fiction bridges the two cultures. It draws its beliefs, its material, its great organizing metaphors, its very attitudes, from a culture that could not exist before the industrial revolution, before science became both an autonomous activity and a way of looking at the world. In short, science fiction is *not* derived from traditional Western literary culture and critics of traditional Western literature have good reason to regard science fiction as a changeling in the literary cradle.

Perhaps science fiction is one symptom of a change in sensibility (and culture) as profound as that of the Renaissance. Despite its ultra-American, individualistic muscle-flexing, science fiction (largely American in origins and influence)[13] is nonetheless collective in outlook, didactic, materialist, and paradoxically often intensely religious or mystical. Such a cluster of traits reminds one not only of medieval culture, but, possibly, of tendencies in our own, post-industrial culture. It may be no accident that elaborate modern statements of the aesthetic *of the didactic* are to be found in places like Brecht's "A Short Organum for the Theatre."[14] Of course, didactic art does not necessarily mean propaganda or political Leftism. But there are similarities between Samuel Delany's insistence that modern literature must be concerned not with passion, but with perception,[15] Suvin's definition of science fiction as a literature of "cognitive estrangement,"[16] George Bernard Shaw's insistence on art as didactic, Brecht's definition of art as a kind of experiment, and descriptions of science fiction as "thought experiments."[17] It is as if literary and dramatic art were being asked to perform tasks of analysis and teaching as a means of dealing with some drastic change in the conditions of human life.

Science fiction is the only modern literature to take work as its central and characteristic concern.

Except for some modern fantasy (e.g. the novels of Charles Williams) science fiction is the only kind of modern narrative literature to deal directly (often awkwardly) with religion as process, not as doctrine, i.e. the ground of feeling and experience from which religion springs.

Like much "post-modern" literature (Nabokov, Borges) science fiction deals commonly, typically, and often insistently, with epistemology.

It is unlikely that science fiction will ever become a major form of literature. Life-as-it-is (however glamorized or falsified) is more interesting to most people than the science-fictional life-as-it-might-be. Moreover, the second depends on an understanding and appreciation of the first. In a sense, science fiction includes (or is parasitic on, depending on your point of view) non-science fiction.

However, there is one realm in which science fiction will remain extremely important. It is the only modern literature which attempts to assimilate imaginatively scientific knowledge about reality and the scientific method, as distinct from the merely practical changes science has made in our lives. The latter are important and sometimes overwhelming, but they can be dealt with imaginatively in exactly the same way a Londoner could have dealt with the Great Plague of 1665 ("Life is full of troubles") or the way we characteristically deal with our failures in social organization ("Man is alienated"). Science fiction is also the only modern literary form (with the possible exception of the detective puzzle) which embodies in its basic assumptions the conviction that finding out, or knowing about something—however impractical the knowledge—is itself a crucial good. Science fiction is a positive response to the post-industrial world, not always in its content (there is plenty of nostalgia for the past and dislike of change in science fiction) but in its very assumptions, its very form.

Criticism of science fiction cannot possibly look like the criticism we are used to. It will—perforce—employ an aesthetic in which the elegance, rigorousness, and systematic coherence of explicit ideas is of great importance.[18] It will therefore appear to stray into all sorts of extra-literary fields, meta-physics, politics, philosophy, physics, biology, psychology, topology, mathe-matics, history, and so on. The relations of foreground and background that we are so used to after a century and a half of realism will not obtain. In-deed, they may be reversed. Science-fiction criticism will discover themes and structures (like those of Olaf Stapledon's *Last and First Men*) which may seem recondite, extra-literary, or plain ridiculous. Themes we customarily regard as emotionally neutral will be charged with emotion. Traditionally "human" concerns will be absent; protagonists may be all but unrecognizable as such. What in other fiction would be marvelous will here be merely accurate or plain; what in other fiction would be ordinary or mundane will here be astonishing, complex, wonderful. (For example, allusions to the death of God will be trivial jokes, while metaphors involving the differences between telephone switchboards and radio stations will be poignantly tragic. Stories ostensibly about persons will really be about topology. Erotics will be intra-cranial, mechanical [literally], and moving.)[19]

Science fiction is, of course, about human concerns. It is written and read by human beings. But the culture from which it comes—the experiences, attitudes, knowledge, and learning which one must bring to it—these are not at all what we are used to as proper to literature. They may, however, be increasingly proper to human life. According to Professor Suvin, the last century has seen a sharp rise in the popularity of science fiction in all the leading industrial nations of the world.[20] There will, in all probability, be more and more science fiction written, and therefore more and more of a need for its explication and criticism.

Such criticism will not be easy. The task of a modern critic of science fiction might be compared to the difficulties of studying Shakespeare's works armed only with a vast, miscellaneous mass of Elizabethan and Jacobean plays, a few remarks of Ben Jonson's, some scattered eulogies in Richard Burbage, Rowe's comments on *Othello*, and a set of literary standards de-rived exclusively from the Greek and Latin classics—which, somehow, do not quite fit.

Some beginnings have been made in outlining an aesthetics of science fiction, particularly in the work of Lem and Suvin, but much remains to be done. Perhaps the very first task lies in discovering that we are indeed dealing with a new and different literature,. Applying the standards and methods one is used to can have only three results: the dismissal of all science fiction as non-literature, a preference for certain narrow kinds of science fiction (be-cause they can be understood at least partly in the usual way), or a miscon-ceiving and misperception of the very texts one is trying to understand. The first reaction seems to be the most common. In the second category one might place the odd phenomenon that critics inexperienced in the field seem to find two kinds of fiction easy to deal with: seventeenth century flights to the moon and dystopias. Thus *Brave New World* and *1984* have received much more critical attention than, say, Shaw's late plays or Stapledon's work. The third category has hitherto been rare because academic consideration of science fiction has been rare, but it could become all too common if the in-creasing popularity of college courses in the subject is not accompanied by criticism proper to the subject. Futurologists, physicists, and sociologists may use science fiction in extra-literary ways but they are not literary critics. If the literary critics misperceive or misconceive their material, the results will be to discourage readers, discourage science fiction writers (who are as serious about their work as any other writers), destroy the academic import-ance of the subject itself, and thus impoverish the whole realm of literature, of which science fiction is a new—but a vigorous and growing—province.

NOTES

[1]"Environments" and similar examples of contemporary art seem to lend themselves to science fiction. For example, as of this writing, an "archeological" exhibit of the fictional Civilization of Llhuros is visiting our local museum. Strictly speaking, the exhibit is fantasy and not science fiction, since the creator (Professor Norman Daly of Cornell University) makes no attempt to place this imaginary country in either a known, a future, or an extraterrene history.

[2]See particularly "On the Poetics of the Science Fiction Genre," *College English* 34(1972):372-82.

[3]For example, "On The Structural Analysis of Science Fiction," SFS 1(1973):26-33.

[4]"About Five Thousand One Hundred and Seventy-Five Words," *Extrapolation* 10(1969):52-66.

[5]At least not immediately. Major changes in scientific theory may lead to major re-evaluation in the fiction, but most science fiction hasn't been around long enough for that. I would agree with George Bernard Shaw that didactic literature does (at least in part) wear out with time, but most science fiction can still rest on the Scottish verdict of "not proven."

[6]Suvin (Note 2), p377.

[7]Damon Knight, *In Search of Wonder* (2nd edn 1967). The phrase is used throughout.

[8]From time to time what might even be called quasi-essays appear, e.g., Larry Niven, "The Theory and Practice of Teleportation," *Galaxy*, March 1969.

[9]A dictum attributed to Theodore Sturgeon, science-fiction writer, is that 90% of anything is bad.

[10]As of this writing, SUNY Binghamton is presenting a summer course in science fiction taught by a graduate student who is—a medievalist.

[11]Bernard Bergonzi, *The Early H.G. Wells* (1961), p52ff.

[12]Eric Bentley, *The Playwright as Thinker* (New York 1967), p224.

[13]Kingsley Amis emphasizes that 20th-century science fiction is predominantly an American phenomenon: *New Maps of Hell* New York 1960), p17 (or Ballantine Books edn, p17), q.v.

[14]In *Brecht on Theatre*, trans. John Willett (New York 1962), pp179-205.

[15]In a talk given at the MLA seminar on science fiction, December 1968, in New York.

[16]Suvin (Note 2), p372.

[17]This phrase has been used so widely in the field that original attribution is impossible.

[18]Suvin (Note 2), p381, as follows: The consistency of extrapolation, precision of analogy, and width of reference in such a cognitive discussion turn into aesthetic factors...*a cognitive—in most cases strictly scientific—element becomes a measure of aesthetic quality.*"

[19]In turn, James Blish's *Black Easter* (which I take to be about Manicheanism), Stapledon's *Last and First Men* (the Martian invasion), A.J. Deutsch's "A Subway Named Moebius" (frequently anthologized), and George Zebrowski's "Starcrossed" (In *Eros in Orbit*, ed. Joseph Elder, 1973).

[20]Suvin (Note 2), p372.

Stanislaw Lem

The Time-Travel Story and Related Matters of SF Structuring

(from SFS *1:143 - 154, Spring 1974)*

Let's look at a couple of simple sentences which logic, by virtue of a "disconnected middle" or by virtue of a tautology, asserts are always true, and let's investigate whether there can be worlds in which their veracity ceases. The first will be the ever real disjuncture: "John is the father of Peter or John is not the father of Peter." Any logician would acknowledge that this disjuncture satisfies at all times the requirement for truth since *tertium non datur*, it is impossible to be 40% father and 60% non-father.

Next, let's work with a complex sentence: "If Peter has sexual relations with his mother, then Peter commits incest." The implication is a tautological one since, according to the semantic rules of language, to have sexual relations with one's mother is tantamount to committing incest. (Our conjunction is not a complete tautology since incest constitutes a concept broader than sexual relations with a mother, referring rather to relations with any person of such close kinship. We could bring the sentence to a perfect tautology, but this would necessitate complexities which would in no way alter the essence of the matter and merely make the argumentation more difficult.)

To simplify matters we shall investigate first the impact of changes on the veracity or falsity of the statement "John is the father of Peter." We should point out that what is involved here is a truly causative biological relation to the birth of a child, and not the ambiguous use of the designation "father" (since it is indeed possible to be a biological father and not be a baptismal father, or conversely, to be a godfather, but not a parent).

Suppose John is a person who died three hundred years ago, but whose reproductive cells were preserved by refrigeration. A woman fertilized by them will become Peter's mother. Will John then be Peter's father? Undoubtedly.

But then suppose the following: John died and did not leave reproductive cells, but a woman asked a genetic technician to make up in laboratory a spermatozoon of John from a single preserved cell of John's epithelium (all the cells of the body having the same genetic composition). Will John, once fertilization is complete, now also be Peter's father?

Now suppose the following case: John not only died, but did not leave a single bodily cell. Instead, John left a will in which he expressed the desire that a genetic technician perform the steps necessary to enable a woman to become the mother of a child of John, i.e. that such a woman give birth to a child and that the child be markedly similar to John. In addition, the genetic technician is not permitted to use any spermatozoa. Rather, he is supposed to cause a parthenogenetic development of the female ovum. Along with this he is supposed to control the genic substance and direct it by embryogenetic transformations in such a way that the Peter born is "the spit and image of John" (there are photographs of John available, a recording of his voice, etc.). The geneticist "sculptures" in the chromosomal substance of the woman all the features John craved for in a child. And thus, to the question "Is John the father or not the father of Peter?" it is now impossible to give an unequivocal answer of "yes" or "no." In some senses John is indeed the father, but in others he is not. An appeal to empiricism alone will not in itself furnish a clear answer. The definition will be essentially determined by the cultural standards of the society in which John, Peter's mother, Peter, as well as the genetic technician, all live.

Let's assume that these standards are fixed, and that the child realized in strict accordance with John's testamental instructions is generally acknowledged to be his child. If, however, the genetic technician either on his own or at the instigation of others made up 45% of the genotypical features of the child not in accordance with the stipulations of the will, but in accordance with an entirely different prescription, it would then be impossible to maintain that John, in agreement with the standards of a given culture, either is or is not the child's father. The situation is the same as when some experts say about a picture reputed to be a work of Rembrandt: "This is a canvas by Rembrandt" while others say: "This is not a canvas by Rembrandt." Since it is quite possible that Rembrandt began the picture, but that some anonymous person finished the work, then 47% of the work could be said to originate from Rembrandt, and 53% from someone else. In such a situation of "partial authorship," *tertium datur*. In other words, there are situations in which it is possible to be a father only in part. (It is also possible to achieve such situations in other ways, e.g., by removing a certain number of genes from a spermatozoon of John and substituting another person's genes for them.)

The possibilties of the transformations mentioned above, which entail a change in the logical value of the disjunction—"John is the father of Peter or John is not the father of Peter"—lie, one may judge, in the bosom of a not too distant future. Thus a work describing such a matter would be fantastic today, but thirty or fifty years hence it might indeed be realistic. However, the work by no means needs to relate the story of a definite, concrete John, Peter, and mother of Peter. It could describe fictitious persons in a manner typical of any form of literary composition. The relational invariables between father, mother, and child would not have at that time the fictitious nature they have in the present. The invariables that concern paternity are today different from those of a time when genetic engineering would be realized. In this sense a composition written today and depicting a given situation without a "disconnected middle" in the predication of paternity, may be considered a futurological prognosis or a hypothesis which may prove to be true.

For a real tautology to become a falsehood, the device of *travel in time* is necessary. Suppose Peter, having grown up, learns that his father was a very vile person, *viz.* that he seduced Peter's mother and abandoned her only to disappear without a trace. Burning with the desire to bring his father to account for so despicable an act and unable to locate him in the present, Peter boards a time vehicle, sets out for the past and seeks out the father in the vicinity of the place where his mother was supposed to have resided at that time. The search, although very thorough, turns out to be in vain. However, in the course of establishing various contacts related to his expedition,

Peter meets a young girl who attracts him. The two fall in love and a baby is conceived. Peter, however, cannot remain permanently in the past; he is obliged to return to his old mother, for whom he is the sole support. Having been convinced by the girl that she has not become pregnant, Peter returns to the present. He has not succeeded in finding traces of his father. One day he finds in one of his mother's drawers a thirty-year-old photograph and to his horror recognizes in it the girl whom he loved. Not wishing to impede him, she committed a white lie, and hid her pregnancy. Peter thus comes to understand that he did not find his father for the simple enough reason that he himself is the father. So, Peter journeyed into the past to search for a missing father, assuming the name of John to facilitate his search by remaining incognito. The upshot of this journey is his own birth. Thus, we have before us a circular causal structure. Peter is his own father, but, as against a superficial judgment, he did not commit incest at all, since, when he had sexual intercourse with her, his mother was not (and could not be) his mother. (From a purely genetic point of view, if we forget that—as is today believed—the causal circle is impossible, Peter is genotypically identical with his mother. In other words, Peter's mother for all practical purposes gave birth to him parthenogenetically since, of course, no man inseminated her who was alien to her.)

THIS STRUCTURE constitutes the so-called time loop, a causal structure characteristic of an enormous number of SF compositions. The composition which I described is a "minimal" loop, yet there is one still "smaller," created by Robert Heinlein in the story "All You Zombies" (1959).[1] Its plot is as follows: a certain young girl becomes pregnant by a man who then promptly disappears. She bears a child, or more correctly, gives birth to it by Caesarean section. During the operation, the doctors ascertain that she is a hermaphrodite and it is essential (for reasons not explained by the author) to change her sex. She leaves the clinic as a young man who, because he was until quite recently a woman, has given birth to a child. She seeks her seducer for a long time, until it comes to light that *she herself* is he. We have the following circular situation: one and the same individual was in time T1 both a girl and her partner since the girl, transformed into a man by surgical intervention, was transferred by the narrator to time T1 from a future time, T2. The narrator, a time traveller, "removed" the young man from time T2 and transferred him to time T1 so that the latter seduced "himself."

Nine months after time T1 the child was born. The narrator stole this child and took it back in time twenty years, to moment T0, so he could leave it under the trees of a foundling home. So the circle is completely closed: the same individual comprises "father," "mother," and "child." In other words, a person impregnated himself and gave birth to himself. The baby, born as a result of this, is left behind in time, bringing about in twenty years the growth of a girl who has in time T1 sex with a young man from time T2. The young man is she herself, transformed into a man by a surgical operation. The fact that a sexual hermaphrodite should not be able to bear a child is a relatively small hindrance, since the puzzling situation of a person's giving birth to himself is considerably "more impossible." What we are dealing with here is an act of *creatio ex nihilo*. All structures of the time-loop variety are internally contradictory in a causal sense. The contradictoriness, however, is not always as apparent as in Heinlein's story.

Frederic Brown writes about a man who travels into the past in order to punish his grandfather for tormenting his grandmother. In the course of an altercation he kills his grandfather before his father has been engendered. Thus the time traveller cannot then come into the world. Who, therefore, in fact killed the grandfather, if the murderer has not come into the world at all? Herein lies the contradiction. Sometimes an absent-minded scientist, having left something in the past which he has visited, returns for the lost object and encounters his own self, since he has not returned exactly to the moment after his departure for the present, but to the time-point at which he was before. When such returns are repeated, the individual is subject to multiple reproduction in the form of doubles. Since such possibilities appear to be pointless, in one of my stories about Ion Tichy (the "7th Journey"),[2] I maximalized "duplication" of the central character. Ion Tichy's spaceship finds itself in gravitational whirlpools that bend time into a circle, so that the space-ship is filled with a great number of different Ions.

The loop motif can be used, for instance, in the following ways: someone proceeds into the past, deposits ducats in a Venetian bank at compound interest, and centuries later in New York demands from a consortium of banks payment of the entire capital, a gigantic sum. Why does he need so much money all of a sudden? So that he can hire the best physicists to construct for him a thus far nonexistent time vehicle, and by means of this vehicle go back in time to Venice where he will deposit ducats at compound interest... (Mack Reynolds, "Compounded Interest" [1956]). Or another example: in the future someone comes to an artist (in one story to a painter, in another to a writer) and gives him either a book dealing with painting in the future or a novel written in the future. The artist then begins to imitate this material as much as possible, and becomes famous, the paradox being that he is borrowing from his own self (since he himself was the author of that book or those pictures, only "twenty years later").

We learn, further, from various works of this sort how the Mesozoic reptiles became extinct thanks to hunters who organized a "safari into the past" (Frederic Brown), or how, in order to move in time in one direction, an equal mass must be displaced in the opposite direction, or how expeditions in time can reshape historical events. The latter theme has been used time and again, as in one American tale in which the Confederate States are victorious over the North (Ward Moore's *Bring the Jubilee* [1952/1953]). The hero, a military historian, sets out for the past in order to investigate how the Southerners gained victory near Gettysburg. His arrival in a time machine, however, throws General Lee's troop formations into disarray, which results in victory for the North. The hero is no longer able to return to the future, because his arrival also disturbed the causal chain upon which the subsequent construction of his time machine depended. Thus, the person who was supposed to have financed the construction of the machine will not do this, the machine will not exist, and the historian will be stuck in the year 1863 without the means to travel back into the original time. Of course here also there is an inherent paradox—just how did he reach the past? As a rule, the fun consists in the way the paradox is shifted from one segment of the action to another. The time loop as the backbone of a work's causal structure is thus different from the far looser motif of journeys in time per se; but, of course, it is merely a logical, although extreme, consequence of the general acceptance of the possibility of "chronomotion." There are actually two possible authorial attitudes which are mutually exclusive: either one deliberately demonstrates causal paradoxes resulting from "chronomotion" with the greatest possible consistency, or else one cleverly avoids them. In the first instance, the careful development of logical consequences leads to situations as absurd as the one cited (an individual that is his very own father, that procreates himself), and usually has a comic effect (though this does not follow automatically).

EVEN THOUGH a circular causal structure may signalize a frivolous type of content, this does not mean that it is necessarily reduced to the construction of comic antinomies for the sake of pure entertainment. The causal circle may be employed not as the goal of the story, but as a means of visualizing certain theses, e.g. from the philosophy of history. Slonimski's story of the Time Torpedo[3] belongs here. It is a belletristic assertion of the *"ergo*ness" or ergodicity of history: monkeying with events which have had sad consequences does not bring about any improvement of history; instead of one group of disasters and wars there simply comes about another, in no way better set.

A diametrically opposed hypothesis, on the other hand, is incorporated into Ray Bradbury's "A Sound of Thunder" (1952). In an excellently written short episode, a participant in a "safari for tyrannosaurs" tramples a butterfly and a couple of flowers, and by that microscopic act causes such perturbances of causal chains involving millions of years, that upon his return the English language has a different orthography and a different candidate—not liberal but rather a kind of dictator—has won in the presidential election. It is only a pity that Bradbury feels obliged to set in motion complicated and unconvincing explanations to account for the fact that hunting for reptiles, which indeed fall from shots, disturbs nothing in the causal chains, whereas the trampling of a tiny flower does (when a tyrannosaur drops to the ground, the quantity of ruined flowers must be greater than when the safari participant descends from a safety zone to the ground). "A Sound of Thunder" exemplifies an "anti-ergodic" hypothesis of history, as opposed to Slonimski's story. In a way, however, the two are reconcilable: History can as a whole be "ergodic" if not very responsive to local disturbances, and at the same time such exceptional hypersensitive points in the causal chains can exist, the vehement disturbance of which produces more intensive results. In personal affairs such a "hyperallergic point" would be, for example, a situation in which a car attempts to pass a truck at the same time that a second car is approaching from the opposite direction.

As is usually the case in SF, a theme defined by a certain devised structure of occurrences (in this instance pertaining to a journey in time) undergoes a characteristic cognitive-artistic involution. We could have demonstrated this for any given theme, but let's take advantage of the opportunity at hand.

At first, authors and readers are satisfied by the joy of discerning the effects of innovations still virginal as far as their inherent contradictions are concerned. Then, an intense search is begun for initial situations which allow for the most effective exploitation of consequences that are potentially present in a given structure. Thus, the devices of chronomotion begin supporting, e.g., theses of history and philosophy (concerned with the "ergodicity" or non-ergodicity of history). Then, grotesque and humorous stories like Frederic Brown's "The Yehudi Principle" (1944) appear: this short story is *itself* a causal circle (it ends with the words that it began with: it describes a test of a device for fulfilling wishes; one of the wishes expressed is that a story "write itself," which is what just happened).

Finally, the premise of time travel serves frequently as a simple pretext for weaving tales of sensational, criminal, or melodramatic intrigue; this usually involves the revival and slight refurbishment of petrified plots.

Time travel has been used so extensively in SF that it has been divided into separate sub-categories. There is, e.g., the category of *missent parcels* that find their way into the present from the future: someone receives a "Build-a-Man Set" box with "freeze-dried nerve preparations," bones, etc.; he builds his own double, and an "inspector from the future," who comes to reclaim the parcel, disassembles instead of the artificial twin, the very hero of the story; this is William Tenn's "Child's Play" (1947). In Damon Knight's "Thing of Beauty" (1958) there is a different parcel—an automaton that draws pictures by itself. In general, strange things are produced in the future, SF teaches us (e.g., polka-dotted paint as well as thousands of objects with secret names and purposes not known).

Another category is *tiers in time*. In its simplest form it is presented in Anthony Boucher's "The Barrier" (1942), a slightly satiric work. The hero, travelling to the future, comes to a state of "eternal stasis," which, to protect its perfect stagnation from all disturbances, has constructed "time barriers" that foil any penetration. Now and then, however, a barrier becomes pervious. Rather disagreeable conditions prevail in this state which is ruled by a police similar to the Gestapo (Stapper). One must be a slightly more advanced SF reader to follow the story. The hero finds his way immediately into a circle of people who know him very well, but whom he does not know at all. This is explained by the fact that in order to elude the police he goes somewhat further back in time. He at that time gets to know these very people, then considerably younger. He is for them a stranger, but he, while he was in the future, has already succeeded in getting to know them. An old lady, who got into the time vehicle with the hero when they were fleeing from the police, meets as a result her own self as a young person and suffers a severe shock. It is clear, however, that Boucher does not know what to do with the "encountering oneself" motif in this context, and therefore makes the lady's shock long and drawn out. Further jumps in time, one after another, complicate the intrigue in a purely formal way. Attempts are begun to overthrow the dictatorial government, but everything goes to pieces, providing in the process sensationalism. *Anti-problematic escapism into adventure* is a very common phenomenon in SF: authors indicate its formal effectiveness, understood as the ingenious setting of a game in motion, as the skill of achieving uncommon *movements*, without mastering and utilizing the problematic and semantic aspects of such kinematics.

Such authors neither discuss nor solve the problems raised by their writing, but rather "take care" of them by dodges, employing patterns like the happy ending or the setting in motion of sheer pandemonium, a chaos which quickly engulfs loose meanings.

Such a state of affairs is a result of the distinctly "ludic" or playful position of writers; they go for an effect as a tank goes for an obstacle: without regard for anything incidental. It is as if their field of vision were greatly intensified and, simultaneously, also greatly confined. As in Tenn's story, the consequences of a "temporal lapse" in a postal matter are everything. Let us call such a vision *monoparametric*. At issue is a situation which is bizarre, amusing, uncanny, logically developed from a structural premise (e.g., from the presupposition of "journeys in time," which implies a qualitative difference in the world's causal structure). At the same time such a vision does not deal with anything more than that.

This can be seen readily from an example of "maximal intensification" of the subject of *governments in time* or "chronocracy," described by Isaac Asimov in his novel *The End of Eternity* (1955). "The Barrier" showed a single state isolating itself in the historical flow of events, as once the Chinese attempted to isolate themselves from the disturbing influences by building the Chinese wall (a spatially exact equivalent of a "time barrier"). *The End of Eternity* shows a goverment in power throughout humanity's entire temporal existence. Inspector-generals, travelling in time, examine the goings on in individual epochs, centuries, and millenia, and by calculating the probability of occurrences and then counteracting the undesirable ones, keep in hand the entire system—"history extended in a four-dimensional continuum"—in a state of desirable equilibrium. Obviously, presuppositions of this sort are more thickly larded with antinomies than is the scrawniest hare larded with bacon. While Asimov's great proficiency is manifested by the size of the slalom over which the narrative runs, it is, in the end, an ineffably naive conception because no issues from philosophy or history are involved. The problem of "closed millenia," which the "tempocrats" do not have access to, is explained when a certain beautiful girl, whom an inspector falls in love with, turns out to be not a lowly inhabitant of one of the centuries under the dominion of the tempocracy, but a secret emissary from the "inaccessible millenia." The time dictatorship as a control over the continuum of history will be destroyed, and a liberated humanity will be able to take up astronautics and other select suitable occupations. The enigma of the inaccessible millenia is remarkably similar to the "enigma of the closed room" found in fairy tales and detective stories. The various epochs about which the emissaries of the chronocracy hover also recall separate rooms. *The End of Eternity* is an exhibition of formal entertainment to which sentiments about the fight for freedom and against dictatorship have been tacked on rather casually.

WE HAVE already spoken about the "minimal time loop." Let us talk now, simply for the sake of symmetry, about the "maximal" loops.

A.E. van Vogt has approached this concept in *The Weapon Shops of Isher* (1949/1951), but let's expound it in our own way. As is known, there is a hypothesis (it can be found in Feynman's physics) which states that positrons are electrons moving "against the tide" in the flow of time. It is also known that in principle, even galaxies can arise from atomic collisions, as long as the colliding atoms are sufficiently rich in energy. In accordance with these presuppositions we can construct the following story: in a rather distant future a celebrated cosmologist reaches, on the basis of his own research as well as that of all his predecessors, the irrefutable conclusion that, on the one hand, the cosmos came into being from a single particle and, on the other, that such a single particle could not have existed—where could it have sprung from? Thus he is confronted with a dilemma: the cosmos has come into being, but it could not come into being! He is horrified by this revelation, but, after profound reflections, suddenly sees the light: the cosmos exists exactly as mesons sometimes exist; mesons, admittedly, break the law of conservation, but do this so quickly that they do not break it. The cosmos exists on credit! It is like a debenture, a draft for material and energy which *must* be repaid immediately, because its existence is the purest one hundred percent liability both in terms of energy and in terms of material. Then, just what does the cosmologist do? With the help of physicist friends he builds a great "chronogun" which fires one single electron backward "against the tide" in the flow of time. That electron, transformed into a positron as a result of its motion "against the grain" of time, goes speeding through time, and in the course of this journey acquires more and more energy. Finally, at the point where it "leaps out" of the cosmos, i.e. in a place in which there had *as yet* been no cosmos, all the terrible energies it has acquired are released in that tremendously powerful explosion which brings about the Universe! In this manner the debt is paid off. At the same time, thanks to the largest possible "causal circle," the existence of the cosmos is authenticated, and a person turns out to be the actual creator of that very Universe! It is possible to complicate this story slightly, for example, by telling how certain colleagues of the cosmologist, unpleasant and envious people, meddled in his work, shooting on their own some lesser particles backwards against the tide of time. These particles exploded inaccurately when the cosmologist's positron was producing the cosmos, and because of this that unpleasant rash came into being which bothers science so much today, namely the enigmatic quasars and pulsars which are not readily incorporated into the corpus of contemporary knowledge. These then are the "artifacts" produced by the cosmologist's malicious competitors. It would also be possible to tell how humanity both created and depraved itself, because some physicist shot the "chronogun" hurriedly and carelessly and a particle went astray, exploding as a nova in the vicinity of the solar system two million years ago, and damaging by its hard radiance the hereditary plasma of the original anthropoids who therefore did not evolve into "man good and rational" as "should have happened" without the new particle. In other words, the new particle caused the degeneration of Homo sapiens—witness his history.

In this version, then, we created the cosmos only in a mediocre fashion, and our own selves quite poorly. Obviously a work of this sort, in whichever variant, becomes ironical, independently of its basic notion (i.e. the "self-creative" application of the "maximal time loop").

As one can see, what is involved is an intellectual game, actually fantasy-making which alters in a logical or pseudo-logical manner current scientific hypotheses. This is "pure" Science-Fiction, or Science-Fantasy as it is sometimes called. It shows us nothing serious, but merely demonstrates the consequences of a reasoning which, operating within the guidelines of the scientific method, is used sometimes in unaltered form (in predicting the "composition percentage of paternity" we have in no way altered the scientific data), and sometimes secretly modified. And thus SF can be responsibly or irresponsibly plugged into the hypothesis-creating system of scientific thought.

The example of "self-creation" reveals first of all the "maximal proportions" of a self-perpetrating paradox: Peter gave birth only to himself, whereas in the universal variant, mankind concocted itself, and, what is more, perhaps not in the best manner, so that it would be even possible to use "Manichaean" terminology. Furthermore, this example at the same time demonstrates that the conceptual premise of essential innovations in the structure of the objective world presented is central to a science-fictional work (in the case of journeys in time, a change in causality is involved, by admitting the reversibility of that which we consider today as universally and commonly irreversible). The qualities of fictional material which serve a dominant concept are thus subject to an assessment based on the usefulness to this concept. Fictional material should in that case be an embodiment of a pseudo-scholarly or simply scholarly hypothesis—and that's all. Thus "pure" SF arises, appealing exclusively to "pure reason." It is possible to complicate a work with problems lying beyond the scope of such an intellectual game: when, e.g., the "Manichaeism of existence" is interpreted as due to an error of an envious physicist, then an opportunity for sarcasm or irony arises as a harmonic "overtone" above the narrative's main axis. But by doing this, we have forced SF to perform "impure" services, because it is then not delivering scientific pseudo-revelations, but functioning in the same semantic substratum in which literature has normally operated. It is because of this that we call SF contaminated by semantic problems "*relational* SF."

However, just as "normal" literature can also perform high and low services—produce sentimental love stories and epics—*relational* SF shows an analogous amplitude. As was noted, it is possible to interpret it allegorically (e.g., Manichaeism in relation to the creation of the cosmos)—and this will be the direction of grotesque or humorous departures from a state of "intellectual purity" which is somewhat analogous to "mathematical vacuity." It is also possible to overlay the history of creating the cosmos with melodrama, e.g., to make it part of a sensational, psychopathological intrigue (the cosmologist who created the Universe has a wicked wife whom he nonetheless loves madly; or, the cosmologist becomes possessed; or also, faced with his deeds, the cosmologist goes insane and, as a megalomaniac, will be treated slightingly in an insane asylum, etc.).

THUS , in the end, the realistic writer is not responsible for the overall—e.g., the causal—structure of the real world. In evaluating his works, we are not centrally concerned with assessing the structure of the world to which they nonetheless have some relation.

On the contrary, the SF writer is responsible both for the world in which he has placed his action, and for the action as well, inasmuch as he, within certain limits, invents both one and the other.

However, the invention of new worlds in SF is as rare as a pearl the size of a bread loaf. And so 99.9% of all SF works follow compositionally a scheme, one of the thematic structures which constitute the whole SF repertoire. For a world truly new in structural qualities is one in which the causal irreversibility of occurrences is denied, or one in which a person's individuality conflicts with an individual scientifically produced by means of an "intellectronic evolution," or one in which Earthly culture is in communication with a non-Earthly culture distinct from human culture not only nominally but *qualitatively*, and so forth. However, just as it is impossible to invent a steam engine, or an internal combustion engine, or any other already existing thing, it is also impossible to invent once more worlds with the sensational quality of "chronomotion" or of "a reasoning machine." As the detective story churns out unweariedly the same plot stereotypes, so does SF when it tells us of countless peripeties merely to show that by interposing a time loop they have been successfully invalidated (e.g. in Thomas Wilson's "The Entrepreneur" [1952] which talks about the dreadful Communists having conquered the USA, and time travellers who start backwards at the necessary point, invalidating such an invasion and dictatorship). In lieu of Communists, there may be Aliens or even the Same People Arriving from the Future (thanks to the time loop, anyone can battle with himself just as long as he pleases), etc.

If new concepts, those atomic kernels that initiate a whole flood of works, correspond to that gigantic device by which bioevolution was "invented"—i.e., to the constitutional principle of types of animals such as vertebrates and nonvertebrates, or fish, amphibians, mammals, and birds—then, in the "evolution of SF," the equivalent of type-creating revolutions were the ideas of *time travel*, of *constructing a robot*, of *cosmic contact*, of *cosmic invasion*, and of *ultimate catastrophe for the human species*. And, as within the organization of biological types a natural evolution imperceptibly produces distinctive changes according to genera, families, races, and so forth—similarly, SF persistently operates within a framework of modest, simply variational craftsmanship.

This very craftsmanship, however, betrays a systematic, unidirectional bias: as we stated and demonstrated, great concepts that alter the structure of the fictional world are a manifestation of a pure play of the intellect. The results are assessed according to the type of play. The play can also be "relational," involved with situations only loosely or not at all connected with the dominant principle. What connection is there, after all, between the existence of the cosmologist who created the world, and the fact that he has a beautiful secretary whom he beds? Or, by what if not by a retardation device will the cosmologist be snatched away before he fires the "chronogun"? In this manner an idea lending itself to articulation in a couple of sentences (as we have done here) becomes a pretext for writing a long novel (where a "cosmos-creating" shot comes only in the epilogue, after some deliverers sent by the author have finally saved the cosmologist from his sorry plight). The purely intellectual concept is stretched thoroughly out of proportion to its inherent possibilities. But this is just how SF proceeds— usually.

On the other hand, rarely is a departure made from "emptiness" or "pure play" in the direction of dealing with a set of important and involved problems. For in the world of SF it is structurally as possible to set up an adventure plot as a psychological drama; it is as possible to deal in sensational happenings as it is to stimulate thought by an ontological implication created by the narrative as a whole. It is precisely this slide toward easy, sensational intrigue which is a symptom of the degeneration of this branch of literature. An idea is permitted in SF if it is packaged so that one can barely see it through the glitter of the wrapping. As against conventions only superficially associated to innovations in the world's structure and which have worn completely threadbare from countless repetitions, SF should be stimulated and induced to deviate from this trend of development, namely, by involution away from the "sensational pole." SF should not operate by increasing the number of blasters or Martians who impede the cosmologist in his efforts to fire from the "chronogun"; such inflation is not appropriate. Rather, one should change direction radically and head for the opposite pole. After all, in principle the same bipolar opposition also prevails in ordinary literature, which also shuttles between cheap melodrama and stories with the highest aesthetic and cognitive aspirations.

It is difficult, however, to detect in SF a convalescence or outright salvation of this sort. An odd fate seems to loom heavily over its domain, which prompts writers with the highest ambitions and considerable talent, such as Ray Bradbury or J.G. Ballard, to employ the conceptual and rational tools of SF in an at times admittedly superb way, yet not in order to ennoble the genre, but instead to bring it toward an "optimal" pole of literature. Aiming in that direction, they are simultaneously, in each successive step, giving up the programmatic rationalism of SF in favour of the irrational; their intellect fails to match their know-how and their artistic talent. In practice, what this amounts to is that they do not use the "signalling equipment" of SF, its available accessories, to express any truly, intellectually new problems or content. They try to bring about the conversion of SF to the "creed of normal literature" through articulating, by fantastic means, such non-fantastic content which is already old-fashioned in an ethical, axiological, philosophical sense. The revolt against the machine and against civilization, the praise of the "aesthetic" nature of catastrophe, the dead-end course of human civilization—these are their foremost problems, the intellectual content of their works. Such SF is as it were a priori vitiated by pessimism, in the sense that anything that may happen will be for the worse.

Such writers proceed as if they thought that, should mankind acknowledge the existence of even a one-in-a-million or one-in-a-billion chance— transcending the already known cyclical pulsation of history, which has oscillated between a state of relative stabilization and of complete material devastation—such an approach would not be proper. Only in mankind's severe, resolute rejection of all chances of development, in complete negation, in a gesture of escapism or nihilism, do they find the proper mission of all SF which would not be cheap. Consequently they build on dead-end tragedy. This may be called into question not merely from the standpoint of optimism, of whatever hue and intensity. Rather, one should criticize their ideology by attempting to prove that they tear to shreds that which they themselves do not understand. With regard to the formidable movements which shake our world, they nourish the same fear of *misunderstanding* the mechanisms of change that every ordinary form of literature has. Isn't it clear what proportions their defection assumes because of this? *Cognitive* optimism is, first of all, a thoroughly non-ludic premise in the creation of SF. The result is often extremely cheap, artistically as well as intellectually, but its principle is good. According to this principle, there is only one remedy for imperfect knowledge: better knowledge, because more varied knowledge. SF, to be sure, normally supplies numerous surrogates for such knowledge. But, according to its premises, that knowledge exists and is accessible: the irrationalism of Bradbury's or Ballard's fantasy negates both these premises. One is not allowed to entertain any cognitive hopes—that becomes the unwritten axiom of their work. Instead of introducing into traditional qualities of writing new conceptual equipment as well as new notional configurations relying on intellectual imagination, these authors, while ridding themselves of the stigma of cheap and defective SF, in one fell swoop give up all that constitutes its cognitive value. Obviously, they are unaware of the consequences of such desertion, but this only clears them morally: so much the worse for literature and for culture, seriously damaged by their mistake.

—*Translated from the Polish by Thomas H. Hoisington and Darko Suvin.*

NOTES

[1]The dates given in this essay are either for first publication whether in serial or book form or for serial/book publication. —RDM.

[2]"The Seventh Journey of Ion Tichy" is available in several Polish editions, such as *Dzienni qwiazdowe* (Cracow 1966); it has not yet been published in English. —DS.

[3]Antoni Slonimski, born in 1895, Polish poet and essayist; his *Torpeda czasu* (i.e., Time Torpedo) was first published in 1967. —THH.

Fredric Jameson

Generic Discontinuities
in SF: Brian Aldiss' *Starship*

(from SFS *1:57 - 68, Fall 1973)*

The theme or narrative convention of the lost-spaceship-as-universe offers
a particularly striking occasion to observe the differences between the
socalled old and new waves in SF, since Aldiss' *Starship* (1958) was
preceded by a fine treatment of the same material by Robert A. Heinlein
in *Orphans of the Sky* (serialized 1941 as "Universe" and "Common
Sense").[1] Taken together, the versions of the two writers give us a synoptic
view of the basic narrative line that describes the experiences of the hero
as he ventures beyond the claustrophobic limits of his home territory into
other compartments of a world peopled by strangers and mutants. He
comes at length to understand that the space through which he moves is
not the universe but simply a gigantic ship in transit through the galaxy;
and this discovery--which may be said to have in such a context all the
momentous scientific consequences that the discoveries of Copernicus and
Einstein had in our own--takes the twin form of text and secret chamber.
On the one hand, the hero learns to read the enigmatic "Manual of Electric Circuits of Starship," a manual of his own cosmos, supplemented by
the ship's log with its record of the ancient catastrophe--mutiny and
natural disaster as Genesis and Fall--which broke the link between future
generations of the ship's inhabitants and all knowledge of their origins.
And on the other, he makes his way to the ship's long vacant control room
and there comes to know, for the first time, the shattering experience of
deep space and the terror of the stars. The narrative then terminates with
the arrival of the ship--against all expectation--at its immemorial and
long forgotten destination and with the end of what some indigenous star-
ship-philosopher would no doubt have called the "prehistory" of the
inhabitants.
       But this series of events constitutes only what might be called the
horizontal dimension of the thematic material in question. On its basis a
kind of vertical structure is erected which amounts to an account of the
customs and culture that have evolved within the sealed realm of the lost
ship. Both Heinlein and Aldiss, indeed, take anthropological pains to note

the peculiar native religion of the ship, oriented around its mythical founders, its codified survival-ethic, whose concepts of good and evil are derived from the tradition of the great mutiny as from some primal disobedience of man, its characteristic figures of speech and ritualistic formulae similarly originating in long-forgotten and incomprehensible events and situations ("Take a journey!"= "Drop dead!"; "By Huff!"= "What the devil!" in allusion to the ringleader of the mutiny; and so on). With this anthropological dimension of the narrative, the two books may be said to fulfill one of the supreme functions of SF as a genre, namely the "estrangement," in the Brechtian sense,[2] of our culture and institutions--a shocked renewal of our vision such that once again, and as though for the first time, we are able to perceive their historicity and their arbitrariness, their profound dependency on the accidents of man's historical adventure.

Indeed, I propose to reverse the traditional order of aesthetic priorities and to suggest that this whole theme is nothing but a pretext for the spectacle of the artificial formation of a culture within the closed situation of the lost ship. Such a hypothesis demands a closer look at the role of the *artificial* in these narratives, which takes at least two distinct forms. First, there is the artificiality of the mile-long spaceship as a human construct used as an instrument in a human project. Here the reader is oppressed by the substitution of culture for nature (a substitution dramatically and unexpectedly extended by Aldiss in the twist ending that we shall speak of later). Accustomed to the idea that that human history and culture obey a kind of organic and natural rhythm in their evolution, emerging slowly within a determinate geographical and climatic situation under the shaping forces of events (invasions, inventions, economic developments) that are themselves felt to have some inner or "natural" logic, he feels the supreme influence of the ship's environment as a cruel and unnatural joke. The replacement of the forests and plains in which men have evolved by the artificial compartments of the spaceship is in itself only the external and stifling symbol of the original man-made decision (a grim caricature of God's gesture of creation) which sent man on such a fatal mission and which was at the source of this new and artificial culture. Somehow the decisive moments of real human history (Caesar at the Rubicon, Lenin on the eve of the October revolution) do not come before us with this irrevocable force, for they are reabsorbed into the web of subsequent events and "alienated" by the collective existence of society as a whole. But the inauguratory act of the launchers of the spaceship implies a terrible and godlike responsibility which is not without serious political overtones and to which we will return. For the present let us suggest that the estrangement-effect inherent in such a substitution of culture for nature would seem to involve two apparently contradictory impulses: on the one hand, it causes us obscurely to doubt whether our own institutions are quite as natural as we supposed, and whether our "real" open-air environment may not itself be as confining and constricting as the closed world of the ship; on the other hand, it casts uncertainty on the principle of the "natural" itself, which as a conceptual category no longer seems quite so self-justifying and common-sensical.

The other sense in which the artificial plays a crucial role in the spaceship-as-universe narrative has to do with the author himself, who is called on, as it were, to reinvent history out of whole cloth, and to devise, out of his own individual imagination, institutions and cultural phenomena which in real life come into being only over great stretches of time and only as a result of collective processes. Historical truth is always stranger and more unpredictable, more unimaginable, than any fiction: whatever the talent of the novelist, his inventions must always of necessity spring from extrapolation of or analogy with the real, and this law emerges with particular force and visibility in SF with its generic attachment to "future history." This is to say that the cultural traits invented by Aldiss and Heinlein always come before us as *signs:* they ask us to take them as equivalents for the cultural habits of our own daily lives, they beg to be judged on their intention rather than by what they actually realize, to be read with complicity rather than for the impoverished literal content. But this apparently inevitable failure of the imagination is not so disastrous aesthetically as one might expect: on the contrary, it projects an estrangement-effect of its own, and our reaction is not so much disappointment at the imaginative lapses of Aldiss and Heinlein as rather bemusement with the limits of man's vision. Such details cause us to measure the distance between the creative power of the individual mind and the unforeseeable, inexhaustible fullness of history as the collective human adventure. So the ultimate inability of the writer to create a genuinely alternate universe only returns us the more surely to this one.

So much for the similarities between these two books, and for the narrative structure which they share. Their differences begin to emerge when we observe the way in which each deals with the principal strategic problem of such a narrative, namely the degree to which the reader is to be held, along with the hero, in ignorance of the basic facts about the lost ship. Now it will be said that both books give their secret away at the very outset--Aldiss with his title, and Heinlein with the initial but retrospective "historical" motto which recounts the disappearance of the ship in outer space. Apparently, therefore, we have to do in both cases with an adventure-story in which the hero discovers something we know already, rather than with a cognitive or puzzle-solving form in which we ourselves come to learn something new. Yet the closing episodes of the two books are different enough to suggest some significant structural distinctions between them. In Heinlein's story, indeed, the lost ship ultimately *lands,* and the identity of the destination is not so important as the finality of the landing itself, which has the effect of satisfying our aesthetic expectations with a full stop. Of course, the book could have ended in any one of a number of other ways: the ship might have crashed, the hero might have been killed by his enemies, the inhabitants might all have died and sailed on, embalmed, into intergalactic space like the characters in Martinson's poem and Blomdahl's opera *Aniara.* The point is that such alternate endings do not in themselves call into question the basic category of an ending or plot-resolution; rather, they reconfirm the convention of the linear narrative with its beginning (*in medias res* or *navigationis*), middle, and end.

The twist ending of Aldiss' novel, on the other hand, turns the whole concept of such a plot inside out like a glove. It shows us that there was a mystery or puzzle to be solved after all, but not where we thought it was; as it were a second-degree puzzle, a mystery to the second power, tran-

scending the question of the world as ship which we as readers had taken
for granted from the outset. The twist ending, therefore, returns upon the
opening pages to transform the very generic expectations aroused there. It
suddenly reidentifies the category of the narrative in a wholly unexpected
way, and shows us that we have been reading a very different type of book
than the one we started out with. In comparison with anything to be
found in the Heinlein story, where all the discoveries take place *within*,
and are predicated on the existence and stability of, the narrative frame,
the new information furnished us by Aldiss in his closing pages has structural consequences of a far more thorough-going kind.

The notion of *generic expectations*[1] may now serve as our primary
tool for the analysis of *Starship*--at the same time that such a reading
will define and illustrate this notion more concretely. I suppose that the
reader who comes to Aldiss from Heinlein is impressed first of all by the
incomparably more vivid "physiological" density of Aldiss' style. In spite
of everything the title tells us of the world we are about to enter, the
reader of *Starship*, in its opening pages, finds himself exploring a mystery
into which he is plunged up to the very limits of his senses. In particular,
he must find some way of reconciling, in his own mind, the two contradictory terminological and conceptual fields which we have already
discussed under the headings of nature and culture: on the one hand, indications of the presence of a "deck," with its "compartments,"
"barricades," and "wooden partitions," and on the other hand, the
organic growth of "ponic tangle" through which the tribe slowly hacks its
way as through a jungle, "thrusting forward the leading barricade, and
moving up the rear ones, at the other end of Quarters, a corresponding
distance" (§1:1). Such an apparently unimaginable interpenetration of
the natural and the artificial is underscored by a sentence like the
following: "The hardest job in the task of clearing ponics was breaking up
the interlacing root structure, which lay like a steel mesh under the grit,
its lower tendrils biting deep into the deck" (§1:1). Such a sentence is an
invitation to "rêverie" in Gaston Bachelard's sense of the imaginative exploration of the properties and elements of space through language; it
exercises the function of poetry as Heidegger conceives it, as a non-
conceptualized meditation on the very mysteries of our being-in-the-
world. Its force springs, however, from its internal contradictions, from
the incomprehensible conflict between natural and artificial imagery,
which arouses and stimulates our perceptual faculties at the same time
that it seems to block their full unfolding. We can appreciate this
mechanism more accurately in juxtaposition with a later book by Aldiss
himself, *Hothouse* (1962),[1] in which a post-civilized Earth offers only the
most abundant and riotous purely organic imagery, the cultural and artificial with few exceptions having long since vanished.

This is not to say that Heinlein's book does not have analogous
moments of mystery, but they are of a narrative rather than descriptive
kind. I think, for example, of the episode near the beginning of "Universe"
in which Hugh and his companion, lost in a strange part of the ship, sight
a "farmer":

> "Hey! Shipmate! Where are we?"
> The peasant looked them over slowly, then directed them in

reluctant monosyllables to the main passageway which would lead them back to their own village.

A brisk walk of a mile and a half down a wide tunnel moderately crowded with traffic--travelers, porters, an occasional pushcart, a dignified scientist swinging in a litter borne by four husky orderlies and preceded by his master-at-arms to clear the common crew out of the way--a mile and a half of this brought them to the common of their own village, a spacious compartment three decks high and perhaps ten times as wide.

One thinks of Rabelais' narrator climbing down into Pantagruel's throat and chatting with the peasant he finds there planting cabbage; and it ought to be said, in Heinlein's defense, that the purely descriptive intensity of Aldiss' pages should be considered a late phenomenon stylistically, one which reflects the breakdown of plot and the failure of some genuinely narrative gesture, subverting the classical story-telling function of novels into an illicit poetic one which substitutes objects and atmosphere for events and actions. On the other hand, it is true that what characterizes a writer like Aldiss--and in the largest sense the writer of the "new novel" generally--is precisely that he writes *after* the "old novel" and presupposes the latter's existence. In an Hegelian sense one can say that such "poetic" writing includes the older narrative within itself as it were canceled and raised up into a new type of structure.

Yet the point I want to make is that the Aldiss material determines generic expectations in a way in which the Heinlein episode does not. The latter is merely one more event among others, whereas Aldiss' pages programme the reader for a particular type of reading, for the physiological or Bachelardian exploration, through style, of the properties of a peculiar and fascinating world. That such phenomenological attention is for the moment primary may be judged by our distance from Complain, the main character, who in this first section of the book may be said to serve as a mere pretext for our perceptions of this strange new space, and in fact to amount, with his unaccountable longings and rages, to little other than one more curious object within it, which we observe in ethnological dispassion from the outside. Indeed, the shifting in our distance from the characters, the transformations of the very categories through which we perceive characters, are among the most important indices of what we have called generic expectation. This concept may now perhaps be more clearly illustrated if we note that the opening pages of *Starship* (roughly to the point in §1:4 where Complain is drawn into Marapper's plot to explore the ship) project a type of narrative or genre which is not subsequently executed. *Hothouse*, indeed, provides a very useful comparison in this context, for it may be seen as a book-length fulfillment of the kind of generic expectation aroused in this first section of *Starship*. *Hothouse* is precisely, from start to finish, a Bachelardian narrative of the type which *Starship* ceases to be after Complain leaves his tribe, and is for this reason a more homogenous product than *Starship*, more prodigious in its stylistic invention, but by the same token more monotonous and less interesting formally.

For the predominant formal characteristic of *Starship* is the way in which each new section projects a different kind of novel or narrative, a fresh generic expectation broken off unfulfilled and replaced in its turn by a new and seemingly unrelated one. Such divisions are of course approximative and must be mapped out by each reader according to his own responses. My own feeling is that with the onset of Marapper's plot, the novel is transformed into a kind of *adventure story* of the hostile-territory or jungle-exploration type, in which the hero and his companions, in their search for the ship's control room, begin to grapple with geographical obstacles, hostile tribes, alien beings, and internal dissension. In this section, lasting for some twenty pages, the reader's attention is focussed on the success or failure of the expedition, and on the problems of its organization and leadership.

With the discovery, in the middle of the night, of the immense Swimming Pool (§2:2)--a sight as astounding, for the travellers, as the Europeans' first glimpse of Lake Victoria and the source of the Nile--our interest again shifts subtly, returning to the structure of the ship itself, with its numbered decks through which the men slowly make their way. The questions and expectations now aroused seem once more to be of a *cognitive* type, and suggest that the mere certainty of being in a spaceship does not begin to solve all the problems we may have about it, and in particular does not explain why it is that the ship, thus mysteriously abandoned to its destiny, continues to *run* (e.g., its generators still produce electricity for the lighting system).

But the result of this new kind of attention to the physical environment is yet another shift in tone or narrative convention. For the unexpected appearance of hitherto unknown beings--the Giants and the army of intelligent mind-probing rats--seems to plunge us for the moment into a story line of almost supernatural cast. With the rats in particular we feel ourselves dangerously close to the transition from SF to fairy tale or fantasy literature in general, and visions of the Nutcracker or even the comic-book variety. (This new shift, incidentally, is proof of the immense gulf which separates SF from fantasy and which might therefore be described in terms of generic expectations.)

With the entry, in §3, of the explorers into the higher civilization of the Forwards area, Marapper's plot proves a failure, and once again a new generic expectation replaces the earlier one: with the enlargement of the focus, we find ourselves in the midst of a collective-catastrophe novel, for now we have a beleaguered society struggling for its life against real and imagined enemies--the Outsiders, the Giants, the rats, and the lower barbarians of the Deadways. Once again the generic shift is signalled by a change in our distance from Complain, who from a mere team member is promoted to romantic hero through his love affair with Vyann, one of the political leaders of the Forwards state. Our new proximity to and identification with Complain is reinforced by his discovery that the chieftain of the barbarian guerilla force is none other than his long-missing brother (a discovery which perhaps sets in motion minor generic expectations of its own, recalling last-minute denouements of the Hellenistic story a la Heliodorus, or family reunions in orphan or foundling plots, as in *Tom Jones* or *Cymbeline*).

At length, in the apocalyptic chaos with which the novel ends, the fires and melees, the invasion of the rats, the breakdown of the electrical system and impending destruction of the ship itself, we reach the twist ending already mentioned. Here the supernatural elements are, as it were reabsorbed into the SF (one is tempted to say, the realistic) plot structure, for we discover that the Giants and Outsiders actually exist and can be rationally explained. The mechanism of this final generic transformation is a physical enlargement of the context in which the action is taking place: for the first time the inner environment of the ship ceases to be the outer limit of our experience. The ship acquires an outer surface, and a position in outer space; what has hitherto been a complete world in its own right is now retransformed into an immense vessel floating within an even larger system of stable and external coordinates. At the same time, the very function of the ship is altered, for with the momentous final discovery, the endless, aimless journey through space proves to have been an illusion, and the inhabitants discover themselves to be in orbit around the Earth. It is an orbit that has been maintained for generations, so that the discovery returns upon the past to transform it as well and to turn the "tragic" history of the ship into a sort of grisly masquerade. So at length we learn that the main characters in the story, the characters with whom we have identified, are mutants administered "for their own good" by a scientific commission from Earth, a commission whose representatives the ship-dwellers have instinctively identified as Giants or Outsiders.

Thus in its final avatar, *Starship* is transformed, from a pseudo-cosmological adventure story of explorations within the strange world of the ship, to a *political fable* of man's manipulation of his fellow man. This ultimate genre to which the book is shown to belong leads our attention not into the immensities of interstellar space, but rather back to the human inte tions underlying the ghastly paternalism which was responsible for the incarceration within the ship, over so many generations, of the descendants of the original crew. If my reading is correct, the twist ending involved here is not simply the solution to a puzzle confronted unsuccessfully since the opening pages of the book; rather, the puzzle at the heart of the work is only now for the first time revealed, by being unwittingly solved.

This revelation has the effect of discrediting all our previous modes of reading, or generic expectations. Over and above the story of the characters and of the fate of the ship, one is tempted to posit the existence of a second plot or narrative line in that very different set of purely formal events which govern our reading: our groping and tentative efforts to identify, during the course of the reading, the type of book being read, and our ultimate solution to the puzzle with the discovery of its social or political character.

Such a description will not surprise anyone familiar with the aesthetics of modernism and aware of the degree to which modern writers in general have taken the artistic process itself as their "subject matter," assigning themselves the task of foregrounding, not the objects perceived, not the *content* of of the work, but rather the very act of aesthetic reception and perception. This is achieved on the whole by tampering with the perceptual apparatus or the frame, and the notion of generic discontinuity suggests that in *Starship* the basic story-line may be varied as much by shifts in our receptive stance as by internal modifications of the content. One recalls the well-known experiment, in the early days of Soviet film, in which a single shot of an actor's face seemed to express now joy, now irony, now hunger, now sadness, depending on the context developed by the shots with which it was juxtaposed. Indeed the very notion of generic expectation requires us to distinguish between the sense of the individual sentences and our assessment of the whole to which we assign them as parts and which dictates our interpretation of them (a process often described as the "hermeneutic circle"). Aldiss' *Starship* confirms such a notion by showing the results of a systematic variation and subversion of narrative context; and that such a structure is not merely an aesthetic freak, but stands rather in the mainstream of literary experimentation, may be demonstrated by a comparison with the structure of the French *nouveau roman*, and particularly with the stylistic and compositional devices of Alain Robbe-Grillet, whose work Aldiss has himself ranged in the SF category, speaking of *"L'Année dernière à Marienbad,* where the gilded hotel with its endless corridors--*énormes, sompteux, baroques, lugubres*--stands more vividly as a symbol of isolation from the currents of life than any spaceship, simply by virtue of being more dreadfully accessible to our imaginations."[5]

What Aldiss does not say is that such symbols are the end-product of a whole artistic method or procedure: in the narrative of Robbe-Grillet, for instance, our reading of the words is sapped at the very base: as the narrative eye crawls slowly along the contours of the objects so minutely described, we begin to feel a profound uncertainty as to the very possibilities of physical description through language.[6] Indeed, what happens is that the words remain the same while their referents shift without warning: the bare names of the objects are insufficient to convey the unique identity of a single time and place, and the reader is constantly forced to reevaluate the coordinates of the table, the rocking chair, the eraser in question, just as in Resnais' film the same events appear to take place over and over again, but at different times and in different settings. Such effects are quite different from what happens in dream or surrealist literature, where it is the object itself that is transformed before our eyes, and where the power of language to register the most grotesque metamorphoses is reaffirmed: thus in Ovid, language is called upon to express the well-nigh inexpressible and to articulate in all their fullness things that we doubt our real eyes could ever see. In the *nouveau roman*, on the contrary, and in those SF works related to it (e.g., the hallucinatory scenes in such Philip K. Dick novels as *The Three Stigmata of Palmer Eldritch*), it is the expressive capacity of words and names that is called into question and subverted, and this is not from within but from without, by imperceptible but momentous shifts in the context of the description.

Yet there is a way in which the characteristic material of SF enjoys a privileged relationship with such effects, which seem to be common to modernist literature in general. One would like to avoid, in this connection, a replay of the well-worn and tiresome controversies over literary realism. Perhaps it would be enough to suggest that, in so-called realistic works, the reference to some shared or "real" objective outside world serves the basic structural function of unifying the work from without. Whatever the heterogeneity of its materials, the unity of the "realistic" work is thus assured *a priori* by the unity of its referent. It follows then that when, as in SF, such a referent is abandoned, the fundamental formal problem posed by plot construction will be that of finding some new principle of unity. Of course, one way in which this can be achieved is by taking over some ready-made formal unity existing in the tradition itself, and this seems to be the path taken by so-called mythical SF, which finds a spurious comfort in the predetermined unity of the myth or legend which serves it as an organizational device. (This procedure goes back, of course, to Joyce's *Ulysses*, but I am tempted to claim that the incomparable greatness of this literary predecessor comes from its *incomplete* use of myth: Joyce lets us see that the "myth" is nothing but an organizational device, and his subject is not some fictive unity of experience which the myth is supposed to guarantee, but rather that fragmentation of life in the modern world which called for reunification in the first place.)

Where the mythological solution is eschewed, there remains available to SF another organizational procedure which I will call *collage:* the bringing into precarious coexistence of elements drawn from very different sources and contexts, elements which derive for the most part from older literary models and which amount to broken fragments of the outworn older genres or of the newer productions of the media (e.g., comic strips). At its worst, collage results in a kind of desperate pasting together of whatever lies to hand; at its best, however, it operates a kind of foregrounding of the older generic models themselves, a kind of estrangement-effect practiced on our own generic receptivity. Something like this is what we have sought to describe in our reading of *Starship*.

But the arbitrariness of collage as a form has the further result of intensifying, and indeed transforming, the structural function of the author himself, who is now felt to be the supreme source and origin of whatever unity can be maintained in the work. The reader then submits to the authority of the author in a rather different way than in the conventions of realistic narrative: it is, if you will, the difference between asking to be manipulated, and agreeing to pretend that no human agency is present in the first place.

It would be possible to show, I think (and here the works of Philip K. Dick would serve as the principal exhibits), that the thematic obsession, in SF, with manipulation as social phenomenon and nightmare all in one may be understood as a projection of the form of SF into its content. This is not to say that the theme of manipulation is not, given the kind of world we live in, eminently self-explanatory in terms of its own urgency, but only that there is a kind of privileged relationship, a pre-established harmony, between this theme and the literary structures which characterize SF. To restrict our generalization for the moment to *Starship* itself, it seems to me no accident that the fundamental social issue in a book in which the author toys with the reader, constantly shifting direction, baffling the latter's expectations, issuing false generic clues, and in general using his official plot as a pretext for the manipulation of the reader's reactions, should be the problem of the manipulation of man by other men. And with this we touch upon the point at which form and content, in *Starship*, become one, and at which the fundamental identity between the narrative structure previously analyzed, and the political problem raised by the book's ending, stands revealed.

That Mr. Aldiss is well aware of the ultimate political character of his novel is evident, not only from his Preface, but also from occasional reflections throughout the book. But it seems clear from his remarks that he understands his fable--which illustrates the disastrous effects of large-scale social decisions upon individual life--to have an anti-bureaucratic and anti-socialist thrust (bureaucracy being the way socialism is conceived by those it threatens). "Nothing," he tells us, "but the full flowering of a technological age, such as the Twenty-fourth Century knew, could have launched this miraculous ship; yet the miracle was sterile, cruel. Only a technological age could condemn unborn generations to exist in it, as if man were mere protoplasm, without emotion or aspiration." (§3:4). And his Preface underscores the point even further: "An idea, which is man-conceived, unlike most of the myriad effects which comprise our universe, is seldom balanced. . . . The idea, as ideas will, had gone wrong and gobbled up their real lives." We glimpse here the familiar outlines of that most influential of all counter-revolutionary positions, first and most fully worked out by Edmund Burke in his *Reflections on the French Revolution*, for which human reason, in its fundamental imperfection, is incapable of substituting itself and its own powers for the organic, natural growth of community and tradition. Such an ideology finds confirmation in the revolutionary Terror (itself generally, it should be added, a response of the revolution to external and internal threats), which thus appears as the humiliation of man's revolutionary *hubris*, of his presumption at usurping the place of nature and traditional authority.

But this reading by Mr. Aldiss of his own fable is not necessarily the only interpretation open to us. I would myself associate it rather with a whole group of SF narratives which explicitly or implicitly raise a political and social issue of a quite different kind, which may be characterized as belonging to the ethical problems of utopia, or to the political dilemmas of a future in which politics has once again become ethics. This issue turns essentially on *the right of advanced civilizations or cultures to intervene into the lower forms of social life with which they come into contact.* (The qualifications of higher and lower, or advanced and underdeveloped, are here clearly to be understood in a historical rather than a purely qualitative sense.) This problem has of course been a thematic concern of SF since its inception: witness H. G. Wells's *War of the Worlds,* patently a guilt fantasy on the part of Victorian man who wonders whether the brutality with which he has used the colonial peoples may not be visited on him by some more advanced race intent, in its turn, on his destruction. In our time, however, such a theme tends to be reformulated in positive terms that lend it a new originality. That the destruction of less advanced societies is wrong and inhuman is no longer, surely, a matter for intelligent debate. What is at issue is the degree to which even benign and well-intentioned intervention of higher into lower cultures may not be ultimately destructive in its results. Although the conventions of SF may dramatize this issue in terms of galactic encounters, the concern clearly has a very terrestrial source in the relations between industrialized and so-called underdeveloped societies of our own planet.

During the 1950s and early 1960s, a safe liberal anti-colonialism, analogous to the U.S. condemnation of the decaying British and French colonial empires, seems to have been quite fashionable in American SF. In one whole wing of it, interstellar law prohibiting the establishment of colonies on planets already inhabited by an intelligent species became an accepted convention. However, the full implications of this theme, with a few exceptions such as Ursula Le Guin's *The Left Hand of Darkness* (1969), were explored only in the SF written within socialist horizons, in particular in the works of Stanislaw Lem and in the Strugatsky Brothers' *It's Hard to be a God* (1964).[7] In Western SF, this theme is present mainly as a cliché or as an unconscious preoccupation, and manifests itself in peculiarly formalized ways. So I would suggest that visions of extragalactic intervention, such as Arthur C. Clarke's *Childhood's End*, belong in this category, as well as many of the intricate paradoxes of time travel, where the hero's unexpected appearance in the distant past arouses the fear that he may alter the course of history in such a way as to prevent himself from being born in the first place. In all these traits of Western SF one detects the presence, it seems to me, of a virtual *repression* of the ethico-political motif in question, although it should be made clear that it is a repression which SF shares with most cultural and artistic activities pursued in the West. Indeed, such unconscious concealment of the underlying socio-economic or material bases of life with a concomitant concentration on purely spiritual activities, is responsible for the ways of thinking which classical Marxist theory designates as *idealism*. It amounts to a refusal to connect existential or personal experience, the experience of our individual private life, with the system and suprapersonal organization of monopoly cpaitalism as an all-pervasive whole.

In the present instance--to restrict ourselves to that alone--it is our wilful ignorance of the inherent structural relationship between that economic system and the neo-colonialistic exploitation of the Third World which prevents any realistic view or concept of the correct relationship between two distinct national or social groupings. Thus we tend to think of the relations between countries in ethical terms, in terms of cruelty or philanthrophy, with the result that Western business investments come to appear to us as the bearers of progress and "development" in backward areas. The real questions--whether "progress" is desirable and if so which kind of progress, whether a country has the right to opt out of the international circuit, whether a more advanced country has the right to intervene, even benignly, in the historical evolution of a less advanced country; in sum, the general relationship between indigenous culture and industrialization--are historical and political in character. For our literature to be able to raise them, it would be necessary to ask ourselves a good many more probing and difficult questions about our own system than we are presently willing to do. I should add that this comparison between the formal capacities of Western and Soviet SF is not intended to imply that the Soviet Union has in any sense solved the above problems, but merely that for the Soviet Union such problems have arisen in an explicit and fully conscious, indeed agonizing fashion, and that it is from the experience of such dilemmas and contradictions that its best literature is being fashioned.

The thematic interest of *Starship* lies precisely in the approach of such a dilemma to the threshold of consciousness, in the way in which the theme of intercultural influence or manipulation is raised almost to explicit thematization. In this sense, it makes little difference whether the reader chooses to take Mr. Aldiss' own rather reactionary political interjections at face value, or to substitute for them the historical interpretation suggested above; the crucial fact remains that the political reemerges in the closing pages of the book. The structural inability of such material to stay buried, its irrepressible tendency to reveal itself in its most fundamental historical being, generically transforms the novel into that political fable which was latent in it all along, without our knowing it. So it is that en route to space and to galactic escapism, we find ourselves locked in the force field of very earthly political realities.

NOTES

[1]The British (and original) title of *Starship* is *Non-Stop*; the book *Orphans of the Sky* was published in book form in 1963.

[2]See Bertolt Brecht, *Brecht on Theatre*, ed. and tr. by John Willett (US 1964), especially pp191-93.

[3]Any reflection on genre today owes a debt--sometimes an unwilling one--to Northrop Frye's *Anatomy of Criticism* (1957); we should also mention, in the renewal of this field of study, the Chicago Neo-Aristotelians represented in R.S. Crane's anthology *Critics and Criticism* (1952). For a recent survey of recent theories, see Paul Hernadi, *Beyond Genre* (1972), and for the latest discussion of "generic expectations," E.D. Hirsch, Jr., *Validity in Interpretation* (1967). On SF as a genre, the essential statement is of course Darko Suvin's "On the Poetics of the Science Fiction Genre," *College English*, December 1972; while the seminal investigation of the relationship between genre and social experience remains that of Georg Lukács (see for example his *Writer and Critic* [1970], and *The Historical Novel* [new edn 1969], or for a more general discussion, my "Case for Georg Lukács," in *Marxism and Form* [1972].

[4]Published in US as *The Long Afternoon of Earth*.

[5]Harry Harrison and Brian W. Aldiss, eds., *Best SF: 1969* (US 1970), p217.

[6]I have discussed this phenomenon from a different point of view in "Seriality in Modern Literature," *Bucknell Review*, Spring 1970.

[7]This is a working hypothesis only, since the basic thematic spadework--as in so many other aspects of SF--has not yet been done. A bibliography of such writings should be compiled as a first step toward further investigation.

Sunken Atlantis and the Utopia Question:
Parry's *The Scarlet Empire* and Coblentz's *The Sunken World*

(from SFS *1:290 - 297, Fall 1974)*

C.R. LA BOSSIERE. *THE SCARLET EMPIRE*: TWO VISIONS IN ONE

Oscar Wilde's well-known pronouncement—"A map of the world that does not include Utopia is not even worth glancing at, for it leaves out the one country at which Humanity is always landing. And when Humanity lands there, it looks out, and seeing a better world, sets sail. Progress is the realization of Utopias."—with its glaring *non sequitur* and *petitio principii*, provides many students of 20th-century utopian (i.e., in the main, dystopian) literature with final-chapter hope. Dystopias, it would appear, leave too little hope. D-503's return to equations and obedience in *We*, Winston's abdication to terror in *1984*, the Savage's suicide in *Brave New World*, the inanity of the Pelphase and the cannibalism of the Gusphase in *The Wanting Seed*, and the apparent inevitability of *fiat voluntas tua* in *A Canticle for Leibowitz*, do not satisfy the evidently continuing need for a vision of earthly perfection. It is indeed difficult to have one's cake and eat it too. As Dostoevski reminds us, bread and freedom are incompatible. An analogous and immediately related problem exists in utopian literary criticism. No one, I think, would deny that *Huckleberry Finn*, *The Time Machine*, and *Major Barbara* are, as works of the literary imagination, clearly superior to *The Strange Republic of Bangour*, *A Modern Utopia*, and *Back to Methuselah*, respectively. The reason is quite simple: forms in blueprints of ideal states lack any appreciable individuation. Utopias tend to argue discursively: dystopias, to argue movingly. *News from Nowhere* appears to be the sole significant exception in the past hundred years, largely because its vision incorporates the mythical-romantic view of man, with its emphasis on the life of the imagination. Infrequently do we recognize in visions of earthly perfection any "real" individuals; characters tend to be either diaphanous or merely argumentative, forms who little resemble men and women as we know them. And yet, J.C. Garrett, having underlined the dangers inherent in utopianism, and having mentioned the dubious literary merit of *Looking Backward* and *Walden II*, the two most influential literary utopias ever written in the United States, concludes his *Utopias in Literature Since the Romantic Period* (Christchurch 1968) on this note: "The Utopian dream is as old as mankind; it is unlikely to die as long as men yearn for a better world." Mustapha Mond proves a more perceptive and persistent critic when he argues that Shakespeare has no place in man's earthly paradise.

    An explicitly optimistic dystopia, it would seem, would satisfy all needs. In such a work the author would avail himself of the resources of the satirist, but would at the same time present a vision of perfection: Bellamy inverted and turned novelist. Such a work would score attempts to reduce men to robots, but would at the same time present a permanently stable world of free and creative individuals dedicated to self-fulfillment and progress. David McLean Parry's *The Scarlet Empire* (1906) is a rare attempt to fuse the two visions; his areas of success and his areas of failure in this work are symptomatic.

The story begins with an unsuccessful suicide attempt by an avid young socialist. Man's inhumanity to man crushes him; "possessed with bitterness," he leaps from a pier. Through the intervention of 713, the young man suddenly finds himself in the Social Democracy of Atlantis, the Scarlet Empire. He is elated: "A social democracy—exactly what I have been dreaming of for years!" Here all men, he is told, are treated equally. No more than a few minutes pass, however, before the hero begins to suspect that this state may not be exactly what he had hoped for: 713 informs him that all citizens of Atlantis must carry a "verbometer," a device ensuring that no citizen excedes his daily word-quota. Physicians, he learns soon after, much to his chagrin, are incompetent; diagnosis and medication are by numbers. Gradually he discovers that the people of Atlantis have also been reduced to numbers. The government is dedicated to concretizing the metaphor "all men are created equal": the tall must marry the short, the beautiful the ugly, the yound the old, the intelligent the stupid. Everyone wears the prescribed garb, and eats the same portions of the same food at the same time. Any deviation incurs swift and severe punishment. Selected by lot for the legislature, the hero maliciously pursues this logic by proposing that all citizens chew their food the same number of times, and that all walk at the same pace. Abundant supplies of "lethe-weed" keep the people content with their drab existence. The state persecutes all "atavars," throwbacks to primitive individualism; and yet, as the hero eventually learns, the state itself is controlled by a clique of atavars—a deformed dwarf, a disgusting hag, and two equally repulsive colleagues. Periodic public executions satisfy the citizens' occasional lust for excitement, and serve to keep them in a state of fear-induced conformity.

Zamiatin, Orwell, and Huxley have presented us with similar nightmares, reductions to absurdity of utopian dreams. Prescience alone, however, does not make for literary excellence. The atavars in control of the Scarlet Empire are relatively powerful characters, as grotesque, as insidious, as cunning as Quilp, Fagin, and Madame Defarge (a citizen who has the temerity to ask for a second portion of food is likened by the narrator to Oliver Twist). The hag, proud of her ugliness, allows the ingenuous hero, whom she suspects of political subversion, to ensnare himself in his own passions. She carefully notes his reactions at the trial of a beautiful atavar, places temptation in his path, and waits patiently. The dwarf, equally suspicious, offers a share of political power, hoping to damn him through either acceptance or refusal. The hero and his beloved Astraea, the atavar he had seen at the trial, fade in comparison: they are mere collages of ideal qualities, recipes for perfection. He is the archetypal Yankee individualist, honest, strong, resourceful, kind to his friends, ruthless to his enemies, courageous, and appreciative of the merits of gunpowder and six-gun. She is the ravishingly beautiful maid, obedient to her man, tender, and helpless. Without knowing it, Parry was of the party of the dwarf and hag (Bonario and Cecilia seem transparent next to Volpone and Mosca). In the end the hero shoots his way out; and, accompanied by Astraea, 713, and a doctor befriended early in the story, returns to the surface via a submarine filled with treasure stolen from a museum. A stray torpedo smashes through the barrier that holds back the sea, and thus ends the nightmare.

Whatever merit as literature this novel possesses lies in its satire; its affirmation is downright naive. The urge to project patterns of earthly perfection seems to mitigate against wit, complexity, and individuation. In the conclusion of *The Scarlet Empire*, the utopian theme emerges clearly: perfection exists here and now in the 1906 USA. The hero, who has recounted his adventures and conversion for our edification, informs us that after his escape he, Astraea, and their companions fulfilled themselves completely: he as a wealthy industrialist and philanthropist (the loot from Atlantis proved useful); Astraea as his mate, a perfect wife, hostess, and mother; 713 as an "ultra individualist" and eminent doctor of medicine; and the other doctor as a brilliant researcher-entrepreneur dedicated to the progress of mankind. All enjoyed peace, happiness, wealth, and civil liberties in the land of capitalism and progress—a satisfying conclusion for a writer who had parlayed a small hardware business into a factory employing 2800 men in 1904, and who had been elected president of the National Association of Manufacturers in 1902.

The greatest good for the greatest number may appear a reasonable and attractive doctrine, but, one suspects, only to those who belong to the greatest number. Meritorious writers and their creations have always been unfortunately few. Parry, insofar as he is a utopian, would have us believe he is of the majority; he and critics who would have worthwhile books of the literary imagination *and* utopia prove less consistent philosophers and less perceptive critics than the Grand Inquisitor and Mustapha Mond. The following lines from Cousin-Jacques' *Nicodème dans la lune*, a play performed in Paris in 1790-91, might be adapted to serve as an epilogue to *The Scarlet Empire*: "Tous ceux qui n's'ront pas contens/ En France d'leux fortune:/ Afin d'mieux leur temps,/ Pourront v'nir avec moi dans la lune."

R.D. MULLEN. *THE SUNKEN WORLD*: ALSO TWO VISIONS IN ONE

Stanton A. Coblentz's *The Sunken World* (*Amazing Stories Quarterly*, Summer 1928; book form 1949) resembles, contrasts with, and presumably derives from *The Scarlet Empire*. Coblentz's sunken Atlantis fascinated me so greatly when I first read the story at 13 that I have never forgotten it. Having reread it, I still find it interesting and only wish that the author's command of language and understanding of thought, character, nature, and plot had been sufficient for him to have realized his purposes more fully. My intention here is to argue briefly against the widespread notion presented so vigorously above by Professor La Bossiere, the notion that it is simply not possible to write utopias that are comparable to dystopias in literary distinction or even in ordinary SF interest. My method will be the comparison of the two books in their treatment of diction, thought, character (differences between things of the same species), nature (differences between species), and plot, in an effort to show that Coblentz's novel is superior to Parry's and that its superiority has nothing to do with the fact that it is a utopia and Parry's novel a dystopia.

The two are like each other, like most SF novels, and indeed like most fiction of any kind in being quite undistinguished in diction. Except for a few stabs at lower-class dialect by Coblentz, no appreciable effort is made in either book to distinguish the language of one person from that of another or even to differentiate conversational dialogue from the running narrative of the protagonist-narrator. Since neither author is a master of language, neither is able to render either thought or character with any precision or vividness.

What we get in the way of thought consists simply of conventional arguments—for or against socialism, for or against capitalism, for or against the concept of man as inherently indolent, etc. The rendering of character is equally crude: in Parry's story the hero and heroine and their two allies are good by definition since they seek to escape the oppression of the bad people, of whom some are bad in that they manipulate the law in their efforts to victimize heroine and hero while others are bad merely in that they abide by and seek to enforce the foolish laws of a foolish society; in Coblentz' story there are no good-bad distinctions, the conflicts being intellectual and comic rather than moral and melodramatic.

We are thus left, as we are in nearly all SF novels, with matters of nature and plot. In both novels the physical environment differs so greatly from our own—or from that of the authors—that it must be said to be a difference in nature rather than in character. We have in each story a world that sank beneath the sea 3000 years ago but that somehow survived with roofs and walls that hold back the water and with sources of light, heat, and air that replace the sun and the atmosphere. In *The Scarlet Empire* the survival was accidental in a way that is never adequately explained: "these gigantic columns which you admire so much are the petrified forests of the Garden of Eden. You cannot see their branches here below, but if you could ascend...you would find that great limbs spread out in all directions, supporting a dome which seems a mass of foliage and mineral matter impervious to water" (§7). In *The Sunken World* the submergence was planned: a dome of glass was constructed over a large area and "intra-atomic heat" was used "to sink the whole island to the bottom of the sea" (§12). Each of the narrators is taken on a tour of the enclosed world, but whereas the Coblentz world is described in considerable detail, the Parry world is hardly described at all: *The Sunken World* is thus a more rewarding novel than *The Scarlet Empire* on the basis of the interest that science-fiction readers take in the attributes of any imaginary world.

In each book the political and socioeconomic environment also differs in nature from our own (i.e., the United States of 1903, 1928, or 1974) in that it is socialist and equalitarian rather than capitalist and graded, and in character if not in nature from modern socialist states in that the equality has a completeness far beyond anything known in our world: in Coblentz the Atlanteans live in comfort and plenty supplied by two hours of work a day, and devote their leisure to artistic and intellectual endeavors; in Parry they live in abject poverty, with four-fifths of the people working fifteen hours a day under whips wielded by the other fifth, who are not much better off since they must wield the whips for the same fifteen hours, must eat the same food, etc., and even the members of what Professor La Bossière calls the ruling clique gain only venial rewards by their rule. The government of Coblentz's utopia is a direct democracy (the population being held at 500,000 to make this possible), with the few administrators being chosen by examination; the government of Parry's dystopia is representative democracy, with legislators and administrators being chosen and all work-assignments (including the wielding or the working under the whips) being made by lot. Although neither novel gives us anything more than the banalities of routine utopian/dystopian exposition, Coblentz's world is again detailed with greater fullness and coherence and therefore is superior in ordinary SF interest—or, to say it in a different way, would surely be of much greater interest to any bright 12-year-old just becoming aware of utopian/dystopian possibilities.

Finally, there *should* be in each novel a spiritual environment resulting from the isolation of the society from the rest of humanity, but only Coblentz makes anything of this, Parry being content to attribute all the evils of his Atlantis simply to socialism. The utopian Atlantis came into being as a result of the decision of the Atlanteans that they could create and maintain a just society only if they isolated themselves from the wicked world, but now after 3000 years the political parties of utopian Atlantis include an Industrial Reform Party, a Party of Artistic Emancipation, a Party of Birth Extension, and even a Party of Emergence whose members argue that although the plans of the founders were almost perfect, they were deficient in that they "did not leave room enough in Atlantis for adventure" (§§22-23). In sum, Coblentz' story is superior to Parry's in that whereas the latter is simplistic enough for its dystopia to be perfectly bad, the former is sufficiently complex for its utopia not to be perfectly good.

Both novels are somewhat incoherent in plot. (In the analysis used here, plot is defined as the interaction of protagonist and environment, with the environment of the protagonist including the personal [his friends and enemies], the sociocultural, the sociophysical, the geophysical, or whatever, and with the organizing principle of the plot being a change in the thought, character, or nature of the protagonist or environment, or in their relationship.) *The Scarlet Empire* begins with a change-in-thought plot, but our hero has already learned his lesson by the end of §6, whereupon the plot of §§7-41 becomes one of melodramatic adventure in which our hero rescues a maiden in distress, wins her love, plunders a museum of great wealth (pagan temples in unenlightened lands being fair game for enlightened adventurers from the civilized world), shoots his way free, destroys his enemy (some five million people), and escapes to happiness ever after as a rich man with a beautiful and adoring wife in the best of worlds, the USA. Having said all this in full agreement with Professor La Bossiere's statement that Parry's "affirmation is downright naive," we must add that there is an ugly development in the character of the protagonist—who goes from simple greed at the sight of the jewels stored in the museum (§11) to the self-righteousness of declaring that the five million people killed by a torpedo from his submarine were "overwhelmed by the wrath of God," were a "nation that through its worship of Social Equality went down to destruction" (§41)—a development which is probably merely a reflection of the naive self-righteousness of the author but which might possibly be read as the overall plot of a novel that has self-righteous robber-baron greed as its ultimate object of satire.

In §§1-14 of *The Sunken World* the plot seems to center on a conflict between the narrator and his commanding officer for the leadership of the crew of submariners who have accidentally arrived in a country which they are told they will never be permitted to leave, but from §15 on the commander and crew simply cease to figure in any important way in the story. Forced to back up and start over, we find that in §§11-32 the story is concerned chiefly with the inability of the obtuse narrator to grasp the realities of his sociocultural environment, and with the resulting foolishness of his behavior. From the beautiful Aelios, who serves as his cicerone and as the expounder of Atlantean orthodoxy, he learns that in the centuries before the submergence, the Atlanteans applied themselves less and less to "the pursuit of the beautiful" and more and more to "construction of huge and intricate machines, of towering but unsightly piles of masonry, of swift means of locomotion, and of unique and elaborate systems of amusement," and that with their "lightning means of travel and lightning weapons of aggression" they "began to swoop down occasionally upon a foreign coast, picking a quarrel with the people and finding some excuse for smiting thousands dead." But of the Atlanteans, "not all...were savages, and not all approved of [the] policy of international murder," and so an "Anti-Mechanism" party of beauty-lovers arose to argue that Atlantis's "best human material was being used up and cast aside like so much straw," that "its best social energies were being diverted into wasteful and even poisonous channels," that "its too-rapid scientific progress was imposing a wrenching strain upon the civilized mind and institutions," and that there was "only one remedy, other than the natural one of oblivion and death, and that remedy was in a complete metamorphosis, a change such as the caterpillar undergoes when it enters the chrysalis, a transformation into an environment of such repose that society might have time to recover from its overgrowth and to evolve along quiet and peaceful lines" (§13).

But the fact that he is in a society that has achieved and abjured a triumph over nature, that has renounced the pursuit of power and glory, and that has isolated itself from the rest of the world so that it might follow the ways of peace and art, does not prevent our hero from continuing to assume the universal validity of the values of his own world. And so at the first opportunity he rises in a public assembly to deny that he and his companions are the "barbarians" the Atlanteans take them to be, and to claim that they are instead "representatives of the highest of modern civilizations":

> My description of the growth and attainments of the modern world was listened to with interest, but with a lack of comprehension that I thought almost idiotic. Thus when I declared that the United States was a leading nation because of its population of a hundred million, its rare inventions and its prolific manufactures, my hearers merely looked blank and asked how the country ranked in art; and when I stated (what is surely self-evident to all patriotic Americans) that New York is the greatest city on earth because of its tall buildings and its capacity for housing a million human beings in one square mile, my audience regarded me with something akin to horror, and one of the men—evidently a dolt, for he seemed quite serious—asked whether no steps had been taken to abolish the evil.
>
> But it was when describing my own career that I was most grievously misunderstood. Had I confessed to murder, the people could not have been more shocked than when I mentioned that I was one of the crew commissioned to ram and destroy other ships; and I felt that my prestige was ruined beyond repair when I stated that I had entered the war voluntarily. (§13)

There are a number of incidents that illustrate the obtuseness of our hero, but since we have heard it all before, in Brobdingnag and Houyhnhnmsland, we can content ourselves with three examples. At the annual Pageant of the Good Destruction, where films are shown of pre-Submergence Atlantis (films that cause one of his companions to exclaim, "By the holy father, if we're not back in the old U.S.A.!"), he muses to himself that he "had never known anything quite so ugly as the scenes we now witnessed" (§15). When he has completed the course of study that qualifies him for citizenship, and has been made the Official Historian of the Upper World, he sets himself to write "a grand resume of modern achievement...to show the steps by which that achievement had been consummated, and to picture in general the course of those social fluctuations, those invasions, battles, slave-raids, civil conflicts, religious persecutions, crusades, economic revolutions, industrial tumults and international blood-feuds that had brought civilization to its present high estate" (§25). And when he sees in a museum a display of weapons used by the Atlanteans in their war-making days, he exults "at the proof of or superiority:...the bayonets were fully half a foot shorter than our own; the machine guns...had obviously not half the killing capacity of ours," etc. (§26).

But although this conflict between protagonist and environment gives us the utopian dual vision by opposing Atlantis to the United States (with our twin, ancient Atlantis), it does not develop as a plot but instead merely runs on an even course until it peters out in what can hardly be called a climax but must still serve as the only evidence of any change of thought in the protagonist: when attempting to write on "Social Traditions and Institutions in the Upper World" he finds that the "the further I proceeded the harder the work became, for the more I learned of Atlantis the more difficult it appeared to represent the earth in a light that was not merely pitiable" (§33).

Our second plot having faded away, we must once again back up and start over. That our hero is an unreliable narrator is obvious from the beginning, and near the end of §22 we learn with disconcerting suddenness what should have been made evident by diction but was not: that the beautiful Aelios is also unreliable, for if happiness and freedom were as complete in Atlantis as she claims, there would surely be no need for such political organizations as the Industrial Reform Party, the Party of Artistic Emancipation, the Party of Birth Extension, and the Party of Emergence. It soon becomes obvious that this incident, together with the following chapter (in which our hero is instructed in the principles of the Party of Emergence by its leader, a "fiery spirit, audacious thinker, and trustworthy friend"), is a prelude to the concluding action of the novel (§§27-35), in which the people of Atlantis assume the role of protagonist.

The appearance of a crack in the great dome shatters the calm of the people of Atlantis: "most of them [were] so transformed that I could hardly recognize them as citizens of the Sunken World; for they were chattering wildly, or pacing distractedly back and forth, or uttering half-hysterical exclamations; and one or two of them were muttering or mumbling to themselves, or moving their lips silently in what might have been prayer" (§27). The crack is soon repaired to the complete satisfaction of the majority of the committee of scientists and engineers assigned to the problem, and calm returns. One member of the committee submits a minority report holding that the repairs will prove adequate for only five or six years, and urging "the immediate erection of a new glass bulwark against the affected portion of the wall," which can probably be completed in time, "prodigious though the effort will necessarily be," but the other members of the committee testify at length on "the scientific unsoundness of Peliades' theories," and disprove "his views to their own satisfaction and that of the people" (§28). Even so, the Party of Emergence wins many new supporters for its policy of allowing a portion of the population to emigrate to the surface, and seems to be headed for victory in a referendum on the matter until the publication of our hero's *History of the Upper World* turns the entire country against making any contact with the barbarians of the upper world (§§29-31). And so for six years the unadventurous descendants of the builders of the great dome do nothing whatever to ensure that it will continue to make life possible in their enclosed and isolated world, and make no plans for escape if the dome should fail—as fail it does (§§32-35).

TO THE BEST of my no doubt limited knowledge in this field, no utopographer has ever defined utopias as either "perfect" worlds or "permanently stable" worlds; this strawman is the creation of those who deride any belief in the possibility of improving the human condition. Since the utopian world, even though much more nearly perfect than our own, is still imperfect, there is room in it for conflict of various kinds and hence for the kinds of action portrayed in plotted as opposed to simply expository fiction. Just as we find in dystopian fiction a conflict between protagonist and environment in which the protagonist is in the right, so we would expect to find in utopian fiction a conflict in which the protagonist is in the wrong or a conflict which tests the strength of the society—and such conflicts we do find in *The Sunken World*, even though they are poorly handled. My proposition in this essay has been that it is quite possible to write utopian novels of literary distinction or, at least, of considerable SF interest. When I began writing it seemed necessary to argue the proposition in the abstract, but that is no longer necessary (and this essay may have lost its purpose), for the proposition has been triumphantly demonstrated by Ursula K. Le Guin in her 1974 novel, *The Dispossessed*.

An Exchange on Marxism
(And Other Things)

FRANZ ROTTENSTEINER. ON AN ESSAY BY JAMES BLISH

(from SFS *1:84 - 98, Fall 1973)*

In the essay "Future Recall"[1] James Blish is playing the old game of finding a function for SF. He quite rightly demolishes some of its claims:

> Thus far then, I have said that science fiction is not notably prophetic; that it is not educational in the usual sense; that it is steadily writing itself out of the business of suggesting inventions, or careers in science; and that even the free-wheeling speculation which used to be its exclusive province can now be found in many other places, including the pages of *Nature*. I have only to add that even as fiction most of it is poor--and it will appear that I have pulled the rug out from under the genre entirely.

But not so, continues Mr. Blish, for SF is the literature of change. It "attempts to help us prepare for the changes" that the real world is undergoing. Now as we know, "change" is the *om mani padme hum* in the prayer mills of SF authors, repeated there *ad nauseam*. Perhaps we need to look at some principal considerations.

How can change be shown in literature? In two ways: by static contrast, or as a dynamic process. The second way, of course, is the more difficult and intellectually the more sophisticated. Therefore most SF is conspicuously silent concerning the rules that govern and motivate change, and offers only the cliché of the "progress of science and technology" instead of useful analyses. When SF attempts to show motivations, it falls hopelessly behind the theoretical level achieved by contemporary philosophical and sociological thought on the subject. When sociologists have written about SF, they have mostly diagnosed its static, conservative nature.

Therefore most SF shows change by way of contrast; another strange and alien world is presented; some other time, space and society, with nothing to explain how these worlds came about. The reader can only accept the premises of such stories. But then SF does only what any historical novel or any "mainstream" book from another era does. And while it is true that "mainstream" fiction does not emphasize change, a sampling of world literature makes it quite obvious that the world is changing and has always been changing, at least in the field of social attitudes, cultural norms and mores, and so on. One of the major themes of literature is the struggle between generations, between the old and the young, because the old can no longer understand the quite different views of the young. But you don't find this conflict in SF (e.g. Heinlein depicts different, but quite static societies, where children believe exactly what their daddies tell them, with no back-chat), nor character development. In SF there can be no development of character, because there are no characters. If a "character's" ideas change, then we are forced to believe in miracles, since we are shown no other psychological motivation.

But I have still not looked at the main question about the "therapeutic" value of SF as postulated by Blish. Are readers of SF really better equipped to face change than the people who refuse to read the stuff? What really can ESP powers, feudal societies, time travel, worlds in the atom, intelligent robots, invaders or monsters from space, and all the other paraphernalia and worn-out gambits of SF, contribute to our preparation for the future? Anyone who reads contemporary SF to help him survive in the future would, to put it mildly, be wasting his time. After reading widely in SF, the disinterested observer will find a total innocence of SF writers as far as real problems and likely developments of the future are concerned. He will find that the "changes" SF envisions bear no relationship whatever to the real course of the world, as they are only resurrections of old clichés, dead modes of life, dim myths and popular superstitions firmly rooted in the subconscious of mass-man. SF is not a branch of epistemological fiction, but a new kind of opium for the people, offering wish-fulfillment instead of cognition.

The best indicator of the intellectual degradation of English-language SF and its resistance to radical and real change can perhaps be found in its attitude or rather silence towards Marxism. It must make you think when you realize that no American or English author has written a story that would endorse a Marxist view of change, or at least contain an intelligent discussion of it. Now those authors would probably all claim that they consider Marxism to be wrong. However, rightness and wrongness is irrelevant in this context, for SF authors endorse views or incorporate views into their stories that most certainly are wrong: the Bates method of eye-training, for instance, dianetics, the tarot, or astrology. Even on statistical expectations, one would expect at least a few authors to be familiar with socialism. For Americans, Marxism is probably a most alien system of thought, therefore those authors who say they describe change and other possible societies should leap upon Marxism as an example of radical change. That they don't recognize this direction of thought is a clear indication of their conservatism. Also, wrong or not, Marxism is one of the most important philosophical and economic systems of our time, the official doctrine of millions of this planet's inhabitants, the hope of several hundred million more in the undeveloped countries, and it is heatedly discussed by intellectuals all over the world. It just isn't possible to dismiss such a system out of hand, even if you consider it wrong, for it will certainly help to shape the future. The main difference between the ready acceptance of crank theories by SF and its neglect of socialism seems to be this: the more banal a system is, the more easily it can be assimilated and digested by trivial fiction. An example: note the crusade-like manner in which even the most trifling stylistic innovations are quarreled about by the fans. This seems to show that SF readers are ill-equipped to realize the various claims for their acceptance of "change." For when they react so violently to such unimportant matters, how will they react to changes involving their personal lives?

To sum up: to stress change is but a fairly useless cliché. It is far more important to look at the specific qualities of change, and this SF does not do. For in the future we will find no galactic races offering gifts to us; no talking human-like robots; no "spindizzies" with the physical properties of flying carpets, but lacking their charm; there will be neither time-travel nor extrasensory perception; and Poul Anderson's naive belief in the fine art of fencing won't help anyone.

There is another point which Mr. Blish should have considered, but did not touch upon: why must SF be a fiction of change? With so many popular journals, newspapers, books of futurology, and so on, to tell you about change, how does SF justify itself, especially as the other media reach a much wider audience than SF, and are much more precise in their descriptions of change?

JAMES BLISH. A REPLY TO MR. ROTTENSTEINER

Having first read Mr. Rottensteiner's review in *Quarber Merkur* filtered through my bare acquaintance with his beautiful native language, and now having read it again in his better command of mine, I must admit at the outset that I can still only guess at his objections to my essay. There seems to me to be two: (1) he does not agree that SF is "the literature of change"; and (2) he thinks that SF in the West ought to pay more attention to Marxism.

(1) The fact, which he points out, that I did not invent the notion that SF uniquely prepares the reader for our present situation of almost exponential change is an *ad hominem* argument which may be dismissed forthwith as such. I never claimed I did; moreover, many people have stated it better than I have, and I have made some attempts since 1969, when I wrote the essay he attacks, at qualifying it and setting limits upon it which apparently have not come to his attention. All that matters here is that I still subscribe to it and that I think his case against it is flabby.

I so think because he uses "literature" in two senses without allowing that there is any difference between them. One of these senses allows the term to cover any published work of substance, including works in philosophy, sociology, popular journals, newspapers and now futurology (not a collection I would lump under "works of substance," but since he implies that he does, I take it as read). In this sense, it's not difficult to recognize that there are only a few great minds, and that the followers of each derive, dilute, break up into small schools, and eventually disappear into niggling, feuding little brackish backwaters of no importance whatsoever to the history of thought or the life of the mind. I adduce Freud; he wrote not one word that I admire except aesthetically, yet it should be easy to see that, whether one agrees with him or not, his whole scholium goes downhill from him and follows the natural history of the degeneration of an original idea to the inevitable useless quibbling within a pack of doctrinaire idiots. I further adduce such other marvels as Plato,

Christ, Duns Scotus, Roger Bacon, Hume, Berkeley, Nietzsche, Marx, Spengler, Pareto, and Wittgenstein; Mr. Rottensteiner will have his own pick of pernicious thinkers among these, as I have mine, but neither of us' will find it difficult to see that every one has had no followers who haven't been lesser men than they were.

In the second sense, "literature" is limited to the world of poetry, drama, fiction and various secondary arts such as criticism. Those who enjoy and value this do so because it supplies them with a number of things not obtainable from works of philosophy or sociology. It is to this world that SF belongs. One of the things *good* SF does is to show how given individual human beings might react to a postulated environmental (including social and technological) change. I will grant that not many SF stories actually do this, and still fewer do it well, but this is simply to grant that most SF also is bad, which has no bearing on the main argument. Contrary to Mr. Rottensteiner's sweeping dismissal, there are some good examples, and their existence shows that the possibility of doing it is inherent in the medium. The improbability of most of the postulated changes is another side-issue, first because it's impossible to weigh them -- the world I live in now would have seemed an almost solid mass of improbabilities to the one I was born in half a century ago -- and second because we are not talking about any specified proposed changes, but the process of change itself.

(2) It has always been my impression that Marxism had a deep and visible influence upon the work of Olaf Stapledon, to cite one English-language SF author Mr. Rottensteiner's other blanket dismissal cannot sweep away. In America in the 1930's quite a number of SF authors were sympathetic toward socialism, and one group in New York City, the Futurian Society, was formed exclusively for those who were either actual members of the Communist Party or espoused the Party's policies. Later, the barriers were lowered a little to admit Trotskyites as well as Stalinists. The aim of this group, proclaimed publicly at a World-Con by John B. Michel with a pamphlet to back him up, was to use SF to help bring about what they believed to be *the* future. They wrote and published SF stories with this intent. The stories were bad, which is doubtless why Mr. Rottensteiner has never encountered them -- even I, who knew all the authors at the time and read the stories, can't cite any of the titles from memory--but they did endorse the Marxist view of change, or whatever version of it the American CP was wedded to at the time, so Mr. Rottensteiner's "statistical expectations" are in fact satisfied. And of course the badness of the stories was the fault of the authors, not of the subject, for good SF stories with socialist assumptions also exist; that these assumptions found their way only into bad stories in the U.S.A. is unfortunate, but again, irrelevant. Contrary to Mr. Rottensteiner's statement, they exist, which should be quite enough to "make you think" twice.[2]

In my opinion, the minor (*not* non-existent) role Marxism has played in English-language SF may be due to the very fact he cites, that it is "the official doctrine of millions of this planet's inhabitants." Nazism was the official doctrine of (fewer) millions for a while, and while some tags and attitudes of Fascism have popped up, sometimes fairly consistently, in the works of some English-language authors, only one, M. P. Shiel, can in fairness be described as espousing the Nazi version of it (before the

Nazis were in power), and it's equally unfortunate from a non-literary point of view that as a novelist he is quite as good as Stapledon; and I can think of only two American stories, both good,[3] that adopted Fascist economic theory. We may be tempted to attribute this dearth to human decency, but then we might well use the same point against Stalinism. It seems to me far more likely that most SF writers in the West are fundamentally antipathetic toward "official doctrine" no matter what form it takes, and when they have made any use of it at all, it has been as material for satire. We do not, in fact, like closed systems of any sort, and if we use them, do so only for the sake of the story in hand. Let us take one of the most conspicuous examples, A. E. van Vogt. He has adopted Spengler, Nietzsche, Bates, Korzybski, Graves and both halves of Hubbard (and I may have missed a few others), and unless I completely mistake Mr. Rottensteiner, the latter cannot believe that there is anything good to be said for any of these theorists; and with various reservations, a few of which are serious, I would agree with him. But what is much more important is that all of these untenable, antithetical or just plain ill-understood assumptions have been advocated by *a single author* (restlessness within closed systems), and that every one of these source-authors, though one of them is not banal and has influenced millions and another is the simplest kind of crank, is a would-be revolutionary (antipathy to "official doctrine"). Though we may be detected carrying placards now and then, most of us find the posture acutely uncomfortable, as most writers of any sort of fiction do, and should; and as writers whose fundamental sympathy lies with continuous and unexpected change, we would find ourselves drowned out if we got trapped into beating the same drum over and over again. In SF, no notion, not even Bates eye-exercises, is so monstrously trivial as having a mind closed to all ideas but one, no matter how important and complex that one may be. A failure to understand this implies incomprehension of *any* sort of creative enterprise.

I may not believe a word of this tomorrow. This would surprise me, but it would also please me.

URSULA K. LE GUIN. SURVEYING THE BATTLEFIELD

In attacking the achievements and potentialities of SF as he does, Mr Rottensteiner is in a very strong position. The massed armies of Lit. Crit. are behind him; he has enlisted the storm-troops of Futurology; he holds all the advantage of the ground, of strategy, and of recognized legitimacy. Mr. Blish, speaking for a ragged crew of dissidents, very few of whom are even willing to be represented by him, their main concern being quarrelling with one another, stands on the shakiest ground, and with resolute gallantry defends the all but indefensible.

It is only too easy for a bystander (like Pierre at Borodino) to point out the weaknesses in Mr. Blish's arguments. If, for all Marxist influence in any lasting or meaningful sense in English-language SF, one can point *only* to Stapledon--scarcely an orthodox Marxist!--perhaps that point were better conceded altogether. If one reduces all philosophy, theology, social thought, etc. to the works of "a few great minds" and a mess of squabbles among their "doctrinaire idiot" followers, perhaps it were better not to mention these topics at all. On these issues, it almost seems that Mr. Blish seeks deliberately to make his position more untenable than it already is.

But what does our Napoleon, Mr. Rottensteiner, do? How does he deploy his magnificent artillery? With wonderful consistency: He spikes every gun he's got.

The technique is familiar. With, ummistakably, the purest motives, the most earnest, honest admiration, Mr. Rottensteiner has done more to build up antipathy towards his friend Stanislaw Lem among English-speaking readers, these past couple of years, than Lem's worst enemy could have done. He has overpraised Lem, oversold him, used him to make invidious and otiose comparisons, translated his difficult, vigorous, genial style into pedantic, ham-handed English, and in short done everything possible to make his books disliked before they are read. Fortunately, Lem is so very good a writer that his works, as they appear in English, will survive this introduction. Nothing can hold a talent like that down; but Mr. Rottensteiner, with the best intentions in the world, has certainly tried. And in this essay, he's at it again.

Personally, I agree with most of his main points: and, having read them as he states them, am ready to deny them all categorically. I think that if I was told in this tone of voice that energy equals mass times the square of the velocity of light, I would deny it. This is not, however, a mere matter of tone of voice, of manners or "taste." The solidest idea, if presented by a bigot, loses its solidity; it becomes, not an idea any more, but a dogma--a much more tenuous, and less interesting, thing. Mr. Rottensteiner is not a bigot. Rather, he is passionately, and admirably, concerned. But an unbalanced concern, or an overly polemical one, becomes fanaticism; and so we see this intelligent man suddenly ascending the pulpit and speaking ex cathedra. Those of us (possibly including Mr. Blish) whose conscience insists that we mistrust any statement that sets itself above debate, must wince to see sound arguments thus rendered, if not untenable, certainly intolerable.

I do not wholly subscribe to Mr. Blish's ideas of the usefulness of SF, if indeed I understand it. I am extremely suspicious of any usefulness at all being ascribed to literature: in fact, of the whole criterion of usefulness as applied to literature, music, oak trees, oceans, persons, etc. -- unless a great many other criteria, of equal or superior value, are applied at the same time. But this idea of a "literature of change" is not the main drift of his reply to his critic. He states his main idea plainly and cogently: the idea of *the open system.* (It is an idea, by the way, with which I believe Stanislaw Lem agrees; in a very closely equivalent context -- talking about the faults and potentialities of SF -- he calls the same thing *the open universe.*)

I only wish that Mr. Blish had remarked (thus undercutting his opponent on his own ground--sawing through his pulpit, as it were) that the dislike of and restlessness within the closed system also characterizes the best Soviet/Communist-nation SF. The supreme example is probably Zamyatin's *We. (We,* of course, has never been printed in Russia. Ardent anti-Communists may take comfort in that fact, though I do not see how they can take comfort in the fact that it was, after all, *written* in Russia, and by an old Bolshevik at that.) Zamyatin's novel perfectly exemplifies Blish's central point, that SF operates *effectively* only in an open system.

The open system is not, cannot be, merely the writer's society; essentially, it exists in his mind.

"Marxism" can be accepted as an open system (Marx) or a closed one (Stalin). "American democracy" can be taken as an open system (Jefferson) or a closed one (Nixon). What must be remembered is that, if the individual has decided to opt for the open system, he is free to *go beyond it*. If his society or his government forbid him to do so, and if he accepts that decree, then he is living in a larger, but not an open, system. He has let the door be shut again.

The intellectual crime for which Zamyatin was reviled and silenced was that of being an "internal emigre." (The American equivalent would be "un-Americanism.") This smear-word is a precise and noble description of the finest writers of SF, in all countries.

Mr. Rottensteiner is altogether justified in criticising SF writers who, living in nations without overt censorship, yet choose to shut the door, to close their minds into hermetic ideological systems such as free-enterprise capitalism, Social Darwinism, Catholicism, or pseudo-ideologies like dianetics, and thus to cripple their imagination and their intellect. But what is lacking in his criticism is humanity. He says, "Stop! You are wrong!"--but he does not say, "Look around--you are free." His critique is authoritarian, not libertarian. The idea of simply opening the door and leaving it open seems not to occur to him. And this is why Mr. Blish, with his shaky arguments, making his hopeless defense of a lot of shoddy writers, finally appears as the only man left standing upright in a shambles of verbiage. For he is speaking, across all national and ideological boundaries, for the liberty of the mind. Mr. Rottensteiner has all the artillery; but if there are any angels around, they are on Mr. Blish's side.

H. BRUCE FRANKLIN. A RESPONSE FROM A MARXIST

Franz Rottensteiner criticizes Anglo-American SF for its failure to give any expression to a Marxist outlook. This is extremely mild criticism, for in fact Anglo-American SF does not merely ignore Marxism, but is profoundly hostile to it. The main body of English-language SF writers range from conscious anti-Communist propagandists such as Ayn Rand, Aldous Huxley, George Orwell, and Robert A. Heinlein, to writers who are politically ignorant and so thoroughly conditioned by anti-Communist assumptions that they echo their rulers and masters without even knowing what they are doing.

As a Marxist myself, I would go considerably further, to a more fundamental criticism. To me--as to the vast majority of intellectuals in Asia, Continental Europe, and Latin America--Marxism is the only science one can intelligently bring to bear on any overall discussion of humanity's future, near or far. *Only* in Great Britain, the United States, and the English-language regions of Canada is Marxism not generally regarded as *the* science of human history--past, present, and future. To most of the world's intellectuals, the philosophical bases of Anglo-American SF seem like bizarre anachronisms. It is as though a section of the world insisted on trying to build a science of matter by relying on medieval metaphysics while pretending that experimental physics had not been invented (or that Isaac Newton was the mastermind of a sinister global conspiracy aimed at reducing humanity from glorious beings to mere machines). Most of the SF of Great Britain and the U.S. seems as irrational as the societies that produced it. This should be no surprise. Anglo-American SF does not project the future of the world; it merely reflects the realities of these two dying empires. Imaginary inter-galactic wars of conquest against alien beings are natural products of societies whose entire history has flowed from genocidal wars against people of color throughout the world. And the grotesque worlds of Anglo-American SF in general are not too far removed from the social worlds of Great Britain and the U.S., whose vast productivity, instead of being used to satisfy human needs and desires, debauches human existence and poisons the environment, creating anarchic urban jungles built on exploitation, drugs, sex for sale, and every conceivable form of predatory relationship. And what could be more improbable than the fact that these vast empires are ruled by gangs of master criminals, who command armed forces capable of annihilating all life and who deploy involuted networks of uniformed and secret police utilizing the most advance electronic surveillance systems?

James Blish's responses to Rottensteiner's criticism are mere reflex actions. The key sentence in the debate is Rottensteiner's timid understatement: "Also, wrong or not, Marxism is one of the most important philosophical and economic systems of our time, the official doctrine of millions of this planet's inhabitants, the hope of several hundred million more in the undeveloped countries, and it is heatedly discussed by intellectuals all over the world." Blish ignores all the main points of this conservative declaration of fact. Instead he obediently leaps at the words "official doctrine." Like all loyal citizens of the Anglo-American Free World, he loudly proclaims his scorn for the slavish Communist "official doctrine" (and all other foreign ideologies). Of course *we* have no ideology, and nothing controls or determines *our* thinking, particularly if we happen to be such free, creative, individualistic beings as SF writers and critics.

Of course, being a liberal, Blish has to show that he's just as tolerant of Marx as he is of other "great minds." So he puts Marx in a hodge-podge list in the free academic marketplace of solitary geniuses. Pick your favorite "pernicious thinker," he offers, and do with him what you will. But among these, Marx alone provides the basis for a serious, intelligent, *scientific* science fiction. And of far more fundamental importance, the hundreds of millions of people who are determining humanity's future are not and will not be guided by a metaphysical maniac like Bishop Berkeley, a theorist for an ideal conformistic police state like Plato, or any embodiment of ancient superstition, even Christ.

"We do not," declares James Blish, "like closed systems of any sort." Well, Marxism is the opposite of closed. It is not the reflections of some solitary genius, but rather a developing science which puts into the hands of the people the control over their own destiny. Blish fails to see that it is we in the U.S. who function within a system as closed as that of the Greek slave empire that also called itself a "democracy."

In fact the interlocking Anglo-American empires have decayed so far that they have produced some SF that does indeed border on a Marxist analysis. Advanced state capitalism has now given birth to a whole body of SF works that project the next stages of its monstrous cancer. Kurt Vonnegut's *Player Piano*, Frederik Pohl and C. M. Kornbluth's *The Space Merchants*, Pohl's "The Midas Plague," Robert Silverberg's "The Pain Peddlers" and "Company Store," Robert Sheckley's "Something for Nothing," J. G. Ballard's "Subliminal Man," John D. MacDonald's

"Trojan Horse Laugh" and "Spectator Sport"--all these are good projections of what capitalism might become if it were not destroyed. But capitalism is in the process of extinction, and those who are wiping it out and replacing it with a decent human society are guided by the science of Marxism.

My criticism of James Blish is not intended to be an attack against him personally, but rather against the all-too-common ideas he expresses. We Marxists believe in vigorous and forthright debate of these issues of life and death. On the other hand, the apologists for the "Free World" usually conduct their side of the debate by exclusion, repression, open terror, and mass violence. The methods used to silence us, including my firing from Stanford University for giving political speeches, are typical of those employed against all who express revolutionary Marxism. Like many other comrades who try to base their lives on this philosophy, I have been deprived of my livelihood, arrested several times, beaten by the police, and most recently, had my door kicked in by two dozen agents of the federal secret police (F.B.I.) who held my wife and three children at gunpoint while they kidnapped me on charges they later had to drop. But this terroristic repression only increases our determination to expose and change the exclusion of Marxism from our lives. To me, the exclusion of Marxism from SF is intimately connected to the world-wide campaign of terror and suppression being waged by this frenzied dinosaur empire.

CHANDLER DAVIS. THESIS, ANTITHESIS, SYNTHESIS

Thesis (Blish): SF is the literature of change. Antithesis (Rottensteiner): No, it's not.

And yet Mr. Rottensteiner agrees that it ought to be, and at its best, is. He complains that it mostly doesn't do the job Mr. Blish assigns it; but that, Mr. Blish concedes. There is still a real issue here. But in defining it, let me treat not the mass of mostly undistinguished SF, but rather an ideal type abstracted from the best of it--or even a desired new literature for which something in SF raises hopes.

A whole generation of young English-speaking fans--Mr. Blish's generation and mine--surely came to SF seeking a literature of change. Whimsy, intellectual playfulness, we had. It merged into a Faustian intellectual arrogance: we were god-like, since we could contemplate so many worlds. For many fans that was as far as it went. But our generation too had those--Mr. Blish and me among them--who opposed as Mr. Rottensteiner does the merely playful in SF. For "our" literature, even when it was light or satirical, we had serious aspirations.

We believed in the mutability of the assumptions integral to the inherited social order. We welcomed the writer who exposed their evitability--whether it was Karl Marx or Jonathan Swift or Ruth Benedict or Olaf Stapledon.

We believed the future just as real as the present. We welcomed the writer who attacked the illusion that nothing will happen--whether it was Karl Marx or H. G. Wells. We welcomed (to the extent that we could find it) the kind of future fiction that fit Heinlein's epithet: "more realistic than most historical and contemporary-scene fiction."

We believed in a human responsibility to *act*, to make history. We welcomed the rare writer who pictured different roads, both possible, and called us to take part in choosing--whether it was the Marxist Jack London or the anti-Marxist Aldous Huxley. Granted that the hours we devoted to SF were not our most activist hours, were perhaps even escape, still we saw in SF more than horrid or radiant futures, or worlds of what if: we sought real problems truly posed.

Marxism seemed neither absent from SF (Rottensteiner) nor peripheral to it (Blish). Marxism seemed to treat questions which were of SF's essence. And our then view of SF's essence underlies Mr. Blish's present view: "It is in stretching the mind to accommodate this multiplicity of possible futures that science fiction has its reason for being."

We must admit to Mr. Rottensteiner and to ourselves that we failed to create an SF which lived up to our vision, and that even the vision faded. What happened?

We starry-eyed youth came to accept more and more the flip whimsy of the other fans among whom we found ourselves. First because we did find ourselves among them, reason enough; too, some of us may have soured because our millennium failed to arrive on schedule; but other things were eroding our seriousness.

There was this technical limitation: Whereas the real future incorporates a profusion of simultaneous novelties, whose effects can scarcely be disentangled, the fictional future must bring out a few, to avoid swamping the finite readers, and to allow tracing effects. I am not resisting this necessity; but it did militate against our fidelity to *real* future and for a rapprochement with the fantasy-writer's arbitrary *contrary-to-fact* hypothesis.

Another reason was our genuine eclecticism. Though mostly socialists, we found that Zamiatin, Huxley, and Heinlein, who were not, had something to teach us--even something to teach us about socialism. We ought to have been prepared by John Stuart Mill (and Marx!) to understand that the truth is many-sided and imperfectly known, so our doctrine must be dialectical and evolving. To our discredit, we tended rather to the non-dialectical eclecticism which accepts contradictory ideas without confronting them. Marx, Spenser, Freud, Jung, Bates--who cares, as long as there's a story in it? We ought not to have decided, just because we saw that true ideas may come from unexpected sources, that there are no false ideas.

A final reason was the pose of innocuousness. When the inquisitor looked in on the Renaissance humanist, he was assured, "Ah, but though my book sets forth the heresies reason has taught me, I retract them all on its last page, for when reason and the Church conflict then reason must be in error." When the inquisitor looks in on the SF writer, on the other hand, he is assured, "Ah, but the revolutions and utopias in my stories are mere escape fantasies, and even my social satires are mere jokes. Everything is grist for the SF mill. You'll see--my next story will be about a witch who's allergic to broomsticks, ha-ha." This disguise had done good service to our precursors, and was easily available to us in the 50's when we needed it. How natural that the mask should now seem part of our face. Natural, and pitiful. Let's express contentious ideas obliquely when we must, but let's dare to have them, and express them.

The future is still real, still coming at us, and at least as unknown as we thought it. Let's face it with the respect it deserves.

Marxism *as an official philosophy* is also important for SF, just as Catholicism is (witness Blish's excellent *A Case of Conscience*) but more so: it is a weightier social fact in the world of the real near future. So yes, let's admit it to our fictional futures. But caution! For SF, however Marxist, official Marxism can't be the right stance. No official philosophy can. Governmental apologetics are not always false, but they are always one-sided; usually their time-scale is in months not centuries, though they claim otherwise.

By all means let SF stretch the people's minds to accommodate a multiplicity of possible futures. Not just futures into which they may be herded. Futures they urgently have to see coming, and struggle to avert or to realize.

NOTES (BY RDM)

[1] Mr. Blish's essay appeared in George Hay, ed., *The Disappearing Future* (London: Panther, 1970). Mr. Rottensteiner's present article is from his review of that book, which appeared, in German, in his fan magazine, *Quarber Merkur* No. 26.

[2] For some reminiscences of this group, see Robert A.W. Lowndes, "A Eulogy for the Dying Science-Fiction Magazines," *Riverside Quarterly*, 6 (1973):34-35.

[3] Mr. Blish has written us that the books he had in mind were Robert A. Heinlein, *Beyond This Horizon* (1942) and L. Sprague de Camp, *The Stolen Dormouse* (1941). He might well have added James Blish and Norman L. Knight, *A Torrent of Faces* (1967).

Franz Rottensteiner

Playing Around with Creation: Philip José Farmer

Writing in *The Magazine of Fantasy and Science Fiction* for March, 1961, Alfred Bester singled out Philip José Farmer as one of seven SF authors meriting special praise: "Mr. Farmer's is the true courage, for he has the strength to project into the dark where no pre-formed attitudes wait to support him . . . . Mr. Farmer often shocks because he has had the courage to extrapolate a harmless idea to its terrible conclusion" (p80). Let's take a look at such extrapolating; and *To Your Scattered Bodies Go*, the first of a series of stories, might be an appropriate subject, having won a "Hugo" as the most popular SF novel of 1971 among American fans.

The basic idea of that novel is imaginative enough, and does justice to Mr. Farmer's reputation of daring to handle controversial topics. All human beings that ever lived up to the year 2002, when all but a few were destroyed by extra-terrestrial visitors, have been resurrected along the banks of a river 25 million miles or so long, which zigzags its way in a narrow valley on some artificial alien planet. All these humans, from the Neanderthals to the moderns, thirty-six billion, six million, nine thousand and thirty-seven in number (Mr. Farmer has industriously counted them), find themselves exactly twenty-five years of age, stark naked, totally hairless, the females all virgins, the men circumcised. Why this should be so is anybody's guess, but one assumes that Mr. Farmer threw in the circumcision as a joke on Jew-haters. The virgins seem to be a special bonus for characters that like to deflorate, so that the state of virginity is soon. remedied--but without much explicit description.

Population is distributed in different areas of the river valley according to a fixed ratio: 60% of a particular nationality and century, 30% of some other people, usually of a different time, and 10% from any time and place. Food is no problem, since every individual is equipped with a "grail" that delivers to him sustenance, such as beefsteaks, and other commodities, including cigarettes: as far as food is concerned, this afterlife is a Land of Cockayne if you are careful not to lose your "grail". But in most other respects it is a jungle, with men preying on each other, and warfare among the various groups and small states, and "grail slavery." In fact, this episodic novel is a chain of various battles, adventures (mostly of a bloody kind) and fights that the heroes experience while travelling in this world--and what better excuse for a quest than a gigantic meandering river?

With all beings awakening naked, there are initially some problem of decorum (among Victorians, say), and the author manfully pleads for a breaking of taboos; and since the function of the grails isn't obvious at once, and there are no animals, a few good words are put in for cannibalism, a favorite pastime among more "iconoclastic" SF authors. But while there is no food, and no clothes, luckily there are stones to batter heads in with, and bamboo to make spears for impaling bodies.

Aside from these familiar concerns and dutiful motions of any adventure story, in or out of SF, there is a Big Philosophical Question. Why have all humans been resurrected? Are they in heaven, hell, purgatory or whatever? It soon transpires that it wasn't God who lent a helping hand but rather a race of superior beings, called the "Ethicals" though they appear to be villains. The purpose of their actions is unclear, but there are conflicting theories. One of them is advanced by the "Church of the Second Chance", among whose more illustrious members is a sympathetically portrayed Hermann Goering (who seems to hold a special appeal for American SF writers, to judge from the number of SF stories in which he has figured). It holds that the riverworld is a sort of purgatory to cleanse humans of all impurities, and prepare them for an eternal bliss, which some saints are supposed to have already achieved. This happens also to be the official doctrine of the "Ethicals," as we discover when the book's protagonist, Richard Francis Burton, the 19th Century adventurer and translator of the *Thousand and One Nights,* is brought before a tribunal in celebration of his 777th death. For death in the riverworld is not final, but an act repeatable at will, although turning dying into a hobby isn't advisable, since, the reader is told, the soul or "psychomorph" might get lost. Its ties with the body are weakened by too many deaths, and one might truly die.

The other theory is advanced by a renegade Ethical called The Mysterious Stranger--an allusion to a story by Mark Twain, whose name is taken in vain for the hero of the second novel in the series, *The Fabulous Riverboat* (1971). He contends that the riverworld is a gigantic experiment, a scientific test for finding out the reaction of human beings in various situations, and for increasing the knowledge of history by interviewing the resurrected humans. This Mysterious Stranger pretends to want to help people, but he might lie, as might the other Ethicals. Aside from the fact that there is no interviewing in the novel, this theory is nonsense, since any race able to restore every person that ever lived, atom by atom, with all memories intact, already knows so much about them as to be in no need of interviewing them. What can you tell a being that knows every atom of your structure, which is infinitely more than any man can know about himself?

In any case, Richard Burton determines to find out the Truth, to arrive at the dark Grail Tower where the mysterious grail masters dwell. To do so, he travels around, until he discovers a more original method of transportation: teleportation by suicide. Since the resurrections occur at different "grailstones" along the river, obeying a random principle, dying is a method of statistical travel. Now I have no idea what Burton or the heroes of the other books in the series, existing or forthcoming, will finally find out about the Ethicals, but on the evidence we have so far I am prepared to bet that it is something not worth knowing, and just as banal as what has passed before. For I contend that *To Your Scattered Bodies Go* doesn't tell us anything meaningful about life, death, or the hereafter. Rather, it presents little children playing with the marbles of space, time and resurrection; its "afterlife" is merely one more stage for the same old set of events which have been recounted in any number of novels of adventure.

What little value the novel has lies wholly in the fact that it presents in an almost pure form the particular method of mass-market SF--that is, playing around with a limited set of elements that are combined and recombined to infinity. A kaleidoscope of oddities that is simultaneously derivative, self-perpetuating and incestuous; a *mixtum compositum* of almost unlimited assimilative powers, ahistorical and devaluating; readily accepting what is intellectually bankrupt, and bankrupting what initially had some value, before it was drawn into the gigantic junk-yard of SF, where everything is but a pretext for another cops-and-robbers story--regardless how the figures are called, and whether the background is the earth, some other planet, the galaxy, past, present or future, some other dimension, or indeed the afterlife. Without paying notice to historical context, environment or character, such SF throws together the customs and institutions of different pasts, usually jazzed up with some hyperbolic technology of the future (a never described technique of resurrection in Mr. Farmer's case). What SF in general does metaphorically, Mr. Farmer presents literally as his subject: the river-world is quite factually a world where past, present and future meet, where historical context no longer exists, and knowledge of milieu is no longer necessary, since all figures in the story share the same uniform and artificial background. Even the psychology of individuals and character development has given way to mere name-dropping: Mark Twain, Hermann Goering, Richard Francis Burton, the "original" Alice. None of these humans has, as lively as some of them are, any real relation to their historical "prototypes": what Mr. Farmer has to offer is at best some commonly known lexicographical information. A revival on such a gigantic scale would have offered a chance of a unique meeting of minds; but all Mr. Farmer presents is the old trite quarrel of survival and petty warfare. People who were noted for their sharp minds are here reduced to pages and pages of inane mutterings, and to playing at the old game of imprisonment and escape.

This series is also further proof, if such proof were needed, that present-day SF, far from being *the* literature of change, is as a rule, very conservative in methods as well as content. While paying lipservice to change, and offering some background slightly changed in relation to the author's environment, it actually comforts the reader with the palliative that nothing will ever really change, that we'll always be again what we have been before, in this world or the next; as below, so above; as on Earth, so in the afterlife, Amen.

Ever since *The Lovers* (1961)--his first and, for all its faults, still most interesting SF novel, along with *Night of Light* (1966)--three components, intermixed in different ways and degrees, occur again and again in Mr. Farmer's work: religion, sex, and violence. Religion most often takes the form of a fascinated,secularized preoccupation with creation. His creators, however, lack any dignity or higher purpose; they appear childlike in their creative omnipotence, playful, scheming, lying, deceitful--and not very bright. In *Outside Inside* (1964), for instance, the hero, a social climber, finds himself in a nightmare miniature world that presents the reverse side of the riverworld coin. It delineates not a world after death, but a prenatal world, where artificial souls, created again by a race of "Ethicals" (perhaps the same as in *To Your Scattered Bodies Go)*, are conditioned for life in our world. Or so at least the hero is told in the end, which may or may not be a lie (it seems likely that it is only a cruel joke of the "gods" to further torment the characters of the story). For, again, the "explanation" makes very little sense: if the Ethicals create immortal souls out of benevolence, why "condition" those souls in a purgatory? This seems to indicate a very poor engineering job, for why not create souls that have the desired qualities in the first place? And the straightening out job seems as poor. Sexual perverts, for instance, are treated in the following way: "So, the Exchange castrated them, cut out their tongues, amputated all four limbs, and thus made them unable to offend or harm anybody, even themselves." The Ethicals really must have very curious educational theories, and Mr. Farmer is aware of the irony of the situation: he has a "demon" comment in the story that the perverts, to spite their creators, get more vicious all the time.

Equally cruel is the afterlife pocket-universe in "A Bowl Bigger than Earth," a short story in Mr. Farmer's collection *Down in the Black Gang* (1971). There, human beings find themselves thrown into an intestine-shaped world, imprisoned in identical sexless bodies, and subjected to mindless drudgery. This world is truly hell, and they are punished if they so much as utter the word; insult is added to injury in that they are required to exclaim that they positively like their toiling and that things couldn't be better.

What does this all suggest? Farmer presents hellish worlds, before birth and after it, into which a vague hope is introduced only as an additional torture. They depict various degrees of degradation of man, and reject the autonomy of human values and human beings. These stories proclaim the Fortean doctrine that man is only property, utterly at the mercy of beings with remarkable powers, "gods" or "ethicals," who appear to be childlike, prankish, sadistic dimwits, taking delight only in causing pain and suffering. Even death offers no escape from the torturers, since it has lost its uniqueness and become a playful act that can be reversed or repeated at will. "As flies to wanton boys, are we to the gods, / They kill us for their sport."

The author of such "gods" does in fiction what they are supposed to do in reality: he plays around with shocking situations and possibilities, without justifying them or giving them a larger meaning. Sometimes these creations are, in their vividness of description, remarkable as fruits of a grotesque imagination; but I think they are never of any importance as speculative thought, as intellectual effort. Of the three components, religion, sex and violence, the last seems by far the strongest, and to be gaining in strength with time. Sex if often restricted to a few puns, some "bad" language (which hardly seems anything but cursory), and a few acts deviating from what is considered "proper"; more essential in these stories are the many acts of maiming, mutilating, torturing and killing. The most significant argument for this is perhaps the fact that Mr. Farmer unabashedly continued one of his most far-out sex-books, the hardcore pornography *A Feast Unknown* (1969), in two "clean" novels: *Lord of the Trees /The Mad Goblin* (Ace Double, 1970). Does it not seem strange that a writer in whose work sex is said to be so central, should find it so easy to delete all sex in a sequel? Such an act, one would assume, would change the whole nature of a story, turn it into something else altogether. That Mr. Farmer did it so effortlessly, seems typical of him and SF in particular, and the civilization it mirrors in general. Sex can come and go, as commercial considerations make it necessary; the atrocities and violence are constant, for nobody objects to *that*. At least not the editors, the publishers, or the Hugo Award voters.

Notes by Several Hands

(from SFS *1:135 - 136, Fall 1973)*

SF WRITERS, THE GREAT CONSENSUS, AND Non-ALIGNMENT. It is only fair to assume that any article printed in SFS has in the editors' opinion-- even where they disagree with it--some significant redeeming aspects. Thus I personally think that Dr. Rottensteiner's robust polemics on Mr. Farmer's "riverworld" cycle make a salutary point. But as was said in my little dialogue in our first issue, the critic should be *for* the creative writer, not against him. Since in this imperfect world very few writers are either totally creative or totally non-creative, but various shades of in-between, it seems to me that the most fruitful strategy is to condemn trashy and unhealthy writings, and very rarely the author. Mr. Farmer is after all the writer who extended the closed world of American SF thematics with such stories as "Father," "My Sister's Brother," and above all "Riders of the Purple Wage," which even his sternest critic, Stanislaw Lem, has called "no mean piece of prose" (see Lem's very significant essay, "SF: A Hopeless Case--With Exceptions," *SF Commentary* No. 35-37, 1973). Where Dr. Rottensteiner talks of "Farmer," therefore, I take the name to mean not the actual citizen of Peoria, but the authorial *persona* that has allowed economic and psychological pressures to turn him from "Riders" to the works that Dr. Rottensteiner criticizes, the *persona* that has allowed the ruling system--represented in SF by the publishing circuit, the fan-voters, and the whole mutual-admiration club--to become internalized as the norm for such "aligned" or *gleichgeschaltet* writing. Very little has actually been changed by the supposedly "dangerous" themes of sex and blasphemy that Mr. Farmer has pioneered in American SF, for in their actual use within conformist structures these "new" themes appear only as the obverse of the puritanism and agnosticism of the old SF. In other words, whatever the wishes of an SF writer may be, whatever his opinions as a private citizen may be, if his writings portray intelligent beings facing a new world as isolated individuals without significant new relationships to other intelligent beings and to the totality of their institutions, he is aligned with the powers-that-be.

In present power circumstances, a writer, as Ms. Le Guin says in this issue, can save his soul, whether in the USSR or the USA, only by refusing to become so aligned. The fact that US writers, such as Blish, Clement, Delaney, Dick, Disch, Knight, Le Guin, Leiber, Miller, Oliver, Pohl, Sheckley, Simak, etc., have to an important extent managed to escape such aligning proves that despite the pressures it is a matter of choice. But this choice determines the writer's aesthetics as well as his ethics. Most SF writers have fooled themselves for far too long that they are a vanguard educating the American people (and then all other peoples) for the space age, for inner space, or what not. Sadly, the basic ideological pull seems to have drawn the other way: the price of success--such as it is--has been the educators' becoming educated into a subdivision of the great American consensus (see also Dr. Davis's contribution to this issue). So to my mind, writers like Mr. Farmer, capable of better work if given better financial support and better normative systems, should be regarded with sorrow at least as much as with anger: so many wasted opportunities, so much wasted talent! If villains need be, the anger should be directed at the writers' submitting to such publicity systems of reinforcement as the Hugo award, rapidly becoming the measure of what is immature in SF.--DS.

(from SFS *1:219 - 220, Spring 1974)*

A REACTION TO SFS #2. It seems to me a mistake to treat Franz Rottensteiner as a serious critic or to respond to him more elaborately than by pointing out his errors, e.g., "that no American or English author has written a story that would endorse a Marxist view of change, or at least contain an intelligent discussion of it." Mack Reynolds, in a long series of stories published in *Analog* in the sixties, has done just what is demanded in the second clause. Rottensteiner also says "the disinterested observer [Are his initials F.R.?] will find a total innocence of SF writers as far as real problems and likely developments of the future are concerned." Again, this is just plain wrong—see recent work by Edward Bryant, Richard E. Peck, Dave Skal, Charles Platt, and Kate Wilhelm.

I was disappointed in the discussions of Aldiss, Heinlein, and Farmer. Jameson's article is interesting, but the jargon in it is awful—worse than anything in SF. I don't find anything to quarrel with in Rottensteiner's essay on Farmer, but it doesn't take much critical intelligence to notice that a lot of Farmer's work is crude, etc. What would be really interesting, and much more difficult, would be to try to find out why these crude efforts are so popular. That could not be done in a vacuum—the critic would have to examine published responses to the work, talk to readers, perhaps even interview the author. I left a similar job undone when I wrote my essay on van Vogt in the forties. Van Vogt has just revealed, for the first time as far as I know, that during this period he made a practice of dreaming about his stories and waking himself up every ninety minutes to take notes, This explains a good deal about the stories, and suggests that it is really useless to attack them by conventional standards. If the stories have a dream consistency which affects readers powerfully, it is probably irrelevant that they lack ordinary consistency.

Thus I am bothered by what seems to me a tendency to treat SF stories as if they were another kind of essay—as if only the content mattered. When this is done, everything that is alive in the story slips through the critic's fingers. In fact, in a lot of cases it's a mistake even to take the content as primary—what looks like content may be something the author whipped up on the spur of the moment to fill a hole in the story. It may be what Hitchcock calls a McGuffin—some gadget or plot device that has to be there or the machinery wouldn't work, but it doesn't matter at all which gadget or device it is. This is the case in the Asimov story, "Little Lost Robot," cited by Plank on page 75. The parallels between robots and black slaves are there quite explicitly, but are there purely as a plot device in a formal puzzle story. —DAMON KNIGHT.

ROBERT SCHOLES. NOVELS BY BRUNNER AND LEVIN

(from SFS *1:213 - 216, Spring 1974)*

Two recent, strong works of SF should be mentioned in relation to your ongoing discussion of change and Marxism: Ira Levin's *This Perfect Day* (1970) and John Brunner's *The Sheep Look Up* (1972).

Though it is the weaker of the two (and degenerates badly at the end), Levin's book is interesting because it contemplates a specifically Marxist "utopian" society ("Christ, Marx, Wood, and Wei / led us to this perfect day.") and rejects it. In doing so, it follows a familiar path traced by Zamyatin, Orwell, and Huxley, but its Marxian "utopia" is more interesting than theirs in some ways, because it is more gently and kindly perceived. It is by no means altogether horrible, though it makes clear the price in lost individuality exacted by the perfection of its socioeconomic arrangements. Beyond this, Levin's work surprised and pleased me by presenting the capitalist island of freedom in the novel as a place at least as odious as the socialist paradise.

Levin's criticism of capitalism as it functions on the island of "Liberty" is devastating, and might quite properly be called Marxist. Thus his book criticizes socialism from the perspective of individualism, and individualism from the perspective of socialism—and this is a genuine achievement. If Levin has no final answer, this is because final answers are very difficult to come by. And I should add that they are especially difficult to come by in fictional form, for reasons that are very interesting in themselves.

When a utopia is imagined concretely, as it must be in fictional form, the price it exacts for its improvements in the human situation becomes clear. Thus all utopias, however ideally intended, have something repellent about them, and even the most generously conceived socialist or individualist utopia in fictional form will reveal certain repellent features as the price for its utopian qualities. This same principle applies with much greater force to attempts to realize utopian dreams in actual societies. What is America today but the fictional intentions of Jefferson and Hamilton, realized and shaped by the interaction of social forces with individual men of power from Washington to Nixon? And what is Russia but the similar ideals of Marx and Engels as enacted by Lenin, Stalin, and others? Mr. H. Bruce Franklin has received treatment in America which is shameful. (It makes me ashamed, anyway.) Others, like Solzhenitsyn, have been treated at least as badly in Russia. Are we to blame Jefferson and Marx for this? I think not. Both Jeffersonian democracy and Marxian socialism are noble ideals which seem difficult to enact and sustain even in fiction, let alone life.

In fiction, it seems clear, both socialistic and individualistic ideas function better when used critically than when used for utopian projection. Thus Marxism is most useful to writers of SF who aim at producing a critique of capitalism, and individualism is most useful to writers criticizing socialism. This presents a special problem for writers in socialist countries.

Robert M. Philmus

A Dialogue Between Ideaphilos and Philologos
(Intended to Prove Little and Clarify Much)

NOTE. In the following dialogue, no correspondence is intended between the fictitious characters therein and any particular students of literature, living or dead. It is admissible, however, to read the general term *literature* as a surrogate for the more specific *science fiction*.

> The opposite of a true statement is a false statement. But the opposite of a profound truth may be another profound truth. —Niels Bohr.

Ideaphilos. I confess to being more than a little annoyed with you for your refusal to take sides in my argument with that no-good Idiokrasios over the outright reactionary tendencies of so much modern literature.
　Philologus. I explained to you the reason for my refusal.
　I. So you did. And I must say I am a bit more puzzled by it than I was chagrined by your not expressing the sympathy I know you have for my point of view. What is this distinction between criticism and interpretation

that so obsesses you?

P. It is, my dear Ideaphilos, quite simple, really. Criticism, as I see the enterprise, orients itself primarily and overtly towards value judgments, which may have—in a more or less narrow sense of the terms—a moral, esthetic, or ideological basis—and bias. As an interpreter, on the other hand, I aim principally at understanding literature rather than imposing normative criteria on it.

I. You will, I hope, excuse the bluntness of my observing that what you say is as naive as it is pretentious. Surely this pretense of neutrality on your part is just that: a pretense. You will not be so disingenuous as to deny that the interpretative effort is hardly value-free, as you call it.

P. Admittedly, the dividing line between criticism and interpretation is in practice sometimes as obscure—or obscured—as that separating pedantry from precision. Still, from the fact that the distinction is not always clear it is fallacious to infer that it altogether doesn't exist. You will not contend that it is pointless to distinguish music from noise merely on the grounds that the one occasionally modulates into the other?

I. Is that to say you concede the difference to be a matter of degree rather than of kind?

P. If you wish.

I. Well then, let me press the point. What is the degree of difference between criticism and interpretation? Surely if you elect to give your time and attention to a work of literature you imply a judgment of value? And if you choose to attend to this work rather than that you are making a normative discrimination?

P. True enough.

I. In which case, your professed neutrality is really hypocritical. You assume certain values but don't bring them out into the open.

P. If a hypocrite is anyone who assumes some things without explicitly saying what they are, I shall have to accept the epithet. And indeed it is true that the profession of neutrality is a hypocritical evasion in all too many instances. But I did not claim, you may recall, that an interpreter is neutral: what I said is that the interpreter, unlike the critic, does not deal in overt value judgments. Moreover, if I am a hypocrite, you may be one also—or something worse.

I. What do you mean?

P. Exactly this: you admit that you have a weakness for literature that is good by literary standards? That just as I have some sympathy for your politics you have some for my aesthetics (excuse my using the terms loosely; we both understand that epistemology, ethics, and aesthetics tend to shade into one another)?

I. I suppose I can make that admission.

P. You suppose so? I certainly hope that is true, for otherwise you would be something of a hypocrite yourself, wouldn't you? After all, it is a bit hypocritical to devote your life to the study of literature, as you do, and not be interested in the stuff at all? Do you begin to see how the other side of the argument you used a moment ago begins to cut you?

I. I guess so. But look here, I don't see that there's any problem or difficulty in being concerned with literary and non-literary values at the same time.

P. Maybe not. But let's examine the matter. When you were arguing with Idiokrasios, you remember, you denounced the ideological bent of certain literary works, thinking it your duty as a critic to do so.

I. Yes, though by the way your distinction does not seem strictly valid here, since criticism in this instance requires interpretative understanding.

P. In this instance, perhaps—though that is not always true. But I will grant the point for the moment since I am trying to get at something else. Now: the works you inveighed against you disapprove of, of course?

I. Of course.

P. You think them pernicious and would not want others to read them and be influenced by them: It would be well if they were consigned to oblivion?

I. True.

P. But isn't that end more likely to be effected by ignoring them altogether instead of carping about them and thus preserving their names for posterity as well as giving them currency in our time? [*Pause*] I assume your silence indicates assent, and will therefore proceed to another, related matter. Do you suppose that your concern with the ideas expressed in a work of literature will persuade our writers to adhere to high literary standards and increase the demand for such standards on the part of their readers?

I. Isn't that self-evident? Obviously an insistence on well thought out and responsible ideas will ultimately produce great literature.

P. No doubt Idiokrasios would go along with you there, though the two of you could never get together on the meaning of your terms. But if your assumptions were correct, any of our philosophers should have produced works of greater literary value than have our poets; and on the same grounds treatises on, say, law or economics should be preferred by your would-be literary criteria to works of "pure literature" themselves. If you are not willing to accept that consequence, you must, I fear, admit to the error of your critical ways, which ignore what makes literature literature.

I. I shall admit no such thing. Apart from the fact that you seem to be reformulating the anathema of literature for literature's sake, the kind of literature I am interested in does deal with ideas, clearly and undeniably.

P. I have not denied it. What I have said, however, is that critics should not expect that by insisting on ideas they encourage good literature—indeed, they may discourage it. As for your anathema, I consider it equally heretical to divorce what a work of literature means from how it means—in effect, your practice when you abstract what you judge to be its ideational content.

I. But surely that is the function of criticism: to identify and elucidate the ideas in a literary work.

P. The function of criticism, possibly, but not of interpretation—unless *idea* is defined in a very special sense, one which connects it with structure and so on. In any other sense, literary merit has no essential relation to ideational content *per se*.

I. I cannot accept that, but I begin to see that the differences between us are greater than I had supposed.

Change, SF, and Marxism: Open or Closed Universes?

(from SFS *1:269 - 276, Fall 1974)*

NOTE. This exchange, begun in SFS #2 by a discussion between Franz Rottensteiner and James Blish and the intervention into that discussion by Ursula K. Le Guin, H. Bruce Franklin, and Chandler Davis, and continued in SFS #3 by Robert Scholes's essay, Damon Knight's letter, and, obliquely, Robert M. Philmus's dialogue, ends here with the contribution by Mack Reynolds and the final reply by Franz Rottensteiner (James Blish chose not to exercise his right to reply). The editors, finally, asked Fredric Jameson to sum up the discussion and comment on it. We hope that, for all its meanders, this debate—if taken as a whole—will have clarified what can legitimately be meant by the concepts in its title and their interactions. —DS.

MACK REYNOLDS. WHAT DO YOU MEAN—MARXISM?

While I agree that most SF writers are woefully ignorant about Marxism and hence have handicaps when dealing with socioeconomic subjects, I am afraid that the charges made have been too sweeping. One of the difficulties with Franz Rottensteiner's and also H. Bruce Franklin's contributions is that they don't tell us exactly what they mean by Marxism. A century after Marx and Engels did their work, the term has become somewhat elastic. One of the reasons for this is that the founders of scientific socialism never drew a blueprint of the new society. Marx's work was largely a critique of classical capitalism, and he never finished it. It gives one who wishes to call himself a Marxist a great deal of leeway.

I hope that Rottensteiner and Franklin do not equate Marxism with any of the so-called communist parties, including that of the Soviet Union, the various Trotskyites, the Maoists, the Castroites, or the Titoists, not to speak of Allende's alleged Marxism in Chile. I would briefly define socialism as a society replacing capitalism in which the means of production are democratically owned and operated by and for the people and in which the state has been replaced by a democratically elected government whose main task is to plan production. Now I have travelled extensively in all the "communist" countries of Europe save Albania, where they wouldn't let me in, and in none of them found such Marxian socialism. And I have read of none of it in China, Cuba, or any of the other "communist" countries. The nearest thing to it, perhaps, is Yugoslavia—and that's not very near. Certainly, the state has not withered away in any of them, as called for by Marx and Engels. Indeed, it has been strengthened beyond anything known in the capitalistic West at this time.

I was born into a Marxian Socialist family. I am the child who, at the age of five or six, said to his parent, "Mother, who is Comrade Jesus Christ?"—for I had never met anyone in that household who wasn't called Comrade. While still in my teens, I joined the Marxist Socialist Labor Party and remained, very active, in it for many years, though I have since resigned, believing their program inadequate in the modern age. I have been a life-long radical and, so far as I know, have read everything written by Marx that has been translated into English, along with a great many other socialist classics. I have even taught the subject and lectured extensively in colleges, over radio, etc. In short, I think I am competent to handle the Marxian viewpoint, even though at present day I think much of Marx's work has become antiquated. (Much of the program presented in the *Communist Manifesto* [1848] has already been adopted by capitalist society.)

I began writing on a full-time basis in 1949. Early in the game I realized that I was much too shaky in the physical sciences to deal with them adequately, so I began specializing in stories with social-science themes, especially socioeconomics. Since 1949 I have sold some forty books and several hundred shorter works. I have been translated into at least nine languages, including German. I would estimate that at least half my stories are based on political-economy themes. I simply can't understand Mr. Rottensteiner reading much SF without running into at least some of these, including some that "endorse a Marxist view of change," for example, "Ruskies Go Home!" (*F & SF* Nov 1960), soon to be published in enlarged form by Ace as *Tomorrow May Be Different*, which foresees a future in which the Soviet Union has realized all its goals and has become the most affluent country in the world. If you are interested in an attack on the Soviet Union from the Marxian viewpoint, try "Freedom" (*Analog* Feb 1961), in which a new Russian underground is attempting to overthrow the "communist" bureaucracy to form a new government more in line with the teachings of Marx. Or read "Utopian," in Harry Harrison's *The Year 2000* (Doubleday 1970), in which a Marxian Socialist is thrown forward by a time-travel gimmick into the world he has worked for all his life. Believe me, I could go on and on. (*Mercenary from Tomorrow* and *Time Gladiators* have been published in German by Moewig. Both are attacks on capitalism and its present-day trends; both call for the institution of a more advanced society.)

Others have listed some of the other English-language writers who have written from the Marxist viewpoint, including Jack London (who once belonged to the same SLP I did) and Olaf Stapledon, so I won't go into this, though I'll mention the fact that two of my SF writer friends fought in the International Brigades in Spain. I didn't, though I was in the age group, for I had already become disgusted with the Stalinists, as my friends later did in the course of the civil war.

I was surprised to see Mr. Franklin refer to George Orwell as an anti-Communist propagandist. Of course, it's a matter of what you mean by communist, Orwell might have been anti-Soviet Union, and so am I, but he wasn't anti-Marxist. Only by calling the Soviet Union a communist country does that accusation hold water.

Marx and Engels (the names cannot be separated) used the terms *socialism* and *communism* interchangeably, in spite of the manner in which Soviet writers have used them since. And, going by their teachings, the Soviet Union is by no means communist, or socialist. The most apt label I can think of is "State Capitalism," since they retain all the aspects of capitalism save that ownership of the means of production is in the hands of the state (the Communist Party) rather than in private hands.

FRANZ ROTTENSTEINER. IN REBUTTAL

It seems to me that many of the contributors to your symposium answer points that I did not make. I did not, for instance, particularly point out that Blish did not invent the notion that SF uniquely prepares the reader for change; in fact, I think that priority here is of no importance, and I could have discussed dozens of other writers instead. I wrote about Blish's essay simply because I happened to be reviewing George Hay's book, and because his essay provided me with a springboard to say some things I had wanted to say for some time.

I also do not ask of SF writers that every one (or even one) of them be a Darwin, Freud, or Marx, nor do I hold that no intellectual achievement smaller than theirs counts; I should be quite content if SF writers managed to incorporate intelligently in fiction what greater men thought first. But obviously there is an ocean between Mr. Blish's (or Mr. Knight's) notions of what constitutes intelligence in a writer, and my own.

Contrary to Ms. Le Guin's belief I did not say a word about the *potential* of the SF form; and it need hardly be pointed out that my anger would be totally inexplicable if I weren't aware of the abyss between the potential of the form and its actual state.

I have also been accused of not knowing Stapledon or Jack London's *The Iron Heel*, and only wonder that nobody threw old Bellamy at me. There were, of course, a couple of Anglo-American writers with socialist convictions, Upton Sinclair, for instance, who wrote a few utopian stories, or, in more recent times, Thomas McGrath with a novel like *The Gates of Ivory, the Gates of Horn* (tellingly published by "Masses & Mainstream Inc."), but I was speaking about the SF field, the mass-produced SF of today, and what have these isolated men to do with the condition of American or British SF?

I even know Mack Reynolds, and have read about one-third to one-half of his stories, and while I don't question the honesty of his political convictions, I am afraid that I have a very low opinion of his judgment, and I have always thought his "social SF" to be just another brand of the variety cops-and-robbers, at times undistinguishable from the work of his ideological opposite, H. Beam Piper. Nominally though, he may indeed deal with Marxism, much in the same manner as van Vogt has dealt with "general semantics."

Mr. Knight's second proof of my factual wrongness is just funny. I don't see how I, not being the happy possessor of a time machine, could possibly have known the "recent work" of such eminent writers as Richard E Peck or Dave Skal when I wrote my review of George Hay's book—in February 1971. I believe that some of the writers mentioned by Damon Knight were then still unpublished. Apparently Mr. Knight was unable to find even one story dealing with "real problems" (and so far as I know we haven't yet reached a consensus on what a "real problem" is; I didn't define the term in my polemics) before the revolutionary advent of Messrs. Bryant, Peck, Platt, etc. I could well name him some authors and stories that deal with what I would consider real problems—but I do not think that those rare instances are statistically relevant.

FREDRIC JAMESON. IN RETROSPECT

Quite as frequently as those about SF, debates about Marxism often turn out to be sham disputes in which each party means something else by the term at issue; it is therefore not surprising that, compounded, such an exchange gives us a feeling that the participants have jumped on their hobby-horses only to ride off in all directions. It is not, for instance, helpful to find Robert Scholes confusing communism (or socialism) as a type of socioeconomic organization with Marxism as a system of thought, even though I welcome his appreciation of the critical power of the latter. I would want to go on to make a more fundamental distinction than this, however, and to suggest that we must first of all make up our minds whether we are talking about the writer of SF, and the usefulness of Marxism to him, or about the reader and the critic, and the way in which a Marxist approach can sharpen their understanding of SF works which exist already.

Rottensteiner and Franklin, for instance, are speaking primarily to the writers of SF, and suggesting that their work will improve in power and in relevance if they come to some awareness of the things that Marxism has to teach us about the world we live in. I would agree, of course, although I don't imagine anyone feels that Marxist convictions could be a substitute for what is called talent, nor would they deny that works either innocent of

Marxism or hostile to it might be interesting ones (Mr. Blish mentions Shiel, and one of Rottensteiner's points is obviously that there are lots of examples in American SF). Yet this second qualification then clearly shifts the argument to reader and critic, and the attitude they are to take to already existing works of SF. Before I turn to this question, I would simply add a final word on prescribing to the creative writer: the idea is probably not as shocking any more as it was during the fifties, when the critical establishment worked hard to foster the notion that literature was "autonomous" and that the best writers were those "whose minds were too fine to be violated by an idea" (T.S. Eliot's tribute to Henry James). Still, one of the basic emphases of Marxism has always been on the primacy of the situation itself—on the unique requirements of a given historical moment and a given socioeconomic conjuncture; this means that even a militant writer would recognize that the nature of the work to be produced has to vary according to the needs of its public. In a middle-class country like the U.S., effective political writing will be very different from what is wanted in a peasant society in the process of building socialism and learning to read. Even that kind of assessment, moreover, does not begin to answer the question of the effectiveness of SF itself as opposed to other types of militant literature. In the Soviet Union, for instance, it seems that great SF has served the positive and utopian function of keeping the basic goals of socialism alive (see for example Efremov's *Andromeda*), while in a country like our own we would expect a militant SF to serve that far more negative, critical, destructive purpose which Scholes has underscored.

Mack Reynolds seems to me to shift the focus of this particular debate by suggesting that Marxism "gets into" SF, not by way of the author's political intent or conscious ideology, but rather by the nature of the literary materials he uses, which Reynolds designates, in the occurrence, as "socioeconomics." This is, I suppose, a useful fallback position: we may argue at length over whether a book like *The Space Merchants* is genuinely radical, or ultimately merely liberal, in its effect on the audience, but if we limit ourselves to the question of raw material, then the innovative nature of that particular novel—compared, e.g., to space opera—becomes unmistakable. The same holds true for a story like Ballard's "Subliminal Man," yet Franklin's example strikes me as most unfortunate in another sense and raises issues which will ultimately lead into our second theme, namely the need of ideological criticism in the reading of SF. For every reader of Ballard knows that the lush and diseased, apocalyptic world of that great writer is the very opposite of a committed literature, and that it is by sheerest accident that his private obsessions (entropy, illusion, the shrinkage of space itself towards some deathly center) happened, in "The Subliminal Man," to have intersected with a piece of genuinely sociopolitical raw material. Ballard's work is one immense attempt to substitute nature for history, and thus a kind of dizzying and ecstatic feeling of inevitable natural eschatology for that far more troubled sense of collective historical death which someone so steeped in the British colonial experience must of necessity feel. That part of Ballard we surely cannot recuperate by attaching it to "socioeconomics" (and I hope I have not given the impression—following Mr. Reynolds—that Marxists wish to limit SF to this kind of material exclusively; I for one would be sorry to lose the very distinctive work of a writer like Larry Niven); we must therefore envisage a different kind of approach, some deeper kind of reading which makes the relationship between Ballard's talent and his concrete experience of history more accessible and visible to us.

At this point, of course, we have already shifted from prescription to description, from the question of what kind of SF the writer ought to produce to that equally urgent one of the way in which the reader of SF ought to use that corpus of existing works which already surrounds us. Here a Marxist critic clearly has several tactical options: he may feel that a work is likely to exercise some particularly pernicious effect ideologically, and in that case, he will want to denounce it by making it clearer to a relatively unfore-warned audience what the particular work is really up to. Such culture criti-cism, however, will inevitably single out recent works, and works, moreover, which have had enough popular success to be worth taking on. It is unlikely, in other words, that at the present day Marxists will want to denounce the undoubted ideological ambiguities of H.G. Wells with the same passion they would bring to, say, Heinlein. Criticism like this forms a public by forcing it to be a little more lucid about its enthusiasms, and by reminding it of the sometimes sorry connections between some of its favorite products and the culture industry from which they issue, by furnishing concrete demonstrations of the various ways in which such products can reinforce the status quo and discourage political action and meaningful change.

So no Marxist critic would want to rule out the option of some really negative and destructive criticism of misleading and ideologically pernicious works (although I would tend to agree with Suvin in wondering whether Farmer as a writer deserves Rottensteiner's attack, and with Franklin in wondering whether, if he does, the attack is really critical *enough*). But per-haps it would be helpful to people who, like Mr. Philmus, find themselves locked in the sterile antithesis between analysis and evaluation (or criticism and interpretation), to point out that not all so-called ideological analysis need be of this wholly negative kind.

Indeed, SF more than most types of literature relies heavily on conceptual schemes (which is to say, on ideological materials) for its construction of future or alternate universes: the term extrapolation is of course simply another word for this process, whereby elements of our own world are se-lected in accordance with this or that abstract concept or model. John Brun-ner's recent works may indeed serve as a textbook illustration of the de-pendence of SF plots on what are essentially ideological choices; for he seems to have decided to furnish us with a series of "near futures" based on systematically varied extrapolations, *Stand on Zanzibar* offering a near future seen through the lens of the genetic theme, *The Sheep Look Up* providing an alternate version in terms of ecology. (*Total Eclipse* may then be seen as kind of finger exercise in which Mr. Brunner's genetic theme, ingeniously combined with an older economic determinism, is projected into the classical SF tra-dition of space travel and alien contact...) Such works might then be seen as functioning somewhat like Zola's "experimental novel," giving us a kind of small-scale experimental model of various versions of what classical Marxism calls "ultimately determining instances," now genetic, now ecological, now technological, etc. But the reader would have to be aware of the nature of the experiment, which otherwise is scarcely an innocent one ideologically. Now it is true that Mr. Brunner mentions the intent of his "genetic determi-nism" somewhere along the way: " 'We're all Marxists now' is a common cry among the world's intellectuals... But today's commonplace is often tomor-row's fallacy, and arguments from biology are increasing both in scope and precision. J. Merritt Emlen...puts forward the view that modern genetic theory can provide more subtle interpretations of human behavior than is generally realized," etc. (*Stand on Zanzibar*, Context 15). But one wonders whether this is enough to be make the reader aware of the quite systematic effort Brunner has made, in organizing *Stand on Zanzibar*, to put across this viewpoint, which of course involves the substitution of "natural" and "Scientific" considerations for political and historical ones.

Yet ideological analysis can also shed light on the purely artistic structure of such a work. If, indeed, one subjects the plot structure of the overrated *Stand on Zanzibar* to close examination, it becomes clear that its three sub-plots come from wholly different and unequal generic traditions. The New York section, with its overpopulation and its riots and its berserk and homicidal rampages, stems directly from the classic near-future line of books like *Make Room, Make Room!* The episode on Yatakang, on the other hand with its totalitarian Asiatic dictatorship and its oppressed scientists, far from being SF, is simply classic espionage melodrama, even to the final reversal (become a commonplace in the works of writers like Le Carre) in which it turns out to be the "free world" rescuers who are in reality the more evil of the two adversaries. Meanwhile, the picture of the backward and peaceful African nation with its wise and kindly ruler and its mutating human species (shades of Arthur C. Clarke!), springs right out of the long SF preoccupation with superhuman and future powers. The first point to be made about such an analysis is that these three stories don't really go together, since each one demands a completely different kind of reading (a different type of generic reception, if you excuse the jargon), while their juxtaposition involves awkward shifting of intellectual gears. Such a view goes a long way towards accounting for what is unsatisfactory about the book (and another part of the explanation would underscore Brunner's unequal manipulation of the three traditions—expert in the first, relatively realistic plot, and full of wit and inventiveness in his projection of future media, his spy story is perfunctory and uninventive, while the whole African episode is so frankly bad as to make one squirm).

The other point to be made is that these three plots correspond to an underlying political and ideological scheme and, once unveiled as such, offer quite unacceptable political stereotypes: they amount, indeed, to nothing but the most conventional and shopworn images of the First, Second and Third Worlds respectively, and perpetuate the picture of an advanced world in which the problems are decaying cities and crime in the streets (all resulting, mind you, from overpopulation), of a second sphere of old-fashioned communist dictatorship, and finally of the enviably precapitalist and archaic rhythms of those pastoral and tribal societies of the Third World, over which the first two worlds are bound to struggle.

Thus what is wrong with Brunner's book aesthetically is a direct consequence of what is wrong with it ideologically; and it would seem to me that if such demonstrations were more systematically practiced (of the best, not of the worst, contemporary SF) they might well be more effective in persuading the writers of SF to reexamine their philosophical positions than the relatively terroristic threats of Mr. Rottensteiner.

I would conclude by basing the necessity of ideological analysis on the very nature of SF itself: for me it is only incidentally about science or technology, and even more incidentally about unusual psychic states. It seems to me that *SF is in its very nature a symbolic meditation on history itself*, comparable in its emergence as a new genre to the birth of the historical novel around the time of the French Revolution. Thus, I am perhaps not so far from the position of James Blish, provided his deliberately neutralized word "change" is replaced with the substantive one of history (which may involve stasis, or imperceptible transformation, as well as the rapid change he himself tends to associate with science and technology). If this is the case, then, surely we have as readers not been equal to the capacity of the form itself until we have resituated SF into that vision of the relationship of man to social and political and economic forces which is its historical element.

(from SFS *1:305, Fall 1974)*

A Response to Damon Knight. I cannot share Mr. Knight's conviction that it would be very interesting or very difficult fo find out why crude efforts are so popular in the SF field (see SFS 1:220). Knight apparently is of the persuasion—which strikes me as naive—that there is a definite correspondence between literary quality and popularity, and that the popularity of bad work is therefore an unusual and difficult problem. Whereas I think that while there certainly is a positive correlation with such factors as readability, story-telling or day-dreaming, there is no such positive correlation between the total literary quality of a story and its popularity. Indeed, I am convinced that a very high literary quality would be quite detrimental to popularity, that mediocrity is the safe road to success in SF, and that good work can become really popular only if it also has strong virtues of old-fashioned story-telling (such as Le Guin's work). The results of the various popularity contests and Mr. Knight's own criticism seem to be ample proof of this. What Mr. Knight seems to want now is not criticism but market research. I for one certainly see no reason why I should travel to the U,S.A. just in order to find out why an unimportant writer is relatively popular. And before asking the readers, a critic should ask himself. If I followed Mr. Knight's logic, the most interesting critical problem in SF just now would be "Perry Rhodan"—for this series is really so much more popular than Farmer's work, besides being so much worse. —**Franz Rottensteiner.**

On Nineteenth-Century
Science Fiction

Darko Suvin

Radical Rhapsody and Romantic Recoil in the Age of Anticipation: A Chapter in the History of SF

(from SFS 1:255 - 269, Fall 1974)

> Let's be realistic—let's demand the impossible.
> —Anonymus Sorbonensis, May 1968.

> The really philosophical writers invent the true,
> by analogy....   —Balzac.

It seems most useful to define SF not by its thematic field, potentially unlimited, but by aspects that are always present in it. For any SF story these aspects are *radically different agents (figures, dramatis personae) and/ or a radically different scene (existential context, locus)*. To use a key term of the formalist critics, most successfully developed by Brecht, such radically different aspects of a narrative make it appear strange; implying the possibility of new technological, sociological, biological, even philosophical sets of norms, the narrative in turn estranges the author's and reader's own empirical environment. As opposed to "naturalistic" ("mimetic" or "mundane") fiction, which aims at holding the mirror up to nature, SF is an *estranged* literary genre. The reason for its existence is a radically different, strange and estranging, newness.

Since certain other genres use the attitude of estrangement, they are sometimes hybridized with SF and sometimes confused with it. The mythological tale sees fixed, supernaturally determined relations under the flux of human fortunes. This mythical static constancy is to SF an illusion, usually a fraud, at best only an arrested realization of the dynamic possibilities of life. Myth asks ahistorically about The Man and The World. SF asks, What kind of man?, In what kind of world?, and Why such a man (or indeed non-man) in such a world? Myth absolutizes apparently constant relationships from periods of sluggish social development. SF builds on variable processes from the great whirlpool periods of history, such as the 16-17th and 19-20th centuries. It is committed to a *cognitive* and critical approach which is blood brother to the scientific method; though SF could and did appear long before Descartes, this commitment is the rational kernel to the assertion that it is a "scientific fiction."

If SF is defined by the interaction of cognition and estrangement, if it is a literature of possible and reasonable wonder or *cognitive estrangement*, then—notwithstanding all sterile hybridizations—it is fundamentally different from the genres derived from myth: the fairy tale, the horror story, or what is now called heroic fantasy, which are all concerned with the irruption of anti-cognitive laws into the author's empirical environment or with worlds in which such laws hold sway. SF, on the other hand, shares with "naturalistic" fiction the basic rule that man's destiny is man—other humans (or psychozoa) and their devices and institutions, powerful but understandable by reason and methodical doubt and therefore changeable. In SF, then, the radically different agents and scenes are still agents and scenes of the human world.[1]

Historically SF arose from the blending of utopian hopes and fears with popularizations of the social and natural sciences in the adventure-journey, the "extraordinary voyage," with its catalogue of wonders that appear along Ulysses' or Nemo's way. Modern SF thus has its antecedents in such historical forms as the Blessed Island Tale, the utopia, the "planetary novel" of the 17th and 18th centures, the Rationalist "state novel," the Romantic blueprint and anti-utopia, the Vernean "scientific novel," and the Wellsian "scientific romance." In spite of their differences, this sequence of types amounts to a coherent tradition (the writers in the line of, say, Lucian, More, Rabelais, Cyrano, Swift, M. Shelley, Verne, Wells, Zamiatin, Stapledon were aware of its unity).[2] It constitutes a literature of cognitive estrangement or wonder, an SF genre with various sub-genres, all of which use the old rhetorical trope of "the impossibilities" (*impossibilia*) in a new and triumphant fusion with the equally old notion of the wished-for land or time; a genre in which autonomous worlds are opposed to the author's empirical environment either in explicit detail, as a "world upsidedown" (existentially in the Cockaigne tales, politically in the utopias, etc.), or in implicit parallel, as satirical or playful wonder testifying to radical other possibilities, or both. Its significant texts group themselves in distinct clusters, where different historical purposes developed the basic SF form into different sub-genres, from the oral tales and ancient classics, through the clusters of 1510-1660, 1770-1830, and 1880-1910, to the cluster of the last 35 years. In between, for this is a subversive tradition, it was driven underground (e.g., the oral literature and hermetical apocrypha of the Middle Ages), or into exile (e.g., French SF after the Fronde), or into the disreputable organs of sub-literature (e.g., the U.S. pulp magazines of the period between the wars). SF thus belongs— like many types of humor—to that popular literature which spread through centuries by word of mouth and other unofficial channels, penetrating into officially accepted literature only at rare favorable moments; when it did penetrate, however, it produced masterpieces which were sufficient to establish a tenuous yet potent intellectual tradition. Having been sustained by subordinate social groups, with whom it achieved and then lost historical legitimacy, this iceberg character of SF, only a fraction showing above the silent surface of officially recorded culture, is thus the result of class tensions.

If SF is historically part and parcel of a submerged or popular "lower literature" expressing the yearnings of repressed social groups, it is understandable that its major breakthroughs to the cultural surface should happen in the periods of sudden social convulsion, such as the age of the bourgeois-democratic and industrial revolutions, incubating in western Europe since More and Bacon, breaking out at the end of the 18th century, and continuing into the 19th. The imaginative horizon or *locus* of estrangement in SF shifts radically at this time. Hitherto located in a *space* existing alongside the author's empirical environment (i.e., an alternative island whose radical otherness and/or debunking parody put that environment into question), SF in the 18th century turns increasingly to a *time* into which the author's age might evolve. A wished-for or feared future becomes the new space of the cognitive imagination, no doubt in intimate connection with the shift from the social power of land to that of capital based on labor sold and profit gained in that time which—as the new slogan said—is money. In the 19th century, time finally froze "into an exactly delimited, quantifiable continuum, filled with quantifiable 'things' [and thus] it becomes space";[3] and quantified natural science made social change in one lifetime the rule rather than the exception. In this essay we shall see that the high price of a success of the industrial revolution which was linked to a failure of social revolutions led SF from the radical blueprints and rhapsodies of Mercier, Condorcet, Babeuf, Saint-Simon, Fourier, Blake, and Shelley to the Romantic recoil from harsh reality and internalization of suffering in Mary Shelley, Hawthorne, Poe, and Melville.

1. RADICAL RHAPSODY. When time is the ocean on whose further shore the alternative life is situated, Jerusalem can be latent in England:

> I will not cease from mental strife,
> Nor shall by sword sleep in my hand,
> Till we have built Jerusalem
> In England's green and pleasant land.

Blake's Preface to *Milton* fuses a strong collective activism with the Biblical tradition of such future horizons: "Jerusalem is called Liberty among the children of Albion" (*Jerusalem* §54). In the Bible, old Hebraic communism—the desert tradition of prizing men above possessions—intermittently gives rise to expectations of a time when everyone shall "buy wine and milk without money and without price" (Isaiah) and when "nation shall not lift up sword against nation...but they shall sit every man under his vine and under his fig tree; and none shall make them afraid" (Micah), even to "a new Heavens and a new Earth: and the former shall not be remembered, nor come into mind" (Isaiah). Christ's communism of love was resolutely turned toward such a millenium. Throughout the intervening centuries, heretic sects and plebeian revolts kept this longing alive. Joachim Di Fiore announced a new age without church, state, or possessions, when the flesh shall again be sinless and Christ dissolved into a community of friends. By way of the 17th-century religious revolutionaries this tradition led to Blake. His age witnesses a new, lay prophetic line from Babeuf and Shelley to Marx, fusing poetry and politics and inveighing against the great Babylon of class-state, "the merchants of the earth" and "the kings of the earth who have committed fornication with her" (Revelations). As of then, the future is a new existential horizon corroding what Blake calls the "apparent surfaces" of the present, etching it in as unsatisfactory. As in Virgil's Fourth Eclogue, "the great succession of ages begins anew."

Apart from insignificant precursors, SF anticipation began as part and parcel of the French Enlightenment's confidence in cognitive progress. Its "drawing-room communists" Mably and Morelly drew up blueprints transferring Plato's argument against private property from heavenly ideals into nature's moral laws. At the conservative end of the oppositional political spectrum, MERCIER's hero, who wakes up in *Year 2440* (1770),[4] dwelt in the first full-fledged utopian anticipation: in it progress had led to constitutional government, moral and technical advances (e.g., a phonograph with cries of wounded is used to educate princes), and a substitution of science for religion. The noblest expression of such an horizon was CONDORCET's *Sketch...of the progress of human mind* (written in 1793) which envisaged a turning point in human history—the advent of a new man arising out of the "limitless perfectibility of the human faculties and the social order." Perfected institutions and scientific research would eradicate inhumanity, conquer nature and chance, extend human senses, and lead in an infinite progression to an

Elysium created by reason and love for humanity. Condorcet tried to work hard toward such a state within the Revolution, just as did "Gracchus" BABEUF, in whom culminates the century of utopian activism before Marx. Equality, claimed Babeuf, was a lie along with Liberty and Fraternity as long as property (including education) is not wholly equalized through gaining power for the starved against the starvers. An *association* of men in a planned production and distribution without money is the only way of "chaining destiny," of appeasing "the perpetual disquiet of each of us about our tomorrows." For a great hope was spreading among the lower classes that the just City was only a resolute hand's grasp away, that—as Babeuf's fellow conspirators wrote in *The Manifesto of the Equals*—"The French Revolution is merely the forerunner of another Revolution, much greater and more solemn, which will be the last." Even when Babeuf as well as Condorcet was executed by the Jacobins and the revolution taken over by Napoleon, when anticipatory SF turned to blueprints of all-embracing systems eschewing politics, it remained wedded to the concept of humanity as association. This applies to Blake as well as to Saint-Simon and Fourier.

These two great system-builders of utopian anticipation can here be mentioned only insofar as their approaches are found in and analogous to much SF. In a way, the whole subsequent history of change within and against capitalism has oscillated between Saint-Simon's radical social engineering and Fourier's radical quest for harmonious happiness, which flank Marxism on either side. Henri de SAINT-SIMON anticipated that only industry, "the industrial class" (from wage-earners to industrialists) and its organizational method are pertinent in the new age. The "monde renversé" where this "second nation" is scorned must be righted by standing the world on its feet again. This full reversal means, in terms of temporal orientation, "the great moral, poetic, and scientific operation which will shift the Earthly Paradise and transport it from the past into the future," constituting a welfare state of increasing production and technological command of the whole globe by a united White civilization. This "Golden Age of the human species" is to be attained by "a positive Science of Man" permitting predictive extrapolation. Saint-Simon is the prophet of engineers and industrial productivity, usable equally for a regulated capitalism or an autocratic socialism. The Suez Canal as well as Stalin, and all SF whose hero is the "ideologically neutral" engineering organizer, from Verne to Asimov, or Bellamy to the feebler, utopian Wells, are saintsimonian.

For all his rational organizing, Saint-Simon had forsaken 18th-century Rationalism by answering the Swiftian question "What is man?" in terms of economic life rather than of "nature" and "natural rights," even if he then retreated to positing three separate human natures or psychophysiological classes—rational, administrative, and emotive—whose representatives would form the ruling "Council of Newton," the college of cardinals of his "New Christianity." Charles FOURIER based a radically humanized economy entirely upon a complex series of desires. Civilization "thwarted and falsified" them whereas it could and should have increased the gratification of all passions—sensual, collective (desires for respect, friendhsip, love, and a reconstituted family), or "serial" (desires for faction, variety, and unity). It is a world turned inside out (*monde à rebours*) in which the physician has to hope for "good fevers," the builder for "good fires," and the priest for "the good dead"; in which family means adultery (and Fourier enumerates with glee 49 types of cuckold), riches bankruptcy, and work a constraint; in which property ruins the proprietor, abundance leads to unemployment, and the machine to hunger. Against this Fourier elaborated a method of "absolute deviation" which was to lead to a world where both work and human relations would be a matter of "passionate attraction." Men and their passions are not equal but immensely varied, like notes in the harmonic scale, colors in the spectrum, or dishes at a gastronomic banquet, and have to be skilfully composed in a "calculus of the Destinies." Corresponding to the potential harmony of the "social movement" are series of animal, vegetable, geometric, and cosmic relationships. Thus there will be 18 different creations on Earth in this passional cosmology; ours is the first and worst, having to traverse five horrible stages from Savagery down to Civilization before ascending through "Guarantism" (the economico-sexual welfare state of federated productive associations or *phalanstères*) to Harmony. At that point humanity will have cleansed the Earth of sexual and economic repression, illnesses, nations, the sundering of production from consumption, and the struggle for existence; and the Earth—itself a living being in love with another bisexual planet—will respond by melting the polar ice, turning the oceans into something like lemonade (all this elaborately justified by physics), and producing useful "anti-beasts" such as the anti-lion, as well as new senses for men. The blessed life of Harmony and the succeeding 16 creations (the last one seeing the end of the globe) will turn the procedures of class and power inside out: courts and priests will be Courts of Love and priesthoods of sex; armies will clean, plant, and reconstruct; work will become play and art, and "abnormality" the mainspring of society. Fourier's shattering interplay of maniacal poetry and ironical dialectics, rooted in the deep longings of the classes crushed by commerce and industry, in a genuine folk imagination with its immense strengths and foibles, will reappear in garden cities and kibbutzin, communes and "retribalization." In his exemplary scenes and characters—such as Nero becoming a respected butcher in Harmony, much like Rabelais's King Anarch—he is himself writing warm SF. It will be followed in the rare but precious visions fusing relativist sociopolitics, erotics, and cosmology in SF, from Shelley through Stapledon to Le Guin.

Blake's and Shelley's imaginations, in spite of their dissimilar traditions, often run astoundingly parallel to this contemporary of theirs. They too rejected the orthodox division of man into body versus soul and of society into classes, as well as the merely given "human form." BLAKE championed Man's individual and collective "imaginative body" rising as a giant into a projected free fulfillment simultaneously economic, sexual, and creative. The hypocritic and cruel civilization of Church, Army, Palace, and Merchant, with its principle of selfhood, creates jealous possessiveness over children and women, shame of sexual love, and slavery to hunger and toil. Money, the cement of this fallen society, murders the poor by stunting and the rich by corrupting their imaginative needs, thus engendering sterility. Therefore Blake sang the American and French revolutions in his Promethean "Orc cycle" of the 1790s—from *The French Revolution, America*, and *Europe* to *The Four Zoas*—which announced the end of post-Genesis history and the advent of a new divine Man in a realm of freedom (a term Marx too was to use). Revolution is identical with imagination and life, and absolutely unavoidable; but if its beginning is in politics, its end is in a joyous Joachimite Jerusalem where the body personal and the body politic shall have been redeemed. However, as the American and French experiences turned to bourgeois rule and aggressive conquests, and as English repression grew virulent, Blake's earlier work remained unpublished and unfinished. Orc aged into his Rationalist sky-god antagonist Urizen, and Blake came to stress timeless religious apocalypse and pragmatic compensation through art in place of the imminent passage through the Earthly Paradise of sexuality and benevolent nature to the Eden of creativity. His fantasies of cosmogonic history read like a gigantic inventory of later "far out" SF, from Stapledon and E.E. Smith to Arthur Clarke and van Vogt. But as different from their impoverished strainings into cosmic sensations, even the most opaque pseudomythology of the later Blake retains the estranging principle of "twofold vision" which sees the unfallen world within the fallen one, and the cognitive orientation of an "Innocence [that] dwells with Wisdom." In his last year, amid the bread riots, he persisted in his Biblical communism: "Give us the bread that is our due and right, by taking away money, or a price, or tax upon what is Common to all in thy Kingdom."

SHELLEY, younger than Blake and from a higher social class, and irrevocably opposed to Christianity, which he saw as tyranny, marked the orienting of revolutionary toward political parable and vision rather than mythical form, toward Hellenic, Shakespearean, and scientific rather than Biblical or Miltonic traditions. His first major work, *Queen Mab* (1813), is an embattled vision of humanity's past, present, and future which draws on contemporary natural sciences, the *philosophes* such as Condorcet, and their English systematizer William Godwin for the future ideally perfectible society. Godwin's *Political Justice*, invoking Plato, More, and Swift's Houyhnhnms, pleaded for the equalization of property so that men could change their character, abandon war and monogamous family, and finally become immortal by the control of mind over matter. Shelley fleshes out such a Rationalist anarchism in his anticipation of a harmonious Earth rejoicing in the perpetual Spring of a fertile and gentle Nature, where "All things are recreated, and the flame / Of consentaneous love inspires all life" (§8:106-08). In the notes to *Queen Mab*, Shelley develops his views both on labor as the sole source of wealth, which could be reduced to two hours daily, and on the change of Earth's axis and the speeding up of the mind's perception to vanquish time by "an infinite number of ideas in a minute." Such horizons, as well as the poem's forceful attacks on the ruling political tyranny, capitalist selfishness and corruption, and church and religion, made *Queen Mab*, in spite of legal persecution, the bible of English working-class radicalism from Owenites to Chartists and beyond.

Queen Mab is the concluding chord in the great sequence of societal and cosmic anticipations accompanying the democratic revolutions in America and France. From Diderot and Condorcet to Blake and almost all the European romantics, two generations shared the expectation of an imminent millenium of peace, freedom, and brotherhood:

> Not in Utopia—subterranean fields—
> Or some secreted island, Heaven knows where!
> But in the very world, which is the world
> Of all of us—the place where, in the end,
> We find our happiness, or not at all!
> —Wordsworth, *The Prelude* §11:140-44.

But the revulsion from the results of the revolutions "was terrible," observed Shelley in the Preface to *The Revolt of Islam* (1818): "Thus, many of the most ardent and tender hearted...have been morally ruined by what a partial glimpse of the events they deplored appeared to show as the melancholy desolation of all their cherished hopes. Hence gloom and misanthropy have become the characteristics of the age in which we live, the solace of a disappointment that unconsciously finds relief only in the wilful exaggeration of its own despair." The shift of SF location from space to the present or immediate future, we can now see, was arrested and re-channelled either back into timelessness or into the staking out of anticipation in distant futures. These alternatives develop into different, twin but opposed, genres and atmospheres. A *fantasy* more tenuous, internalized, and horrific than that of the later Blake emerges as a new shudder and genre in Romantic melodrama, tale, and narrative poem. (In particular, Coleridge's *Ancient Mariner*, using both scientific observations and the polar voyage as metaphor for the breakdown of human relationships in an alienating society, had a profound effect on Mary Shelley and Poe, and through them on much subsequent SF.) On the other hand, Shelley is (together with Fourier) the great poetic forerunner of the SF *extrapolative anticipation* saved from arid political or natural-science didacticism by also being a *parabolic analogy*. In the hands of poets, whether in verse or prose, such analogy, simultaneously collective and intimate, has cosmic pretensions over and beyond sociopolitical (later also technological) anticipation.

   The Revolt of Islam itself is an "alternative history," the account of a loving pacifist-revolutionary couple who are defeated politically but not ruined morally because they keep faith with their personal love as well as with the future vision of "divine Equality" (§5:3). Laon and Cythna must die in this "Winter of the world," but "Spring comes, though we must, who made / The promise of its birth" (§9:25). Parallel to the satirical comedy *Swellfoot the Tyrant,* a sarcastic political travesty of *King Oedipus* as beast-fable, Shelley's culminating statement comes in *Prometheus Unbound* (1820). This "lyrical drama" is a delicately tough parable in which Prometheus stands for Humanity that created evil in the shape of its oppressor Jupiter, but also for intellect and intellectuals as champions of the oppressed. In order to escape the fate of the French Revolution, or of Blake's Orc, Prometheus renounces hate in spite of the torments by Furies, who stand for the forces of court, church, war, commerce, and law, but also for ethical torments and despondency: political and ethical tenor are convertible in this multiply woven "fable." Jupiter is thereupon toppled by Demogorgon (the subterranean and plebeian titanic Necessity of nature and society, associated with subversive volcanic and earthquake imagery), who has been contacted by Prometheus's bride Asia, standing for Love or overriding human sympathy. Necessity, Love, and Hercules (Strength and armed insurrection) liberate Prometheus, and thus bring about the transformation of society to "Fortunate isles," a renewed life where evil and ugly masks have been stripped off all nature, and man remains

> Scepterless, free, uncircumscribed, but man
> Equal, unclassed, tribeless, and nationless,
> Exempt from awe, worship, degree, the king
> Over himself; just, gentle, wise.... (§3:4:194-98)

In the final act, even this Earthly Paradise is after "an hundred ages" superseded by Time stopping in a full unfolding of human psychic and cosmic potentiality. The universe too becomes Promethean, and the newly warmed and habitable Moon sings a paean of praise to redeemed Earth in a lyrical finale of surpassing power, imbued with the peculiarly Shelleian "Liquid splendour," often in images of vivifying electricity.

Shelley's expressionist lyricism, using poetic abstraction as an "intelligible and beautiful analogy" with the most precise apprehensions of mind and nature and their most sensitive historical oscillations, gives poetry the power to comprehend all knowledge. Politics, cosmology, and natural sciences such as chemistry, electricity, and astronomy are potential liberators of humanity, equally based on labor and Promethean thought:

> Our toil from thought all glorious forms shall cull
> To make this Earth, our home, more beautiful,
> And Science, and her sister, Poesy,
> Shall clothe in light the fields and cities of the free!
> *Revolt of Islam* §5:51:5.

And humanity cannot be whole again (he resolutely agreed with Mary Wollstonecraft) until the state is abolished where "Woman as the bond-slave dwells / Of man a slave; and life is poisoned in its wells" (Ibid. §8:13). Parallel to this poetry of cognition, Shelley's estrangement is the most delicate yet vigorous personal emotion at the sight of life enslaved, approaching it always "with a fresh wonder and an insatiable indignation";[5] e.g., the line "Hell is a city much like London" (*Peter Bell the Third* §3:1) is quite Swiftian. Often at the limits of the expressible—"With thoughts too swift and strong for one lone human breast" (*Revolt of Islam* §9:33)—Shelley's insight into scientific and political thought as strife and sympathy between man, planetary nature, and time, makes *Prometheus Unbound* "one of the few great philosophical poems in English."[6] The opus culminating in this poem—strongly imbued with political anticipation, Lucretian cosmic and anthropological speculation, and utopian romance such as Paltock's *Peter Wilkins* (1750) and J.H. Lawrence's feminist *Empire of the Nairs* (1801)—is proof that SF can be supreme poetry, and vice versa.

2. ROMANTIC RECOIL. Although MARY SHELLEY was the daughter of two radical writers, Godwin (mentioned above) and the feminist Mary Wollstonecraft, and wrote *Frankenstein, or The Modern Prometheus* even while her husband was preparing himself for *Prometheus Unbound*, yet in this revealingly flawed hybrid of horror-tale and philosophical SF she expresses with considerable force the widespread recoil from Promethean utopianism, the "disappointment that unconsciously finds relief only in the wilful exaggeration of its own despair," which was to become a dominant tendency in subsequent English-language SF. The novel's theme is twofold: Frankenstein's creation of artificial life is the vehicle for a parable on the fate of an alienated representative individual—his Creature (called "monster" only twice, I think, in the entire book). A series of paradoxes and contradictions emerges from the opposition of these two themes and characters.

Victor Frankenstein's theme shapes a horror tale about the attitudes of modern "objective" science. It is not quite anti-scientific, but is recounted as an awful warning to Walton, the explorer of icy polar regions, not to pursue discovery unless solitary imagination is allied to warm fellow-feeling. Walton's "belief in the marvellous," though fed by Romantic poetry, science, and utopian travel dreams, merely hurried him "out of the common pathways of men" and rendered him friendless; parallel to this, Frankenstein has spurned the study of language and politics, recapitulating in his personal history the exclusion of "human sciences" from post-Baconian science. Just as Walton is ruthlessly prepared to sacrifice his crew and his own life for "the acquirement of knowledge" equated with dominion over nature in the name of an abstract mankind, so Frankenstein had quite scientifically concluded that "to examine the causes of life, we must first have recourse to death," and proudly gone about creating a human being with the aid of science instead of the traditional "divine spark" (bestowed by God or stolen from him by Prometheus) or the alchemical, magic elixir of life. For Percy (and presumably Mary) Shelley, electricity was vital energy imbued with natural human sympathy; Frankenstein used it instead with mathematics and charnel-house surgery. That his desire to break through the boundary between life and death boomerangs, in the Creature's killing all his dear ones and thus desolating his life, is in the best theological tradition; his horror and disgust when seeing his creature come alive would thus, as in a Gothic story, prefigure its behavior, just as its hideous looks would testify to its corrupt essence.

But the Creature's pathetic story of coming to sentience and to conscious-ness of his untenable position provides an almost diametrically opposed point of view. His theme is both the compositional core and the real novelty or SF element that lifts Frankenstein above a grippingly mindless Gothic story. Far from being foul within, the Creature starts as an ideal 18th-century "noble savage," benevolent and good, loving and yearning for love. His ter-rible disappointment and alienation is that of the typical Romantic hero— of, as he himself points out, Goethe's Werther or a Romantically justified Miltonic Satan—wandering through mountains and glaciers. In the Creature this outcast status is projected from historical practice into biological necessity: he is caught between his vital spark of freedom and the iron grip of scorn and persecution that arises from his racial alienness. We are back on the shores of Houyhnhnmland as seen by Godwin: for in the Creature a "sensitive and rational animal" (§24), less guilty than man, is again showing up human his-tory, politics, psychology, and metaphysics. These are explained in the four books the Creature overhears being discussed during his strange education by proxy:

> The strange system of human society was explained to me.... I learned that the possessions most esteemed by your fellow creatures were high and unsullied descent united with riches. A man might be respected with only one of these advantages; but without either, he was considered ...as a vagabond and a slave, doomed to waste his powers for the profits of the chosen few! And what was I?... I knew that I possessed no money, no friends, no kind of property. I was, besides, endued with a figure hideously deformed and loathsome; I was not even of the same nature as man.... Was I then a monster...? (§13)

But the addition of "sensitive" to the 18th-century definition of man as a rational animal points to a great shift across the watershed of the failed democratic and the costly industrial revolution. Humanity is being shown up not only as irrational but also as cruel, in impassioned rather than satirical accents, by a suffering and wronged creature who wants to belong rather than be a detached and wondering observer. This shift exactly corre-sponds to the shift from far-off places to a present that should be radically transformed, from More's or Swift's static juxtaposition of islands and cities to the dynamic mutual pursuit of Frankenstein and his Creature across the extreme landscapes of lifeless cold and desolation, from behaviorist to senti-mental psychology, from general human nature to historical human relation-ships. Life, the central category of the Romantics, "is opposed to being in the same way as movement to immobility, as time to space, as the secret wish to the visible expression."[7]

This hallowed status of sentient life and its genesis was threatened by a capitalist use of physical sciences which substituted "mechanical or two-way time for history, the dissected corpse for the living body, dismantled units called 'individuals' for men-in-groups, or in general the mechanically measurable or reproducible for the inaccessible and the complicated and the organically whole."[8] This led to a growing relevance of and fascination with *automata* as puzzling "doubles" of man. Before Mary Shelley, such a semi-alien twin had been treated either as a wondrously ingenious toy (in the 18th century) or as an unclean demonic manifestation (in most German Romantics); in the first case it belonged to "naturalistic" literature, in the second to horror-fantasy. The nearest approximation to an artificial creature seen both as perfect human loveliness and (later) as a horrible mechanical construct was provided by Hoffman in *The Sandman* (1816). But even he oscillated between fiends and physics, and his Olimpia was seen solely through a dazzled observer. Mary Shelley's Creature is not only undoubtedly alive though alien, and fashioned out of human material instead of the inorganic wires of puppetry, he is also allowed to gain our sympathy by being shown from the inside, as a subject degradingly treated like an object. However, because of the "exaggerated despair" which Shelley accurately diagnosed, not only is human society monstrous in its dealing with the Creature, but he too is "objectively" a monster—living though unnatural, sentient and intelligent though inhuman.

Clearly, the two main themes and viewpoints of the novel contradict each other. The Creature is the moral focus of this parable, so that the reader cannot treat him as a Gothic monster merely vouched for by science instead of the supernatural. But vice versa, if one is to look at this as SF, important unresolved questions appear—and fundamentally, why did the Creature have to be hideous? Conceivably, though unconvincingly, the contrived accident of Frankenstein's creative haste might be discounted as just one more among the melodramatic contrivances and technical clumsinesses of this novel; even so, why should alienness have to be automatically equated with hideousness? The tenor and the vehicle of the parable are here startlingly discrepant— a signal that some strong psychic censorhip is at work. As Shelley suggested in the Preface to *The Revolt of Islam*, we are here dealing with a gloom and misanthropy rooted in the moral ruin of the revulsion from the French Revolution. The hypothesis that, just as in Blake and Shelley, the relationships in *Frankenstein* are symbolic both of individual psychology and collective politics explains the curious contradictions found in the novel. Frankenstein and the Creature are in some ways comparable to Freud's Ego and Id, but they are not reducible to such a Jekyll-Hyde relationship. The Creature is warmer and finally more intelligent than his creator, like Milton's Adam and Satan; nor can Freudism explain why the lower psychological class of Id must always be thought of as lawless and destructive. However, Frankenstein can be seen as an overhasty and half-baked Shelleyan intellectual, the Godwinian *philosophe*-scientist who "animates" the popular masses with "no kind of property" in hopes of a new and glorious creation, only to find—in a parable of the French Revolution—that persecution and injustice exacerbate them to the point of indiscriminate slaughter and that his Prometheanism has desolated his "most cherished hopes." This supplies an historical explanation for the Creature's only partly successful fashioning and the universal revulsion felt for it. It also clarifies why at the end Frankenstein can exclaim "I have myself been blasted in these hopes, yet another may succeed." In this view he was an improper Prometheus or revolutionary intellectual—a truly new one, with more patience and love, will be presented in *Prometheus Unbound*.

Mary Shelley's other SF novel, *The Last Man* (1826), is a renewed reversal of the perspectives in *Prometheus Unbound*. It retains and interestingly details its prospects of political liberation, but reverses its cosmic optimism by having mankind collapse in a plague which leaves the sole survivor finally even more isolated than Frankenstein or his Creature. The shift of the locale into the future (the "tale of the future" becomes six times more frequent after 1800) translates Mary's usual Gothic background into a *black SF anticipation*, already adumbrated in several works that followed the debacle of 18th-century hopes and often posited a new ice age (Grainville's poem *Le dernier homme*, 1805; the "romance-in-futurity" *Last Men*, 1806; Byron's poem "Darkness"; etc.). This makes *The Last Man* a precursor of the SF "physics of alienation" from Poe to *The Time Machine* and beyond. But *Frankenstein* remains her permanent contribution, claiming for SF the concern for a personal working out of overriding sociological and scientific dilemmas. It compromised with horror-fantasy taste by returning these dilemmas largely to biology, thus announcing the legions of menacing aliens and androids from Wells and Capek on. Yet the stress on sympathy and responsibility for the Creature transcends the sensational murders and purple patches of Mary's own novel and most SF writing on this theme (not to mention the Hollywood movies which revert to one-dimensional Gothic monsters). The urgency in *Frankenstein*, situated in an exotic present, interweaves intimate reactions with social destiny, enthusiasm for Promethean science with a feeling for its human results, and marries the exploratory SF parable with the (still somewhat shaky) tradition of the novel. This indicated the way SF would go in meeting the challenge of the cruel times, and of Swift's great question about man—relocated into body and history.

However, the way proved long and thorny. A number of scattered SF writings appeared in Europe in the 1830s and 1840s with the revival of utopian expectations and Romantic dreams. In Russia, V. Odoevsky wrote a mild anticipation, *The Year 4338*.[9] In France, Souvestre disguised a sermon on the immorality of mechanized progress, which had torn down the old pieties and would therefore be destroyed by God, as possibly the first anti-utopian anticipation in *The World as It Shall Be* (1846), and Cabet disguised an authoritarian version of Fourier and Owen as fiction in *A Journey to Icaria* (1840), both only less insipid than Lamartine's liberal United Europe of *France and England* (1843). As a last interesting echo of the 1848 wave, C.I. DEFONTENAY revived in *Star* (1854) the planetary novel with a vivid description, in prose mixed with verse, of a whole planetary system with different man-like species, their physics, politics, and ethics. A utopian humanism and sensibility, which created even samples of Starian literature, vivifies his narration of their history, passing through a cosmic exodus and return—a lone work looking forward to Stapledon. In Britain, J.F. Bray's *A Voyage From Utopia*,[10] halfway between Owen and Bellamy, attempted to merge Swiftian techniques with radical egalitarian propaganda. Utopias in the U.S.A., which had been published since the turn of the century, also gave some signs of reviving. But tries at colonies such as Cabet's and the Brook Farm failed, and the distance from—indeed enmity to—the everyday world increased in the North American writers of the mid-19th century. Living in the country where the bourgeois way of life progressed most rapidly, they recoiled from its optimism most thoroughly, and came to treat the wondrous novelty not in terms of Prometheus the revolutionary, but in terms of Faust, the overreacher who sold his soul to the Devil and whom Goethe had already adopted as symbol of the permanent dynamism accompanying the bourgeois. The most prominent of such recoilers were Hawthorne, Melville, and Poe. The first often used allegorical fantasy, the second a more or less imaginary voyage, and the third both. In some cases, admittedly marginal to the ensemble of their works, their fictions bordered on or passed into SF.

One of the strong American literary traditions was that of the world supplying moral symbols for the writer, and in particular of the adventurous voyage as an inner quest. It flowed from various updatings of *Pilgrim's Progress*, from Morgan's *History of the Kingdom of Basaruah* (1715) to C.B. Brown, Irving (whose *History of New York*, 1809, has a satirical SF sketch, midway between Voltaire and Wells, of Lunarians dealing with Earthmen as Whites did with Indians), and Cooper (who wrote two rather bad satirico-utopian novels) and it culminated in Hawthorne's fiction as the working out of a hypothesis with a symbolically collective rather than individualist main character. In short, there was almost "no major 19th-century American writer of fiction, and indeed few of the second rank, who did not write some SF or at least one utopian romance."[11] HAWTHORNE usually equivocates between the natural and the supernatural, so that the hypnotism and other controlling influences in his major romances are never more than an undercurrent. Even in the stories that turn on the scientist-artist, the somewhat melodramatic allegory suggests that his Faustian urge is unnatural—at worst criminal, as in "The Birthmark," and at best useless except for his inner satisfaction, as in "The Artist of the Beautiful." Only in "Rappaccini's Daughter" (1846) is Hawthorne prepared to envisage a counter-creation for a moment on its own merits. Though Beatrice is not given as spirited a defense as Frankenstein's Creature, she is at least an innocently wronged alien who exercises considerable passionate attraction—rather similar to the Fourierist ideas that Hawthorne was to renounce as senseless and wicked after his Brook Farm experience, itself comparable to a poisoned Eden. But finally, her father's revolutionary creation is dismissed in an ending more akin to exorcism than to SF.

On the contrary, POE took to an exemplary extreme both the autonomy of his imaginary worlds and the isolation of the individual who does not relate to a coherent community but to some metaphysical principle. Poe was more exposed than Hawthorne to a civilization that was finding the artist unnecessary except as a leisure-time entertainer for marginal social strata. History and society meant to him merely a rapidly expanding "dollar-manufacture," a hateful democracy or Mob rule, so that his protagonist—raising the stakes in comparison with the revolts of the first Romantic generation—ignores almost all human interaction, not only in politics and work but also in sex and knowledge. Science, technology, and all knowledge have become Mephistophelean instead of Promethean powers, fascinating but leading only to dead-ends and destruction: "Poe confronts and represents, as few authors before him, the alienated and alienating quality of the technological environment."[12]

Therefore he constructed a compensatory fantasy-world connecting an exacerbated inner reality directly to the universe. But this fantasy is a kind of photographic negative of his environment. Feeling is dissociated from the intelligence and will that normally acted upon a socially recognizable reality, and a subjective timelessness (indeed a dream or nightmare-time) or instant apprehension of horror efface any objectively measurable progress of time: personality and consciousness are here disintegrating. In the actuality "timekeeping had merged with record-keeping in the art of communication."[13]

Poe, the first significant figure in this tradition to live from commercial work for periodicals (even writing a story to fit a magazine illustration, as often in present-day SF), concentrated on the obstacles to communication. To him it is a maze of masks, hoaxes and cryptograms, exemplified by the recurrent manuscript in a bottle, falsely sent or mysteriously received, revealing truth ambiguously if at all.

Most of Poe's tales existing within the horizons of terror, of flight from life and time, are horror-fantasies pretending to a private supernatural reality which is in fact based upon pre-scientific lore. In this light, Poe is the originator of what is least mature in the writing commercially peddled as SF—an adolescent combination of hysterical sensibility and sensational violence, and dissociation of symbol from imaginative consistency of any (even imaginary) world, a vague intensity of style used for creepy incantation. His protagonist is often "the perpetual American boy-man...[who] must, to express himself, go above, or away from, or beyond our commoner range of experience."[14] T.S. Eliot, acknowledging his "very exceptional mind and sensibility," has even suggested that Poe's intellect was that "of a highly gifted young person before puberty."[15] Though this may not be fair to Poe, who at his best knew how to present his limitations with ironic distancing, it accurately pinpoints the emotional age of his imitators in the No-Man's-Land of fantasy passed off as SF from Haggard and Lovecraft to Bradbury and further.

Three groups of Poe's works have a more direct claim to attention in this survey: those marginally using some SF conventions, those using SF for comic comment or ideological revelation, and the cosmological speculations. The first group comprises the poem "Al Aaraaf," the dialogues "Eiros and Charmion" (which mentions the destruction of Earth by a comet-caused conflagration) and "The Power of Words," and the tales of oceanic descent culminating in *The Narrative of Arthur Gordon Pym* (1838). *Pym* appropriates the extraordinary-voyage tradition for a metaphysical (and in the Tsalal episode passably racist) quest for purity or the unknown, presents an interesting use of correspondences between the world and the protagonist, and possibly ends with the Pole being an entrance to the hollow earth popularized in *Symzonia* (1820). The second group features anticipations like balloon-flights across the Atlantic and to the Moon or suspended animation (in "The Balloon Hoax," "The Unparalleled Adventures of One Hans Pfaall," "Some Words With a Mummy," "Mellonta Tauta," "Van Kempelen and His Discovery") as hoaxes or satires on present-day certainties of progress; it includes in "The Man That Was Used Up" (1840) the first instance of a man almost totally composed of artificial organs. The most substantial among them, "Pfaall" (1840) and "Mellonta Tauta" (1850) are most strongly science-fictional. The interplanetary flight prepared by an amateur inventor in his back yard, the verisimilar flight perils and observations, and the glimpses of grotesque yet kindred aliens in the first story gave the cue to much later space-travel SF. More subtly, so did the future inventions, political satire, and cultural incomprehension of the reader's times in the second story (as also, retrospectively, in "The Thousand and Second Tale of Scheherazade") to later time-travel SF. The three "mesmeric tales" culminating in the scientifically motivated horrors of "The Facts in the Case of M. Valdemar" (1845), whether used for revelation of Poe's cosmology or tongue-in-cheek sensationalism, are ancillary to his fantastic system of correspondences. Finally, *Eureka* (1848), his crowning piece of essayistic SF, explicates this highly heretical, complex web of analogies and conversions by which in Poe life does not end with death, sentience is not confined to organic matter, cosmogony is analogous to individual sensibility and creativity (see "The Power of Words"), and the universe is God's coded monologue. Such mechanistic metaphysics lead finally to solipsism: whatever the writer can imagine is as good as created, and conversely all that is created is imagined. No wonder he appealed to later lonely writers.

Poe's influence has been immense in both Anglo-American and French SF (the latter has yet to recover from it). Though his ideology and time-horizon tend to horror-fantasy forms, the pioneering incompleteness of his work provided SF with a wealth of hints for fusing the rational with the symbolical, such as his techniques of gradual domestication of the extraordinary, and of the "half-closed eye" estrangement just glimpsing the extraordinary. With Poe, the tradition of the moral quest became urbanized, escapist, and unorthodox. His influence encompasses on the one hand the mechanical marvels of Verne and the dime novels, and on the other the escapist strain in some of the "straightest" U.S. SF, e.g., Heinlein's time-travelling solipsism. Both are blended in the Wellsian grotesque tradition, from some of Wells's cumulations of believable terrors to, say, the symbolical tales of Blish or Knight. Poe's notes stressing verisimilitude, analogy, and probability for the wondrous story made him also the first theoretician of SF.

MELVILLE's whole opus is a "major contribution to the literature of created societies,"[16] for he had an ingrained tendency to expand almost any subject into an allegorical microcosm of its own, and he took the Faustian quest more seriously than Hawthorne and less necrophiliacally than Poe. *Mardi* (1849), though somewhat formless, is an iconoclastic "extraordinary voyage" among islands of unsatisfactory mythologies, politics, and philosophies which blends Rabelais with memories of Polynesia. "The Tartarus of Maids," a revulsion against industrial and sexual exploitation of women, with sexual physiology masked as factory organization, is on the margins of SF by virtue of its sustained parallel between production of babies and that of paper. Most interestingly, in "The Bell-Tower" (1856), the "practical materialist" merchant-mechanician protagonist, "enriched through commerce with the Levant," rising as a new force in a feudal society and raising his tower with the clock and the "state-bell," is a potent symbol for rising capitalism and the emblematic American Liberty Bell. But his bell has been cast with an admixture of workman's blood, and the automaton created by him to be the bell's ringer, the "iron slave" who stands for all servitude from that of Negroes to that of workers, finally slays his master. The complex—even if not always congruous—religious, sexual, and political symbolism make this the nearest that mid-century narrative-prose SF has come to a Blakean approach. The American SF story continued to be well represented into the second half of the 19th century, as in some stories by Fitz-James O'Brien culminating in the somber tale of microscopic fatality and elective affinity, "The Diamond Lens" (1858). But O'Brien was killed in the Civil War, and the ensuing Gilded Age was not propitious to sustained SF, which would revive only with Bellamy.

Thus the period that opened with universal anticipations of liberation, with Blake's and Shelley's rhapsodies, found its central expression in the anguished immediacy of Frankenstein's costly failure, and ended in the symbolic gloom of representative creators from what began as liberty's first and last frontier but turned out to be a Liberty Bell cracked by the blood of the toilers. As Wordsworth precisely noted: "We poets in our youth begin in gladness; / But thereof comes despondency and madness" ("Resolution and

Independence"). This can be used as a characterization of the age more than of the poets it moulded, turning them from Shelley's unacknowledged legislating to Melville's passionate witnessing.

NOTES

[1] I have discussed this approach to SF in "On the Poetics of the Science Fiction Genre," *College English* 34(1972):372-82, and "Science Fiction and the Genological Jungle," *Genre* 6(1973):251-73. For Bertolt Brecht's practice and theory of estrangement, see *Brecht on Theatre*, ed. and tr. John Willett (NY 1964), especially pp 96 and 192 (where *Verfremdung*, "estrangement," is wrongly translated as "alienation").

[2] For Lucian's influence down to Rabelais and Voltaire, see John E. Sandys, *A History of Classical Scholarship* (Cambridge 1903-08) and Basil L. Gildersleeve, *Essays and Studies* (Baltimore 1908).

[3] Georg Lukács, *History and Class Consciousness* (Boston 1971), p 90, and the whole essay-chapter "The Phenomenon of Reification" on pp 83 seqq. For the epistemological shift from spatial to temporal imagination see also the insights in *Capital* and other writings by Marx, developed by Lukács as well as by Ernst Bloch, *Das Prinzip Hoffnung* I-II (Frankfurt 1959) Lewis Mumford, *Technics and Civilization* (NY and Burlingame 1963), and Edmund Wilson, *To the Finland Station* (1940).

[4] All the dates in the body of this essay are for first book publication.

[5] H.N. Brailsford, *Shelley, Godwin, and Their Circle* (L 1930), p 221.

[6] Carl Grabo, *A Newton Among Poets* (Chapel Hill 1930), p 198.

[7] Michel Foucault, *The Order of Things* (L 1970), p 278.

[8] Mumford (Note 3), p 50.

[9] Odoevsky's text, written in 1837-39 as an epistolary novel, was never completed, presumably because of the dim prospects of its being published in Tsarist Russia, where only one fragment ever appeared (in the magazine "Utrennyaya Zarya" for 1840). It was first published in book form in 1926 (Moscow: Bibl. "Oronek").

[10] Bray's book was written in 1840-41. A year later, the pressures on this radical labor leader and Chartist induced him to emigrate to the USA, and the book was first published only in 1957 (L: Lawrence and Wishart).

[11] H. Bruce Franklin, *Future Perfect: American Science Fiction of the Nineteenth Century* (NY 1966), p x.

[12] David Halliburton, *Edgar Allan Poe* (Princeton 1973), p 247.

[13] Mumford (Note 3), p 136.

[14] E.H. Davidson, *Poe* (Cambridge, Mass. 1957), p 214.

[15] T.S. Eliot, in Eric W. Carlson, ed., *The Recognition of Edgar Allan Poe* (Ann Arbor 1966), pp 212-13.

[16] Franklin (Note 11), p 135.

Aija Ozolins

Dreams and Doctrines: Dual Strands in *Frankenstein*

(from SFS *2:103 - 112, July 1975)*

In her *Journal* the entry made by Mary Shelley for February 22, 1815, records the birth of a seven-month baby that was "not expected to live." The laconic entry for March 6, "Find my baby dead," understates the impact of the child's death, as is indicated by the entry for March 9: "Still think about my little baby—'tis hard indeed for a mother to lose a child." How deeply Mary brooded on her loss is apparent from the entry for March 19: "Dream that my little baby came to life again; that it had only been cold, and that we rubbed it before the fire and it lived. Awake and find no baby."[1] This dream of reanimation apparently lodged in Mary's subconscious and eventually blended with the more famous dream of the following year, the one described in the Introduction to the 1831 edition of *Frankenstein*: "I saw—with shut eyes, but acute mental vision,—I saw the pale student of unhallowed arts kneeling beside the thing he had put together. I saw the hideous phantasm of a man stretched out, and then, on the working of some powerful engine, show signs of life, and stir with an uneasy, half vital motion."[2]

Having thus found "her story" in a dream, Mary began her contribution to that famous set of ghost stories with what is now the opening of §5—"It was on a dreary night of November"—and with the intention of writing only "a short tale." But Shelley urged her to develop the idea at greater length, which she did, by rationalizing and moralizing the spontaneous core of horror.

This twofold process of composition—subconscious generation and conscious elaboration—has resulted in an obviously layered work: e.g., the monster's narrative is embedded in Frankenstein's narrative, which in turn is framed by Walton's Letters and Continuation. Knowing that §5 was part of the original kernel, critics have reached divergent conclusions on the subsequent accretions: some hold the Gothic core of the dream as central and object to the didacticism of the monster's narrative, while others approve of the social and moral themes and thus regard the monster's narrative as central.[3] I propose to examine both the oneiric and the didactic components, beginning with a survey of the dreams that figure in the novel and a discussion of the doppelgänger motif, continuing with the didactic component as expressed in the monster's narrative, and concluding with the didacticism of the Frankenstein and Walton narratives.

1. THE MONSTER AS DOPPELGÄNGER. The word *dream* is used in the novel in various senses. It can be a synonym for the ideals of Frankenstein and Walton, who both refer to their lonely quests as dreams or daydreams (§§ 01, 02, 3, 4, 5). It can also signify what is illusory or insubstantial: before the creation of the monster, and especially afterward, Frankenstein often speaks of how unreal his life seems (§§ 3, 7, 17, 21). Finally, there are actual dreams: Frankenstein has a premonitory dream of his fiancée's death (§5); he has nightmares after the monster has killed Henry Clerval (§21); and sometimes he finds solace in dreams in which he is united with all his loved ones (§§23-24). In most instances dreams are associated with illusoriness or with ideals that turn into nightmares of horror and guilt, but at the same time they all indirectly point back to Mary's seminal dream.

Let us return to that original dream to examine another element that informs the novel—the motif of the doppelgänger. Whatever we call it—shadow, objectified id, or double of the ego personality[4]—this motif of a second self constitutes the chief source of the novel's latent power. Occasionally the double in literature is an embodiment of good (as in Poe's "William Wilson"), but more often he is an image of man's innate propensity toward evil.

There is ample evidence in the novel that the creature functions as the scientist's baser self. Frankenstein's epithets for him consistently connote evil: *devil, fiend, daemon, horror, wretch, monster, monstrous image, vile insect, abhorred entity, detested form, hideous phantasm, odious companion,* and *demoniacal corpse.* Neutral terms like *creature* and *being* are comparatively rare. Most important, there is Frankenstein's thinking of him as "my own vampire, my own spirit let loose from the grave, and forced to destroy all that was dear to me" (§7). And after each murder Frankenstein acknowledges his complicity: "I not in deed, but in effect, was the true murderer" (§9); cf §§ 8, 21, 22).

One sure sign of the double is his haunting presence. Maria Mahoney characterizes the feeling as "someone or something behind you, an ominous adversary dogging your footsteps...[a] sinister and truly evil figure lurking in the dark."[5] Even though Frankenstein initially flees from his creature and even though their direct confrontations are few, the monster is nevertheless a ubiquitous presence in his life. Wandering about the city in order to evade his creature, Frankenstein compares himself to Coleridge's Mariner, who also walks "in fear and dread,/...Because he knows a frightful fiend/Doth close behind him tread" (§5). When he agrees to fashion a mate for his creature he is told to expect constant surveillance: "I shall watch your progress with unutterable anxiety; and fear not but that when you are ready I shall appear" (§17). After breaking his promise he is even more oppressed by a sense of the monster's presence; even his days take on a nightmarish quality: "although the sun shone," he felt only "a dense and frightful darkness, penetrated by no light but the glimmer of two eyes that glared" at him (§21).

The psychological motif of the double is reinforced by several visual tableaux that hint at a secret sympathy between the monster and his maker. At the beginning of her dream Mary saw "the pale student of unhallowed arts kneeling beside the thing he had put together," but at its conclusion the positions are reversed, with the "horrid thing" standing at the student's bedside and "looking on him with yellow, watery, but speculative eyes" (§I). This picture is repeated at the end of the novel when the monster stands sorrowfully over the corpse of Frankenstein (§C). Similarly, there are three moonlight encounters between the two. Although meetings by lightning and moonlight are a conventional part of the Gothic landscape, Mary's conjunction of man, moon, and monster is traceable to her dream and serves to emphasize the close relationship between them. Also, because most of these moonlight encounters are preceded by a crime, they spotlight the creature's jeering, malevolent form.

The last and most important point regarding the double is the necessity to confront and recognize the dark aspect of one's personality in order to transform it by an act of conscious choice. Ideally, the Shadow diminishes as one's awareness increases. "Freedom comes," according to Mahoney, "not in eliminating the Shadow...but in *recognizing him in yourself.*"[6] Prospero acknowledges Caliban—"This thing of darkness I acknowledge mine"—but Frankenstein's typical reactions are first to flee, then to kill. His rejection of his creature is crucial, both in the present psychological context and in the sociological context we shall consider later. Frankenstein, as Philmus says, is always "fleeing from self-knowledge," always seeking "to lose himself in the external world."[7] and thus denying, in Nelson's words, the "nether forces for which he should have accepted a fully aware responsibility."[8]

2. THE DEFENSE OF POLYPHEMUS. The duality of the novel's didactic component is foreshadowed in the juxtaposition of the subtitle referring to Frankenstein, "The Modern Prometheus," and the epigraph from *Paradise Lost*, which applies to the creature's predicament: "Did I request thee, Maker, from my clay/To mould me man? Did I solicit thee/From darkness to promote me?" In Frankenstein's narrative the creature constructed from parts of cadavers and vivified by electricity is an "artificial man," but when Mary traces the social implications of the experiment, when she humanizes the monster and elicits sympathy for him, and when she allows him to tell his own story, summarizing his life from his first day of consciousness to his encounter with Frankenstein many months later, he takes on the aspect of the "natural man" who recapitulates the stages between man in the state of nature and man in civilized society. As such, he is often the mouthpiece for Lockean, Godwinian, and Shelleyan ideas.[9]

In the six chapters told from the creature's point of view we learn how he acquired knowledge and benevolence and why he became malevolent. The agents of his education were his sensations, his observations of the De Lacey family, and his reading. Faithful to the Lockean concept that there are no innate ideas, all knowledge being derived from experience, the creature's monologue begins with the Lockean progression from inarticulate feelings and indistinct perceptions to conceptualized emotions and ideas:

It is with considerable difficulty that I remember the original era of my being: all the events of that period appear confused and indistinct. A strange multiplicity of sensations seized me, and I saw, felt, heard, and smelt, at the same time; and it was, indeed, a long time before I learned to distinguish between the operations of my various senses.... No distinct ideas occupied my mind; all was confused. I felt light, and hunger, and thirst, and darkness.... [after about a week] I began to distinguish my sensations from each other.... [About a month later] my sensations had...become distinct, and my mind received every day additional ideas. (§11)

The De Lacey family, a society in miniature, is the creature's school for studying human language and human nature: from "my beloved cottagers.... I learned to admire their virtues, and to deprecate the vices of mankind," for "benevolence and generosity were ever present before me, inciting within me a desire to become an actor in the busy scene where so many admirable qualities were called forth and displayed" (§15). When he realizes that stealing food from them increases their distress, he satisfies himself with nuts, roots, and berries; moreover, he succeeds in lightening their toil by secretly supplying them with firewood: "I observed with pleasure that he [Felix] did not go to the forest that day, but spent it in repairing the cottage and cultivating the garden" (§12). The creature has by now ascended high on the Godwinian scale of pleasure: at first he took delight in birdsong and moonlight, then in learning, and finally in sympathy with others—all in accord with Godwin's belief that the pleasures of "intellectual feeling...sympathy, and self-approbation" are nobler than the pleasures of the senses.[10]

The scope of the creature's education is broadened by reading: *Werther* stirs his private feelings, awakening "despondency and gloom"; Plutarch extends his thoughts to "new and mighty scenes of action" in the realms of public affairs; and portions of *Paradise Lost* reflect his own outcast state (§15). Volney's *Ruins*, "a widely read compendium of meditations on history... strongly coloured by the author's radical and deist views,"[11] evokes a mixed reaction which is at the same time an oblique Godwinian criticism of society: "Was man, indeed, at once so powerful, so virtuous, and magnificent, yet so vicious and base?... For a long time I could not conceive how one man could go forth to murder his fellow, or even why there were laws and governments; but when I heard details of vice and bloodshed, my wonder ceased, and I turned away with disgust and loathing" (§13).

The course of the creature's education brings out another Godwinian concept central to the novel: "the actions and dispositions of mankind are the offspring of circumstances and events, and not of any original determination that they bring into the world."[12] Although some of the Romantics ascribe innate goodness to natural man, Mary follows her father in stressing the formative influence of "circumstances and events." For example, the creature suggests that whereas Plutarch aroused and strengthened his desire for good, a less edifying volume might have had a different effect:

> I felt the greatest ardour for virtue rise within me, and abhorrence for vice, as far as I understood the significance of those terms.... Induced by these feelings, I was of course led to admire peaceful lawgivers, Numa, Solon, and Lycurgus, in preference to Romulus and Theseus. The patriarchal lives of my protectors caused these impressions to take a firm hold on my mind; perhaps, if my first introduction to humanity had been made by a young soldier, burning for glory and slaughter, I should have been imbued with different sensations. (§15)

And the benevolence learned from excellent models in literature and life does indeed turn to hatred and violence when the creature suffers social rejection: "I was benevolent and good; misery made me a fiend. Make me happy and I shall again be virtuous" (§10); "I cannot believe that I am the same creature whose thoughts were once filled with sublime and transcendent visions of the beauty and majesty of goodness. But it is even so; the fallen angel becomes the malignant devil" (§C).

In the series of rejections that causes this demonic transformation (Frankenstein's flight at the moment of the creature's awakening, Felix's driving him from the door of the cottage, the attempt on his life by the rustic whose child he has saved from drowning), in the series of crimes with which the creature responds to his rejection, and in the creature's demand that Frankenstein create a female to be his mate ("My vices are the children of a forced solitude that I abhor; and my virtues will necessarily arise when I live in communion with an equal" [§17]), Mary follows her father and her husband in insisting on the causal connection between social acceptance and virtue, between social rejection and crime.[13] The failure of some modern scholars to recognize this connection has led them to recast the creature as a Noble Outlaw, a champion of violence and rebellion,[14] but such an interpretation is surely inconsistent with the creature's own attitude toward his deeds: "Polluted by crimes, and torn with the bitterest remorse, where can I find rest but in death?" (§C).

One final piece of extra-textual evidence that indicates how Mary intended her creature to be viewed has been generally overlooked. To a remark in a letter from Leigh Hunt, "Polyphemus...always appears to me a pathetic rather than a monstrous person, though his disappointed sympathies at last made him cruel,"[15] Mary replied (April 6, 1819), "I have written a book in defence of Polypheme have I not?"[16] The reference must be to the story of Polyphemus and Galatea as told in §12 of Ovid's *Metamorphoses*. In 1815, day by day with scarcely a break from April 8 to May 13, Mary had diligently applied herself to the translation of Ovid's fables. Consider the parallels between the predicaments of Frankenstein's creature and the giant, uncouth, one-eyed Polyphemus, who falls in love with a beautiful nymph. Disdained by Galatea, the Cyclops composes a lovelorn song: "But didst thou know me well, thou wouldest repine to have fled...."[17] This plaint is echoed in the Monster's words to Walton: "Once I falsely hoped to meet with beings, who, pardoning my outward form, would love me for the excellent qualities which I was capable of unfolding" (§C). Preferring the handsome Acis,

Galatea spurns the suit of Polyphemus, who, having one day seen them in each other's arms, tosses a ton of rocks at Acis and thus buries him. When we recall the monster's chagrin that "the gentle words of Agatha, and the animated smiles of the charming Arabian were not for [him]," his envy upon seeing the sleeping Justine ("Here...is one of those whose joy-imparting smiles are bestowed on all but me"), and, above all, his bitterness when Frankenstein and Elizabeth sought "enjoyment in feelings and passions from the indulgence of which [he] was for ever barred" (§§ 13, 16, 24), we can understand why Mary Shelley spoke of her book as a "defence of Polypheme."

3. THE DEFENSE OF THE MODERN PROMETHEUS. A created being has certain rights and needs—hence Mary Shelley's defense of her Polyphemus. But the morality of Frankenstein's endeavor is more open to question, as is that of Walton's search for a northern passage and of scientific research in general. I find that, on the whole, Mary sanctions Frankenstein's and Walton's Promethean quests, but does so with vacillations and with a particular view of morality in mind. The fact that these scientific endeavors are alternately presented as culpable and laudable may stem from Mary's intensely dualistic temperament: "I see things pretty clearly, but cannot demonstrate them. Besides, I feel the counter-arguments too strongly.... besides that, on some topics...I am far from making up my own mind.... I may distrust my own judgment too much—be too indolent and too timid."[18]

It is perilous to assume that with respect to morality Mary was writing within an orthodox Christian framework. Her childhood had been spent in an atmosphere of determinism, and she was widely read in Godwin, Voltaire, Rousseau, Holbach, Volney, and other deistic or materialistic *philosophes* of the Enlightenment, whose spirit pervades *Frankenstein* so thoroughly that Aldiss terms it a "dark and atheistic work."[19] Godwin rejected "Love thy neighbor as thyself," for he doubted that a man and his neighbor were likely to be of equal worth, and instead measured a person's moral worth by his contribution to the general good. Thus he was able to declare morality an exact science concerned with "nothing else but a calculation of consequences."[20] Although Mary at times shows an insight into the non-quantifiable essence of morality, she generally agrees with Godwin that virtue is a contribution to the general welfare and that vice is an infraction of the social law. The quests of Frankenstein and Walton, therefore, should be judged in terms of their intended and actual effects. Mary is at pains to stress the humanitarian motives of both men. Frankenstein seeks the elixir of life in order to "banish disease from the human frame, and render man invulnerable to any but a violent death" (§2), while Walton dreams of conferring "inestimable benefit...on all mankind to the last generation, by discovering a passage near the pole...or by ascertaining the secret of the magnet" (§01).

With Mary's dualistic temperament and moral biases in mind, let us examine her attitudes toward these scientific projects. At first she appears to be pointing an explicit moral against presumption. Frankenstein recounts his tale to Walton as an exemplum to dissuade the latter from continuing his Arctic expedition:

"Unhappy man! Do you share my madness? Have you drank also of the intoxicating draught? Hear me, let me reveal my tale, and you will dash the cup from your lips!... You seek for knowledge and wisdom, as I once did.... When I reflect that you are pursuing the same course, exposing yourself to the same dangers which have rendered me what I am, I imagine that you may deduce an apt moral from my tale...." (§04)

"Learn from me, if not by my precepts, at least by my example, how dangerous is the acquirement of knowledge, and how much happier that man is who believes his native town to be the world, than he who aspires to become greater than his nature will allow." (§4)

Through statements such as these Mary is clearly endorsing the traditional taboo against seeking forbidden knowledge but with the important qualification that the search for knowledge is dangerous and unlawful only if it impairs the social affections:

A human being in perfection ought always to preserve a calm and peaceful mind, and never allow passion or transitory desire to disturb his tranquillity. I do not think that the pursuit of knowledge is an exception to this rule. If the study to which you apply yourself has a tendency to weaken your affections, and to destroy your taste for...simple pleasures...then that study is certainly unlawful. (§4)

Although Walton is usually assumed to be as guilty as Frankenstein of sacrificing human ties for knowledge, he seems to me less culpable. After all, he writes home regularly to his sister, he expresses great longing for a friend, and he shows concern for the welfare of his crew, even to the point of yielding to their entreaties to abandon the enterprise. Nevertheless the alienating connotations of ice and snow, of sailing farther and farther away from human habitation, do tacitly impugn the morality of his mission.[21]

This emphasis on human feelings is traceable to the writings of Godwin and his disciple Shelley. Godwin is commonly associated with the stern rationalism of the first edition of *Political Justice* (1793), but the subsequent editions of this work (1796, 1798) along with his novels show a revaluation of the importance of feeling, largely because of his own brief, happy marriage to Mary Wollstonecraft. Thus he argues that "Even knowledge, and the enlargement of the intellect, are poor, when unmixed with sentiments of benevolence and sympathy," and that the exercise of "domestic and private affections" is a prerequisite for effectively displaying benevolence in society at large.[22] This humanistic ethic, as Goldberg points out, is quite prevalent among Mary's contemporaries, notably Shelley, Byron, and Paine: in their hierarchy of values love or sympathy is a higher good than abstract knowledge, and their criterion for establishing this priority is human, not divine.[23]

The lesson of Frankenstein's tale to Walton is thus that man should avoid temptation of knowledge lest it lead to estrangement from family and society, but it turns out that after implanting this idea so firmly in our minds, Mary Shelley has Frankenstein completely reverse himself—a crucial point that scholars have generally overlooked—in his exhortation to Walton's mutinous crew:

"You were hereafter to be hailed as the benefactors of your species.... And now, behold, with the first...mighty and terrific trial of your courage, you shrink away...; ye need not have come thus far, and dragged your captain to shame and defeat, merely to prove yourselves cowards. Oh! be men, or be more than men.... Do not return to your families with the stigma of disgrace marked on your brows. Return, as heroes who have fought and conquered." (§C)

The sudden bravado of this speech is soon negated by Frankenstein's dying words—"Farewell, Walton! Seek happiness in tranquility, and avoid ambition, even if it be the apparently innocent one of distinguishing yourself in science and discoveries"—and then partly reconfirmed!: "I have myself been blasted in these hopes, yet another may succeed."

What are we to make of these divergent pronouncements? Are they intended to reflect Frankenstein's confused state of mind as he nears death, or do they mirror the author's indecisiveness?

The same ambiguity of conception afflicts Frankenstein's role as "the modern Prometheus." On the one hand, some of his utterances imply guilt for overstepping human limitations: he feels as if his "soul were grappling with a palpable enemy" (§3); he calls himself the "living monument of presumption and rash ignorance" (§7); he grieves over the work of his "thrice-accursed hands" as he beholds the graves of William and Justine, "the first hapless victims of [his] unhallowed arts" (§8); he shudders at "the mad enthusiasm that hurried [him] on to the creation of [his] hideous enemy" (§21); and he regards the making of the second creature as an "unearthly occupation" (§18). On the other hand, these expressions of *mea culpa* seem merely perfunctory against the novel's general cast of scientific naturalism: Frankenstein speaks of "the mechanism of my being" (§3); he considers man a complex and wonderful animal (§4); and Mary's Introduction contains an obviously deistic phrase: "the stupendous mechanism of the Creator of the world."[24] Thus it seems that Mary Shelley on the whole defends her "modern Prometheus." If the consequences of his experiment were disastrous, his goal of discovering "the secrets of heaven and earth" was nonetheless legitimate for a man of science.

Although scholars tend to assume that Mary shares Byron's and Shelley's conception of Prometheus as the adversary of Jove, the benefactor and suffering champion of mankind,[25] I believe that she focuses on the often overlooked role of Prometheus as the maker of natural man and hence a prototype for any maker of artificial man. In classical mythology this Titan is a deeply enigmatic figure, acting both as lawful creator and as usurper of divine prerogative. To the Greeks, notably Aeschylus, he was Prometheus *pyrphoros*, the fire-bringer; to the Romans, however, he was Prometheus *plasticator*, the creator of man; by the second or third century the two roles were fused, "so that the fire stolen by Prometheus was also the fire of life with which he animated his man of clay."[26]

Although Frankenstein's animation of an artificial being is sufficient to account for his epithet "the modern Prometheus," there is a highly probable source for the phrase itself. I agree with Mario Praz, who suggests that Frankenstein may be an answer to La Mettrie's call for "un nouveau Prométhée." Praz believes that "the similarity of the *Frankenstein* theme to the attempts made in France to create an artificial man may not be due to mere coincidence," and such scholars as Cohen, Ebeling, and Swoboda, less cautious than Praz, emphasize the work of 17th-century horologists and mechanists as precedents for Frankenstein's project.[27] The makers of automata and experimenters in spontaneous generation saw themselves as gaining legitimate control over nature rather than impiously delving into the mysteries of God. Their experiments, which indicated that the causes of all organic and inorganic developments were to be sought within nature, not in God or chance, were immensely important to the 18th-century materialist *philosophes*. In 1740 Abraham Trembley discovered that when a certain kind of fresh-water polyp is cut into pieces, each piece becomes a new polyp. Julien Offray de La Mettrie used the self-regenerating property of the polyp to support his doctrine of materialism: if an animal's soul or vital principle is divisible with its body, then the same might be true of the human soul—i.e., man has no soul apart from his material organization. After rejecting "immateriality" or "spirituality" as a final cause, La Mettrie postulated that "matter possesses intrinsically the causes of its activity and organization."[28]

Le Mettrie's materialist ideas culminate in *Man a Machine* (i.e., *L'Homme machine*, 1748):

[Man] is to the ape, and to the most intelligent animals, as the planetary pendulum of Huyghens is to a watch of Julien Leory. More instruments, more wheels and more springs were necessary to mark the movements of the planets than to mark or strike the hours; and Vaucanson, who needed more skill for making his flute player than for making his duck, would have needed still more to make a talking man, a mechanism no longer to be regarded as impossible, especially in the hands of another Prometheus [d'un nouveau Prométhée].[29]

La Mettrie has singled out the leading mechanists. The French watchmaker Julien Leroy excelled in the construction of large clocks and pendulums. In the application of mechanical laws he was superseded by Huyghens, the Dutch mathematician, physicist, and astronomer renowned for improving the telescope, developing the wave theory of light, and inventing a pendulum clock which was a miniature model of the solar system, measuring the movements of the planets. Yet he was eclipsed by the ingenuity and skill of Vaucanson, whose three celebrated automata—a flute player, a drummer, and a digesting duck—were shown throughout Europe and (in 1742) in London.[30] The duck was a three-dimensional working model of the functions of eating, drinking, digesting, and swimming, with the internal mechanisms fully exposed to view. The wooden flutist played twelve melodies while moving the fingers, lips, and tongue. Vaucanson was as meticulous with the flute as with the flutist: he made 300 flutes before he was satisfied with the tonal quality. He even "cherished a secret ambition to make an artificial man. At the instigation of Lous XV he did indeed attempt to make a model with heart, veins, and arteries, but he died before completing his task."[31]

Frankenstein's defiant, pro-science stance at the end of the novel is directly in line with the experimental outlook exhibited by the alchemists, the 17th-century mechanists and horologists, the 18th-century biologists, and most modern behavioral scientists and futurists. This is undoubtedly one reason why the novel has remained popular to this day. Though with part of her mind Mary Shelley may have endorsed Frankenstein's warning against *libido sciendi*, she felt the claims of the opposite viewpoint strongly enough to reverse the moral at the end and, more subtly, to permeate the entire book with materialistic and mechanistic assumptions.

Frankenstein, as we have seen, is a markedly dualistic work, full of contrasts, conflicts, and even contradictions. Mary's hero vacillates between rejection and advocacy of modern Prometheanism in science. His creature is equally protean as he acts out his various roles of horrific monster, evil alter ego, and pitiful Polyphemus. I surmise that what makes *Frankenstein* so enduringly interesting is precisely the tension between the claims of reason and imagination that it exhibits. To borrow William Madden's comment on Chaucer, Mary Shelley's first novel is instinct with that duality which lies at the very heart of life.

NOTES

1. Frederick L. Jones, ed., *Mary Shelley's Journal* (1947).

2. The text followed here is that of Mary W. Shelley, *Frankenstein; Or, The Modern Prometheus*, edited with an Introduction by M.K. Joseph (1969). References are to chapter, with the "Letters" cited as §01, §02, etc., "Walton's Continuation" as §C, and the 1831 Introduction as §I.

3. The following scholars regard the dream-derived narrative as central and thus deprecate amplification: Ernest A. Baker, *The History of the English Novel* (1934), 5:217-19; Edith Birkhead, *The Tale of Terror: A Study of the Gothic Romance* (1921), pp 161, 164; Milton Millhauser, "The Noble Savage in Mary Shelley's 'Frankenstein'," *Notes and Queries* 191(1946):248-50; D.J. Palmer and R.E. Dowse, " 'Frankenstein': A Moral Fable," *The Listener* 68(1962):284. The following approve of amplifying the

dream-vision with social and moral themes: Harold Bloom, "Afterword," in *Franken-stein* (Signet 1965), pp 219, 221; M.A. Goldberg, "Moral and Myth in Mrs. Shelley's *Frankenstein*," *Keats-Shelley Journal* 8(1959):27-29.

4. The following studies of the double are useful: Albert J. Guérard, "Concepts of the Double," in *Stories of the Double* (1967); Carl F. Keppler, *The Literature of the Second Self* (1972); Masao Myoshi, *The Divided Self* (1969); Robert Rogers, *The Double in Literature* (1969); Ralph Tymms, *Doubles in Literary Psychology* (1949).

5. Maria F. Mahoney, *The Meaning in Dreams and Dreaming: The Jungian View-point* (1966), p109.

6. Ibid., pp 108, 110, 114.

7. Robert M. Philmus, *Into the Unknown: The Evolution of Science Fiction from Francis Godwin to H.G. Wells* (1970), p88.

8. Lowry Nelson, Jr., "Night Thoughts on the Gothic Novel," *Yale Review* 52(1963): 247-48.

9. For Mary's reading before and during the period of the composition of *Franken-stein*, see the *Journal* (Note 1); see also Katherine Richardson Powers, "The Influence of William Godwin on the Novels of Mary Shelley" (University of Tennessee Disser-tation 1972).

10. William Godwin, *Enquiry Concerning Political Justice and Its Influence on Morals and Happiness*, ed. F.E.L. Priestley (1946), 1:xxiii, 3:15.

11. Joseph (Note 2), p239, C.F. Volney, *The Ruins; Or, Meditations on the Revo-lutions of Empires, to which is Added the Law of Nature* (1857; first English edition, 1795).

12. Godwin (Note 10), 1:26.

13. Compare Goldberg (Note 3), pp33-35.

14. See the following: Stephen Crafts, "*Frankenstein*: Camp Curiosity or Premo-nition?" *Catalyst* 3(1967):96-103; Milton A. Mays, "*Frankenstein*: Mary Shelley's Black Theodicy," *Southern Humanities Review* 3(1969):146-53; John L. McKenney, "Nietzsche and the Frankenstein Creature," *Dalhousie Review* 41(1961):40-48. Peter Thorslev's study, *The Byronic Hero: Types and Prototypes* (1962), pp65-70, contains a valuable dis-cussion of how the Gothic villain of the 18th century emerged as the Noble Outlaw of the 19th.

15. Elizabeth Nitchie, *Mary Shelley: Author of Frankenstein* (1953), p17; also James Rieger, *The Mutiny Within: The Heresies of Percy Bysshe Shelley* (1967), p247.

16. Frederick L. Jones, ed., *The Letters of Mary W. Shelley* (1944), 1:66.

17. *Ovid's Metamorphoses, Translated into English Prose by Joseph Davidson* (1797), p472.

18. *Journal* (Note 1), pp204-05.

19. Brian W. Aldiss, *Billion Year Spree: The True History of Science Fiction* (US 1973), p199.

20. Godwin (Note 10), 1:126-29, 1:342, 3:17. Volney (Note 11) expresses a similar concept in his Preface to *The Ruins*.

21. For the novel's symbolic geography see William Walling, *Mary Shelley* (1972), pp36-37, and Rieger (Note 15), pp81-89. Rieger compares Frankenstein's exhortation to Ulysses' speech to his crew in §26 of Dante's *Inferno*, the implication being that both are evil counselors.

22. Godwin (Note 10), 1:311; Godwin's Preface to *St. Leon* (1799) and to *Fleet-wood* (1805).

23. Goldberg (Note 3), p33.

24. Mary Shelley's second work of fantasy, *The Last Man* (1826), contains the following mechanistic references to man and the world: "shattered mechanism," "earthly mechanism," "animal mechanism," "animal machine," "automation of flesh," "mortal mechanism," "wheels and springs of life," "mechanism of senses," and "the uni-versal machine."

25. Scholars who stress the rebellious nature of Prometheus include Bloom, Gold-berg, Palmer, and Dowse.

26. Joseph (Note 2), p. viii.

27. Mario Praz, "Introductory Essay" in *Three Gothic Novels*, ed. Peter Fair-clough (Penquin Books 1968), p30; John Cohen, *Human Robots in Myth and Science* (1961), pp 61, 68-88; Hermann Ebeling, "Hachwort," in *Frankenstein: oder der neue Prometheus* (Munich 1970), pp325-26; Helmut Swoboda, *Der künstliche Mensch* (Munich

1967), pp 12, 87-98, 220-22.

    28. Aram Vartanian, "Trembley's Polyp, La Mettrie, and Eighteenth-Century French Materialism," *Journal of the History of Ideas* 11(1950):271. My discussion is based on this article, which covers pp259-86.

    29. Julian Offray de la Mettrie, *Man a Machine* (1912), pp 70, 140-41. Also see Aram Vartanian, *La Mettrie's L'Homme machine: A Study in the Origins of an Idea* (1960).

    30. Ibid., pp202-03; Praz (Note 27), p28. Mary Shelley, in her *Rambles in Germany and Italy* (1844), 1:49, mentions seeing a "self-acting" musical instrument at Lenzkirch.

    31. Cohen (Note 27), pp86-88; Swoboda (Note 27), p93.

J.-P. Vernier

The SF of J.H. Rosny the Elder

(from SFS 2:156 - 163, July 1975)

While Wells and Verne are today considered the founders of modern SF, J.H. Rosny Aîné (Rosny the Elder) remains virtually unknown, in spite of the fact that he was a prominent figure in French literary life at the turn of the century and produced a number of extremely interesting works in this genre. His first tale, "Les Xipéhuz" (The Xipehuz) one of the most original examples of early SF, was published in 1887, eight years before *The Time Machine*, and he continued writing SF all his life (1866-1940—see the appended list). However, his literary reputation declined sharply after his death. Like Wells he was over-prolific, and the value of many of his novels is very dubious. He made his name with the "prehistoric" novels—*La Guerre du feu* (The Fire War, 1909) being the best known. All his other works were ignored or forgotten. Much of his "realistic" fiction is nowadays almost unreadable, and even his best works are not entirely free from prolixity, maudlin sentimentality and awkward stylistic mannerisms. However, among the books discarded by critics and readers alike were some excellent and very original SF stories. The recent publication of a collection comprising the finest of these[1] points to a revival of interest in his SF work. In spite of resemblances, he seems to have had no influence on Wells; on the other hand, it is likely that Rosny's later work partly reflects the interest aroused by French translations of Wells's SF. Unlike Wells, who was attracted by the imaginative potentialities of biological evolution and by the workings of the scientific mind considered as a means of triumphing over the waste in his contemporary world, Rosny, though very interested in other forms of life, was attracted not only by descriptive biology and ethnology but also by physics, chemistry and astronomy. His main concern was less with the Wellsian "mankind in the making" and more with possibilities of life in the universe.

Rosny was born in Belgium, but after a visit to England pursued his uneventful career of a professional man of letters in Paris. He was first a follower of Zola, whose influence he publicly repudiated in 1887, then a respectable member of the Académie Goncourt"—yet exceptionally fascinated by the vistas science had opened up. His real name was Joseph Henri Böex. He had a younger brother, Justin Böex, who was also a novelist, and both used the same pen-name. Until 1892, Joseph Henri published his works under the name of "J.H. Rosny"; then, between 1893 and 1907, this pseudonym was used for books written by the two brothers in collaboration. This ended in 1907 when they decided to use the respective names of "J.H. Rosny Aîné" and "J.H. Rosny Jeune." Thus, the works published in 1893-1907 and now attributed to Rosny the Elder, were in fact written together with his brother; however, the stylistic traits they have in common with those written earlier or later show that Rosny the Elder was probably responsible for most of the writing.

Rosny's SF can be divided into four categories which represent different aspects of the same vision: (1) those dealing with wholly alien forms of life, in the past or future of mankind or on other planets; (2) those dealing with parallel worlds or unexplained natural beings and phenomena impinging on the narrator's and original reader's present; (3) those based on the "undiscovered island" pattern, in which the human protagonists suddenly find themselves cut off from society and placed in an alien setting which is presented as an autonomous world, though it does not have to be an island in the geographical sense; (4) novels dealing with the life of man and animals in prehistory.

I have excluded from this classification not only Rosny's "realistic" books, but also stories and novels with fantastic themes such as witchcraft, vampirism or doppelgängers. I have also left out works in which an SF element appears only incidentally and is not central to their development. Further, the question whether works describing adventures set in an imaginary prehistory are SF remains, in Rosny's case, open. One finds in them familiar SF themes, but the emphasis is largely an adventure for its own sake and a sort of high-flown lyricism rather than on logical exploitation of the situation created. In short, the cognitive element seems to have been made largely subservient to the pleasures of escapism. Of course, some of his stories are on the border-line where my categories overlap.

IN ROSNY'S FIRST STORY, "Les Xipéhuz," nomadic tribes in the land that was to become Mesopotamia, the cradle of mankind, are confronted with mysterious creatures shaped like translucent cones of living matter fraught with magnetic energy. Their sudden appearance on Earth and proliferation threatens the very existence of the human species. The Xipéhuz are living minerals and so fundamentally different from men that no communication can ever be established with them. Contrary to Wells's Martians, who are shown as a further development in man's evolution, the Xipéhuz represent a form of life for which there is no precedent or conceivable model in the human mind. Eventually the invaders are annihilated due to the ingenuity of an exceptional man, Bakhoûn—an outsider who refuses the accepted norms of society. Bakhoûn's life represents a more advanced stage of human civilization, or conversely, it is reminiscent of Edenic perfection—a comparison explicitly drawn by Rosny. A sedentary life, which he shares with four wives and thirty children, enables him to devote all his energy to intellectual pursuits.... Bakhoûn's reasonings rely on measurable data, and he opposes the religion of his age by believing in a single God and emphasizing wisdom as man's fundamental moral principle.

This first story reveals Rosny's constant assumptions that other forms of life, of coherently organized energy, could coinhabit the universe without our being aware of it, and that the man capable of coping with such problems is a character harmoniously combining science, faith and art, a superman who shares with a small elite of disciples the secrets of the universe.

In "La Mort de la Terre" (The Death of the Earth, 1910), Rosny describes not the death of our planet but that of mankind. The Earth has undergone tremendous geological changes, and when the story starts, 500 centuries in the future, there is an irreversible shortage of water. The few men left have returned to small independent communities in which the birth-rate is deliberately kept very low. Posthistorical men have reinvented tribal life, but as different from prehistory men now know that they are a doomed species, and their behaviour is utterly passive: "The creature spirit has gone; it reappears, atavistically, only in a few individuals. Through a selective process, the race has acquired a spirit of automatic and therefore perfect obedience to new immutable laws."[2] Instead of human consciousness and of the animal kingdom in general, the Earth now favours the mineral kingdom. A new form of "ferromagnetic" life has arisen; it will soon come into its own and supersede animal life. Symbolically, the last man refuses euthanasia and lies on Earth where the minerals will cause his death by anemia: "Then, humbly, some particles of the last human life entered the New Life."[3] The last men accept the new form of life which will cause their extinction, but which also implies a mysterious design governing the evolution of life.

This sense of *a basic unity in the universe* is a major motif in Rosny. It reappears in the short novel Les Navigateurs de l'infini (The Navigators of the Infinite, 1925),[4] where estrangement is spatial rather than temporal. Three Earthmen land on Mars which they find inhabited by creatures whose shape is based on a ternary symmetry: the tripeds have six eyes, and they reproduce by parthenogenesis. This enables Rosny to expatiate on the advantages of a method which does away with the grossness and vulgarity of sex.... But the Martians have reached the same stage of evolution as the men in "The Death of the Earth": they are threatened by the "zoomorphs," a new form of flat protoplasmic life, and have lost all creative spirit; it is the Earthmen's technology and energy that wins the struggle against the alien creatures and ensures the survival of the Martian tripeds. The main weakness of the book lies in a love affair between the narrator and a female Martian triped; it often verges on the ridiculous, but it also enables Rosny to suggest that our aesthetic appreciation can be aroused by things or beings possessing no common point with man. In the same way, the discovery on Mars of the Ethereals, luminous networks of phosphorescent matter who are an entirely alien form of life, appeals to the explorers' keen aesthetic sense. Men are not equipped to fully understand this phenomenon, but they are filled with a sense of beauty and wonder at the sight. All this is a consequence and proof of the mysterious design and unity at work in the universe. The sense of a universe extending far beyond our ordinary faculties of perception was probably the source of Rosny's imaginative powers.

THE SECOND GROUP of stories and novels deals with strange (though not supernatural) *unexplained beings and phenomena*. As Rosny explained in *La Force mysteriéuse* (The Mysterious Power, 1913), the existence of parallel worlds leaves two alternatives: either they constantly permeate our world and are thus diffiuclt to perceive since they do not disrupt the customary course of things, or their interaction with us is only occasional and the collision of two worlds gives rise to the most terrible catastrophes.

Two stories deal with the first alternative: "Un autre monde" (Another World, 1895) and "Dans le monde des Variants" (In the World of the Variants, 1939). In both, an exceptional individual living in our world can perceive and exist in a different parallel universe too. In "Another World" a young Dutchman, held for debile, is in fact born with an organism geared to a different rhythm: he moves much faster than ordinary men, speaks so quickly that his words have to be recorded and slowed down to become understandable, and what is opaque to ordinary men is transparent to him and vice versa. These peculiarities enable him to see a world populated by mysterious beings entirely different from ourselves and living alongside us, ignoring men and ignored by them, and yet modifying our environment as we modify theirs. Here again Rosny is concerned with expanding imaginatively the limits of our universe: our limited perception may be the only explanation for the assumption that man is a superior creature and the focus of the whole world.

The same hypothesis is the basis of his short story "Le Cataclysme" (The Catastrophe, 1888) and his novel *The Mysterious Power*. In both Rosny exploits the theme of the Earth accidentally encountering an unknown source of energy from outer space. In the short story a "stellar shower," falling on an isolated French tableland of peculiar bolide origins, modifying the physical properties of matter and realizing thus an old popular prophecy, is presented with remarkable imaginative power. *The Mysterious Power* is a more elaborate use of the catastrophe theme: a mysterious zone of energy crosses the trajectory of Earth and suddenly alters the properties of the light spectrum. Chaos spreads over Earth, communications and industrial production come to a halt. (Strangely enough, a few months after the publication of this novel, Conan Doyle's *The Poison Belt* appeared in *The Strand Magazine*; the similarities between the two works were so striking that in 1924 Rosny suggested the possibility of plagiarism. However, the device was a familiar one: it had been used by Verne in *Hector Servadac*, by Wells and by a number of popular writers.) Rosny's novel works out the implications of this device through neat scientific explanation. Unfortunately, it is marred by a sentimental and melodramatic subplot, and also by the fact that the events are seen from the point of view of another very unconvincing ideal scientist. This stereotyped character, who reappears in many of his works, may be one of the reasons for Rosny's lapse from literary fame.

THE IDEAL SCIENTIST plays a particularly important role in the "undiscovered island" stories, where he is as a rule the protagonist, and often also the narrator. The stories follow the same pattern: an explorer discovers some hitherto unknown part of the globe, where he is made to confront creatures whose existence calls into question some basic assumption concerning mankind or reveals some hidden aspect of the human personality. The observer is placed into a situation where social relationships are reduced to a minimum, so that the impact of discovery falls on his isolated personality, usually representative of what Rosny considered the best qualities of the human species.

A few examples will show the common characteristics of these discoveries. In "Nymphée" (1893) the hero narrates how during an expedition to the Far East he found a strange country of marshes, islands and caves inhabited by several different tribes of "Men of the Water," human creatures biologically adapted to their exceptional environment and representing the living proof of the reality on which ancient legends were founded. Rosny devotes several stories to variations on the physical shapes acquired by different types of hominidae who, by some accident of nature, have been kept apart from the development of the modern world. In "Les Profondeurs de Kyamo" (In the Depths of Kyamo, 1896), the explorer Alglave—who reappears in several stories—finds and aids giant gorillas in whom he recognizes the ancestors of man. Another expedition takes him to a world of mysterious caves ("La Contrée prodigiuese des cavernes"—The Prodigious Cave Country, 1896) where strange animals live in a primitive society ruled by intelligent vampire-bats. But the most significant stories may well be "Le Voyage" (The Journey, 1900) and "Le Trésor dans le neige" (The Treasure in the Snow, 1922). In the first one Rosny inverts a number of generally accepted notions concerning biological evolution: in it primitive men are found living in friendship with and subordination to elephants, whose decisions give an example of wisdom as opposed to the murderous folly of men. Similarly, in "The Treasure in the Snow" Alglave discovers, amidst barren expanses of polar ice, a temperate oasis where a last family of primitive men has survived with the last mammoths. He saves our ancestors from extinction, and conveys the survivors to North Africa. There he creates a kind of prehistoric reservation where the virtues of the first men are allied to the knowledge brought by divilization. At the end of the story, a new miscegenated race is being created.

THIS SUMMARY of Rosny's main forms suggests the scope and originality of his imagination. Although his thought is not systematic, the recurrence of patterns and motifs points to certain ideological standpoints.

In 1899 Rosny published La Légende sceptique (The Skeptical Legend) which he described as a "fictionalized essay." In this strange work, of the family of Poe's Eureka, scientific concepts are blended with passages of somewhat hazy lyrical mysticism in an attempt at a comprehensive vision of creation and the development of life. It shows that, for Rosny, science was essentially a means to an end situated beyond the realm of knowledge, "a poetical passion."[5] He proceeds from subjective aesthetic appreciation considered as an absolute—hence his insistence that beauty can be perceived independently of any reference to past experience. His characters fall under the spell of Martian tripedettes or prehistoric females regardless of the fact that such experiences are outside known aesthetic enjoyment. Rosny assumed that there is such a thing as an innate sense of the beautiful, and that it has a positive value. Thus aesthetics was associated with ethics, because it reflected the individual's perception of the mysterious great design at work in the universe. This personal, intimate aesthetic reaction to the outside world is a way of achieving a direct knowledge of reality, a cognitive process—which at first sight seems hardly reconcilable with the rational demonstration of science. Yet Rosny saw no contradiction between this blind faith in the direct apprehension of the universe and a scientific knowledge of its multiform aspects which increased man's cosmic sense. Scientific knowledge was neither an end in itself nor a means of establishing Man's mastery over nature, it was simply another element increasing our perception of the basic unity and mystery of creation. Thus, his SF did not aim to create imaginary structures based on scientific hypotheses. It blended the logical deductive process of scientific research with a vague meditation, interspersed with daydreams on the mysterious nature of the universe. Rosny's imagination apparently worked in two contrary and yet complementary directions: on the one hand it expanded almost indefinitely, suggesting the possible existence of boundless parallel worlds, survival and development of ancient forms of life, or universal catastrophes due to unforeseen cosmic vagaries; on the other hand, all these diverging elements were kept under control, and chaos prevented, by a blind act of faith in the existence of a significant unifying principle in the universe. This ideological conception manifests itself in the recurrence of certain elements in Rosny's fiction. His main characters are usually scientists cum philosophers cum priests cum poets: they are mystic explorers of the unknown, always outside society, and little concerned with the rest of mankind. Consequently, Rosny almost never achieves Wells's effect of subversive estrangement due to the contrast between the unexpected and the norms of the everyday world, and thus putting these norms into question. In Rosny's work, the world of normality hardly ever appears, and when it does—as in "Another World" or *The Mysterious Power*—it is ispopulated by brutish louts, bloodthirsty rabble, dumb but faithful servants, and other stereotypes whose sole function is to exist as a foil to the protagonist. Only a small élite approaches the sense of religious unity with the world, although it is true that secular power is not their goal: when these supermen, thanks to their knowledge and superior spiritual qualities, have saved the world, they usually withdraw in splendid isolation after advising their less gifted brethren to cultivate wisdom....

This attempt at reconciling the rational and the irrational con be explained only if one realizes that Rosny's vision is permeated with the Edenic myth, i.e. with nostalgia for an imaginary period when the universe was characterized by the organic union of opposite and contradictory elements. Or, to put it differently, Rosny was fascinated by the notion of an ahistorical era, of a time when the complexities of modern society were unknown, and in which brute strength determined evolution. Hence the part played by prehistoric times in his fiction: they provided him with a setting in which he could outline the concept of a fundamental link uniting men and animals, and also express his ambivalent response to primal urges.

Rosny's attitude toward love affords a revealing illustration of this ambivalence. When one of his protagonists falls in love, the result is a series of conventional sentimental scenes, but when one of the partners does not belong to the ordinary, contemporary world the result is far more interesting. Rosny is disgusted by and fascinated with sex, that competing principle of unity. In "Les Hommes-sangliers" (The Wild-Boar Men, 1929) a Dutch girl is captured by primitive boar-like men and repeatedly raped by their leader. She reacts with shame and horror but also with fascination and sexual yearning; the primeval instinctual urge which has thus been revealed makes a return to civilized life appear as an intolerable anticlimax, and she commits suicide as the only way out of her dilemma. This union of individuals belonging to different species illustrates Rosny's interest in the possibility of creating new beings that would reconcile apparently conflicting traits. Sympathetic parthenogenesis—the reproductive system of Martians in *The Navigators of the Infinite*—is an ideal because in it the biological urge is transmuted into a perfect fusion of two selves. In "The Treasure in the Snow" Alglave copulates with a prehistoric female, thus creating a race that will unite the fundamental qualities of primitive life and the more sophisticated knowledge of modern man.

Rosny always emphasizes unity: man is not the centre of the universe, but his world may be intimately associated with other parallel worlds; primitive life fills the modern observer with a sense of perfect harmony; Eden may not mean peace but it certainly means a natural order of things. And science enables modern man to see, beyond appearances, that the diversity of the world is but part of its fundamental oneness. Scientific knowledge is the discovery, by logic and deduction, of the fact hinted at by mythical and popular lore that life in all its aspects springs from a basic unifying urge. Because it is a sort of revelation, it has to be pursued in isolation, outside of the social and historical context.

This is why Rosny could equate science with poetic enthusiasm: like the Romantic poets, the scientists worked toward the recreation of the lost original oneness. Their function was religious since it led to a metaphysical interpretation of the world and sprang from a subjective sense of wonder at the spectacle of the universe. In a world in which God was dead, science was to take over the role of traditional religion and show that there *was* a purpose—even if not completely intelligible to man—in the universe. In the light of the French literary scene at the end of the 19th Century, Rosny's work appears thus as a reaction to nautralistic fiction and mechanical materialism, yet one that does not return to a refurbished Roman Catholicism.

Rosny has largely been ignored by modern criticism because his best work is contained in his SF (especially in the short stories). I am not suggesting that his fiction has the same symbolic power as Wells's: his failure to refer to the ordinary social scene of his day otherwise than through vapid abstraction does much to undermine his artistic achievement. But his imagination was extremely original, and his best stories are historically pioneering and still valuable contributions to modern SF. In spite of the rather pseudo-romantic lyricism which mars a good many of his descriptions, his conception of parallel worlds inhabitated by beings with whom no communication would ever be possible and the way he inverted generally accepted notions on evolution remain, even today, a considerable achievement.

Rosny had the misfortune of being a contemporary of both Verne and Wells, who overshadowed his reputation. But there is no reason why the fate of his vision should not parallel theirs. It is different but just as fascinating. His powers were probably more uneven, but at his best he could certainly rival either.

NOTES

[1]J.H. Rosny Aîné, *Récits de science-fiction*, edited by J. Baronian with an introduction by J. Van Herp (Verviers: A Gérard-Marabout 1973); this is the best available collection of Rosny's stories.

[2]"La Mort de la Terre," in *Récits* (Note 1), p148 (my translation).

[3]Ibid., p188.

[4]It was followed by a second part, *Les Astronautes*, published posthumously (Paris: Rayon fantastique 1960).

[5]J.H. Rosny Aîné, *Torches et lumignons* (Paris 1921), p11.

SELECT BIBLIOGRAPHY. Only the SF stories and novels are mentioned. As they were all published in Paris and, in the case of the short stories, frequently reprinted in various collections, only the date of first publication is given. Novels not discussed above are briefly characterized.

My thanks are due to M. Pierre Versins for indications about the secondary bibliography. The following books by Rosny also contain useful material on him: *Torches et lumignons* (2921), *Les Sciences et le pluralisme* (1922), *Portraits et souvenirs* (1945, with biographical note by R. Borel).

*The stories marked by an asterisk appear in *Récits* (Note 1).

S1. H.P. Thieme. *Bibliographie de la littérature francaise*. Paris 1933. Volume 2, pp663-66, contains a fairly complete bibliography of works by and on Rosny up to 1930.

#1. Les Xipéhuz.* 1887.

#2. Le Cataclysme.* 1888.

#3. *La Legénde sceptique*.* 1889. Essay.

#4. *Vamireh*. 1892. Prehistoric novel.

#5. *Eyrimah*. 1893. Prehistoric novel.

#6. Nymphée.* 1893.

#7. Un Autre Monde.* 1895.

#8. La Contrée prodigieuse des cavernes.* 1896.

#9. Les Profondeurs de Kyamo.* 1896.

#10. Le Voyage.* 1900.

#11. *La Guerre du feu*. 1909. Prehistoric novel.

#12. La Mort de la Terre.* 1910.

#13. La Force mystérieuse. 1913.

#14. *Le Félin géant* (The Giant Cat). 1918. Prehistoric novel.

#15. *La Grande énigme*. 1920. Another variation on the discovery of an unknown land, in which the relationships between living beings are inverted, thus calling into question man's place.

#16. Le Trésor dans la neige."* 1922.

#17. *L'Etonnant voyage de Hareton Ironcastle*. 1922. Mainly an adventure in which the explorers discover that part of an alien planet, with its fauna and flora, has become welded to Earth; the device is reminiscent of Verne.

#18. *Les Navigateurs de l'infini*.* 1925. For Part II see #24.

#19. Les Hommes-sangliers.* 1929.

#20. *Helgvor de fleuve bleu* (Helgvor of the Blue River). 1930. Prehistoric novel.

#21. *Les Compagnons de l'univers* (Kinghts of the Universe). 1934. A lengthy reflection on the mysteries not so much explained as revealed by science; rather than a novel proper, it is in the line of #3, *La Légende sceptique*.

#22. La Sauvage aventure (The Wild Adventure). 1935. A development of the theme exploited in #19, "Les Hommes-sangliers" (The Wild-Boar Men).

#23. "Dans le monde des Variants.* 1939.

#24. *Les Astronautes*. 1960. Part II of the 1925 book—posthumous.

S2. J. Moog. "Un disciple de Zola," *Nouvelle Revue* 82(1893):554-71.

S3. R. Doumic. "Les romans de Rosny," *Revue des Deux-Mondes* 129(1895):936-47.

S4. Vernon Lee. "Rosny and the Analytical Novel in France," *Cosmopolis* 7(1897):289-96.

S5. G. Rodenbach. "Les Rosny," *Nouvelle Revue* 105(1897):289-96

S6. Zadig (pseud.). "J.H. Rosny," *Revue Bleue* 13(1900):533-35.

S7. M.A. Leblond. "L'épopée évolutionniste de l'énergie humaine." *Revue des Revues* 46(1903):641-55.

S8. G. Casella. *Les Célébrites d'aujourd'hui: J.H. Rosny. Biographie critique*. Paris 1907.

S9. M.C. Poinsot. "J.H. Rosny," *Grande Revue* 41(1907):449-59, 595-604.

S10. J. Sageret. "La sociologie de Rosny Aîné," *Revue du Mois* 9(1910):270-85.

S11. C. Berton. "Souvenirs de la vie littéraire de J.H. Rosny," *La Vie des peuples* 4(1921):385-95.

S12. J. d'Ivray. "Rosny Aîné," *Revue des Revues* 150(1922): 394-405.

S13. J. Morel and P. Massé. "Rosny Aîné et la préhistoire," *Mercure de France* 168(1923):5.

S14. J. Sageret. *La Révolte philosophique et la science*. Paris 1925.

S15. J. Morel. "Rosny Aîné et le merveilleux scientifique," *Mercure de France* 187(1926):82.

S16. J.J. Bridenne. *La Littérature francais d'imagination scientifique*. Paris 1950. Pp 191-98.

S17. J.J. Bridenne. "J.H. Rosny Aîné, romancier des possibles cosmiques," *Fiction*, Feb. 1956.

S18. P. Domeyne. *Le Merveilleux scientifique, ses sources et ses prolongements dans les romans et nouvelles de J.H. Rosny Aîné*. Diss. Lyon 1965.

Six Twentieth-Century Writers

David N. Samuelson

Childhood's End: A Median Stage of Adolescence?

(from SFS *1:4 - 17, Spring 1973)*

Arthur C. Clarke's *Childhood's End* is one of the "classics" of modern SF, and perhaps justifiably so. It incorporates into some 75,000 words a large measure of the virtues and vices distinctive to SF as a literary art form. Technological extrapolation, the enthronement of reason, the "cosmic viewpoint", alien contact, and a "sense of wonder" achieved largely through the manipulation of mythic symbolism are all important elements in this visionary novel. Unfortunately, and this is symptomatic of Clarke's work and of much SF, its vision is far from perfectly realized. The literate reader, especially, may be put off by an imbalance between abstract theme and concrete illustration, by a persistent banality of style, in short, by what may seem a curious inattention to the means by which the author communicates his vision. The experience of the whole may be saved by its general unity of tone, of imagery, and of theme, but not without some strain being put on the contract implicit between author and reader to collaborate in the "willing suspension of disbelief".

Although much of Clarke's SF is concerned with sober images of man's probable future expansion of technological progress and territorial domain, often despite his own worst nature, in a number of stories and at least three novels he conjures up eschatological visions of what man may become, with or without his knowing complicity. *Against the Fall of Night* (1948) is a fairy tale of a boy's quest for identity in a sterile technological society far in our future; confined in setting and narrative focus, it provides adolescent adventure, a veritable catalogue of future technology, and a cautionary parable in a pleasant blend. *2001: A Space Odyssey* (1968, "based on a screenplay by Stanley Kubrick and Arthur C. Clarke")

This article appeared in different form in Mr. Samuelson's University of Southern California dissertation "Studies in the Contemporary American and British Science Fiction Novel," which is Copyright 1969 by David N. Samuelson.

credits a mysterious device of alien manufacture with two quantum jumps in man's evolution, from pre-man, and to super-man; its choppy structure, detailed technology, sparse suggestiveness of the evolutionary process, are all admirably suited to cinematic presentation, but not untypical of Clarke's work on his own, as a close examination of *Childhood's End* should demonstrate.

From the moon-bound rockets of the "Prologue" to the last stage of the racial metamorphosis of mankind, familiar science fictions guide us gradually if jerkily through *Childhood's End*. Besides futuristic technological hardware, we are shown three rational utopian societies and mysterious glimpses of extra-sensory powers. Reducing all of these, however, practically to the status of leitmotifs, the theme of alien contact is expanded to include something close enough to the infinite, eternal, and unknowable that it could be called God; yet even this being, called the Overmind, is rationalized, and assumed to be subject to natural laws.

Two stages of advanced technology are shown us, one human, one alien. The first, ca. 2050 A.D., is said to consist mainly in "a completely reliable oral contraceptive . . . an equally infallible method of identifying the father of any child. . .[and] the perfection of air transport"(§6). Other advances vary in seriousness and significance: a mechanized ouija board, a complete star catalog, "telecaster" newspapers, elaborate undersea laboratories, plastic "taxidermy", and central community kitchens. The technology of the Overlords, the guardians of man's metamorphosis, includes non-injuring pain projectors, three-dimensional image projectors, cameraless television spanning time as well as space, vehicles that move swiftly without the feeling of acceleration, interstellar travel, and the ability to completely transform the atmosphere and gravity of their adopted home planet. In this book, none of these developments is treated in any detail, and together they amount to no more than a suggestive sketch, serving as the merest foundation for the hypotheses built up from and around them.

Technology accounts in part for the utopian social organizations projected in this book, and also for their failings. Technologically enforced law and order, technology-conferred freedom of movement and sexuality, help to establish a worldwide "Golden Age", but the elimination of real suffering and anguish, combined with the humans' sense of inferiority, results in mild anxiety, resentment, and lethargy. To make utopia really utopian, an artists' colony is established, on the traditionally utopian, locale of an island, but the colonists don't regard their creations as having any real value. Whether Clarke could imagine predictable great art is irrelevant, since their futility underscores the insignificance of New Athens in the larger context: for the Overlords, the island is a gathering-point for them to observe the most gifted human children in the first stages of metamorphosis. Besides being unimportant, however, utopia is unreachable; just as technology can not make everyone happy on Earth, so is it insufficient for the supremely rational and scientific Overlords. Their placid orderliness, their long lives, may excite our envy, but they in turn envy those species which can become part of the Overmind.

Thus *Childhood's End* is not really utopian, as Mark Hillegas contends,[1] so much as it is a critique of utopian goals. Whatever the social machinery, and Clarke is extremely sketchy about how this society is run, peace and prosperity are inadequate; the people of New Athens need something more to strive for. This particular "utopia" is only a temporary stage in man's development. Theoretically, he could go in the direction of enlarging his storehouse of empirical knowledge; this is the way of the Overlords, without whom man could not have defused his own self-destructive tendencies. Yet, paradoxically, the Overlords are present in order to cut man off from entering their "evolutionary *cul de sac*", to insure that he takes the other road, parallelling the mystical return of the soul to God.

On the surface, Clarke seems to commit himself to neutral extrapolation. Science and technology may have their limitations, but they can increase our knowledge and improve our living conditions. The technological power of the Overlords may be totalitarian, but their dictatorship is benevolent and discreet. From the "scientific" viewpoint of speculative biology, even the predestined metamorphosis of mankind could be seen simply as an evolutionary step, proceeding according to natural law, with no necessary emotional commitment, positive or negative. There is a value system implicit in this reading, of course, which the narrator seems to share with the characters. The supreme representatives of reason and science, the Overlords, are thinkers and observers in general, and manipulators and experimenters in their role as mankind's guardians. The few human characters with whom we have any chance to identify also exhibit a scientistic attitude, i.e. the belief that science can discover everything. Stormgren resists the fear that the as-yet invisible Overlords may be Bug-Eyed-Monsters, and muses on man's absurd superstitions: "The mind, not the body, was all that mattered" (§3). Jean Greggson's clairvoyance is supported by Jan Rodricks' researches, and counterpointed by the study of parapsychological literature by the Overlord Rashaverak. George Greggson, when his son begins to dream of alien planets, is reassured by Rashaverak when he confides "I think there's a rational explanation for everything" (§18). Even Jan Rodricks retains his faith in reason in the face of the inexplicable glimpsed on the Overlord's home planet. Only hysterical preachers and befuddled women apparently have any doubts.

Yet there is some doubt about reason's power, engendered by the basic science fictions of the book, the aliens, both those who guard and guide mankind, and that toward which man is evolving. The Overlords' espousal of scientific knowledge is open to suspicion. They admit they can not comprehend the Overmind and that certain mental faculties (intuition, e.s.p.) are closed to them. They are repeatedly deceptive about their appearance and their mission. First they say they have come to prevent man's self-destruction, and that man is doomed never to reach the stars. They later proclaim being sent by the Overmind to oversee man's metamorphosis, and then admit engaging in scientific observation of that transformation for their own purposes. Meanwhile one man does reach the stars, returning to find that the children of man will indeed reach, and perhaps inherit, the stars, but only by means of a kind of self-destruction. Only toward the end do the Overlords confess that their name, made up by their human subjects, is an ironic one, given their own subject circumstances.

It may be that their duplicity is necessary, that man must be readied for closer approximations of the truth; science and reason both deal with the world by means of approximations. But even their closest approximations may be far from the truth. because of their inability to comprehend, because of further duplicity, or both. They resemble physically that figure of European folklore known as the "Father of Lies", their names are suitably devilish, and even their home planet is reminiscent of Hell: the light from its sun is red, the inhabitants fly through the dense atmosphere, Jan sees their architecture as dystopianly functional and unornamented. If he were better versed in literature, he might also recognize the Miltonic parallel of the Overlords' having conquered this world after being forced to leave another. The Overlords are certainly well-versed in human mythic thinking: they require their first contacts to "ascend" to their ship, they assume a guise of om-nipotence and omniscience, and Karellen makes his first physical ap-pearance in the Christ-like pose of having "a human child resting trust-fully on either arm" (§5).

Starkly contrasting with the Overlords' anthropomorphic shape and thinking processes is the totally alien Overmind, evoking images of unlimited power used for unknowable purposes. To the human observer it appears as a living volcano on the Overlords' planet; its power is also made visible in the actions of the children of Earth, who convert their planet to energy in order to propel themselves to an unknown destination. Yet these visible manifestations seem to be mere side-effects, insignificant to the purposes of the being. The Overlords claim to know something of its behavior and composition, from having observed other metamorphoses, as Karellen indicates: "We believe--and it is only a theory--that the Over-mind is trying to grow, to extend its powers and its awareness of the universe. By now it must be the sum of many races, and long ago it left the tyranny of matter behind. It is conscious of intelligence, everywhere. When it knew that you were ready, it sent us here to do its bidding, to prepare you for the transformation that is now at hand." The change always begins with a child, spreading like "crystals round the first nucleus in a saturated solution" (§20). Eventually, the children will become united in a single entity, unreachable and unfathomable by any in-dividual, rational mind. This is the extent of the Overlords' knowledge, and it may not be reliable; but the metaphor of crystallization can hardly be adequate to describe the transformed state. All they can really know, when the Overmind summons them, is that they are to serve as "mid-wives" at another "birth", and they go like angels at God's bidding, but "fallen angels" unable to share in the deity's glory.

On the surface, this inability to understand the Overmind is merely a sign of its strangeness and vastness, which may some day become com-prehensible to reason and science--after all, how would a human writer describe something totally alien?--but underneath we feel the tug of the irrational, in familiar terms. The Overmind clearly parallels the Oversoul, the Great Spirit, and various formulations of God, while the children's metamorphosis neatly ties in with mystical beliefs in Nirvana, "cosmic consciousness", and "becoming as little children to enter the Kingdom of God". It is therefore fitting that the Overmind be known only vaguely and indirectly, and the confidence of any individual in isolation that he will come to understand this being rings as hollow as the boasts of Milton's Satan. Thus the interplay between the Overlords and the Overmind may be seen as a reworking of the old morality-play situation of the Devil trying to steal away from God the souls of men. These Devils appear to be devoted servants carrying out God's orders, but the Overlords also never stop trying to bring Him down to their level, and they manage to convince the reason-loving men of the story that, just as our faith in science tells us, everything has a natural explanation. Those men are doomed, however, and only the "children of man" may be saved in this Last Judgment and Resurrection, leaving the continuing struggle between two faiths to reverberate in the mind of the reader.

If the reader is thoroughly indoctrinated in the simple paradigms of ostensibly neutral but implicitly scientistic popular SF of the Verne-Gernsback-Campbell tradition (and Clarke can hardly have anticipated a much larger audience in 1949-53), he can be expected to take the side of reason, science, and Western man, with perhaps a slight anxiety over their alliance with Devilish aliens. But the reception *Childhood's End* received from mainstream reviewers suggests quite a different reading; for them the eschatological theme was what made the book worthwhile, not the Overlords' continuation of man's tradition of systematic inquiry, or the successive approaches to technological utopia.[2] They, and many readers since, have sensed in Clarke a streak of sentimental mysticism, which makes some of his SF quite congenial to their own views, unconstrained by the scientist's straitjackets of skepticism, proof, and unbending rules.[3] For all of Clarke's reputation for conservative extrapolation, quite justified by much of his fiction as well as his non-fiction, he apparently pushes more buttons when he strays from confident expectation of technological change into what may be termed watered-down theological speculation.[4]

Even if a work of SF could be totally neutral in its extrapolations from the findings and theories of the physical and/or social sciences, those extrapolations would have to reach the reader by means of characters, events, situations described in words which offer at least analogies to his own experience. Every word, and every word-construct, picks up meanings from other contexts in which we have seen it, and the more perceptive the reader is to his own psychology, and to a wide range of literature, the more meanings and patterns will accrue to his interpretation. The less a work of SF is anchored in incremental extrapolation from actual experience, the freer we can expect the reign given to a mythologizing tendency.[5] Positive reactions to imaginary situations will be associated not only with utopia, and its heretical premise of man's perfectibility, but also with the mythological parallel between utopia and Heaven, whereas negative reactions will summon up dystopian and Hellish contexts. The situation is complicated further by the alliance in medieval Christian tradition between the Devil and forbidden knowledge, including science, and by the post-Romantic reversal of values which opposes an oppressive Judeo-Christian God to ideals of progress, growth, and process. For Blake perhaps the ringleader of this revolt, the oppressive God was allied with Newtonian science, an "absentee landlord" of an unjust social order, and the Devil's strength was passion, disorder, wilfulness, refusal to accept the rules as absolute limitations. Accordingly, Blake depicted Milton as on Satan's side, Shelley sympathized with Prometheus, and Goethe with Mephistopheles (before letting Faust "cop a plea" because he meant well); Zamyatin's underground, which seeks to overthrow the perfect order of the "United State", clearly has reason for calling itself "MEPHI".[6]

Clarke seems quite aware of the affinity between alien beings in science fiction and the apocalyptic and demonic imagery of mythological fantasy.[7] By deliberately choosing devil-figures as spokesmen for scientific, or scientistic, thought, he establishes a growing tension between conflicting emotions as the climax of the novel nears, and the reader is almost forced to make a choice between two extreme positions. If he is scientifically-oriented, he is offered the possibility of being like the Overlords, individualistic, isolated, able to understand things only by approximations from the outside; this is the way of "the Devil's party", but not in a Blakean, rather in a medieval sense. If the reader is more-mystically-oriented, he is offered the possibility of giving up the responsibilities of maturity, giving himself over to imagination and the irrational, and submerging his individuality in a oneness with God. This is not the only choice available to man outside the medieval tradition, and Clarke's awareness that this choice might be untenable for a work of SF, may be partly responsible for his prefacing the paperback edition of *Childhood's End* with the cryptic statement: "The opinions expressed in this book are not these of the author". But this is certainly not the only work in which his "normal" skepticism toward technocracy has modulated into myth.

In dealing with any theme of larger scope than ironing out the bugs in advanced technological hardware, it may be difficult for an SF writer to avoid mythic structures.[8] And some have argued, like Samuel Delany, that "to move into an 'unreal world' demands a brush with mysticism".[9] Despite the continuing antagonism between devotees of science and myth, our age has seen numerous creative and critical attempts to link the two, such as by opening up the definition of myth to a flexibility undreamt by a true believer.[10] But the critically sensitive reader does have the right to expect the writer of SF to use the myth, rather than be used by it, i.e. to make the whole book work on science-fictional terms. The Universe may or may not be comprehensible to reason, but the mythico-religious presentation of the Overmind and the children's metamorphosis does not seem to me consonant with serious exobiological speculation. It may be probable, as Clarke writes elsewhere, that alien beings superior to us exist, but it seems highly improbable that they are so analogous to the gods and devils of our imagination.[11] Systematic inquiry and testing may yet turn up scientific verification of e.s.p., but a quasi-religious explanation, tied to the Stapledonian fantasy of a group-mind and to the fruitless "researches" of spiritualism, turns the reader away from disinterested speculation toward simple wish-fulfillment.[12] Not limited to verified fact, scientific speculation, in or out of narrative fiction, normally tries to domesticate the unknown in theoretical terms not so openly contradictory of known realities. In turning his critique of scientism into a supernatural fable, Clarke has considerably stretched the limitations of science, if not of SF.

His mechanical wonders and quasi-utopian communities are familiar conventions; aliens, too, are acceptable as science fictions. The Overlords are obviously present to the senses, and psychologically human, and through them we receive the theory that almost explains the Overmind. This science-fictional domestication. however. is undercut bv failings in literary domestication. For example, it is not reasonable that aliens should be so similar to long-established European (and European only) folklore. And this is tied to another affront to credibility in Clarke's use of e.s.p. Contradicting himself in successive paragraphs, Karellen declares that man's science could not encompass e.s.p., and that he was sent to put a stop to apparently successful studies of e.s.p. (§20). Such research having been kept from fruition, Karellen is apparently forced to use traditional spiritualist terms to explain e.s.p., i.e. these powers are real, have long been labelled but not verified, and have some connections with the Overmind. Clarke's own demonstrations are similarly vague, and decidedly un-scientific: the children's dreams, powers, and cosmic dance are responses to the Overmind, while Jean's clairvoyance, accomplished by means of a ouija board (!), is "explained" by her being a "sensitive". Perhaps if we can accept at face value the Overmind. we should not cavil at a little spiritualism, but it does seem a bit unfair to explain one "impossibility" (e.s.p.) by means of another (Overmind), in turn comprehended only partially by yet another (Overlords). This use of the *deus ex machina* may have a noble history, and it may be convenient in daydreams and fresh-man themes on God, but it is at least suspicious in an art form dedicated to projecting "possibilities". Even if we accept all of these improbabilities in the context of the story, giving in to the fable, Clarke has another sur-prise for us. A reader who is aware, as Damon Knight is for example, of the evidence for Satan's medieval *European* origin out of bits and pieces of pagan myth, may well object to the rewriting of history needed to make the Devil part of the mythology of *all peoples,* caused by a racial memory (or premonition) of the future.[13]

Gaffes of this magnitude not only upset all but the most hypnotic suspension of disbelief at the moment, but they also raise doubt as to the reliability of the narrator, and the credibility of the whole narrative. Clarke may want us to question the omniscience of science and the adequacy of the Overlords; Karellen's speech denigrating the ability of human science to deal with e.s.p. can be fitted into either pattern, or both. But undermining the veracity of the narrator is a dangerous game to play with a reader already aware that the subject matter is tenuously anchored fantasy.

Why does Clarke even attempt this explanation of mythology? Why, in an SF novel, does he fill several pages with a spiritualistic seance? Neither was necessary to the theme it would appear, or to the book as a whole. The Overlords' parallel with the Christian Devil could have been left unexplained, without impairing them as alien beings or as literary symbols; the explanation given is worse than none at all. The seance func-tions peripherally to show the similarity between human and Overlord minds, and to foreshadow the role of Jean Greggson's children as first contacts with the Overmind. It also serves to point up man's boredom with the Golden Age and the ridiculous ends which his technology can be made to serve, namely the production of mechanized ouija boards, but Rupert Boyce, whom the party characterizes, is an unimportant figure, and the success of the seance undercuts the satire. The least important purpose the seance serves is to provide Jan Rodricks with the catalogue number of the Overlords' home star; his visit to the museum to consult the catalogue is equally irrelevant to his stowing away on the starship, which will go where it will, with or without his knowledge of its destination. The problem which seems to exist on an SF level is essentially a literary one: not fully in control of his materials, Clarke has attempted more than he can fulfill.

The "cosmic viewpoint" which Clarke praised in 1962 in a speech accepting UNESCO's Kalinga Prize for the popularization of science[14] is common in SF, as is its negative corollary, inattention to details. Besides leading writers into multi-volumed "future histories", the cosmic viewpoint encourages close attention in smaller works only to the major outlines and the background. The characters are frequently left to fend for themselves, as it were, in a jungle of disorderly plots, melodramatic incidents, and haphazard image-patterns, which are symptomatic of an unbalanced narrative technique. Unity, if there is any in such a composition, frequently is maintained only by an uninspired consistency of style and tone, and by the momentum built up in the unwary reader by the breakneck pace of events. *Childhood's End,* like many books inferior to it, suffers from just such a disproportionate emphasis on the large, "significant" effects, at the expense of the parts of which they are composed.

Structurally, disproportion is evident in *Childhood's End* in several ways. The three titled sections are balanced in length, but not in space, time, or relationships between characters and events. Each succession of actions breaks down into almost random fragments of panoramic chronicle, desultory conversation, and tentative internal monologue. Part of the problem may be that the novel "just growed" from a novelette,[15] but that is symptomatic of Clarke's failure to bring his theme down to manageable human dimensions. The effect might be similar if he had written several stories of varying length and intensity, then tried to connect them up to an outline-summary of future history. The point-of-view is uniformly third-person-omniscient, yet the narrative duties seem divided between an awe-struck spectator at a cosmic morality play, and a disinterested observer of ordinary human events. The historian-spectator is at least involved in his theme, which he attempts to match in grandeur by panoramic wide-angle photographs and impressive-sounding generalizations or *sententiae.* But the detached observer gives us "slices of life"--political negotiating sessions, a party, a visit to a library, a press conference, a group meeting, a counseling session, a sightseeing trip-- which haven't much life, and fails to reveal the principles behind his slicing. Individual episodes stubbornly resist integration with the whole, but they can not stand up independently, because they are "illustrations" insignificant in themselves. Clarke's intent seems to be to counterpoint the great, slow movement toward metamorphosis with the everyday activities that people, ignorant of their contribution to the whole, carry on independently, activities such as he often treats in his fiction of the predictable future, where plot is a peg on which to hang the background, and melodrama adds a little spice. But where the background is a large expanse of space and time, and the context involves the larger mysteries of life, such stagey effects as Stormgren's kidnapping, the Overlords' intellec-

tual striptease, and the explanation of one mystery by another, are unnecessary, irrelevant, annoying, and finally self-defeating.

Either a unified plot or a more carefully developed poetic structure
might have been preferable to the awkward misfit of this particular essay
in counterpoint. But Clarke is apparently unable to imagine a plot
adequate to the scope of his framework; his "predictive" novels are
equally plotless and even his tale of the far future is made up of a series of
accidental occurrences, set into motion almost haphazardly by the
adolescent hero's desire for change and adventure. So the counterpoint
structure was attempted for *Childhood's End*, and the result is a
hodgepodge of pretentious chronicle, apologetic melodrama, and superficial sketches of static unrelated, individual scenes. Even if we regard the
book as an elegy for mankind, for the end of personal and racial
"childhood", the elegiac tone is inconsistent, and insufficient to maintain
unity over 75,000 words without a more carefully wrought "poetic structure", and the lame, pedestrian style of the novel seems particularly in-
congruous for a poem.

As it is practically plotless, the novel is also almost characterless.
Against the ambitious theme and tremendous scope, individuals and their
merely personal problems are bound to look somewhat insignificant. The
unknown bulks extremely large, and the attitude of the characters is
stereotyped, not in the heroic mold, whose calculated respect for size and
power allows for action, but in the passive mold, whose awe and reverence
we normally term "religious". Man the Creator, acting, progressing, continually making changes in his environment, whom I would consider the
ideal (if not the most common) protagonist of SF, gives way to man the
Creature, full of fear and wonder and more than willing to follow orders
when an encounter with an incalculable unknown power forces him to admit how small he is and how little he knows.[16] Although the fear of racial
annihilation is counterbalanced by pride in man's being "chosen", this
revaluation of the inevitable as somehow "good" has an orthodox
religious ring to it, contrasting sharply with the heresy and *hubris* which
have characterized science in modern civilization.[17] Puny on an absolute
scale, man's achievements are respectable measured against the present;
his potential, symbolized by the Overlords, is by no means slighted. To
preserve this respectability, despite the awesome realities beyond, Clarke
does show us representative moments of the better, i.e. rational selves of
certain men.

Stormgren, George, Jan, and Karellen are the only major characters;
one of them is involved in every episode we are shown, not merely told
about. All males, actively questing for knowledge, they all appear confident and rational, unless belief in rationality in the face of the incomprehensible is itself irrational. Even their mental processes are shown to
us in formal, grammatical sentences, with no trace of irrational stream-of-
consciousness. Given little to do, however, they seem no more than
marionettes in this cosmic puppet-show. Only Karellen, long-lived,
revisiting a familiar pattern of events, scientifically detached and curious,
has any real stature. Behind his posturing, lecturing, and deceit, his sense
of tragedy makes him the most human of all; his intellectual stubbornness
is like that which doomed his prototype, Milton's Satan, to a similarly
tragic and isolated immortality.

A resigned acceptance, common to all four characters, is largely responsible for the elegiac tone pervading the book. Stormgren knows he will never see the Overlords, George knows man has lost his future as man, Jan knows he can not survive cut off from humankind, and Karellen knows he will never find the kind of answers that he seeks. It is the reader's knowledge of impending doom that makes the characters' inconsequential behavior and sunny dispositions seem ironic; juxtaposition, a "cinematic" technique, accomplishes what style does not. Although Clarke sometimes stumbles over awkward circumlocutions, trite *sententiae*, pedantic speech-making, and labored humor, the pedestrian lucidity and uncomplicated vocabulary of his style seldom draw the reader's attention away from the events being described. I feel the author's presence only toward the end, where his style does manage to impart a sense of melancholic majesty to the spectacle. His attempt at generating a "sense of wonder", which ranges from "gee-whiz" impressions of the Overlords to awed contemplation of man's fate, is most successful as the children grow more confident in the testing of their powers, and it culminates in the cataclysmic shock witnessed by Jan up close, then by Karellen far in the distance. The note of regret, though cloying and sentimental at times (Jeff Greggson's dog mourning his master lost in dreams, his parents' final farewell just before their island community blows itself up), also gains in depth with this echoing crescendo.

The major source of unity, besides the figure of Karellen and the basic consistency of style and tone, seems to lie in certain image-patterns and the repetition of significant motifs. The dozen or so allusions to figures from folklore and history, while they may be intended to add depth to the narrative, are so haphazardly chosen and introduced as to seem unrelated to the whole. On the other hand, the apocalyptic and demonic imagery of the Overlords and the Overmind is so persistent as to lay down at the symbolic level a morality play contradicting the rational message on the surface. The majority of patterns function somewhere in between these two extremes, mainly as unifying factors. The power of Stormgren, and his superiority over the human masses, are echoed by the Overlords' power and superiority over him, and by the Overmind's power and superiority over them. Karellen's reference to humans as beloved pets reminds us of his attitude toward Stormgren, and is reinforced by the dog's loneliness. A widening perspective is seen in the Overlords' intellectual striptease, in the emphasis given e.s.p., in Jan's discovery of what lies beyond the solar system, in frequent panoramic views of space and time, of Earth and human society. The frustrated takeoff of the Prologue's moon-rockets is echoed by Karellen's edict that "the Stars are not for Man", and by Jan's discovery of the edict's essential if not literal truth (are the children still "man"?). This frustration is counterbalanced by Stormgren's "ascent" to Karellen's ship, by flights of Overlord ships away from Earth (including the one Jan stows away on), and by the final departures of both children and Overlords. And the final transformation of the children into a fully symbiotic, super-organic life form is foreshadowed by images of other kinds of togetherness, progressively becoming more compressed: the fifty starships hovering over world capitals that turn out to be projections of just one, the mob demonstration broken up by Stormgren, the gangsters' "conference" broken up by Karellen, the entrance of

Karellen with the children, the party where the seance is held, the artists' colony whose sense of community rests on its individual members, and a single family dissolving as its children become something else.

If *Childhood's End* is not a fully satisfying literary experience, it does illustrate certain characteristics of SF at its best, and it does exhibit literary virtues. Respect for rational thought, construction of a cosmic perspective, relentless pursuit of extrapolative hypotheses, and a genuine evocation of the sense of wonder are each positive achievements, on their own terms. The whole, however, is flawed, not only by deficiencies in style, characterization, and narrative structure, which could presumably be corrected by revision, but also by a fundamental dichotomy between opposing goals.[18]

Algis Budrys sees Clarke's problem as commercial wilfulness; after identifying him as the author of "a clutch of mystical novels", Budrys chides Clarke for his "fixed and pernicious idea of how to produce a saleable short story [and presumably a novel]. That idea is to introduce an intriguing technological notion or scientific premise, and then use it to evoke frights or menaces. [Thus he can] raise a formidable reputation for profundity by repeating, over and over again, that the universe is wide and man is very small."[19] Budrys' criticism is pertinent as far as it goes, but it is limited; Clarke has shown more variety, and capacity for growth than Budrys would allow, and the flaws in *Childhood's End* are only partly, I think, due to the author's eye for a dollar.

Certainly, Clarke is a commercial writer, a member of the second generation of pulp magazine writers consciously turning out SF. Thus he has one foot firmly planted in the SF magazines of the 1920's and 1930's, with their infantile dependency on Bug-Eyed Monsters, slam-bang action, and technological artifacts treated as objects worthy of awe and wonder. But he is also rooted in a "respectable" British literary tradition. Blake, Shelley, Mary Shelley, Hardy, Butler, Morris, Wells, Doyle, Stapledon, Huxley, C. S. Lewis, and Orwell all wrote works in which they showed science and technology as demonic, at least potentially. This tradition is, I believe, still entrenched in Anglo-American humanistic circles, affecting like blinders many academics and reviewers, and that part of the literate public for whom they remain arbiters of literary taste.[20] Rather than a critical appreciation for science, they tend to inculcate fear and hostility toward it; by abdicating their function as a knowledgeable, foreseeing counterbalance, they make more likely the technocratic state they profess to anticipate with abhorrence.[21]

Given these traditions, neither of which I would call mature, Clarke and other second generation writers for the SF magazines had little that was adequate out of which to construct a coherent critique of science and scientism. If *Childhood's End* is a "classic", it is partly because it is a hybrid, a respectable representative of that period during which SF magazine writers were first trying to reach out to a literary audience, as well as to their more habitual readers. An ambitious effort, better than people outside the pulp field thought it capable of achieving, it is also an abortive effort, an impressive failure, the flaws of which are indicative of the problems frequently attendant upon the literary domestication of SF. It has a high seriousness that sets it apart from the ordinary pulp science fiction novel of any generation, but it barely lives up to its name. An attempt at maturity, *Childhood's End* is no more than a median stage of adolescence.

California State University, Long Beach

NOTES

¹Mark R. Hillegas, *The Future as Nightmare: H.G. Wells and the Anti-Utopians* (1967), pp153-54.

²For reviews of *Childhood's End* after publication, see James J. Rollo, *Atlantic Monthly* Nov 1953, p112; William Du Bois, *NY Times* Aug. 27, 1953, p23; Basil Davenport, *NYTBR* Aug. 23, 1953, p19; Groff Conklin, *Galaxy* Mar. 1954, pp118-19; H.H. Holmes (Anthony Boucher [W. Anthony White]), *NY Herald-Tribune Book Review* Aug. 23, 1953, p9; P. Schuyler Miller, *Astounding* Feb. 1954, pp51-52.

³A compendium of reviews, among other things, of a later work may be found in Jerome Agel, ed., *The Making of Kubrick's 2001* (New American Library 1970). The propensity of humanistic, and scientific, critics of SF to see it through different-colored glasses I have explored in some detail in "Science Fiction and the Two Cultures: A Study in the Theory and Criticism of Contemporary Science Fiction with Reference to the Cultural Division Between the Sciences and the Humanities," B.A. Thesis, Drew University, 1962.

⁴Not only has Clarke been publicly lionized for his quasimystical novels, but of his short stories that have been anthologized by both academic and commercial editors, theological speculation seems more rewarded than technological extrapolation. Cf W.R. Cole, *A Checklist of Science Fiction Anthologies* (1964, privately printed). A survey of more recent anthologies, especially those intended as textbooks, bears out this predominance.

⁵This argument is derived from Northrop Frye, *Anatomy of Criticism* (US 1957), esp pp141-150.

⁶Blake's *Milton*, Shelley's *Prometheus Unbound*, Goethe's *Faust*, and Zamyatin's *We* are just a few of the works that reflect this Romantic tradition. For a further discussion of the Romantic hero as, among other things, a "fallen angel", see W. H. Auden, *The Enchafed Flood: or the Romantic Iconography of the Sea* (1950).

⁷This subject has been explored in some depth by Robert Plank in *The Emotional Significance of Imaginary Beings: A Study of the Interaction Between Psychopathology, Literature, and Reality in the Modern World* (1968).

⁸Northrop Frye sees these structures as underlying even the most realistic fiction; see *Anatomy of Criticism* (US 1957), pp131-40 and *passim*.

⁹Samuel R. Delany, "About Five Thousand One Hundred and Seventy-Five Words," in Thomas D. Clareson, ed., *SF: The Other Side of Realism* (1971), p144. Cf Alexei Panshin, "Science Fiction in Dimension," in Clareson. For opposing views see Stanislaw Lem, "Robots in Science Fiction," in Clareson, and Darko Suvin, "On the Poetics of the Science Fiction Genre," *College English* 34(1972):372-82.

¹⁰Cf Joseph Campbell's discussion of the functions of myth in *The*

Hero With a Thousand Faces (1949), esp "Prologue: The Monomyth"; Northrop Frye, *The Modern Century* (Canada 1967), esp pp105-20; Joseph Campbell, *The Masks of God* (4v 1959-68), *passim.*

[11]Clarke's sober speculations may be found, for example, in *The Promise of Space* (1968), §29 "Where's Everybody?", and in *Voices from the Sky: Previews of the Coming Space Age* (1965), §[17] "Science and Spirituality", where in both instances he draws comparisons to what might be "godlike" qualities in the aliens. Cf Plank (¶7).

[12]Again, Clarke has paid more serious attention to e.s.p. and the idea of the group mind in his non-fiction; see *Profiles of the Future* (1962; 1973 with addenda), §17 "Brain and Body"; *Voices from the Sky* (1965), §[18] "Class of '00". He has also attacked "The Lunatic Fringe" for their gullibility, as in a chapter of that name (§[20]) in *Voices.* The relationship of e.s.p. to wish-fulfilment is also explored by C.E.M. Hansel, *E.S.P.: A Scientific Evaluation* (1966), which debunks the notion made popular by Rhine that e.s.p. has been empirically verified, and by Robert Plank, "Communication in Science Fiction," in Samuel I. Hayakawa, ed., *Our Language and Our World* (1958).

[13]Damon Knight, *In Search of Wonder: Essays on Modern Science Fiction*, rev ed (US 1967), p188. Knight wrongly accuses Clarke of having the Overlords encounter man in prehistory; Clarke writes that people assumed this (§6), but later corrects this impression with the future-memory explanation (§23). On the amalgamation of the Devil image, in the particular shape Clarke chose for his Overlords, in the late European Middle Ages, see Bernard J. Bamberger, *Fallen Angels* (US 1952), pp208-32; Maurice Garçon and Jean Vinchon, *The Devil: An Historical, Critical and Medical Study,* tr Stephen Haden Guest (1930); Pennethorne Hughes, *Witchcraft* (1952), §8; Ernest Jones, *Nightmare, Witches, and Devils* (US 1931), pp154-59. The theory of prehistoric encounters with aliens has, of course, been given wide dissemination quite recently by Erich von Däniken in *Chariots of the Gods? Unsolved Mysteries of the Past* (1969) and *Gods from Outer Space* (1971), both tr by Michael Heron. By a quirk of fate, the original title of von Däniken's first book translates literally as "Memories of the Future".

[14]Reprinted from *UNESCO Courier* as "Kalinga Award Speech" in Arthur C. Clarke, *Voices from the Sky: Previews of the Coming Space Age* (1965).

[15]"Guardian Angel," *New Worlds,* Winter 1950, is basically the same story as Part One of *Childhood's End;* revision removed some poor repartee, added more background, and diminished slightly the dependence on melodramatic effect.

[16]Cf Algis Budrys' comments on the "inertial school" of SF, with specific reference to Aldiss, Ballard, Disch, and Knight, in *Galaxy* Dec 1966, pp128-33.

[17]This is not to say that Clarke is an orthodox adherent to any religion; his caricatures of the true believer, Wainwright, in the early pages of *Childhood's End*, and of the lunatic fringe in *Voices from the Sky* (¶12), seem sincere enough, and his non-fiction writing is steadfastly on the side of man's continued exploration and expansion of knowledge. But his flirtation with the mythic imagination is also continuous, even in his non-fiction, suggesting at least a humble regard for the limitations of

science and a dependency upon an anti-scientific literary tradition as a source of imagery.

[18]In revising the early drafts of *2001: A Space Odyssey* (see *The Lost Worlds of 2001* [1972]), in adapting "Guardian Angel" for inclusion in *Childhood's End* (see ¶15), and in revising *Against the Fall of Night* for republication as *The City and the Stars* (1956), which he declared to be the "final, definitive version" in his introduction to the omnibus volume *From the Ocean, From the Stars* (1958), Clarke showed some ear for style and tone, but seems to have concentrated primarily on logical or aesthetic consistency of scenes in context.

[19]*Galaxy* Oct 1967, p190.

[20]Although it has now been over ten years since the publication of that *cause célèbre*, C.P. Snow's *The Two Cultures and the Scientific Revolution* (1960), many of its accusations still ring true.

[21]Two notable exceptions are Jacques Barzun, *Science: The Glorious Entertainment* (1964), and Martin Green, *Science and the Shabby Curate of Poetry* (1965). The best critiques of science and technology, however, seem to be written by scientists, e.g. Nigel Calder, *Technopolis* (1969).

Robert H. Canary

Utopian and Fantastic Dualities in Robert Graves's *Watch the North Wind Rise*

(from SFS 1:248 - 254, Fall 1974)

For nearly sixty years Robert Graves has thought of himself as primarily a poet; for nearly thirty years, he has publicly identified himself as a poet-servant of the eternal Muse, the White Goddess worshipped under many names in antiquity. But Graves is more familiar to the reading public as the author of historical novels like *I, Claudius* (1934) and of the classic autobiography of World War I, *Good-bye to All That* (1929). Some critics have argued that Graves' prose works deserve as much serious consideration as his poetry, but little has been done; especially surprising is the general neglect of *Watch the North Wind Rise* (1949), a utopian novel about a future society which has returned to the worship of the Goddess.[1] I would like to suggest that the framework of this novel exhibits a duality characteristic of the genre of the "fantastic," that it provides an example of the way in which similar dualities may be found in utopian works, and that it is the very existence of such dualities which makes this novel a satisfactory vehicle for Graves's reflections on the nature of poetry, the Muse, and the women in whom she is seen incarnate.

The term "fantastic" here is taken from Todorov, who sees the genre as defined by the reader's hesitation between a natural and a supernatural explanation for the events he observes; the fantastic is thus midway between the uncanny and the marvellous (which is often called "fantasy").[2] *Watch the North Wind Rise* begins with the protagonist summoned into the future by the poet-magicians of New Crete and ends when he recovers consciousness to find himself naked outside his own door back on the night on which he had left. The dream journey can be explained either by magic or by sleepwalking. The protagonist is an English poet, Edward Venn-Thomas, who might naturally dream of a utopia managed by poets; on the other hand, Venn-Thomas professes to be convinced of the reality of the journey—and Graves, his creator, had recently published a long work testifying to the historical power of the Goddess, *The White Goddess* (London: Faber and Faber, 1948).

Traditional tales of the fantastic have been situated within known history; alternative worlds have usually been thought of as giving complete allegiance to natural laws (science fiction) or as openly allowing for the supernatural (fantasy, fairy tale). Although set in a future alternative world, *Watch the North Wind Rise* maintains a certain tension between natural and supernatural explanations for what Venn-Thomas sees in New Crete, as well as for the dream-journey which takes him there. The poet-magicians who have summoned him believe implicitly in their own magic powers, but the magic which Venn-Thomas actually observes is explainable in terms of psychological suggestion and common sense; Venn-Thomas himself, as a poet, is a member of the magician caste and can work some minor feats of suggestion, which he regards with suitable skepticism: "If one used the right formula, the commons could be hypnotized into doing any ridiculous thing" (§22). Venn-Thomas meets the Goddess herself, incarnate in an old crone and perhaps in other forms as well, but the possibility that these are merely mortal women remains open. His attitude toward her worship remains ambivalent: "Such fantastic ingenuousness of faith! Yet, without such ingenuousness, what strength had religion?" (§19). On balance, Venn-Thomas seems to believe in the Goddess, but the reader is not required to do so.

IT MIGHT BE THOUGHT THAT the uncertainties of the fantastic would be incompatible with the demands of utopia as a literary genre, for the latter would seem to call for an ideal society constructed within the realm of natural possibility. But utopias have always been both "the good place" and "no place," and few literary utopias of any merit have failed to deal in some fashion with the obvious question of whether the ideal proposed is a possible one for natural men. Even in B.F. Skinner's positivist, small-scale, contemporary utopia, *Walden Two* (1948), the author has his protagonist wonder whether the utopian community's success derives from its principles or from the temporary influence of a charismatic founder.

The existence of such hesitations between the possible and impossible is, in fact, one of many such dualities in utopias, which cannot be reduced to mere blueprints for attainable social reforms. While sketching one possible ideal society, literary utopias also serve as criticisms of the author's own society, of other utopias, and often of themselves.

Almost by definition, utopias mediate between the ideal they propose and the actualities of the author's own society. While in dystopias the criticism of the author's society takes the form of explicit exaggeration of present trends, in utopias the criticism is more often by implicit presentation of better alternatives. The contrast with the present is their reason for being, and it may be argued that the "literary value of utopian fiction depends largely upon its satiric potential."[3] Graves, for example, contrasts New Crete, where the ritual murder of the Victim-King makes murder for less sacred ends seem unthinkable, and his own world, where millions die in the senseless slaughter of war; the force of the comparison does not depend on the specific likelihood of the alternative presented, only upon its relative correspondence to our own ideals. The criticism of the author's own society may also be explicit, in the fashion of dystopias. In New Crete, we are told, priests are drawn from the more stupid members of the servant class. Incidental touches of this sort are not really out of key in a work whose principal reference point is inevitably the author's own society.

The opposition between the utopia and the author's society is not, however, the only duality found in literary utopias. Utopias breed counterutopias, and most literary utopias stand in some defined relationship to the utopian tradition itself. In *Watch the North Wind Rise*, we learn that New Crete was a deliberate creation of a world council, influenced by the author of a *Critique of Utopias*, who concluded "we must retrace our steps, or perish" (§4). Anthropological enclaves were formed, recreating earlier periods from history. New Crete was the most successful of these enclaves and now, five hundred years later, has spread its system "over a great part of the still habitable world" (§4). New Crete has thus been chosen over all utopias which extrapolate man's technological progress and has proved itself in competition with other archaic patterns.

New Crete shares with many other utopias a caste system, and *Watch the North Wind Rise* includes both implicit and explicit satire on this feature of utopias. Implicitly, Graves criticizes those utopias in which the caste structure is hereditary; individuals are assigned to castes on the basis of their childhood behavior, and captains (the warrior caste) are not allowed to marry. Even more importantly, the highest ranking caste is that of the poet-magicians, in contrast to the intellectual or managerial elites of other utopias. Poets are here the acknowledged legislators of the human race, and poetic values rule even in economic matters: there is no money in New Crete, goods being given to those who need then in return for free gifts; no machines are allowed that are not hand-crafted, made with the hands of "love." For Graves, at least, love is a poetic value.

Some of the other castes are objects of satire. We see relatively little of the commoners (the masses) or the servants (who do menial chores for higher castes). The recorders are an upper caste, but most are presented as fussy pedants. The captains ride about giving moral exhortations, much in the style (as Leiber says) "of head-boys at a British school." Venn-Thomas nicknames one captain Nervo the Fearless. Both the recorders and captains are objects for satire against the intellectual and military classes so often given high rank in utopian societies—and our own. But explicit satire of this sort is also at the expense of the structure of Graves's own utopia.

The self-critical side of utopias is by no means at odds with their function as implicit criticism of the author's own time. In their focus on alternatives

opposed to society as it is, utopias become societies of humors; when their
authors are men of sense, the ridiculous side of the ideal is apt to be shown.
Venn-Thomas decides that the lack of a money economy has dulled the wits
of the people of New Crete. He has no doubts that New Crete is a more
perfect society—"if I had to choose between New Cretan half-wittedness and
American whole-wittedness, I was simpleton enough to choose the former
and avoid stomach ulcers, ticker tape and Sunday best" (§19)—but he finds
New Crete a bit bland, a bit boring. The author and the Goddess apparently
agree, for Venn-Thomas has been brought to New Crete to help destroy it.
His presence helps re-introduce the inhabitants to lying, jealousy, murder, and
suicide. The North Wind is rising, and soon all New Crete will suffer from
"an itching palm, narrowed eyes and a forked tongue" (§22), characteristics of modern whole-wittedness. New Crete has brought man happiness,
innocence, and goodness, but at a price in other human qualities, notably
reason.

The world of the utopia may thus be seen as existing in opposition to
the author's own society, to other utopias, and (again) to an implicit notion
of human possibilities. New Crete may also be seen as both a reproduction
and an idealization of Late Bronze Age Crete, a Golden Age or lost Eden—
though Graves's destruction of his own utopia at the end suggests that he believes in the Fortunate Fall. Beyond this ambiguous relationship to a specific
period, New Crete stands in an uneasy relationship with the idea of history itself—clocks are forbidden, and few records are kept. Societies which aspire to
be perfect, as utopias do, are almost inevitably static, and New Crete seems
to have been created as an escape from the consequences of man's history.
But to be human is to change, and change is coming to New Crete at the
end of the novel. The dualities of time and timelessness, stasis and change,
history and perfection are linked to those set up by the utopia's opposition
to other societies by the very ambiguity that surrounds its status as a possible/
impossible world.

THE TENSION SET UP by the dualities of the novel's structure is parallel to
that generated by its emotional and thematic content. At some level, *Watch
the North Wind Rise* is a projection of the conscious concerns and latent
impulses of the poet Venn-Thomas-Graves. To begin with, it is obviously
concerned not only with the kind of society implied by Graves's poetic
values but also with the kind of society ideal for poets. The two are not
identical, for the poetry of New Crete—and its music as well—is insipid and
academic.

In some ways, New Crete deals with poets in ways which we know (from
other writings) Graves approves of. Although poets are honored as a caste,
few are afforded immortality. All poetry must begin as oral poetry, for there
is no paper. The best of a poet's poems may be inscribed on silver plates.
The best poems of an age may be inscribed on golden plates and kept in
the *Canon of Poetry*, which has been reduced to fifteen volumes. The details
of a poet's life are kept only in verbal tradition, which re-arranges them
freely. The inhabitants of New Crete do not admire poets but the Goddess
who inspired them. All this sounds very Gravesian, although Venn-Thomas
does not seem very pleased to find a poem of his in the Canon—"but
clumsily rewritten and attributed to 'the poet Tseliot' " (§18).

The failure of New Crete is the failure of the utopian ideal itself. The
soft, good life which it provides its inhabitants does not arouse the strong

emotions which Graves thinks necessary for true poetry. Poetry is to act as a mediator between innocence and experience, good and evil, but here is only innocence and good. It is significant that the only good poet Venn-Thomas meets is Quant, a recorder. Because he is a recorder, Quant is closer to history than his fellows. Because he is a member of one caste who follows the discipline of another, Quant is a marginal man, set apart from his society; the implication is that poets are better off in worlds not run by poets. Venn-Thomas can take with equanimity a future which implies the destruction of his own non-poetic age, but he is the very agent of the destruction of the anti-poetic utopia run by poets.

It is significant that it is the Goddess who has summoned Venn-Thomas to perform this task. Graves has always insisted on the cruel side of the Muse. His ideal figure of the poet has not been the poet-magician but the royal lover, who accepts his eventual fate in return for the privilege of her love:

> Dwell on her graciousness, dwell on her smiling
> Do not forget what flowers
> The great boar trampled down in ivy time.
> Her brow was creamy as the crested wave,
> Her sea-gray eyes were wild
> But nothing promised that is not performed.
> ("To Juan at the Winter Solstice")

The love the Muse offers the poet is like the dream of New Crete itself, a momentary idyll; the poet will suffer jealousy and loss, even death, just as New Crete must undergo fearsome change at the Goddess's hands.

Graves's early criticism, written before his submission to the Goddess, casts some light on his fascination with the double-edged promises of the Muse.[4] He held that poetry was a product of internal conflict between "the rival sub-personalities" of the poet, holding "apparently contradictory emotional ideas" (*On English Poetry*, pp. 123, 13). Graves himself has written of the opposition between reason and emotion in his own inheritance, between the Classical and Romantic traditions of poetry. Poetry resolves such conflicts by integration. *Watch the North Wind Rise* can be seen as fulfilling a similar function. Even the doubts allowed to remain about the real existence of the Goddess can be seen as satisfying Graves's latent rationalism.

To see how this process of integration is achieved, we must look at the plot which unifies this novel. Soon after his arrival, Venn-Thomas begins a platonic affair with one of his host witches, Sapphire, but his sleep with her is troubled by mysterious voices that sound like his wife, Antonia. The other witch, Sally, seems to be involved with at least two of the three men at Magic House, but she treats Venn-Thomas coldly. Venn-Thomas's old flame, an adventuress named Erica, makes the first of several unexplained appearances and tells him that Sally is jealous of Sapphire. Erica is probably the Goddess in disguise, and her interpretation of Sally is naturally correct. Sally arranges for her lover Fig-bread to be killed by his horse, so that she can spread her cloak across his grave and demand that Venn-Thomas sleep with her. This local custom is supposed to afford the dead man's spirit rebirth in the child so conceived, but Venn-Thomas refuses her. Later that night, his wife Antonia shows up in his bedroom; he sleeps with her, only to discover that it was not Antonia but Sally working her magic on him. He

goes to Sapphire, who has fled the house, and she says that she will not
sleep with him until she can spread her cloak on Sally's grave. Instead,
Sally arranges for Sapphire to undergo ritual death by swallowing a per-
sonality-destroying drug; Sapphire does so and is reborn as a commoner
named Stormbird, but first she kills Sally. Of the remaining inhabitants of
the Magic House, one becomes an "elder" (spending his remaining days in the
Nonsense House) and the other dies of heartbreak or suicide on hearing of
Sally's death. The village is left without a poet-magician caste for protection;
this fulfills a prophecy, and means that the North Wind is about to be loosed
on New Crete. Venn-Thomas finds Stormbird, only to realize that he does
not desire her sexually but as the daughter he and Antonia have never had.
After he returns to his own time, waking to make love to Antonia, Stormbird
returns as the daughter to be born from that act of love, announcing her
coming in New Cretan style, by knocking three times on the door.

As a utopia, *Watch the North Wind Rise* involves choices among opposed
social ideas; as a novel, it presents its protagonist with choices among women.
There are really two choices, one of which has already been made. Venn-
Thomas could never really have chosen to keep Erica, for Muses cannot be
kept, but in marrying Antonia he chose to temper his pursuit of the Muse
with a quieter, familial love. Now Erica appears in his dream of the future,
though secondary elaboration explains her presence as an incarnation of the
Goddess, and Antonia seems to be present, though we are given the delayed
explanation that her form was taken by Sally. Sapphire also looks a bit
like Antonia—"Who are you really?" he asks her, and she replies, "The woman
you love" (§3). The opposition between the attractive but evil Sally and the
gentle Sapphire is, in fact, parallel to that between Erica and Antonia, and
between sexual passion and familial love in general.

Chapter Seventeen of the novel, "Who is Edward?" makes it quite clear
that the choices involved are also choices among the rival sub-personalities
of Venn-Thomas himself. He wonders whether his true self is the Ward who
loved an American girl, the Teddy who loved Erica, the Ned who loves Antonia,
the Edward who loves Sapphire, or none of these. Venn-Thomas's dream-
solution makes a distinction between choices made as a poet and as a man.
As a poet, he chooses the Erica-Muse and accepts the destruction and suffering entailed by such a choice; as a man, he escapes from the whirlwind and
returns to his stable home, sanctifying his sexual love for his wife by his
paternal love for his yet unborn daughter. To do this is to reject the static
utopia of New Crete while attempting to incorporate its values (represented
by Sapphire) into his own life, to reject the necessity for evil in society
(represented by Sally) while serving as its involuntary agent. On the emotional,
artistic, and social level, the conflicting ideals of his rival sub-personalities
are balanced and integrated in the structure of the novel.

Watch the North Wind Rise has many of the characteristics of the "fantastic" genre, which is to be located in an area of tension between the natural
and the supernatural. As a utopian fiction, it also presents oppositions between notions of the possible, between social ideals, and between the idealiz-
ing and satiric impulse. Such formal dualities make it a particularly appropriate vehicle for the reflections of a poet who has always seen poetry as
the result of mastering conflicting impulses. The congruence of the formal
structure of the novel with the internal dynamic of its plot gives *Watch the
North Wind Rise* an organic unity unusual in Graves's fiction and entitles it
to greater attention than it has hitherto received.

NOTES

[1]George Steiner, for example, sees Graves as closer to first-rank as a historical novelist than as a poet—"The Genius of Robert Graves," *Kenyon Review*, 22 (1960), 340-65. The lack of detailed work on Graves's novel is obvious from David E. Pownall, "An Annotated Bibliography of Articles on Robert Graves," *Focus on Robert Graves*, no. 2 (December 1973), 17-23. *Watch the North Wind Rise* (N.Y.: Creative Age, 1949) appears as the first edition in Fred H. Higginson's authoritative *Bibliography of the Works of Robert Graves* (London: Nicholas Vane, 1966), but some readers may know the novel from the English edition, which was published as *Seven Days in New Crete* (London: Cassell, 1949). The only extended treatment of this novel with which I am familiar is Fritz Leiber, "Utopia for Poets and Witches," *Riverside Quarterly*, 4 (June 1970), 194-205, a sympathetic summary which stresses the fantasy elements in the book. Graves's critics have seldom given the novel more than a passing sentence, and it is completely ignored by several critics otherwise particularly interested in Graves's view of the Goddess: John B. Vickery, *Robert Graves and the White Goddess* (Lincoln: U. of Nebraska, 1972); Daniel Hoffman, *Barbarous Knowledge, Myth in the Poetry of Yeats, Graves, and Muir* (N.Y.: Oxford, 1967); and Randall Jarrell, "Graves and the White Goddess," *The Third Book of Criticism* (N.Y.: Farrar, Straus & Giroux, 1969), 77-112. With the honorable exception of Leiber, critics of utopian fiction and "speculative fiction" have also neglected *Watch the North Wind Rise*, perhaps because because it is the only Graves novel to fall into these categories. Robert C. Elliott, *The Shape of Utopia* (Chicago: University of Chicago, 1970) devotes a few pages to Graves, arguing that Graves's apocalyptic ending is an arbitrary response to the "formal and experiential limitations of utopia" (p. 117); in what follows I hope to suggest that Elliott is wrong about both utopian fiction and Graves's novel.

[2]Tzvetan Todorov, *The Fantastic* [1970], trans. Richard Howard (Cleveland: Case Western Reserve, 1973), p. 33. Jane Mobley, "Defining Fantasy Fiction; Focus and Form," paper presented to MMLA Speculative Fiction seminar, 1973, identifies true fantasy with magic-using other worlds (a subgenre of Todorov's "marvellous"). Darko Suvin, on the other hand, has identified fantasy with Gothic, horror, and weird tales, categories which are excluded by Mobley's definition and which overlap Todorov's genres—"On the Poetics of Science Fiction," *College English*, 34 (December 1972), 372-82, and "Science Fiction and the Genological Jungle," *Genre*, 6 (September 1973), 251-73. Todorov's "fantastic" might, however, be thought of as existing on the borderline between Suvin's cognitive and non-cognitive estrangement. So long as the criteria used are made clear there is probably no great harm in such terminological confusion, though it remains a nuisance.

[3]David Ketterer, *New Worlds for Old* (Bloomington: Indiana University, 1974), p. 101. On utopia as a literary genre, Darko Suvin, "Defining the Literary Genre of Utopia: Some Historical Semantics, Some Genology, A Proposal and a Plea," *Studies in the Literary Imagination*, 6 (Fall 1973), 121-45.

[4]I have discussed this at greater length in "The Making of the Graves Canon: The Case for the Early Criticism," paper presented to the MLA Graves seminar, 1973. The most important early works are *On English Poetry* (N.Y.: Knopf, 1922), *The Meaning of Dreams* (London: Cecil Palmer, 1924), and *Poetic Unreason* (London: Cecil Palmer, 1925).

Roy Arthur Swanson

Nabokov's *Ada* as Science Fiction

(from SFS 2:76 - 88, *March 1975)*

In his "first collection of public prose," entitled *Strong Opinions*, Vladimir Nabokov catalogues his loathings: "stupidity, oppression, crime, cruelty, soft music" (3).[1] He loathes dictatorships (149) and Freudians (*passim*) as, perhaps, respective examples of oppression and stupidity. He identifies Van Veen as "the charming villain" of *Ada or Ardor: A Family Chronicle* and says, "I loathe Van Veen" (120). In an equally declarative but less subtle sentence, he states, "I loathe science fiction with its gals and goons, suspense and suspensories" (117). Although criticism, as an object of loathing, is not a part of his catalogue, Nabokov's antipathy to criticism in general is strongly evident in *Strong Opinions*, which title does not keep him from asserting that he is "immune to any kind of opinion" (173). Against all this, one has to risk Nabokov's contempt and his charge of stupidity in drawing up a critique to buttress one's opinions that Nabokov subscribes to Van Veen's concepts of time and that *Ada* may be viewed as science fiction.

One may begin by noting that, in 1969, the year of *Ada*'s publication, Nabokov was at least undecided whether he agreed with Van Veen "in all his views on the texture of time" (143) and that two years later he was still willing to admit that his "conception of the texture of time somewhat resembles its image in Part 4 of *Ada*. The present is only the top of the past, and the future does not exist" (184).

With regard to science fiction, Nabokov does express "the deepest admiration" for H.G. Wells; and he names as special favorites five of Wells's stories, all of which had been identified, generically, as science-fiction works well before *Ada* came to be written: *The Time Machine, The Invisible Man, The War of the Worlds, The First Men in the Moon*, and "The Country of the Blind" (175). Against his identification of these works as "romances" instead of SF it would be pointless to argue: the works are, quite clearly, SF romances. In any case, he speaks elsewhere of Aleksey Tolstoy as "a writer of some talent," who "has two or three science fiction stories or novels which are memorable" (87).

Additionally, the fiction-writer Nabokov is himself, as a lepidopterist, also a scientist; and he is of the opinion, to which he is nonetheless presumably immune, "that in a work of art there is a kind of merging between... the precision of poetry and the excitement of pure science" (10). Poetry, in his strong opinion, "includes all creative writing," and he has "never been able to see any generic difference between poetry and artistic prose" (44). Concurring with these opinions, we could label almost all of Nabokov's narrative art as SF; but to do so would be specious and would obscure the point that Nabokov loathes, not SF, with which he clearly has an affinity, but routine SF.

Finally, one may follow the lead given in Nabokov's comment that "Every original novel is 'anti-' because it does not resemble the genre or kind of its predecessor" (173). *Ada*, for all its attention to "Antiterra" and to anagrammatic satire (for example, "Osberg" for "Borges"), is not an "anti-novel"; but it is "anti-": it does not resemble SF, but it may be studied as being of that genre or kind, especially if the study centers on that SF element which, for the sake of convenience, we may term "eversion." The term would denote a double reversal or a turning-inside-out; and *Ada*'s eversions of time, earth, and sexual gender can be called, respectively, "transtemporality," "transterrestriality," and "transsexuality."

The first sentence of the novel is an eversion of the first sentence of Tolstoy's *Anna Karenin*;[2] in Nabokov's words, "the opening sentence of *Anna Karenin*...is turned inside out" (285). Throughout the novel things are turned inside out. The dominant eversions are those of time, the planet Earth, and sexual gender. Time is turned inside out, so that much of the present becomes the past: the mid-20th century and the late 19th century are anachronistically confused. The planet Earth appears now and then as Antiterra, on which the eastern and western hemispheres are transposed, so that Asia and North America are turned into each other, producing Amerussia, and on which the inhabitants speculate upon the actual existence of Terra, just as inhabitants of our world now speculate upon the reality, or actual existence, of Heaven or of extraterrestial life: "they are all in heaven or on Terra," Marina Veen muses in nostalgic reference to old roomy limousines and professional chauffeurs (257/§1:38).[3] The male is turned outwardly into the female: Adam becomes the female Ada, and Eve becomes the male Ivan (Van Veen). Eversions of this type are common in science fiction.

In science fiction eversion is itself one form of a constant for which the best term would be "version," that is, "a turning." Other forms, then, would be conversion, inversion, obversion, reversion, and the like—that is, a turning into, upside down, over, back, and so forth. "Version" is initially a change of perspective and ultimately a change, or even a loss, or possibly even a creation, of function. In Samuel Butler's *Erewhon*, for example, the reactions to sickness and crime are reversed to produce what has proved to be a prophetic change of perspective. Archibald Marshall toys with perspective in his utopian work, *Upsidonia* (1915). The androgyny in Ursula K. Le Guin's *The Left Hand of Darkness* is a conversion of humanoid life from an investiture in two sexes to a hermaphroditic investiture in one. The material and anti-material worlds (the universe and the para-universe) in Isaac Asimov's *The Gods Themselves* reflect speculative inversion; in one respect, the universe's advantages in energy intake are inversely proportional to those of the para-universe. The time travelling and time "warps" of H.G. Wells's *The Time Machine*, Vonnegut's *Slaughterhouse-Five*, Andre Norton's *Operation Time Search*, or various of the *Star Trek* episodes on television, are perversions or reversions of time. In works like these, the shiftings of physical and psychological perspectives predispose readers (or viewers) to contemplate the function, or, to use Sartre's term, the essence of the human being. "Version" is one of the distinctive features of speculative fiction, and of science fiction especially.

Broadly speaking, serious science fiction offers analogies to the first man and the last man from the paleontology and teleology of humankind; and it may compound this challenge to academic thinking, as *Ada* does, by everting the analogies or by subjecting them to other forms of "version."

In Nabokov's *Ada* human concepts, notably those of the first and last man and woman, are everted. The sense of this may be that man (the species) creates himself in his own concepts, that he gains an understanding of his own concepts by turning them inside out, that he uncreates himself by this turning-inside-out, and that he is ultimately survived by his own concepts, which, in themselves, are not destroyed by eversion. Myths, for example, are concepts; in Samuel R. Delany's *The Einstein Intersection* (1967), myths survive the humans who have conceived them, not only myths like that of Orpheus and Eurydice or that of Theseus and Phaedra but also myths like those of Elvis Presley and "the great rock and the great roll" (§2). *Ada* everts myth and fact, or *mythos* and *logos*, and, in doing so, establishes that they are one and the same. Etymologically, both *mythos* and *logos* have the same meaning, namely, "word." In *Ada*, the words "thank God" become "thank Log" (33, 43/§1:4, 6), as they do now and then in the writings of Robert Graves and Anthony Burgess. In one passage, Van is said to have "wondered what really kept him alive on terrible Antiterra, with Terra a myth" (452/§3:1). Antiterra, as *logos*, and Terra, as *mythos*, are one and the same; they differ only as concepts. Classical myths hover about and intrude into the lives of the characters in *Ada*; and myths of the 1960's emerge in phrases like "blue suede shoes" (306/§1:42), "a musician called Rack" (313/§1:42) (pronounced "rock"), and "the rock and the roll" (492/§3:5), or in a prose collage of "Lucy in the Sky with Diamonds" (193-194/§1:31). Physically, a human being may be survived by the child that he or she conceives. Psychologically or spiritually, a human being may be survived by his or her own concepts. The childless Ada and Van are survived by their concepts of their love on earth and in time. Nabokov's conspectus is that each human being is psychologically both male and female and is both physically human and spiritually divine: each human being is a Tiresian solipsism, or, to use the words reported in *Strong Opinions*, an "indivisible monism" (124; cf. *Ada*, 314/§1:42, "man, by nature a monist").

The progenitor of Ada and Van is D. Veen, which name can be read as both "divine" and "Duveen,"[4] man as spiritual and man as materialistic. We combine "divine" and "Duveen" by combining Walter Dementiy (Demon) Veen with his eversion, his cousin Walter Daniel Veen: Demon is *daimon*, or "spirit"; Daniel is identified as "a Manhattan art dealer" and as Van's "art-collecting uncle" (4, 588/§1:1, §5:6). Demon Veen is, in the novel, associated with air; his paramour and cousin-in-law Marina with fire; his second-cousin Lucette with water; and Ada and Van, his illegitimate children (by Marina), with earth.

The association of characters with elements is made by the narrator in reference to the deaths of three specific characters: "Three elements, fire, water, and air, destroyed, in that sequence, Marina, Lucette, and Demon. Terra waited" (450/§3:1).[5] Terra had already claimed Aqua, Van's putative mother. When Van was thirteen, she had taken an overdose of sleeping pills in an Arizona gulch, where she was found, survived by her suicide note, lying "as if buried prehistorically, in a *fetus-in-utero* position" (28-29/§1:3). But Terra waits again, this time to claim Van and Ada. The explicit association of Marina and Lucette with the elements by which they die reverses their appropriate-name identification with elements: the name "Marina," like that of Marina's twin sister Aqua, identifies "water"; and the name "Lucette" identifies "light" or "fire." The name "Demon," as "spirit," remains appropriate to "air." The names "Ada" and "Van" contextually identify "earth." Van is to be equated with earth by his *Letters from Terra*, the novel which is to be taken as "literature from Van," in keeping with his *nom de plume* Voltemand (an anagram for "Van told me"). To identify Terra, or earth, as Ada, we must attend upon Ada as the eversion of the Adam who was formed of the earth and resident in Eden; Ada's Eden is Ardis Park, an anagrammatical "Paradise."[6] An added word-play, on the androgynous Norse deity Vanadis, can be detected. This old name for the fertility goddess Freya is a compound of "Vanr," the name of a male fertility god, and "dis," meaning "goddess." Fertility deities, like the bearded Aphrodite, or Venus, of Cyprus, are necessarily earth deities. The androgynous Venus and the androgynous Vanadis are mythological cognates anagrammatically rehearsed in the names "Van," "Ada," "Ardis," and "Veen." The concepts of God the Father, of man the collector, and of the elemental universe of Classical myth (air, fire, water, and earth) are here all incorporate in human beings and, by inference, in each human being.

Nabokov also reminds us that "Ada" is the Russian word for "hades" or "Hell"; e.g., "*teper' iz ada* ('now is out of hell')" (29/§1:3). Paradise and Hell are implicit in the human being; and the human being in this novel is the composite of Ada and Van on and as everted earth. Ada says that she will be with Van "in the depths *moego ada*, of my Hades," that is, in herself. "As lovers *and* siblings," she tells Van, "we have a double chance of being together in eternity, in terrarity. Four pairs of eyes in paradise" (583-84/§5:6). Van and Ada are a schizoid John Shade, the poet of Nabokov's *Pale Fire*: the Russian equivalent of "John" is "Ivan," and "Shade" is not only referent to an inhabitant of Hades but also an anagram of the word "Hades." John Shade is mentioned, and quoted, shortly after Ada utters the words just cited (585-586/§5:6), and we are presently informed that, if Ada and Van "ever intended to die they would die, as it were, *into* the finished book, into Eden or Hades, into the prose of the book or the poetry of its blurb" (587/§5:6). They have conceived the book as a means of understanding themselves. Self-understanding is, figuratively at least, a form of suicide in which one is survived by the very means by which that understanding has been gained. If Ada and Van die into the book, they will be survived by the concepts they have spawned.

Nabokov touches upon the long-standing idea that the quest for Heaven is actually a quest for the fullness of life on Earth: one is in Hell without knowing it, like Marlowe's Faustus or Pär Lagerkvist's Tobias, and cannot adjust to Hell until the Kingdom of Heaven is discovered within one's heart; with this discovery comes the realization that the Kingdom of Heaven is Hell-plus-love; the discovery cannot be made so long as one externalizes, or extra-terrestrializes, Heaven and Hell, to do which is to extraterrestrialize Earth— to view Terra as Antiterra. In this context Nabokov proves to be closer to Kurt Vonnegut, Jr. than to other writers. Like Vonnegut, he turns human existence inside out in an effort to show people what they are looking for; and his vehicle of eversion, like Vonnegut's amounts to science fiction, given the definition of science fiction as the extrapolative and/or analogical paleontology and teleology of humankind.

Vonnegut, interestingly, shares Nabokov's distaste for science fiction. His professed loathing of science fiction is the subject of the opening essay in his first collection of public prose, which is parenthetically subtitled "Opinions." He berates some of the "boomers of science fiction" for being "crazy enough to try to capture Tolstoy."[7] Others, to be sure, are crazy enough to swing their nets at works like *Ada* and *The Sirens of Titan*.

It is probably coincidence that the dog Kazak in *The Sirens of Titan* (1959) has the same name as the title of a palindromic poem by Nabokov (see *Strong Opinions*, 293; the word itself is Russian for "cossack"); and it may be coincidence that Vonnegut and Nabokov develop similar themes in similar vehicles, however different the exterior appearances of those vehicles. The coincidences at least warrant a brief digression on Vonnegut.

Vonnegut's *The Sirens of Titan* opens with this sentence: "Everyone now knows how to find the meaning of life within himself." The novel then explores times prior to this stipulated present when mankind, "ignorant of the truths that lie within every human being, looked outward," when only "the human soul remained terra incognita" (§1). Mankind is the malcontent, *Malachi Constant*. In being "pushed ever outward"—to Mars and Mercury, for example—he becomes a machine, a thing that is unknowing and unknown: he becomes *Unk*, who mates with Bee (or Being) and conceives a son, Chrono (or Time). He *finds* his self, tentatively, during a brief return to Earth, only to be pushed outward again—this time to Titan, a moon of Jupiter. On his final return to Earth he finds his paradise *in* himself as he sits on a bus-stop bench on the outskirts of Indianapolis; moments later, he dies. He had managed to learn that, without love and friendship, which are found only in the human heart, he was a mere robot. He had known that the name "Malachi Constant" meant "faithful messenger"; but he had not known to whom he was faithful or whose messenger he was; he had not known his self, that is.[8] On Titan he had met his eversion, the faithful messenger Salo of Trafalmadore, a machine that became human through love and friendship. The name "Salo" is, alter-egoistically, an anagram of "also" and an attenuated eversion of "Malachi Constant." The Trafalmadorians could be the completion of that Darwinian evolution of machines which Butler projects in the "Book of the Machines" section of *Erewhon*.

Vonnegut claims to be contemptuous of people who are "scrogging the universe." He deplores mankind's outward push and its destruction of inner being. The attraction of the Sirens is the attraction of anticipation, the attraction of the future, the false revelation that draws mankind out of its own humanity. Likewise Nabokov: through revelation, says the narrator of *Ada*, sick minds identify "the notion of a Terra planet with that of another world and this 'Other World' [gets] confused not only with the 'Next World' but with the Real World in us and beyond us" (20/§1:3). Vonnegut intimates that the quest for a God beyond and outside of mankind is the quest for a God that is utterly indifferent and a surrender to the "Universal Will to Become" or to "Mankind's wish to improve itself." By either coincidence or design, Vonnegut takes issue with Heidegger, who propounds an attunement to *Sein und Zeit* (Being and Time) which consists in transforming *Dasein* (Being There) into *Sein zum* (Being Toward), that is, a doctrine of living for the future.

Dasein itself is a state of unknowing; it is the haphazard status of manipulable objects.[9] Vonnegut and Nabokov create a science fiction which intimates that people achieve subjectivity, not through mere Being There or through Being Toward, but through consciously being what they have learned they are and through love. Malachi Constant comes to understand "that a purpose of human life, no matter who is controlling it, is to love whoever is around to be loved" (*Sirens*, Epilogue). Van Veen tells Ada, whose name as a homonym of "ardor" is the antonym of "apathy" or "indifference," that the hopeless fallacy of an imagined hereafter is that "you cannot bring your friends along—or your enemies for that matter—to the party" (586/§5:6).

Van insists that "to be" means to know one "has been." He dismisses the future as sham time. "Life, love, libraries," he says, "have no future." There are, according to him, only "two panels" of Time: "The Past (everexisting in my mind) and the Present (to which my mind gives duration and, therefore, reality)" (559-560/§4). In *The Sirens of Titan* Vonnegut dismisses the future by purging the solar system of the future's immaterial force in the form of Winston Niles Rumfoord, who admits that futurity is no more than a perpetuation of past and present: "Everything that ever was always will be, and everything that ever will be always was" (§12).[10]

When Vonnegut speaks of "the thrill of the *fast reverse*" (§10), and when he makes it patent that Unk's passing his intelligence test amounts to his turning his space ship upside down as the only means of egress from the caves of Mercury, the nature of "version" in science fiction is illustrated. Nabokov, his admiration of Wells's *The Time Machine* notwithstanding, objects to "Technology Fiction" in which relativity is exploited for the purpose of depicting time travel (see 543/§4); yet he illustrates science fiction "version" when he says, in the character of Van,

My aim was to compose a kind of novella in the form of a treatise on the Texture of Time, an investigation of its veily substance, with illustrative metaphors gradually increasing, very gradually building up a logical love story, *going from past to present*, blossoming as a concrete story, and just as gradually *reversing analogies* and disintegrating again into bland abstraction. [562-63/§4; emphases added]

Nabokov reverses analogies of Time and he reverses analogies of Travel, but he does not construe time and travel as an analogue of space-time. He explains in *Strong Opinions* that the metaphors "in the Texture-of-Time section of *Ada*...gradually and gracefully...form a story—the story of a man traveling by car through Switzerland from east to west" (122). The movements from past to present, from east to west, and from concretion to abstraction are reversed and turned inside out, but not as metaphors of anything like a space-time continuum.

The entire novel goes from past to present and from present to past, not by way of time travel, but through what we may call "transtemporality" or "metachronism," a complex form of anachronism in which the present can antedate the past. For example, Ada's mother, Marina, is following a typewritten shooting script in the making of a color movie, of which she is the star (197, 203/§1:32). The movie has the Fitzgeraldian title, *The Young and the Doomed* (see, e.g., 424/§2:9); it is to be completed and released in 1890. The typescript would be a possibility at this time, although the front-stroke typewriter was not in practical use before 1897; but the very first one-reel motion pictures did not appear until 1903, and the historic cinematograph of Louis and August Lumière was not a reality until 1895, the year before the presentation of Thomas Armat's *vitascope* at Koster and Bial's music hall in New York. The advent of color movies belongs to the mid-1930's. Nabokov appears to have reversed the late 1880's and the mid-1940's (cf. 580/§5:5: "1940 by the Terranean calendar, and about 1890 by ours"); but the appearance is somewhat deceptive in that the generation *preceding* that of Ada and Van is inclusive of what Van, in a reference to early photography and as a pun on "enlightenment," calls "The Twilight before the Lumières" (399/§2:7; see also 43/§1:6).

To follow Nabokov in his reversing of time-analogies, we may, with this movie-making episode, picture time as a pocket, the opening of which is 1840 (or the past), the outside bottom of which is 1940 (or the "future"), and the inside bottom of which is 1890 (or the present). The "future" and the present, then, are simply the obverse and reverse of the same cloth; and time consists exclusively of past and present, its material or texture being the cloth. Nabokov here not only turns the pocket inside out but he also turns it upside down.

The movie scene is being filmed at a "pool-side patio," again a setting that is more 1946-ish than 1888-ish, especially if one recalls the pool-side musical-play rehearsal in the 1946 color movie *Night and Day* (with Cary Grant, Alexis Smith, and, among others, Eve Arden). Ada, Lucette, and the eighteen-year-old Van are present, and, as they move away from the pool, Van "out of charity for the sisters' bare fee,...changed his course from gravel path to velvet lawn (reversing the action of Dr. Ero, pursued by the Invisible Albino in one of the greatest novels of English literature)" (203/§1:32). In this accolade to a science-fiction work, the Dr. Kemp of Wells's *The Invisible Man* becomes Dr. Ero in a double anagrammatic play.[11] With a double reversal of letters the English word "order" becomes "Dr. Ero"; and the names "Ero" and "Kemp" provide an anagram of the Russian phrase *po merke*, which means "...to measure" or "...to order" in a phrase like "made to order."

"Order" is a concealed pun on "Ardor" and also on "Ardis," which, as will be noted below, means "the point of the arrow"; and "arrow" is a homonym of "Ero." There is also a temporal double reversal in this passage, not unlike that of the 1840-1890-1940 eversion already noted. Van reverses Dr. Ero's action; but Van's action (in 1888) antedates the action of Dr. Ero (or Dr. Kemp), insofar as *The Invisible Man* was published in 1897. If Van, as the "author" of this third-person narrative, is writing in the 1960's, as indeed he is, then we have a parallel 1888-1897-1966 eversion. The last date is for the year during which Van redictated his memoirs to Violet Knox, who, with Ronald Oranger, her husband-to-be, edits the memoirs which survive Van and Ada (578/§5:4). (The "epilogue" to *Ada* is written by Van in his ninety-seventh year, that is, in 1967. Characteristic of the novel itself, this "epilogue" is actually the "true introduction" [567/§5:1].)

Transtemporality, or the eversion of time, also accounts for Van's anachronistic "quoting" in 1922 from Martin Gardner's *The Ambidextrous Universe*, published in 1964: "'Space is a swarming in the eyes, and Time a singing in the ears,' says John Shade, a modern poet, as quoted by an invented philosopher ('Martin Gardiner' [sic]) in *The Ambidextrous Universe*, page 165 [sic]" (542/§4; for date, 536/§4). John Shade, the poet invented by Nabokov in his 1962 novel, *Pale Fire*, is quoted by the very real Martin Gardner on page 168 of *The Ambidextrous Universe*. An uninformed reader, however, would not learn from Gardner's *Pale Fire* quotation or from his note on page 177 identifying the quotation that John Francis Shade is a fictional character. Gardner makes no mention whatsoever of Shade's inventor, Vladimir Nabokov. The eversion, or double reverse, here is as follows: first, the dates 1922-1964 are turned inside out; second, citation is turned inside out: the composition in 1922 of *Texture of Time*, the book within the novel *Ada*, involves a reference to *Pale Fire*, the poem within the 1962 novel of that name, as cited in *The Ambidextrous Universe*, the 1964 work which is cited in *Ada* as antecedent to *Texture of Time*.

Van is engaged with *Texture of Time* in 1922, and the work is presented as having been published in 1924. The first date is important because it links Nabokov's transtemporality to a second science-fiction element, which we may call "transterrestriality" or "metageism," the already mentioned eversion of Earth's eastern and western hemispheres.

We are to imagine "that 'Russia,' instead of being a quaint synonym of Estoty, the American province extending from the Arctic no longer vicious Circle to the United States proper, was on Terra the name of a country, transferred as if by some sleight of *land* across the ha-ha of a doubled ocean to the opposite hemisphere" (17-18/§1:3).[12] This figurative spatial transference produces Amerussia, an amalgam of not only spatial but also temporal complications "because a gap of up to a hundred years one way or another existed between the two earths; a gap marked by a bizarre confusion of directional signs at the crossroads of passing time not *all* the no-longers of one world corresponding to the not-yets of the other" (18/§1:3). If we begin the "hundred years" with the birth of Ada in 1872, the "crossroads of passing time," as, say, the half-way mark, is 1922, the year in which Van started "a new life with Ada" (573/§5:3), and the year, to be sure, in which T.S. Eliot's *The Waste Land*, the crossroads point for modern poetry, was published. "Estoty" or "Estotia" is Russian for "Waste Land." The admixture of space to time and commixture of present and past in Eliot's *Waste Land* lend themselves to the science fiction of Nabokov's Estotiland. The preoccupation with space and time that Eliot carried into his *Four Quartets* (1943) informs much of the novel *Ada*, especially the metaphoric traveling by car in Part Four. Eliot's "point of intersection of the timeless/With time" is consonant with Nabokov's "crossroads of passing time," where, as Eliot says, "the impossible union/Of spheres of existence is actual." Nabokov's "Ada or Ardor" corresponds to Eliot's notion that the apprehension of this point of intersection is "something given/And taken, in a lifetime's death in love,/ Ardour" (see "Little Gidding" V). Nabokov makes a point of pointing out that "Ardis," in Greek, means "point," specifically "the point of an arrow" (225/§1:36). At Ardis Hall in 1888, Ada suffers the ardor of a girl who does not want to "lose her only true love, the head of the arrow, the point of the pain" (192/§1:31). Nabokov's arrow, incidentally, would fit the metaphoric bow of Heraclitus or that of the mythic Eros. Heraclitus conceived of world-order as eternal fire, and his bow was an analogy for the complementary character of opposing tensions. Eros, as we first learn in Euripides' *Iphigenia in Aulis*, has two arrows for his bow, one productive of love and the other of death. Heraclitus's *order* is rational burning, and Eros's *ardor* is an irrational burning.

Nabokov's allusions to Eliot's poetry and drama are numerous. So, for that matter, are his allusions to Shakespeare, Byron, Chateaubriand, Poe, Stendhal (e.g., "Ruby Black"), de Maupassant, Proust, and others, including Joyce, whose *Finnegans Wake* is cited by Ada in 1884, two years after Joyce's birth.[13] The first allusion to Eliot is ironic: "Mr. Eliot, a Jewish business man" (5/§1:1); Eliot satirized Jewish businessmen in some of his earlier poems.

Among other of the more noticeable allusions are the following. Ada loses her virginity to Van in 1884 and makes love with him for the third time in 1888 (see 440/§2:11), a pivotal year in the novel and the year of Eliot's birth; she marries Andrey Vinelander in 1893 and is widowed in the *Waste Land* year of 1922. Chapter 38 of Part One is a Family Reunion scene set in 1888; the chapter, which alludes to Eliot by way of one of his play titles and, again, by way of his birth year, includes the "echt deutsch" phrase (261/§1:38) which Eliot uses in *The Waste Land*. Elsewhere there is mention of "the author of Agonic Lines and Mr. Eliot,"[14] and of "old Eliot...and solemn Kithar Sween," in allusion to Eliot's character Sweeney and to Eliot's *Sweeney Agonistes*. The roles of "Sweeney" and Eliot are everted. Kithar Sween is accredited with having "produced *The Waistline*...and *Cardinal Grishkin*" (505-506/§3:7). "Cardinal Grishkin" would be a transformation of the Russian woman, Grishkin, in Eliot's "Whispers of Immortality."

Eliot's *Waste Land* entertains a movement in time from present to past and in space from west to east, from the mountains of the West, for example, to those of the East, from London to Jerusalem to India and the Orient. Nabokov's *Ada* shows these movements in reverse, and the presentation is evocative of science fiction in that the past is eversively moved *to* the present and the East is eversively moved *to* the West.

In many forms of literature time and space are juggled or fractured; but eversive movements of time and space are most commonly apparent in science fiction. The same observation applies, with some qualification, in the matter of sexual gender. Eversions of sexual gender are not peculiar to science fiction. Sophocles' and Ovid's Tiresias, T.S. Eliot's Tiresias, Virginia Woolf's Orlando, Genet's "Our Lady of the Flowers," Joyce's Bloom at Bella Cohen's—these and others like these are not characters in science fiction. In contrast, Ursula K. Le Guin's Estraven, Isaac Asimov's Estwald, and Nabokov's Ada-and-Van *are* science-fiction characters because they serve as analogies to the first and last man. To the terms "transtemporality" and "transterrestriality" we may now add this third, "transsexuality." The terms represent the three factors of the science-fiction product in Nabokov's *Ada*. The Greek-derived equivalent of "transsexuality" would be "metaphysistism";

and this overture of everted sex to metaphysics is somehow playfully in tune with Nabokov's relentless word-play. Turn a celibate male, like a Cardinal, inside out, and there is a sexy female, like the Red-Russian Grishkin, whose chair, according to Eliot, "even the Abstract Entities/Circumambulate," while "our lot," if we take it to be that of an uneverted Cardinal, "crawls between dry ribs/To keep our metaphysics warm."[15]

The first sentence of *Ada* includes the assignment of the masculine patronymic "Arkadievitch" to "Anna Karenin." Nabokov has insisted that this is one of three blunders which were deliberately planted in the first paragraph of the novel and which were "meant to ridicule mistranslations of Russian classics" (*Strong Opinions*, 285). The effectiveness of the ridicule is all but nullified by the ugliness of the blemish; and the grotesquerie is perhaps best justified as a perverse contribution to the transsexuality that informs the "Adam (Ada) and Eve (Ivan)" theme of the novel, a theme implicit in a name like "Cardinal Grishkin" or in the presentation of Mlle Ida Larivière as the author of a work that was written by de Maupassant.[16] When Nabokov says, "Antiterra happens to be an anachronistic world in regard to Terra—that's all there is to it" (*Strong Opinions*, 122), one must assume his dissimulation; and when he explains the perversion of a patronymic as a device of ridicule, one would do best to assume his simulation and to read his breach of taste as a thematic breach of sexual gender.

The sexuality in the novel includes marital relations, adultery, bisexuality, lesbianism, and incest. Dementiy and Daniel Veen are first-cousins, both born in 1838; Aqua and Marina Durmanov are twin sisters born in 1844. Dementiy, or Demon, marries Aqua in April 1869. Van is born illegitimately to Demon and Marina in 1870 and is apparently given to the mentally ill Aqua, in lieu of her stillborn six-month-old male fetus, "to be registered as her son Ivan Veen" (25/§1:3). Daniel Veen marries Marina in December 1871. The first child of this marriage, Adelaida, or Ada, born in July 1872, is actually the second illegitimate child of Demon and Marina; Daniel is her "putative father." Her sister Lucinda, or Lucette, born in January 1876, is the actual and legitimate daughter of Daniel and Marina. The fourteen-year-old Van deflowers his blood-sister, the twelve-year-old nymphet Ada, in 1884. Their subsequent life-long affair of death in love is interrupted by the marriage of Ada to Andrey Vinelander, that is, from 1893 to 1922, and it is complicated by Van's infidelities and by Ada's erotic affairs with Philip Rack, Percy de Prey, a certain Johnny ("a young star from Fuerteventura" [380/§2:5]), and with Ida Larivière and Lucette. Moreover, Lucette's unrequited love for Van ends with her suicide by drowning in 1901.

Transsexually, Lucette is the Byron who pursues Van as Augusta (Byron's half-sister). Van plays Gertrude to Marina's Hamlet in chapter 37 of Part One. In this scene Marina adds to the sexuality-catalogue by mentioning the pederasty of Van's uncle (i.e., Daniel), the incidence of "dreadful perverts in our ancestry," and the sodomy of one of her forebears (233-234/§1:37). But it is as the transsexual Adam and Eve that Ada and Van reflect the first and the last of humanity. Their Tree of Knowledge is "the glossy-limbed shattal tree at the bottom of the garden" (94, 95/§1:15) in Ardis Park.[17] The Satan of this Eden of theirs takes the form of a mosquito, the *female* of the "*Culex chateaubriandi* Brown" (105/§1:17). They have no children, no issue other than their writings. Van, for example, is "pregnant" (325/§1:43) with *Letters from Terra* during the period (1888-1890) of Ada's "Very Private Letters" to him. Lacking physical progeny, Ada herself plays Cain to Lucette's Abel. "Adam and Eve" is a concept of human beginnings; everted to "Ada and Van," the concept completes a circle; and the circle is like that of the opening of a pocket which is turned inside out. The Veen-

Durmanov line ends with Ada and Van, who compose "letters" during the same biennium and later collaborate on a book (*Information and Form*, published in 1957 [578/§5:4]), and who merge into a composite of the first and last human being, the Qayin (or Cain, or creature) who begins in earth, time, and love and is survived by his concepts of Antiterra (also known as Demonia), the Imperfect Present, and Sex.

Earth, time, and love are perennial subjects of fiction; but it is mainly in science fiction that these subjects are turned inside out as a means of showing Man that he is his own fullness, his own beginning and the agent of his own end. Such eversion is enjoyably exciting but unpleasantly precise. Vonnegut's Francine Pefko, tentatively identified in *Cat's Cradle* (1963) "as an appropriate representative for almost all mankind," complains that Dr. Horvath is "maybe talking about something that's going to turn everything upside-down and inside-out like the atom bomb" (§15). H. Lowe Crosby, the Ugly American in the same novel, complains of Philip Castle: "You can't say a damn thing to him that he won't turn inside out" (§69).[18] Mr. Plunkett, Van Veen's tutor in sleight-of-hand, is shown to have cautioned Van that "secret pockets were useful but could be turned inside out and against you" (85/§1:13).

Eversion is, in science fiction, a means of communication; and in *Ada* it communicates, among other things, the very nature of a communication gap. We are led to consider that during the 1960's the great loss of subjective verbal contact between generations was brought about by the beginning of modern civilization's ability to extend communication through galactic space. The duration of this ability has been labeled the "L factor." This factor, as it is identified and outlined in Walter Sullivan's *We Are Not Alone*,[19] poses the paradox that for civilizations which are technologically advanced enough to communicate across galactic space there is a tendency either to be destroyed by the technology that has made the communication possible or to be so changed by the technology as to lose interest in the communication, in either of which cases the L factor becomes a small number (indicating short duration of the ability). In *Ada* the Terra-Antiterra dichotomy represents the phenomenon of the 1960's, namely, the inception of the ability to achieve extraterrestrial communication: the beginning of the Space Age, which will be the period during which this ability is sustained. As the pocket of communication is turned outward, its contents of intraterrestrial communication are lost proportionately; as they disappear, Terra, relegated to nostalgia, becomes as fanciful a myth as the Estotiland on the late sixteenth-century map in the Zeno brothers' *Scoprimento*.[20] The L factor in *Ada* is the "L disaster" (17/§1:3) or "Lettrocalamity" (147/§1:24) and the reaction to it is a prohibition of that electronic communication which extended verbal contact at the cost of subjective verbal contact.

The "L" is to be associated with the Twilight of the Lumières, as the darkness produced by enlightenment; with Van's *Letters from Terra*, as evidence of the mythification of Terra; and with Lucette's suicide-death by water, as an eversion of the Drowned Phoenician Sailor ritual.[21] Aqua, before her suicide, had hit upon a method of transmitting speech by water; and this method brought about a simplification of the elaborate and expensive "hydrodynamic telephone" (hydrophones, dorophones, clepsydrophones, etc.) which had replaced the electronic telephones of the ante-L years.[22] The Erewhonian-style outlawry of electronic machines induces a reverse nostalgia, and, as in *Erewhon Revisited*, "after great anti-L years of reactionary delusion have gone by...our sleek little machines, Faragod bless them, hum again" (17/§1:3). Aqua, who devises a means of communication, commits suicide, ironically, because she cannot communicate with her husband and family. This inability to communicate with one's own kind, as a concomitant of the ability to communicate beyond one's own kind, is the paradox of the L factor. Both Aqua and Lucette are denied love; ritual cleansing, in the form of Aqua herself and her water language and in the form of Lucette's drowning, is an attempt to restore the love-communication that has been wiped out by space-communication—or, to restore the Love factor that has been superseded by the L factor.

In Nabokov's science fiction, the communication *gap* is, analogically, a *pocket* turned inside out: by eversion the pocket is fully discovered, but its contents are lost; the full discovery of the pocket results in the loss of the pocket's function.

Since 1939, one of the more dramatic scientific theories of eversion has been the "black hole" in space, the best example of which is a collapsed giant star whose density or mass, following its collapse, becomes so great that its gravity prevents the escape even of light. If this collapsed giant star were one of a binary, or two-star, system, its gravity would turn its uncollapsed companion inside out by pulling away and to itself the·layers of gases of which its "twin" is composed. (Two years after the publication of *Ada*, Cygnus X-1, hitherto taken to be a pulsar, was identified as a black hole, an invisible pocket turned against a star in the Cygnus constellation and turning that star inside out.) A black hole can be detected by astronomers only because of the bright star in its company, the same bright star which initially attracts attention to itself and away from its unseen mate. Nabokov toys cleverly with this bit of astronomy: Mr. Plunkett teaches Van, not only about secret pockets, but also about the sleight-of-hand expert who distracts his audience with mirrors and reflectors, "the cheater with bright objects around him" (173/§1:28).

Van meets such a cheater, one Dick, who is emptying the pockets of the French twins, Jean and Jacques. Van becomes Dick's "twin" by cheating Dick in the way that a black hole, devoid of "twinkle," cheats its twin: and Dick "did not 'twinkle' long .after that" (173-177/§1:28). In the episode immediately following the chapter given over to Van's card-sharp curriculum and practice, Van, at the inn of Malahar, "some twenty miles from Ardis," finds that the "toilet on the landing was a black hole, with traces of a fecal explosion, between a squatter's two giant soles" (179/§1:29). Nabokov fills six pages of his text here with enough terminological suggestions of the black-hole theory to satisfy any science fiction reader. Even "giant soles" is terminologically suggestive, inasmuch as *soles* is the Latin for "suns," which are stars. The section may be taken as a microcosm of the astronomical phenomena in question.

As literary devices, both paradox (as in the case of the L factor) and microcosm (as in the case of Nabokov's diminution of the black-hole theory) are forms of "version." A paradox is an assertion that turns itself inside out by self-contradiction. A microcosm is an analogical turning of the very large into the very small. The Greek term for "version" is "trope" (a turning). Tropes are turns of thought, figures of noesis (according to "Longinus"), conceits or concepts, and, in general, the speech of imagination or visionary dreams; Nabokov exemplifies his eversive use of them by stating, "Tropes are the dreams of speech" (416/§2:8).

It is safe to say that lengthier exegesis could disclose many more science fiction elements in *Ada*, including, for example, phrases like "Star Rats," "Space Aces," and "physics fiction," which are significant even in their adverseness because they tie in with "Space, the impostor" (338, 339/§2:2; 540/§4). But, in running its limited course, this essay has sought merely to establish that *Ada* may be viewed as science fiction because it exploits the

science fiction element of eversion in the forms of transtemporality, transterrestriality, and transsexuality; because its science fiction parallels
with Vonnegut's *The Sirens of Titan* are striking; because it translates T.S.
Eliot's notions of time and space into science fiction; and because to its
analogies from paleontology and teleology it adds analogies from, for
example, the science of astronomy.

The question here has been "Can *Ada* be viewed as science fiction?" If
the foregoing argument in the affirmative is accepted, other questions must
follow: Why does Nabokov make use of science fiction elements? Does he
consider science to be, when unblended with poetry, a form of incest which
transforms humans into insects, as his insect-scient-nicest-incest anagram
indicates? (85/§1:13) Does he consider that science ruins the towers and
breaks the bridges it has built precisely because it has found the means to
build them, that science turns "real things" (facts, *logoi*) into "ghost things"
(abstractions, fictions, mists, *mythoi*) precisely because it has achieved the
means of discovering "real things?"[23] These questions and others like them
must lead to other essays, and those essays in turn to further studies, until
the meaning of *Ada* disappears because it has been discovered, and until
the novel, like its inbred agonists, is survived by its own concepts.

NOTES

[1](3) = Page 3 of *Strong Opinions* (New York: McGraw-Hill, ©1973).

[2]"'All happy families are more or less dissimilar; all unhappy ones are more or
less alike'"; cf. Tolstoy (in the Constance Garnett translation): "Happy families are
all alike; every unhappy family is unhappy in its own way."

[3](257/§1:38) = Page 257 of the First Edition of *Ada or Ardor: A Family Chronicle*
(New York: McGraw-Hill, ©1969; identified as First Edition on title-page verso) or
Part 1, Chapter 39 of any edition.

[4]Joseph Duveen, first Baron Duveen of Millbank (1869-1939), the famous English
art-collector and dealer.

[5]If we were to read "destroyed" as both transitive verb and participial adjective,
"Terra waited" would govern two understood infinitives, namely, "to destroy" and
"to be destroyed." The passage, then, as both sentence and sentence fragment, would
be poetic in its ambiguity: it would identify humankind and Terra with the elements of
which both are composed; and, in identifying humankind with its terrestrial habitation, it would emphasize the terrestrial nature of humankind.

[6]One of the editors of *Science-Fiction Studies* has reminded the writer that
"'Ardis' is also the name of a wonder city in Jack London's *The Iron Heel* (1907),
in which the future historian of the Age of Brotherhood writes his preface to the MS
found from the revolutionary Ages. The wonder cities are modelled on the oligarchic
retreats in Wells's *When the Sleeper Wakes* (1899)."

[7]*Wampeters, Foma & Granfalloons (Opinions)* (New York: Delacorte Press, 1974),
p. 4.

[8]Cf. Robert Charroux, *Forgotten Worlds*, tr. Lowell Bair (New York: Popular
Library, 1973), p. 354: "On the hypothesis that the universe is a vast living organism
and that each planet is a part of that organism, we may assume that man has a
great and unknown function, perhaps similar to that of DNA, the *messenger of
cellular life*."

[9]Cf. Jerzy Kosinski's *Being There* (1971), the title of which novel relates to the
manipulability of its main character, Chance the gardener, whose total susceptibility
to externals renders him incapable of independent action.

[10]William Irwin Thompson, in *Passages About Earth* (New York: Harper & Row,
1973), p. 128, takes *The Sirens of Titan* to be a fun-filled, if not comic, view of the
kind of history now made popular by Robert Charroux (see note 8 above), Erich von
Däniken, and other proponents of the "ancient astronauts" brand of science fiction
posing as archaeology.

[11]Note that this paragraph ends with the words "Double take, double exposure."

[12]Cf. James Robert Enterline's definition of "the Grand Misunderstanding," in *Vi-*

king America (Garden City, N.Y.: Doubleday), p. 79: "a misconception that the unrecognized North American continent was actually the known Eurasian continent seen from the opposite end. In maps...the pictures of the American lands were attached to the Old World map at their actual relative positions on the North American continent."

[13]"Did he like elms? Did he know Joyce's poem about the two washerwomen?" (54/§1:8) See *Finnegans Wake*, pp. 196-216.

[14](459/§3:3) The first name of "Mr. Eliot" is, ironically, "Milton." The allusion is to Eliot's initial antipathy to the effects of Milton's poetry; see Eliot's essay "Milton I" (1936).

[15]"Whispers of Immortality," Lines 29-32.

[16]Namely *La Parure*, first published in 1884, the year during which Mlle Larivière (also referred to as "Mlle Laparure") typed out her *La Rivière de Diamants*; see *Ada*, pp. 83,87. Both *parure de diamants* and *rivière de diamants* mean "diamond necklace"; note especially 61/§1:10, 257/§1:38, and also §1:31.

[17]The temptation to provide a gloss on "shattal" cannot be resisted. This so-called "apple tree" is perhaps a tropical acacia, with limbs that are "glossy" from the exudation of gum arabic. There is doubtless a hidden pun on "acacia," from Greek *akē* (point, cf. "Ardis"), and on the Hebrew term for a species of acacia, namely, *shittah* cf. the excremental association, "shit, shat," and Nabokov's choice of the word "bottom," shortly followed by the prospect of Ada's bare bottom). A North American variety of acacia is the locust (N.B. "the first cicada of the season") or pseudoacacia. The tree has been imported from "Eden National Park" in Iraq, where "no apple trees grow." In Iraq, the Tigris and Euphrates rivers, borders of the legendary site of Eden, are now in confluence; that is, the *two* rivers of ancient times no longer flow separately into the Persian Gulf: their confluence at Qurna has produced *one* river, the *Shatt-el-Arab* (or Shat-al-Arab, or Shat[t]-el-Arab). Further, the above-mentioned *akē* denotes "thorn," which, taken with the Edenic "apple" permits an association with "thorn-apple," the Russian for which is *durman* (cf. "Durmanov").

[18]Cf. Alexei Panshin's *Rite of Passage* (New York: Ace Books, 1968), p. 135: the author assigns to the space suits worn by his characters and to the space ship in which they live "an adaptation of the basic discontinuity principle"; he explains that the "discontinuity effect, as far as the Ship is concerned, grabs the universe by the tail and turns it inside out so as to get at it better." Note also that David Bowman's passage through the Star Gate in *2001: A Space Odyssey* concludes with a universe turned inside out, as the eversion of the first man (Moon-Watcher) and the last man (Bowman) is completed.

[19]New York: McGraw-Hill, 1964; revised ed., Signet Books, 1966, pp. 246-253.

[20]See, for example, Samuel Eliot Morison, *The European Discovery of America: The Northern Voyages A.D. 500-1600* (New York: Oxford, 1971), pp. 87-89, 609. Andrey Vinelander, as "an Arizonian cattle-breeder whose fabulous ancestor discovered our country" (588/§5:6), links Amerussia to the abortive Norse colonizations of North America and to the mediaeval cartographic confusions of Siberia/Alaska with Siberia/Lapland.

[21]Cf. Eliot's *The Waste Land* IV ("Death by Water"), "Dans le Restaurant," and "Marina." There is also an "L-shaped bathroom" (144/§1:23), which anticipates the "black hole" toilet (see 179/§1:29) and thematically ties the L factor to the black-hole theory.

[22](17-23/§1:3) Note the phrase used in answering the dorophone: "*A l'eau!*" (= "'Allo! = "Hello!") (261/§1:38).

[23]Cf. Eliot's *The Waste Land*, lines 383, 427.

Edward Balcerzan

Seeking Only Man: Language and Ethics in Solaris

Translated from the Polish by Konrad Brodziński

(from SFS 2:152 - 156, July 1975)

Lem's Solaris cannot be assessed within that system of values which the 20th-century avant-garde has evolved and implanted in our consciousnesses.

The present-day literary innovator tends to be an isolated figure, misunderstood by the general reader. He experiments as one of a group of experimenters. As a rule he "belongs" to a movement, accomodates himself within a school of thought, enters into the crossfire of various "isms." The opposite is true of the author of Solaris: today Stanislaw Lem is read, reprinted, discussed, translated, even filmed. And yet this writer works on his own. He moves almost in a "perfect vacuum," outside the current "isms," in a peculiar stratum of contrariness[1] in the literary consciousness of our times. It would be futile to seek a place for Solaris in the topography of Polish post-war prose; the critical pointers are negative: lack of contexts, absence of narrative forms corresponding to the order of development, a kind of "uprootedness" of the novel as a whole. Lem himself makes sure that he stays on just such an indefinite plane: always beside or above. This is confirmed by his statements in the mass media.

In 1970 Lem published his two-volume study Fantastyka i futurologia (SF and Futurology). One might suppose that this would be the book in which he admitted his affiliation to a certain movement, with which he is prepared to share success and failure. After all, he belongs—ostensibly—to the ranks of SF writers. However, he deals and polemicises mainly with non-Polish realizations of that genre, with texts unknown to Polish readers. He presents them in "summarized" form: summarized, and perhaps at the same time parodied? One is led to suspect that it is not Lem defining himself in relation to some "ism," but an alien "ism" defining itself in relation to Lem. His next book, Doskonala próżnia (Perfect Vacuum—Warsaw: Czytelnik, 1971), confirmed such conjectures. The actual state of affairs in current fiction—earlier so perceptively analyzed in the essays of Lem's book Wejście na orbitę (Entering Into Orbit—Cracow: Wyd. Literackie, 1962)—is of less and less concern to him. He does not see his own writing directly in terms of contemporary structures and sign-posts. He invents his own. Doskonala próżnia contains "reviews" of unwritten works.

Naturally, Lem as theoretician is aware of the literary battlefields, and knows the objectives and means of battles fought by the multifarious avant-gardes. In practice, however—and this is particularly true of Solaris—his knowledge of the conflict between the avant- and arrière-gardes does not influence the shape of his story.

The contemporary avant-gardist needs continually to question and contest. He needs to take apart stereotypes, to break down automatisms, to dissolve conventions. Thrown into a tradition, he endeavours first of all to question the language of his predecessors. He wants his writing to be an interplay of "the old" and "the new," but the result of the game is a foregone conclusion: the "new" wins. Lem's approach is different. The structure of Solaris accomodates and reconciles the Languages of two eras: those of the 19th and 20th centuries. Reading Lem's novel we feel that all the crises, rebellions, seasonal dictatorships and similar eruptions which continually destroyed and re-formed the narrative art did not manage to violate the essential identity of the genre: the story has remained the story. Changes have turned out to be superficial: the "new" has not eliminated the "old," it functions *side by side* with it; the cataclysms were not fatal. These language revolts, riots and outrages are reduced in *Solaris* to the rôle *neutral matter*. Systems hitherto in conflict begin here to gravitate towards each other; they are fused into a whole.

Let us begin with "the old." Granted a great deal of over-simplification, it can be said that the prose which we now feel to be "old"—traditional or traditionalistic—and whose possibilities, if the avant-gardists are to be believed, have been exhausted, regulated reality in the novel according to the rules of common sense. Here the world-order, established by common experience and by the current state of scientific research, went unquestioned. It constituted the primary condition of a relationship between the author and his readers. Time was linear; space three-dimensional; the sequence of events continuous (or simulating continuity); the characters explained through biography; the language.... The language we shall consider later. Lem has written a phantasmagorical novel, but in actual fact the world of *Solaris* is seen in a traditional perspective. What has changed? Time has been extended—it has run on into the future; space has been broadened—up to the furthest crannies of the cosmos. These changes are nonetheless only *quantitative*. The basic system of orienting and measuring has remained the same. Two suns shine on the planet Solaris—this complicates the rhythm of life, but not to such an extent as to render the situations in which the heroes of the novel have got entangled untranslatable into the language of ordinary, earthly, human experience.

17:20 hours: in fog. Altitude 200. Visibility 20-40 metres. Silence. Climbing to 400.
17:45: Altitude 500. Pall of fog to horizon. Funnel-shaped openings through which I can see ocean surface. Something is happening there. Shall try to enter one of these clearings. (§6)[2]

The gam gliding over the "thinking" ocean, in a landscape of strange objects: "extensors," "fungoids," "mimoids," "asymmetriads" and "symmetriads" (§8), moves about like each of us would in familiar surroundings—in the mountains, say, in a skyscraper, in an elevator. Time and space here contain none of the compressions and attenuations to be found in the contemporary novel, no umplumbed depths; everything runs according to the calendar, there is no "thirteenth month," no psychological or metaphysical labyrinths.

Lem has written an SF novel; in this peculiar genre even the boldest visions are timely entrenched in common sense, equipped with ocular and objective. They have no right to be otherwise. We perceive them as fantastic for the very reason that they exist in a non-fantastic environment, in an ocean of normality. In fact, a practical intelligence means more here than it does in "realistic" writing: it is not merely a capacity appreciated passively, without comment, it receives special protection. Thus, for example, "visitors" begin to pay calls on the members of the solaris expedition. Who are they?—"'Hallucinations, you mean.' 'No...it's real...'" (§1).

Kris, the hero of *Solaris*, would nonetheless prefer them to be just hallucinations. A *healthy* mind seeks explanation in *illness*. He can accept deviation from the norm, but he cannot believe that there are orders transcending the antinomy of "health" and "illness" by means of completely unexpected deviations *within* the system. "Then a curous change came over me," says Kris; "at the thought that I had gone mad, I calmed down." This makes good sense: "Assuming that I was ill, there was reason to believe that I would get better, which gave me some hope of deliverance—a hope in no way to be found in the tangled nightmares of those few hours I had just experienced, on Solaris" (§4).[3]

Tangled nightmares which cannot be disentangled at the given point of time, but which nevertheless *are* being disentangled continuously and at all cost, present a threat to the sovereignty of common sense. A game offers a form of defence: the game of common sense, or pretence that everything is as it should be. A "visitor," Harey,[4] calls on Kris. This is—real. She is a girl in a white dress, betrayed only by one detail: the dress has no fastener. The game begins. Kris slits open the material—"As though it were the most normal way of going about it" (§5). The game does not end there. The "visitors" go through a process of humanisation. The more human character-istics they acquire, the more sensibly they reason. A new Harey arrives, wiser, more determined. The scene with the dress is re-enacted. "This time she herself tore the stitch apart with a pair of scissors. She said that the fastener had probably got stuck" (§7).[5]

The power of common sense (this likewise has a somewhat antiquated air about it, foreign to present trends) finds its basis in the conceptualization of character and organisation of the plot. Thus the characters' actions have plausible motives, and the plot has a clear beginning and end. A character, particularly a subordinate one, may have a fossilized personality, acting according to the same script in each situation and reproducing the same com-plex of characteristics (Sartorius). He may evolve (Kris, Harey), but only if such a change stays within the sphere of "real-life" feasibility. There is nothing here of Witkacy or Schulz.[6] In Witkacy, protagonists change suddenly, in one leap, without explanation: "The old man changes from a meek man into a rabid psychopath and murders a little girl who has only just crept in Stage Left." Such leaps are out of the question in the convention of *Solaris*. Un-questionably, here too the gentle turn degenerate and the bestial become angels. If, however, they encounter an incident analogous to the old man and the little girl, they do not give in, but, recalling all their specialist reading, armed to the teeth with the latest scientific apparatus, they try to explain (to the reader and to themselves) how such a horrendous crime could have come about, why (to continue our analogy) the girl "crept" in instead of just walking in, why she crept in from the left and not from the right, and so on. All the Solarists behave in this manner: Kris, Gibarian, Snaut,[7] Sartorius....

Given such a framework, the *language* of the narrative is surprising. The "old" novel embodied its vision of the world in a language which was maximally self-assured, unambiguous and translucent. This was a *sine qua non* of the *art of confirmation*. The narrator of *Solaris*, on the other hand, has at his disposal a language which he cannot trust—just as 20th-century avant-garde writers do not trust it. However, the sub-codes of scientific cognition turn out to be quite insecure, and their ostensible purity problematic; they are liable to decay just as much as the vernacular. They become antiquated, or stray from their precise subject, or combine with alien sub-codes such as that of sensationalist journalism, or become prey to the antics of cranks and maniacs of all kinds. "Every science engenders some pseudo-science," says Kris (§6), and it has to go on as a *confused* language, in which it is difficult to separate truth from falsehood. He has, moreover, to use a tongue which is *foreign*, second-hand, even "third-hand" and "fourth-hand." It is not surprising, therefore, that "any scientist...has the indelible impression that he can discern fragments of an intelligent structure, perhaps endowed with genius, hap-hazardly mingled with outlandish phenomena, apparently the product of an unhinged mind" (§2).

The whole novel is *search for a language*—in its "uniqueness and truth."

The search ends in failure. Neither elaborate systems, which incapacitate through surfeit of words, nor sparse ones, which in turn lose the "subtle complexity of thought," satisfy the narrator. Each new phenomenon arouses a speech-forming passion, finding its place in the language as a collection of names. The "visitors" appear. In what word can one embody their existence, their extraordinariness: polytheria, succubi, phantoms, Phi-creatures? "But ultimately no terms will convey what happens on Solaris,"[8] says Kris: all the terms turned out to have been "inadequate" (§8). As in the modern literary currents, the narrative constantly reviews and revises itself, reveals itself in a speech which is uncertain, contained within inverted commas, capricious, turbid.

On the fly-leaf of the first edition of *Glos Pana* (*His Master's Voice*—Warsaw: Czytelnik, 1968), Lem wrote that he himself did not understand *Solaris* completely. "I do not understand" means here: "My novel is not written in a language which meets with my complete approval."—"'Does your word still possess any value for you?' 'Good God, Snaut, still going on about *that*? It does. And I have given it to you...'" (§14).[9] The "word of honour" may still have some value, but it is a subjective value, private and ethical rather than cognitive. It may be my word on any subject, but fails to become my word on something outside of me. We thus have a *paradoxical novel*: the world seen simultaneously in a "new" and an "old" way. Why, though, does this hybrid creature not break down, and why is such a combination of fire and water at all conceivable and admissible?

It is conceivable within a system of compromises. We are witnessing a continuous relay-race of two poetics. In some sections of the text, in episodes of concentrated action in which there is no time for reflection, the language becomes translucent as the world reverts to its norm. In other parts of the novel the opposite is true: the world constructs itself outside the norm. Then the action dies out—Kris shuts himself away in a library—and the more the language is analysed, the more violently it crumbles away and gives birth to monstrosities, symmetriads and asymmetriads, various mimoids and surrealia.... Then again: action, tempo, clarity. And so it goes on until the end of the book.

Is this good or bad? The structure of *Solaris* imitates *the structure of the human personality*, especially that of an intellectual like Kris or Snaut. Lem's novel "behaves" as everyone behaves who sees the difference between the language of empirical life and the language set apart for analytic purposes. The first must be common-sense and realistic; the second is often irrational and twisted; and yet we use both of them almost concurrently. Lem knows this: time after time he plays the critic. He cannot be subservient to the literary canons of either the 19th or 20th centuries, because his loyalty lies first and foremost with his protagonists.

This, I think, is good.

The case of Harey and Kris was known to literature long before *Solaris* was written, in various stories about the man-phantom encounter in a context of different sexes by, e.g., Mickiewicz, Slowacki or Syspiański. It is difficult to discuss such a theme in terms of old-fashioned versus avant-garde. A different set of concepts comes into play here: that of "originality" against "unoriginality." Lem is original. He is original in the classical sense of the word, as the author of a text which takes a theme out of its historical and literary order and radically updates it (so radically that bringing up the names of the great Romantics may seem no more than a joke on the part of the critic). To put it another way: *whenever the KNOWN is perceived by us as NEW, we are dealing with originality.*

The case in question is the drama of a man who is in love with *someone's image* and lives with it as with a "flesh and blood" person: an image deeply rooted in the memory, sketched in one's fantasies, appearing in day-dreams. Lem is not interested in the pathological aspect of this phenomenon. He is admittedly presenting an extraordinary situation, but at the same time he employs all his energy and inventiveness to convey to the reader that *every-one* experiences what happened to the helpless, desperate Solarists. Kris has lost a fiancée: Harey died—she did not have to die, he could simply have lost immediate contact with her; and now it appears that *contact* has not been lost because it still remains in Kris's memory, without Harey, but in connection with her. More than that: it emancipates itself within him, it evolves, it has periods of activity and of stagnation. What does this mean? If we are involved in a dialogue with the absent, who, or what, is our interlocutor?

"We are only seeking Man," says Snaut in chapter 6.

This is the key sentence in *Solaris*. Only seeking Man. If this is so, then even the image of a person (which after all has no matter, or is material in a different way) becomes not just an epistemological puzzle but a *moral problem*. Does not—Lem asks—demoralisation perhaps begin at the point when—in a supposedly "make-believe" way, bloodlessly, in a void—we murder *the thought about another person*? Just the thought, the reflection, a "Phi-creature".... These are the questions Lem asks. The rest is a fantastic story, which forces the reader to project the fictitious story of Kris the Solarist through the prism of his own biography.

NOTES BY DS

[1]The Polish *mimoism*, Balcerzan's own neologism, means literally "contrary-to-ism," or "athwart-ism"; since he was probably trying to pun on Lem's "mimoids," the translator and editor throw up their hands in despair and settle for the next best.

[2]Changed from the Kilmartin-Cox translation of the UK and US editions to conform with the original.

[3]Slightly emended from the Kilmartin-Cox translation.

[4]In the French and English translations for unclear reasons called Rheya.

[5]Changed from the Kilmartin-Cox translation.

[6]Famous 20th-century Polish fantasy writers.

[7]In English translation Snow.

[8]Changed from the Kilmartin-Cox translation.

[9]Changed from the Kilmartin-Cox translation of: "'Can I rely on your word?' 'Still fretting? Yes, you can....'"

Douglas Barbour

Wholeness and Balance in
the Hainish Novels of Ursula K. Le Guin

(from SFS 1:164 - 173, Spring 1974)

The five stories by Ursula K. Le Guin with which this essay is directly concerned—*Rocannon's World* (1966), *Planet of Exile* (1966), *City of Illusions* (1967), *The Left Hand of Darkness* (1969), and "The Word for World is Forest" (1972)[1]—are all set in what may be called the Hainish universe, for it was the people of the planet Hain who originally "seeded" all the habitable worlds of this part of the galaxy and thus produced a humanoid universe that is single, expanding, and historically continuous, but at the same time marvelous in its variety, for each planetary environment caused specific local mutations in its humanoids as they adapted and developed. The result is a universe full of "humans" who display enough variety to provide for any number of alien encounters, and since any possible stage of civilization can be found on some particular planet, new definitions of "civilization" can be made in a narrative rather than a discursive mode.

In *Rocannon's World* and *Planet of Exile* Le Guin sketches in the background of the League of All Worlds, which is preparing to fight an Enemy from some distant part of the galaxy, and prepares the reader for *City of Illusions*, which is the story of the man who will eventually "rescue" humanity from the Shing, the mind-lying aliens. *The Left Hand of Darkness* is set in an even further future when the Shing have been defeated and most of humanity has once again united, this time in the Ekumen of Known Worlds—a subtler and humbler title than the former one. "The Word for World is Forest," being set in the first year of the League, brings the Hainish universe comparatively close to our own time.

Besides the continuous time-space history, these narratives are bound together by a consistent imagery that both extends and informs meaning. Although Le Guin has used particular images which emerge naturally from the cultural and ecological context of her imagined worlds as linking devices within each work, she has also consistently used light/dark imagery as a linking device for the whole series. Again and again, good emerges from ambiguous darkness, evil from blinding light. Thus there is a specific local imagery in each novel, and a pervasive light/dark imagery in all of them.

In *Rocannon's World* the local image is the "Eye of the Sea." This jewel, the efficient cause of Semley's actions in the "Prologue," appears throughout Rocannon's adventures until, when he has accomplished his task, he gives it, as a final sign that he has found his home, to the Lady Ganye, who, at the end of the story, appears as "his widow, tall and fair-haired, wearing a great blue jewel set in gold at her throat."

The light/dark imagery is more pervasive and more complex. From the very beginning the interdependence of light and darkness are made clear. Take Kyo's explanation of the difference between his people and the Gdmiar: the Fiia chose to live only in the light, the Clayfolk chose "night and caves and swords" (§7), and both lost something by their choice. The image of the Fiia dance, "a play of light and dark in the glow of the fire" (§7), reflects a pattern which Rocannon realizes had existed between Kyo and himself. This *dance* of shadows and light is the proper image for their interplay in all Le Guin's work: both the light and the dark are necessary if any pattern is to emerge from chaos (see *Left* §16). When Rocannon meets the Ancient One, he must enter the "dark place" to gain the gift of mind-hearing (§8). Later he enters the FTL ships on "a night when of all the four moons only the little captured asteroid...would be in the sky before midnight" (§9). The success of his mission, the explosion destroying the enemy base, is marked by "not the light but the darkness, the darkness that blinded his mind, the knowledge in his own flesh of the death of a thousand men all in one moment" (§9). Clearly and consistently light/dark images dance through the whole novel.

The title of the first chapter in *Planet of Exile*, "A Handful of Darkness," refers to Agat's dark hand against Rolery's white one. The alliance of farborns and hilfs, of black and white, is touched on throughout the novel: Agat's and Rolery's growing love is imaged in these terms. As Rolery "seemed to hold against her palm a handful of darkness, where his touch had been" (§1), so Agat "recalled briefly...the light, lithe, frightened figure of the girl Rolery, reaching up her hand to him from the dark sea-besieged stones" (§3). Rolery feels a "little rush of fear ·and darkness through her veins" (§5) because she is a natural telepath and has been "bespoken" by Agat; later, when Agat is attacked and wounded and sends out calls for help, "Rolery's mind went quite dark for a while" (§6) and she is the one to find him. Both are young and fear the Winter, for they have only "known the sunlight" (§5). That oncoming 5000-day cold spell provides some of the local image patterns of this novel, as do the customs of the Askatevar, but the light/dark imagery weaves its way from book to book.

"Imagine darkness. In the darkness that faces outward from the sun a mute spirit woke. Wholly involved in chaos, he knew no pattern." Thus begins *City of Illusion*, and thus begins Falk's book-long search for the correct pattern, one made up of light and darkness as all good patterns must be. Naturally enough, in a story of lie and paradox, light and dark seldom carry ordinary meanings. Falk begins and ends in darkness, yet the two darknesses are opposed: the first a mental chaos, the last an important part of the whole pattern he has sought. As the images gather, we begin to see the pattern, and the play of paradox and illusion within it. The old

Listener's warning about "the awful darkness of the bright lights of Es Toch" (§3) presents one of the central paradoxes, one Falk must resolve if he is to survive. In Es Toch it is "the word spoken in darkness with none to hear at the beginning, the first page of time" to which Falk turns as he tries to outmaneuver the Shing (§8).

The two major local images are the "patterning frame" (§§1, 5) and the "Way" of the "Old Canon" (i.e., the *Tao-te ching*). References to Falk as a stone within the frame appear throughout the story, as do quotations from and allusions to the *Tao*. Falk-Ramarren's final recognition that "there's always more than one way towards the truth" (§10), which is his personal resolution of the dark/light pattern, is an "open" one. Yet it has been implicit in the imagery of the patterning frame and the *Tao*, which has been very carefully organized, and which leads directly to the novel's final paragraph:

On the screen dawn coming over the Eastern Ocean shone in a golden crescent for a moment against the dust of the stars, like a jewel on a great patterning frame. Then frame and pattern shattered, the barrier was passed, and the little ship broke free of time and took them out across the darkness.

"Tormer's Lay," from which *The Left Hand of Darkness* takes its title (§16), suggests the importance of the light/dark image pattern in that novel. When Ai finally comes to accept and love Estraven as a whole person, he shows him the Yin-Yang symbol: "Light, dark. Fear, courage. Female, male. It is yourself, Therem. Both and one. A shadow on snow." (§19). This list of opposites yoked together expresses precisely the deep meaning that the image pattern points to; it clearly owes much to the Tao sensibility of Chuang Tzu who similarly yokes opposites together on the Way.[2]

When Estreven says that the word *Shifgrethor*, which Ai has found impossible to understand, "comes from an old word for *shadow*" (§18), a clear light is cast back across the novel, illuminating passage after passage where shadows or the lack of them are mentioned with particular emphasis— even Ai himself had said of the Orgota that it was "as if they did not cast shadows" (§10). This sequence of images is solidly grounded in Gethenian psychology and philosophy, yet it simultaneously fits into the larger pattern that connects all the novels. In *Left Hand* shadow images concerned with personal integrity indicate what kind of person is being referred to; they are also deeply embedded in the ecology of the planet, the warm shadows of the hearths opposing the snow, the terrible cold, so bright with danger: no wonder the Handdara is a "fecund darkness" (§5).

The essential unity of light and darkness is always implicit in the imagery, as in the description of the Foretelling: "Hours and seconds passed, the moonlight shone on the wrong wall, there was no moonlight only darkness, and in the center of all darkness Faxe: the Weaver: a woman, a woman dressed in light" (§5). The Foretelling emerges from the Darkness, the very darkness the Handdara rely on, as is shown by their "short and charming grace of invocation, the only ritual words" Ai ever learns of them: "Praise then darkness and Creation unfinished" (§18). "Dothe," the special strength Handdarata can call up in their bodies, is the "strength out of the Dark," and "thangen," the sleep of recovery, is "the dark sleep" (§14). Yet Faxe the Weaver shines with his own light, even in noon sunlight (§5). As the Lay says, "Two are one ... like the end and the way" (§16).

Having heard Estraven recite Tormer's Lay, Ai speaks of the difference between Gethenians and Terrans:

"You're isolated, and undivided. Perhaps you are as obsessed with wholeness as we are with dualisms."

"We are dualists too. Duality is essential, isn't it? So long as there is *myself* and *the other*."

"I and Thou," he said. "Yes, it does, after all, go even wider than sex...." (§16)

As wide as the universe of meaning itself, the images say: wholeness and duality, together and separate at once, a pattern of life itself, woven through an artist's fictions, the matrix of her vision.

AS THE DISCUSSION of imagery has shown, Le Guin's artistic vision is multiplex, dualistic, and holistic. That she has never sought simplistic philosophical solutions for the human problems she explores in her narratives, could be demonstrated in her first three books, but I wish to concentrate here on her artistic handling of balance as a way of life in *The Left Hand of Darkness* and "The Word for World is Forest."

Very few SF books have succeeded as well as *The Left Hand of Darkness* in invoking a whole environment, a completely consistent alien world, and in making the proper extrapolations from it. Le Guin has chosen a form that allows for various kinds of "documentation": six of the twenty chapters (not to mention the Appendix) are documents separate from the actual narrative—three "Hearth tales" (§§ 2, 4, 9), a report on Gethenian sexuality (§7), excerpts from a sacred book (§12), and "An Orgota Creation Myth" (§17)—each placed so as to aid our understanding of the narrative at a particular point in its progression. And the narrative itself is a document, consisting partly of Ai's transcription of passages from Estraven's notebook and partly of Ai's direct report to his superiors in the officialdom of the Ekumen. The whole is a masterful example of form creating content.

Quite early in the story, immediately after a "hearth tale" concerned with their Foretellings, Ai spends considerable space reporting on his experiences at a Handdara Fastness, and it soon becomes obvious that he considers the Handdara a religion of considerable profundity. I think it is safe to assume that Le Guin means us to agree with this opinion, partly because of the way in which Handdara thought reflects the *Tao-te ching*, which is explicitly drawn upon in *City of Illusions*. In *Left Hand* the basic Handdara religious philosophy is influenced by the specific paraverbal talent the Gethenians have, yet there are many allusive connections between this invented religion and Taoism.

"The Handdara," says Ai, "is a religion without institution, without priests, without hierarchy, without vows, without creed; I am still unable to

say whether it has a god or not. It is elusive. It is always somewhere else."
(§5). Similarly, the *Tao-te ching*:

> The thing that is called Tao is eluding and vague.
> Vague and eluding, there is in it the form.
> Eluding and vague, in it are things.
> Deep and obscure, in it is the essence.
>   (§21; translation by Wing-tsit Chan)[3]

Although Taoist-influenced Zen Buddhism has many points in common with
the Handdara, Le Guin has created in this "elusive"religion something that
is still alien as well as very human. The Handdara's "only fixed manifestation
is in the Fastnesses, retreats to which people may retire and spend the night
or a lifetime" (§5). Ai visits the Otherhord Fastness to investigate the "foretellings" for the Ekumen; these predictions, which must be paid for, are
apparently completely true. Ai arrives a skeptic and departs a believer, having participated unwillingly in the Foretelling by virtue of his own paraverbal talent. He remarks that although the humanoids of the Ekumen have
certain paraverbal abilities, they have not yet "tamed hunch to run in harness;
for that we must go to Gethen." But this chapter also reveals basic Handdara
beliefs and attitudes which later clarify Estraven's behavior, for he has been
Handdara trained. The response of young Goss to what Ai intends as an
apology for being "exceedingly ignorant"—"I'm honored!...I haven't yet
acquired enough ignorance to be worth mentioning."—is important in that
it introduces the central doctrine of Handdara life:

It was an introverted life, self-sufficient, stagnant, steeped in that singular
"ignorance" prized by the Handdarata and obedient to their rule of inactivity
or non-interference. That rule (expressed in the word *nusuth*, which I have
to translate as "no matter") is the heart of the cult, and I don't pretend to
understand it. (§5)

Most readers will sympathize with Ai's last small complaint, but these ideas
have much in common with the Tao of both Lao Tzu and Chuang Tzu. *Tao*
§37 says, "Tao invariably takes no action, and yet there is nothing left
undone," and Chuang Tzu writes: "I take inaction to be true happiness, but
ordinary people think it is a bitter thing.... the world can't decide what is
right and what is wrong. And yet inaction can decide this. The highest happiness, keeping alive—only inaction gets you close to this."[4] The time that
Ai spends at the Otherhord Fastness is the happiest he has known.

The Handdarata, Estraven tells Ai, are perhaps, in comparison with the
Yomeshta of Orgoreyn, who are somewhat further into the pattern of the
ecology-breaking cultures of other worlds, "less aware of the gap between
men and beast, being more occupied with likenesses, the links, the whole
of which living things are a part" (§16). This preoccupation with wholeness
and likenesses is found throughout the *Tao*, for the Way unites all things.
Tormer's Lay, which Estraven recites for Ai in §16, brings to a focus the
light and dark imagery which has operated which such poetic subtlety

throughout; it also expresses in highly charged and culturally consistent imagery the ideas of wholeness and balance which have been implicit in the language of the novel:

> Light is the left hand of darkness
> and darkness the right hand of light.
> Two are one, life and death, lying
> together like lovers in kemmer,
> like hands joined together,
> like the end and the way.

LIGHT AND DARKNESS sharing the world and our apprehension of it: this is a deeply Taoist insight, but it is also a deeply holistic/artistic one. On Athshe, the world of "The Word for World is Forest," it is one of the bases of life for the natives, and a lost fragment of old knowledge for the Terran colonists. Here Le Guin departs from any obvious use of Taoism; instead, she approaches the theme of balance, of the light and darkness joined together, through a highly dense and specific creation of an ecology and culture inextricably entwined, and through the ideas of Dement and Hadfield on the nature of dreams.[5] In creating a culture in which people balance their "sanity not on the razor's edge of reason but on the double support, the fine balance of reason and dream" (§5), she has also created a powerful image of holistic duality. The sanity and balance of Athshean society, the Athshean's awareness of "the whole of which living things are a part" (*Left Hand* §16), stands in stark contrast to the emotional and mental imbalance of the Earth-imperialist colonial culture which represents a logical extension of certain present-day technological and political trends. Despite the fact that the Earthmen come from all parts of the globe (ironically, their leader, Colonel Dongh, is from Viet Nam), they are all imbued with the attitudes of the "Judeao-Christian-Rationalist West," as Haber will so fondly call it in §6 of *The Lathe of Heaven* (1972).

The Terran colonists are xenophobic despite their knowledge of other star-traveling humanoid races (the story is set in the period in which the league of All Worlds is first founded): they still believe they are kings of the universe. They have no desire to understand, or, more important, learn from, the hilfs. With the sole exception of Lyubov, the military men of the colony see the Athsheans as "creechies," animal-creatures; that is, as non-human and therefore to be treated as animals. Although the group is presented in general terms, the foci of interest are the individual psychologies of Davidson and Lyubov. These are extreme types, at opposite ends of the Earth-human spectrum, and in each we can see those attitudes and behavioral mannerisms which, in a mixed way, are the heritage of a civilization given over to the acquisition of material goods and power, the attitudes of which are fixed in the Hobbesian vision of man. Davidson's nearly incoherent "reasoning" provides a spectacular instance of how a man's psychosis (in this case, paranoia) correlates to the excessive exploitation of a world's inhabitants and natural resources. Lyubov's tortured soul-searching, eager reaching out to others for knowledge, and final refusal of Selver's proffered gift of dreaming, reveal a mild, humane, liberal, and finally weak man. Selver, the Athshean who becomes a "god" and acts with violence to protect his people when necessity so dictates, reveals by contrast the weakness of Lyubov's position.

These contrasts of character are partially exposed in light/dark imagery and partially translated into balance/imbalance imagery. The brightness of Don Davidson's mind, intense, paranoid, and in love with the fire that kills others, especially "creechies," is frighteningly unbalanced. Seeing "water and sunlight, or darkness and leaves" only as opposites, he chooses to "end the darkness, and turn the tree-jumble into clean sawn planks, more prized on Earth than gold" (§1). Earthmen, trying to balance their sanity "on the razor's edge of reason," fail to comprehend "the fine balance of reason and dream" and thus live in fear of the dark forests of the Athsheans, where "into wind, water, sunlight, starlight, there always entered leaf and branch, bole and root, the shadowy, the complex" (§2). The complex is that fusion of light and darkness which represents wholeness. The concept of living in both dream-time and world-time reflects this wholeness. Lyubov's reflection on his original fear of the forest and his gradual acceptance of it reveals how much the Earthmen, from a technological, well-lit, treeless Earth, have lost in their relentless pursuit of power. They would clean out the forest, burn it off, to let the light shine on the barren ground that they mistakenly believe will bear growth again. Driven by the "yumens" to struggle for survival, the Athsheans have "taken up the fire they feared into their own hands: taken up the mastery over the evil dream: and loosed the death they feared upon their enemy" (§8). Truth is complex, dark and light at once, and the various images attached to the forest, that place of no revelation, "no certainty," all contribute to our understanding of this. The Athsheans are at home in the complex, and sit under a big tree to meet with the yumens: "The light beneath the great tree was soft, complex with shadows" (§8). This complexity is deeply embedded in their culture, in which everyone lives in both times, that of the dream and that of the world.

Although specific references to darkness and light are not as numerous as in some of the other stories, the pattern is definitely there, in the ambiguous forest, behind the words and images that do appear. In a very important sense, the disturbed balance of dream-time and world-time is the local image-system in this work.

Selver, recognizing the necessity of armed resistance (of fighting a war of liberation that has obvious parallels with Third World struggles, especially that in Viet Nam), is the dreamer who becomes a god, translating to his people the terrible but necessary new dream of killing one's own kind (for the Athsheans, unlike the yumens, have recognized the essential oneness of the two races). Their survival depends upon it, but their innocence has been forever lost, and he recognizes what a terrible price that is to pay for freedom (§8). Le Guin's handling of this specific political problem is remarkable, at least in the world of popular SF, for its intellectual toughness: Lyubov's death results directly from his "liberal" inability to face the reality of the situation as the Athsheans have seen it. Selver survives, together with his people, because he rigorously follows the logic of the situation to its necessary conclusion: fight or be exterminated.

Le Guin's fictions are all imbued with great sympathy for the strange "human" cultures they present. Nevertheless, the Athshean culture of "Forest" is her clearest example yet of a culture presented as in basic and violent conflict with present-day "Earth-normal" standards but still as unequivocally the saner of the two. Thus the culture of the Athsheans, the ecology of Athshe, and the profound connections between them, are the focus of this novella. The ecological balance of Athshe, though not quite precarious, is delicate, as is revealed in §1 by the complete devastation of an entire island and indirectly by Davidson's thoughts on the exploitative value of this "New Tahiti." The Athshean vision emerges in a thick poetic prose at the beginning of the first Selver chapter (§2) in a description whose beauty and complexity stand in stark contrast to the prose associated with Davidson or even Lyubov. The forest is presented in a series of concrete images; then there is this:

Nothing was dry, arid, plain. Revelation was lacking. There was no seeing everything at once: no certainty. The colors of rust and sunset kept changing in the hanging leaves of the copper willows, and you could not say even whether the leaves of the willows were brownish-red, or reddish-green, or green.
Selver came up a path beside the water, going slowly and often stumbling on the willow roots. He saw an old man dreaming, and stopped. The old man looked at him through the long willow-leaves and saw him in his dream.

We have been introduced to the ecology from within, and to the major aspect of the culture: all that follows will merely fill out the sketch before us until it is a full portrait.

The clan system that is tied into tree names, the small village systems, the special male and female roles that have been devised to maintain the society, the major part that dreaming plays in the lives of the Athsheans, their use of "a kind of ritualized singing to replace physical combat" (§3), and many other aspects of their culture, are all brought out as the novella progresses. Lyubov explains the Athsheans in this way:

"They're a static, stable, uniform society. They have no history. Perfectly integrated, and wholly unprogressive. You might say that like the forest they live in, they've attained a climax state. But I don't mean to imply that they're incapable of adaptation." (§3)

But even though he sees that the Athsheans might be able to adapt to meet the challenge of the Earthmen, he does not really know their culture.

The most important aspect of Athshean culture is the use of dreams. Selver says that Lyubov, despite his attempts to understand Athshean ways, "called the world-time 'real' and the dream-time 'unreal,' as if that were the difference between them" (§2). Le Guin's extrapolations from Hadfield's theories have resulted in a marvellously different culture in "Forest." If it lacks "progress," Athshean culture possesses in abundance the sanity Earth culture so obviously lacks. Lyubov's thoughts on this matter in §5 add some interesting scientific "facts" to the speculative enterprise, yet all he can see is that the Athsheans have learned to dream in a brilliant and complex fashion. The Athsheans, however, see the situation in different terms: they have learned to *live*, sanely, in both times.

The whole question of sanity, or balance, is argued in the concrete terms of fiction throughout the novel. There are two forms of art on Athshe, dreaming and singing, and both are specialized cultural activities which serve to nullify aggression against other humans. The Athsheans recognize a necessity for controlling one's dreams, for dreaming properly, but the devastating impact of the Terrans has resulted in a deep cultural trauma:

"And all men's dreams," said Cora Mena, cross-legged in shadow, "will be changed. They will never be the same again. I shall never walk again that path I came with you yesterday.... It is changed. You have walked on it and it is utterly changed.... For you have done what you had to do, and it was not right. You have killed men. (§2)

Having done what "was not right," Selver has become a god—"a god that knows death, a god that kills and is not himself reborn"—and for the Athsheans such a person is "a changer, a bridge between realities" (§2). The concept is clarified further by Lyubov's hesitant articulation of the implications of "sha'ab, translator" to the point where he sees that Selver is "A link: one who could speak aloud the perceptions of the subconscious. To 'speak' that tongue is to act. To do a new thing. To change or to be changed, radically, from the root. For the root is the dream." (§5). Although Selver's godhead enables him to lead the Athsheans to victory over the Terrans, it is a burden that brings him nothing but pain, loss, and insanity, and at the end he renounces it. That he should be allowed to do so is a significant example of the sanity of his culture.

His culture's sanity—the awareness that balance must be sought where dark and light meet and mix, in the ambiguous center where simple-minded "we-they" solutions fail—emerges organically from its total context in the fictional world of the novel. Yet that balance, though no longer clearly Taoist, is paralleled in the Taoist insights of *City of Illusions* and *The Left Hand of Darkness*, in the teachings of the Handdarata in the latter book, in the joining of the races in *Planet of Exile*, and in the lessons learned by Rocannon in *Rocannon's World*. For Le Guin's artistic vision, her deep understanding of the real meaning of culture, has always been ambiguous, multiplex, subtle, and dualistic/holistic in the sense that it has always recognized the cultural relativity of "truth." Always, in her work, the representatives of different cultures meet, interact, and, in the cases that count, learn of each other (often through love) that they are equally human, part of the great brotherhood of "man."

NOTES

[1]The first three of these books have been published only in paperback; "The Word for World is Forest" appears in Harlan Ellison's anthology, *Again Dangerous Visions* (1972).

[2]Burton Watson, tr., *Chuang Tzu: Basic Writings* (US 1964), pp32-33, 38, 39-40, 70.

[3]The version of the *Tao-te ching* followed here is that of Wing-tzit Chan, ed., tr., *The Way of Lao-Tzu* (1963).

[4]Watson, p112.

[5]See J.A. Hadfield, *Dreams and Nightmares* (Harmondsworth 1966), pp 66, 72; and various of Dement's articles. Further on Dement's researches, see Brian Aldiss, *The Shape of Further Things* (UK 1970), pp 37-39, 42, with its pertinent discussion of how the lack of REM sleep leads to insanity.

Ursula K. Le Guin

On Norman Spinrad's *The Iron Dream*

(from SFS *1:41 - 44, Spring 1973)*

Adolf Hitler's Hugo-winning novel of 1954, *Lord of the Swastika,* presented by Norman Spinrad as *The Iron Dream* (Avon 1972), is an extraordinary book. Perhaps it deserves the 1973 Hugo, as well.

On the back cover Michael Moorcock compares the book with "the works of J.R.R. Tolkien, C.S. Lewis, G.K. Chesterton, and Sir Oswald Mosley. . . . It is the very quintessence of sword and sorcery." None of the authors mentioned is relevant, except Mosley, but the reference to sword and sorcery is exact. *The Iron Dream* can be read as a tremendous parody of the subgenre represented by Moorcock's own Runestaff saga, and by Conan the Barbarian, and Brak the Barbarian, and those Gor books, and so on--"heroic fantasy" on the sub-basement level, the writing of which seems to be motivated by a mixture of simple-minded escapism and money-minded cynicism.

Taken as a parody of S&S, the book hits all its targets. There is the Hero, the Alpha Male with his muscles of steel and his clear eyes and his manifest destiny; there are the Hero's Friends; there are the vile, subhuman enemies; there is the Hero's Sword, in this case a truncheon of interesting construction; there are the tests, quests, battles, victories, culminating in a final supernal super-victory of the Superman. There are no women at all, no dirty words, no sex of any kind: the book is a flawless example of clean obscenity. It will pass any censor, except the one that sits within the soul.

A parody of S&S, however, is self-doomed. You cannot exaggerate what is already witlessly exaggerated; you cannot distort for comic effect something that is already distorted out of all reality. All Spinrad can do is equal the crassest kind of S&S; no one could surpass it. But fortunately he has larger game in mind.

There is another kind of book of which this can be said to be a parody or oblique criticism, and that is the Straight SF Adventure Yarn, as it is called in manly-modest disclaimer of its having any highfalutin philosophical/intellectual message, though, in fact, it usually contains a strong dose of concentrated ideology. This is the kind of story best exemplified by Robert Heinlein, who believes in the Alpha Male, in the role of the innately (genetically) superior man, in the heroic virtues of militarism, in the desirability and necessity of authoritarian control, etc., and who is a very persuasive arguer for all these things. Here *The Iron Dream* may have an effect as a moral counterweight: for in reading it, reading all the familiar things about the glory of battle, the foulness of enemies of the truth, the joys of obedience to a true leader, the reader is forced to remember that *it is Hitler saying these things*--and thus to *question* what is said, over and over. The tension and discomfort thus set up may prove salutary to people who are used to swallowing the stuff whole.

And, of course, the book is not merely satirising the machismo of certain minor literary genres, but the whole authoritarian bag. It is, like all Spinrad's serious works, a moral statement.

The beauty of the thing is the idea of it: a novel by an obscure hack named Hitler. The danger, the risk of it is that that idea is embodied in 255 pages of--inevitably--third-rate prose.

This may not bother Spinrad. There are obvious parodic elements in the style, which is prudish, slightly stiff, and full of locutions such as "naught but"; but in fact the style is seldom very much worse than Spinrad's own, before Hitlerisation. Since he is one of the best short story writers in SF, perhaps the best, I doubted my own instinct here, and checked back with the stories in the collection *The Last Hurrah of the Golden Horde* (Avon 1970). Vivid, imaginative, and powerful, the stories make their impact through their ideas and despite their prose. They are mostly written on about the level of this sentence from "Once More, With Feeling": "There was an expectant tension in her voice that he couldn't fathom but that rippled the flesh of his thighs." Like most prose described as "punchy," "gutsy," "hard-hitting," Spinrad's is actually a highly over-intellectualised style. Nobody who responds sensually and perceptually to the sound and meaning of words could write or can read that sentence with satisfaction. How do you fathom a tension? with a plumb-line? How does her tension ripple his thighs? does it make little waves like grass in the wind on the skin, or little ridges like a washboard?--Of course one isn't expected to ask such questions, one isn't supposed to react, to the false concreteness of the verbs except in the most generalised and fuzzy way--just as with political slogans and bureaucratese. What Spinrad is after is an idea, a moral idea; of the world of emotions and sensations, nothing exists but a vague atmosphere of charged violence, through which the reader is hurled forward breakneck towards the goal. To read a Spinrad short story is to be driven at top speed across the salt flats in a racing car. It's a powerful car and he's a great driver. He leaves the other racers way behind.

But a novel isn't a racing car. It is much more like a camel caravan, an ocean liner, or the Graf Zeppelin. It is by essence large, long, slow, intricate, messy, and liable to get where it is going by following a Great Circle. Variety of pace, variety of tone and mood, and above all complexity of subject, are absolutely essential to the novel. I don't think Spinrad has faced that yet. His three long books are over-extended short stories. And they have been relative failures, because you do not make a novel by just stretching out a story.

But, in this case, does it matter? How can a novel by Adolf Hitler be well-written, complex, interesting? Of course, it can't. It would spoil the bitter joke.

On the other hand, why should one read a book that isn't interesting?

A short story, yes. Even a book of a hundred or a hundred and twenty pages. At that length, the idea would carry one through; the essential interest of the distancing effect, the strength of the irony, would have held up. And all that is said in 255 pages could have been said. Nobody would ask Spinrad to sacrifice such scenes as the winning of the Great Truncheon by the hero Feric and the subsequent kissing of the Great Truncheon by the Black Avengers, or the terrific final scene. These are magnificent. They are horribly funny. They are totally successful tours de force. But the long build-ups to them are not necessary, as they would be in a novel; rather they weaken the whole effect. Only the high points matter; only they support the ironic tension.

As it is, the tension lags; and I am afraid that those who read the book clear through may do so because their insensitivity allows them to ignore the distancing which is the book's strength and justification. They will read it just as they read Conan, or *Starship Troopers,* or *Goldfinger* -- as good, clean fun. What's the harm in that? it's all just made up, it's all just fantasy, isn't it?--And so they will agree with "Homer Whipple" of N.Y.U., who provides, in the Afterword, the last twist of Spinrad's knife. After all it can't, Dr. Whipple says, happen here.

This--the misplaced suspension of disbelief--is the risk Spinrad ran, and surely knew he was running. If he loses, he loses the whole game. And that will be a disaster, for he is (unlike most of the cautious practitioners now writing SF) playing for high stakes. His moral seriousness is intense and intelligent, but he does not moralise and preach at us. He gambles; he tries to engage us. In other words, he works as an artist.

He has done, in *The Iron Dream,* something as outrageous as what Borges talks about doing in "Pierre Menard" (the rewriting of *Don Quixote,* word for word, by a twentieth-century Frenchman): he has attempted a staggeringly bold act of forced, extreme distancing. And distancing, the pulling back from "reality" in order to see it better, is perhaps the essential gesture of SF. It is by distancing that SF achieves aesthetic joy, tragic tension, and moral cogency. It is the latter that Spinrad aims for, and achieves. We are forced, in so far as we can continue to read the book seriously, to think, not about Adolf Hitler and his historic crimes-- Hitler is simply the distancing medium--but to think about ourselves: our moral assumptions, our ideas of heroism, our desires to, lead or to be led, our righteous wars. What Spinrad is trying to tell us is that it *is* happening here.

Portland, Oregon

The Science Fiction of
Philip K. Dick

Edited by Darko Suvin

(from SFS *2:3 - 75, March 1975)*

I cannot now recall with any precision the reason which prompted SFS to announce a special issue on Philip K. Dick and Ursula K. Le Guin, except that we had been getting all kinds of signals from our students and colleagues that the proof of SF criticism is in making sense of the major contemporary SF writers in its main domain, the USA, and that two of these are Mr Dick and Ms Le Guin. The quantity and quality of the response to our announcement has, I believed, confirmed that we were on the right track, so much so that we have had to change our plans to allow for two special issues—the present one for Dick and SFS #7 (November 1975) for Le Guin. This has also meant that some interesting proposals have had to be turned down for lack of space and time or because of thematic overlap. But I hope that SFS readers will agree that quite enough remains to make for a searching and provocative issue. I am particularly pleased that through the kind cooperation of Mr Dick and Professor Willis E. McNelly we are able to present here both an unpublished essay by Dick himself and a survey of the Dick manuscripts at CSU Fullerton.

Several of our Editorial Consultants have urged me to comment on the fact that Dick is a prophet honoured much more abroad than in his own country. The contributions to this special issue attest to that too. Not counting the bibliographies and Dick's own contribution, there are seven essays, four written by prominent European SF scholars (of whom three are also prominent SF writers, a happy union!), and three by North American academics strongly influenced by European, especially French and German, criticism, and leaning more toward comparative literature or theory of literature than toward classical Eng. Lit. Particularly in France, but increasingly in Britain and other European countries, Dick seems to be the center of a small hurricane of discovery and praise (in France there is already at least one dissertation on him). I don't know whether this means that North American critics are too close to Dick to see him steadily and see him whole, or that no heretic who subverts the accepted norms of a genre as wholeheartedly as Dick can expect to be a prophet in that genre's heartland. Whatever the cause, it is true (as Dr Lem has charged in the to date most impressive though to my mind also somewhat one-sided article on Dick, "SF: A Hopeless Case—With Exceptions," *SF Commentary* ##35-37, September 1973) that North American SF critics have lagged behind not only their European colleagues but also US fans in recognizing the merits of Dick's writing. I could have also said "the merits *in* Dick's writing": for it is only when one has articulated what merits can arguably be found in an opus, that one can also argue about the reasons, scope, and specific weight of the weaknesses also in that opus: for a special issue is not an embalming laudation but a recognition that a subject is significant enough to be painted with care, warts and all.

Perhaps I should not fail to mention that my own contribution—although written as a first approximation to that overview of Dick's opus which I could not persuade any contributor to undertake, and therefore printed at the beginning—was written last, and has thus profited from reading, and sometimes discussions at length with, all the other contributors, even those with whom I do not wholly agree. My editorial and personal thanks go to all of them for patience when faced with editorial nagging, and for what I believe the readers of SFS will learn from their essays about Dick, about SF, and about our times.

Philip K. Dick: Manuscripts and Books

WILLIS E. MC NELLY. THE MANUSCRIPTS AND PAPERS AT FULLERTON

In 1972 Philip K. Dick donated his manuscripts and papers to the Special Collections Library, California State University, Fullerton. These include completed manuscripts, carbon copies, setting copies, first drafts, and so on for both published and unpublished novels and stories, together with an extensive correspondence, commonplace books, copies of critical articles on his work, and copies of various ephemera relating to his career as one of the world's foremost science-fiction writers.

This entire collection, unquestionably the best single source for the study of Dick's work, is open to any student of science fiction for research or consultation, but because of the special nature of the collection, its materials are not available on inter-library loan. The manuscripts and papers are gathered into 24 document boxes. The following record of their contents, presented in shelf-list order and with cross references to the list of books that follows, gives some idea of the extent and nature of the holdings and their value to students of science fiction. (L = leaves; the items within each box are in random order.)

D1. §1. The man whose teeth were all exactly alike (unpublished). Ms (carbon, 358 L). §2. Mary and the giant (unpublished). Ms (carbon, 315 L).

D2. Gather yourselves together (unpublished). Ms (481 L).

D3. Do androids dream of electric sheep! (See #25). Ms (225 L of earlier version entitled The electric toad [sheep]). Ms (carbon, 244 L). A few pages of corrections and a synopsis.

D4. Puttering about in a small land (unpublished). Ms (carbon, 416 L in two spring binders).

D5. Ubik (see #26). Ms (236 L; entitled Death of an anti-watcher). Ms (carbon, 248 L).

D6. Eye in the sky (see #5). Ms (carbon, 2 copies, 305 L; with earlier title, With opened mind).

D7. Confessions of a crap artist (see #35). Ms (294 L). Ms (carbon, 295 L).

D8. The unteleported man (see #21, which = first half; second half unpublished). Ms (125 L). Ms (carbon, 106 L).

D9. The man who japed (see #4). Ms (carbon, 216 L).

D10. §1. In Milton Lumky territory (unpublished). Ms (carbon, 293 L). §2. The broken bubble of Thisbe Holt (unpublished). Ms (350 L).

D11-12. Counter-clock world (see #22). Ms (231 L; entitled The dead grow young). Ms (carbon, 238 L; entitled The dead grow young). Setting copy (238 L; Berkley Publishing Corporation).

D13. Galactic pot-healer (see #28). Ms (98 L; outline with title The glimmung of Plowman's planet). Ms (carbon, about 214 L). Ms (setting copy?, 214 L).

D14. Dr. Bloodmoney, or, How we got along after the bomb (see #18). Ms (46 L of short story, A Terran odyssey, original version of novel). Setting copy (298 L; Ace Books).

D15. The zap gun (see #23). Ms (320 L; "uncut version" published as #23). Tear sheets (from Worlds of Tomorrow, as Project plowshare). Ms (carbon, outline, 9 L).

D16. Voices from the street (unpublished). Ms (carbon, 652 L).

D17. Flow my tears, the policeman said (see #33). Working papers: deleted sections, first part of novel, outline.

D18. Clans of the Alphane moon (see #17). Setting copy (244 L; Ace Books).

D19. Our Friends from Frolix 8 (see #30). Ms (carbon, 278 L). Outline (carbon, 24 L). Character list (1 L).

D20. The man in the high castle (see #11). 2 original illustrations. Japanese paperback edition.

D21. §1. Return match (Galaxy, Feb 1967). Ms (carbon, 22 L). §2. Holy quarrel (Worlds of Tomorrow, May 1966). Ms (carbon, 34 L). §3. Not by its cover (Famous Science Fiction, Summer 1967). Ms (carbon, 13 L). §4. What the dead men say (see #27§14). Ms (carbon, 76 L; original title, Man with a broken match). §5. Oh, to be a Blobel! (see #27§13). Ms (carbon, 30 L; working title, Well, see, there were these Blobels). §6. If there were no Benny Cemoli (see #27§10). Ms (carbon, 30 L; working title, Had there never been a Benny Cemoli). §7. Orpheus with clay feet (unpublished). Ms (carbon, 21 L). §8. Retreat syndrome (see #27§11). §9. No ordinary guy (unpublished). Ms (carbon, 31 L). §10. The days of Perky Pat (Amazing, Dec 1963). Ms (carbon, 36 L; working title, In the days of Perky Pat). §11. Top stand-by job (see #27§6). Ms (carbon, 26 L). §12. Sir Waldo and Sir Lunchalot (unpublished). Ms (14 L). §13. The Pre-Persons (Magazine of Fantasy and Science Fiction, Oct 1974). Ms (34 L).

D22. Correspondence.

D23. Unsorted manuscript papers.

D24. §1. The evolution of a vital love (unpublished critique of #31, We Can Build You). Ms (19 L). §2. Warning: we are your police (unpublished). Ms (16 L; tv outline, 4800 words). §3. Foreword ([unpublished] to The preserving machine, #27). Ms (5 L). §4. A good Savoyard is a dead Savoyard (unpublished article). Ms (14 L). §5. A. Lincoln (see #31). Incomplete reproduced copy of proof sheets (71 columns). §6. The android and the human (see #40). Ms (carbon, 38 L). §7. The kneeling legless man (rough draft of unfinished novel, collaboration with Roger Zelazny). Ms (corrected, LL 5-48).

R.D. MULLEN. BOOKS, STORIES, ESSAYS

The list of books (##1-35) derives from a list compiled by Robert Greenberg, a member of the Los Angeles Science Fantasy Society, for distribution at Westercon 1974, supplemented by information from S1 and standard library sources. The intention is to include all US and UK editions but not reprintings of the same edition (e.g., most if not all of the Ace pb editions have been reprinted a number of times), but is doubtless deficient, especially with respect to UK editions. Stories published in "original" anthologies, the most recent magazine story, and a number of miscellaneous items have been added as ##36-44. For Dick's uncollected magazine stories the reader is referred to items S2-S4. In ##1-35, dates for magazine publication are given in parenthesis.

S1. Donald H. Tuck, *The Encyclopedia of Science Fiction and Fantasy*, Vol. 1. $20.00. Advent Publishers, PO Box A3228, Chicago, Ill. 60690.

S2. Erwin S. Strauss, *Index to the SF Magazines 1951-1965*; Anthony Lewis, *Index to the Science Fiction Magazines 1966-1970*; Anthony Lewis and Andrew H. White, *The NESFA Index: Science Fiction Magazines and Original Anthologies 1971-72*. $8.00, $5.00, and $3.00 respectively. The New England Science Fiction Association, PO Box G, MIT Branch PO, Cambridge, Mass. 02139.

S3. Walter R. Cole, *A Checklist of Science Fiction Anthologies*. Brooklyn, 1964. Scheduled for reprinting by Arno Press in February 1975.

S4. Frederick Siemon, *Science Fiction Story Index*. Chicago: American Library Association, 1971.

#1a. Solar Lottery. 1955 (Ace pb). NOTE. ## 1a and 1b, according to a note from Dick, are "different versions of the same novel."

#1b. World of Chance. 1956 (UK; Rich hb). 1957 (UK: SFBC hb). 1972 (as Solar Lottery, but still #1b, UK: Arrow pb).

#2. A Handful of Darkness. 1955 (UK: Rich hb). 1957 (UK: SFBC hb). 1966 (with §§7-8 omitted, UK: Panther pb). §1. Colony (1953). §2. Imposter (1953). §3. Expendable (1953). §4. Planet for Transients (1953). §5. Prominent Author (1954). §6. The Builder (1954). §7. The Little Movement (1952). §8. The Preserving Machine (1953). §9. The Impossible Planet (1953). §10. The Indefatigable Frog (1953). §11. The Turning Wheel (1954). §12. Progeny (1954). §13. Upon the Dull Earth (1954). §14. The Cookie Lady (1953). §15. Exhibit Piece (1954).

#3. The World Jones Made. 1956 (Ace pb). 1968 (UK: Sidgwick hb). 1970 (UK: Panther pb).

#4. The Man Who Japed. 1956 (Ace pb). See D9.

#5. Eye in the Sky. 1957 (Ace pb). 1971 (UK: Arrow pb). See D6.

#6. The Cosmic Puppets (1956, as A Glass of Darkness). 1957 (Ace pb).

#7. The Variable Man and Other Stories. 1957 (Ace pb). 1969 (UK: Sphere pb). §1. The Variable Man (1953). §2. Second Variety (1953). §3. The Minority Report (1956). §4. Autofac (1955). §5. A World of Talent (1954).

#8. Time out of Joint (1959-60). 1959 (Lippincott hb). 1961 (UK: SFBC hb). 1965 (Belmont pb). 1969 (UK: Penguin pb).

#9. Dr. Futurity (1954, shorter version as Time Pawn). 1960 (Ace pb). 1970 (with #19 and #21 in *A Philip K Dick Omnibus*, UK: Sidgwick 1970).

#10. Vulcan's Hammer (1956). 1960 (Ace pb).

#11. The Man in the High Castle. 1962 (Putnam hb; also Putnam hb for SFBC). 1964 (Popular pb). 1965 (UK: Penguin pb). 1974 (Berkley pb). See D20.

#12. The Game-Players of Titan. 1963 (Ace pb). 1969 (UK: Sphere pb).

#13. Martian Time-Slip (1963, shorter version as All We Marsmen). 1964 (Ballantine pb). Scheduled for 1975 (UK: Eyre Methuen SF Master Series).

#14. The Three Stigmata of Palmer Eldritch. 1964 (Doubleday hb). 1965 (Doubleday hb for SFBC). 1966 (UK: Cape hb). 1966 (Macfadden pb). 1973 (UK: Penguin pb).

#15. The Simulacra. 1964 (Ace pb).

#16. The Penultimate Truth. 1964 (Belmont pb). 1967 (UK: Cape hb).

1967 (UK: Penguin pb).

#17. Clans of the Alphane Moon. 1964 (Ace pb). See D18.

#18. Dr. Bloodmoney, or How We Got Along After the Bomb. 1965 (Ace pb). See D14.

#19. The Crack in Space (1964, shorter version as Cantata 140). 1966 (Ace pb).

#20. Now Wait for Last Year. 1966 (Doubleday hb). 1968? (Doubleday hb for SFBC). 1968 (Macfadden pb). 1974 (Manor pb).

#21. The Unteleported Man (1964). 1966 (Ace pb). See D8.

#22. Counter-Clock World. 1967 (Berkley pb). 1968 (UK: Sphere pb). See D11-12.

#23. The Zap Gun (1965-66, as Project Plowshare). 1967 (Pyramid pb). See D15.

#24. The Ganymede Takeover. With Ray Nelson. 1967 (Ace pb). 1971 (UK: Arrow pb).

#25. Do Androids Dream of Electric Sheep? 1968 (Doubleday hb). 1969 (New American Library pb). 1969 (UK: Rapp hb). 1972 (UK: Panther pb). See D9.

#26. Ubik. 1969 (Doubleday hb, also Doubleday hb for SFBC). 1970 (UK: Rapp hb). 1970 (Dell pb). See D3.

#27. The Preserving Machine and Other Stories. 1969 (Ace pb). 1970 (Ace hb for SFBC). 1971 (UK: Gollancz hb). 1972 (UK: Pan pb). See D24§3 for unpublished foreword. §1. The Preserving Machine (1953). §2. War Game (1959). §3. Upon the Dull Earth (1954). §4. Roog (1953). §5. War Veteran (1955). §6. Top Stand-By Job (1963, as Stand-By; See D21§11). §7. Beyond Lies the Wub (1952). §8. We Can Remember It For You Wholesale (1966). §9. Captive Market (1955). §10. If There Were No Benny Cemoli (1963; see D21§6). §11. Retreat Syndrome (1965; see D21§8). §12. The Crawlers (1954). §13. Oh, to Be A Blobel (1964; see D21§5). §14. What the Dead Men Say (1964; see D21§4). §15. Pay for the Printer (1956).

#28. Galactic Pot-Healer. 1969 (Berkley pb). 1971 (UK: Gollancz hb). 1972 (UK: Pan pb). See D13.

#29. A Maze of Death. 1970 (Doubleday hb). 1971 (Paperback Library pb). 1972 (UK: Gollancz hb). 1973 (UK: Pan pb).

#30. Our Friends from Frolix 8. 1970 (Ace pb). 1971 (Ace hb for SFBC). See D19.

#31. We Can Build You (1969-70, as A. Lincoln, Simulacrum). 1972 (DAW pb). See D24§5.

#32. The Book of Philip K. Dick. 1973 (DAW pb). §1. Nanny (1955). §2. The Turning Wheel (1954). §3. The Defenders (1953). §4. Adjustment Team (1954). §5. Psi-Man (1955, as Psi-Man, Heal My Child!). §6. The Commuter (1953). §7. A Present for Pat (1954). §8. Breakfast at Twilight (1954). §9. Shell Game (1954).

#33. Flow My Tears, the Policeman Said. 1974 (Doubleday hb). 1974 (UK; Gollancz hb).

#34. A Scanner Darkly. Scheduled for 1975 (Doubleday hb).

#35. Confessions of a Crap Artist. To be published by Paul Williams and David Hartwell. See D7.

#36. Jon's World. Story in *Time to Come*, ed. August Derleth (Farrar, Straus, and Giroux, 1954).

#37. Foster, You're Dead. Story in *Star Science Fiction Stories*, No. 3., ed Frederick Pohl (Ballantine pb. 1955).

#38. Faith of Our Fathers. Story in *Dangerous Visions*, ed. Harlan Ellison (Doubleday, 1967).

#39. Anthony Boucher. Requiem statement in *The Magazine of Fantasy and Science Fiction*, August 1968.

#40. The Android and the Human. Speech delivered in Vancouver, Canada, printed in *SF Commentary* #31, December 1972. See D24§6.

#41. Interview with photos, by Arthur Byron Cover. *Vertex*, February 1974.

#42. A Little Something for Us Tempunauts. Story in *Final Stage*, ed. Edward L. Ferman and Barry N. Malzberg (Charterhouse 1974, an edition repudiated by the editors; new edition scheduled by Penguin for early 1975).

#43. The Pre-Persons. Story in *The Magazine of Fantasy and Science Fiction*, October 1974.

#44. Who is a Science Fiction Writer? Essay in *Science Fiction: The Academic Awakening*, ed. Willis E. McNelly (1974, College English Association, c/o Professor Herbert V. Fackler, Department of English, University of Southwestern Louisiana, Lafayette, La. 70501, $2.00 postpaid).

Darko Suvin

P.K. Dick's Opus: Artifice as Refuge and World View (Introductory Reflections)

I would divide Dick's writing[1] into three main periods: 1952-62, 1962-65, and 1966-74. The first period is one of apprenticeship and limning of his themes and devices, first in short or longer stories (1952-56) and then in his early novels from *Solar Lottery* to *Vulcan's Hammer* (1955-60), and it culminates in the masterly polyphony of *The Man in the High Castle* (1962). Dick's second, central period stands out to my mind as a high plateau in his opus. Following on his creative breakthrough in *MHC*, it comprises (together with some less successful tries) the masterpieces of *Martian Time-Slip* and *Dr. Bloodmoney*, as well as that flawed but powerful near-masterpiece *The Three Stigmata of Palmer Eldritch*. The latest phase of Dick's writing, beginning in 1966, is in many ways a falling off. It is characterized by a turning from a fruitful tension between public and private concerns toward a simplified narration increasingly preoccupied with solitary anxieties and by a corresponding concern with unexplainable ontological puzzles; and it has clearly led to the creative sterility of 1970-74 (*We Can Build You*, though published in 1972, had appeared in magazine version by 1970). However, *Ubik* (1969), the richest and most provocative novel of this phase, testifies to the necessity for a closer analysis of even this downbeat period of Dick's. Thus, an overview of his opus can, I trust, find a certain logic in its development, but it is not a mechanical or linear logic. Dick's work, intimately influenced by and participating in the great processes of the American collective or social psychology in these last 20 years, shares the hesitations, the often irrational though always understandable leaps backwards, forwards and sideways of that psychology. It is perhaps most understandable as the work of a prose poet whose basic tools are not verse lines and poetic figures but (1) relationships within the narrative; (2) various alternate worlds, the specific political and ontological relationships in each of which are analogous to the USA (or simply to California) in the 1950's and 60's; and (3)—last not least—the vivid characters on whom his narration and his worlds finally repose. In this essay, I propose to deal with these three areas of Dick's creativity: some basic relationships in Dick's story-telling—a notion richer than though connected with, the plotting—will be explored by an analysis of narrative foci and power levels; Dick's alternate worlds will be explored in function of his increasing shift from mostly political to mostly ontological horizons; finally, Dick's allegorically exaggerated characters will be explored in their own right as fundaments for the morality and cognition in his novels.

1. PILGRIMAGE WITHOUT PROGRESS: NARRATIVE FOCI AND POWER LEVELS

> Amazing the power of fiction, even cheap popular fiction, to evoke. —*MHC* §8.

In order to illuminate the development of Dick's story-telling, I shall follow his use of characters as *narrative foci* and as indicators of *upper and lower social classes or power statuses*. The concept of narrative focus seems necessary because Dick as a rule uses a narration which is neither that of the old-fashioned all-knowing, neutral and superior, narrator, nor a narration in the first person by the central characters. The narration proceeds instead somewhere in between those two extreme possibilities, simultaneously in the third person and from the vantage point of the central or focal character in a given segment. This is always clearly delimited from other segments with other focal characters—first, by means of chapter endings or at least by double spacing within a chapter, and second, by the focal character being named at the beginning of each such narrative segment, usually after a monotony-avoiding introductory sentence or subordinate clause which sets up the time and place of the new narrative segment. The focal character is also used as a visual, auditive, and psychological focus whose vantage point in fact colours and limits the subsequent narration. This permits the empathizing into—usually sympathizing with but always at least understanding—all the focal characters, be they villains or heroes in the underlying plot conflict; which is equivalent to saying that Dick has no black or white villains and heroes in the sense of Van Vogt (from whom the abstracted plot conflicts are often borrowed). In the collective, non-individualist world of Dick, everybody, high and low, destroyer and sufferer, is in an existential situation which largely determines his/her actions; even the arch-destroyer Palmer Eldritch is a sufferer.

The novels before 1962 are approximations to such a technique of multi-focal narrative. Its lower limit-case and primitive seed, the one-hero-at-the-center narrative, is to be found in *Eye in the Sky* and, with a half-hearted try at two subsidiary foci, in *The Man Who Japed*. *Solar Lottery* has two clear foci, Benteley and Cartwright, with insufficiently sustained strivings toward a polyphonic structure (Verrick, Wakeman, Groves). Similarly, though there are half a dozen narrative foci in *Time Out of Joint*, Ragle is clearly their privileged center; in fact, the whole universe of the book has been constructed only to impinge upon him, just as all universes impinged upon the protagonist of *Eye in the Sky*. *Vulcan's Hammer* is focussed around the two bureaucrats Barris and Dill, with Marion coming a poor third; the important character of Father Fields does not become a narrative focus, as he logically should have, nor does the intelligent computer though he is similar, say, to the equally destructive and destroyed Arnie in *MTS*. However, in *MHC* there is to be found for the first time the full Dickian narrative articulation, surpassed only in *MTS* and *Dr. B*. With some simplifying of secondary characters and sub-plots, and taking into account the levels of social—here explicitly political—power, *MHC* divides into two parallel plots with these narrative foci (marked by caps, while other important characters are named in lower case):

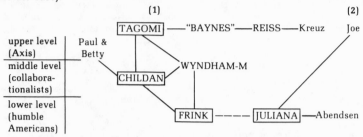

The upper level is one of politico-ethical conflict between murderous Nazi fanaticism and Japanese tolerance (the assumption that a victorious Japanese fascism would be radically better than the German one is the major political blunder of Dick's novel). In (1), the San Francisco plot, the two sympathetic focal characters are Frank Frink, the suffering refugee Jew and creative little man, and Mr. Tagomi, the ethical Japanese official. In (2), the locomotive plot, the sole focal character is Juliana. Tagomi helps "Baynes" in trying to foil the global political scheme of Nazi universal domination, and incidentally also foils the extradition of Frink to the Nazis, while Juliana foils the Nazis' (Joe's) plot to assassinate Abendsen, the SF writer of a book postulating Axis defeat in World War 2; they both turn out to be, more by instinct than by design, antagonists of the fascist politico-psychological evil. But the passive link between them is Frink, Juliana's ex-husband, and his artistic creation, the silvery pin mediating between earth and sky, life and death, past and future, the *MHC*-universe and the alternate universe of our empirical reality. Tagomi's reality-change vision in §14. induced by contemplating Frink's pin, is a Dickian set scene which recreates, through an admittedly partial narrative viewpoint, the great utopian tradition that treats a return to the reader's freeways, smog, and jukebox civilization as a vision of hell—exactly as at the end of *Gulliver's Travels*, *Looking Backward*, or *News From Nowhere*. But it is also an analogue of the vision of Abendsen's book: the book and the pin come from chthonic depths but become mediators only after being shaped by the intellect, albeit an oracular and largely instinctive one. For Dick, a writer (especially an SF writer) is always first and foremost an "artificer," both in the sense of artful craftsman and in the sense of creator of new, "artificial" but nonetheless possible worlds. Frink and Abendsen, the two artificers—one the broodingly passive but (see the diagram) centrally situated narrative focus of the book, the other a shadowy but haunting figure appearing at its close—constitute with Tagomi and Juliana, the two instinctive ethical activists, the four pillars of hope opposed to the dominant political madness of Fascism. Though most clearly institutionalized in German Nazism, it can also be found in middle-class Americans such as Childan, the rascist small shopkeeper oscillating between being a helper and a deceitful exploiter of creative artificers such as Frink.

The second or plateau period of Dick's opus retains and deepens the *MHC* narrative polyphony. It does so both by increasing the number of the narrative foci and by stressing some relationships among the focal characters as privileged, thereby making for easier overview with less redundancy and a stronger impact. The two culminations of such proceeding are *MTS* and *Dr. B.* In *MTS*, three of the focal characters stand out (underlined):

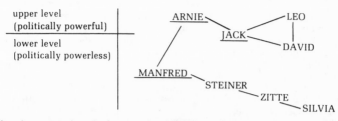

Of the three privileged characters, the labour boss Arnie is powerful and sociable, the autistic boy Manfred politically powerless and asocial, while the central character, Jack Bohlen, mediates between the two not only in his sociopolitical status but also in his fits of and struggle against psychosis. However, Jack and Manfred, the time-binding precog and the manual craftsman, are allied against the tycoon Arnie. This is the first clear expression in Dick's opus of the alliance and yet also the split between Rousseauist personal freedom, realized in Manfred's final symbiosis with the totally asocial, noble-savage Bleekmen, and an ethical communal order, implied in Jack. The politically powerless turn the tables on the powerful—as did Juliana in MHC—by means of their greater sensitivity. This allows them a much deeper understanding of people and things, inner and outer nature (which they pay for by greater suffering). Therefore, the set-piece or obligatory situation in MTS is again a visionary scene involving Manfred, Jack and Arnie in several interdependent versions of nightmarish reality-change (§§10-11).

The oppositions are aggravated and therefore explored more fully in Dr. B, Dick's narratively most sophisticated work. Nine personal narrative foci are here, astoundingly, joined by two choral groups—the secondary characters who get killed during the narrative but help decisively in Hoppy's defeat, such as Fergesson, and the post-Bomb-community secondary characters, such as June. The double division in MTS (powerful/powerless plus personal freedom/ethical order) is here richly articulated into (1) the destructive dangers which are opposed to the new prospects of life and vitality, further subdivided into (2) the search for a balanced community, and (3) the search for personal happiness. Very interestingly, Dangerfield, the mediator of practical tips and past culture, provides the link between all those who oppose the destroyers. In this most optimistic of Dick's novels, Bloodmoney's Bomb was a Happy Fall: the collapse of American sociopolitical and technological power abolishes the class distinctions, and thus makes possible a new start and innocence leading to the defeat of the new, anti-utopian would-be usurpers by the complementary forces of a new communal and personal order. These forces are aptly symbolized by the homunculus Bill—perhaps Dick's most endearing character—who is both person and symbiotic creature:

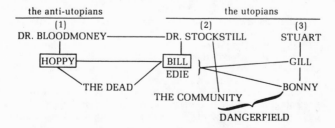

In this light, the ideological movement of the book is complete when Bonny, the all-embracing Earth Mother figure, has forsaken the old danger, Bloodmoney, and when her son Bill—coeval with the innocence and power of the new order (much as his feebler prototype, Mrs Grayles in *A Canticle for Leibowitz*)—has defeated the new danger, Hoppy. Professor Jameson identifies (in this issue) the new danger convincingly with a neo-pragmatic stance connected with modern electronics and the USA, just as the old danger was the classical mad scientist of the Dr. Strangelove type connected with nuclear physics and Germany. Jameson's essay, as well as the analyses of *MTS* by Mr. Aldiss and Professor Pagetti, make it possible to cut short here the discussion of narrative foci in these two masterpieces of Dick's. It only remains to notice that a Rousseauist utopianism cannot finally fuse personal happiness and harmonious community—at the utmost it can run them in tandem.

2. AM-WEB: POLITICS AND ONTOLOGY

> The disintegration of the social and economic system had been slow, gradual, and profound. It went so deep that people lost faith in natural law itself.—*Solar Lottery* §2.

There remains, in Dick's middle period, the important if ambiguous *3SPE*, the discussion of which will require shifting the emphasis to what are for Dick the horizons of human destiny. *3SPE* is the first significant Dick novel to allot equal weight to politics and ontology as arbiters of its microcosm and its characters' destinies. I shall deal first with politics.

Up to the mid-60's Dick could be characterized as a writer of anti-utopian SF in the wake of Orwell's *1984* and of the menacing world-war and post-Bomb horizons in the pulp "new maps of hell" by Bradbury, Heinlein, Blish and Pohl (to mention those who, together with Vanvogtian plotting and Besterian Espers, seem to have meant most to him). The horrors of Cold War politics, paranoiac militarism, mass hysteria organized by politicians, and encroaching government totalitarianism are broached in the stories of the mid-50's such as "Breakfast at Twilight," "War Veteran" or "Second Variety"; in one of the best, "Foster, You're Dead," the militarist craze for bomb-shelters is further seen as a tool for commercial twisting of the everyday life of little people. In Dick's early novels the dystopian framework is developed by adding to a look at the dominated humble people an equally inside look at the ruling circles—the telepaths and quizmasters in *Solar Lottery*, the secret police in "The Variable Man" and *The World Jones Made*, the mass-media persuaders in *The Man Who Japed*, the powerful bureaucrats in *Vulcan's Hammer*. Indeed, *Eye in the Sky* is the formalization of a literally "inside" look at four variants of dystopia, and carries the message that in the world of modern science we are all truly members of one another. Up to *3SPE*, then, the novels by Dick which are not primarily dystopian (*The Cosmic Puppets, Dr. Futurity, The Game-Players of Titan*) are best forgotten. Obversely, political dystopia has remained a kind of zero-level for Dick's writing right to the present day (e.g. in *Flow My Tears, the Policeman Said*), at times even explicitly connecting the early stories to the later second-line novels by taking over a story's theme or situation and developing it into the novel's mainstay (e.g. "The Defenders" and *The Penultimate Truth*, or "Shell Game" and *Clans of the Alphane Moon*).

The culmination and transmutation of political horizons occurs in Dick's "plateau tetralogy," from *MHC* to *Dr. B. MHC*, with its superb feel of Nazi psychology and of life in a world of occupiers, occupied, and quislings overshadowed by it, is the high point of Dick's explicitly political anti-utopianism. Paradoxically if precariously balanced by ethical optimism, it is, because of that confident balance and richness, in some ways Dick's most lucid book. It is also the first culmination of the Germanic-paranoia-turning-fascist theme which has been haunting Dick as no other American SF writer (with the possible exception of Vonnegut) since "The Variable Man" with its Security Commissioner Reinhart, and the seminal *Man Who Japed* with its German-American Big Brother in the person of Major Jules Streiter, founder of the Moral Reclamation movement. The naming of this shadowy King Anti-Utopus is an excellent example for Dick's ideological onomastics: it compounds allusions to the names and doctrines of Moral Rearmament's Buchman, Social Credit's Major Douglas, and the fanatic Nazi racist Julius Streicher. The liberalism of even the seemingly most hard-nosed dystopian SF in the American 1940's-50's, with its illusions of Back to the Spirit of 1776, pales into insignificance beside Dick's pervasive, intimate and astoundingly rich understanding of the affinities between German and American fascism, born of the same social classes of big speculators and small shopkeepers. This understanding is embodied in a number of characters who span the death-lust spectrum between political and psychological threat. Beginning with the wholly American Childan (who is, correspondingly, a racist out of insecurity rather than fanaticism, and is allowed a positive conversion) and the German assassin Joe masquerading as an American in *MHC*, through Norbert Steiner and Otto Zitte as well as the vaguely Teutonic-American corrupt bigwigs Leo Bohlen and Arnie Kott in *MTS*, such a series culminates in Dr. Bruno Bluthgeld/Bloodmoney (descended from Von Braun, Teller, et sim., both through newspapers and through Kubrick's mad German scientist Dr. Strangelove). It finally leads to a German takeover of the Western world by means of their industries and androids in *The Simulacra*, and of the whole planet through the UN in *The Unteleported Man*. In this last novel, the revelation that UN boss Horst Bertold (whose name and final revelatory plea are derived from Bertolt Brecht, the anti-fascist German whose name would be most familiar to the music and drama lover Dick) is a "good" German, on the same side of the political fence as the hounded little man Rachmael ben Applebaum, effects a reconciliation of powerful German and powerless Jew.

These politico-national roles or clichés had started poles apart in *MHC*. But by the end of Dick's German-Nazi theme and cycle the year was 1966, and the sensitive author quite rightly recognized that the world, and in particular the USA, had other fish to fry: the ubiquitous fascist menace was no longer primarily German or anti-Jewish. Already in *MTS*, the lone German killers Steiner and Zitte were small fry compared to the Americans of Teutonic descent Leo and Arnie. In *Dr. B*, therefore, the Bluthgeld menace is supplanted by the deformed American obstinately associated with the product of Bluthgeld's fallout—the Ayn Rand follower and cripple Hoppy, wired literally up to his teeth into the newest electronic death-dealing gadgets. Clearly, Bluthgeld relates to Hoppy as the German-associated World-War-2 and Cold-War technology of the 1940's and 50's to the Vietnam-War technology of the 60's. It is the same relation as the one between the Nazi-treated superman Bulero and the reality manipulator Eldritch, and finally between the Krupps and Heydrichs of *MHC* and the military-industrial complex of American capitalism: "it was Washington that was dropping the bombs on [the American people], not the Chinese or the Russians" (*Dr. B* §5). The transformation or transubstantiation of classical European fascism into new American power is also the theme of two significant stories Dick wrote in the 60's, "If There Were no Benny Cemoli" (read—Benito Mussolini) and

"Oh, To Be A Blobel" (where an American tycoon turns Alien while his humbler employee wife turns human). The third significant story, "What the Dead Men Say"—which stands halfway between *3SPE* and *Ubik*—features half-life as a non-supernatural hoax by American economic and political totalitarians on the make.

By the *MTS* phase, Dick's little man is being opposed not only to political and technological but also to economic power in the person of the rival tycoons Leo (representing a classical big speculators' syndicate) and Arnie (whose capital comes from control of big trade-union funds), while on the horizon of both Terra and Mars there looms the big cooperative movement, whose capital comes from investments of members. In the corrupt microcosm of *MTS* these three variants of capitalism (classical laissez-faire, bureaucratic, and demagogically managerial), together with the state capitalism of the superstate UN disposing of entire planets, constitute what is almost a brief survey of its possible forms. The slogan of the big cooperative-capitalist movement, which Manfred sees crowning his horrible vision of planetary future in decay, is AM-WEB, explained in Dick's frequent record-jacket German as "Alle Menschen werden Brüder"—"All men become brothers" (from Schiller through Beethoven's Ninth). But of course this explanation is half true and half disingenuous—the proper acronym for the slogan would, after all, be AMWB with no "E" and no hyphen. Thus, within Dick's normative Germano-American parallelism, AM-WEB is also, and even primarily, an emblem of the ironic reversal of pretended liberty, fraternity, and equality—it is the *American Web* of big business, corrupt labour aristocracy, and big state that turn the difficult everyday life of the little man into a future nightmare. As Mr. Aldiss remarks in this issue, the whole of *MTS*—and beyond that, most of Dick—is a maledictory web. The economico-political spider spinning it is identified with a clarity scarcely known in American SF between Jack London's Oligarchy and Ursula Le Guin's Propertarians. The Rousseauist utopianism of *Dr. B* is an indication that the urge to escape this cursed web is so deep it would almost welcome an atomic holocaust as a chance to start anew: "We are, Adams realized, a cursed race. Genesis is right; there is a stigma on us, a mark" (*The Penultimate Truth*, §13).

The three stigmata of Palmer Eldritch, the interplanetary industrialist who peddles dope to enslave the masses, are three signs of demonic artificiality. The prosthetic eyes, hands, and teeth, allow him—in a variant of the Wolf in Little Red Riding Hood—to see (understand), grab (manipulate), and rend (ingest, consume) his victims better. Like the tycoon in "Oh, To Be A Blobel," this eldritch palmer or uncanny pilgrim towards the goal of universal market domination is clearly a "mad capitalist" (to coin a term parallel to mad scientist), a miraculous organizer of production wasted through absence of rational distribution (§1) who turned Alien on a power trip. But his peculiar terrifying force is that he turns his doped manipulees not only into a captive market (see Dick's early story of that title) but also into partial, stigmatized replicas of himself by working through their ethical and existential weaknesses. The Palmer Eldritch type of super-corporative capitalism is in fact a new religion, stronger and more pervasive than the classical transcendental ones, because "GOD PROMISES ETERNAL LIFE. WE CAN DELIVER IT," (§9). What it delivers, though, is not only a new thing under the Sun but also false, activating the bestial or alien inhumanity within man: "And—we have no mediating sacraments through which to protect ourselves.... It [the Eldritch Presence] is out in the open, ranging in every direction. It looks into our eyes; and it looks out of our eyes" (§13). Dick moves here along jungle trails first blazed by William S. Burroughs: for both, the hallucinatory operators are real.

The narrative structure of *3SPE* combines multifocality with a privileged protagonist-antagonist (Mayerson-Eldritch) axis and with the division into power levels:

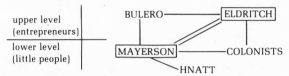

However, the erstwhile normal conflict between the upper and the lower social levels is here superseded by the appearance of a new-type antagonist, Eldritch, who snares not only the little people—Mayerson and other Mars colonists—but also the established power of Bulero, and indeed subverts the whole notion of monadic, Individualistic characters of the 19th Century kind upon which Dick's, like most other, SF had so far reposed. The appearance of Eldritch, signalized by his stigmata, *inside* the other characters shifts the conflict into their psyches—can they trust their reality perceptions? The political theme and horizon begin here to give way to the ontological. While the ontological dilemmas have a clear genesis in the political ones, they shift the power relationships from human institutions to mysterious entities, never quite accounted for or understood in the narration. *3SPE* is thus that first significant station in Dick's development where the ontological preoccupations begin to weigh as heavily as, or more heavily than, the political dystopianism.

Such preoccupations can, no doubt, be found in Dick's writing right from the beginning. "Foster, You're Dead," the story of a boy alienated by conformist social pressures, is already halfway between Pohl's satires (it was published by Pohl in *Star SF 3*) and the suffering alienated boy Manfred in *MTS* who erects an alternative reality as refuge, and can serve as a key to Dick's theme of mental alienation connected with reality changes. Parallel to that, "Adjustment Team" is a first tentative try at evolving the "Tunnel Under the World" situation of total manipulation—also the kernel of *3SPE*—toward metaphysics. The mysterious failure of memory, or missing interval of consciousness accompanied by headache, which is a sign of dissolving realities and is often found in combination with drug-taking, recurs from *The Man Who Japed* through *MTS* to *3SPE*. Tagomi's great vision in *MHC* and Manfred's AM-WEB vision in *MTS* can already be interpreted not only as trance-like insights but also as actual changes in collective reality. These are changes in being (ontological, as already in *Eye in the Sky*) rather than only in foreknowledge (gnoseological, as in *The World Jones Made*) or, even more simply, fraudulent-cum-psychotic ones (as in *Time Out of Joint*). Indeed, the story-telling microcosms, the depicted planetary realities of both *MHC* and *MTS*, are analogies for reality changes immanent in the author's here-and-now and already showing through it, like Eldritch's stigmata. *MHC* is an alternative world explicating a California, USA, and globe fallen prey to fascism. *MTS* substitutes the more general physical category of entropy for its political particular case; Dick's Mars is a run-down future, "a sort of Humpty-Dumpty" where people and things have decayed "into rusty bits and useless debris" (§6), a space and time leading—in ironic repudiation of Bradbury's nostalgia for the petty-bourgeois past and Clarke's confidence in liberal scientism—to the dialectical interplay between Manfred's devolutionary vision of "gubble" (rubble, rubbish, crumble, gobble) invading everybody's reality and vitality and Jack's struggle against it. The totalitarian manipulation and the entropic human relations are to be found in *3SPE* together with and flowing into a false, profit-making religion.

However, the shift from politics to ontology, which was only hinted at in *MHC* and will culminate in *Ubik*, is in *3SPE* not consistent. The referents of this lush novel are over-determined: Eldritch, the allegorical representative of neo-capitalism, is at the same time the bearer of an "evil, negative trinity of alienation, blurred reality and despair" (§13) of demonic though unclear origin. An orthodox religious and an orthodox politico-economic reading of *3SPE* can both be fully supported by the evidence of the novel; but neither of these complementary and yet in some ways basically contradictory readings can explain the full novel—which is to boot overburdened with quite unnecessary elements such as Mayerson's precog faculties, the garden-variety theological speculations, etc. Politics, physics and metaphysics combine to create in *3SPE* a fascinating and iridescent manifold, but their interference also, to my mind, makes for an insufficiently economical novel. It starts squarely within the political and physical field (clash of big drug corporations, temperature rise, colonization of Mars) and then drags across it the red herring of ontologico-religious speculations grafted upon Vanvogtian plot gimmicks (here from Leigh Brackett's *The Big Jump*, 1955) which shelve rather than solve the thematic problems.

3. ALL WE MARSMEN: CHARACTEROLOGY AS MORALITY AND COGNITION

> We do not have the ideal world, such as we
> would like, where morality is easy because
> cognition is easy. —*MHC* §15.

In Dick's anthropology, the differentiation between upper and lower politico-economic power statuses is correlative to a system of correspondences between profession, as relating to a specific type of creativity, and ethical goodness or evil. This reposes on a more general view of human nature and species-specific human conduct, for which morality and cognition are closely allied, and which will be discussed in this section. Such an alliance breaks down in *Ubik*; this is to my mind the explanation of Dick's difficulties after 1966.

From Dick's earliest writings, aggressiveness is identified not only with militarism but also with commercialism (as in "Nanny"), and villainy with either totalitarian or capitalist rulers (as in "A Present for Pat," and in the stories of the 60's mentioned in section 2). Opposed to the unscrupulous tycoons and other bigwigs (Verrick in *Solar Lottery*, the terrifying roster of Führer candidates in *MHC*, Leo Bohlen and Arnie Kott in *MTS*, Leo Bulero and Palmer Eldritch in *3SPE*, the Yancy Men in *The Penultimate Truth*, etc.) are the little people. The two ends of the politico-economic and power scale relate as "havenots" to "titans" (*The Unteleported Man* §4), but also as creators to destroyers. For, Dick's protagonists are as a rule some variant of immediate producer or direct creator. They are not industrial workers engaged in collective production—a class conspicuous by its absence here as in practically all modern SF. On the contrary, Dick's heroes are most often the new individual craftsmen, producers of art objects or repairmen of the most sophisticated (e.g. cybernetic) Second-Industrial-Revolution products. They are updated versions of the old-fashioned handyman (who is celebrated in the "Fixit-cart," non-statistical, unquantifiable, "variable man" of the eponymous story) for a contemporary, or near-future, highly industrialized society; and their main trait is a direct and personalized relationship to creative productivity as opposed to standardized mass-production with its concomitant other-directedness, loss of self-reliance, and shoddy living (a key to this is to be found in the story "Pay for the Printer," a finger-exercise for *Dr. B*).

This characterology is not yet quite clear in the earlier novels, which deal more with the Ibsenian theme of social deceit versus individual struggle for truth than with the theme of destruction vs. creation. Of *Solar Lottery's* two heroes one, Benteley, is a classical "cadre," a biochemist, and only the other, Cartwirght, is "electronics repairman and human being with a conscience" (§2). Similarly, the hero of *Eye in the Sky* turns only at the end of the book from chief of missile lab to builder of phonographs, switching from Dick's chief dislike, militarism, to his chief love, music. But already in his early works there appears a populist or indeed New Left tendency to distrust rational intelligence, contaminated as it is by its association with "the cult of the Technocrat...run by and for those oriented around verbal knowledge" (*Vulcan's Hammer* §14), and to oppose to it spontaneous action guided by intuition—a politics of the "do your own thing" type. Thus, in *Time Out of Joint* Ragle is a creative personality who dislikes the nine-to-five drudgery of the huge conformist organizations, regimented like armies (§1), and who can "sense the pattern" of events through his artistic abilities (§14). Though the traces of this dichotomy can be felt even in the *MHC* heroes Tagomi and Frink—who are juxtaposed as mind and hand, intellectual visionary from the upper power level and intuitive creator from the powerless depths—it is fortunately absent from his most mature creations, the "plateau masterpieces" in which his ethico-professional pattern of characters emerges most clearly. In *MTS*, Steiner and Zitte are small speculators who exploit the work of others, just as the small shopkeeper Childan in *MHC* exploited the creativity of the artificer Jew-Gentile pair, Frink and McCarthy; like him, Steiner and Zitte are unable to face reality and so resort to sexual fantasies alternating with suicidal/homicidal moods. At the other end of the power scale, Arnie fuses the financial role of big speculator, represented in pure form by Leo, with Zitte's role of sexual exploiter.

This quasi-robotic role of a sexually efficient but emotionally uncommitted *macho*, for Dick an ethical equivalent of economic exploitation, is to be found in his negative characters from the android of "Second Variety" to such "titans" as Verrick in *Solar Lottery* or Arnie in *MTS* who use their female employees and mistresses as pawns in power manoeuvers. Opposed to them are the sincere little people, here the repairman Jack Bohlen, who fight their way through the sexual as well as the economic jungle step by laborious step. In *3SPE*, the character spread runs from the capitalist destroyer Eldritch to the suffering artist-creator Emily; and the central hero Mayerson's fall from grace begins by his leaving Emily for success's sake and is consummated when he refuses her creations for personal revenge, thus becoming an impediment to human creativity and falling into the clutches of Eldritch's false creations. Emily's husband Hnatt is midway between her and Mayerson: he is her co-worker, the vendor of her products, but his ambiguous position in the productive process finally brings about his creative regression in the novel's rather underdeveloped sub-plot of false creativity through forced intellectual evolution (this sub-plot is carried by Bulero, the old-fashioned tycoon). Similarly, in *The Penultimate Truth* the weak and less sympathetic characters are the wordsmiths who have forsaken personal creativity to be abused for the purposes of a regressive political apparatus (Lindblom). This novel divides into two plots, the ruling-class and the subterranean one. The first centers, alas, around a Vanvogtian immortal and the intrigue from *The House That Stood Still* (1950), marring one of Dick's potentially most interesting books. For the hero of the other plot, Nick, is the democratically elected president of an oppressed community, whose creativity is manifested by political persistence in securing the rights of an endangered member. Thus, Dick's concept of creativity, though it centers on artists, encompasses both erotical and political creative ethics.

Beside the professional roles, Dick has three basic female roles, also clearly present in *3SPE* as Roni, Emily, and Anne around Mayerson. The first role is that of castrating bitch, a female *macho*, striving to rise in the corporative power-world (also Kathy in *Now Wait for Last Year*, Pris in *We Can Build You*, etc.); the second that of weak but stabilizing influence (also Silvia in *MTS*, etc.); and the third, crowning one that of a strong but warm sustaining force. Although Dick's female characters seem less fully developed than his male ones, such an Earth Mother becomes the final embodiment of ethical and political rightness in his most hopeful novels, *MHC* and *Dr. B* (Juliana and Bonny); conversely, the Bitch is developed with increasing fascination in his third phase.

As suggested above, the totally unethical and therefore inhuman person is often an android, what Dick, with a stress on its counterfeiting and artificial aspect, calls a *simulacrum* (see his very instructive Vancouver speech in *SF Commentary* #31). Already in his first novel, this is associated with modern science being manipulated by power-mad people, who are themselves the truly reified inhumans and therefore in a way more unauthentic than their simulacra. An interesting central anthropological tenet is adumbrated here, halfway between Rousseau and Marx, according to which there is an *authentic core* identical with humanity in Homo sapiens, from which men and women have to be alienated by civilizational pressures in order to behave in an unauthentic, dehumanized way, so that there is always an inner resistance to such pressures in anybody who simply follows his or her human(e) instinct of treating people as ends, not means. That is why Dick's heroes rely on instinct and persistence (several of them, such as Jack in *MTS* or Nick in *The Penultimate Truth* are characterized as permanently "going to keep trying"). That is why social class is both a functionally decisive and yet not an exclusive criterion for determining the humanity of the characters: the more powerful one is, the more dehumanized one becomes, and Dick's only real heroes tend to be the creative little people, with the addition of an occasional visionary; yet even the literally dehumanized alien such as Eldritch has inextinguishable remnants of humanity within him which qualify him for suffering, and thus for the reader's partial, dialectical sympathy for his (now alienated) human potentialities. That is why, finally, there emerges the strange and charmingly grotesque Dickian world of semi-animated cybernetic constructs, which makes stretches of even his weaker novels enjoyable light reading: e.g. the fly-size shrilling commercial and the hypnotic surrogate-"papoola" of *The Simulacra*, the Lazy Brown Dog reject carts in *Now Wait for Last Year*, the stupid elevators and grumpy cybernetic taxis such as Max the auto-auto in *The Game-Players of Titan*, etc. Together with a few interesting aliens, the all-too-human inhumans culminate in the menace of *3SPE* and in Dick's richest spectrum of creatures in *Dr. B*, which runs from the stigmatic psi-powers of Bluthgeld and cyborg booster-devices of Hoppy to the zany and appealing new life-cycle of homeostatic traps and evolved animals. At the center of *Dr. B* is the homunculus Bill, who is in touch with humans, animals and even the dead, and unites the kinaesthetic and verbal powers in the universe of that novel.

I have left *Ubik* for the end of this discussion both because it seems to me Dick's last major work to date and because in it the analogies between morality and cognition suffer a sea-change. The Dickian narrative model, as discussed in this essay, is in *Ubik* extremely simplified and then recomplicated by being twisted into a new shape. The character types remain the same and thus link the new model with Dick's earlier work: the bitch Pat, the redeemer Ella, the bewildered old-fashioned tycoon Runciter, the shadowy illusion creator Jory, losing in precision but gaining in domination in comparison to Eldritch, and, most important, the buffeted but persistent *schlemiel* Joe Chip. But the shift from social to ontological horizons around the axis connecting the two main narrative foci of Runciter and Chip results in a world without stable centers or peripheries, where the main problem is to find out who is inside and who outside the unstable circles of narrative consciousness, liable to an infinite receding series of contaminations from other—often only guessed at—such centers. The characterological equivalent of this uncertainty is the half-life, a loss of sovereignty over one's microcosm. After the explosion on the Moon, is Chip, or Runciter, or neither, or both in that state? The most all-embracing explanation would be that both are in the moratorium with different degrees of control, and acted on by the rival forces of destruction and redemption of Jory and Ella. However, no explanation will explain this novel, about which I have to differ fundamentally with what seem to me the one-sided praises of Dr. Lem and Professor Fitting in this issue. No doubt, as they convincingly point out, *Ubik* is a heroic effort with great strengths, particularly in portraying the experiences of running down, decay, and senility, the invasion of entropy into life and consciousness, amid which the little man yet carries on: *impavidum ferient ruinae*. This experience of manipulated worlds, so characteristic of all our lives, is expressed by a verbal richness manifest, first, in a whole fascinating cluster of neologisms connected with the half-life, and second, in the delicious satire centered on the thing Ubik—the principle of food, health, and preservation of existence, of anti-entropic energy—which is promoted in kitschy ad terms parodying the unholy capitalist alliance of science, commercialism, and religious blasphemy. Dick's basic concern with death and rebirth, or to put it briefly with *transubstantiation*, has here surfaced perhaps more clearly than anywhere else in his opus. Yet it seems to me that—regardless of how far one would be prepared to follow Dick's rather unclear religious speculations—there is a serious loss of narrative control in *Ubik*. The "psi-powers" signifier has here become not only unnecessary but positively stultifying—e.g., has anybody in the book ever got back on the original time-track after Pat's first try-out?; did Pat engineer also her own death? etc. Further questions arise later: why isn't Pat wired out of the common circuit in the moratorium?; why isn't Jory?; etc. There is a clumsy try at subsidiary narrative foci with Vogelsang and Tippy (§§1 and 5); Jory "east" Wendy just when Pat was supposed to have done it; etc. The net result seems to me one of great strengths balanced by equally great weaknesses in a narrative irresponsibility reminiscent of the rabbits-from-the-hat carelessness associated with rankest Van Vogt if not "Doc" Smith: the false infinities of explaining one improbability by a succession of ever greater ones.

The deconstruction of bourgeois rationality for which Professor Fitting argues seems thus not to result in a new form but in a nihilistic collapse into the oldest mystifying forms of SF melodrama, refurbished, and therefore rendered more virulent, by some genuinely interesting new experiences. This is, of course, not without correlation to Dick's ideologies after the mid-60's, his drug-taking experiences, and his (often very ingenious) God-constructions; and one must assume that this was validated by the feeblest and least useful aspects of the late-60's counterculture, by the mentality despising reason, logic, and order of any kind—old or new. Thus, the heroic effort of *Ubik* seems to me, in spite of its many incidental felicities, to be the *3SPE* experience writ large: in some ways among the most fascinating SF books of its time, it is finally, I fear, a heroic failure. In art, at least (and I would maintain in society too), there is no freedom without order, no liberation without controlled focussing. A morality cut off from cognition becomes arbitrary; as Dick's own words in the epigraph to this section imply, it becomes in fact impossible.

My argument may perhaps gain some additional strength if it is accepted that Dick's writing around and after *Ubik* has not been on the order of his first-rate novels. From *Now Wait for Last Year* on, it has withdrawn from the earlier richness into an only fragmentary use of his already established model, it has centered on one protagonist and his increasingly private and psychoanalytic problems, or, as the other side of the same coin, on a Jungian collective unconscious. In *We Can Build You*, e.g., the erstwhile characteristic Dickian theme of the simulacrum Lincoln is left to fizzle out in favour of the Jungian theme of Pris—though the conjuring up of the past probity from the heroic age of the U.S. bourgeoisie against its present corruption cries out for more detailed treatment. While the touch of the master shows in incidental elements of these late novels (e.g., the comics society of *The Zap Gun*, or the imitations of Chaplin's *Great Dictator* in *Now Wait for Last Year*) there are also outright failures, such as *Do Androids Dream of Electric Sheep?*, with its underlying confusion between androids as wronged lower class and as inhuman menace. Indeed, Dick's last novel, *Flow My Tears....*, raises to my mind seriously the question whether he is going to continue writing SF or change to "realistic" prose, for its properly SF elements (future Civil War, the reality-changing drug, the "sixes") are quite perfunctory in comparison to its realistic police-state situations.

4. THE TIME IS OUT OF JOINT: INSTEAD OF A CONCLUSION

> "Oh no," Betty disagreed, "no science in it. Science fiction deals with future, in particular future where science had advanced over now. Book fits neither premise."
>
> "But," Paul said, "it deals with alternate present. Many well-known science fiction novels of that sort." —MHC §7.

A number of very tempting subjects have to be left undiscussed here: the uses and transubstantiations of stimuli from movies and music (especially vocal music concerned with transcending the empirical world, e.g. in Bach, Wagner, or Verdi); the uses of literature—from Shakespeare, Aesop, and Ibsen through Hemingway, Wells, Orwell and the comics to the SF of the 40's and 50's; the strange co-existence of dazzling verbal invention with sloppiness and crudities; etc. Also, no conclusion will be attempted here. That would be rather an impertinence in the case of a writer hopefully only in the middle of his life's path, who has grown and changed several times so startlingly, outstripping consistently most of his critics (so that he will, hopefully, also prove my gloomy opinions about his latest phase wrong). For a conclusion, the reader is referred to this whole issue, and to a re-reading of Dick. But instead of it, I would like to indicate that in his very imperfections Dick seems typical. All his near futures and alternate presents are parabolic mirrors for our time, which he has always deeply felt to be out of joint. His political acumen was a good dozen years in advance of his fellow-Americans, not so much because he mentions Nixon both as President and as FBI Chief in his earliest works as because, for example, in his first novel he asked: "But what are you supposed to do in a society that's corrupt? Are you supposed to obey corrupt laws? Is it a crime to break a rotten law...?" (§14). His ontologico-religious speculations, while to my mind less felicitous, have the merit of taking to some logical SF limits the preoccupations a great number of people have tried to express in more timid ways. It is when Dick's view is trained both on Society and Reality in their impact upon human relationships, with the ontology still clearly grounded in the sociology, that I believe Dick's major works, from *MHC* to *Dr. B*, have been written. His concerns with alienation and reification, with one-dimensional humans, parallel in SF terms the concerns of a whole generation, expressed in writings such as those of Marcuse or Laing. His concerns with a social organization based on direct human relations parallel the movements for a radical democracy from the Berkeley Free Speech movement (the scene of his most fully utopian work, *Dr. B*) to the abortive youth-New Left movement of the late 60's. His deep intuitive feeling for decline and entropy raises the usual Spenglerian theatrics of space-opera SF to the "Humpty-Dumpty" landscapes of *MTS*, *3SPE* and *Ubik*. He always speaks directly out of and to the American experience of his generation, most so when he uses the parabolic mirror of Germans and Nazis. He has the strengths and limitations of his existential horizons, which are identical to that of his favourite hero—the artificer, including the verbal craftsman. His books are artefacts, refuges from and visions of reality—as are Abendsen's book *The Grasshopper Lies Heavy* in *MHC* and Lederman's *Pilgrim Without Progress* in *3SPE*. In fact, only a fiction writer could have embarked on the Pirandellian ontology of *Ubik*, whose characters search not only for their Author but also for their world. Explicating the message in terms of the form, half a dozen works by Dick, at least, are SF classics. That is equivalent to saying that they are significant humanistic literature.

NOTE

[1]The chronology of Dick's *publications*, taking into account only his books, looks as follows (S means stories collected or otherwise published in books, namely ##2, 7, 27, 32, 36, 37, 38, and 42 in R.D. Mullen's bibliography in this issue, with the lead story from #7 somewhat arbitrarily classified as a novel; N means novels; the 1967 *Ganymede Take-Over*, written in collaboration, is counted as one half of a novel and will not be further considered here):

	1952	1953	1954	1955	1956	1957	1958	1959	1960	1961	1962
S	2	12	13	6	2	--	--	1	--	--	--
N	--	--	--	1	2	3	--	1	2	--	1

	1963	1964	1965	1966	1967	1968	1969	1970	1971	1972	1973	1974
S	2	2	1	1	1	--	--	--	--	--	--	1
N	1	5	1	3	2½	1	3	1	--	1	--	1

Though I rather enjoy some of Dick's stories, from "The Preserving Machine" (1953) and "Nanny" (1955) to "Oh To Be a Blobel" (1964), they are clearly secondary to his novels, where the themes of the most interesting stories are developed more fully. The novel format allows Dick to develop his peculiar strength of alternate-world creation by means of arresting characters counterposed to each other in cunningly wrought plots. Therefore, after 1956 Dick returned to writing notable stories only in his peak 1962-65 period; his later tries at forcing himself to write them are not too successful, e.g. the story in *Dangerous Visions* (though I have not read his 1974 story yet). In this article I shall concentrate on discussing his novels.

The most frequently used titles of Dick's will be abbreviated, after their first mention, as follows: *MHC* for *The Man in the High Castle*, *MTS* for *Martian Time-Slip*, *3SPE* for *The Three Stigmata of Palmer Eldritch*, and *Dr. B* for *Dr. Bloodmoney*.

My thanks for help in procuring books by Dick are due to Professor Fredric Jameson, Mr. L.W. Currey, Mr. Martinas Ycas, and to Doubleday and Co. for *Flow My Tears, the Policeman Said*; and for first forcing me to look closer at Dick to Ms. Allison Gopnik, McGill student. I have also profited from all the other contributions to this issue, both where I largely agree (as with Professor Jameson) and where I largely disagree (as with Dr. Lem and Professor Fitting).

Philip K. Dick

(Unpublished) Foreword to *The Preserving Machine*

The difference between a short story and a novel comes to this: a short story may deal with a murder; a novel deals with the murderer, and his actions stem from a psyche which, if the writer knows his craft, he has previously presented. The difference, therefore, between a novel and a short story is not length; for example, William Styron's *The Long March* is now published as a "short novel" whereas originally in *Discovery* it was published as a "long story." This means that if you read it in *Discovery* you are reading a story, but if you pick up the paperback version you are reading a novel. So much for that.

There is one restriction in a novel not found in short stories: the requirement that the protagonist be liked enough or familiar enough to the reader so that, whatever the protagonist does, the readers would also do, under the same circumstances...or, in the case of escapist fiction, would like to do. In a story it is not necessary to create such a reader identification character because (one) there is not enough room for such background material in a short story and (two) since the emphasis is on the deed, not the doer, it really does not matter—within reasonable limits, of course—*who* in a story commits the murder. In a story, you learn about the characters from what they do; in a novel it is the other way around: you have your characters and then they do something idiosyncratic, emanation from their unique natures. So it can be said that events in a novel are unique—not found in other writings; but the same events occur over and over again in stories, until, at last, a sort of code language is built up between the reader and the author. I am not sure that this is bad by any means.

Further, a novel—in particular the SF novel—creates an entire world, with countless petty details—petty, perhaps, to the characters in the novel, but vital for the reader to know, since out of these manifold details his comprehension of the entire fictional world is obtained. In a story, on the other hand, you are in a future world when soap operas come at you from every wall in the room...as Ray Bradbury once described. That one fact alone catapulted the story out of mainstream fiction and into SF.

What a SF story really requires is the *initial premise* which cuts it off entirely from our present world. This break must be made in the reading of, and the writing of, *all* good fiction...a made-up world must be presented. But there is much more pressure on an SF writer, for the break is far greater than in, say, "Paul's Case" or "Big Blonde"—two varieties of mainstream fiction which will always be with us.

It is in SF stories that SF action occurs; it is in SF novels that worlds occur. The stories in this collection are a series of events. Crisis is the key to story-writing, a sort of brinkmanship in which the author mires his characters in happenings so sticky as to seem impossible of solution. And then he gets them out...usually. He *can* get them out; that's what matters. But in a novel the actions are so deeply rooted in the personality of the main character that to extricate him the author would have to go back and rewrite his character. This need not happen in a story, especially a short one (such long, long stories as Thomas Mann's *Death in Venice* are, like the Styron piece, really short novels). The implication of all this makes clear why some SF writers can write stories but not novels, or novels but not stories. It is because *anything* can happen in a story; the author merely tailors his character to the event. So, in terms of actions and events, the story is far less restrictive to the author than is a novel. As a writer builds up a novel-length piece it slowly begins to imprison him, to take away his freedom; his own characters are taking over and doing what they want to do—not what he would like them to do. This is on one hand the strength of the novel and on the other, its weakness.

When I look over this collection of my stories I can see what has been lost to me in the several years of strictly novel writing. These stories range in time and space; situations bubble up to the surface; characters struggle, and then the struggle is resolved and a new story begins. Relationships are made, broken. Persons appear, speak their piece, and then go away. The momentum of writing fades out briefly and then a new cast of people, and a new crisis, materializes.

In choosing these particular stories, Terry Carr has done a superb job. To start with he read the stories which I supplied as my idea of what a collection of Philip K. Dick stories ought to be like. Terry, however, went to incalculable trouble in getting together *all* my published stories; it took four years of work for him to finalize on the stories here contained. It includes, for example, the first story I ever sold: "Roog," to Tony Boucher's *F & SF*. It contains my first published story, "Beyond Lies the Wub." Then there are middle period stories such as "Pay for the Printer," "War Veteran," "Upon the Dull Earth." And, at last, recent stories, such as "If There Were no Benny Cemoli," "What the Dead Men Say," or "We Can Remember It for You Wholesale."

It would not be politic for me to say that I think this is a "superb collection by a master craftsman of the field," as the blurbs say about one author after another. What I do think—and want to say—is this. No better collection of my stories could be made. Terry Carr missed nothing. I myself—I couldn't have done as well. It contains stories from every period of my writing, which covers a period of seventeen years. It is, to be blunt, definitive. (An English collection which appeared a number of years ago was decidedly not.) A brilliant editor can do so much to help an author, more than the reader realizes. "I must have read three hundred thousand words by you," Terry told me when the collection was half finished. I wonder how many it finally come to.

One more thing: I would like to list my favorite two or three stories in the book. To me, "Beyond Lies the Wub" is pleasing; then "If There Were no Benny Cemoli," and finally "The Preserving Machine," which, like "Roog," was a very early story (1952) that I sold to Tony Boucher.

Tony Boucher—what is the field going to do without him? It was his encouragement that got me to try submitting my stories; I had never imagined that they might sell. Consider this collection as dedicated to Tony and everything he represented. We shall never see another of his like. *Te amo*, Tony. Forever.

Carlo Pagetti

Dick and Meta-SF

Translated by Angela Minchella and D. Suvin

Some years ago I wrote that "in an obsessive crescendo, Dick's fiction is increasingly becoming a reflection on the subjective nature of reality, culminating in The Man in the High Castle (the disintegration of history) and The
Three Stigmata of Palmer Eldritch (the disintegration of planetary reality)."[1]
The first of these dates back to 1962; the second, together with The Simulacra
and Martian Time-Slip, is from 1964; indeed, the period 1962-64 can perhaps
be considered the highest moment in Dick's fiction both in the quality of
the works and the richness of their motifs. At this time Dick reached a
maturity—as did, incidentally, Anglo-American SF in general: Robert Sheckley's Journey Beyond Tomorrow and J.G. Ballard's The Drowned World appeared in 1962, Kurt Vonnegut's Cat's Cradle in 1963, etc. From the very beginning, Dick's extraordinary narrative skill is manifested in his ability to
adapt the principal themes and conventions of the Ameridan SF tradition to
his own basically tragic and pessimistic conception of reality and of American society. All the motifs that can be traced from Dick's first short stories
and novels, dating back to the early 1950s—the perfect mechanisms that prevail over man and take over his functions, the presence of mutants or of men
endowed with extrasensory qualities, the ruthless struggle for power in
which the dictatorial leaders of the future are engaged—are undoubtedly
drawn from the works of Asimov, Van Vogt, Heinlein. Nonetheless, there is
a subtle deviation in respect to their conception, a difference in the use of
these motifs, which is both critical interpretaions and personal probing. The
anthropomorphic robots of Asimov become in Dick images of an incubus un-
bounded by any simplisitc "robotic laws"; the prodigious mutants of Van
Vogt are transformed into human beings tortured by the awareness of a
useless struggle against fate; and Heinlein's supermen, no longer at the center
of the representation, are reduced to supporting roles and presented from
the point of view of the hunblest of characters. Reality being no longer one,
"objective," it is extremely difficult to find in Dick one protagonist acting as
privileged mediator between author and reader. Points of view are different,
fragmentary, often contradictory to each other. In Martian Time-Slip, for
example, the survivors of the ancient Martian civilization are seen through
the compassionate eyes of Jack Bohlen as well as through the pitiless eyes
of Arnie Kott; the harsh, desperate love scene between Jack and his mistress
at the home of Kott is experienced not only by these two but also by Manfred,
the autistic child who lives in another dimension of reality. For Dick, reality
has the configuaration of a magic mirror that reflects marvellous images at
the moment when, being struck by something which we define as "chance"
or "destiny" (or science?), it crumbles into a thousand fragments.

Undoubtedly, at the beginning of Dick's career one could find a greater
optimism. In what is probably his first significant attempt, the short novel
"The Variable Man" (1953), that "democratic" vision of SF of which Asimov
and Simak had become bearers is apparent. The protagonist of "The Variable
Man" is a humble artisan, dragged in spite of himself into a fantastic future
to act as arbiter in a conflict of colossal proportions, involving the whole universe (a similar situation occurs in Asimov's Pebble in the Sky, 1950). Already
in "The Variable Man" we note the unconstrained use of scientific data. The
description of the machines of the future, e.g., remains always vague, im-

pressionistic—exactly as in H.G. Wells; it always concentrates on the *effects* of the scientific discoveries and not on the discoveries themselves. Here is Dick's description of the lethal bomb that should give victory to the Earth in the intergalactic war:

> Rising up in the center of the chamber was a squat small cylinder, a great ugly cone of dark gray. Technicians circled around it, wiring up the exposed relay banks. Reinhart caught a glimpse of endless tubes and filaments, a maze of wires and terminals and parts criss-crossing each other, layer on layer. (§1).

The mechanical structure is transformed into an impressionistic and subjective "vision" through the eyes of an outsider. To his question "What is it?" someone very aptly replies, "An *idea* of Jamison Hedge."

Another characteristic of Dick's narrative, already evident in "The Variable Man," is the use of the sensationalistic element, in part drawn from traditional "space opera." The Centaurian starships engage the Terrestrial fleet in a colossal battle (which is, however, only reported rather than directly shown). The villain Reinhart, once exposed, does not hesitate to point the gun, in accordance with the best "thrilling" tradition, at the political assembly that rules the New World Order, threatening a massacre which, naturally, will be averted by the stratagem of the hero. This hero, the scientist Sherikov, does not disdain a sentimental idyllic love affair, fortunately just hinted at, with the lady President of the Assembly. But all these elements have scarcely any weight in the train of events, which has at its center a theme dear to Asimov—the struggle between a fanatic and Machiavellian political power and a scientific power dedicated exclusively to the improvement of the human race. In this context it is significant that the political warmonger has a German name (Reinhart), while his scientist-antagonist is given the name Sherikov and operates in the Urals. The time is 1953, when anticommunist frenzy—fed by ambitious young political adventurers, among whom the future president Nixon—had overwhelmed the United States. Dick will react to this neo-Puritan climate, displaying the same civil commitment as the best "social science fiction," in *The Man Who Japed* and especially in that gem of SF stories, *Eye in the Sky*—a pretext to ridicule the neurosis of American society in the 50's, but at the same time a reaffirmation of that relativistic vision of reality which was becoming ever more central to Dick's fiction. In so doing, Dick was partly abandoning the objectives of "social science fiction." In Dick, in fact, criticism of American society does not presuppose the faith that after all evil can be exorcised. His pessimism is not only social, but concerns itself with all of man's existence. Though always based on an analysis of American reality, it is metaphysical and existential.

Dick's fiction in the 50's moves along the double track of civil commitment and metaphysical representation of the struggle for power and of a destiny that transcends the will even of the most powerful of men. In *Solar Lottery*, the mysticism of the humble is opposed to the violence of the arrogant. However, both are subject to the implacable wheel of fate, which here has assumed social dimensions because a principle of chance has become the law in the improbable world state postulated by Dick. At times, behind the forces of "chance" strong organizations are hidden, that manipulate reality; but in their turn these organizations are shattered when faced with the imponderable events that they have not foreseen. Thus, the image of the future that Dick transmits is of an extraordinary complexity. The scientific miracle is an integral part of it; but when the novel begins it has already occurred, it is a discounted and unquestionable event that merits no description whatsoever. But as scientific progress opens new prospects to man (immortality, voyages in time and space, control over the psyche), man finds himself more and more at the mercy of uncontrollable and colossal forces that mould his life, give him an illusionary vision of reality, and falsify his memories. Science modifies society and therefore the reality of man. Dick is among the few writers of SF who think of the future in terms of *total* change. Even the psychic, religious, sentimental sphere of man is modified, and the more man is insecure, dazzled, confused, the more he is in need of faith, of a trust in something absolute and transcendental. But the great forces that dominate his life will by the logic of domination procure false religious images, false myths, false illusions of salvation...and so the process of the disintegration of reality begins again, and on the ashes of a futuristic society—which is yet always set in the U.S.A., always unmistakably *American*—man's tragedy, often investing even his sentimental sphere, is played out. This is another characteristic that distinguishes Dick inside Anglo-American SF: the presence of couples in a perpetual crisis, unable to live together, condemned to sterile relationships in a universe without mercy and morality, dominated by chance.

This process of dissolution of the technological in the apocalyptic, of futuristic convention in existential anguish, took shape in Dick's novels of the 50's (among which it is necessary to mention at least *Time Out Of Joint*). It finds full expression in *The Man in the High Castle* where the expedient of imagining the United States dominated by the forces of the Axis is not a pretext for a "false" reconstruction of history, but the sign of an *arbitrariness* that has contaminated history—as in the more recent *Counter-Clock World*, where it overthrows even biological laws. In *The Man in the High Castle* we witness, in fact, the disintegration of American society when faced with other dominant cultural forces, and the emergence of violence and chance as principal factors in the destiny of every individual. The victory of the Axis during the Second World War is symbolical of a historical reality in which American society no longer possesses values to oppose to an apparently defeated adversary. One of the main characters in the novel publishes a book dealing with an inverted historical dimension in which the Axis troops have been actually defeated: even a great act of justice—the Nuremberg trial—has been accomplished. The mirror of fiction reveals an image of truth: the artist is the only one who knows the answer. Hawthorne Abendsen, the author, is right, but his creator is also right. Nazi violence, the historical equivalent of the spiritual futility and chaos of modern America, rules the world, and the Nuremberg trial is only a dream.

In *The Man in the High Castle* Mr. Tagomi, the main Japanese character, is treated by Dick with peculiar kindness. To him Dick atrributes a deep awareness of the elusive quality of reality, a sharp sense of displacement ("We're blind moles. Creeping through the soil, feeling with our snoots. We know nothing. I perceived this...now I don't know where to go. Screech with fear, only. Run away." [§6]), which allows Tagomi to belong to both dimensions of reality and experience the repulsive ugliness of the "other" San Francisco in a terrifying nightmare.

IT IS AT THIS POINT THAT DICK WROTE the "Martian" novels, The *Three Stigmata of Palmer Eldritch*, a vision of planetary reality fallen prey to drug hallucination, and *Martian Time-Slip*. The very beginning of this novel, with the laborious reawakening of Silvia Bohlen from the artificial sleep of barbiturates, is almost identical to the opening of *The Three Stigmata of*

Palmer Eldritch: "His head unnaturally aching, Barney Mayerson woke to find himself in an unfamiliar bedroom, in an unfamiliar conapt building...." In *Martian Time-Slip* Dick's narrative method has reached a peculiar perfection of its own, which consists of using different techniques and semantic levels. Even here, Dick does not reject commercial SF, but develops his novel following seemingly conventional schemes. Thus, the representation of Mars with the canals of classic SF, studded with UN colonies leading a difficult life and traversed by the last representatives of the dying native civilization, echoes the famous *Martian Chronicles* of Ray Bradbury. If we look closely, however, Dick's dry language, functional to the limits of triviality, his rejections of any lyricism and decorative language, is at the antipode of Bradbury. Dick does not hesitate to refer even to the "Western" models, applied shallowly to the "space opera" of the 30's on. In the crucial scene of the novel we find, strangely enough, a gun duel, in which the rocky desert of Mars in 1994 AD could easily be replaced by that of Arizona one century earlier.

But even the (apparent) chaos in the plot should, as always when Dick is concerned, put the reader on his guard. To an intentionally traditional basis he applies a Ballardian concern for "inner space" and discontinuous conception of time and, at the same time, his own, fundamentally tragic vision of life.

At a closer look, in fact, the planet of *Martian Time-Slip* is revealed as a replica of budding American society not only with its generous pioneers, but also with phenomena from the formation of a capitalist society dominated by the inexorable law of profit and speculation. Will the "melting pot of races" (White, of course, in spite of the presence of a Chinese entrepreneur) colonizing Mars make the same fatal errors as the U.S. pioneers? The incubus that torments Manfred—the monstrous ruined buildings swarming on the barren expanse of the planet—seems to indicate that it will. But, it would be much too simple to interpret the novel exclusively in terms of an anti-utopia.

The values that dominate Martian reality, are again the ruthless struggle for power: violence, deceit, and, finally, the spiritual aridity of man. All the characters of the novel are implacably impelled toward neurosis, madness, homicide, suicide, adultery. In terms of traditional narrative, outside SF, the reality described by Dick is devastating. We pass from suicide toward which is driven a despairing character unable to endure the pain of life (like Manfred's father) to adultery committed almost simultaneously by Silvia Bohlen and her husband, both prisoners of their universe of sterile and psychopathic anguish, and we arrive finally to the real protagonist of the novel, Manfred, an autistic child inexorably cut off from any communication with the outside world and tormented by terrifying visions.

Mars is, therefore, another of the many images of the Waste Land that 20th Century culture proposes to us with obsessive repetitiousness. If for T.S. Eliot (and for the Dick of *The Man in the High Castle*) history is a labyrinth without an exit, for the author of *Martian Time-Slip* the future is an incubus evoked by the mind of an autistic child, who projects into already nightmarish reality his terror of life and his inability to communicate with others. In this context perhaps only death preserves a tragic concreteness. Arnie Kott, the ambiguous syndicalist-capitalist in search of absolute power, mortally wounded by an enemy, can deceive himself in believing that he is prisoner of a malignant but relative illusion: "You can't fool me, Arnie thought. I know I'm still in Manfred's mind; pretty soon I'll wake up and I won't be shot, I'll be O.K. again, and I'll find my way back to my own world, where things like this don't happen..."; but instead: "During his flight back to Lewistown, Arnie Kott died" (§16).

Thus, the disintegrated vision of Martian reality determines the breakdown of the myth of space pioneering, on which *Martian Time-Slip* may appear to be constructed. It is precisely this internal tension of meanings that makes Dick's narrative so complex and difficult, and explains the limited popularity of this author until the success of *The Man in the High Castle*, a novel based on a sensational plot able to attract even the most unsophisticated American reader.

Moreover, if a last proof of the revolutionary quality of the SF of *Martian Time-Slip* was required, it would be enough to compare the character of Manfred to other figures endowed with extrasensory powers, created by more conventional authors—like Van Vogt's in *Slan* and Sturgeon's in *More Than Human*—who conduct their narration by means of sensationalistic psychology. In *Martian Time-Slip* Manfred is beyond any psychological description, being the living emblem of a cosmic loneliness and a total incommunicability expressed only through a vision of metaphysical horror: "He saw a hole as large as a world; the earth disappeared and became black, empty, and nothing.... Into the hole the men jumped one by one, until none of them were left. He was alone, with the silent world-hole." (§12).

DICK RETURNS TO A "TERRESTRIAL" THEME in *The Simulacra* (1964) and to a more direct, although no less fantastic, representation of American society. In Dick, in fact, unlike the other authors that emerged in the 60's, the triumph of hallucination does not imply escapism, flight from reality and refuge in myth, but is rather an attempt to stretch to the extreme limit of SF a narration that remains substantially anchored to American society. It is not by chance that the classic figure of the Alien is almost totally absent in Dick's fiction; instead, his humans are often endowed with paranormal qualities or they are poor madmen lost in a cruel and incomprehensible world or again, mechanisms, androids that reproduce not only the physical but also the psychological structure of man.

The dissolution of the scientific datum which becomes increasingly stronger in the last works, coincides on the collective level with the breakdown of society and on the individual level with the crisis of emotional values associated with the family. As the scientific factor becomes more and more problematic, Dick takes increasingly as his model a society which is essentially that of 20th Century U.S.A. In *The Simulacra* the central plot is the manipulation of the mass information centers controlled by the authorities; In *Do Androids Dream of Electic Sheep?* (1968) society must defend itself against the overwhelming power of an industry of mechanical devices that introduces to the market automata so perfect as to be confused with men and take their place; in *Counter-Clock World* (1967) the social structure is still, grotesquely, the capitalist one; other U.S. problems of the 60's (control over culture, Black revolts, etc.) also appear punctually. In these last novels the believability of premised scientific data has become nil. In *The Simulacra* we had immortal characters and the possibility to go back in time, fantastically enough, to make a deal in favor of the Jews with Nazi Germany. In *Counter-Clock World* science (the "Hobart phase") is introduced simply to classify—certainly not to explain—a miraculous event, i.e. the inversion of the biological rhythm that causes the dead to resurrect and the living to retreat in time towards the womb. In *Do Androids Dream of Electric Sheep?* the androids are so perfect that, apparently, only a complex psychological test can reveal their mechanical nature. Dick annihilates the traditional relationship between natural science and SF, that is, the positivistic assumption that science, for better or worse, is the conditioning element of contemporary society. With his relativistic and pessimistic vision of reality Dick calls in question the gnoseological foundations of science, of our mental categories and of scientific methods.

We may ask what is left to man in this disintegrated universe, seeing that Dick is certainly not so naive as to believe that a bucolic return to nature is possible, but postulates rather, precisely because he does not believe in science, an eternal technological hell in which humanity has been condemned. In social terms, *the great capitalist forces and the authoritarianism innate in state apparatus tend to extend their power in an ineluctable process that leaves less and less liberty to the individual.* At the end of the road the authoritarian super-state, master of an immeasurably sophisticated technology, will defy any opponent, not actually suppressing him, but enveloping him in a net of subtle hallucinations, from which he will never emerge (*The Three Stigmata of Palmer Eldritch*), through which his mental power will be ruthlessly exploited (*Time Out Of Joint*).

In Dick's last novels there emerges the presence of a supernatural mysticism which seems to preach a kind of cosmic resignation as the last alternative to spiritual chaos and social dissolution. The message of Wilbur Mercer in *Do Androids Dream of Electric Sheep?*—naturally a pre-fabricated deity—springs, nonetheless, from intense and desolate truth: "Any place that you go you will be asked to err. This is the condition of life: to be forced to violate one's own identity. Sooner or later every living creature must do it. It is the final shadow, the defeat of creation: it is the curse at work, the curse fed by life. All over the Universe." (§15). Wilbur Mercer (note the pun on "mercy") is represented, in this religious iconography of the future, in the act of ascending a hill while unknown assassins hurl rocks at him and drive him inexorably back to the bottom. Mercer is, therefore, an analogue to Christ climbing Golgotha. *Do Androids Dream of Electric Sheep?*, probably the most important, and perhaps overall the most intense among the recent Dick novels, presents a U.S.A. disintegrated psychologically more than materially by the Third World War, where the possession of one of the few animals that escaped nuclear extermination is a symbol of social prestige, a cure for the neurosis of mechanized life and the terror of the implacable atomic "fall-out." This novel suggests a partial alternative to the chaos. What differentiates, after all, the androids from men and justifies their elimination, is the lack of religious spirit, their cold cruelty and determination. The most human of the human beings is perhaps the semi-deficient Isidore, who first offers to help a group of androids without bothering about the consequences, and then assists horrified at the torture they inflict on a spider.

At the end of the novel, the main character, in order to understand life better in all its negative totality (just like Mrs. Moore in the Marabar Caves in E.M. Forster's *A Passage to India*), climbs up a radioactive hill and is stoned: "Here there existed no one to record his or anyone else's degradation, and any courage or pride which might manifest itself here at the end would go unmarked: the dead stones, the dust-stricken weeds dry and dying, perceived nothing, recollected nothing, about him or themselves" (§21). But he survives, after all, not to fulfill an impossible redemption, but to accept the true essence of life. Life is a sequence of illusions, just as the holy toad on the hill is not a divine gift, but an artificial toy. To realize that, to refuse the desperate attitude of the characters in *The Simulacra*, blindly lost behind the everlasting puppet of Nicole Thibodeaux ("What's unreal and what's real? To me she's more real than anything else; than you, even. Even than myself, my own life." [§9]). is perhaps the beginning of a new consciousness, the search for the truest *self*: the death of Wilbur Mercer is emphatically *not* the death of man.

The spiritual element is even more evident in *Counter-Clock World*, a rather confused and perhaps not quite successful novel, in which Dick represents a universe not only symbolically but actually apocalyptic, in which the dead, according to the prophecy, resurrect from their tombs. In this disturbed universe emerges the figure of Anarch Peak, a Black preacher resurrected and then again killed without having been allowed to communicate his religious message, who nonetheless, in the few days in which he remains alive, preaches the forgiveness for one's own enemies and salvation for the humble and helpless. In *Counter-Clock World* we assist at the successive violent deaths of all the principal characters—Anarch Peak and two men and a woman tied by a strong bond of love. Thus at the end another landscape of total and terrifying desolation emerges. Yet from the bottom of this abyss of death can perhaps be seen a possibility of building new values.

Again the final episode is highly significant and possibly one of the best scenes written by Dick. Sebastian, the hero of the novel, is bleeding to death. After the death of Lotte, his lover, and of Anarch Peak no hope is left. But hearing the "deaders" (dead reverting to life) calling from the soil under his feet, Sebastian refuses to be taken to hospital. He feels his individual life is not important any longer, he wants to help all the buried humanity struggling for a physical, but also spiritual resurrection. After all the false gods, we have perhaps here a genuine Christ-like figure:

> "The deaders?" Lindy gripped him around his waist, lifted him to his feet. "Later," he said. "Can you walk at all? You must have been walking, your shoes are covered with mud. And your clothes are torn."...
>
> "They need help," Sebastian said.... "It wasn't just one I heard this time; I heard them all." He had never heard anything like it before. Ever. So many at once—all of them together. (§21)

According to Brian Aldiss "throughout Dick's books and titles blows the horn of freedom,"[2] but this is possibly true only in the early fiction (*The Man Who Japed, Eye in the Sky*). Later Dick discovers that freedom too can be manipulated easily. Mercy, pity, love have a stronger substance: They can exist even in a world without freedom.

On the narrative level, in the last novels Dick proceeds on the road of aggravating the sensationalistic motifs. We have already mentioned the resurrection of the dead in *Counter-Clock World;* *Do Androids Dream of Electric Sheep?* includes an erotic scene between one of the protagonists and an android girl, a hunting of the android accomplished by a police "bounty killer," and a kind of magic box through which the inhabitants of the future U.S.A. put themselves in direct contact with Wilbur Mercer. Dick's narrative line is always within the conventions of SF, and for this reason he will always be less popular in the eyes of orthodox literary criticism than writers like Bradbury and Vonnegut, who use SF within a wider narrative tradition, or indeed than Asimov, who is always substantially faithful to the Wellsian paradigm which corresponds to the image of SF that the public still clings to. Dick is by the same token also different from J.G. Ballard who devotes more attention to the use of experimental literary devices, such as the "stream of consciousness," and makes large use of elements drawn from psychology and psychoanalysis. In Dick we find "only" a coarse SF plot, pushed to the extreme limits of sensationalism. Yet the unique quality of his narrative has been fully appreciated by the same British "new wave" SF writers[3] who have tried, not always successfully, to give a new literary and avant-garde dignity to SF. In fact, while J.G. Ballard seems too often interested in the disturbed activity of a decadent individual mind in an empty world, the great strength of Dick's fiction lies in the solid relationship between the individual world of the psyche and the grotesque concreteness of the society, however bizarre and mystified, that engulfs his heroes.

Acting within SF, accepting the popular element which has always constitiued one of its foundations, Dick is, nonetheless, placing into jeopardy the conception of reality on which all of SF was based. He is challenging the narrative and cultural values of SF not by denying them flatly, but by exploiting them to their extreme formal and ideological consequences.[4] Dick is actually writing SF about SF. In other words, he is conducting a critical inquiry on the meanings of SF through the narrative devices that SF puts at his disposal, distorting and modifying them in a search which pushes him always closer towards a meta-SF that does not exhaust itself in an intellectual game, but is simultaneously a coherent interpretation of the crisis that troubles the technological man and the American society of the 20th century.

NOTES

[1]Carlo Pagetti, Il Senso del Futuro: La Fantascienza nella Letteratura Americana (Roma: Edizioni di Storia e Letteratura, 1970), p. 255.

[2]Brian W. Aldiss, Billion Year Spree (1973), p. 313.

[3]Perhaps the first really good critical survey of Dick's fiction was John Brunner's "The Work of Philip K. Dick" in New Worlds, Sept 1966, pp. 142-49.

[4]In short, Dick seems to have critically realized that "jsut like technocracy SF dispossesses the human subject from his human reality and reifies him. We get thus a progress whose movement depends on individuals, on its subjects, yet which is at the same time independent of them because of a superior principle. This is a pre-established cyclical movement which results from an activity outside and in spite of men—a superior power known variously as Fortune, Destiny, Chance, Providence, God" (from the excellent and too little known study by Franco Ferrini, Che Cosa E' La Fantascienza [Roma: Ubaldini, 1970], p. 55).

Fredric Jameson

After Armageddon: Character Systems in Dr. Bloodmoney

Dick's voluminous work can be seen as falling into various distinct thematic groups or cycles: there is, for instance, the early Vanvogtian game-playing cycle, the Nazi cycle (e.g. The Man in the High Castle, The Unteleported Man), a relatively minor Jungian cycle (of which the best effort is undoubtedly Galactic Pot-Healer), and, of course, the late "metaphysical" cycle which includes his most striking novels, Ubik and The Three Stigmata of Palmer Eldritch. In such a view, Dr. Bloodmoney (1965) can be assigned to a small but crucial middle group of eschatological novels, along with its less successful companion-piece, The Simulacra. In these two works, for the first time, there emerges that bewildering and kaleidoscopic plot structure we associate with Dick's mature production. At the same time, this cycle helps us to understand the origins and the function of this sudden and alarming proliferation of sub-plots, minor characters, and exuberantly episodic digressions, for both of these works dramatize the utopian purgation of a fallen and historically corrupted world by some final climactic overloading, some ultimate explosion beyond which the outlines of a new and simpler social order emerge. But in the two cases the "coding" of the evil, as well as its exorcism, is different: in *The Simulacra*, this is political and economic, and it is a big-corporation but also entertainment-industry-type power elite which invites purgation, while in *Dr. Bloodmoney* the historical crisis is expressed in terms of the familiar counterculture denunciation of an evil or perverted science (compare Vonnegut in *Cat's Cradle*), only too emblematically exposed by the invention of the atomic bomb.

In this particular book, indeed, for the first and last time in the Dick canon, we are given to witness an event which serves in one way or another as the precondition and the premise of other books but which already lies in the past by the time the latter begin: the atomic cataclysm, World War III, the holocaust from which all the peculiar Dick near-futures spring and in which they find their historical sustenance. Here alone are we able to see the bombs actually fall and the towers topple; indeed, an untypical flashback isolates the moment itself and draws our attention to it with hallucinatory intensity. So we would want to ask, at the outset, why such a vision of catastrophe, on which other SF writers have not shown the same reluctance to dwell, should be so infrequently represented by a writer not otherwise known for his squeamishness; or, to reverse the order of priorities, what in the construction of *Dr. Bloodmoney* enables it to present this vision.

In the context of Dick's world, for his aesthetic and the narrative line that is so unmistakably his own, the raw material of atomic destruction presents artistic problems unlike any other, problems of a delicate and strategic kind, that involve the very scaffolding of Dick's novelistic construction. Nowhere else, indeed, is the fundamental ambivalence of his imagination revealed so clearly, an ambivalence which is however the very source of his strength elsewhere and the formative mechanism of his invention. For the point about the atomic cataclysm in *Dr. Bloodmoney* is not merely that Bluthgeld takes it to be a projection of his own psychic powers, but that, as the book continues, we are ourselves less and less able to distinguish between what I am forced to call "real" explosions, and those that take place within the psyche. Every reader of Dick is familiar with this nightmarish uncertainty, this reality fluctuation, sometimes accounted for by drugs, sometimes by schizophrenia, and sometimes by new SF powers, in which the psychic world as it were goes outside, and reappears in the form of simulacra or of some photographically cunning reproduction of the external. In general, the effect of these passages, in which the narrative line comes unstuck from its referent and begins to enjoy the bewildering autonomy of a kind of temporal Moebius strip, is to efface the boundary between real and hallucinatory altogether, and to discredit the reader's otherwise inevitable question as to which of the events witnessed is to be considered "true."

In such moments, Dick's work transcends the opposition between the subjective and the objective, and thereby confronts the dilemma which in one way or another characterizes all modern literature of any consequence: the intolerable and yet unavoidable choice between a literature of the self and a language of some impersonal exteriority, between the subjectivism of private languages and case histories, or some nostalgia for the objective that leads outside the realm of individual or existential experience into some reassuringly stable place of common sense and statistics. Dick's force lies in the effort to retain possession and use of both apparently contradictory, mutually exclusive subjective and objective explanation systems all at once. The causal attribution, then, of the hallucinatory experiences to drugs, to schizophrenia or to the half-life, is not so much a concession to the demands of the older kind of reading for explanation as it is a refusal of that first, now archaic solution of symbolism and modernism—the sheer fantasy and dream narrative. To attribute his nightmares to drugs, schizophrenia or half-life is thus a way of affirming their reality and rescuing their intolerable experiences from being defused as an unthreatening surrealism; a way of preserving the resistence and the density of the subjective moment, of emphasizing the commitment of his work to this very alternation itself as its basic content. And this discontinuity is at one with our fragmented existence under capitalism; it dramatizes our simultaneous presence in the separate compartments of private and public worlds, our twin condemnation to both history and psychology in scandalous concurrence.

Now, however, it becomes apparent what is unique about the atomic blast as a literary event in such a world: for with it the question about the referent, about the truth value of the narrative, returns in force. It becomes impossible for Dick to do what he is able to do elsewhere: to prevent the reestablishment of the reality principle and the reconstitution of experience into the twin airtight domains of the objective and the subjective. For unlike the time warps and the time sags, the hallucinations and the four-dimensional mirages of the other books, atomic holocaust is a collective event about whose reality the reader cannot but decide. Dick's narrative ambiguity can accomodate individual experience, but runs greater risks in evoking the materials of world history, the flat *yes* or *no* of the mushroom cloud. And behind this difficulty, perhaps, lies the feeling that America itself and its institutions are so massively in place, so unshakeable, so unchangeable (save by total destruction), that the partial modification available in private life through drugs and analogous devices is here unconvincing and ineffectual. How, then, does *Dr. Bloodmoney* manage to assimilate something which apparently by definition lies outside the range of Dick's aesthetic possibilities?

THE OVERALL PLOT OF THE NOVEL is rather conventional: we follow several survivors of the blast in thier various post-atomic adventures which all appear to reach some climax in the death of Bluthgeld, and which all have a kind of coda in the return to Berkeley as to a gradual reemergence of civilization. Yet it seems to me that the content of the individual adventures, and the detail of the novel, cannot really be understood until we become aware of the operative presence within it of a certain number of *systems* of which the surface events are now seen as so many combinations and articulations.

Chief among these, as is so often the case in non-realistic narratives, narratives not dependent on common sense presuppositions and habituated perceptions, is that formed by a whole *constellation of peculiar characters*.

The revelation—made in passing, without any great flourishes—that the initial point-of-view figure (Stuart) happens to be a Negro has the function of staging the appearance of the first really unusual figure—the thalidomide cul-de-jatte or phocomelus Hoppy Harrington—in the still fairly "realistic" and everyday perspective of social stigma: both work for a businessman who prides himself on providing jobs for people otherwise excluded from the normal white American society with which we are all familiar. It is only later on, after the bomb blast, that the real mutants begin to flourish; yet it seems to me that these opening pages have the function of slowly beginning to separate us from our ordinary characterology, and of deprogramming our typological reactions, preparing us for a narrative space in which new and unfamiliar systems of classifying characters can operate at full throttle, unimpeded by cultural and personal presuppositions on the part of the reader.

A first hint that these various characters do not exist as mere isolated curiosities, as unrelated monsters of various kinds, is provided by the fate of the "first man on Mars," immobilized in eternal orbit by the outbreak of the war and circling Earth henceforth as a kind of celestial vaguely leftist disk jockey whose task it is to provide a communications relay between the stricken areas over which he passes, and otherwise to play hours of taped music and read aloud the few available surviving texts—Somerset Maugham's *Of Human Bondage*, for instance—which remain of the cultural patrimony at the dawn of these new dark ages. Dangerfield is, of course, a more or less ordinary human being, yet aspects of his situation slowly—and improbably—begin to impose an analogy with Hoppy's. Consider, for instance, Stuart's reflexion on the latter character: "Now, of course, one say many phoces, and almost all of them on their 'mobiles', exactly as Hoppy had been, placed dead center each in his own little universe, like an armless, legless god" (§8). This image might also characterize Dangerfield's sacred isolation as he circles the earth; but a childhood memory of Hoppy's reinforces the parallel: " 'One time a ram butted me and flew through the air. Like a ball.'... They all laughed, now, himself and Fergesson and the two repairmen; they imagined how it looked, Hoppy Harrington, seven years old, with no arms and legs, only a torso and a head, rolling over the ground, howling with fright and pain—but it was funny; he knew it" (§2). This power of Hoppy's to project bodies into the air like soccer balls later becomes lethal (the death of Bluthgeld), but it suggests a kinesthetic affinity for Dangerfield's fate as well—the live being housed in a cylindrical unit soaring through empty space. And when it is remembered that this plot-line reaches its climax in Hoppy's attempt to substitute himself, through his own voice and powers of mimicry, for the ailing Dangerfield, the analogy between the two positions becomes unmistakable.

Yet they are not exactly symmetrical. Subsequent events, and the introduction of newer and even stranger characters, seem to make the point that Hoppy is, if anything, *insufficiently* like Dangerfield. At this stage, indeed, in the increasing post-atomic prosperity of the West Marin collective, it is as though Hoppy, with his complicated prostheses and his remarkable skills in repair and invention, has become far too active a figure to maintain the analogy with the imprisoned disk jockey. The episode-producing mechanism of the novel then produces a new being, a more monstrous and more adequate replica in the form of the homunculus Bill, carried around inside his sister's body and emitting messages to her and to others on the outside, but as decisively insulated from the world as Dangerfield himself.

Indeed, it may be suggested that the entire action of the novel is organized around this sudden shift in relationships, this sudden rotation of the axis of the book's characterological system on the introduction of the new being. We may describe it as a problem of substitutions: Hoppy's error is to believe that he is Dangerfield's opposite number, and, as such, destined in some way to replace him. In fact, however, his mission in the plot is quite different, for he is called upon to eliminate the ominous Bluthgeld, who has not yet figured in our account and whose anomaly (schizophrenic paranoia) would not seem to be a physical disability of the type exemplified by Hoppy or Bill, or, by metaphoric extension, by Dangerfield himself.

But before trying to integrate Bluthgeld into our scheme, let us first rapidly enumerate the other freaks or anomalous beings that people this extravagant work. We have omitted, for one thing, the realm of the dead themselves, to which Bill has special access—"trillions and trillions of them and they're all different.... Down in the ground" (§10). Here then, already the half-life world of *Ubik* is beginning to take shape; yet as entities the dead are quite distinct from either Bill or Dangerfield in that—equally isolated—they have no mode of action or influence on the outside world, and cannot even, as do the former, emit messages to it: "After a point the dead people down below weren't very interesting because they never did anything, they just waited around. Some of them, like Mr. Blaine, thought all the time about killing and others just mooned like vegetables" (§12).

Finally, among the extreme varieties of mutant fauna in the post-atomic landscape, we must not forget to mention the so-called "brilliant animals," creatures with speech and organizational ability, like Bluthgeld's talking dog or the touching subjects of the following anecdotes: " 'Listen, my friend,' the veteran said, 'I got a pet rat lives under the pilings with me? He's smart; he can play the flute. I'm not putting you under an illusion, it's true. I made a little wooden flute and he plays it through his nose.'... 'Let me tell you about a rat I once saw that did a heroic deed,' the veteran began, but Stuart cut him off" (§8). These gifted animals, indeed, provide Stuart with his livelihood, the sale of Hardy's Homeostatic Vermin Traps, mechanical contrivances scarcely less intelligent than the prey they are designed to hunt down, and which may therefore lay some equal claim to being yet another variety of new creature.

I will now suggest that all of these beings, taken together, organize themselves into systematic permutations of a fairly limited complex of ideas or characteristics which turns around the notion of *organism and organs*, of mechanical contrivances, and (in the case of the phocomelus) of protheses. But the results of these combinations are a good deal more complicated than a simple opposition between the organic and the mechanical, and A.J. Greimas's semantic rectangle[1] allows us to map the various possibilities inherent in the system as follows:

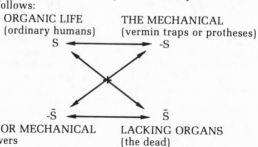

ORGANIC LIFE   THE MECHANICAL
(ordinary humans)   (vermin traps or protheses)

NEITHER ORGANIC NOR MECHANICAL   LACKING ORGANS
(abnormal spiritual powers   (the dead)
—the gifted animals)

The four self-generating terms of the graph represent the simplest atomic units of the characterological system of *Dr. Bloodmoney*. yet it will be noted that, with the possible exception of S itself (or in other words, of all the *normal* human characters in the book), all are in another sense merely part of the background of the work, providing a kind of strange new living environment for the action in it, and marking out the life coordinates of this post-atomic universe, fixing the limits within which the plot will unfold, without themselves really participating in it. In particular, it will have become clear that none of the really aberrant characters described above can be accomodated neatly within any given one of the four basic terms.

Yet the generative capacity of the semantic rectangle is not exhausted with these four primary elements. On the contrary, its specific mode of conceptual production is to construct a host of complex entities out of the various new combinations logically obtainable between the simple terms. These new and more complicated, synthetic concepts correspond to the various sides of the semantic rectangle, so that the complex term designates an idea or a phenomenon able to unite in itself both terms of the initial opposition S and -S, while the neutral term accordingly governs the negatives of both, a synthesis of the bottom terms -$\overline{S}$ and $\overline{S}$. The respective combinations of the left-hand and right-hand sides of the rectangle are technically known as the positive and negative deictic axes. A little experimentation now shows that these four combinations correspond exactly to the four principal anomalous characters or actors of the book.

The complex term, for instance, a being which would unite a normal human body (S) with a machine or mechanical prostheses (-S), can only be Dangerfield himself, as he circles the Earth forever united to his satellite. The negative deixis which emerges from the union of a prosthesis with a crippled being ($\overline{S}$, lacking organs) is of course Hoppy Harrington, the phocomelus. The neutral presents perhaps greater problems, insofar as it involves the enigmatic fourth position, -$\overline{S}$, itself the negation of a negation and thus apparently devoid of any positive content. Yet if we read this particular term, which is neither an organism not a machine, as something on the order of a *spiritual prosthesis*, a kind of supplement to either organic or mechanical existence which is qualitatively different from either, then we sense the presence of that familiar realm in Dick's works in which, under the stimulus of drugs or schizophrenic disorder, vision, second sight, precognition, hallucination, are all possible. If this reading is accepted, then the neutral term would be understood as a combination between just such a spiritual prosthesis or supplementary power and a being lacking organs; and it becomes clear that what is thus designated can only be the homunculus Bill, with his access to the realm of the dead and his absence from the world of physical existence.

Our scheme has the added advantage of allowing us now to integrate Bluthgeld himself into a more generalized system of anomalous characters. As long as our basic traits or characteristics were limited to the opposition of organic to mechanical, the system seemed to bear no particular relevance to the figure of Bluthgeld. With the idea of spiritual powers, his position with relation to the other characters is now more easily defined, and it would seem appropriate to assign him the as yet unfilled function of the so-called positive deixis, or in other words, the synthesis of S (ordinary human) and -$\overline{S}$ (spiritual prosthesis). Now his privileged relationship to Hoppy Harrington also becomes comprehensible: to the phocomelus alone will fall the power to destroy Bluthgeld, because Hoppy is the latter's reverse or mirror-image. (Indeed, their relationship is still more complicated than this; for in appearance Hoppy is Bluthgeld's creature, and the other characters believe him to be the genetic result of the notorious 1972 fall-out catastrophe for which the the scientist was responsible. In reality, however, he is a thalidomide birth from an earlier period—1964—and owes nothing to the latter, whom he is thus free to annihilate.)

We may now articulate this new system of combinations as follows:

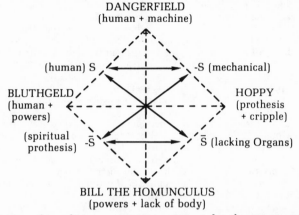

DANGERFIELD
(human + machine)

(human) S   -S (mechanical)

BLUTHGELD   HOPPY
(human +   (prothesis
powers)   + cripple)

(spiritual
prothesis)   -S̄   S̄ (lacking Organs)

BILL THE HOMUNCULUS
(powers + lack of body)

Not only does this scheme permit us to account for the construction of the main characters of *Dr. Bloodmoney* and to understand their relationship to each other, it provides us with material for grasping their symbol-value as well, and thus eventually for an interpretation of the bizarre events which the novel recounts. The systematic arrangement here proposed, for instance, suggests that the four characters are distinguished by distinct functions or realms of activity and competency. If for example we take *knowledge* as a theme, and interrogate the various positions accordingly, we find that each corresponds to a different and specific type of cognitive power: Hoppy thus possesses knowledge about the future as well as a practical kinaesthetic knowledge and control of inorganic matter; Bill the homunculus possesses (verbal) knowledge about the dead and kinaesthetic knowledge/control of organic matter. Meanwhile, the final long-distance psychoanalysis of the ailing Dangerfield suggests that the particular type of knowledge associated with him is (verbal or theoretical) knowledge of the past, and he is, of course, the guardian of an almost annihilated Earthly culture. As for Bluthgeld, his province is surely Knowledge in general, the theoretical secrets of inorganic matter (and kinaesthetic control of it), i.e. of the universe itself.

But as we enrich the thematic content of the four positions, it seems possible to characterize them in a more general way, one which may ultimately allow us to see them in terms of some basic overriding thematic opposition. So to each position or combination would seem to correspond a particular type of *professional activity* as well: Dangerfield is thus, as we already noted, a kind of celestial DJ, one version among many of the characteristic Dick entertainment-celebrity, whose most recent incarnation is the Jason of *Flow My Tears, the Policeman Said*. Opposed to this valorization of the word, Hoppy takes his place as an embodiment of the other characteristic form of creative activity in Dick's world, namely the practical handiman or artisan-inventor. The other two figures do not at first glance appear to fit very neatly into this scheme of things; Bluthgeld is of course the prototypical mad scientist, but more directly, during the course of the book's action, the psychotic and visionary; while Bill—judging from the endless conversations carried on with him by his sister Edie, much to the dismay of her elders— would seem best described as an imaginary playmate.

Still, even these approximations suggest some larger thematic oppositions: there is a sense in which both Hoppy and Bluthgeld have as their privileged object the world of things, which they divide up between them along the traditional and familiar axis of contemplative and active attitudes. Bluthgeld, whether as a scientist or a madman, sees into the structure of the world in a contemplative fashion; and this suggests that his great sin was to have passed, whether voluntarily or inadvertently, from the realm of contemplation to that of action (the fall-out from the tests of 1972, World War III itself). As for Hoppy, his knowledge of the future is, like his mechanical skill, simply part of the equipment necessary for survival; but his increasing psychic powers suggest an abuse of his particular position not unlike that of Bluthgeld's, and fraught with similar dangers.

Insofar as he forms a structural pendant to Dangerfield, I am tempted to describe the homunculus Bill in terms of the well-known axis that information theory provides between sender and receiver. Bill sends messages also, to be sure, but in relationship to the realm of the dead his principal function is surely that of receiving them, that of the absent listener to imaginary conversations, that open slot which is the function of the interlocutor in all discourse, even that of absolute solitude. There thus is articulated around the character of Bill the whole communicational syntax of interpersonal relationships, so that at this point the vertical axis which includes the positions of both Bill and Dangerfield seems by its linguistic emphasis quite sharply distinguished from the other axis which governs the world of objects:

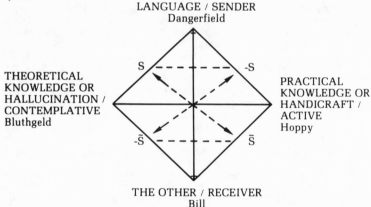

The verbal axis which includes the positions of Bill and Dangerfield is now seen to be primarily a linguistic one, and sharply distinguished from the horizontal axis which includes the positions of Bluthgeld and Hoppy and which is concerned with physics. Furthermore, the vertical Bill-Dangerfield axis is one of the use of knowledge for community well-being (prefigured in the "just" killing for the community's sake), whereas the horizontal Bluthgeld-Hoppy axis is one of the perversion of knowledge or its manipulation (even literally in the case of Hoppy's "handling" at a distance), which threatens to destroy the human community. The organic or communicational Bill-Dangerfield axis bringing together the past and the present, the living and the dead, is thus the locus and bearer of life-enhancing activities in the novel, whereas the inorganic or physical Bluthgeld-Hoppy axis is the locus of individualistic madness which would, if unchecked, certainly enslave and most probably destroy human life on Earth. Clearly, Dick's solution of the fundamental politico-existential problems facing humanity is here slanted toward art and language rather than toward an explicit scientific diagnosis which would meet the political problem head on. Nonetheless, Dick seems to realize that the verbal, linguistic or communicational field cannot by itself provide a solution. The playful character of Bill rises therefore, by his at least approximate synthesis of verbal and kinaesthetic powers, of communications and active physical intervention, to the status of final mediator, arbiter and one could almost say saviour in the microcosm of *Dr. Bloodmoney*.

WITH THE CHARACTEROLOGICAL SYSTEMS of the book thus revealed, we may now perhaps attempt a reading of its *action as a whole*. Briefly, it may be suggested that the book is organized around two narrative lines, one following Bluthgeld himself and the people who knew him, the other involving Hoppy Harrington and his respective acquaintances. The privileged narrator or "point of view" for the first plot is Bonnie, that of the second Stuart McConchie. Hence the arrival of Stuart in the West Marin County commune where Bonnie lives and where Bluthgeld is in hiding serves to trigger off the explosive interaction between the two plot lines, the lethal encounter between Hoppy and Bluthgeld, and the final *dénouement*.

The end or object of the action's development is evidently the neutralization of the dangerous and sinister Bluthgeld and his removal from the human scene in general; the complexity of the intrigue results from the difficulty of accomplishing this. For Bluthgeld is after all seen as the cause, in person, of World War III; yet this personalized and Manichaean view of history involves us in some curious conceptual antinomies which the narrative may be seen as a symbolic attempt to work through. It would seem appropriate, then, here to follow the example of Lévi-Strauss[2] in his analysis of myth as a narrative construction of symbolic mediations or syntheses whose purpose is the resolution, in story form, of a contradiction which the culture in question is unable to solve in reality. In the present context, this contradiction may be formulated as follows: How can you get rid of the cause of something as devastating as atomic war, when—in order to function as its cause in the first place—that ultimate causal determinant must be all-powerful and thus by definition impossible to get rid of? To put it in terms of the plot, the only way that an isolated individual like Bluthgeld can be imagined to be the "cause" of World War III is by endowing him with a power so immense that it is thereafter impossible to imagine any other power capable of matching him. If you like, the contradiction is more one inherent in liberal thought than in reality: if world politics is seen, not as the expression of class and national politico-economical dynamics which have an inner logic of their own, but rather as the result of the decisions of free conscious agents, some of whom are good (us) and some of whom are evil (the enemy, whoever he happens to be), then it is clear that the problem of the evil adversary's sources of power will return again and again with a kind of agonizing and incomprehensible persistence. Like any good American "leftist," of course, Dick sees the enemy as the American power elite and in particular its nuclear physicists; yet that point of view, as attractive as it may be, remains a prisoner of the same basic contradictions as the liberal ideology it imagines itself to be opposing.

In the novel itself, the solution lies in the development of a counterforce, an adversary powerful enough to neutralize Bluthgeld's magic and thus to destroy him. This is Hoppy Harrington's role, and the phocomelus grows in power as the book continues—objectively because the needs of the new post-atomic community encourage the growth and diversification of his special talents, and subjectively insofar as his self-confidence keeps pace with the immense range of new contrivances and weapons he has been able to evolve (some of them psychic). Along with this new self-confidence, however, his resentment has intensified as well. By the time of the confrontation with Bluthgeld, Hoppy is himself a dangerously paranoid figure, potentially as harmful to the community as the man he is now able to destroy. Thus a kind of interminable regression is at work here, in which any adversary powerful enough to blast the evil at its source becomes then sufficiently dangerous to call forth a nemesis in his own right, and so forth (see Dick's early novel *Vulcan's Hammer*). The basic contradiction, in other words, has not been solved at all, but merely displaced onto the mechanism devised to remove it, where it continues to function without any prospect of resolution.

The elegance of Dick's solution to this apparently insoluble dilemma makes of his novel a kind of textbook illustration of that mechanism which Structuralism has taken as its privileged object of study and which has seemed to underscore a basic parallelism between the workings of kinship systems and those of language, between the rules governing gift-giving in primitive societies and those at work in the market system, between the mechanisms of political and historical development and those of plot. This is the phenomenon of *exchange*, and nowhere is the flash between contrary poles quite so dramatic as in the moment in *Dr. Bloodmoney* when the circle is squared and the mind of the homunculus substituted for that of the malevolent Hoppy, on the point of taking over the world: " 'I'm the same; I'm Bill Keller,' the phocomelus said. 'Not Hoppy Harrington.' With his right manual extensor he pointed. 'There's Hoppy. That's him from now on.'—In the corner lay a shriveled dough-like object several inches long; its mouth gaped in congealed emptiness. It had a human-like quality to it, and Stockstill went over to pick it up" (§16). What makes the exchange possible is the peculiar status of the homunculus's body, both in and outside the world; Bill was attached to something real, a foetal body which died rapidly on exposure to the atmosphere; but in another sense, he was the only one of the four characters to be *without a body* and thus able to switch places without the development of an elaborate counterforce which might then—as in the infinite regression described above—become a threat in its own right. Hoppy fights Bluthgeld, in other words, on the latter's own terms, while Bill's replacement of Hoppy amounts to a shift from that system to a new one; and this is made possible by Hoppy's own violation of his particular system and powers. For he meant to replace Dangerfield by mimicry, that is, by the use of a verbal and linguistic skill quite different from the kinaesthetic one with which he had beaten Bluthgeld. But at this point, then, he is vulnerable to the superior use of the same purely verbal power by Bill, who intimidates and demoralizes him by his own use of the voices of the dead, and then finishes him off by wholesale personality transference—combining verbal and kinaesthetic power.

The basic shift in question we are now able to understand as a substitution of one axis for another, of that of Dangerfield and the homunculus for that of Bluthgeld and Hoppy, of that of language for that of existence—either practical or contemplative—in the world of objects. The latter axis—the horizontal one, in our schematic representation above—is of course marked negatively, both of its extremes being evil or malevolent in terms of the narrative. It does not, however, follow that the other axis is in contrast completely positive: in fact, in most of the novel both Bill and Dangerfield are immobilized or paralyzed. Even at the end, both remain under a depressing restriction in mobility and human potentialities in general, which serves to deprive the resolution of the book of tones that might otherwise be complacent or unacceptably aestheticizing.

For it seems clear that the basic event envisaged by *Dr. Bloodmoney* is the substitution of the realm of language for the realm of things, the replacement of the older compromised world of empirical activity, capitalist everyday work and scientific knowledge, by that newer one of communication and of messages of all kinds with which we are only too familiar in this consumer and service era. In reality, this shift seems to me to contain many negative and doubtful elements, and to welcome too unqualifiedly developments which are not necessarily an unmixed blessing. It is of course the very distinctness of these two axes—itself predicated on the "fact" of atomic war—that allows the exchange in *Dr. Bloodmoney* to take place in so striking and exemplary a fashion. But even in this novel, there is a hint of fusing concern about language and concern about objects in Bill, so that the exchange solution is only a provisional one, and relatively unstable. We would want at this point to return from this novel to Dick's other works in order to determine whether the priority of language over objects is there maintained. It would seem, for instance, that in some of the other works (*Galactic Pot-Healer*, for example, or most recently *Flow My Tears, The Policeman Said*), handicrafts, and particularly pot-making, are understood as a different kind of synthesis between art and work, developing more explicitly the trend in the present book.

Our analysis is in any case not complete until we return from this as it were super-human level of the narrative—the interactions between the various synthetic or complex terms of the characterological system—to the more pedestrian reality of the ordinary human characters like Bonnie or Stuart, who constitute, as we have suggested earlier, merely one simple term among others in the original system. Now it can be confidently asserted, it seems to me, that what held for the other simple terms (machines, the dead, the animals) holds true for the human population of *Dr. Bloodmoney* as well, namely that they provide the background and furnish the spectators and onlookers for a drama largely transcending them in significance. Thus the novel betrays a formal kinship with earlier works of Dick, such as the deservedly forgotten *Cosmic Puppets*, in which ordinary humans are the playthings of cosmic forces of some mythological type: the difference being that here those forces are not theological or Jungian in content but correspond to the very realities of modern history itself (scientific technique on the one hand and the communicational network on the other).

As far as the ordinary human characters of the book are concerned, then, the drama enacted not so much above as among them amounts to a purification of society and its reestablishment, to the rebirth of some new and utopian Berkeley on the ruins of the old one in whose streets ominous Bluthgelds might have from time to time been glimpsed (and surely the choice of the site of that dress rehearsal of May 1968 which was the Free Speech Berkeley of 1963—two years before the publication of Dick's novel—is no accident and has historical implications that largely transcend whatever autobiographical motives may also be involved). To say that the social form to which Dick's work corresponds is the small town would convey something anachronistic in the present social context; or at any rate, we should add that it is to be understood as the university town which never knew the provincialism nor the claustrophobia of the classical Main Streets of the American Middle West. Nor is Dick's pastoral a purely agricultural one, like that achieved in a kind of desperate exhilaration by the survivors of John Wyndham's various universal cataclysms. As different from him, or from the small-town pastoral in the best works of Ray Bradbury and Clifford Simak, it is an artisanal world against the scarcity of which the various commodities once more recover their true taste and reassert a use-value to which the jaded sensibilities of the affluent society, brainwashed by advertising, had become insensitive: so now there is something precious about the individual cigarette, made of real tobacco, and the glass of real pre-war Scotch, while even the language of Somerset Maugham becomes something we have to treasure. The vision of freshening our own stale and fallen universe, of a utopian revitalization of the tired goods and services all around us, their projection into some genuinely Jeffersonian commonwealth beyond the bomb, is the ultimate recompense for all those complicated struggles and interchanges we have been describing; and they go far towards compensating for what we would otherwise have to see as an ideological imbalance in Dick's work in general, a status defense on the part of the artist and an idealistic overemphasis on language and art in the place of political action. The typically American and "liberal" hostility to politics is outweighed, it seems to me, by just such glimpses into a reestablished collectivity, glimpses which, at the heart of all Dick's obligatory happy endings, mark him as an anti-Vonnegut, as the unseasonable spokesman for a historical' consciousness distinct from and superior to that limited dystopian and apocalyptic vision so fashionable in Western SF today.

NOTES

¹This forbidding apparatus is based on the idea that concepts do not exist in isolation but are defined in opposition to each other, in relatively organized clusters; and on the further refinement that there is a basic distinction between the opposite, or contrary, of a contradictory, S̄. Thus if S is the Good, then -S is Evil, while S̄ is that somewhat different category of things "not good" in general. The determination of the negative of -S is more complicated, as we show in the text; and as is also demonstrated further on, there is the further possibility of more complicated terms which unite these simple ones in various ways. See for further discussion of this schema, A.J. Greimas, "The Interaction of Semiotic Constraints," *Yale French Studies*, #41, 1968; and also my *Prison-House of Language* (Princeton 1972), pp. 162-68.

#See "The Structural Study of Myth," in *Structural Anthropology* (Anchor 1967), pp. 202-28.

Brian W. Aldiss

Dick's Maledictory Web: About and Around *Martian Time-Slip*

Arnie Kott is on his way back into a schizoid variant of the recent past:

> The trail levelled out and became wider. And all was in shadow; cold and damp hung over everything, as if they were treading within a great tomb. The vegetation that grew thin and noxious along the surface of the rocks had a dead quality to it, as if something had poisoned it in its act of growing. Ahead lay a dead bird on the path, a rotten corpse that might have been there for weeks; he could not tell. (§14)

The setting is Mars, which is now partly colonised. Colonists live along the water system, where conditions of near-fertility exist.

This web of civilization is stretched thin over utter desolation. There is no guaranteeing that it can be maintained. Its stability is threatened by the Great Powers back on Earth. For years they have neglected Mars, concentrating dollars and man-hours on further exploration elsewhere in the system; now they may interfere actively with the balance of the colony.

Behind this web exists another, even more tenuous: the web of human relationships. Men and women, children, old men, bleekmen (the autochthonous but non-indigenous natives of Mars) all depend, however reluctantly, on one another. When poor Norbert Steiner commits suicide, the effects of the event are felt by everyone.

Behind these two webs lies a third, revealed only indirectly. This is the web connecting all the good and bad things in the universe. The despised Bleekmen, who tremble on the edge of greater knowledge than humanity, are acutely aware of this web and occasionally succeed in twitching a strand here and there, to their advantage; but they are as much in its toils as anyone else.

These three webs integrate at various coordinate points, the most remarkable point being AM-WEB, a complex structure which the UN may build some time in the future in the F.D.R. Mountains. The structure is visible to Steiner's autistic son, Manfred, who sees in it an advanced stage of decay. Its function in the novel is to provide a symbol for the aspirations and failures of mankind. The structure will be a considerable achievement when completed; which is not to say that it is not ultimately doomed; and part of that doom may be decreed by the miserable political and financial maneuverings which form one of the minor themes of this intricately designed novel.

MARTIAN TIME -SLIP COMES FROM THE MIDDLE of one of Dick's most creative periods. *The Man in the High Castle* was published in 1962. In 1963 came *The Game-Players of Titan* and then, in 1964, *The Simulacra, The Penultimate Truth, Clans of the Alphane Moon,* and the present volume. Although Dick is a prolific author, with some thirty novels appearing in fifteen years, his production rate is modest when compared with many other writers in the prodigal field of SF.

One of the attractions of Dick's novels is that they all have points at which they inter-relate, although Dick never introduces characters from previous books. The relationship is more subtle—more web-like—than that. There is a web in *Clans of the Alphane Moon,* made by the "world-spider as it spins its web of determination for all life." The way in which Mars in the present novel is parcelled up between various nationalities is reminiscent of the parcelling up of Earth into great estates in *The Penultimate Truth,* and *The Game-Players of Titan.* The horrifying corrupt world of Manfred's schizophrenia, the realm of Gubble, reminds of the tomb world into which John Isidore falls in *Do Androids Dream of Electric Sheep* or of one of the ghastly fake universes of Palmer Eldritch in *The Three Stigmata of Palmer Eldritch.* When Jack Bohlen, in the first few pages of the novel, awaits the arrival of his father from Earth, change is about to creep in; and change is often paradoxically embodied in someone or something old, like the Edward M. Stanton lying wrapped up in newspaper in the back of Maury Rock's Jaguar, in the opening pages of *We Can Build You.*

Such building blocks are by no means interchangeable from book to book; Dick's kaleidoscope is always being shaken, new sinister colours and patterns continually emerge. The power in the Dickian universe resides in these blocks, rather than in his characters; even when one of the characters has a special power (like Jones's ability to foresee the future in *The World Jones Made),* it rarely does him any good.

If we look at two of the most important of these building blocks and observe how they depend on each other for greatest effect, we come close to understanding one aspect of Dickian thought. These blocks are the Concern-With-Reality and the Involvement-with-the-Past.

Most of the characteristic themes of SF are materialist ones; only the concern-with-reality theme involves a quasi-metaphysical speculation, and this theme Dick has made peculiarly his own. Among his earliest published stories is "Imposter" (1953), in which a robot believes himself to be a man; the faking is so good that even he cannot detect the truth until the bomb within him is triggered by a phrase he himself speaks. Later, Dickian characters are frequently to find themselves trapped in hallucinations or fake worlds of various kinds, often without knowing it or, if knowing it, without being able to do anything about it. In *The Man in the High Castle*, the world we know—in which the Allies won World War II and the Axis Powers lost—is itself reduced to a hypothetical world existing only in a novel called *The Grasshopper Lies Heavy*, which the victorious Japanese and Germans have banned.

And it is not only worlds that are fake. Objects, animals, people, may also be unreal in various ways. Dick's novels are littered with fakes, from the reproduction guns buried in rock in *The Penultimate Truth* which later are used, and so become "genuine fakes," to the toad which can hardly be told from real in *Do Androids Dream of Electric Sheep?* and the androids masquerading as human in the same novel. Things are always talking back to humans. Doors argue, medicine bags patronize, the cab at the end of *Now Wait for Last Year* advises Dr. Eric Sweetscent to stay with his ailing wife. All sorts of drugs are available which lead to entirely imaginary universes, like the evil Can-D and Chew-Z used by the colonists on Mars in *Palmer Eldritch*, or the JJ-180 which is banned on Earth in *Now Wait for Last Year*.

The colonists in *Martian Time-Slip* use only the drugs available to us, though these are generally at hand—in the very opening scene we come across Silvia Bohlen doped up on phenobarbitone. Here the concern-with-reality theme is worked out through the time-slip of the title, and through the autistic boy, Manfred.

Manfred falls into the power of Arnie Kott, boss of the plumbing union which, because water is so scarce, has something of a stranglehold on Mars (a typical piece of wild Dickian ingenuity). Arnie worries a lot. He asks his Bleekman servant, Helio, if he has ever been psychoanalyzed.

> "No, Mister. Entire psychoanalysis is a vainglorious foolishness."
> "Howzat, Helio?"
> "Question they never deal with is, what to remold sick person like. There is no what, Mister."
> "I don't get you, Helio."
> "Purpose of life is unknown, and hence way to be is hidden from the eyes of living critters. Who can say if perhaps the skizophrenics are not correct? Mister, they take a brave journey. They turn away from mere things, which one may handle and turn into practical use; they turn inward to meaning. There, the black night-without-bottom lies, the pit...." (§6)

Of course, there are many ways of falling into the pit, one of which is to have too much involvement-with-the-past. In a published interview with Philip Purser, Dick admits to a fascination with the past, quoting lines of Henry Vaughan, "Some men a forward motion love / But I by backward steps would move...." Whilst saying how much he enjoys the junk of the past, Dick adds, "But I'm equally aware of the ominous possibilities. Ray Bradbury goes for the Thirties, too, and I think he falsifies and glamourises them" (*Daily Telegraph Magazine*, 19th July 1974).

Arnie Kott has an innocent fascination with objects of the past—he possesses the only spinet on Mars. In the same way, Robert Childan's trading Mickey-Mouse watches and scarce copies of Tip Top Comics to the victorious Japanese (in *The Man in the High Castle*) is represented as entirely innocuous. Trouble comes when the interest with the past and all its artifacts builds into an obsession, like Virgil Ackerman's Wash-55, a vast regressive babyland which features in *Now Wait for Last Year*.

And this is indeed where Dick parts company with Ray Bradbury, and with many another writer, in or out of SF. If he sees little safety in the future, the past is even more insidiously corrupting. So dreadful is Manfred's past that you can die in it. The past is seen as regressive; one of the most striking Dickian concepts is the "regression of forms" which takes place in *Ubik*, that magnificent but flawed novel in which the characters try to make headway through a world becoming ever more primitive, so that the airliner devolves into a Ford trimotor into a Curtis biplane, while Joe's multiplex FM tuner will regress into a cylinder phonograph playing a shouted recitation of the Lord's Prayer.

In *Martian Time-Slip*, the involvement-with-the-past is general, as well as being particularised in Manfred's illness. Mars itself is regarded by Earth as a has-been, and is patterned with has-been communities based on earlier versions of terrestrial history. Here it is especially difficult to escape damnation.

With the past so corrupting, the present so uncertain, and the future so threatening, we might wonder if there can be any escape. The secret of survival in Dick's universe is not to attempt escape into any alternate version of reality but to see things through as best you can; in that way, you may succeed if not actually triumphing. The favoured character in *Martian Time-Slip* is Jack Bohlen, whom we last see reunited with his wife, out in the dark garden, flashing a torch and looking for someone. His voice is business-like, competent, and patient; these are high-ranking virtues in the Dickian anthropology. It is significant that Jack is a *repairman* ("an idiot who can fix things," says Kott)—a survival-rich job, since it helps maintain the status quo. Similar survivors in other novels are pot-healers, traders, doctors, musical instrument makers, and android-shooters (since androids threaten the status quo).

The characters who survive are generally aided by some system of knowledge involving faith. The system is rarely a scientific one; it is more likely to be ancient. In *Martian Time-Slip*, it is the never-formulated paranormal understanding of the Bleekmen; Bohlen respects this vague eschatological faith without comprehending it, just as Kott despises it. The *I Ching*, or *Book of Changes*, the four-thousand-year-old Chinese work of divination, performs a similar function in *The Man in the High Castle*, whilst in *Counter-Clock World* Lotta Hermes randomly consults the Bible, which predicts the future with an alarming accuracy. In both Dick's two early masterpieces, *Time-Slip* and *High Castle*, this religious element—presented as something crumbling, unreliable, to be figured out with pain—is well-integrated into the texture of the novel.

Dick's next great book, *The Three Stigmata of Palmer Eldritch*, was written very soon after *Martian Time-Slip*, and the two are closely related, not only because Mars is in both cases used as a setting. To my view, *Eldritch* is a flawed work, over-complicated, and finally disappearing into a cloud of quasi-theology; whereas *Martian Time-Slip* has a calm and lucidity about it. But in *Eldritch* we also find an ancient and unreliable meta-structure of faith, in this case embodied in the ferocious alien entity which fuses with

Eldritch's being.

> Our opponent, something admittedly ugly and foreign that entered one of our race like an ailment during the long voyage between Terra and Prox...and yet it knew much more than I did about the meaning of our finite lives, here; it saw in perspective. From its centuries of vacant drifting as it waited for some kind of life form to pass by which it could grab and become...maybe that's the source of its knowledge: not experience but unending solitary brooding. (§12)

So muses Barney Mayerson. Jack Bohlen desperately needs a transcendental act of fusion; he is estranged from his wife, sold by his first employer, threatened by his second, invaded by the schizophrenia of the boy he befriends. He sees in this mental illness, so frightenly depicted in the book, the ultimate enemy. From this ultimate enemy come the time-slip of the title and that startling paragraph which seems to condense much of the feeling of the book—and, indeed, of Dick's work in general, when Bohleñ works out what Manfred's mental illness means:

> It is the stopping of time. The end of experience, of anything new. Once the person becomes psychotic, nothing ever happens to him again. (§11)

This is the maledictory circle within which Dick's beings move and from which they have to escape: although almost any change is for the worse, stasis means death, spiritual if not actual.

A NY DISCUSSION OF DICK'S WORK makes it sound a grim and appalling world. So, on the surface, it may be; yet it must also be said that Dick is amazingly funny. The terror and the humor are fused. It is this rare quality which marks Dick out. This is why critics, in seeking to convey his essential flavour, bring forth the names of Dickens and Kafka, earlier masters of ghastly comedy.

Martian Time-Slip is full of delightful comic effects, not least in the way in which Steiner and the lecherous Otto Zitte ship illegal gourmet-food items from Earth in unmanned Swiss rockets. Dick's fondness for oddball entities and titles is much in evidence, notably in the surrealist public school, where the Emperor Tiberius, Sir Francis Drake, Mark Twain, and various other dignitaries talk to the boys. Below this easy-going humour lies a darker stream of wit. Arnie Kott's terrible and fatal mistake of believing that reality is merely another version of the schizoid past is also part of the comedy of mistakes to which Dick's characters always dance.

There is a deeper resemblance to the works of Dickens and Kafka. Dick, like Dickens, enjoys a multi-plotted novel. As the legal metaphor is to *Bleak House*, the world-as-prison to *Little Dorrit*, the dust heap to *Our Mutual Friend*, the tainted wealth to *Great Expectations*, so is Mars to *Martian Time-Slip*. It is exactly and vividly drawn; it is neither the Mars as adventure-playground of Edgar Rice Burroughs nor the Mars as parallel of Pristine America of Ray Bradbury; this is Mars used in elegant and expert fashion as metaphor of spiritual poverty. In functioning as a dreamscape, it has much in common with the semi-allegorical, semi-surrealist locations used by Kafka to heighten his Ghastly Comedy of bafflement. (Staring at his house in the meagre Martian desert, Bohlen smiles and says, "This is the dream of a million years, to stand here and see this" [§9]).

Dick's alliance, if one may call it that, with writers such as Dickens and

Kafka makes him immediately congenial to English and European readers. It may be this quality which has brought him reputation and respect on this side of the Atlantic before his virtues are fully recognized in his own country.

Peter Fitting

Ubik: The Deconstruction of Bourgeois SF

Philip K. Dick's Ubik (1969) is, for this reader, one of the most important SF works of the 1960s, for it is both deconstruction and a hint at reconstruction: it lays bare the principal ways that SF is used for ideological ends, in terms of science and of fiction, while tentatively looking towards a future freed from the restraints it has exposed. In this novel Dick has exploded and transcended the SF genre and the "representational novel" of which it is a part.

Two general criteria are most commonly used to screen out the "trash" from those SF works which are deemed worthy of critical attention and may be included in the university curriculum. The first refers to a work's scientific or philosophic intentions and content, by virtue of which it is described as fictionalized science (vulgarisation), or as a paradigm of the scientific method (extrapolation) which may be used to probe our contemporary problems—for instance, SF as Utopian Literature. A pedigree of academic worth may also be granted on the basis of formal criteria, involving the discovery of esthetic or literary qualities: attention to style, imagery and metaphor, and to the work's striving towards the status of High Art.[1] These attempts to make SF respectable through its co-optation into some larger literary tradition effectively strip it of its specific or generic qualities. Thus, they also fulfill an important role in the preservation of the literary status quo and, in corollary fashion, of the society it is the university's function to support. But such conformist critical recuperation cannot make sense of much that is best within SF, and in particular, of the writing of Philip K. Dick.

Dick's writing is not easily included within traditional academic limits, for his novels are, in appearance, badly and carelessly written, with superficial characterization, confusing plots and similar deviations from "good writing." This apparent inattention to writing, along with an overabundance of traditional SF details and conventions have earned him the neglect of the proponents both of high art and of the New Wave; while his sprawling, chaotic near futures and his total disregard for the traditional SF virtues of rationality and futurological plausibility have caused him to be overlooked by the proponents of the more traditional extrapolative SF.[2] However, this paper will attempt to set out, through the example of Ubik, how Dick's SF presents a model of a more subversive form of writing which undermines rather than reconfirms the repressive system in which it has been produced, and acts as a critique of the ideological presuppositions of the SF genre and of the traditional novel in general.

A S WITH HIS OTHER FICTIONS, from Eye in the Sky (1957) and Man in the High Castle (1962) through The Three Stigmata of Palmer Eldritch (1964) and Maze of Death (1970), Ubik is centered on the the "reality problem"— on the efforts of a group of people to grasp an elusive, changing, sometimes hallucinatory and often hostile reality. The novel divides readily into two parts. The events which lead up to the explosion take place primarily on a single reality plane involving the business rivalry between Hollis Talents' psi agents and Runciter Associates' "inertials" (anti-psis). Then, following the explosion and death of Runciter, reality begins to lose its consistency and integrity. Although Joe Chip and the other inertials succeed in transporting Runciter to the Blessed Brethren Moratorium where the dead are preserved in "half-life"—a state between "full-life and the grave" (§2) in which the subject may be revived and communicated with as long as the waning "cephalic activity" is retained—attempts to revive Runciter fail and are superseded by the inertials' own anxious efforts to understand what is happening to them. Faced with a disintegrating, hostile reality, they surmise that there are two opposing forces at work: a "process of deterioration" in which their reality ages and decays, and another force which counteracts the first and involves inexplicable manifestations of the dead Runciter.

Their attempts at comprehension can be seen in the different hypotheses which they develop and which occupy much of the novel: they think that Runciter has pre-recorded messages to them before his death; that Runciter is alive trying to contact them in half-life; or that Pat (Joe Chip's wife) is an agent of Hollis and has succeeded in trapping them in a mental illusion. But as Joe Chip concedes, they can't make it all add up; finally, he "meets" Runciter who assures him that they—not he—were killed in the explosion and are now linked together in half-life where he has been trying to communicate with them. And the inertials' shared awareness of Des Moines in 1939 is the mental construct of the boy Jory who maintains his own half-life by feeding on the vitality of other half-lifers. Yet this final explanation is first modified, when Chip inadvertently summons into this illusion a living person from the future who replenishes his supply of Ubik, the "reality support" which protects him from Jory; and then destroyed when Runciter, upon leaving the Moratorium, discovers that all his coins and bills bear the likeness of Joe Chip.

From the first mention of half-life—a phenomenon which, according to Runciter, has "made theologians out of them all" (§2)—to the inertials' quest for the meaning of their existence and their awareness of the forces of life and death, the narrative of Ubik continuously plays with a metaphysical dimension. Half-life is not presented as a realistic future possibility (that is to say, the novel does not explain how half-life might be possible, nor does it explore the possible moral, ethical or scientific problems raised). Thus the reader might begin by envisaging half-life as the fictional transposition of the world of ghosts and spirits into an SF novel, where the explanation is provided by pseudo-scientific assertions rather than by reference to the supernatural. Within this context both the quest for meaning and the never ending struggle between the forces of life and death have traditionally a metaphysical significance. The quest would usually rouse the reader to expect not only that there is some discernible meaning in reality, but that this meaning lies beyond or behind observable reality (teleology) and that man sometimes receives messages from the beyond about the meaning of reality (divine revelation). Jory, the negative force of illusion and death, is the devil in this Manichean allegory, while the Runciters are the agents of Ubik, the life-preserving force which is clearly analogous to God: by its name (from the Latin ubique, the root of ubiquity, one of the attributes of the Christian God), by its functions and, most explicitly, by the epigraph to the last chapter which recalls John's "In the beginning was the Word...":

> I am Ubik. Before the universe was, I am. I made the suns. I made the worlds. I created the lives and the places they inhabit; I move them here,

I put them there. They go as I say, they do as I tell them. I am the word and my name is never spoken, the name which no one knows. I am called Ubik, but that is not my name. I am. I shall always be. (§17)

Although the reality problem is thus posed in metaphysical terms, such expectations by the reader are ultimately frustrated, and metaphysics is rejected. The characters are unable to discover any final, comprehensive meaning, and Joe Chip realizes, when he meets Jory, that there is nothing *behind* that reality: "Well, he thought, that's one of the two agencies who're at work; Jory is the one who's destroying us—has destroyed us, except for me. Behind Jory there is nothing: he is the end" (§15). And again, when he meets Ella, he exclaims "*You're the other one*, Jory destroying us, you trying to help us. Behind you there's no one. I've reached the last entities involved" (§16).

Yet Joe Chip's discovery of the "last entities involved" is not that of a final or first cause. Jory and Ubik, although they may be seen as allegorical representations of God and the Devil, are limited, nonetheless, in several crucial ways which weaken this allegory; or rather, which suggests a criticism of such idealistic concepts as "God" or "the Devil." In fact, Jory only "speeds up" the "normal cooling off" and death of things which is the "destiny of the universe" (§13). Nor does Jory think of himself as evil: his own half-life, he tells Chip, depends on his ability to prey on weaker half-lifers (§15) a dependance which is very similar to Joe Chip's "ecological" argument in defence of Runciter Associates and the anti-Psis "neutralising" of Psis: "[anti-Psis] are life forms preying on the Psis, and the Psis are life forms that prey on the Norms...Balance, the full circle, predator and prey. It appears to be an eternal system; and frankly I don't see how it could be improved" (§3).

In metaphysical terms, the thing Ubik is also an analogue to Christian "grace," the divine assistance given man to help him through the earthly vale of tears into which he is fallen, towards the afterlife and his heavenly reward. Chip's quest becomes, in large part, a search for Ubik (as Perceval's quest was for the Grail, symbol of Christian grace and redemption), which will protect him from the forces of evil and death (Jory). However, Ubik's significance as a mediating agency or signpost of metaphysical reality is undermined in several critical ways. First, it protects Chip by maintaining him an illusory reality, while covering up the "real" reality of the Moratorium. In similar fashion the established Christian religions have glossed over the human problems and injustices of reality while affirming that this existence is but the shadow of and preparation for an immaterial, ideal reality. Second, Ubik is de-sacralized through the ironic use of epigraphs, which I shall discuss in a moment, and within the narrative itself. For as Chip learns (§16), Ubik is a *human* invention, an image of humankind's own struggle against entropy, rather than an image of divine assistance or guidance in that struggle. And the final reference to Ubik in the narrative is an ironical comment on divine intervention: after the attractive young woman who has materialized from the future to bring Joe Chip a spray-can of Ubik disappears, leaving him in the middle of trying to invite her to dinner, he discovers a message on the can: "I THINK HER NAME IS MYRA LANLEY. LOOK ON REVERSE SIDE OF CONTAINER FOR ADDRESS AND PHONE NUMBER" (§16).

AN EPIGRAPH IN THE FORM of an advertising jingle opens each chapter of Ubik, except that the last chapter has the epigraph quoted above, which can, however, be read as a theological super-ad, confirming the novel's strange identification of religion and capitalist consumerism. These commercials, which have little or nothing to do with the narrative, sell Ubik as the best beer, the best instant coffee, the best shampoo....

> Friends this is clean-up time and we're discounting all our silent, electric Ubiks by this much money. Yes we're throwing away the bluebook. And remember: every Ubik on our lot has been used only as directed. (§1)

> The best way to ask for beer is to sing out for Ubik. Made from select hops, choice water, slow aged for perfect flavor, Ubik is the nation's number one choice in beer. Made only in Cleveland. (§2)

> If money worries have you in the cellar, go visit the lady at Ubik Savings & Loan. She'll take the frets out of your debts. Suppose, for example, you borrow fifty-nine poscreds on an interest-only loan. Let's see, that adds up to— (§8)

These "commercial messages" provide a restatement of Marx's description of value, for Ubik is a *universal equivalent* (the embodiment of exchange value), which can represent or replace any other commodity: under capitalism everything has its price; while the presentation of Ubik through these ads stresses the obligation of capitalism to produce needs (use-values) in the consumer.

Furthermore, the epigraphs, by their non-pertinence to the narrative (where Ubik is a "reality-support" which comes in a spray-can and is not mentioned until chapter 10), may also be seen as a further subversion of the metaphysical concept of representation. An epigraph, like a title, is expected to serve as a comment and/or digest of the contents of a chapter, as if meaning were *contained* in the writing and could be summed up in the way that labels tell us what is inside a can at the supermarket. Impertinent or facetious epigraphs (or chapter headings, as in *Maze of Death*) are a deliberate mislabeling which violates the commercial contract at the basis of the traditional novel.

The ironically inappropriate epigraphs to each chapter are thus a prelude to a more complex refutation of teleology and metaphysics in *Ubik* which depends upon recognizing the metaphysical presuppositions of the novel form itself. The classical bourgeois novel has been described in recent French literary theory as itself a metaphysical construct: traditionally, the novel has been a representative medium, and the concept of representation implies that the text is a restatement of some pre-existent meaning.[3] This attitude reduces reading to a *looking through* the text to the "real" meaning, whether that meaning be empirical reality, the author's conscious design or his unconscious intentions. Such a transcendental bias valorizes the meaning (the *signified*) while reducing the *signifier* to a means; it thereby masks and mystifies the text itself, both in its materiality (its texture) and in its production (the act of writing), in much the same way that—as Marx has shown—exchange value effects a masking and mystification of an object's use-value as well as of the concrete human labor invested in it.[4]

The traditional "representational novel" functions in this way as an ideological support for capitalism: it reinforces a transcendental conception of reality which mystifies the actual reality of the capitalist mode of production and the resultant repression and alienation. And although SF stories depict an imaginary reality, they have traditionally been concerned with the representation of a "fictional alternative to the author's empirical environment" which is usually consistent and regulated by knowable laws.[5] As in other novels, there is a discernible, comprehensible meaning which informs the SF novel. (And this quite apart from any criticism one could make of the "contents" of the traditional SF novel.) But the reader of *Ubik* is refused any such final, definitive interpretation. At the end of the novel the reader seems to have at last achieved a complete explanation of the events according to which Joe Chip and the others are in half-life while Runciter is alive trying to contact them. The reader's usual satisfaction in finishing a novel and looking back over how everything fits together derives from the formal confirmation of his conception of reality and, in the case of *Ubik*, from his relief at having finally resolved the disquieting tension between fictional reality and illusion. But this satisfaction is short-lived, for as Runciter leaves the Moratorium he discovers that the coins and bills in his pocket all bear the likeness of Joe Chip (as, at the beginning of the second part of the novel, Joe Chip and the other inertials' money bore the likeness of Runciter)—an indication that this reality is also an illusion. And the novel concludes, as Runciter looks disbelievingly at his money: "This was just the beginning": the beginning of an endless series of illusory realities, but for the careful reader, also the beginning of an end to a number of illusions about both reality and the novel. There is no satisfactory single interpretation of *Ubik*, my own included; and the reader's traditional response—the discovery of that interpretation—is frustrated. However, that frustration was planned; this kind of text is no longer a window opening onto a transcendental meaning, but a mirror which reflects the reader's look, forcing him out of his familiar reading habits while drawing his attention to the functioning of the novel as a form of manipulation.

UBIK IS NOT ONLY A DECONSTRUCTION of the *metaphysical ideologies* and the *metaphysical formal implications of the classical bourgeois novel*, but also of what (in *Solaris*) Lem has described as the *anthropomorphic presuppositions of science and of SF*. Science is expressly demystified, first of all, through the disregard for scientific plausibility and through the single "scientific" description of a technological device in the novel:

> A spray can of Ubik is a portable negative ionizer, with a self-contained, high-voltage, low-amp unit powered by a peak-gain helium battery of 25kv. The negative ions are given a counterclockwise spin by a radically biased acceleration chamber, which creates a centripetal tendency to them so that they cohere rather than dissipate. A negative ion field diminishes the velocity of anti-protophasons normally present in the atmosphere; as soon as their velocity falls they cease to be anti-protophasons and, under the principle of parity, no longer can unite with protophasons radiated from persons frozen in cold-pac; that is, those in half-life. The end result is that the proportion of protophasons not canceled by anti-protophasons increases, which means—for a specific time, anyhow—an increment in the net put-forth field of protophasonic activity...which the affected half-lifer experiences as greater vitality plus a lowering of the experience of low cold-pac temperatures. (§16)

This passage parodies scientific jargon which is often used to conceal ignorance rather then to convey information or knowledge (try reading a textbook description of cancer, for instance, a "disease" which science can "describe" without understanding it).

More importantly, *Ubik* is a critique of the *a priori* modes of perception which inform scientific thinking and which science often claims as objective empirical principles.[6] Dick undertakes this critique of scientific imperialism and tunnel-vision by carrying subjectivity to an extreme, by reminding us—as he has done perhaps most effectively in *The Clans of the Alphane Moon* and in *Maze of Death*—that the position of the observer is an extremely subjective perspective from which to deduce universal laws; that "reality" is a mental construct which may be undermined at any time.

Dick's writing has often been labeled schizophrenic, but it is time to recognize that this is not necessarily a criticism, that schizophrenia may be, in R.D. Laing's words from *The Politics of Experience*, a "breakthrough" rather than a "breakdown." Philip K. Dick's writing is an example of such a breakthrough, not only in the sense of a deconstruction of the SF novel, but also of a breaking through the psychological and perceptual confines imposed on us by capitalism.

For the repression of the individual under capitalism goes beyond the obvious economic and military machinery of imperialism or the internal police control which Dick has frequently denounced in his public letters and speeches. It also functions in a more subtle and dangerous way through the control and direction of our forms of perception and thought, making a radically different reality either unthinkable or horribly monstrous. The well-known SF film, *The Forbidden Planet* (1956), for instance, is a classic presentation of the theme of the "monsters of the id," those libidinal energies which (from the notion of "original sin" to the contemporary theories of man's innate aggressiveness), we have been taught to fear and distrust, which society seeks to dominate and control, and which are unleashed from the unconscious whenever the individual's conscious vigilance is relaxed. Unlike this film which contains an explicit warning against the unbinding of those forces, Van Vogt's *Voyage of The Space Beagle* reveals a more ambiguous attitude towards that repression. For what is striking about Van Vogt's novel (especially in view of his expressed political philosophy) is not so much the voyage, which is both a voyage of self-discovery and the familiar SF theme for the need for synthesis and integration of different scientific methods and disciplines in order to meet the challenges of a changing world, but the narrative of a series of contacts between humans and hostile space creatures. Like the monsters of *The Forbidden Planet*, these creatures are symbols of the raw, unrepressed libidinal energies which threaten the fabric and smooth functioning of capitalism. Yet in his presentation of these monsters we can detect as well an implicit (or illicit) desire for their force and power which contradicts the novel's explicit message of science containing those threats. During each confrontation in Van Vogt's novel, the reader looks for a time through the monster's eyes, feeling and perceiving reality as the monster experiences it. This identification, however brief, provokes our admiration and envy. To an even higher degree, this is the case in the emphatic understanding of what it would be like to be a Loper in Simak's *City*, where almost the entire population of Earth emigrates to Jupiter when offered the chance of becoming such a monster.

The SF of Philip K. Dick concentrates less on the actual unbinding of these forces (Dick's use of parallel worlds, his exteriorisation of internal reality) or on the "real" shape they might take than on attacking the forms of control which I have discussed—the presuppositions of the novel form and of science. Although the metaphysical solution is rejected, although there seems to be no final answer then to the question of what reality is, and although for Dick there can be no single, final reality, there is little pessimism in the endings of Dick's novels when compared to the facile pessimism of the currently fashionable literature of despair. Although *Ubik* does mark the end of some of our illusions, it is hopeful in its refusal to close the conflicts by a pat happy or unhappy ending in much the same way as another important SF novel of the 1960s, Delany's *The Einstein Intersection*. In Delany's post-cataclysmic world, strange mutated beings roam the Earth and speak of a different and unknowable future, but one towards which they move deliberately, with hope and longing. *Ubik*, through the figure of Ella Runciter, also holds out the promise of a different, unknowable future. Ella is leaving half-life for a "new womb" to be "reborn." This rebirth begins with the dissolution of the personality, as can be seen in Ella's description of the intermingling and "growing together" of different personalities in half-life. But this rebirth is not described as reincarnation; it does not involve becoming something specific, something which has been designed or programmed: rather it is an opening towards new forms and new collective possibilities.

NOTES

[1]The most recent such study is David Ketterer's *New Worlds for Old* (1974), which argues SF's pedigree by attributing it to a "form of accepted literature" which Ketterer identifies as "apocalyptic" (p. ix): "If more teachers of literature are to be convinced that science fiction is a viable area of study, it must be demonstrated to them that a novel such as *The Martian Chronicles* can open up to intense critical scrutiny just as *Moby Dick* can" (p. x). And to accomplish this accreditation he will employ a "critical strategy [which] involves the comparative, hopefully mutually illuminating consideration of science-fictional and non-science-fictional or 'classic' manifestations of the apocalyptic imagination" (p. x).

[2]See the counterblast of S. Lem, "Philip K. Dick, czyli fantomatyka mimo woli" in his *Fantastyka i Futurologia* (Krakow 1973), 1:174-92. A modified version of this study appears in *SF Commentary* ##35-36-37 (Sept 1973) as "Science Fiction: A Hopeless Case—With Exceptions." The exception is Dick, of whom Lem writes (pp. 22-23): "The surface of his books seem quite coarse and raw to me, connected with the omnipresence of trash.... Dick cannot tame trash; rather he lets loose a pandemonium and lets it calm down on its way. His metaphysics often slip in the direction of cheap circus tricks. His prose is threatened by uncontrolled outgrowths, especially when it boils over into a long series of fantastic freaks, and therefore loses all its functions of message."

[3]This discussion is based largely on the critical theories of the Tel Quel group: *Tel Quel: Théorie d'ensemble* (Paris 1968), in particular the critical and theoretical writings of Roland Barthes, Jacques Derrida, Julia Kristeva, Jean Ricardou and Philippe Sollers. For a critical appreciation of their work see Frederic Jameson, *The Prison House of Language* (Princeton 1972), pp. 172-186.

[4]Marx's theory of value is set out in Part I, Vol. I of *Capital*, "Commodities and Money," In 1914 Lenin summed that theory up as follows: "A commodity is, in the first place, a thing that satisfies a human want; in the second place, it is a thing that can be exchanged for another thing. The utility of a thing makes it a *use-value*. Exchange value (or simply, value) is first of all the ratio, the proportion, in which a certain number of use-values of one kind can be exchanged for a certain number of use-values of another kind...Their common feature is that they are *products of labour*.... The production of commodities is a system of social relations in which the individual producers create diverse products (the social division of labour), and in which all these products are equated to one another in the process of exchange. Consequently, what is common to all commodities is not the concrete labour of a definite branch of production, not labour of one particular kind, but *abstract* human labour—human labour in general.... After making a detailed analysis of the twofold character of the labour incorporated in commodities, Marx goes on to analyse the *form of value* and *money*. Here, Marx's main task is to study the *origin of the money form of value*, to study the *historical process* of the development of exchange, beginning with individual and incidental acts of exchange..., passing on to the universal from of value, in which a number of different commodities are exchanged for one and the same particular commodity, and ending with the money form of value, when gold becomes that particular commodity, the universal equivalent. As the highest product of the development of exchange and commodity production, money masks, conceals, the social character of all individual labour, the social link between individual producers united by the

market." *Collected Works* (Moscow 1964), 21:59-61.

The specific parallel between *value* and *meaning* is developed by J.-J. Goux, "Marx et l'inscription du travail" in *Tel Quel*, op. cit.: "The phonic or scriptural materials become simply signs, simple signifiers (of an exterior, transcendant meaning); but their transforming function (as a means of production) and their transformed character-istics (as a product) are denied. The fact is that any meaning is but the product of work on and the work of real signs—the result of textual production—is hidden, as is the original use (or merchandise) value of money (gold or silver whose value comes from the work invested in its extraction) in order to reduce it to an arbitrary secondary sign, only a sign" (p. 193).

⁵Darko Suvin, "On the Poetics of The Science Fiction Genre," *College English* 34(1972):375.

⁶In Lem's *Solaris*, the narrator describes the theories of the Solarist Grastrom who "set out to demonstrate that the most abstract achievements of science, the most advanced theories and victories of mathematics represented nothing more than a stumbling one- or two-step progression from our rude, prehistoric, anthropomorphic understanding of the universe around us. He pointed out correspondences with the human body—the projection of our senses, the structure of our physical organization, and the physiological limitations of man—in the equations of the theory of relativity, the theorem of magnetic fields and the various unified field theories" (§11).

The investigation of the metaphysical or ideological presuppositions of science and scientific method as well as the demystification of science's claims for its neutrality and objectivity have been the subject of a number of interesting and very different studies in recent years, from Boris Eizykman's important *Science Fiction et capital-isme: critique de la position de désir de la science* (Paris 1974) to Arthur Koestler's *The Sleepwalkers* (1968) and Daniel Greenburg's *The Politics of Pure Science* (1967). For a look at the interrelationships of science, Marxism and political goals and the resulting successes and failures in the Soviet Union, see Loren Graham's very valuable *Science and Philosophy in the Soviet Union* (1972).

Stanislaw Lem

Philip K. Dick: A Visionary Among the Charlatans

Translated from the Polish by Robert Abernathy

No one in his right mind seeks the psychological truth about crime in detec-tive stories. Whoever seeks such truth will turn rather to *Crime and Punish-ment*. In relation to Agatha Christie, Dostoevsky constitutes a higher court of appeal, yet no one in his right mind will condemn the English author's stories on this account. They have a right to be treated as the entertaining thrillers they are, and the tasks Dostoevsky set himself are foreign to them.

If anyone is dissatisfied with SF in its role as an examiner of the future and of civilization, there is no way to make an analogous move from literary oversimplifications to full-fledged art, because there is no court of appeal from this genre. There would be no harm in this, save that American SF, exploiting its exceptional status, lays claim to occupy the pinnacles of art and thought. One is annoyed by the pretentiousness of a genre which fends off accusations of primitivism by pleading its entertainment character and then, once such accusations have been silenced, renews its overweening claims. By being one thing and purporting to be another, SF promotes a mystification which, moreover, goes on with the tacit consent of readers and public. The development of interest in SF at American universities has, contrary to what might have been expected, altered nothing in this state of affairs. In all candor it must be said, though one risk perpetrating a crime *laesae Almae Matris*, that the critical methods of theoreticians of literature are inadequate in the face of the deceptive tactics of SF. But it is not hard to grasp the reason for this paradox: if the only fictional works treating of problems of crime were like those of Agatha Christie, then to just what kind of books could even the most scholarly critic appeal in order to demonstrate the intellectual poverty and artistic mediocrity of the detective thriller? Qualitative norms and upper limits are established in literature by concrete works and not by critics' postulates. No mountain of theoretical lucubrations can compensate for the absence of an outstanding fictional work as a lofty model. The criticism of experts in historiography did not undermine the status of Sienkiewicz's *Trilogy*, for there was no Polish Leo Tolstoy to devote a *War and Peace* to the period of the Cossack and Swedish wars. In short, *inter caecos luscus rex*—where there is nothing first-rate, its role will be taken over by mediocrity, which sets itself facile goals and achieves them by facile means.

What the absence of such model works leads to is shown, more plainly than by any abstract discussions, by the change of heart which Damon Knight, both author and respected critic, expressed in SFS #3. Knight declared himself to have been mistaken earlier in attacking books by van Vogt for their incoherence and irrationalism, on the grounds that, if van Vogt enjoys an enormous readership, he *must by that very fact* be on the right track as an author, and that it is wrong for criticism to discredit such writing in the name of arbitrary values, if the reading public does not *want* to recognize such values. The job of criticism is, rather, to discover those traits to which the work owes its popularity. Such words, from a man who struggled for years to stamp out tawdriness in SF, are more than the admission of a personal defeat—they are the diagnosis of a general condition. If even the perennial defender of artistic values has laid down his arms, what can lesser spirits hope to accomplish in this situation?

Indeed, the possibility cannot be ruled out that Joseph Conrad's elevated description of literature as rendering "the highest kind of truth to the visible universe" may become an anachronism—that the independence of literature from fashion and demand may vanish outside SF as well, and then whatever reaps immediate applause as a best-seller will be identified with what is most worthwhile. That would be a gloomy prospect. The culture of any period is a mixture of that which docilely caters to passing whims and fancies and that which transcends these things—and may also pass judgment on them. Whatever defers to current tastes becomes an entertainment which achieves success immediately or not at all, for there is no such thing as a stage-magic exhibition or a football game which, unrecognized today, will become famous a hundred years from now. Literature is another matter: it is created by a process of natural selection of values, which takes place in society and which does not necessarily relegate works to obscurity if they are *also* entertainment, but which consigns them to oblivion if they are *only* entertainment. Why is this so? Much could be said about this. If the concept of the human being as an individual who desires of society and of the world something more than immediate satisfactions were abolished, then the difference between literature and entertainment would likewise disappear. But since we do not as yet identify the dexterity of a conjurer with the personal expression of a relationship to the world, we cannot measure literary values by numbers of books sold.

But how does it ever happen that something which is less popular can, in the historical long run, hold its own against that which scores prompt successes and even contrives to silence its opponents? This results from the aforementioned natural selection in culture, strikingly similar to such selection in biological evolution. The changes by virtue of which some species yield place to others on the evolutionary scene are seldom consequences of great cataclysms. Let the progeny of one species outsurvive that of another by a margin of only one in a million, and by and by only the former species will remain alive—though the difference between the chances of the two is imperceptible at short range. So it is also in culture: books which in the eyes of their contemporaries are so alike as to be peers part company as the years go by; facile charm, being ephemeral, gives way at last to that which is more difficult to perceive. Thus regularities in the rise and decline of literary works come into being and give direction to the development of the spiritual culture of an age.

Nevertheless, there can be circumstances that frustrate this process of natural selection. In biological evolution the result will be retrogression, degeneration, or at the very least developmental stagnation, typical of populations isolated from the outside world and vitiated by inbreeding, since these are most lacking in the fruitful diversity that is guaranteed only by openness to all the world's influences. In culture an analogous situation leads to the emergence of enclaves shut up in ghettos, where intellectual production likewise stagnates because of inbreeding in the form of incessant repetition of the selfsame creative patterns and techniques. The internal dynamics of the ghetto may appear to be intense, but with the passage of years it becomes evident that this is only a semblance of motion, since it leads nowhere, since it neither feeds into nor is fed by the open domain of culture, since it does not generate new patterns or trends, and since finally it nurses the falsest of notions about itself, for lack of any honest evaluation of its activities from outside. The books of the ghetto assimilate themselves to one another, becoming an anonymous mass, while such surroundings thrust whatever is better downward toward the worse, so that works of differing quality meet one another halfway, as it were, in the levelling process forced upon them. In such a situation publishing success not only may but must become the sole standard of evaluation, since a vacuum of standards is impossible. Hence, where there are no ratings on the merits, these are replaced by ratings on a commercial basis.

Just such a situation reigns in American SF, which is a domain of herd creativity. Its herd character manifests itself in the fact that books by different authors become as it were different sessions of playing at one and the same game or various figures of the selfsame dance. It should be emphasized that, in literary culture as in natural evolution, effects become causes by virtue of feedback loops: the artistic-intellectual passivity and mediocrity of works touted as brilliant repel the more exigent authors and readers, so that the loss of individuality in SF is at once a cause and an effect of ghetto seclusion. In SF there is little room left for creative work that would aspire to deal with problems of our time without mystification, oversimplification, or facile entertainment: e.g., for work which would reflect on the place that Reason can occupy in the Universe, on the outer limits of concepts formed on Earth as instruments of cognition, or on such consequences of contacts with extraterrestrial life as find no place in the desperately primitive repertoire of SF devices (bounded by the alternative "we win"/"they win"). These devices bear much the same relation to serious treatment of problems of the kind mentioned as does the detective story to the problems of evil inherent in mankind. Whoever brings up the heavy artillery of comparative ethnology, cultural anthropology and sociology against such devices is told that he is using cannon to shoot sparrows, since it is merely a matter of entertainment; once he falls silent, the voices of the apologists for the culture-shaping, anticipative, predictive and mythopoeic role of SF are raised anew. SF behaves rather like a conjurer pulling rabbits from a hat, who, threatened with a search of his belongings, pretends to think we are crazy to suggest this and indulgently explains that he is just performing tricks—after which we promptly hear that he is passing himself off in public for an authentic thaumaturge.

IS CREATIVE WORK WITHOUT MYSTIFICATION possible in such an environment? An answer to this question is given by the stories of Philip K. Dick. While these stand out from the background against which they have originated, it is not easy to capture the ways in which they do, since Dick employs the same materials and theatrical props as other American writers. From the warehouse which has long since become their common property, he takes the whole threadbare lot of telepaths, cosmic wars, parallel worlds, and time travel. In his stories terrible catastrophes happen, but this too is no exception to the rule, for lengthening the list of sophisticated ways in which the world can end is among the standard preoccupations of SF. But where other SF writers explicitly name and delimit the source of the disaster, whether social (terrestrial or cosmic war) or natural (elemental forces of nature), the world of Dick's stories suffers dire changes for reasons which remain unascertainable to the end. People perish not because a nova or a war has erupted, not because of flood, famine, plague, draught, or sterility, nor because the Martians have landed on our doorstep; rather, there is some inscrutable factor at work which is visible in its manifestations but not at its source, and the world behaves as if it has fallen prey to a malignant cancer which through metastases attacks one area of life after another. This is, be it said forthwith, apposite as a castigation of historiographic diagnostics, since in fact humanity does not as a rule succeed in exhaustively or conclusively diagnosing the causes of the afflictions which befall it. It is sufficient to recall how many diverse and in part mutually exclusive factors are nowadays adduced by experts as sources of the crisis of civilization. And this, be it added, is also appropriate as an artistic presupposition, since literature which furnishes the reader with godlike omniscience about all narrated events is today an anachronism which neither the theory of art nor the theory of knowledge will undertake to defend.

The forces which bring about world debacle in Dick's books are fantastic, but they are not merely invented *ad hoc* to shock the readers. We shall show this on the example of *Ubik*, a work which, by the way, can also be regarded as a fantastic grotesque, a "macabresque" with obscure allegorical subtexts, decked out in the guise of ordinary SF.

If, however, it is viewed as a work of SF proper the contents of *Ubik* can be most simply summarized as follows:

Telepathic phenomena, having been mastered in the context of capitalistic society, have undergone commercialization like every other technological innovation. So businessmen hire telepaths to steal trade secrets from their competitors, and the latter for their part defend themselves against this "extrasensory industrial espionage" with the aid of "inertials," people whose psyches nullify the "psi field" that makes it possible to receive others' thoughts. By way of specialization, firms have sprung up which rent out telepaths and "inertials" by the hour, and the "strong man" Glen Runciter is the proprietor of such a firm. The medical profession has learned how to arrest the agony of victims of mortal ailments, but still has no means of curing them. Such people are therefore kept in a state of "half-life" in special institutions, "moratoriums" (a kind of "places of postponement"—of death, obviously). If they merely rested there unconscious in their icy caskets, that would be small comfort for their surviving kin. So a technique has been developed for maintaining the mental life of such people in "cold-pac." The world which they experience is not part of reality, but a fiction created by appropriate methods. None the less, normal people can make contact with the frozen ones, for the cold-sleep apparatus has means to this end built into it, something on the order of a telephone.

This idea is not altogether absurd in terms of scientific facts: the concept of freezing the incurably ill to await the time when remedies for their diseases will be found has already come in for serious discussion. It would also be possible in principle to maintain vital processes in a person's brain when the body dies (to be sure, that brain would rapidly suffer psychological disinte-gration as a consequence of sensory deprivation). We know that stimulation of the brain by electrodes produces in the subject of such an operation ex-periences indistinguishable from ordinary perceptions. In Dick we find a perfected extension of such techniques, though he does not discuss this ex-plicitly in the story. Numerous dilemmas arise here: should the "half-lifer" be informed of his condition? is it right to keep him under the illusion that he is leading a normal life?

According to *Ubik*, people who, like Runciter's wife, have spent years in cold sleep are well aware of the fact. It is another matter with those who, like Joe Chip, have come close to meeting with a violent end and have re-gained consciousness imagining that they have escaped death, whereas in fact they are resting in a moratorium. In the book, it must be admitted, this is an unclear point, which is however masked by another dilemma: for, if the world of the frozen person's experiences is a purely subjective one, then any intervention in that world from outside must be for him a phenome-non which upsets the normal course of things. So if someone communicates with the frozen one, as Runciter does with Chip, this contact is accompanied in Chip's experiences by uncanny and startling phenomena—for it is as if waking reality were breaking into the midst of a dream "only from one side," without thereby causing extinction of the dream and wakening of the sleeper (who, after all, cannot wake up like a normal man because he is not a normal man). But, to go a step further, is not contact also possible between two frozen individuals? Might not one of these people dream that he is alive and well and that from his accustomed world he is communicating with the other one—that only the other person succumbed to the unfortunate mishap? This too is possible. And, finally, is it possible to imagine a wholly infallible technology? There can be no such thing. Hence certain perturbations may affect the subjective world of the frozen sleeper, to whom it will then seem that his environment is going mad—perhaps that in it even *time* is falling to pieces! Interpreting the events presented in this fashion, we come to the con-clusion that all the principal characters of the story were killed by the bomb on the Moon, and consequently all of them had to be placed in the mora-torium and from this point on the book recounts only their visions and il-lusions. In a realistic novel (but this is a *contradictio in adiecto*) this version would correspond to a narrative which, after coming to the demise of the hero, would go on to describe his life *after death*. The realistic novel cannot describe this life, since the principle of realism rules out such descriptions. If, however, we assume a technology which makes possible the "half-life" of the dead, nothing prevents the author from remaining faithful to his characters and following them with his narrative—into the depths of their icy dream, which is henceforward the only form of life open to them.

Thus it is possible to rationalize the story in the above manner—on which, however, I would not insist too seriously, and that for two reasons at once. The *first reason* is that to make the plot fully consistent along the lines sketched above is impossible. If all Runciter's people perished on the Moon, then *who* transported them to the moratorium? Another thing which does not yield to any rationalization is the talent of the girl who by mental effort alone was able to alter the present by transposing causal nodes in a past already over and done with. (This takes place before the occurrence on the Moon, when there are no grounds for regarding the represented world as the purely subjective one of any "half-life" character.) Similar misigvings are inspired by Ubik itself, "the Absolute in a spray can," to which we will devote attention a little later on. If we approach the fictional world pedantically, no case can be made for it, for it is full of contradictions. But if we shelve such objections and inquire rather after the overall meaning of the work, we will discover that it is close to the meanings of other books by Dick, for all that they seem to differ from one another. Essentially it is always one and the same world which figures in them—a world of elementally unleashed entropy, of decay which not only, as in our reality, attacks the harmonious arrangement of matter, but which even consumes the order of elapsing time. Dick has thus amplified, rendered monumental and at the same time monstrous certain fundamental properties of the actual world, giving them dramatic acceleration and impetus. All the technological innovations, the magnificent inventions and the newly mastered human capabilities (such as telepathy, which our author has provided with an uncommonly rich articulation into "specialties") ultimately come to nothing in the struggle against the inexorably rising floodwaters of Chaos. Dick's province is thus a "world of pre-established disharmony," which is hidden at first and does not manifest itself in the opening scenes of the novel; these are presented unhurriedly and with calm matter-of-factness, just in order that the intrusion of the destructive factor should be all the more effective. Dick is a prolific author, but I speak only of those of his novels which constitute the "main sequence" of his works; each of these books (I would count among them: *The Three Stigmata of Palmer Eldritch, Ubik, Now Wait for Last Year,* and perhaps also *Galactic Pot-Healer*) is a somewhat different embodiment of the same dramatic principle—the conversion of the order of the universe to rack and ruin before our eyes. In a world smitten with insanity, in which even the chronology of events is subject to convulsions, it is only the people who preserve their normality. So Dick subjects them to the pressure of a terrible testing, and in his fantastic experiment only the psychology of the characters remains nonfantastic. They struggle bitterly and stoically to the end, like Joe Chip in the current instance, against the chaos pressing on them from all sides, the sources of which remain, actually, unfathomable, so that in this regard the reader is thrown back on his own conjectures.

The peculiarities of Dick's worlds arise especially from the fact that in them it is waking reality which undergoes profound dissociation and duplication. Sometimes the dissociating agency consists in chemical substances (of the hallucinogenic type—thus in *The Three Stigmata of Palmer Eldritch*); sometimes in "cold-sleep technique" (as precisely in *Ubik*); sometimes (as in *Now Wait for Last Year*) in a combination of narcotics and "parallel worlds." The end-effect is always the same: distinguishing between waking reality and visions proves to be impossible. The technical aspect of this phenomenon is fairly inessential—it does not matter whether the splitting of reality is brought about by a new technology of chemical manipulation of the mind or, as in *Ubik*, by one of surgical operations. The essential point is that a world equipped with the means of splitting perceived reality into indistinguishable likenesses of itself creates practical dilemmas that are known only to the theoretical speculations of philosophy. This is a world in which, so to speak, this philosophy goes out into the street and becomes for every ordinary mortal no less of a burning question than is for us the threatened destruction of the biosphere.

There is no question of using a meticulous factual bookkeeping to strike a rational balance for the novel, by virtue of which it would satisfy the demands of common sense. We are not only forced to but we ought to at a certain point leave off defending its "science-fictional nature" also for a *second reason* so far unmentioned. The first reason was dictated to us simply by necessity: given that the elements of the work lack a focal point, it *cannot* be rendered consistent. The second reason is more essential: the impossibility of imposing consistency on the text compels us to seek its global meanings not in the realm of events themselves, but in that of their constructive principle, the very thing that is responsible for lack of focus. If no such meaningful principle were discoverable, Dick's novels would have to be called mystifications, since any work must justify itself either on the level of what it presents literally or on the level of deeper semantic content, not so much overtly present in as summoned up by the text. Indeed, Dick's works teem with non sequiturs, and any sufficiently sensitive reader can without difficulty make up lists of incidents which flout logic and experience alike. But—to repeat what was already said in other ways—what is inconsistency in literature? It is a symptom either of incompetence or else of repudiation of some values (such as credibility of incidents or their logical coherence) for the sake of other values.

Here we come to a ticklish point in our discussion, since the values alluded to cannot be objectively compared. There is no universally valid answer to the question whether it is permissible to sacrifice order for the sake of vision in a creative work—everything depends on what kind of order and what kind of vision are involved. Dick's novels have been variously interpreted. There are critics, such as Sam Lundwall, who say that Dick is cultivating an "offshoot of mysticism" in SF. It is not, though, a question of mysticism in the religious sense, but rather of occult phenomena. *Ubik* furnishes some grounds for such a conclusion—does not the person who ousts Ella Runciter's soul from her body behave like a "possessing spirit"? Does not he metamorphose into various incarnations when fighting with Joe Chip? So such an approach is admissible.

Another critic (George Turner) has denied all value in *Ubik*, declaring that the novel is a pack of conflicting absurdities—which can be demonstrated with pencil and paper. I think, however, that the critic should not be the prosecutor of a book but its defender, though one not allowed to lie: he may only present the work in the most favorable light. And because a book full of meaningless contradictions is as worthless as one that holds forth about vampires and other monstrous revenants, since neither of them touches on problems worthy of serious consideration, I prefer my account of *Ubik* to all the rest. The theme of catastrophe had been so much worked over in SF that it seemed to be played out until Dick's books became a proof that this had been a matter of frivolous mystification. For science-fictional endings of the world were brought about either by man himself, e.g. by unrestrained warfare, or by some cataclysm as extrinsic as it was accidental, which thus might equally well not have happened at all.

Dick, on the other hand, by introducing into the annihilation ploy—the tempo of which becomes more violent as the action progresses—also instruments of civilization such as hallucinogens, effects such a commingling of the convulsions of technology with those of human experience that it is no longer apparent just what works the terrible wonders—a *Deus ex machina* or a *machina ex Deo*, historical accident or historical necessity. It is difficult to elucidate Dick's position in this regard, because in particular novels he has given mutually incongruent answers to this question. Appeal to transcendence appears now as a mere possibility for the reader's conjectures, now as a diagnostic near-certainty. In *Ubik*, as we have said, a conjectural solution which refuses to explain events in terms of some verion of occultism or spiritualism finds support in the bizarre technology of "half-life" as the last chance offered by medicine to people on the point of death. But already in *The Three Stigmata of Palmer Eldritch* transcendental evil emanates from the titular hero—that is, by the way, rather lowgrade metaphysics, being akin to hack treatments of "supernatural visitations" and "ghost," and all that saves the thing from turning into a fiasco is the author's virtuosity as a storyteller. And in *Galactic Pot-Healer* we have to do with a fabulous parable about a sunken cathedral on some planet and about the struggle which takes place between Light and Darkness over raising it, so that the last semblance of literalness of events vanishes here. Dick is, so I instinctively judge, perfidious in that he does not give unambiguous answers to the questions provoked by reading him, in that he strikes no balances and explains nothing "scientifically," but rather just confounds things, not only in the plot itself but with respect to a superordinated category: the literary *convention* within which the story unfolds. For all that *Galactic Pot-Healer* leans toward allegory, it does not adopt this position either unambiguously or definitively, and a like indeterminacy as to genre is also characteristic for other novels by Dick, perhaps to an even higher degree. We thus encounter here the same difficulty about genre placement of a work which we have met with in the writing of Kafka.

It should be emphasized that the genre affiliation of a creative work is not an abstract problem of interest only to theorists of literature, but is an indispensable prerequisite to the reading of a work; the difference between the theorist and the ordinary reader reduces itself to the fact that the latter places the book he has read in a specific genre automatically, under the influence of his internalized experiences—in the same way that we employ our native language automatically, even when we do not know its morphology or syntax from specialized studies. The convention proper to a concrete genre becomes fixed with the passage of time and is familiar to every qualified reader; consequently "everybody knows" that in a realistic novel the author cannot cause his hero to walk through closed doors, but can on the other hand reveal to the reader the content of a dream which the hero has and forgets before he wakes up (although the one thing is as impossible as the other from a commonsense point of view). The convention of the detective story requires that the perpetrator of a crime be found out, while the convention of SF requires rational accounting for events that are quite improbable and even seemingly at odds with logic and experience. On the other hand, the evolution of literary genres is based precisely on violation of storytelling conventions which have already become static. So Dick's novels in some measure violate the convention of SF, which can be *accounted to him as* merit, because they thereby acquire broadened meanings having allegorical import. This import cannot be exactly determined; the indefiniteness which originates in this way favors the emergence of an aura of enigmatic mystery about the work. What is involved is a modern authorial strategy which some people may find intolerable, but which cannot be assailed with factual arguments, since the demand for absolute purity of genres is becoming nowadays an anachronism in literature. The critics and readers who hold Dick's "impurity" with respect to genre against him are fossilized traditionalists, and a counterpart to their attitude would be an insistence that prosaists should keep on writing in the manner of Zola and Balzac, and only thus. In the light of the foregoing observations one can understand better the peculiarity and uniqueness of the place occupied by Dick in SF. His novels throw many readers accustomed to standard SF into abiding confusion, and give rise to complaints, as naive as they are wrathful, that Dick, instead of providing "precise explanations" by way of conclusion, instead of solving puzzles, sweeps things under the rug. In relation to Kafka analogous objections would consist in demanding that *The Metamorphosis* should conclude with an explicit "entomological justification," making plain when and under what circumstances a normal man can turn into a bug, and that *The Trial* should explain just what Mr. K. is accused of.

PHILIP DICK DOES NOT LEAD his critics an easy life, since he does not so much play the part of a guide through his fantasmagoric worlds as he gives the impression of one lost in their labyrinth. He has stood all the more in need of critical assistance, but has not received it, and has gone on writing labelled a "mystic" and thrown back entirely on his own resources. There is no telling whether or how his work would have changed if it had come under the scrutinies of genuine critics. Perhaps such change would not have been all that much to the good. A second characteristic trait of Dick's work, after its ambiguity as to genre, is its tawdriness which is not without a certain charm, being reminiscent of the goods offered at county fairs by primitive craftsmen who are at once clever and naive, possessed of more talent than self-knowledge. Dick has as a rule taken over a rubble of building materials from the run-of-the-mill American professionals of SF, frequently adding a true gleam of originality to already worn-out concepts and, what is surely more important, erecting with such material constructions truly his own. The world gone mad, with a spasmodic flow of time and a network of causes and effects which wriggles as if nauseated, the world of frenzied physics, is unquestionably his invention, being an inversion of our familiar standard according to which only we, but never our environment, may fall victim to psychosis. Ordinarily, the heroes of SF are overtaken only by two kinds of calamities: the social, such as the "infernos of police-state tyranny," and the physical, such as catastrophes caused by Nature. Evil is thus inflicted on people either by other people (invaders from the stars are merely people in monstrous disguises), or by the blind forces of matter.

With Dick the very basis of such a clearcut articulation of the proposed diagnosis comes to grief. We can convince ourselves of this by putting to *Ubik* questions of the order just noted: who was responsible for the strange and terrible things which happened to Runciter's people? The bomb attack on the Moon was the doing of a competitor, but of course it was not in his power to bring about the collapse of time. An explanation appealing to the medical "cold-pac" technology is, as we have pointed out, likewise incapable of rationalizing everything. The gaps that separate the fragments of the plot cannot be eliminated, and they lead one to suspect the existence of some higher-order necessity which constitutes the destiny of Dick's world. Whether this destiny resides in the temporal sphere or beyond it is impossible to say. When one considers to what an extent our faith in the infallible beneficence of technical progress has already waned, the fusion which Dick envisages between culture and nature, between the instrument and its basis, by virtue of which it acquires the aggressive character of a malignant neoplasm, no longer seems merely sheer fantasy. This is not to say that Dick is predicting any concrete future. The disintegrating worlds of his stories, as it were inversions of Genesis, order returning to Chaos—this is not so much the future foreseen as it is future shock, not straightforwardly expressed but embodied in fictional reality, it is an objectivized projection of the fears and fascinations proper to the human individual in our times.

It has been customary to identify the downfall of civilization falsely and narrowly with regression to some past stage of history—even to the caveman or downright animal stage. Such an evasion is often employed in SF, since inadequacy of imagination takes refuge in oversimplified pessimism. Then we are shown the remotest *future* as a lingering state of feudal, tribal or slave-holding society, inasmuch as atomic war or invasion from the stars is supposed to have hurled humanity backward, even into the depths of a prehistoric way of life. To say of such works that they advocate the concepts of some cyclic (e.g. Spenglerian) philosophy of history would amount to maintaining that a motif endlessly repeated by a phonograph record represents the concept of some sort of "cyclic music," whereas it is merely a matter of a mechanical defect resulting from a blunt needle and worn grooves. So works of this sort do not pay homage to cyclic historiosophy, but merely reveal an insufficiency of sociological imagination, for which the atomic war or the interstellar invasion is only a convenient pretext for spinning out interminable sagas of primordial tribal life under the pretense of portraying the farthest future. Nor is it possible to hold that such books promulgate the "atomic credo" of belief in the inevitability of a catastrophe which will soon shatter our civilization, since the cataclysm in question amounts to nothing but an excuse for shirking more importnat creative obligations.

Such expedients are foreign to Dick. For him, the development of civilization continues, but is as it were crushed by itself, becoming monstrous at the heights of its achievement—which, as a prognostic viewpoint, is more original than the assuredly unilluminating thesis that, if technical civilization breaks down, people will be forced to get along by returning to primitive tools, even to bludgeons and flints.

Alarm at the impetus of civilization finds expression nowadays in the slogans of a "return to Nature" after smashing and discarding everything "artificial," i.e. science and technology. These pipe dreams turn up also in SF. Happily, they are absent in Dick. The action of his novels takes place in a time when there can no longer be any talk of return to nature or of turning away from the "artificial," since the fusion of the "natural" with the "artificial" has long since become an accomplished fact.

At this point it may be worthwhile to point out the dilemma encountered by futuristically oriented SF. According to an opinion quite generally held by readers, SF ought to depict the world of the fictional future no less explicitly and intelligibly than a writer such as Balzac depicted the world of his own time in *The Human Comedy*. Whoever asserts this fails to take into account the fact that there exists no world beyond or above history and common to all eras or all cultural formations of mankind. That which, as the world of *The Human Comedy*, strikes us an completely clear and intelligible, is not an altogether objective reality, but is only a particular interpretation (of nineteenth-century vintage and hence close to us) of a world classified, understood and experienced in a concrete fashion. The familiarity of Balzac's world thus signifies nothing more than the simple fact that we have grown perfectly accustomed to this account of reality and that consequently the language of Balzac's characters, their culture, their habits and ways of satisfying spiritual and bodily needs, and also their attitude toward nature and transcendence seem to us transparent. However, the movement of historical changes may infuse new content into concepts thought of as fundamental and fixed, as for example the notion of "progress," which according to nineteenth-century attitudes was equivalent to a confident optimism, convinced of the existence of an inviolable boundary separating what is harmful to man from what benefits him. Currently we begin to suspect that the concept thus established is losing its relevance, because the harmful ricochets of progress are not incidental, easily eliminated, adventitious components of it but are rather such a cost of gains achieved as, at some point along the way, liquidates all the gain. In short, absolutizing the drive toward "progress" could prove to be a drive toward ruin.

So the image of the future world cannot be limited to adding a certain number of technical innovations, and meaningful prediction does not lie in serving up the present larded with startling improvements or revelations in lieu of the future.

The difficulties encountered by the reader of a work placed in a remote historical period are not the result of any arbitrariness on the writer's part, any predilection for "estrangements," any wish to shock the reader or to lead him up the garden, but are an ineradicable part of such an artistic undertaking. Situations and concepts can be understood only through relating them to ones already known, but when too great a time interval separates people living in different eras there is a loss of the basis for understanding in common life experiences which we unreflectingly and automatically imagine to be invariant. It follows that an author who truly succeeded in delineating an image of the far future would not achieve literary success, since he would assuredly not be understood. Consequently, in Dick's stories a truth-value can be ascribed only to their generalized basis, which can be summed up more or less as follows: when people become ants in the labyrinths of the technosphere which they themselves have built, the idea of a return to Nature not only becomes utopian but cannot even be meaningfully articulated, because no such thing as a Nature that has not been artificially transformed has existed for ages. We today can still talk of "return to Nature," because we are relics of it, only slightly modified in biological respect within civilization, but try imagining the slogan "return to Nature" uttered by a robot—why, it would mean turning into deposits of iron ore!

The impossibility of civilization's returning to Nature, which is simply equivalent to the irreversibility of history, leads Dick to the pessimistic conclusion that looking far into the future becomes such a fulfilment of dreams of power over matter as converts the ideal of progress into a monstrous caricature. This conclusion does not inevitably follow from the author's assumptions, but it constitutes an eventuality which ought *also* to be taken into account. By the way, in putting things thus we are no longer summarizing Dick's work, but are giving rein to reflections about it, for the author himself seems so caught up in his vision that he is unconcerned about either its literal plausibility or its non-literal message. It is the more unfortunate that criticism has not brought out the intellectual consequences of Dick's work and has not indicated the prospects inherent in its possible continuation, prospects and consequences advantageous not only for the author but for the entire genre, since Dick has presented us not so much with finished *accomplishments* as with fascinating *promises*. It has, indeed, been just the other way round—criticism inside the field has instinctively striven somehow to domesticate Dick's creations, to restrain their meanings, emphasizing what in them is *similar* to the rest of the genre, and saying nothing about what is different—insofar as it did not simply denounce them as worthless for that difference. In this behavior a pathological aberration of the natural selection of literary works is emphatically apparent, since this selection ought to separate workmanlike mediocrity from promising originality, not lump these together, for such a "democratic" proceeding in practice equates the dross to the good metal.

Let us admit, however, that the charms of Dick's books are not unalloyed, so that it is with them somewhat as it is with the beauty of certain actresses, whom one had better not inspect too carefully at close range, on pain of being sadly disillusioned. There is no point in estimating the futurological likelihood of such details in this novel as those apartment and refrigerator doors which the tenant is forced to argue with—for these are fictional ingredients created for the purpose of doing two jobs at once: to introduce the reader into a world decidedly different from the present-day one, and to convey a certain message to him by means of this world.

Every literary work has two components in the above sense, since every one exhibits a given factual world and says something by means of that world. Yet in different genres and different works the ratio between the two components varies. A realistic work of fiction contains a great deal of the first component and very little of the second, as it portrays the real world, which in its own right, that is outside the book, does not constitute any sort of message, but merely exists and flourishes. Nevertheless, because the author, of course, makes particular choices when writing a literary work, these choices give it the character of a statement addressed to the reader. In an allegorical work there is a minimum of the first component and a maximum of the second, seeing that its world is in effect an apparatus signaling the actual content—the message—to the receiver. The tendentiousness of allegorical fiction is usually obvious, that of the realistic kind more or less well-concealed. There are no works whatsoever without tendentiousness; if anyone speaks of such, what he actually has in mind is works devoid of expressly emphasized tendentiousness, which cannot be "translated" into the concrete credo of a world view. The aim of the epic e.g., is precisely to construct a world which can be interpreted in a number of ways—as the reality outside of literature can be interpreted in a number of ways. If, however, the sharp tools of criticism (of the structural kind, for instance) are applied to the epic, it is possible to detect the tendentiousness hidden even in such works, because the author is a human being and by that token a litigant in the existential process, hence complete impartiality is unattainable for him.

Unfortunately, it is only from realistic prose that one can appeal directly to the real world. Therefore, the bane of SF is the desire—doomed from the start to failure—to depict worlds intended at one and the same time to be products of the imagination and to signify nothing, i.e. not to have the character of a message but to be as it were on a par with the things in our environment, from furniture to stars, as regards their objective self-sufficiency. This is a fatal error lodged at the roots of SF, for where deliberate tendentiousness is not allowed involuntary tendentiousness seeps in. By tendency we mean a partisan bias, or point of view which cannot be divinely objective. An epic may strike us as just that objective, because the *how* of its presentation (the viewpoint) is for us imperceptibly concealed under the *what*—the epic too is a partisan account of events, but we do not notice its tendentiousness because we share its bias and cannot get outside it. We discover the bias of the epic centuries later, when the passage of time has transformed the standards of "absolute objectivity" and we can perceive, in what passed for a truthful report, the manner in which "truthful reporting" was at one time understood. For there are no such things as truth or objectivity in the singular; both of these contain an irreducible coefficient of historical relativity. Now, SF can never be on a par with the epic, since *what* the SF work presents belongs to one time (most often the future), while *how* it tells its story belongs to another time, the present. Even if imagination succeeds in rendering plausible *how* it might be, it cannot break completely with the way of apprehending events which is peculiar to the here and now. This way is not only an artistic convention, it is considerably more—a type of classification, interpretation and rationalization of the visible world that is peculiar to an era. Consequently the problem content of an epic can be deeply hidden, but that of SF must be legible, otherwise the story, declining to deal with *nonfictional problems* and not achieving *epic objectivity*, slides fatally down and comes to rest on some such support as the stereotype of the fairy tale, the adventure thriller, the myth, the framework of the detective story, or some hybrid as eclectic as it is trashy. A way out of the dilemma may consist in works for which componential analysis, designed to separate what is "factual" from what forms the "message" ("seen" from a "viewpoint"), proves altogether impracticable. The reader of such a work does not know whether what he is shown is supposed to exist like a stone or a chair, or whether it is supposed also to signify something beyond itself. The indeterminacy of such a creation is not diminished by its author's commentaries, since the author can be mistaken in these, like a man who tries to explain the real meaning of his own dreams. Hence I consider Dick's own comments to be inessential to the analysis of his works.

At this point we might embark on an excursus about the origin of Dick's science-fictional concepts, but let just one example from *Ubik* suffice: to wit, the name which figures as the title of the book. It comes from the Latin *ubique* 'everywhere.' This is a blend (contamination) of two heterogeneous concepts: the concept of the Absolute as eternal and unchanging order which goes back to systematizing philosophy, and the concept of the "gadget"— the handy little device for use on appropriate everyday occasions, a product of the conveyer-belt technology of the consumer society, whose watchword is making things easy for people at whatever they do, from washing clothes to getting a permanent wave. This "canned Absolute," then, is the result of the collision and interpenetration of two styles of thought of different ages, and at the same time of the incarnation of abstraction in the guise of a concrete object. Such a proceeding is an exception to the rule in SF and is Dick's own invention.

It is hardly possible to create, in the way just noted, objects which are empirically plausible or which have a likelihood of ever coming into existence. Accordingly in the case of Ubik it is a matter of a poetic, i.e. metaphorical device and not of any "futurological" one. Ubik plays an important part in the story, emphasized still more by the "advertisements" for it which figure as epigraphs to each chapter. Is it a symbol, and, if so, of just what? This is not easy to answer. An Absolute conjured out of sight by technology, supposed to save man from the ruinous consequences of Chaos or Entropy much as a deodorant shields our sense of smell from the stench of industrial effluents, is not only a demonstration of a tactic typical nowadays (combating, for example, the side effects of one technology by means of another technology), it is an expression of nostalgia for a lost ideal kingdom of untroubled order, but also an expression of irony, since this "invention" of course cannot be taken seriously. Ubik moreover plays in the novel the part of its "internal micromodel," since it contains *in nuce* the whole range of problems specific to the book, those of the struggle of man against Chaos, at the end of which, after temporary successes, defeat inexorably awaits him. The Absolute canned as an aerosol, which saves Joe Chip at the point of death—though only for the time being: will this, then, be a parable and the handwriting on the wall for a civilization which has degraded the Sacred by stuffing it into the Profane? Pursuing such a train of associations, *Ubik* could finally be seen as a take-off on the Greek tragedy, with the role of the ancient heroes, who strive vainly against Moira, assigned to the staff telepaths under the command of a big business executive. If *Ubik* was not actually undertaken with this in mind, it in any case points in such a direction.

The writings of Philip Dick have deserved at least a better fate than that to which they were destined by their birthplace. If they are neither of uniform quality nor fully realized, still it is only by brute force that they can be jammed into that pulp of materials, destitute of intellectual value and original structure, which makes up SF. Its fans are attracted by the worst in Dick—the typical dash of American SF, reaching to the stars, and the headlong pace of action moving from one surprise to the next—but they hold it against him that, instead of unraveling puzzles, he leaves the reader at the end on the battlefield, enveloped in the aura of a mystery as grotesque as it is strange. Yet his bizarre blendings of hallucinogenic and palingenetic techniques have not won him many admirers outside the ghetto walls, since there readers are repelled by the shoddiness of the props he has adopted from the inventory of SF. Indeed, these writings sometims fumble their attempts; but I remain after all under their spell, as it often happens at the sight of a lone imagination's efforts to cope with a shattering superabundance of opportunities—efforts in which even a partial defeat can resemble a victory.

Ian Watson

Le Guin's Lathe of Heaven and the Role of Dick: The False Reality as Mediator

Ursula K. Le Guin's work to date has been remarkable for its overall thematic consistency—both in the "outer space" of the Hainish cycle and in the inner lands of the Earthsea trilogy (to quote a distinction she herself makes in an autobiographical essay).[1] *The Lathe of Heaven* (1971) at first sight seems to represent something of an anomaly—a sport from the true stock—as though in this one particular instance she has been becharmed by that master trickster of false reality states, Philip K. Dick. Not to write a poor book, I hasten to add, for *Lathe* is splendid—but let's say a *tour de force* in the Dick mode, something out of key with the rest of her opus; perhaps even, the suspicion lurks, contradicting the general drift of it? It is as though while writing of those inner lands with her left hand, and of outer space with her right, a third hand has mysteriously intruded on the scene, attached to Palmer Eldritch's prosthetic arm, and it is this hand that has tapped out *Lathe* on the typewriter. Obviously good writers only break new ground (delighting or horrifying their readers, as the case may be) by changing, growing, "pushing out toward the limits—[their] own, and those of the medium," to quote Le Guin again; and I've no wish to fit her with a straitjacket in the guise of a critical essay. But equally clearly an important question of internal consistency arises here with *Lathe*: that deeper consistency of aims and method which is the hallmark of the great, as opposed to the merely good, artist. It is the question of the authentic "voice," which Sartre finds Tintoretto—who could paint anybody's pictures but his own—so tragically deprived of.[2] This hallmark appears with increasing clarity from Le Guin's earlier, slighter novels through to the triumphant *Dispossessed*. And *Lathe* seems anomalous. But is it really so? Let us try to locate *Lathe* in the context of Le Guin's progression as a writer, and see what happens.

Lathe is about paranormal[3] events impinging on an initially realistic Earth of the near future—about a dreamer whose dreams can change the whole fabric of reality. They replace history with false histories that become objective truth, only to be overthrown and modified by further dreams as his well-intentioned yet power-hungry psychiatrist manipulates him, and the whole objective world along with him, trying to steer it away from pollution, overpopulation, social evil, yet only producing successive devastations as a consequence: plague, "citizen arrest" of the sick, alien invasion. And all along the irony lurks that we have been in a "false" world from the very start; for, before ever being referred to a psychiatrist for illegally obtaining drugs to stop himself dreaming, George Orr had "effectively dreamt" a nuclear holocaust out of existence; there is in truth no way to go homeward.

It's perhaps easier to see how *Lathe* meshes with the magic-regulated world of Earthsea than to bring it into line with the Hainish books and stories (with the apparent exception of "The Word for World is Forest," which is also concerned with dreams). But if we plot the chronology of events depicted in the Hainish stories, and the development of the use of the paranormal there, *against* the order in which the stories were written, an interesting pattern emerges. A chart then for Hainish history and for Le Guin's concern with the paranormal:

	INTERNAL CHRONOLOGY		PARANORMALITY LEVEL	ORDER OF PUBLICATION
1. *The Dispossessed*	AD	2300	Nil except for Alpha-rhythm biofeedback.	6. 1974
2. "The Word for World is Forest"	AD LY	2368 18	Same plus dream consciousness in one "mutant" culture.	5. 1972
3. *Rocannon's World*	AD LY	2684 334	Mindspeech first encountered as a learnable discipline.	1. 1966
4. *Planet of Exile*	AD LY	3755 1405	Mindspeech in normal use by Terrans.	2. 1966
5. *City of Illusions*	AD LY	4370 2020	Mindlying (and the advanced mind control with which it is successfully countered).	3. 1967
6. *The Left Hand of Darkness*	AD LY EY	4870 2520 1491	Foretelling.	4. 1969

LY = League Year; EY = Ekumenical Year.
For details of the chronology see Note 4.

Put into words, Le Guin works *forward* chronologically in her first books and opens up increasingly enlarged possibilities for paranormal experience; then, after *Left Hand*, begins to head *backward* through time toward the present, in an increasingly political, sociological, "normal consciousness" mode. The basic orientation of "The Word for World is Forest" is, in fact, political/social/ecological; the paranormal—dreams magically altering reality—is shunted off into *Lathe*, which can thus in a sense be said to constitute a "goodbye to all that" to the material with which the four early Hainish books seemed increasingly proccupied.[5]

The particular danger inherent in SF treatment of the paranormal—and particularly in adopting a time scheme for a "future history" which indicates increasing prominence of paranormal talents as an index of increasing human wisdom—is that this can too easily become a quasi-mystical escape route from real problems: ethical, psychological, epistemological, and practical. A seductive nonsense supervenes. The meaningful pole in SF is represented by Philip K. Dick, and the nonsense pole by A.E. van Vogt. Dick invariably subsumes the paranormal within a zone of genuine social concerns, and thus avoids mystification. His pre-cogs, time-shifters, and other characters with "wild talents" are presented with tact, zany wit, and, most important of all, in an organically structured relation to society—whether this society is human, quasi-human (android, robot), or alien. Van Vogt's use of the paranormal, on the other hand, is a bag of conjuring tricks, amounting to a negation of any society—alien, human, or "post-human." The climax to Le Guin's *City of Illusions*, with the "double-minded" hero leaping out of tele-pathic ambush, is redolent of the Vanvogtian Superhuman; and though there is no such occult bravura in *Left Hand*, this element nonetheless re-mains embedded in the Hainish cycle, built into its dynamics—lying in am-bush somewhere ahead down the time-line, tempting towards false solutions.

Positing *Lathe* in this way as a summation and discharge of a particular theme that has been gathering momentum in tandem with the forward move-ment of the Hainish cycle—the movement which Le Guin is now negating chronologically—we can perhaps usefully read the books as a use of the Dickian mode to discharge this particular accumulation of energy.

Two objections might be raised from Le Guin's publishing history against such a reading. First, does not the *Earthsea* trilogy represent a definite branching in Le Guin's work: a conscious separating of fantasy from SF? There is much in *Earthsea* about dreams, the minor magical powers of illusion on the one hand, and the major magical powers of altering reality objectively through "renaming" of the world on the other. There is also much emphasis on the vital importance of equilibrium (ignoring which pro-vokes the disasters of *Lathe*)—and equilibrium is a social/ecological concept to be taken up again in quite a different vein in *The Dispossessed*, care-fully distinguished from static conservatism by its dynamic concept of a con-stant, complex remaking of the world, without overloading any variables. Thus, it might seem that Le Guin has already adequately sifted the two strains, the paranormal and the "normal," by the invention of Earthsea and magic as a workable proposition—leaving *Lathe*, again, as a sport. Yet Earth-sea does not exactly discharge the accumulated energy vested in the para-normal theme. With the completion of the trilogy, in *The Furthest Shore*, balance is conserved—yet still within a world of magic. In this context it is hardly possible to effect a full discharge of what, adopting a term from Gregory Bateson, we may call "schismogenic tension"[6]—the increasing em-phasis on the paranormal, fed by the flow of Hainish history itself. For that, we must look to *Lathe*. Its image of "The Break" (the popular name for the discontinuity between Old Reality and New Rality, once affairs have been tidied up and balance restored) is, in a sense, an image of the break in the Hainish cycle between "early" Le Guin and "mature" Le Guin—a break that occurs when the arrow of time is reversed, while simultaneously social and psychological depth increases massively.

Second, it could also be objected that "The Word for World is Forest" is a post-break story in the Hainish cycle, dealing largely with dreams (as well as with the politics of ecology). So is there not some considerable osmosis of the paranormal here? A further eruption of *Lathe* material? Not so. For reality is not altered by the power of dreams in "Forest" in the way it is in *Lathe*, falsifying a whole world-line retrospectively. The world of the dreamers never experiences such a "false-reality" dislocation. But rather, the dreamers are simply in conscious rapport with their dreams; the dream is principally a heuristic tool and—in time of crisis—a decision-making apparatus which permits the total individual to be involved in shaping his destiny. The tragedy of "Forest" is that the dream that has to be dreamt, the new psychological trait that has to be generated (dreamt into being) in response to Terran deforestation and enslavement, is the art of killing one's fellows. Principally, this is an extension of Hadfield's concept of the dream as teaching aid, problem-solving device, and governor of our conscious lives (on a principle of positive feedback: the maximising of a dubious situation in order to discharge awareness of danger and self-deceit across the interface between subconscious and conscious).[7]

Theories more pertinent than Hadfield's or Dement's to the dream situation imagined in *Lathe*, and more in key with a "false reality" premise, can be found collected in Charles Tart's *Altered States of Consciousness*;[8] and the dream background of *Lathe* is today best approached via Tart's book.[9] The temporal setting of *Lathe*, A.D. 2002, seems almost unnecessarily far in the future when we read Tart's speculations on techniques of dream control by post-hypnotic suggestion and other means and in addition learn that the UCLA Brain Information Service already publishes a weekly *Sleep Bulletin* for researchers and that the Association for the Psychophysiological Study of Sleep already convenes yearly meetings. Particularly pertinent are Tart's investigations of the "lucid dream" (the waking to full consciousness of a dreamer within a dream) and the technique for evoking such dreams and for manipulating the fake world.

Also germane to the psychology of *Lathe*'s central character is Tart's observation that "we have no 'choice' about dreaming."[10] To be sure, he is here referring to the proven necessity for dream sleep. Studies of dream deprivation have shown the dire effects of preventing dreaming. Yet, twist this vital concept of the role of the dream through an axis of the imagination —for this is the art of speculation—blend it with Le Guin's ethic of Balance, and we have the given character of her dreamer George Orr: a man who consistently falls in the median range of every personality test and whose prime characteristic is his inability to "choose" in conscious waking everyday life. He is a quiescent-acquiescent type, whose character aligns him with the Joe Normal heroes on whom Philip Dick's false realities characteristically impinge. Barney Mayerson in *The Three Stigmata of Palmer Eldritch*, Joe Chip in *Ubik*, Seth Morley in *A Maze of Death* (though this book was most probably too late to exert any stimula on *Lathe*)—these heroes are all failures in one way or another, foundering in their attempts to manage their lives, yet genuinely *heroic* for all their mistakes, and achieving, or being involved in, the transcendent (with a devilish twist in *Ubik*). Their very inertia contains a potential for strength and heroism—as does George Orr's (in keeping with Le Guin's Taoist dialectic of strength and weakness). Inertia—the tendency of a body to preserve its state of rest or uniform motion in a straight line—may appear like passivity, but is in fact a powerful force. Joe Chip's dogged, nightmare battle to get upstairs to his hotel bedroom while the masquerading Jory drains his body of energy (*Ubik* §13) is almost a mirror image of George Orr's dogged, nightmare journey through a decaying reality to switch off Haber's dream machine (*Lathe* §10); the restoration of vitality as soon as Joe Chip reaches his bedroom, finds Glen Runciter there, and gets sprayed with Ubik, is echoed by George Orr's restoration of vital solidity to the world. Similarly, Barney Mayerson's decision to continue as a colonist on barren Mars and accept its dull reality (*Three Stigmata* §13) seems like defeat, but is really an act of strength and commitment; earlier (§§11-12) Palmer Eldritch traded on this very desire of Barney to become a static object such as a stone or wall plaque, to trick him—only to have his trick rebound. Inertia is strength. Pat Conley, who changes time lines—initially in her dreams (*Ubik* §3), prefiguring Le Guin's George Orr, but subsequently by conscious choice (§5)—also has "unbelievable power" (§5) yet at the same is an "inertial" who feels distressed by her own apparent negativity: " 'I don't do anything; I don't move objects or turn stones into bread.... I just negate somebody else's ability. It seems—' She gestured. 'Stultifying.' " And Joe Chip's response to this remark is a very Le Guinish one: " 'The anti-psi factor is a natural restoration of ecological balance.... Balance, the full circle...' " (§3).

In *Lathe* Le Guin is certainly exploring the Dickian mode; yet she is not exploring it in a contingent, happenstance, *tour de force* way since she is discharging the schismogenic thematic tensions generated by her reversing and deepening the Hainish cycle. On the contrary, *Lathe* fits logically into the set of her ideas as a pivotal work, working out a tension that clears the way for *The Dispossessed*. Moving on from particular details to the general ethos of the two writers, then, what sea-change does Le Guin work on the Dick model?

If we take as representative of this model in its mature form the three Dick novels already mentioned, one rule of Dick's false realities is the paradox that once in, there's no way out, yet for this very reason transcendence (of a sort) can be achieved. The religion of *A Maze of Death* is a construct imposed on the crew of a starship during a voluntary trance state by a computer originally provided as a toy to while away the long years in space, which has become their only form of mental "salvation" once their ship is crippled. Yet the godlike figure of the Intercessor, invented as part of the false reality, reaches into the reality of the ship objectively, to offer salvation of a kind. (Seth Morley's salvation is to be reborn as a desert plant on a world where no one will bother him, where he can be both conscious of life, and yet asleep, enjoying a vegetable dream consciousness [§16]). Thus the human generates God. In *Three Stigmata*, while it's arguable whether any objective reality persists after Leo Bulero enters the primary Chew-Z hallucination, the dominant probability is that while objectively reality is hopelessly contaminated with false realities induced by a godlike alien, yet the human is divinized nonetheless, in opposition to the manipulations of this (pseudo-)God. *Ubik* constructs an even more devious maze in a post-death mind-storage unit, the sting in the tail being that the live helper of the inmates from outside may have been dead, and inside, all along. Yet the struggle of mind (the battle between the "Mentufacturer" and "Form Destroyer" in *Maze of Death* terms) is carried on, and the Ubik substance which has passed through so many consumer product formats during the course of the story finally declares its divinity, and would certainly seem to be the invention of the trapped, and dead, Glen Runciter. Once in, never out; and yet....

The same rule applies to *Lathe*. A nuclear war has already been averted by effective dreaming when the book opens; so the characters are committed to the false reality from the start (else they perish). Subsequent fluctuations in population size, skin colour, and urban geography, due to Dr. Haber's programming of George Orr's dreams, are vast enough, yet all are basically quantitative changes in the structure of Earth reality. The qualitative change, and the haunting mystery of the book, comes with the dreaming into being of the aliens—initially as invaders, later as compassionate if enigmatic friends. Conceivably George dreamt a hostile invasion into a peaceful one; yet the dominant probability is that the aliens are, as they maintain, "of the dream-time" (§10), that their whole culture revolves round the mode of "reality dreaming itself into being," that they have been attracted to Earth like the Waveries in Fredric Brown's story, only by dream-waves rather than radio waves.

Arguably, there is an essential difference between Dick's false realities and Le Guin's, in that Dick's warping of reality is quite Machiavellian in its tricksterism and involves the reader himself ultimately in a dissolution of the sense of reality; whereas Le Guin proceeds from change to change far more definitively, ending up with a solid, unambiguous conclusion (a process that paradoxically makes her book more precarious, since the initial premise has to be swallowed whole, whereas with Dick it's difficult to pin down an initial premise as such, and by the time the reader starts wondering, distortion has metastatized wildly). Yet this doesn't really seem to me to be the case. Consider the thread of continuity-awareness that persists through all transformations of colour and temperament wrought upon Heather LeLache (and compare this slender thread with Joe Chip's equally tenuous intuition of what Pat Conley has brought about, in *Ubik* §5, which provides a kind of inverted kinship model of George's love for Heather). But, particularly, consider Le Guin's aliens. If they are not indeed vectored to Earth, Wavery-like, from an actual Aldebaran dream culture but only seen as manifestations of George Orr's human subconscious, they have still become objective realities in the universe and can set up shop—actually, as well as metaphorically. Dream and reality are inextricably interwoven henceforth, by *their* agency—whatever agency was responsible for their origin. It also follows the Dickian pattern of ultimate, if equivocal, transcendence: both in the sense of a dialectical supersession of a previous state, and also in the luminous sense.

"Everything dreams," George warns Haber, as the psychiatrist prepares to produce effective dreaming in himself:

> "The play of form, of being, is the dreaming of substance. Rocks have their dreams, and the earth changes.... But when the mind becomes conscious, when the rate of evolution speeds up, then you have to be careful. Careful of the world. You must learn the way. You must learn the skill, the arts, the limits. A conscious mind must be part of the whole, intentionally and carefully—as the rock is part of the whole unconsciously." (§10)

When the mind becomes conscious.... Matter is therefore immanent with consciousness, with godhood, teleologically. Dr. Haber's effective nightmare ruptures time-lines disastrously and is only suppressed when George Orr wills the route to the dream machine, and its OFF switch, back into existence. Yet the "real" world remains a chaotic *melange* of different continua; and the aliens of the dream time are still with us objectively, their knowledge available to us. The question whether they "actually" arrived, Wavery-like, from Aldebaran remains as open-ended as any riddle set by the "conclusion" of a Philip Dick novel. Thus, as in Dick, once in, never out, *yet* transcendence occurs: " 'Take evening,' the Alien said, 'There is time. There are returns. To go is to return' " (§11).

The words "True voyage is return" will appear on Odo's grave, in *The Dispossessed*, which can now be written. For the thematic tension has been discharged. *Lathe*, superficially an uncharacteristic *pièce de résistance*, is logically validated as mediator by accepting this discharge. For the book mediates structurally, just as its alien characters mediate, between the real and the parareal.

Lathe, too, might seem to represent a warning against overmuch "scientific meddling" in the world about us, since Dr. Haber demonstrably ends up as the archetypal "mad scientist"—from an initially well-intentioned, albeit ambitious, egoistic stance. However, if we contrast his role with that of the scientist Shevek in *The Dispossessed*, and take into account the suggestion that *Lathe* represents a discharge of tension, then we will see that Haber has to be as he is: both benevolent scientist *and* malign anti-social force. For his is the wasteland to which the paranormal as false solution leads.

In *The Dispossessed* Shevek fights to remain in balance with social necessities and values—he is no "egoizer." His search for a scientific method runs hand in hand with his search for a social method. Consequently, his is a genuine dialectic of science and society—which Haber disastrously attempts to short-circuit. This short-circuit is a pitfall inherent in the SF of the paranormal—responsible for the ridiculous, if pyrotechnic, excesses of a van Vogt: the "brainstorm" solution. Shevek does not fall under the same curse: the curse has been lifted. Yet it could only be lifted effectively, and honestly, by the catastrophic release of thematic tension that *Lathe* so strikingly embodies. The Hainish faultline was under strain. It took a worldquake to set the matter right.

NOTES

[1]"A Citizen of Mondath," *Foundation* #4 (July 1973), pp. 20-24.

[2]Jean-Paul Sartre, "The Venetian Pariah," in his *Essays in Aesthetics*, tr. Wade Baskin (London 1964), p. 41: "But this is precisely the thing that arouses suspicion. Why would he need to play their game and submit to their rules if he could outshine them all by being himself? What resentment in his insolence! This Cain assassinates every Abel preferred over him: 'You like this Veronese? Well, I can do much better when I imitate him; you take him for a man and he is nothing but a technique.' And what humility. From time to time this pariah slips into the skin of another person in order to enjoy in his turn the delight of being loved. And then at times it would seem that he lacks the courage to manifest his scandalous genius; disheartened, he leaves his genius in semi-darkness and tries to prove it *deductively*: 'Since I paint the best Veronese and the best Pordenones, just imagine *what I am capable of painting* when I allow myself to be me.'"

[3]The term "paranormal" is taken as referring to phenomena/events outside our current consensus-reality view of the universe—phenomena which negate our present concepts of cause and effect and the material nature of the universe, and drive a wedge through the causal, material mind-body interface, to split off "mind" as a force in its own right; or which seem to do so, since a material base for these postulated phenomena is as yet unproven (though not necessarily unprovable, in part, if not in whole). Conjectural mental powers such as telepathy, precognition, clairvoyance, teleportation, and psychokinesis all fall within this "mind over matter" zone. George Orr's effective dreaming in *Lathe*—the refashioning of entire world-lines by the force of thought—is an extreme instance of this, as is the "effective magic" of Earthsea.

[4]This chart is based on internal dating in the stories with two provisos. Firstly, League years, Ekumenical years, Terran years, etc. (but not the Werelian Great Years of *Planet of Exile*!) are all assumed to be roughly equivalent. Secondly, the baseline date of AD 2300 for *The Dispossessed* is taken from the description of Earth in that book (§11) as having passed through an ecological and social collapse with a population peak of 9 billion to a low-population but highly centralized recovery economy. Earth's old cities are still visible everywhere, in ruins: the concrete crumbles, though the plastic lingers on, non-biodegradable. There were centuries of mismanagement. (But starting when? With the industrial revolution? Or did the mess continue through the 21st century—and recovery take proportionately longer?) The reader who disagrees with my 2300 dating as wrong by a century or two is invited to alter my chart accordingly, but I don't think it's so far out—and it does establish a baseline. *The Dispossessed* is dated 50 years before the League of Worlds came into being, since the ansible (instantaneous transmitter) theorem would have to be transported physically, or transmitted by conventional radio, at no faster than light speed from Tau Ceti to Earth and Hain, then considerable R & D engaged in (if early ansibles cost the equivalent of a "planetary annual revenue") before the meeting of the ambassadors

mentioned in "The Word for World is Forest" (§3) could take place. The latter story is located in League Year 18 (not, as Douglas Barbour says in SFS #3, in LY 1) by the statement "The League of Worlds.... has existed for 18 years" (§3). *Rocannon's World* is given the date mentioned in the Prologue (the "League Mission of 252-254"), with eighty years added on for the time the necklace has been missing (lost before Semley's father was born, some time during her great grandmother's life). *Planet of Exile* is exactly dated by two systems in §3: it is the "Year 1405 of the League of All Worlds" and also the "45th moonphase of the Tenth Local Year of the [Terran] Colony" on Werel. The Werelian year is equated with 60 league years in this chapter and to 60 Terran years in §7 of *City of Illusions*; in the latter book (§9) we also learn that a Werelian moonphase is approximately equal to a Terran year; which all adds up to LY 820 or AD 3170 for the establishment of the Terran colony on Werel. The events of *City of Illusions* are then dated LY 2020 or AD 4370 by numerous references to 1200 years having passed since that event—or since the coming of the Shing (the "Enemy") five years later. *City of Illusions* ends with Falk-Ramarren's setting out for Werel, 142 light years away, in hope of finding there whatever is necessary to free Terra from the Shing; if we allow him 300 years for this mission, and assume that its success brings the end of the Age of the Enemy, then we can date this last event LY 2320, AD 4670. The events of *The Left Hand of Darkness* can then be dated LY 2520, AD 4870 by Genly Ai's putting the Age of the Enemy "a couple of centuries ago" (§10). Since *Left Hand* is explicitly assigned to Ekumenical Year 1491-92 of Hainish Cycle 93 (we are not told how many years are in a cycle), we are now able to equate EY dates with LY dates and, of course, AD dates. Having said all this, we must grant that Le Guin has left her options wide open with the change from LY to EY dating: the end of the Age of the Enemy could be made to occur not only (as in our chronology) 300 years after the events of *City of Illusions* but also immediately thereafter—or any number of centuries or millenia thereafter. On the other hand, Genly Ai's statement that Terrans "were ignorant until about three thousand years ago of the uses of zero" (§18), while giving us a date a thousand years too early by our chronology for *Left Hand* (i.e., AD 3850 rather than our AD 4870), still suggests that we are right in dating *Left Hand* a few centuries rather than many centuries after *City of Illusions*. Certain dates in Hainish history can now be tabulated, with asterisks to mark those given in Le Guin's text, as follows:

	AD	LY	EY
Invention of the ansible	2300		
Foundation of the League	2350	1	
Events of "The Word for World is Forest"	2368	18*	
Expedition to Fomahault II	2604	254*	
Events of *Rocannon's World*	2684	334	
Terran colony established on Werel	3170	820	
The coming of the Shing or Enemy	3175	825	
Year One of Hainish Cycle 93	3380	1030	1
Events of *Planet of Exile*	3755	1405*	376
Events of *City of Illusions*	4370	2020	991
End of the Age of the Enemy	4670	2320	1291
Events of *The Left Hand of Darkness*	4870	2520	1491*

[5]"The Word for World is Forest"—in Harlan Ellison's anthology, *Again, Dangerous Visions* (1972)—was in fact written about three years earlier than publication date, at the same time as the research leading to *Lathe* (Le Guin's personal communication). However this does not substantially alter my thesis, as the story clearly postdates *Left Hand*. Simply, the release of thematic tension was already under way in the dynamics of Le Guin's creative thought culminating shortly thereafter in the actual physical writing of *Lathe*.

[6]Gregory Bateson, "Bali: The Value System of a Steady State," in his *Steps to an Ecology of Mind* (1972). The term "schismogenesis" is used by Bateson to describe a broad range of potentially harmful human activities—such as boasting, commercial rivalry, arms races—where the actions of group/individual A either generate a sym-

metrical reaction in group/individual B, which provokes a symmetrical or stronger response from A (of the form boasting/more boasting, and so on), or alternatively a complementary opposite reaction (of the form: dominance/submission) which also initiates a new round. The tension between A and B, produced by an interaction from which neither side can withdraw, can only generally be resolved by a release through total involvement, of catastrophic or orgasmic character. In Bateson's view, war, commerce, and even the process of mutual falling in love all betray certain schismogenic features. Thus the phenomenon should by no means be localized within a purely "social anthropology" frame of reference, but rather be located within a general "ecology of mind." In the context of Hainish history, the schismogenic circuit is as follows: the arrow of time (a sequence concept of the universe that Le Guin is only able to supersede, after *Lathe*, in *The Dispossessed*) enforces a progressive revelation of paranormal powers—which leads the action (in a positive feedback circuit) further on into the future in search of even wider paranormal powers, since these seem to represent an inevitable evolutionary progression. (Yet at each stage consensus "reality" is in fact receding further.)

⁷J.A. Hadfield, *Dreams and Nightmares* (Harmondsworth 1954).

⁸Charles T. Tart, ed., *Altered States of Consciousness* (2d edn. NY 1972). Hadfield and Dement—the sources cited by Le Guin in her Afterword in *Again, Dangerous Visions*—serve well enough for an interpretation of "The Word for World is Forest." Even so, there is in Tart an essay by Kilton Stewart, "Dream Theory in Malaya," which tells of the Senoi of Malaya, a people who traditionally practiced dream interpretation on a remarkable level of sophistication; and even engaged in lucid "waking-dream" states while not asleep. Stewart comments: "Observing the lives of the Senoi it occurred to me that modern civilization may be sick because people have sloughed off, or failed to develop, half their power to think. Perhaps the most important half" (p. 168). The Senoi mirror Le Guin's Athsheans, even to the balance of male/female status in a dreamer culture, quite remarkably (but coincidentally!). Since Tart (p. 117) confesses that he has "not been able to locate any other literature on the Senoi other than Stewart's," interested readers may usefully be referred to Robert Knox Denton, *The Semai: A Nonviolent People of Malaya* (NY 1968), a volume in the series Case Studies in Cultural Anthropology, which predates Tart's first edition of 1969 and contains a useful bibliography, recommending *inter alia* H.D. Noone, "Report on the Settlements and Welfare of thePre-Temiar Senoi of the Perek-Kelatan Watershed," *Journal of the Federated Malay States Museums*, Vol. 19, Pt. 1, 1936. That H.D. Noone was reporting on precisely the same group as Kilton Stewart is indicated by Richard Noone, *Rape of the Dream People* (L 1972), which refers in some detail to the dream psychology researches of Stewart and the elder Noone, though this particular book is a ghost-written war memoir in dubious taste. Confusion as to the correct naming of the Senoi arises since the word *senoi* simply means *person* in the Senoi language, and *semai* refers to people who speak dialects of Semai, which is closely related to Senoi (if not, in fact, simply a variant group of dialects!). Together the Senoi-Semai form a linguistic enclave among tribes speaking non-Austro-Asiatic. An ethnic way of dividing the group is to call them all Senoi, and describe the southerners as Semai, the northerners as Temiar. It is this northern group that Stewart and the elder Noone were working with; consequently, adopting Noone's classification, the Malayan dreamers described in Tart's *Altered States* are properly Temiar, or Pre-Temiar Senoi.

⁹Tart is useful as highly relevant information about the current state of the art of dream research (with an invaluable bibliography) rather than as a direct primary source. Le Guin, according to a personal communication to me, was unacquainted with Tart's work as such at the time of writing *Lathe*—although well aware of other areas of this research field, such as the work of Aserinsky, Berger, Oswald, Hartman, *et al* (*Lathe* §2), all of which Tart surveys concisely.

¹⁰Tart, "Introduction to Section 3, Dream Consciousness," in Tart (Note 8), p. 115.

(from SFS *2:89, March 1975)*

A Response to Dr Lem   I'm sorry that Stanislaw Lem misread my letter in SFS #3, I'm often accused of being cryptic, but in this case I don't see how I could have said more plainly what I meant. I said, "...it doesn't take much critical intelligence to notice that a lot of Farmer's work is crude, etc. What would be really interesting, and much more difficult, would be to try to find out why these crude efforts are so popular." I neither said nor meant that whatever is popular is good (& I am a little wounded that Lem, whom I respect, should have believed this of me). But it is equally simplistic to dismiss the problem by saying that popular works are popular works because they are bad. In this field alone, thousands of bad works are published every year, and most of them sink into instant oblivion. What is it about certain bad works that makes them immensely popular? The answer which I suggested in the case of van Vogt is that his early works contain a powerful dreamlike element—some of them, in fact, are nothing but dreams embedded in superficial pseudo-stories. In the case of Farmer (who is not always crude), I think there are equally powerful archetypal elements. I don't propose any general solution. I haven't read the Perry Rhodan novels (and since I understand there are about 300, am not about to), but I think their international success requires some explanation. I would find that more interesting than a disquisition on the Aristotelean ideas in Cyrano. —**Damon Knight.**

The Science Fiction of Ursula K. Le Guin

Edited by Darko Suvin

(from SFS 2:203 - 274, November 1975)

One of the contributors in this issue (see Note 2 in Nudelman's article) has fortunately supplied SFS with an excellent rationale for having taken as the subject of its first special issues the opuses of Philip K. Dick and Ursula K. Le Guin. Both of these leading American SF writers of the last 15 years write out of and react against historically the same human—psychological and sociopolitical—situation: the experience of the terrible pressures of alienation, isolation and fragmentation pervading the neo-capitalist society of the world of the mid-20th century. But while Dick is a "romantic" writer, whose energy lashes out in a profusion of incandescent and interfused narrative protuber-ances, Le Guin is a "classical" writer, whose energy is as fierce but strictly controlled within a taut and spare architectural system of narrative cells. While both have—as any significant writer must—a fixed creative focus, Dick writes centrifugally, as it were in revolving sectors (say of a radar sweep) whose apex is always the same but whose field may differ, whereas Le Guin writes centripetally, in a narrowing spiral (say of a falcon circling to a swoop) delineating ever more precisely the same object. The main strength of the first lies in the recording of breakdowns in the old individualist system of interhuman relationships; of the second, in the quest for, and indeed (in the very midst of such a breakdown) in the first sketching of, a new collectivist system. (Dick's fascination with simulcra or super-aliens and Le Guin's with time or the forest-minds do not at all contradict the assertion that their subject is interhuman relationships, to which—as in any writer—all other relations can only be analogies; I argued that for Dick in SFS #5, and will argue it for Le Guin in this issue.) Conversely, Dick gets less believable when he tries to focus on undegraded human relationships, a new collective (as in *Galactic Pot-Healer*)—he is not a bearer of good news—and Le Guin when she tries to focus on a Dickian world in degradation from which the individual must secede (as in *The Lathe of Heaven* and "Those Who Walk Away from Omelas")—she is not a bearer of bad news. Both writers seem to have felt this, and

Galactic Pot-Healer is finally negated by a down-beat ending just as the Le Guin novel and story are by upbeat ones—types of endings really more congenial to the basic creative vision of each. Characteristically, the three works mentioned are those in which the visions of Dick and Le Guin have been invaded by a not wholly assimilated alien vision: by Jung's in the case of Dick, by Dick's in the case of LoH, and by Dunsany's in the case of "Omelas." Concurrently, the stylistic danger for Dick is murkiness and prolixity, for Le Guin brittleness and curtness. Or, to simplify: Dick sees a world of addition and multiplication, so he reproduces it in his narrative forms; Le Guin sees a world of subtraction and division, and she also started by reproducing it—but it seems to me and many collaborators in this issue that as of *The Left Hand of Darkness* she has increasingly expressed the complementary urge toward integration. At any rate, we need seers of both the Le Guin and the Dick type, for their visions help us to define and thus master our common world.

These and many other points are argued abundantly and I think often splendidly in this special issue. My thanks go to all its contributors (a number of them new to the pages of SFS), and my regrets to those we could not accommodate. I am particularly pleased that we can print the contribution of Rafail Nudelman, not only because it is our first one from the USSR, but even more important, because it shows that Republic of Letters is truly one in spite of all difficulties; my cordial thanks go to Alan G. Myers who translated this delayed addition quickly and yet so well. On the unfulfilled, I'm sorry that we couldn't find anybody to integrate the *Earthsea* trilogy with Le Guin's SF. This and a number of other aspects of Le Guin, a constantly evolving writer, remain to be elucidated. Le Guin—herself a brilliant critic, as witness the items in the General section of Levin's bibliography—will contribute a rejoinder in our next issue.

Jeff Levin. Ursula K. Le Guin: A Select Bibliography.

The following bibliography is a selected and, with respect to the type of data presented, otherwise reduced version of a full Bibliographical Checklist of Le Guin's works which I am preparing for independent publication. Le Guin's published prose fiction is given complete, but no poems are listed other than those included in the book C2 (there would be 14 more items between 1959 and 1974), nor are her translations of Rilke's poems from a French version or her translations of Malaguti's prose from the Italian. The General category is a selection confined, in consultation with the editor of this special issue of SFS, to the most significant of her non-fictional works; omitted are about two dozen letters, notes, and brief articles, mainly in SF fan magazines. In preparing this bibliography I have had the help of Ms. Le Guin herself, who generously put her personal files at my disposal. I would also like to thank for their help Virginia Kidd, Leslie Kay Swigart, and Chuck Jarvis. I would be grateful for any information I might have missed.

C1-C3. Collections

C1. Le monde de Rocannon / Planete d'exil / La cité des illusions. [See ## 9, 10, 11]. Translated by Jean Bailhache. Paris: Opta—Club du Livre d'Anticipation, 1972, Also contains the essay G7, tr. Michel Demuth.

C2. Wild Angels [Poems]. 50p. $2.50. Capra Press (631 State Street, Santa Barbara, CA 93101), 1975. 1) O wild angels.... 2) Coming of Age. 3) There. 4) Footnote. 5) Hier Steh' Ich. 6) Song. 7) Archaeology of the Renaissance.

8) From Whose Bourne. 9) March 21. 10) The Darkness. 11) Dreampoem. 12) The Young. 13) The Anger. 14) Ars Lunga [sic.]. 15) The Molsen. 16) The Withinner. 17) Offering. 18) Arboreal. 19) Dreampoem II. 20) A Lament for Rheged. 21) The Rooftree. 22) Some of the Philosophers. 23) Snow. 24) Flying West From Denver. 25) Winter-Rose. 26) Mount St Helens/Omphalos. 27) For Robinson Jeffers' Ghost. 28) For Bob. 29) Für Elise. 30) For Ted. 31) Elegy. 32) Tao Song.

C3. The Wind's Twelve Quarters. Short Stories. 297p (in proof copy). Harper and Row, 1975 (scheduled October). Contains a Foreword and, with prefatory notes, ## 2, 3, 4, 5, 6, 8, 13, 15, 16, 17, 18, 21, 26, 27, 28, 29, 31.

C4. Dreams Must Explain Themselves. In preparation (perhaps now ready), 1975, at Algol, Box 4175, New York, NY 10017. $3.00. Contains #6, G14, and G23.

##1-35. Stories and Novels

#1. An die Musik (short story). Summer 1961 (in *Western Humanities Review* magazine).

#2. April in Paris (short story). Sept 1962 (in *Fantastic* magazine). 1969 (in *Strange Fantasy* No. 10, magazine). 1973 (in *The Best From Fantastic*, ed. Ted White, Manor Books pb). Collected in C3.

#3. The Masters (short story). Feb 1963 (in *Fantastic* magazine). 1975 (in *Sword & Sorcery Annual* magazine). Collected in C3.

#4. Darkness Box (short story). Nov 1963 (in *Fantastic* magazine). 1970 (in *Weird Mystery* No. 2, magazine). Collected in C3.

#5. The Word of Unbinding (short story). Jan 1964 (in *Fantastic* magazine). 1970 (in *Strange Fantasy* No. 13, magazine). 1973 (in *The Golden Road*, ed. Damon Knight, Simon and Schuster hb). Collected in C3.

#6. The Rule of Names (short story). Apr 1964 (in *Fantastic* magazine). 1969 (in *The Most Thrilling Science Fiction Story Ever Told* No. 13, magazine). 1974 (in *Algol* magazine, No. 21). Collected in C3.

#7. Selection. (short story). Aug 1964 (in *Amazing* magazine). 1970 (in *Science Fiction Greats* No. 17, magazine).

#8. The Dowry of Angyar (short story). Sept 1964 (in *Amazing* magazine). 1970 (in *SF Greats* No. 19, magazine). 1973 (in *The Best From Amazing Stories*, ed. Ted White, Manor Books pb). Incorporated as prologue into #10: *Rocannon's World*. (Author's title: Semley's Necklace—collected in C3 under that title.)

#9. Rocannon's World (novel). 1966 (Ace pb, bound with Avram Davidson's *The Kar-Chee Reign*). 1972 (Ace pb). 1972 (UK: Tandem pb). 1973 (Milano: Delta, as *L'ultimo pianeta al di là delle stelle*, tr. Pier Antonio Rumignani). 1975 (Garland hb). See also C1.

#10. Planet of Exile (novel). 1966 (Ace pb, bound with Thomas M. Disch's *Mankind Under the Leash*). 1971 (Ace pb). 1972 (UK: Tandem pb). 1973 (Utrecht/Antwerpen: Het Spectrum, as *Ballings Planeet*, tr. T. Vosdahmen von Bucholz). 1975 (Garland hb). See also C1.

#11. City of Illusions (novel). 1967 (Ace pb). 1971 (UK: Gollancz hb). 1972 (Utrecht/Antwerpen: Het Spectrum as *De Shing-Begoocheling*, tr. A.B.H. van Bommel-van Terwisga). 1973 (UK: Panther pb). 1975 (Garland hb). See also C1. (Author's title: Two-minded Man.)

#12. A Wizard of Earthsea (novel). 1968 (Parnassus Press hb). 1969 (Parnassus Press hb). 1970 (Ace pb). 1971 (UK: Penguin/Puffin pb). 1971 (UK: Gollancz hb). 1974 (UK: Heinemann Educational Books hb). 1974 (as *Machten van Aardzee*, Utrecht/Antwerpen: Het Spectrum). 1974 (Ace pb). 1975 (Bantam pb).

#13. Winter's King (short story). 1969 (in *Orbit 5*, ed. Damon Knight, Putnam hb and various subsequent edns). 1972 (Frankfurt am Main: Fischer, in *Damon Knight's Collection 6*, as "Winterkönig," pb). Emended version collected in C3.

#14. The Left Hand of Darkness (novel). 1969 (Ace pb). 1969 (Walker hb). 1969 (UK: Macdonald hb). 1969 (SFBC edn as pbd by Walker, hb). 1971 (Paris: Robert Laffont, as *La main gauche de la nuit*, tr. Jean Bailhache, pb). 1971 (Bologna: Libra, as *La mano sinistra delle tenebre*, tr. Ugo Malaguti, hb). 1971 (Amsterdam: Meulenhoff, as *Duisters Linkerhand* pb). 1972 (Tokyo: Hayakawa, as *yami no hidari te*, tr. Fusa Obi, pb). 1973 (UK: Panther pb). 1973 (Buenos Aires: Minotauro, as *La mano izquierda de la oscuridad*, tr. Francisco Abelanda, pb).

#15. Nine Lives (short story). Nov 1969 (in *Playboy* magazine). 1970 (in *Nebula Award Stories 5*, ed. James Blish, Doubleday and various subsequent edns). 1970 (in *World's Best Science Fiction 1970*, ed. Donald A Wollheim & Terry Carr, Ace pb and various subsequent edns). 1970 (in *Best SF: 1969*, ed. Harry Harrison & Brian W. Aldiss, Putnam hb, Berkley pb). 1971 (in *The Dead Astronaut*, Playboy Press pb). 1973 (with afterword—see G12.—in *Those Who Can*, ed. Robin Scott Wilson, Mentor pb). 1973 (in *The Best From Playboy Number 7*, Playboy Press). 1974 (in *As Tomorrow Becomes Today*, ed. Charles William Sullivan III, Prentice-Hall). 1974 (in *Introducing Psychology Through Science Fiction*, ed. Harvey A. Katz et al., Rand-McNally). 1974 (in *Man Unwept: Visions from the Inner Eye*, ed. Stephen V. Whaley and Stanley J. Cook, McGraw-Hill). 1974 (in *Modern Science Fiction*, ed. Norman Spinrad, Anchor Books). 1975 (in *Dreams Awake*, ed. Leslie A. Fiedler, Dell pb). Collected, with some cuts restored, in C3.

#16. The End (short story). 1970 (in *Orbit 6*, ed. Damon Knight, Putnam hb. Berkley pb). 1975 (in *The Best From Orbit*, ed. Damon Knight, Berkley-Putnam hb). (Collected in C3 under author's title, Things.)

#17. The Good Trip (short story). Aug 1970 (in *Fantastic* magazine). 1972 (as "Voyage," tr. Alain le Bussy, in *L'Aube Enclaveé* magazine, No. 4). 1973 (as "Voyage," same tr., in *Derrière le néant*, ed. Henry-Luc Planchat, Verviers: Bibliothèque Marabout). 1974 (in *Dream Trips*, ed. Michel Parry, UK: Panther). Collected in C3.

#18. A Trip to the Head (short story). 1970 (in *Quark/#1*, ed. Samuel R. Delany & Marilyn Hacker, Paperback Library pb). 1974 (in *The Liberated Future*, ed. Robert Hoskins, Fawcett Crest pb). Collected in C3.

#19. The Tombs of Atuan (novel). Winter 1970-71 (in *Worlds of Fantasy* No. 3, magazine). 1971 (Atheneum hb). 1972 (UK: Gollancz hb). 1974 (UK: Penguin/Puffin). 1974 (UK: Heinemann Educational Books hb). 1974 (as *De Tomben van Atuan*, tr. F. Oomes, Utrecht/Antwerpen: Het Spectrum).

#20. The Lathe of Heaven (novel). March & May 1971 (in *Amazing* magazine). 1971 (Scribner's hb). 1971 (SFBC as pbd by Scribner's, hb). 1972 (UK: Gollancz hb). 1973 (Avon pb). 1975 (UK: Panther pb). 1974 (as *La falce dei cieli*, tr. Riccardo Valla, Milano: Nord). 1974 (as *Meester Dromer*, tr. G. Suurmeijer, Utrecht/Antwerpen: Het Spectrum)..

#21. Vaster Than Empires and More Slow (short story). Nov 1971 (in *New Dimensions 1*, ed. Robert Silverberg, Doubleday hb, Avon pb). 1972 (in *The Best Science Fiction of the Year*, ed. Terry Carr, Ballantine pb). 1973 (tr. into Japanese, as "teikoku yorimo okiku yuruyakami", in *S-F* Oct 1973). 1974 (in *Wondermakers 2*, ed. Robert Hoskins, Fawcett pb). 1975 (in *Explorers of Space*, ed. Robert Silverberg, Nelson hb). Collected, slightly cut, in C3.

#22. The Farthest Shore (novel). 1972 (Atheneum hb). 1972 (Junior Literary Guild, as pbd by Atheneum, hb). 1973 (UK: Gollancz hb). 1974 (UK: Puffin/Penguin pb). 1974 (as *Konig van Aardzee*, Utrecht/Antwerpen: Het Spectrum pb). 1975 (UK: Heinemann Educational Books hb). (Author's title:

The Farthest West.)

#23. The Word for World is Forest (long story). 1972 (in *Again, Dangerous Visions*, ed. Harlan Ellison, Doubleday hb). 1973 (in *Again, Dangerous Visions, Volume I*, ed. Harlan Ellison, Signet pb). With "Afterword"—see G5. (Author's title: The Little Green Men.)

#24. Cake & Ice Cream (short story). Feb-Mar 1973 (in *Playgirl* magazine).

#25. Imaginary Countries (short story). Winter 1973 (in *The Harvard Advocate* magazine). [According to a communication by the author, written ca. 1960.]

#26. Direction of the Road (short story). 1973 (in *Orbit 12*, ed. Damon Knight, Putnam hb and various subsequent edns). Collected in C3.

#27. Field of Vision (short story). Oct 1973 (in *Galaxy* magazine). 1974 (in *The Best From Galaxy, Volume II*, Award pb). (Author's title: The Field of Vision—collected in C3 under that title.)

#28. The Ones Who Walk Away From Omelas: Variations on a Theme by William James (short story). Oct 1973 (in *New Dimensions 3*, ed. Robert Silverberg, SFBC as Nelson Doubleday hb, Signet pb). 1974 (in *The Best Science Fiction of the Year #3*, ed. Terry Carr, Ballantine pb). 1975 (as "Ceux qui partent d'Omélas...", tr. by Henri-Luc Planchat, in *La frontière avenir*, ed. H.-L. Planchat, Paris: Seghers pb). Collected in C3.

#29. The Stars Below (short story). 1974 (in *Orbit 14*, ed. Damon Knight, Harper & Row hb). Collected in C3.

#30. The Dispossessed (novel). 1974 (Harper & Row hb). 1974 (Toronto: Fitzhenry & Whiteside hb). 1974 (SFBC as pbd by Harper & Row hb). 1974 (Harper & Row hb). 1974 (UK: Gollancz hb). 1975 (Avon pb).

#31. The Day Before the Revolution (short story). Aug 1974 (in *Galaxy* magazine). 1975 (in *Bitches and Sad Ladies*, ed. Pat Rotter, Harper's Magazine Press hb, & Toronto: Fitzhenry & Whiteside). Collected in C3.

#32. Intracom (short story). 1974 (in *StopWatch*, ed. George Hay, UK: New English Library hb).

#33. The Author of the Acacia Seeds and Other Extracts from the *Journal of the Association of Therolinguistics* (short story). 1974 (in *Fellowship of the Stars*, ed. Terry Carr, Simon & Schuster hb & SFBC as pbd by Simon & Schuster). 1975 (in *Best Science Fiction of the Year #4*, ed. Terry Carr, Ballantine pb).

#34. Schrödinger's Cat (short story). 1974 (in *Universe 5*, ed. Terry Carr, Random House hb and various subsequent edns).

#35. The New Atlantis (short story). 1975 (in *The New Atlantis*, ed. Robert Silverberg, Hawthorn hb and SFBC as pbd by Hawthorn, hb).

G1-G30. General

G1. Review of *Jean Lemaire de Belges: "Le Temple d'honneur et de vertus,"* ed. Henri Hornik. *Romanic Review*, 49(Oct 1948):210-11.

G2. A Scene from an Opera (in verse). *The Minority of One*, 3(Aug 1961):9.

G3. Prophets and Mirrors (essay). *The Living Light* (Fall 1970):111-21.

G4. [Interview & Response to questionnaire]. *Entropy Negative*, No. 3, (1971):(17-26).

G5. [Response to questionnaire on SF]. *Colloquy*, 4(May 1971):7.

G6. "Afterword" to "The Word for World is Forest" (see #23).

G7. The Crab Nebula, the Paramecium, and Tolstoy (essay). *Riverside Quarterly*, 5(Feb 1972):89-96. See also C1.

G8. National Book Award Acceptance Speech. *Horn Book*, 49(June 1973): 239; *SFWA Bulletin*, No. 47-48(Summer 1973):32; *Algol*, No. 21(Nov 1973): 14; *Orbit 14*, ed. Damon Knight, Harper & Row, 1974, p.2.

G9. On Norman Spinrad's *The Iron Dream* (review). *SFS* 1(Spring 1973): 41-44.

G10. From Elfland to Poughkeepsie (essay pbd as chapbook). Portland: Pendragon Press, 1973.

G11. A Citizen of Mondath (essay). *Foundation*, No. 4 (July 1973):20-24.

G12. Surveying the Battlefield (essay). *SFS* 1(Fall 1973):88-90.

G13. On Theme (essay). In *Those Who Can*, ed. Robin Scott Wilson, Mentor, 1973, pp. 203-09.

G14. Dreams Must Explain Themselves (essay). *Algol*, No. 21 (Nov 1973): 7-10, 12, 14.

G15. Why Are Americans Afraid of Dragons? (essay). *PNLA Quarterly*, 38(Winter 1974):14-18; as "This Fear of Dragons," in *The Thorny Paradise*, ed. Edward Blishen, UK: Kestrel Books, 1975, pp. 87-92.

G16. The Staring Eye (essay about Tolkien). *Vector*, No. 67-68 (Spring 1974):5-7.

G18. Science Fiction Tomorrow (essay). *Christian Science Monitor*, July 18, 1974.

G19. Escape Routes (essay). *Galaxy*, 35(Dec 1974):40-44.

G20. Science Fiction and the Future of Anarchy (conversations with Ursula K. Le Guin by Charles Bigelow and J. McMahon). *Oregon Times* (Dec 1974):24-29.

G21. The Child and the Shadow (essay). *The Quarterly Journal of the Library of Congress*, 32(April 1975): (139)-148.

G22. Tricks, anthropology create new worlds (interview by Barry Barth). *Portland Scribe*, 4(May 17-25, 1975):8-9.

G23. Ursula K. Le Guin: Interviewed by Jonathan Ward. *Algol*, 12(Summer 1975):6-10.

G24. SF in a Political-Science Textbook (review). *SFS* 2(March 1975):93-94.

G25. Ketterer on *The Left Hand of Darkness* (essay). *SFS* 2(July 1975): 137-39.

#G26. [Letter]. *Galaxy*, 36(Aug 1975):157.

G27. American SF and the Other. (essay). *SFS* 2(Nov 1975):208-10.

G28. Is Gender Necessary? (essay). (Forthcoming in Susan J. Anderson and Vonda McIntyre eds., *Aurora: Beyond Equality*, Fawcett.)

G29. Science Fiction and mrs. Brown (essay). (Forthcoming in a collection of speeches on SF, ed. Peter Nicholls, UK: Gollancz.)

Ursula K. Le Guin. American SF and the Other

One of the great early socialists said that the status of women in a society is a pretty reliable index of the degree of civilisation of that society. If this is true, then the very low status of women in SF should make us ponder about whether SF is civilised at all.

The women's movement has made most of us conscious of the fact that SF has either totally ignored women, or presented them as squeaking dolls subject to instant rape by monsters—or old-maid scientists desexed by hypertrophy of the intellectual organs—or, at best, loyal little wives or mistresses of accomplished heroes. Male elitism has run rampant in SF. But is it only male elitism? Isn't the "subjection of women" in SF merely a symptom of a whole which is authoritarian, power-worshipping, and intensely parochial?

The question involved here is the question of The Other—the being who is different from yourself. This being can be different from you in its sex; or in its annual income; or in its way of speaking and dressing and doing things; or in the color of its skin, or the number of its legs and heads. In other words, there is the sexual Alien, and the social Alien, and the cultural Alien, and finally the racial Alien. *Alien self too*

Well, how about the social Alien in SF? How about, in Marxist terms, "the proletariat"? Where are they in SF? Where are the poor, the people who work hard and go to bed hungry? Are they ever *persons*, in SF? No. They appear as vast anonymous masses fleeing from giant slime-globules from the Chicago sewers, or dying off by the billion from pollution or radiation, or as faceless armies being led to battle by generals and statesmen. In sword and sorcery they behave like the walk-on parts in a high school performance of The Chocolate Prince. Now and then there's a busty lass amongst them who is honored by the attentions of the Captain of the Supreme Terran Command, or in a space-ship crew there's a quaint old cook, with a Scots or Swedish accent, representing the Wisdom of the Common Folk.

The people, in SF, are not people. They are masses, existing for one purpose: to be led by their superiors.

From a social point of view most SF has been incredibly regressive and unimaginative. All those Galactic Empires, taken straight from the British Empire of 1880. All those planets—with 80 trillion miles between them!—conceived of as warring nation-states, or as colonies to be exploited, or to be nudged by the benevolent Imperium of Earth towards self-development—the White Man's Burden all over again. The Rotary Club on Alpha Centauri, that's the size of it.

What about the cultural and the racial Other? This is the Alien everybody recognizes as alien, supposed to be the special concern of SF. Well, in the old pulp SF, it's very simple. The only good alien is a dead alien—whether he is an Aldebaranian Mantis-Man, or a German dentist. And this tradition still flourishes: witness Larry Niven's story "Inconstant Moon" (in *All the Myriad Ways*, 1941) which has a happy ending—consisting of the fact that America, including Los Angeles, was not hurt by a solar flare. Of course a few million Europeans and Asians were fried, but that doesn't matter, it just makes the world a little safer for democracy, in fact. (It is interesting that the female character in the same story is quite brainless; her only function is to say Oh? and Ooooh! to the clever and resourceful hero.)

Then there's the other side of the same coin. If you hold a thing to be totally different from yourself, your fear of it may come out as hatred, or as awe—reverence. So we get all those wise and kindly beings who deign to rescue Earth from her sins and perils. The Alien ends up on a pedestal in a white nightgown and a virtuous smirk—exactly as the "good woman" did in the Victorian Age.

In America, it seems to have been Stanley Weinbaum who invented the sympathetic alien, in *A Martian Odyssey*. From then on, via people like Cyril Kornbluth, Ted Sturgeon, and Cordwainer Smith, SF began to inch its way out of simple racism. Robots—the alien intelligence—begin to behave nicely, With Smith, interestingly enough, the racial alien is combined with the social alien, in the "Underpeople," and they are allowed to have a revolution. As the aliens got more sympathetic, so did the human heroes. They began to have emotions, as well as rayguns. Indeed they began to become almost human.

If you deny any affinity with another person or kind of person, if you declare it to be wholly different from yourself—as men have done to women, and class has done to class, and nation has done to nation—you may hate it, or deify it; but in either case you have denied its spiritual equality, and its human reality. You have made it into a thing, to which the only possible relationship is a power relationship. And thus you have fatally impoverished your own reality.

You have, in fact, alienated yourself.

This tendency has been remarkably strong in American SF. The only social change presented by most SF has been towards authoritarianism, the domination of ignorant masses by a powerful elite—sometimes presented as a warning, but often quite complacently. Socialism is never considered as an alternative, and democracy is quite forgotten. Military virtues are taken as ethical ones. Wealth is assumed to be a righteous goal and a personal virtue. Competitive free-enterprise capitalism is the economic destiny of the entire Galaxy. In general, American SF has assumed a permanent hierarchy of superiors and inferiors, with rich, ambitious, aggressive males at the top, then a great gap, and then at the bottom the poor, the uneducated, the faceless masses, and all the women. The whole picture is, if I may say so, curiously "un-American." It is a perfect baboon patriarchy, with the Alpha Male on top, being respectfully groomed, from time to time, by his inferiors.

Is this speculation? is this imagination? is this extrapolation? I call it brainless regressivism.

I think it's time SF writers—and their readers!—stopped daydreaming about a return to the Age of Queen Victoria, and started thinking about the future. I would like to see the Baboon Ideal replaced by a little human idealism, and some serious consideration of such deeply radical, futuristic concepts as Liberty, Equality, and Fraternity. And remember that about 53% of the Brotherhood of Man is the Sisterhood of Woman.

Rafail Nudelman

An Approach to the Structure of Le Guin's SF

Translated by Alan G. Myers

> I felt that the book itself had become what it treated of, i.e. a musical construct. —Thomas Mann

Ursula K. Le Guin's early work is marked by an artistic originality as pronounced as it is elusive. The seeming impossibility of defining this originality teases the imagination. It begins to seem urgently necessary to analyze what this aesthetic world "represents" before attempting to speak of what it "expresses."

1. The Textual Structure. The first and most obvious characteristic of Le Guin's early tales—*Rocannon's World* (RW), *Planet of Exile* (PE), *City of Illusions* (CI), and *The Left Hand of Darkness* (LHD)—is their interconnectedness. They have a common subject of narration—a science-fictional "union of space civilizations" (League of All Worlds or Ekumen) to which they all relate as separate episodes.

This is a fairly widespread phenomenon in literature as a whole and particularly in the "younger" literary genres. Le Guin's originality shows clearly already in the characteristic connections each tale has to the others and to the whole. It is normal in SF for a causal connection to exist between episodic tales: the upshot of events of a preceding episode prepares, directly or indirectly, the point of departure for the following tale (e.g., Heinlein, Asimov, the Strugatskys). Accordingly, the episodes are in a simple, chronological order, and take place in a unified space. Such a science-fictional model of *history* is equivalent to a natural-science picture of the *universe* on which the fruitful extrapolations of SF are generally based.

This type of interconnectedness is not the only one possible. In a series of adventure tales (e.g. Fenimore Cooper's, or Harry Harrison's Deathworld series), the causal relationships between the episodes amount, in the main, to a purely chronological sequence; the starting point of one tale ignores what has occurred in the preceding one (trivial details apart). Put in another way, the temporal flow becomes indifferent to the events occurring within that time: qualitative changes are absent from the universe of the adventure novel. Space in such novels is also neutral, whatever the outcome of events. Time and space have features of what Newton termed absolute time or empty duration and empty or absolute space; endless proliferation of episodes is a possibility inherent in the adventure-story series.

The disintegration of space-time is even clearer in the series of detective tales unified by a common hero (Conan Doyle, Agatha Christie, etc.). The peculiarities of that genre require a more rigid replication of the highly formalised structure—including the stereotyped starting situations. This precludes any possibility of a causal link between detective-tale episodes, and at the same time sharply defines their space-time. The concept of a "series" is purely conventional here, since any separate episode implies in its structure an infinite number of possible repetitions.

Le Guin's SF fits none of the categories so far mentioned. Looking at it one way, it seems to be organised on chronological principles, since the various tales can be placed in a certain temporal sequence. At first sight, moreover, they constitute a future history drawn with a dotted line—the rise and fall of the League of All Worlds. On the other hand, however, the starting points of all her tales are virtually identical (will a particular world be enabled to join the League?). Thus, every situation repeats the essential *raison d'être* of the League's activities—a movement from fragmentation toward unity.

At the same time, Le Guin's tales are not linked as episodes of a larger whole either spatially or temporally. This may seem to contradict my earlier assertion of the possibility of a chronological order for the episodes. Strictly speaking, however, that ordering does not depend on any direct connection between the events of various tales, but rather on their indirect relationship: each episode, considered separately, relates to the history of the League as a whole. In and by themselves, Le Guin's tales are sharply isolated from each other. Their temporal relationship is deliberately blurred: though there may be some ostensible indications to the contrary, there exists no common time-scale. Furthermore, close inspection causes League history itself to blur out of focus. We know nothing of its crucial events, their course or their consequences, just as we know nothing of the League itself, either its organisation or its functions—apart from its function as a unifier of worlds. It is no coincidence that in LHD the Ekumen is defined as a mystical idea rather than a concrete organisation. What, then, are these episodes of a non-existent "history" about? It would perhaps be most accurate to say that they tell of the separate stages through which the abstract idea or process of unification must of necessity pass. In actual fact, the first four of Le Guin's tales depict, essentially, four stages in the development of this idea: a world being drawn into the League or Ekumen (LHD); a world in the early stages of such involvement (RW); a world which has virtually lost its former ties with the League (PE), and finally, a world torn away from the League and striving to return to it (CI).[1] One might note that this last episode can be regarded as the first part of a new cycle, a new spiral in the League's history, which is the Ekumen—a fact which serves to emphasize the difficulty of assigning any kind of definite chronology within the sequence of tales. Only the whole has an absolute significance, since it possesses neither beginning nor end.

The episodes' separateness in time is complemented by the isolation of their events in space. The worlds of the various tales are not only lost in time, they are also ignorant of the coordinates, the very existence of each other. The space which the League embraces is united and linked only in the sense that it all makes up the League's space; there is no unified system of coordinates or reference points, no grid of relative distances. The only way of defining each planet's position is in relation to the central planets of the League—usually at a monstrous distance. The events in each episode invariably take place on the very edge of the known cosmos, in fearful isolation from its "centre" and from each other; in other words, on the frontier of League territory and "alien" space. The peripheralness, the frontier nature of the spatial situation in each episode is analogous to the peculiar temporal situation. The stages of "League history" symbolised in the various episodes are also "frontier" stages. They do not cover the central areas of this "history," only its initial and final phases, its frontiers.

We begin to sense an odd law obtaining here: the particular instance is always and in every respect "remote" from the central nucleus, the whole which is being suggested; the actual sign is remote from the general meaning it signifies. The League is never itself shown—it is merely an invariable presence in the given situation, dictating an invariable type of reality. The League has no concrete history of its own—but the universal phases of its development are eternally played out in the histories of real worlds, making up the canvas of their events. The League is not located in observable space, it is always in the unreachable "centre of the universe"—but it is the unchanging centre of reference of each episode. On the common-sense level this is made clear by the fact that the universes of the various episodes are "simply" the same universe. But this simplicity is deceptive. Everything connected with the League has a suspicious touch of ambiguity: the very image of the League is constantly ambivalent, sometimes hardening into the representation of a wholly real social structure, then again blurring into a nebulous universal metaphysical concept. The same thing happens with space and time. With Le Guin, time does not flow on from episode to episode, since the episodes are dissociated and isolated; nevertheless, within the frame of each episode the time-flow is real. Such a peculiar, contradictory temporal reality is, in fact, a concrete instance of a sort of "supra-time" within which the history of the League develops, expanding to the dimensions of the universe's eternal history and only content. As for the space in each episode, it too is, like the duration, totally enclosed and without continuation. In other words, it holds within itself the whole universe, with its centre (the League) materialising, so to speak, in an actual world in any particular episode. The spatial reality of this world is also ambivalent: it is both the reality of a particular concrete world, and simultaneously a symbolic arena containing the whole universum with its unique metaphysical reality—the League, its history, and its destiny.

The sensation we have as if the entire universe were "fed into" the finite, localised, sharply concretised space-time of each episode, originates in the peculiar nature of the interconnection between the episodes—or, more accurately, in the absence of their interconnection. It is this very impossibility of extending local space-time beyond the limits of a particular given universe which gives rise to the feeling that beyond those bounds there is "nothing at all," that the material universe comes to an end: a circle of light and beyond it an impenetrable, endless darkness. The universe of a given episode seems to contain within itself the whole of space and to replicate the eternal history of all there is. Events there take on the character of universal laws. In each succeeding tale they unfold along the same lines—in an analogous area "unique in the universe," lost in space and time; it begins with the same, as it were hallowed situation; it develops towards the same conclusion. This fact can only signify one thing—we are faced with a universal order of things, hallowed by time, obligatory for all worlds.

Without losing its concreteness, reality grows more and more symbolic; behind it appear the lineaments of a universal scheme repeating itself in each episode, a general law of being, an eternally self-replicating order of things, "mystically" embodied in the League of All Worlds. The League is a unity of a peculiar kind—not the sum of its parts but rather a common factor, an essential constant derived from them. The universe described by such a model is not, of course, the non-metaphysical universe of modern science used by the run-of-the-mill SF. Or, to be strictly accurate, it is not only that, for in Le Guin's SF there is indeed a realistic foreground. Clear inspection, however, reveals a second dimension which we must term "mythopoetic." For it is in this "second universe" that objects and phenomena lay bare their hidden universal significance and supra-historical law of being.

Le Guin's SF is thus seen to be not only a narrative concerning real problems, but also an attempt to communicate a higher truth persistently recurring in all of life's ephemeral aspects.

But have we enough evidence to assert the existence of this universal hidden meaning in Le Guin's SF? So far, we have established only one of its main peculiarities—the replacement of the *sequential* linkage "from episode to episode," normal in any chronological series of tales (and tantamount to the formula "the whole is the sum of the parts") by another—distinctly original, it is true—*radial* type of linkage: "from a single centre towards each episode" (tantamount to: "the whole is the essence or common factor of its parts"). This is equivalent to the presence of a structural similarity or analogy of the part (episode) to the whole, as well as of each separate episode to any other episode. This identifies the essential structural principle of this SF—its thorough *iconicity*: in it, the "lower" level of the narrative form is a similarity, an image, the isomorphic sign of a more general or "higher" formal level. This holds good not only for the very highest forms of organisation—the "series of tales" and the separate tales. The actual world of each individual episode is also an equivalent or similarity—in this case, the equivalent of the universe of the League. Thus, lineaments of the omnipresent scheme of Le Guin's appear also in her narrative forms.

The world of each tale is formally one—one planet, in fact. The familiar Le Guin scheme reveals itself in that there is never in this world any actual unity—governmental, cultural, or any other. The planet-world is always presented as a conglomerate of two or more cultures, sometimes merely co-existing, sometimes almost inimical. Genuine unity invariably turns out to be the *goal* toward which the events of the narrative proceed; it is always—to come. If on the preceding level of the universe the goal of events was unity within the League, now the same events as it were replicate an analogous movement toward unity, but this time on a planetary scale.

The starting point too is reiterated, also on a diminished scale. On the previous, more generalised level, the hero or heroes acted as an element in the relationship of the League of All Worlds towards the individual world; he was the League's representative on an alien planet. Now, putting aside this mask, he discovers a second beneath it, exactly similar to the first: he invariably turns out to be the willing or unwilling representative of one of the planetary cultures (the planet has conditionally become "his") in the habitat of another, "alien" culture. Sometimes it transpires as the story develops (RW, LHD), but is is always presented before the plot really gets under way. This is all the easier to recognise since all of Le Guin's plot developments are of the same type—they are without fail worked out as a journey, a travelling through space-time. There are fundamental reasons for this of which more later; even the single exception (PE) merely confirms how real these reasons are. The starting-point mentioned above is always presented as given at the moment when this journey begins. And under this mask too, another lurks: *a man among those who are similar to himself but always "other."*

The world in which the hero undertakes his journey bears a striking resemblance to the universe of the League. It is always a world where separateness, fragmentation, alienation are dominant; lonely farmsteads of Earthmen dotted about an endless forest (CI), aborigine settlements separated by enormous distances (RW) or colonial towns and native stamping grounds (PE), states which co-exist but are isolated by an ice-desert and a sea (LHD). The planetary space too lacks any unified, definite grid of coordinates or reliable landmarks; it is fragmented into isolated islets of life separated by vast, mysterious, lifeless wastes. The life islets are not only not linked, but are not even located relative to one another. The space that divides them is always and emphatically of the same type—an all-embracing forest, or similarly unrelieved ice, sea or snow. If life is organisation and structure, then the wastes that divide the islets of planetary life are the negation of life, shapeless, unstructured, monotonous, same. Their dead uniformity hems in the interspersed dots of organised existence.

It is quite clear that this space, repeated from tale to tale, is analogous to the space of the League universe: the same scattered islets of life lost on the rim of the universe, the same formless murk encroaching on them from every side and seeming to embody the principle of alienation. The space on the planet turns out to be an iconic sign for the universe, and is organised like it, according to the same, universal scheme.

We might descend even lower, to the space of each separate cell on the planet-worlds (the woodland farm in CI; the township in PE; etc.). Each succeeding level reveals fresh details, and the universal similarity, being expressed in other *realia*, becomes less and less exact; yet here too it is possible to recognise familiar, if faded, indications. The motif of separation is repeated with unvarying regularity—this time the cells are enclosed by walls, partitions; visions of empty rooms and enormous halls appear before us, in which there live lonely people—usually apart from one another. Estraven's house, and the Inner Hearth of his father are like this (LHD), as are the houses on the forest farms (CI), and the habitations in the colonists' townships (PE). The Shing "City of Illusion" itself, with its kaleidoscope of unseen walls emphasizing the illusory nature of any kind of human intimacy, becomes a concentrated, almost allegorical expression of this apartness. The opposite phenomenon— the large congregations of people which appear now and again in Le Guin's pages—are most often purely mechanical groupings, united, as a rule, in a negative way (the cave folk in RW, the troglodyte horde in PE, the herdsmen in CI, etc.). Even on the level of human relationships one senses a certain cool aloofness, a certain unsurmounted distance and isolation which makes even closely bound people lonely; it is enough to recall the colonists' council in PE, everyday life in the House of CI, or the Foretellers' monastery in LHD. Man, that final atom of creation, usually appears in Le Guin's SF as a solitary being. Solitude is his involuntary form of existence. His status is equivalent, in the descending order of magnitude, to the status of the League cosmos, of the given planet, and of that islet of life where he lives and whose laws his being reflects. As a microcosm, man is truly similar to the macrocosm, and the same universal law of fragmentation which governs the life forms at all levels, rules him too. The "involuntary" nature of this form of existence, its unnaturalness, is quite obvious—it is not by chance that on every level the scattered elements strive toward oneness. The events of the narrative which form its plot manifest themselves on the level of human destinies as the movement of the hero toward oneness with other human creatures.

Thus, moving from level to level in the thematic structure, we observe a repeating image at every stage: a universe which has lost its unity, and is agonizingly groping its way back to it.

As for time, just as in the universe of the League there exist only local times, without relation to each other, and the endlessly cyclical history of the League itself, so, on the level of the sundered society of each planet, no other unified time exists except the cyclical changes of the seasons. Not a single one of these worlds possesses a coherent chronology of historical events; the reckoning of years is, as a rule, lost; the islets of life are not only separated in space, they are enclosed in their own local temporal flow—they have no common history. The sole form of historical recollection is therefore legend, tradition, myth, and the events in each tale, weaving into this mytho-historical temporal fabric, also take on a mythopoetic colouring. Behind the realistic meaning of the events there appears their second, mythico-universal significance of movement toward Oneness, as toward the natural condition of the World.[2] This movement will however, have to be a directed one. For, normal time in such a world is static and merely reproduces itself over and over as inane activity, marked only by the elementary signs of birth and death. It is not for nothing that in the universe of LHD time-reckoning starts again each new year, which is always the year zero. Its past is legend, its future—only a sequence of repetitions of the past. All that lies on either side of the present, lacking the landmarks of historical events, imperceptibly slides into the amorphous, motionless temporal continuum of myth. It is not only that the time of a given world contains within itself the whole time of the universe; it is not only that the time of any part of that world contains, in its turn, the whole of its time; more than this: every instant contains within itself all of time, it becomes equivalent to a day, a year, a century, eternity.

Thus, Le Guin's SF establishes a vertical hierarchy of similarities or equivalents: the universe—the world of the individual planet—the islets of life on it—the individual person. The structure of all these levels is organised following a single scheme, the universe can be seen in a grain of sand. On every level we see a World or Universe of collapsing bonds, sundered space, arrested time, a World frozen in amorphous eventlessness and awaiting a second creation—the establishment of order.

To a certain extent this world picture is echoed in the purely formal articulation of Le Guin's SF. The series of tales breaks down into major episodes—the tales themselves; these, in turn, break down into a series of episodes threaded along the plot-line; if we can regard the entire tale as being the journey of a League emissary, then the central episode within it is also seen to be a journey, in its turn resolved into a chain of episodes. In these transitions from level to level, the scale of the objects drawn into the events gets smaller and smaller. In the central episode of the "elementary journey" we see the most elementary entity still capable of bearing the two basic principles of fragmentation and oneness. Such an entity is two people. The hierarchy of formal articulation repeats the structural hierarchy, and the formal atom of Le Guin's SF, its tiniest episode and its object, coincides with its structural atom. Spatiotemporal movement—from one life islet to another—takes on, at this final or atomic level, its limit-form. Finally, such an isolated "islet in the universe" is simply man, each man. The way to a united universe goes through the reunification of people; the way to a league between individual people becomes a sign and equivalent for a way to cosmic unification.

This repetition of identical thematic structures in all of Le Guin's tales leads to a parallelism between their formal structures. They coincide in compositional construction, in plot episodes, and even, finally, in the regularity with which similar motifs and situations occur at identical nodal points in the tales. As an example of such regularity we may take the constant background against which the climax of the "Hero's Journey" is played out. In Le Guin's work this is always snow, boundless snowy or icy wastes. Rocannon's friend and travelling companion perishes among icy peaks—through Rocannon's fault; Falk in CI finds his companion and betrayer in a snowstorm; Genly Ai and Estraven find the way to one another (and the gulf between them) on an icy plateau—that very ice on which Estraven will die (LHD). Snow is the culmination of the Way, and by that token, also of the way for people toward each other. Therefore, the most important human relationships, those which bind and sunder people, come into being on the snow—Love and Death, Friendship and Treachery. It is no accident—though it has a purely local significance also—that in LHD, which sums up all the motifs of Le Guin's SF up to that time, Life itself is born on the snows (see the creation myth of the first people, §17).

Summing up, we can say that the artistic originality of Le Guin's SF is first and foremost the originality of a strong musically organised form, frankly thrust into the foreground. The all-prevading "vertical" similarity or equivalence (the iconicity or isomorphic relationship of each sign to its meaning) and the all-pervading "horizontal" parallelism (between corresponding formal elements of different works) resemble musical recurrence, that persistence with which a pervasive theme expresses itself in variations. Placing Le Guin's narratives as it were one on top of the other, we would find something resembling an X-ray picture where the coinciding elements are intensified and stand out more sharply, the differences in local detail are effaced, and the nodes and joints of the "skeletal" universal structure stand out against a ghostly aura of fictional flesh. These pervading motifs—this skeleton of concrete form—create in their interweaving a complex musical structure, conveying a certain message.

Thus, it is characteristic of Le Guin's SF that its structure becomes a sign of its message. Moreover, this structure is an iconic sign, i.e. the properties of the structure are similar or equivalent to the content of the message; the content of the message is translated into the language of the peculiar features of the structure. The essence of what is expressed is indicated by the nature of the means of expression; the form of the sign is its meaning.

We may conclude, therefore, that the dominating principle of Le Guin's SF—the repetition of the universal scheme on all its levels—is a message, expressed in the language of fictional structures, about the universality of a world-order in which, on every level of being, one finds the same laws which govern Le Guin's fictional world. Proceeding from the fictional structure to the Universe encoded by it, we can almost physically sense the way in which the sundered and scattered structure of a world-model, trembling in its surge towards Oneness, by imperceptible degrees shows forth the construction of that very World—a universe of disassociated, agonisingly isolated forms, ever seeking amalgamation. The non-fictive World which stands behind Le Guin's SF is an artistically organised whole where universal relationships of form obtain. Being universal, they are inevitably embodied in the structure of any real phenomenon or event, and therefore in the structure of any "true" fictional narrative concerning them. This reciprocal equivalence guarantees the possibility not only of expressing reality in fictional form, but also of reflecting certain fundamental characteristics of the World as a whole.[3] Such a fictional text, richly reflecting reality, becomes at the same time a sign—equivalent of the universal "Text" or universal "Laws of the World."

Furthermore, Le Guin's message concerning the World exists only in her creative work, taken as a whole, in all the multiplicity of its concrete episodes; it is not fully expressed in any particular instance. This separation between sign and meaning also holds true for all levels. The world of each planet, belonging to the general—to the League of All Worlds—is at the same time emphatically distant and isolated from it. The situation of each hero, being a sign for the general existential situation of man in the world, is a concrete fictional form of an extreme isolation (a Crusoe-like existence on an inhabitable island, solitude among aliens). The same principle of separating and isolating "sign" and "meaning" can be observed in the image-system. The invariable background for the most dramatic plot-climaxes is a monotonous and indifferent expanse of ice or snow. The drama is estranged by the indifferent background, and the feeling by terse speech—for even on the verbal level the distance between the sign (the word) and the meaning (thought-feeling) is preserved. The more "neutral" a segment of text, the more plastic and rich in nuance the verbal texture, leaving virtually nothing unsaid; the closer to the "epicentre of complexity," however, the more routine and ritualised the word becomes—and the more ambiguous the meaning.

Thus, on every level of content and form, corresponding elements—by their similarity to those higher placed "vertically," along with their repetitions and echoes "horizontally"—indicate that they belong to some higher generality, in which their meanings merge. By this, they escape one-dimensional "realism" and leave a margin of ambiguity, room for an indefiniteness which does not permit a living and complex thought to turn into allegorical rationalism.

These relationships of coalescence—noncoalescence which permeate Le Guin's universe of fictional forms make it possible to define them as symbolic forms, in the Hegelian sense. The fragmentation and isolation of individual forms of being, and the urge it engenders for amalgamation—such is the depth-image of the universe which this SF impresses upon us. The immanent aspiration of all forms toward a higher oneness constitutes a kind of cosmic Plot, a History of the Universe, its Way; and the plots of the separate books are the individual manifestations ("signs-equivalents") of that Plot. As always in Le Guin, these particular plots do not cover or exhaust their general meaning. In other words, the general is not fully realised in the particular, the cosmic Plot is never fulfilled. The natural "completion" of each individual plot is, from the viewpoint of the cosmic Way, merely a transitional stage.[4] The separate plots form, therefore, a meaningful series, describing the attainment of ever higher levels of unity for all rational life-forms.[5] And it is this all-pervading inner movement of one idea from tale to tale that sharply distinguishes Le Guin's sequence of tales from the cognitively "empty" character of detective or adventure series.

2. The Plot Structure. A proper examination of Le Guin's fictional structure would entail a further discussion of at least her plot and image structures (and in fact this whole article is the smaller part of an unpublished Ms. in which I examine these aspects too). Here I can only give a succinct approach to an examination of her plot structure.

The movement towards Oneness on the planetary scale is absorption into the League; within the planet, it is the reunification of a fragmented society; on the individual level, it is the striving toward fellow-beings and unification with them. The reunification of a world means not only the restoration of links within a human collective but also the "knitting together" of its physical space-time, since the unity of the collective presumes a consciousness of its spatial integrity and historic continuity. In Le Guin's work, therefore, each stage of cosmic history, regarded as a recurrent reunification, is played out as spatio-temporal movement or Journey. The spatial movements of the hero stitches together, so to speak, the isolated islets of life; this can be clearly seen in the journeys of Falk, Rocannon, or Genly Ai. The history of his wanderings, the temporal aspect of the Journey, introduces direction and irreversibility into a formerly static world, since its eventual result is a qualitative renewal of that world; it brings into the world a fulness of time, historically. The hero's history becomes the beginning of history for a previously ahistorical world. The Journey (the "means") on its space-time level is isomorphic to the universal Way (the "ends") which it embodies. The hero brings into a formerly cyclic world the ends or goal which it previously lacked; since the goal has to be reached by overcoming space and time, movement toward it becomes a spatio-temporal Journey. In this way the plot structure takes on a resemblance to the spatio-temporal structure of the culture-hero myth, and through it, to certain types of later, magical fairy tale.[6]

Le Guin's heroes have the mission of attaching a lower-level culture to a higher (finally—to a universal) one. Culture is here interpreted as a unity retaining variety (i.e. the resistance to absorption shown by all unique life-forms), as a structural unity—in contrast to Nature as an unstructured monotony. The plot structure, therefore, not only has a natural starting point but also a natural conclusion—the attainment of the goal; yet, Le Guin's plot remains in essence open-ended. Superficially, this might seem to bring Le Guin's type of tale close to either the detective or the adventure tale. However, there are fundamental differences. For, in the detective tale the natural conclusion of the plot disposes fully of its logical subject; therefore, the conclusion is an absolute end to the events, a return of the universe to its equilibrium and order. This is only possible in a closed universe, isolated from non-fictional reality, such as the detective-tale universe is. Its plot has, as it were, a circular or cyclical character, which is correlative to the character of that universe. The adventure-tale, on the other hand, had no natural conclusion at all, since to its subject-matter—the overcoming of a given danger, difficulty, et sim.—a second, third, etc., danger can always be added. This results in a potentially infinite linear character of the plot. In each particular episode such a plot movement is akin to the Journey (so that adventure novels often take just that form), but as a whole it differs from the Journey by not being able ever to dispose fully of its logical (as different from its accidental, given) subject.

Thus, the detective tale is both formally and logically a closed structure; the adventure-tale is in each particular episode closed, but in its entirety it is an open-ended structure. In contrast to both, the "Journey tale" of Le Guin's type is formally closed—i.e. a tale with a formal conclusion—but logically open-ended. In Le Guin's tales the initial and final situations are superficially similar: Falk-Ramarren (CI) comes from nowhere and returns to nowhere; Genly Ai (LHD) returns to where he set out from; the colonist city (PE) has weathered the siege. However, essentially the end of such a Way is radically different from its beginning. The difference can be measured in terms of those changes which have come about in the process of journeying. Neither the hero nor the world has been left unchanged—as they would be in a pure detective or adventure tale. Le Guin's hero and world have by the end of each tale gone a part of the Way toward that Oneness the longing for which is the motivating force of the subject-matter. The coming about of a changed personality and/or changed world means that the (formally identical) starting and concluding situations of fragmentation and striving toward Oneness are logically or cognitively different: the final situation happens on a "higher" level. As different from the detective tale, it is not only possible but necessary to continue the Way. The continuation will, however, not be a repetition or copy of the just concluded episode, as it would be in an adventure-tale. We might say that we have here to do with a superposition of the closed, circular plot-structure of the detective tale upon an open, linear adventure-tale plot, resulting in the *spiral* structure of a LeGuinian Journey. Such a journey alters the world and the culture in which it takes place from a spatially sundered and temporally cyclic one into a connected and historic one.

A similarly open-ended meaning distinguishes Le Guin's plots not only from the formally similar "winter journey," but also from the wanderings of fairy-tale heroes, who, like Le Guin's heroes, describe an enormous circle beginning and ending in their "own" world but spent for the most part in alien surroundings. All such plots, involving a formal return to their starting point, may be described as *tautological* ones. Whereas myth or fairy tale (where the cyclic journey corresponds to the cyclic world and does not change its orientation) are genuinely tautological, Le Guin's tales are not such. Her Journeys bring into the world a change, which in turn becomes the source of an endless movement-cum-development, a Way toward the Goal.

The stages of this Way are set out according to Le Guin's persistently recurring scheme, a specific "law of the Universe": fragmentation engendering an urge to union changes into a union engendering new fragmentation. The goal of the individual, the collective, and the rational world as a whole, is to attain a harmonious whole preserving the individuality of its component parts. In this sense, Le Guin's SF can be seen as an artistic quest—estrangement and cognition—for ways out of the contradictions and conflicts of modern fragmented culture, and is deeply committed despite its seeming a-social nature. The initial situations of her tales are therefore permeated with a perfectly legitimate atmosphere of solitude and alienation of each from each: the journey, as a movement toward the identity of each with all (toward the "identity of opposites" as Nicolas of Cusa would have put it), becomes a way *to the self* and simultaneously to union with others, i.e. *from the self*. Everything strives to retain its uniqueness, which is a mark of its individual integrity, and at the same time to become part of a higher integrity. This urge towards the union of opposites is most profoundly disclosed in LHD. As Mircea Eliade has observed, men would like to overcome their existential loneliness and be reintegrated in a supraindividual modality; what inhibits them is fear of self-annihilation, of the loss of personal identity.

The hero's quest of himself, i.e. of his separateness, is accomplished in the process of unification with "the other." The Way to "I" lies through "not-I," through the realisation of his own unity with others and of his opposition to everything that is "not-I," in other words through Culture. The plot repeats the establishing of Culture, the formation of a human collective. "I" and "not-I" here are merely forms of the most profound archetypes of human consciousness ("own" vs. "alien"), while the Way is a mythopoetical plot which eliminates this age-old opposition by altering the boundaries of "own" (while retaining a boundary as such, i.e. renewing it over and over again). Culture is understood as a unity which multiplies separateness—it merely shifts the boundaries between "I" and "not-I," and its limit lies in cosmic supra-unity. That is why the theme of a blending of cultures, which permeates all of Le Guin's SF, is always presented by her in the form of an individual human way toward the alien yet intimate other, and why the way toward mutual understanding always leads through a fantastic unification of creatures and principles. The way to mankind's unity can only lead through the involvement of an ever greater number of "others" in man's "I," through an increasing extension of the boundaries of "own."

Basic to Le Guin's SF is the concept that the world is (and must be) in essence One. Things usually separated are in fact united. The Way of the plot leads to an understanding and realisation of this oneness. It is quite deliberate that in her "summarising" tale of LHD a certain stage of unity is embodied in the androgyne—a creature which in terrestrial myths is traditionally linked with the primordial unfragmented condition of the world. The plot in Le Guin is a symbolic sign for such a mythopoetic Way, in Lévi-Strauss' sense of myth as a search for mediations between opposing orders of being—which is always "androgynous." This is what ancient Chinese philosophy expressed by saying (as Le Guin repeats in LHD): "The Yin (feminine, left), the Yang (the masculine, right, etc.)—this is called Tao (the Way)"; incidentally, the ancient Chinese divinity of light and darkness was also an androgyne.

Le Guin's SF, being mythopoetic, remains nevertheless profoundly contemporary, since she confronts modern culture, with its absolute compartmentalisation and oppositions, and the mythological Origin where lie the sources of the oppressive fragmentation, of all that divides men and cultures. The whole Gethen culture in LHD is based on the abolition of the fundamental dualistic oppositions of terrestrial culture, connected with the division of the sexes; it is based on the inversion of earthly conceptions. Such an inversion or overturning permits the revelation of the invariants of human existence, independent of sexual dimorphism, and becomes an instrument for the cognition of earthly culture (this aspect of LHD has been examined in depth by Lem).[7] The mythological state—the Golden Age—appears in this confrontation in the role of not only the initial but simultaneously the final state—the goal or end of the historical Plot. Myth, as a plot, indicates the form and content of History—the abolition of opposites; it becomes the source of historical optimism. The consciousness, however, that the way is endless and the final goal unattainable, supplies Le Guin's books with a constant elegiac undercurrent.

NOTES

1. Le Guin's "The Word for World Is Forest" and The Dispossessed were not available to me at this writing.

2. In this, Le Guin's SF is, as it were, diametrically opposed to that of Philip K. Dick where the opposite movement predominates—toward the disintegration of all Order and Unity, the destruction of all forms. The idea of having a special issue analysing these two authors seems, therefore, well justified.

3. This type of all-pervading iconicity (the equivalence of the sign to its meaning, the isomorphism of the whole and its parts) is characteristic of medieval culture. There, however, it was looked upon as evidence of the unsovereign nature of the real world, which was regarded as a "sign" of the solely sovereign supernatural reality. In Le Guin's SF the structure of the fictional model serves as the "sign." Reality, therefore, remains wholly sovereign here, while the structure of the fictional model becomes mythopoetic.

4. In this sense, Le Guin's tales differ in principle, from, for example, Stapledon's Last and First Men or Starmaker, where the theme of cosmic amalgamation is taken to an all-embracing conclusion.

5. See, beside the novels analysed, Le Guin's story "Nine Lives."

6. These Journeys are, however, to be distinguished in principle from another type of spatio-temporal plot—the "wanderings" into a supernatural world, characteristic of many myths (e.g. Osiris'), medieval Mysteries, Dante, Rabelais or Gogol. The presence of a number of common traditional elements ("alien" world, "false death" and so on) does not mean that Le Guin is dealing in disguised myths. Professor Ketterer's interpretation of LHD (in his New Worlds for Old, Anchor 1974, §4) as a "winter journey" must be considered erroneous, despite his acute particular observations. A "winter journey" is always cyclic, whereas the plot structure of Le Guin's tales is essentially open-ended. In this openness and general inconclusiveness one might see the essential structural difference between myth as such and Le Guin's SF. Its mythopoetic aspect does not exhaust all aspects of its content; a mythological interpretation of its structure can therefore render only a partial account of it.

7. See Stanislaw Lem, "Lost Opportunities," SF Commentary No. 24 (Nov. 1971).

Fredric Jameson

World-Reduction in Le Guin: The Emergence of Utopian Narrative

Huddled forms wrapped in furs, packed snow and sweaty faces, torches by day, a ceremonial trowel and a corner stone swung into place.... Such is our entry into the *other* world of *The Left Hand of Darkness* (LHD), a world which, like all invented ones, awakens irresistible reminiscences of this the real one—here less Eisenstein's Muscovy, perhaps, than some Eskimo High Middle Ages. Yet this surface exoticism conceals a series of what may be called "generic discontinuities,"[1] and the novel can be shown to be constructed from a heterogeneous group of narrative modes artfully superposed and intertwined, thereby constituting a virtual anthology of narrative strands of different kinds. So we find here intermingled: the travel narrative (with anthropological data), the pastiche of myth, the political novel (in the restricted sense of the drama of court intrigue), straight SF (the Hainish colonization, the spaceship in orbit around Gethen's sun), Orwellian dystopia (the imprisonment on the Voluntary Farm and Resettlement Agency), adventure-story (the flight across the glacier), and finally even, perhaps, something like a multi-racial love-story (the drama of communication between the two cultures and species).

Such structural discontinuities, while accounting for the effectiveness of LHD by comparison with books that can do only one or two of these things, at once raise the basic question of the novel's ultimate unity. In what follows, I want to make a case for a thematic coherence which has little enough to do with plot as such, but which would seem to shed some light on the process of world-construction in fictional narratives in general. Thematically, we may distinguish four different types of material in the novel, the most striking and obvious being that of the hermaphroditic sexuality of the inhabitants of Gethen. The "official" message of the book, however, would seem to be rather different than this, involving a social and historical meditation on the institutions of Karhide and the capacity of that or any other society to mount full-scale organized warfare. After this, we would surely want to mention the peculiar ecology, which, along with the way of life it imposes, makes of LHD something like an anti-*Dune*; and, finally, the myths and religious practices of the planet, which give the book its title.[2]

The question is now whether we can find something that all these themes have in common, or better still, whether we can isolate some essential structural *homology* between them. To begin with the climate of Gethen (known to the Ekumen as Winter), the first Investigator supplies an initial interpretation of it in terms of the resistance of this ice-age environment to human life:

The weather of Winter is so relentless, so near the limit of tolerability even to them with all their cold-adaptations, that perhaps they use up their fighting spirit fighting the cold. The marginal peoples, the races that just get by, are rarely the warriors. And in the end, the dominant factor in Gethenian life is not sex or any other human being: it is their environment, their cold world. Here man has a crueler enemy even than himself. (§7)

However, this is not the only connotation that extreme cold may have; the *motif* may have some other, deeper, disguised symbolic meaning that can perhaps best be illustrated by the related symbolism of the tropics in recent SF, particularly in the novels of J.G. Ballard. Heat is here conveyed as a kind of dissolution of the body into the outside world, a loss of that clean separation from clothes and external objects that gives you your autonomy and allows you to move about freely, a sense of increasing contamination and stickiness in the contact between your physical organism and the surfaces around it, the wet air in which it bathes, the fronds that slap against it. So it is that the jungle itself, with its non—or anti-Wordsworthian nature, is felt to be some immense and alien organism into which our bodies run the risk of being absorbed, the most alarming expression of this anxiety in SF being perhaps that terrible scene in Silverberg's *Downward to Earth* (§8) in which the protagonist discovers a human couple who have become hosts to some unknown parasitic larvae that stir inside their still living torsos like monstrous foetuses.

This loss of physical autonomy—dramatized by the total environment of the jungle into which the European dissolves—is then understood as a figure for the loss of psychic autonomy, of which the utter demoralization, the colonial whisky-drinking and general dissolution of the tropical hero is the canonical symbol in literature. (Even more relevant to the present study is the relationship between extreme heat and sexual anxiety—a theme particularly visible in the non-SF treatments of similar material by Catholic novelists like Graham Greene and François Mauriac, for whom the identification of heat and adolescent sexual torment provides ample motivation for the subsequent desexualization experienced by the main characters.)

Ballard's work is suggestive in the way in which he translates both physical and moral dissolution into the great ideological myth of entropy, in which the historic collapse of the British Empire is projected outwards into some immense cosmic deceleration of the universe itself as well as of its molecular building blocks.[3] This kind of ideological message makes it hard to escape the feeling that the heat symbolism in question here is a peculiarly Western and ethnocentric one. Witness, if proof be needed, Vonnegut's *Cat's Cradle*, where the systematic displacement of the action from Upstate New York to the Caribbean, from dehumanized American scientists to the joyous and skeptical religious practices of Bokononism, suggests a scarcely disguised meditation on the relationship between American power and the Third World, between repression and scientific knowledge in the capitalist world, and a nostalgic and primitivistic evocation of the more genuine human possibilities available in an older and simpler culture. The preoccupation with heat, the fear of sweating as of some dissolution of our very being, would then be tantamount to an unconscious anxiety about tropical field-labor (an analogous cultural symbolism can be found in the historical echo of Northern factory work in the blue jeans and work-shirts of our own affluent society). The nightmare of the tropics thus expresses a disguised terror at the inconceivable and unformulable threat posed by the masses of the Third World to our own prosperity and privilege, and suggests a new and unexpected framework in which to interpret the icy climate of Le Guin's Gethen.

In such a reading the cold weather of the planet Winter must be understood, first and foremost, not so much as a rude environment, inhospitable to human life, as rather a symbolic affirmation of the autonomy of the organism, and a fantasy realization of some virtually total disengagement of the body from its environment or eco-system. Cold *isolates*, and the cold of Gethen is what brings home to the characters (and the reader) their physical detachment, their free-standing isolation as separate individuals, goose-flesh transforming the skin itself into some outer envelope, the sub-zero temperatures of the planet forcing the organism back on its own inner resources and making of each a kind of self-sufficient blast-furnace. Gethen thus stands as an attempt to imagine an experimental landscape in which our being-in-the-world is simplified to the extreme, and in which our sensory links with the multiple and shifting perceptual fields around us are abstracted so radically as to vouchsafe, perhaps, some new glimpse as to the ultimate nature of human reality.

It seems to me important to insist on this cognitive and experimental function of the narrative in order to distinguish it from other, more night-marish representations of the sealing off of consciousness from the external world (as, e.g. in the "half-life" of the dead in Philip K. Dick's *Ubik*). One of the most significant potentialities of SF as a form is precisely this capacity to provide something like an experimental variation on our own empirical uni-verse; and Le Guin has herself described her invention of Gethenian sexuality along the lines of just such a "thought experiment" in the tradition of the great physicists: "Einstein shoots a light-ray through a moving elevator; Schrödinger puts a cat in a box. There is no elevator, no cat, no box. The experiment is performed, the question is asked, in the mind."[4] Only one would like to recall that "high literature" once also affirmed such aims. As antiquated as Zola's notions of heredity and as naive as his fascination with Claude Bernard's account of experimental research may have been, the naturalist concept of the *experimental novel* amounted, on the eve of the emergence of modernism, to just such a reassertion of literature's cognitive function. That his assertion no longer seems believable merely suggests that our own particular environment—the total system of late monopoly capital and of the consumer society—feels so massively in place and its reification so over-whelming and impenetrable, that the serious artist is no longer free to tinker with it or to project experimental variations.[5] The historical opportunities of SF as a literary form are intimately related to this paralysis of so-called high literature. The officially "non-serious" or pulp character of SF is an in-dispensable feature in its capacity to relax that tyrannical "reality principle" which functions as a crippling censorship over high art, and to allow the "paraliterary" form thereby to inherit the vocation of giving us alternate versions of a world that has elsewhere seemed to resist even *imagined* change. (This account of the transfer of one of the most vital traditional functions of literature to SF would seem to be confirmed by the increasing efforts of present-day "art literature"—e.g., Thomas Pynchon—to reincorporate those formal capacities back into the literary novel.)

The principal techniques of such narrative experimentation—of the syste-matic variation, by SF, of the empirical and historical world around us—have been most conveniently codified under the twin headings of *analogy* and *extrapolation*.[6] The reading we have proposed of Le Guin's experimental ecology suggests, however, the existence of yet a third and quite distinct technique of variation which it will be the task of the remainder of this analysis to describe. It would certainly be possible to see the Gethenian en-vironment as extrapolating one of our own Earth seasons, in an extrapolation developed according to its own inner logic and pushed to its ultimate con-clusions—as, for example, when Pohl and Kornbluth project out onto a planetary scale, in *The Space Merchants*, huckstering trends already becoming visible in the nascent consumer society of 1952; or when Brunner, in *The Sheep Look Up*, catastrophically speeds up the environmental pollution already underway. Yet this strikes me as being the least interesting thing about Le Guin's experi-ment, which is based on a principle of systematic exclusion, a kind of surgical excision of empirical reality, something like a process of ontological attenuation in which the sheer teeming multiplicity of what exists, of what we call reality, is deliberately thinned and weeded out through an operation of radical ab-straction and simplification which we will henceforth term *world-reduction*. And once we grasp the nature of this technique, its effects in the other thematic areas of the novel become inescapable, as for instance in the conspicuous absence of other animal species on Gethen. The omission of a whole grid-work of evolutionary phyla can, of course, be accounted for by the hypothesis that the colonization of Gethen, and the anomalous sexuality of its inhabitants, were the result of some forgotten biological experiment by the original Hainish civilization, but it does not make that lack any less disquieting: "There are no communal insects on Winter. Gethenians do not share their earth as Terrans do with those older societies, those innumerable cities of little sexless workers possessing no instinct but that of obedience to the group, the whole" (§13).

But it is in Le Guin's later novel, *The Dispossessed* (TD) that this situation is pushed to its ultimate consequences, providing the spectacle of a planet (Anarres) in which human life is virtually without biological partners:

It's a queer situation, biologically speaking. We Anarresti are unnaturally isolated. On the old World there are eighteen phyla of land animal; there are classes, like the insects, that have so many species they've never been able to count them, and some of these species have populations of billions. Think of it: everywhere you looked animals, other creatures, sharing the earth and air with you. You'd feel so much more a *part* (§6)

Hence Shevek's astonishment, when, on his arrival in Urras, he is observed by a face "not like any human face...as long as his arm, and ghastly white. Breath jetted in vapor from what must be nostrils, and terrible, unmistakable, there was an eye." (§1). Yet the absence, from the Anarres of TD, of large animals such as the donkey which here startles Shevek, is the negative obverse of a far more positive omission, namely that of the Darwinian life-cycle itself, with its predators and victims alike: it is the sign that human beings have surmounted historical determinism, and have been left alone with themselves, to invent their own destinies. In TD, then, the principle of world-reduction has become an instrument in the conscious elaboration of a utopia. On Gethen, however, its effects remain more tragic, and the Hainish experiment has resulted in the unwitting evolution of test-tube subjects rather than in some great and self-conscious social laboratory of revolution and collective self-determination:

Your race is appallingly alone in its world. No other mammalian species. No other ambisexual species. No animal intelligent enough even to domesticate as pets. It must color your thinking, this uniqueness...to be so solitary, in so hostile a world: it must affect your entire outlook. (§16)

Still, the deeper import of such details, and of the constructional principle at work in them, will become clear only after we observe similar patterns in other thematic areas of the novel, as, for instance, in Gethenian religion. In keeping with the book's antithetical composition, to the two principal national units, Karhide and Orgoreyn, correspond two appropriately antithetical religious cults: the Orgota one of Meshe being something like a heresy or offshoot of the original Karhidish Handdara in much the same way that Christianity was the issue of Judaism. Meshe's religion of total knowledge reflects the mystical experience from which it sprang and in which all of time and history became blindingly co-present: the emphasis on knowing, however, suggests a positivistic bias which is as appropriate to the commercial society of Orgoreyn, one would think, as was Protestantism to the nascent capitalism of western Europe. It is, however, the other religion, that of Karhide, which is most relevant to our present argument: the Handdara is, in antithesis to the later sect, precisely a mystique of darkness, a cult of non-knowledge parallel to the drastic reductionism of the Gethenian climate. The aim of its spiritual practice is to strip the mind of its non-essentials and to reduce it to some quintessentially simplified function:

The Handdara discipline of Presence...is a kind of trance—the Handdarate, given to negatives, call it an untrance—involving self-loss (self-augmentation?) through extreme
sensual receptiveness and awareness. Though the technique is the exact opposite of
most techniques of mysticism it probably is a mystical discipline, tending towards the
experience of Immanence. (§5)

Thus the fundamental purpose of the ritual practice of the foretelling—dramatized in one of the most remarkable chapters of the novel—is, by answering
answerable questions about the future, "to exhibit the perfect uselessness of
knowing the answer to the wrong question" (§5), and indeed, ultimately, of
the activity of asking questions in general. What the real meaning of these
wrong or unanswerable questions may be, we will try to say later on; but this
mystical valorization of ignorance is certainly quite different from the brash
commercial curiosity with which the Envoy is so pleasantly surprised on his
arrival in Orgoreyn (§10).

Now we must test our hypothesis about the basic constructional principle
of LHD against that picture of an ambisexual species—indeed, an ambisexual
society—which is its most striking and original feature. The obvious defamiliari-
zation with which such a picture confronts the *lecteur moyen sensuel* is
not exactly that of the permissive and countercultural tradition of male SF
writing, as in Farmer or Sturgeon. Rather than a stand in favor of a wider
tolerance for all kinds of sexual behaviour, it seems more appropriate to insist
(as does Le Guin herself in a forthcoming article) on the feminist dimension of
her novel, and on its demystification of the sex roles themselves. The basic
point about Gethenian sexuality is that the sex role does not color everything else in life, as is the case with us, but is rather contained and defused,
reduced to that brief period of the monthly cycle when, as with our animal
species, the Gethenians are in "heat" or "kemmer." So the first Investigator
sent by the Ekumen underscores this basic "estrangement-effect" of Gethen on
"normally" sexed beings:

The First Mobile, if one is sent, must be warned that unless he is very self-assured, or
senile, his pride will suffer. A man wants his virility regarded, a woman wants her
femininity appreciated, however indirect and subtle the indications of regard and
appreciation. On Winter they will not exist. One is respected and judged only as a human
being. It is an appalling experience. (§7)

That there are difficulties in such a representation (e.g., the unavoidable
designation of gender by English pronouns), the author is frank to admit in the
article referred to.[7] Still, the reader's failures are not all her own, and the
inveterate tendency of students to describe the Gethenians as "sexless" says
something about the limits imposed by stereotypes of gender on their own
imaginations. Far from eliminating sex, indeed, Gethenian biology has the
result of eliminating sexual *repression*:

Being so strictly defined and limited by nature, the sexual urge of Gethenians is really
not much interfered with by society: there is less coding, channeling, and repressing of
sex than in any bisexual society I know of. Abstinence is entirely voluntary; indulgence
is entirely acceptable. Sexual fear and sexual frustration are both extremely rare. (§13).

The author was in fact most careful not merely to *say* that these people are
not eunuchs, but also—in a particularly terrifying episode, that of the penal farm
with its anti-kemmer drugs— to *show* by contrast what eunuchs in this society
would look like (§13).

Indeed, the vision of public kemmer-houses (along with the sexual license
of utopia in TD) ought to earn the enthusiasm of the most hard-core Fourierist
or sexual libertarian. If it does not quite do that, it is because there is another,

rather different sense in which my students were not wrong to react as they did and in which we meet, once again, the phenomenon we have called world-reduction. For if Le Guin's Gethen does not do away with sex, it may be suggested that it does away with everything that is *problematical* about it. Essentially, Gethenian physiology *solves* the problem of sex, and that is surely something no human being of our type has ever been able to do (owing largely to the non-biological nature of human desire as opposed to "natural" or instinctual animal need). Desire is permanently scandalous precisely because it admits of no "solution"—promiscuity, repression, or the couple all being equally intolerable. Only a makeup of the Gethenian type, with its limitation of desire to a few days of the monthly cycle, could possibly curb the problem. Such a makeup suggests that sexual desire is something that can be completely removed from other human activities, allowing us to see them in some more fundamental, unmixed fashion. Here again, then, in the construction of this particular projection of desire which is Gethenian ambisexuality, we find a process at work which is structurally analogous to that operation of world-reduction or ontological attenuation we have described above: the experimental production of an imaginary situation by *excision* of the real, by a radical suppression of features of human sexuality which cannot but carry a powerful fantasy-investment in its own right. The dream of some scarcely imaginable freedom from sex, indeed, is a very ancient human fantasy, almost as powerful in its own way as the outright sexual wish-fulfillments themselves. What its more general symbolic meaning in LHD might be, we can only discover by grasping its relationship to that other major theme of the novel which is the nature of Gethenian social systems, and in particular, their respective capacities to wage war.

It would seem on first glance that the parallelism here is obvious and that, on this particular level, the object of what we have been calling world-reduction can only be institutional warfare itself, which has not yet developed in Karhide's feudal system. Certainly Le Guin's work as a whole is strongly pacifistic, and her novella "The Word for World is Forest" is (along with Aldiss' *Dark Light-Years*) one of the major SF denunciations of the American genocide in Vietnam. Yet it remains an ethical, rather than a socioeconomic, vision of imperialism, and its last line extends the guilt of violence to even that war of national liberation of which it has just shown the triumph: " 'Maybe after I die people will be as they were before I was born, and before you came. But I do not think so'" (§8). Yet if there is no righteous violence, then the long afternoon and twilight of Earth will turn out to be just that onerous dystopia SF writers have always expected it would.

This properly liberal, rather than radical, position in Le Guin seems to be underscored by her predilection for quietistic heroes and her valorization of an anti-political, anti-acitivist stance, whether it be in the religion of Karhide, the peaceable traditions of the "creechies," or in Shevek's own reflective temperament. What makes her position more ambiguous and more interesting, however, is that Le Guin's works reject the institutionalization of violence rather than violence itself: nothing is more shocking in TD than the scene in which Shevek is beaten into unconsciousness by a man who is irritated by the similarity between their names:

"You're one of those little profiteers who goes to school to keep his hands clean," the man said. "I've always wanted to knock the shit out of one of you." "Don't call me profiteer!" Shevek said, but this wasn't a verbal battle. Shevet knocked him double. He got in several return blows, having long arms and more temper than his opponent expected: but he was outmatched. Several people paused to watch, saw that it was a fair fight but not an interesting one, and went on. They were neither offended nor attracted by simple violence. Shevek did not call for help, so it was nobody's business but his own. When he came to he was lying on his back on the dark ground between two tents. (§2)

Utopia is, in other words not a place in which humanity is freed from violence, but rather one in which it is released from the multiple determinisms (economic, political, social)of history itself: in which it settles its accounts with its ancient collective fatalisms, precisely in order to be free to do whatever it wants with its interpersonal relationships—whether for violence, love, hate, sex or whatever. All of that is raw and strong, and goes farther towards authenticating Le Guin's vision—as a return to fundamentals rather than some beautification of existence—than any of the explanations of economic and social organization which TD provides.

What looks like conventional liberalism in Le Guin (and is of course still ideologically dubious to the very degree that it continues to "look like" liberalism) is in reality itself a use of the Jeffersonian and Thoreauvian tradition against important political features of that imperializing liberalism which is the dominant ideology of the United States today—as her one contemporary novel, *The Lathe of Heaven*, makes plain. This is surely the meaning of the temperamental opposition between the Tao-like passivity of Orr and the obsession of Haber with apparently reforming and ameliorative projects of all kinds:

The quality of the will to power is, precisely, growth. Achievement is its cancellation. To be, the will to power must increase with each fulfillment, making the fulfillment only a step to a further one. The vaster the power gained, the vaster the appetite for more. As there was no visible limit to the power Haber wielded through Orr's dreams, so there was no end to his determination to improve the world. (§9)

The pacifist bias of LHD is thus part of a more general refusal of the growth-oriented power dynamics of present-day American liberalism, even where the correlations it suggests between institutionalized warfare, centralization, and psychic aggression may strike us as preoccupations of a characteristically liberal type.

I would suggest, however, that beneath this official theme of warfare, there are details scattered here and there throughout the novel which suggest the presence of some more fundamental attempt to reimagine history. What reader has not indeed been struck—without perhaps quite knowing why—by descriptions such as that of the opening cornerstone ceremony: "Masons below have set an electric winch going, and as the king mounts higher the keystone of the arch goes up past him in its sling, is raised, settled, and fitted almost soundlessly, great ton-weight block though it is, into the gap between the two piers, making them one, one thing, an arch" (§1); or of the departure of the first spring caravan towards the fastnesses of the North: "twenty bulky, quiet-running, barge-like trucks on caterpillar treads, going single file down the deep streets of Erhenrang through the shadows of morning" (§5)? Of course, the concept of *extrapolation* in SF means nothing if it does not designate just such details as these, in which heterogenous or contradictory elements of the empirical real world are juxtaposed and recombined into piquant montages. Here the premise is clearly that of a feudal or medieval culture that knows electricity and machine technology. However, the machines do not have the same results as in our own world: "The mechanical-industrial Age of Invention in Karhide is at least three thousand years old, and during those thirty centuries they have developed excellent and economical central-heating devices using steam, electricity, and other principles; but they do not install them in their houses"(§3). What makes all this more complicated than the usual extrapolative projection is, it seems to me, the immense time span involved, and the great antiquity of Karhide's science and technology, which tends to emphasize not so much what happens when we thus combine or amalgamate different historical stages of our own empirical Earth history, but rather precisely *what does not happen.* That is, indeed, what is most significant about the example of Karhide, namely that *nothing happens,* an immemorial social order remains exactly as it was, and the introduction of electrical power fails—quite unaccountably and astonishingly to us—to make any impact whatsoever on the stability of a basically static, unhistorical society.

Now there is surely room for debate as to the role of science and technology in the evolution of the so-called West (i.e., the capitalist countries of western Europe and North America). For Marxists, science developed as a result both of technological needs and of the quantifying thought-modes inherent in the emergent market system; while an anti-Marxist historiography stresses the fundamental role played by technology and inventions in what now becomes strategically known as the Industrial Revolution (rather than capitalism). Such a dispute would in any case be inconceivable were not technology and capitalism so inextricably intertwined in our own history. What Le Guin has done in her projection of Karhide is to sunder the two in peremptory and dramatic fashion:

Along in those four millennia the electric engine was developed, radios and power looms and power vehicles and farm machinery and all the rest began to be used, and a Machine Age got going, gradually, without any industrial revolution, without any revolution at all. (§2)

What is this to say but that Karhide is an attempt to imagine something like a West which would never have known capitalism? The existence of modern technology in the midst of an essentially feudal order is the sign of this imaginative operation as well as the gauge by which its success can be measured: the miraculous presence, among all those furs and feudal *shift-grethor,* of this emblematically quiet, peacefully humming technology is the proof that in Karhide we have to do not with one more specimen of feudal SF, but rather precisely with an alternate world to our own, one in which—by what strange quirk of fate?—capitalism never happened.

It becomes difficult to escape the conclusion that this attempt to rethink Western history without capitalism is of a piece, structurally and in its general spirit, with the attempt to imagine human biology without desire which we have described above; for it is essentially the inner dynamic of the market system which introduces into the chronicle-like and seasonal, cyclical, tempo of pre-capitalist societies the fever and ferment of what we used to call *progress.* The underlying identification between sex as an intolerable, wellnigh gratuitous complication of existence, and capitalism as a disease of change and meaningless evolutionary momentum, is thus powerfully underscored by the very technique—that of world-reduction—whose mission is the utopian exclusion of both phenomena.

Karhide is, of course, not a utopia, and LHD is not in that sense a genuinely utopian work. Indeed, it is now clear that the earlier novel served as something like a proving ground for techniques that are not consciously employed in the construction of a utopia until TD. It is in the latter novel that the device of world-reduction becomes transformed into a sociopolitical hypothesis about the inseparability of utopia and scarcity. The Odonian colonization of barren Anarres offers thus the most thoroughgoing literary application of the technique, at the same time that it constitutes a powerful and timely rebuke to present-day attempts to parlay American abundance and consumers' goods into some ultimate vision of the "great society."[8]

I would not want to suggest that all of the great historical utopias have been constructed around the imaginative operation which we have called world-reduction. It seems possible, indeed, that it is the massive commodity environment of late capitalism that has called up this particular literary and imaginative strategy, which would then amount to a political stance as well. So in William Morris' *News from Nowhere*, the hero—a nineteenth-century visitor to the future—is astonished to watch the lineaments of nature reappear beneath the fading inscription of the grim industrial metropolis, the old names on the river themselves transfigured from dreary slang into the evocation of meadow landscapes, the slopes and streams, so long stifled beneath the pavements of tenement buildings and channeled into sewage gutters, now reemergent in the light of day:

London, which—which I have read about as the modern Babylon of civilization, seems to have disappeared.... As to the big murky places which were once, as we know, the centres of manufacture, they have, like the brick and mortar desert of London, disappeared; only, since they were centres of nothing but "manufacture," and served no purpose but that of the gambling market, they have left less signs of their existence than London.... On the contrary, there has been but little clearance, though much rebuilding, in the smaller towns. Their suburbs, indeed, when they had any, have melted away into the general country, and space and elbow-room has been got in their centres; but there are the towns still with their streets and squares and market-places; so that it is by means of these smaller towns that we of today can get some kind of idea of what the towns of the older world were alike,—I mean to say, at their best.[9]

Morris' utopia is, then, the very prototype of an aesthetically and libidinally oriented social vision, as opposed to the technological and engineering-oriented type of Bellamy's *Looking Backward*—a vision thus in the line of Fourier rather than Saint Simon, and more prophetic of the values of the New Left rather than those of Soviet centralism, a vision in which we find this same process of weeding out the immense waste-and-junk landscape of capitalism and an artisanal gratification in the systematic excision of masses of buildings from a clogged urban geography. Does such an imaginative projection imply and support a militant political stance? Certainly it did so in Morris's case; but the issue in our time is that of the militancy of ecological politics generally. I would be inclined to suggest that such "no-places" offer little more than a breathing space, a momentary relief from the overwhelming presence of late capitalism. Their idyllic, yet elegiac, sweetness, their pastel tones, the rather pathetic withdrawal they offer from grimier Victorian realities, seems most aptly characterized by Morris' subtitle to *News from Nowhere*: *"An Epoch of Rest."* It is as though—after the immense struggle to free yourself, even in imagination, from the infection of our very minds and values and habits by an omnipresent consumer capitalism—on emerging suddenly and against all expectation into a narrative space radically other, uncontaminated by all those properties of the old lives and the old preoccupations, the spirit could only lie there gasping in the fresh silence, too weak, too new, to do more than gaze wanly about it at a world remade.

Something of the fascination of LHD—as well as the ambiguity of its ultimate message—surely derives from the subterranean drive within it towards a utopian "rest" of this kind, towards some ultimate "no-place" of a collectivity untormented by sex or history, by cultural superfluities or an object-world irrelevant to human life. Yet we must not conclude without observing that in this respect the novel includes its own critique as well.

It is indeed a tribute to the rigor with which the framework has been imagined that history has no sooner, within it, been dispelled, than it sets fatally in again; that Karhide, projected as a social order without development, begins to develop with the onset of the narrative itself. This is, it seems to me, the ultimate meaning of that *motif* of right and wrong questions mentioned above and resumed as follows: "to learn which questions are unanswerable, and *not to answer them*: this skill is most needful in times of stress and darkness." It is no accident that this maxim follows hard upon another, far more practical discussion about politics and historical problems:

To be sure, if you turn your back on Mishnory and walk away from it, you are still on the Mishnory road.... You must go somewhere else; you must have another goal; then you walk a different road. Yegey in the Hall of the Thirty-Three today: 'I unalterably oppose this blockade of grain-exports to Karhide, and the spirit of competition which motivates it.' Right enough, but he will not get off the Mishnory road going that way. He must offer an alternative. Orgoreyn and Karhide both must stop following the road they're on, in either direction; they must go somewhere else, and break the circle. (§11)

But, of course, the real alternative to this dilemma, the only conceivable way of breaking out of that vicious circle which is the option between feudalism and capitalism, is a quite different one from the liberal "solution"—the Ekumen as a kind of galactic United Nations—offered by the writer and her heroes. One is tempted to wonder whether the strategy of *not* asking questions ("Mankind," according to Marx, "always [taking] up only such problems as it can solve")[10] is not the way in which the utopian imagination protects itself against a fatal return to just those historical contradictions from which it was supposed to provide relief. In that case, the deepest subject of Le Guin's LHD would not be utopia as such, but rather our own incapacity to conceive it in the first place. In this way too, it would be a proving ground for TD.

NOTES

1. See my "Generic Discontinuities in SF: Brian Aldiss' *Starship*," SFS 1(1973):57-68.

2. I find justification for omitting from this list the theme of communication—mind-speech and foretelling—in Ian Watson's important "Le Guin's *Lathe of Heaven* and the Role of Dick," SFS 2(1975):67-75.

3. Entropy is of course a very characteristic late-19th-century bourgeois myth (e.g., Henry Adams, Wells, Zola). See, for further justification of this type of interpretation, my "In Retrospect," SFS 1(1974):272-76.

4. Ursula K. Le Guin, "Is Gender Necessary?" In *Aurora: Beyond Equality*, ed. Susan J. Anderson and Vonda McIntyre (in press at Fawcett).

5. I have tried to argue an analogous reduction of possibilities for the historical novel in *Marxism and Form* (Princeton 1971), pp. 248-52.

6. See Darko Suvin, "On the Poetics of the Science Fiction Genre," *College English* 34(1972):372-82, and "Science Fiction and the Genological Jungle," *Genre* 6(1973):251-73.

7. See Note 4. Some problems Le Guin does not notice—e.g., synchronization of kemmer and continuity of sex roles between love partners—are pointed out by the relentlessly logical Stanislaw Lem in "Lost Opportunities," *SF Commentary* No. 24, pp. 22-24.

8. Inasmuch as *The Dispossessed*—sure the most important utopia since Skinner's *Walden Two*—seems certain to play a significant part in political reflection, it seems important to question her qualification of Anarres as an "anarchist" Utopia. Thereby she doubtless intends to differentiate its decentralized organization from the classical Soviet model, without taking into account the importance of the "withering away of the state" in Marxism also—a political goal most recently underscored by the Cultural Revolution and the experimental Communes in China and the various types of workers' self-management elsewhere.

9. William Morris, *News from Nowhere* (London 1903), pp. 91, 95, 96.

10. Karl Marx and Friedrich Engels, *Basic Writings on Politics and Philosophy*, ed. Lewis S. Feuer (Garden City, N.Y., 1959), p.44.

Ian Watson

The Forest as Metaphor for Mind: "The Word for World is Forest" and "Vaster Than Empires and More Slow"

In the Afterword to "The Word for World is Forest" (WWF) Le Guin remarks that writing this story was "like taking dictation from a boss with ulcers. What I wanted to write about was the forest and the dream; that is, I wanted to describe a certain ecology from within, and to play with some of Hadfield's and Dement's ideas about the function of dreaming-sleep and the uses of dream. But the boss wanted to talk about the destruction of ecological balance and the rejection of emotional balance." The story accordingly describes the conflict between the forest-dwelling natives of the planet Athshe—who possess a sane and balanced, if (to a prejudiced eye) "primitive," social order—and the Terran colonists who exploit and brutalize them and their world.

The Terrans, having already reduced Earth to a poisoned wasteland, regard the forests of Athshe purely as a source of lumber, and the native Athsheans as a pool of slave labour. The Bureau of Colonial Administration on Earth may issue benevolent guidelines, and a hilfer (high intelligence life form specialist) such as Raj Lyubov be genuinely concerned with native welfare, woodlands and wildlife; but, till the coming of the ansible instantaneous transmitter, there is no means of investigating complaints or introducing reforms within less than half a century. Thus the tone is set by the Terran military on Athshe, represented at its most paranoid and oppressive by Colonel Davidson. "They bring defoliation and they call it peace," to amend Tacitus.[1]

The analogy between Terran conduct on Athshe and the American intervention in Vietnam is explicit, ironically underlined by the provenance of Earth's Colonel Dongh—and a considerable relief from other reflections of America's war experiences in SF, which, albeit the moral is one of futility and savagery, nevertheless frequently intoxicate the reader with the gungho mood of combat and the lavishly presented technology *per se* (as in Joe Haldeman's widely admired set of stories, collected as *The Forever War*).[2] At the same time, the obvious Vietnam analogy should not blind one to other relevant contemporary analogies—the genocide of the Guyaki Indians of Paraguay, or the genocide and deforestation along the Trans-Amazon Highway in Brazil, or even the general destruction of rain-forest habitats from Indonesia to Costa Rica. Le Guin's story is multi-applicable—and multi-faceted.

The political facet aside, WWF is a vivid presentation of the dynamics of a sane society which lives in harmony with its natural environment because its members are themselves in psychological equilibrium. The Athsheans practice conscious dream control,[3] and having thereby free access to their own subconscious processes, do not suffer from the divorce that Terrans exemplify between subconscious urges and conscious rationalizations. To the Athsheans, the Terrans—deprived of this dream knowledge—seem to be an insane people, their closest approach to self-knowledge being the undisciplined confusion brought on by the hallucinogens they entertain themselves with obsessively (the "drug probelm" faced by American forces in Vietnam is here savagely presented as the military norm).[4]

The Athsheans' proficiency in the dream life is directly imaged by their physical residence in the dark tangled forests of the planet: these latter function metaphorically as a kind of external collective unconscious. The Terrans, whose unconscious is an impenetrable jungle in which they are far from being at home, react to the Athshean forest with confusion, fear and dislike. Deforestation is their technological response to the mysteries of the wood. Indeed, one might fairly argue that the metaphorical significance of the Terran deforestation is primary and the economic or factual significance quite secondary:

men were here now to end the darkness, and turn the tree-jumble into clean sawn planks, more prized on Earth than gold. Literally, because gold could be got from seawater and from under the Antarctic ice, but wood could not; wood came only from trees. And it was a really necessary luxury on Earth. (§1)

The paradox of "necessary luxury" neatly capsulates the confused thinking of the Terrans, and goes some way towards explaining the essential implausibility of hauling loads of wood over a distance of 27 light years; but on balance, just as the metaphorical sense precedes the economic in this passage, so it does in the story as a whole, intensely verisimilar though the story is in presentation.

The metaphorical structure operates on a primary opposition of light and darkness: the arid light outside the forests, where the aggressive and exploitative Terrans feel falsely safe, and the shiftingly many-coloured darkness within, where the integral Athsheans wake and dream. The forest paths are "devious as nerves" (§2)—a neural simile which supports the impression that the forest itself is conscious; that it represents the subconscious mind, the dark side of awareness. Being tangled and dark, no superficial reconnaissance of it is possible—no fast overflight surveys beloved of Herman Kahn's "flying think tanks" (Kahn's thermonuclear catechism is rehearsed by the rabid Colonel Davidson, reflecting "by God sometimes you have to be able to think about the unthinkable" [§7]). "Nothing was pure, dry, arid, plain. Revelation was lacking. There was no seeing everything at once, no certainty" (§2). Lyubov, initially oppressed by the world-forest with its impenetrability and "total vegetable indifference to the presence of mind" (§5), eventually comes to terms with the forest (and its implications), and reflects that, whereas the name "terra" designates the soil of his own world, "to the Athsheans soil, ground, earth was not that to which the dead return and by which the living live: the substance of their world was not earth, but forest. Terran man was clay, red dust. Athshean man was branch and root" (§5). The Athshean word for "dream," indeed, is the same as the word for "root."

Out of the original impetus to write about forest and dream, then, has come a world-forest that—while nonsentient itself—nevertheless functions metaphorically as mind: as the collective unconscious mind of the Athsheans. However, the story (at "the boss's" behests) is oriented politically and ecologically; hence it must be primarily verisimilar rather than metaphorical. Consequently there is a surplus of energy and idea, attached to the central image of a forest consciousness, which cannot find a full outlet here. At the same time, WWF is exploring an alternative state of consciousness, in the conscious dream; yet this is not a paranormal state of mind—something which Le Guin has treated extensively in her previous Hainish-cycle works. The "Forest mind" theme, controlled and tempered to politics and ecology in WWF, finds its independent outlet only within a *paranormal* context, in another long story of this period, "Vaster Than Empires and More Slow" (VTE). The two stories are closely linked thematically—the latter involving a general inversion of the situation of the former. If, as I suggest in SFS #5, Le Guin's 1971 novel *The Lathe of Heaven* represents a discharge of paranormal elements built into the framework of the Hainish cycle, then, outside of that cycle, VTE represents a parallel working-out of a conflict between verisimilitude and metaphor in WWF. VTE uses the paranormal element from the Hainish cycle as a way of validating a forest-mind which is a verisimilar actuality rather than a metaphor.

Whilst Earthmen in general are regarded as insane by the Athsheans, the Extreme Survey team of the second story are of unsound mind by the standards of Earth—and Hain, and any other world. Only people who are radically alienated from society would volunteer for a trip lasting five hundred years, objective time.[5] The most alienated of them, Osden, is paradoxically an empath. He possesses the paranormal skill "to pick up emotion or sentience from anything that felt." Unfortunately, the feelings of his fellows only serve to disgust him. Le Guin adds that properly speaking this faculty could be categorised as a "wide-range bioempathic receptivity"—which seems to be a way of suggesting that this is not in fact a paranormal skill, comparable to telepathy, since all human beings possess a certain degree of what can only be termed, "bioempathic receptivity" in relation to kinesic body-signals and pheromone scent-signals (even though most of the time they are unaware of this consciously). However, the fact that a teachable technique for telepathy exists (on Rocannon's World, otherwise Fomalhaut II—locale of Le Guin's first Hainish novel) is deliberately introduced into the story at this point, to rout the skeptic voice that would separate empathy off from telepathy. As the events of the novel *Rocannon's World* are supposed to take place some 300 years after the events of this story, the paranormal comparison is conceivably more important than strict adherence to chronology. But in any case, sharing "lust with a white rat, pain with a squashed cockroach and phototropy with a moth" is hardly classifiable as a natural talent. Clearly this represents a qualitative leap into the beyond of the paranormal—a movement away from a mere extension of everyday (if rarely noted) experience, to a radically different level of perception.

The psychological disconnectedness of the VTE survey team contrasts sharply with the total connectedness of the vegetation on World 4470. There is nothing but vegetation on this world—tree, creeper, grass; but no bird or beast, nothing that moves. The interconnected roots amid creepers function as slow neural pathways binding the whole complex of forest and prairie into a slow vegetable consciousness, whose awareness is a function of this connectedness.

It is aware; yet not intelligent. Slowly realizing the presence of rootless, mobile intruders in its midst, the vegetable mind reacts with an anxiety that grows to terror in the minds of the survey team as they sense it, and which is only absorbed and transcended by the empath Osden. His only psychological defence against the flood of feelings from others, that threaten to swamp his own personality, is to reject these others, and then masochistically thrive on his own rejection by others which this provokes. Thus rejection becomes his salvation.

One might clearly relate Le Guin's use of the forest as metaphor for a mental state to Henry James' use of a similar image in his story "The Beast in the Jungle."[6] Not only does a lurking "psychic beast" lie in wait for James' protagonist John Marcher, to be sensed also by Le Guin's Porlock as "something moving with purpose, trying to attack him from behind." Not only does John Marcher's response, of hurling himself violently facedown in his hallucination, as though he has been physically leapt upon, pre-echo what happens to Le Guin's Osden. But even the very nature of Marcher's beast—which represents a lifelong atrophy of affect, of emotional cathexis with other people and the outside world—parallels Osden's autism.

At the same time, one can find in previous SF several "forest-minds" and vegetable intelligences. Perhaps the most lucid and insightful are Olaf Stapledon's Plant Men in *Star Maker* (1937; §7:3). Stapledon's "vegetable humanities" are specifically associated with the mystical, and even the redemptory. ("Till sunset he slept, not in a dreamless sleep, but in a sort of trance, the meditative and mystical quality of which was to prove in future ages a well of peace for many worlds.") Stapledon is here closest to Le Guin in mood of the various arboriculturists of SF—and it is Stapledon, that mystical atheist, who remains the writer best able to articulate the sense of cosmic mystery as well as to indicate the nature of possible higher-order intelligences, or superminds, without falling into either naive bravura, or will to power. Van Vogt, who, with his assorted slans, silkies, nexialists, etc. can be relied on for an operatic, mystificatory demonstration of the will to power, has described in his short story "Process"[7] a forest-mind that is slow-thinking, yet fast-growing, a ravening leviathan of hostility, yet slothful and stupid, a forest replete with contradictions which visiting spacemen (who remain invisible) insert·their impervious ship into, from time immemorial, to steal some riches (in the form of uranium) and fly away. This story, by contrast with Le Guin, is *unconscious* metaphor. The tangled, fearsome, stupid forest "reads" quite blatantly as the hidden, unconscious area of the mind, into which the masterful creative consciousness plunges—well-armoured—to extract necessary wealth; and the story remains an absorbing one, for all its contradictions, precisely because it is about the process of creation, and at the same time about Van Vogt's own willful refusal to be analytically aware of this. The story is about the betrayal of full consciousness.

Van Vogt's short story "The Harmonizer"[8] describes a supertree which angrily manufactures a stupefying perfume whenever its "sensitive colloids" catch "the blasts of palpable lust" radiated by any killer—whether carnivorous animal, or hate-drunk soldier. Such trees, deposited on Earth by a spacewreck, are responsible for the disappearance of the dinosaurs. Latterly, their one survivor, re-emerging after 80 million years, halts World War III, introducing a malign, brainwashing pseudo-pacificism. This time, the tree is overtly associated with the militant spread of a form of consciousness. A similar manipulatory—though paranormal—situation occurs in Kris Neville's short story "The Forest of Zil,"[9] where a world-forest responds to Terran intrusion by retrospectively cancelling the time-line of Homo Sapiens, sending a creeping ontological amnesia back along the time axis. Manipulatory, too, is the symbiotic diamond wood forest in James H. Schmitz's short story "Balanced Ecology."[10] It too encapsulates both violence and somnolence—twin associations which link these four stories, suggesting that the subconscious, the time of sleep, is indeed underlying these various tree-minds in one form or another, and that the time of sleep, furthermore—when dreams take place—is feared as a time of ignorance and violence. This can certainly not be said of Stapledon's treatment of the theme—nor of Le Guin's.

Theme and image, event and illusion, bind Le Guin's two forest-mind stories together. The title of "Vaster Than Empires and More Slow" is but one of a series of references to the work of Andrew Marvell, especially his poem "To His Coy Mistress": "My vegetable love should grow/Vaster than empires, and more slow." Another allusion to this same poem occurs at the end of the story ("Had we but world enough and time...") while another familiar line from the poem presides over Lyubov's headache in WWF: "...ow, ow, ow, above the right ear I always hear Time's winged chariot hurrying near, for the Athsheans had burned Smith Camp..." (§3). Again, in VTE, Osen's reflecting that the vegetation of World 4470 is "one big green thought" echoes the famous "a green thought in a green shade" from Marvell's poem "The Garden."

The second story also picks up the military argot of WWF where Colonel Davidson is obsessed with the idea of people going "spla"—crazy. Osden uses the word more than once of the effect the forest is producing; while the comment that "the chitinous rigidity of military discipline was quite inapplicable to these teams of Mad Scientists" recalls the behaviour of the Terran military on Athshe, at the same time as it turns it upside-down.

The hallucinatory quality of Athshe—a world "that made you day-dream" (§1)—recurs in the "Hypnotic quality" of the woods of VTE World 4470, where imagery binding root and dream is reinforced. The woods are dark, connected; nightmare passes through the roots as the visitors are sensed; the visitors themselves relapse increasingly into sleep, to dream dreams that are "pathless" and "dark-branching." When awake, the visitors are still scared "blind." The path leading Osden to his self-sacrifice commences with a fall in the forest that injures his face, and lets his blood mingle with the root-nerves. Thereafter his countenance is "flayed" by scars that parallel the injured face of Selver the Athshean, beaten up by Colonel Davidson. But Selver, the flayed one, becomes thereby a "God" in Athshean terms—dreamer of a powerful new collective dream. Osden, too, through psychic identification with the "immortal mindless" forest—an idiot God absorbed in its own Nirvana beyond Maya, the changes of the world—transcends the human level, and at the same time becomes a "colonist" of World 4470. This word, the very last of the story, would seem an odd choice indeed for Osden's fate as castaway did it not reflect back to the Terran ambition to colonize Athshe—which the Terrans signally fail to achieve, precisely because of their disconnectedness. Osden succeeds where they failed; but only in a mystic apotheosis achieved by a paranormal "wild talent"—a fictive dimension ruled out of court by the politically conscious, this-worldly "boss" of WWF, and henceforth to be purged from the Hainish universe of Le Guin.

However, it is apparent from this story that there is an authentic "mystical" strain in Le Guin—an authentic strain, as opposed to the various gimmick-ridden mystifications that frequently pass for mysticism in our times, from the conjuring tricks of Uri Geller or the "grokking" of Charles Manson, via the musico-hagiology of the pop Orient, to the opening of the third eye of confused Western disciples by cult gurus. Whether this authentic mystical strain is necessarily radically at odds with the socio-political strain, as metaphor may be at odds with verisimilitude, is another matter. It might be truer to say that this mystic element has hitherto been falsely expressed through the traditional paranormal gimmickry of SF and that it is here in the process of breaking free (though it is not yet free). Just as The Lathe of Heaven is discharging the tension generated by use of the paranormal in the Hainish cycle, so VTE, structurally attached as it is to the politically "correct" partner story presided over by the "boss," may be seen now as an attempt to discover a permissible locale for the mystical—stripped, as it were, of a phoney mysticism of supermen and superminds. Hence the caginess as to whether Osden's empathy is paranormal or not; hence the need to remark on this and draw the problem to our attention.

The story opens (in the original version at least)[11] with a meditation on the nature of eternity as experienced during NAFAL time-distortion starflight, which is directly compared to the time, outside time, of dreams: "The mystic is a rare bird, and the nearest most people get to God in paradoxical time is... prayer for release," comments Le Guin, coining a phrase clearly suggested by the "paradoxical sleep" of the dream researchers.[12] The story ends with a return to this same keynote mood. Osden is absorbed into the eternity, the no-time sought by those rare birds, the mystics:

He had taken the fear into himself, and accepting had transcended it. He had given up his self to the alien, an unreserved surrender, that left no place for evil. He had learned the love of the Other, and thereby had been given his whole self. But this is not the vocabulary of reason.

The final sentence is revealing. Le Guin has inverted the main values of WWF to give suppressed material a verisimilar outlet. She has swung as far away as possible from the military domain into the realm of the "speshes" (specialists). Dream has become nightmare, and sleep a form of catatonic withdrawal from reality. She has made her visitors to the stars overtly mad. She has created an alien life-form—as opposed to the various humanoids of Hainish descent, that have been her theme hitherto.[13] She has pushed beyond the limits of Hainish expansion to describe a world that nothing to do with Hain. Forest as metaphor of mind has here been translated into narrative reality. The grudging military surrender of the Terrans on Athshe has become the "unreserved" spiritual surrender of Osden, who thus becomes the only true colonist: not so much of World 4470—for how can one man colonise a world?—as of the Beyond, of the dream time (pace Raj Lyubov's shade stalking Selver's dreams). Yet, in the end, this transcendent territory is unchartable by rational discourse. Stripped to the bare minimum of the paranormal trappings that do duty for it elsewhere (however successfully—one thinks of Genly Ai's encounter with Foretelling in The Left Hand of Darkness, §5), it is inarticulable. Or rather, to draw a distinction that Wittgenstein draws, it may be shown forth, but not stated. The ending of VTE recalls the terminal aphorism of the Tractatus: "What we cannot speak about we must pass over in silence."[14] The essentially silent world-forest of VTE shows forth, yet cannot state, the para-rational elements implied by WWF though sternly suppressed in that story.

It might seem, then, that whilst the mystic area of experience may be an authentic area, there is nothing profound one can say about it. Least of all should one attempt to do so by invoking the paraphernalia of the paranormal from the lumber-room of SF, for this only alienates one from the physical—and from the social—universe.[15] Yet the sense of insight into the infinite is not thereby necessarily lost. It returns, in The Dispossessed, with Shevek's creation of a General Theory of Time—within a context of positive social, political and emotional practice. It returns, having been chastened by the "boss" of WWF, and then by contrast—in the partner story VTE—allowed free rein to test out the mystic Pascalian silences where the vocabulary of reason becomes void. To the world-forests of these two stories, both metaphors for mind—one overt, one covert—corresponds Shevek's Theory: which is, within the verisimilar setting of the book, also metaphorical to a large extent. Yet, whereas the forest-mind is presented as something concrete that lies in wait out there for us, Shevek's Theory arises only out of the complex dialectic of his own life as scientist and utopian. As he discovers his own unity, so his theory becomes possible; and only so. This is the vocabulary of reason—which turns out to have far greater scope and depth than that other vocabulary, of unreason, or parareason. But it is a vocabulary of a subversive reason, which has therefore had first to pass through the false, non-reasonable and by themselves non-cognitive expressions of parareason. The two forest minds of WWF and VTE are—beyond their intrinsic interest as bases for two shrewd and powerful stories—necessary stages in a development from ur-SF to the mystico-political theory of time and society in The Dispossessed.

NOTES

1. The pithy apothegm of Tacitus (Agricola §30)—"They make desolation and they call it peace" ("ubi solitudinem faciunt, pacem appellant")—is worked into the texture of the story"Vaster Than Empires and More Slow," in ironic reference to the alienation of the characters: "They were misfits among men, and what they saw there was not desolation, but peace."

2. Joe W. Haldeman, The Forever War (1975). Appearing originally as separate stories in Analog, the episodes drew such acclaim as "a fine and realistic look at the Future...

reveals the keen eye of a complete science fiction author who looks at the future as a different place with different configurations" (from the editorial epigraph to "We are Very Happy," anthologized in *Best SF 73*, ed. H. Harrison & Brian W. Aldiss [1974]).

3. For a discussion of conscious dreaming, see the present writer in SFS 2(1975):75. In addition to the Senoi dreamers of Malaya discussed there, comparison might also be made with the Iroquois who attached an overriding importance to dreams, dream interpretation and dream fulfillment, and indeed practised a form of psychoanalysis—though the practical consequences were not always as benign and pacific as those of Senoi dream analysis. See A.F.C. Wallace, "Dreams and the Wishes of the Soul: A Type of Psychoanalytic Theory among the Seventeenth Century Iroquois," *American Anthropologist* 60(1958):234-48.

4. The "drug crisis" in the US forces in Vietnam was qualitatively different from the alcoholic intoxication characteristic of conquering armies, insofar as (1) the use of drugs was associated with the ethos of a newsworthy sector of the antiwar protest movement, in a radically different sense from drunkenness being the perennial common soldier's protest at authority; (2) the feedback of drugs (heroin not hallucinogens) and drug addicts to the mother country was one factor, albeit a minor one, in eroding the national will to continue fighting; and (3) drug addiction within the American army eroded military discipline and efficiency in a way that alcoholic indulgence could not possibly have done.

5. The story, in the *New Dimensions* version, is dated "during the earliest decade of the League," but also "Before the invention of the instantaneous transmitter," which is inconsistent (cf. the table in SF 2[1975]:74); however, this is reconciled in the version in *The Wind's Twelve Quarters* (1975).

6. In Henry James, *The Better Sort* (1903).

7. Collected in *The Far-Out Worlds of A.E. Van Vogt* (1968).

8. Collected in A.E. Van Vogt, *Away and Beyond* (1963).

9. In H. Harrison & Brian Aldiss, *The Year's Best Science Fiction No. 1* (1968).

10. In Anthony Cheetham, *Bug-Eye Monsters* (1974).

11. The version included in *The Wind's Twelve Quarters* omits the first 4 paragraphs, i.e. all mention of mystics and paradoxical time.

12. Cf SFS 2(1975):70, 75 n. 9.

13. At the same time, in *The Lathe of Heaven* (1971) Le Guin was experimenting with "dream-time" aliens from Aldebaran as a verisimilar mediator for mystical/pararational experience. A curious coincidence of names links *Lathe* to WWF, also: the central character of *Lathe*, George Orr—the dreamer of alternatives, as his name bespeaks—and Mr. Or, the Cetian emissary in WWF share names, if not roles or personalities. It is interesting, too, to note that the military of WWF are deliberately contrasted with the "Mad Scientists" of VTE—while the archetypal Mad Scientist erupts in *Lathe* in the figure of Dr. Haber, associated with irrational solutions to the world's woes.

14. Ludwig Wittgenstein, *Tractatus Logico-Philosophicus*, new transl. by D.F. Pears & B.F. McGuinness (London: Routledge & Kegan Paul, 1961), prop. 7.

15. SFS 2(1975):73 n. 3, for further discussion.

John Huntington

Public and Private Imperatives in Le Guin's Novels

The typical Le Guin hero is a visitor to a world other than his own; sometimes he is a professional anthropologist; sometimes the role is forced on him; in all cases he is a creature of divided allegiance. As a student of an alien society, he has responsibilities to his own culture and to the culture he visits; he must sympathize with and participate deeply in both, for it is by the experience and analysis of their differences that he hopes to arrive at a deeper understanding of the nature and possibilities of mind and of social organization. In his role of scientist, the anthropologist expects cultural division and has been trained to explore it; but as an individual, he finds that his personal attachments exist to an important degree independent of and at times in conflict with his social duty, so that, almost inevitably in Le Guin's work, he finds that he has difficulty reconciling his public, political obligations with the bonds he has developed as a private individual. Though the cultural division often serves to exacerbate his dilemma, Le Guin's hero, as a moral individual rather than as a scientist, often confronts a universal human problem of—in bald terms—how to harmonize love and public duty. The two divisions the anthropologist hero faces are not completely separate, however; different societies demand and deserve different sacrifices. Therefore, the inquiry into what the individual owes society leads naturally into a study of the nature and possibilities of different political structures.

The political axis of Le Guin's work exists at right angles, if you will, to the powerful vision of unity that recent criticism has been exploring, and an accurate perception of her whole achievement requires us to engage both dimensions. While the recent popularity of her work derives in part, one expects, from the vision of unity, it also probably owes much to her exploration of political issues that have developed a particular urgency over the last ten years: to her attempt, increasingly precise and detailed, to use SF for studying problems that arose from the United States' use of military power in Vietnam and from the experience of an alienating and technologically bloated economic system. Douglas Barbour's study of the relation of Le Guin's novels to the *Tao-te ching* points to an aspiration towards unified being that underlies all the novels.[1] We need to recognize, however, how the structure of a novel like *The Left Hand of Darkness* (LHD), by dividing the moral universe into public and private worlds, frustrates unity and turns what might have become ecstatic perceptions and energies into an awareness of tragic incompleteness. It is this failure to achieve a unity the imagery seems to promise which probably accounts for the frustration David Ketterer experiences in LHD and which he attributes to a discontinuity between the mythic theme of the novel and its plot.[2] In the light of Le Guin's recurrent political interest we can see that the discontinuity experienced serves an important thematic function and expresses an ironic perception of the difficult relation of the private individual to the public world in which he acts. In her early novels this perception gives heightened value to the unified heroic act. But in LHD the awareness of the incongruity between the public and private worlds interrupts the full "mythic" triumph, and in two works published after LHD we can see Le Guin stretching this tension between the public and private worlds to such a pitch that one or the other of the two poles has had to give way. In her latest novel, *The Dispossessed* (TD), she breaks through to a new definition of the problem. In order to appreciate the accomplishment of TD, however, we have to understand the problem defined and confronted in the earlier novels.

In Le Guin's early novels there is usually an element of irony inherent in the heroic activity, for public action demands the sacrifice of a private bond. The success of the heroic quest entails personal loss. This theme is given an explicit, fairy tale concreteness in *Rocannon's World* (RW) when Rocannon makes a contract to give what he holds "dearest and would least willingly give" in return for public victory (§8).[3] In this early novel the conflict between the public triumph and private loss does not pose an ethical problem but serves to give contour to the heroic idea: we can admire the hero because he has made sacrifices and, importantly, because it is implicit that he—and the author—see more to life than just public victory. A hero without such awareness becomes either pompously comic (Superman) or sinister (Conan). In RW the reconciliation of the public and private imperatives is rendered fairly easy, however, by the unambiguous clarity and urgency of the political issue. The "enemy," the Faradayans, have no redeeming qualities; they are seen from a great distance and their acts reveal them to be brutal imperialists and terrorists, so that the private sacrifices necessary, however painful, seem a small price to pay for their defeat. Though Rocannon has moments of doubt— when he thinks he has failed he questions the value of the whole enterprise, and when the enemy is obliterated he is appalled at the death of a thousand men (§9)—these suggestions of moral complexity do not really undermine his heroic act; in fact, like his sacrifice of Mogien, his doubt gives his activity moral value; without these qualifications he might seem merely a butcher.

LHD attains a more difficult balance of public and private imperatives, for this later novel does not offer the earlier one's clear-cut public justification for private sacrifice. The two political systems of Gethen, Karhide's feudal one and Orgoreyn's totalitarian-collectivist one, are both corrupt and destructive of individual values, and if the feudal is favored over the totalitarian it is only because it is the more flexible and the more easily influenced of the two; its inefficiency is its virtue. We find no neat distinction available between the good and bad political systems; Genly Ai faces no absolute enemy against whom any act is permitted or sacrifice justified. Also, Ai's goal of persuading Gethen to join the Ekumen lacks the element of urgent crisis that sanctions Rocannon's public acts. In fact, it is important to Ai's mission that there be no public compulsion that would make Gethen's decision to join seem anything less than completely voluntary.

While the public world of LHD exerts a diminished moral imperative, in the intimacy that develops between Ai and Estraven the private world assumes an importance and value that has no equal in any of Le Guin's other novels. The conventional plot carries the public values while behind it, in a separate set of events, the private values develop. Thus, the bond the two alien beings establish on the Gobrin Ice, especially the "bespeaking," has enormous personal significance but does not directly influence political events. There are, then, in effect, two sub-plots to the novel. One is the adventure which, like Rocannon's, leads to political success; the other is the love story of Ai and Estraven. To be sure, a thematic coherence bridges these two plots: insofar as the political problem in the novel involves overcoming the fear of aliens,[4] the love story depicts the successful healing of that division between beings. This theme of union is repeated on a more general level by the androgyny of the Gethenians which offers a pervasive image of the union of the primary opposition experienced among humans.[5] But though they share common themes, the two sub-plots also move in opposite directions: in the love story Ai begins suspicious of Estraven and learns to trust him; in the political story he begins naively trusting both King Argaven and the Commensals of Orgoreyn and learns to suspect them and be cunning. The main challenge to the suggestions of coherence, however, comes from the death of Estraven, for it points to the gap that continues to exist between the public and the private worlds. Ai finally pays for public success with private loss, and at the end of the novel Le Guin makes us face the disjunction between the two worlds by having Ai force Argaven's hand, but at the cost of breaking the vow he made to Estraven that he would see him pardoned before he brought the ship down.

The Karhidish tale of "Estraven the traitor" serves as an ironic paradigm for the discrepancy between the public and private worlds: in the tale, love ultimately settles a political dispute, but at the cost of the murder of one of the lovers and the branding of the offspring of the lovers' union with the title of *traitor*. Ai and Estraven reenact the tale and transpose it from the primitive political level of a feud between neighboring families to the more complex level of international politics. In both the tale and the larger world of the novel, *traitor* becomes an honorific title, thus pointing to the inability of the political terminology to deal with true value.[6] But at the very end of the novel Le Guin prevents us from settling down easily with such an ironic view: Ai, speaking to Estraven's father and son, says "Therem was no traitor. What does it matter what fools call him?" To which the father replies, "It matters." One cannot escape the significance of the public world's blind destructiveness simply by ignoring it.

In its structure, therefore, LHD balances public achievement against personal cost, and Le Guin, dismissing neither, maintains the dialectical tension between them. In two works published since LHD she explores the problem further by upsetting the balance between the two worlds. In *The Lathe of Heaven* (LoH) all public activity leads to failure, and the novel, almost dogmatically, asserts the total primacy of private, inner peace.[7] Dr. Haber, the scientist who envisions creating a better world, turns out to be the villain, and George Orr, the protagonist whose private dreams change the world, spends the novel trying to relinquish this power. Orr makes things happen, but he is incompetent to predict the consequences of his acts, and the novel makes it clear that such incompetence is inevitable, that given man's ignorance, any public act is liable to do wrong, no matter how well intentioned. But if in LoH Le Guin upsets the balance in favor of passivity and inner peace, in "The Word for World is Forest," she upsets it in the opposite direction and argues[8] for the precedence of the public duty over the private one. In this novella the pressure of political events forces Selver, the alien protagonist, to become an active terrorist and guerrilla in spite of his deep sense of the value of private bonds. In order to free his people from the imperialist tyranny of humans, Selver does not merely lose his friend, a human, he participates in his murder. In the hands of a less honest writer than Le Guin, Selver's extraordinary spirituality might be made to counterbalance sentimentally the pitiless brutality of his political acts, but "The Word for World is Forest" (WWF) does not evade the rigors of the moral question; it studies the savagery of guerrilla warfare and accepts it.[9] The story clearly asserts that the private world can flourish only when the public world is benign, that when the public world becomes oppressive the private world must give way.

In all her work Le Guin probes in various ways for the point at which the public and private imperatives intersect, for the act that will allow them to be unified, if only momentarily. Put in the context of this search, it is clear that the split in attention that Ketterer notes in LHD has the important function of carrying one of the major conflicts of the novel, and whatever discontinuity we experience in terms of plot and theme expresses exactly that discontinuity which is being explored between the values of the public and the private worlds. LHD stands apart from Le Guin's other works, however, in its extraordinary balance and its commitment to both of the rival imperatives. The public world of the novel is neither so overpoweringly meaningful that (as in RW) it can easily and indubitably compensate for private loss, nor so arbitrary that (as in LoH) it can be treated as morally trivial. By observing this dialectical balance we can see how far Le Guin differs from an absurdist like Vonnegut who, while he too sees a discrepancy between the two worlds, in much of his work cheerfully dismisses the public world to its insane and pompous self-destruction. LHD renders a basic allegiance to private, humane values without denying the degree to which public, institutional values influence and limit the private ones.

The balance Le Guin achieves in this novel is not a complacent one; it is precarious and leads to serious questions about man's social obligations. LHD marks the beginning of a period in which Le Guin, while always sympathetic to the private world, has pursued these social questions and has become increasingly concerned to anatomize the political structures of the public world which so powerfully affects the private. As a rule she has modeled her fictional public world on familiar western social institutions. In her earlier novels social organizations, with the important exception of primitive ones, are not explored in specific detail. If they appear at all, they do so in symbolic forms—as in the city of the "Winged Ones" in RW (§6)—or as vague and abstract structures like the Ekumen. The city of Es Toch in *City of Illusions* is an SF convention and has no true political structure. LHD breaks with this essentially literary vision of the political world by treating the destructiveness of Orgoreyn and Karhide as a function of their political organizations. The antagonism of both nations to the private world represented by Ai and Estraven's love is not simply a given; it derives from the nature of power and from the specific mechanisms of the nations' governments. Though Karhide's feudal monarchy owes a good deal to literary convention, it is realized with a detail and with a care for the way politics works in this archaic system which is new to Le Guin. And Orgoreyn, with its prison camps and its tyrannic bureaucracies, is clearly an explicit version of one form of the modern, collectivist nation-state. Thus, Le Guin's work, while it has always had an important political element, now begins to examine the failure of specific political structures to give play and sustenance to private values and desires. The romance quest of Rocannon gives way to a more pessimistic vision in which the protagonist seeks, not for victory, but for meaning and value itself in the face of a dominant and alienating public context. This tendency to treat the public world in terms of known and explicit models becomes even more pronounced after LHD. In LoH, set in Le Guin's home city of Portland, Oregon, and WWF, in which Selver fights an organization that is compared to the U.S. Army in Vietnam, Le Guin depicts the alienating public world as the capitalist-imperialist world of the modern U.S.A.

In spite of the fact that her analysis of the public world has become more specific and more contemporary, Le Guin has continued through this period to envision a primitive economy as the main salvation from the modern, technological, imperialist state. Her heroes usually discover in the primitive cultures they visit values and parapsychological powers which, in one way or another, sustain rather than contradict the private world. But in all cases this primitive unity, while it holds out possibilities for meaningful and integrated social life, is vulnerable to outside threats. Even the primitive sages, whose spiritual accomplishments might seem to allow them to avoid the political dilemma altogether, must step out of the retired life and in one way or another confront the complex and generally destructive public world. Kyo aids Rocannon; Faxe leaves his mountain fastness and enters Karhide politics; Selver becomes a general. But, as Le Guin's vision of the public world changes, this act of commitment to the public world assumes different consequences; what in Kyo's and Faxe's cases is a generous and ennobling act, in Selver's entails a spiritual self-mutilation. For Selver to lose part of his wholeness, even for a brief while, changes him permanently; he cannot, as Kyo apparently expects to do, regain primitive innocence at will. WWF, therefore, differs significantly from RW and even from LHD in its perception of the corrupting power of the technological imperialism that threatens the primitive world. Kyo and Rocannon can fight the Faradayans without being tainted, but for Selver to fight his human enemies is, to some extent, to become like them. Thus, the invasion motif, such a staple of SF, begins to take on an important new aspect in Le Guin's hands: the threat is not simply conquest, it is the corruption of the primitive innocence, the violation of spiritual wholeness by the presence of insanely powerful and greedy forces that have no vision at all of a life in which private and public imperatives are truly in harmony.

So long as the options for social life and action are limited to a physhically rich but fragile primitivism and a crudely powerful but spiritually destitute technology, there would seem to be no escape from private tragedy and no possibility of truly voluntary and ethical public action. Le Guin's new novel, *The Dispossessed*, however, sets up what is for her a new definition of the political problem and thus offers a way out of the bind represented by the modern-primitive conflict of her middle period. In this latest novel Le Guin has focused entirely on modern political systems (or possible systems) and has studied them without the nostalgia for the primitive and the parapsychological machinery that constitute the alternatives to the modern state in her earlier novels. Furthermore the racial differences that in all of her earlier works parallel but also dilute the more explicit political theme have been abandoned. TD differs from earlier Le Guin novels in seeing the private world almost totally as a function of specific political systems. The intimate bonds which in her early novels exist apart from any social organization and often in spite of society and which represent an absolute source of value, are here seen as inherently conditioned by the shape of the society. What is in LHD conceived of as a problem of dialectical conflict between two sources of value, love and society, has been transformed into a conflict between two forms of society, anarchist and capitalist, and the question is, not what does the individual owe to society, but what kind of society makes possible valid human bonds? And just as the vision of the political world has been reshaped, the vision of love, of the valid bond itself, has changed. From the vantage of TD we can see how much the valued private bonds of the earlier works, those between Rocannon and Mogien, Ai and Estraven, are rich expressions, not of man as a social animal, but of man alone in a hostile nature. It is significant that the love of Ai and Estraven reaches its height, not in society, but in the utter desolation of the Gobrin Ice. The failure of the public and private worlds to coalesce, therefore, may be in part the fault of an idea of love that does not allow for a social dimension. Thus, as Le Guin has made the political issues more precise and detailed, she has forced an analysis of the specific political systems themselves, which has, in turn, led her to a reinterpretation of the source of value of the private world. TD is important because, though it generates its own ambivalances and problems, it renews the possibilities for viable social action.

NOTES

1. Douglas Barbour, "Wholeness and Balance in the Hainish Novels of Ursula K. Le Guin," SFS 1(1974):164-73.

2. David Ketterer, *New Worlds for Old* (New York: Anchor, 1974), pp. 80, 194.

3. In *City of Illusions* this trade is put in terms of two aspects of a single individual: "To revive Ramarren you must kill Falk" (§8). Falk finally evades the sacrifice, however, by rigging a way of preserving his Falkian memory when he becomes Ramarren.

4. Fear of the alien is a common source of political problems in Le Guin's early and middle work, and she tends to envision some kind of solution in loving the "other." The complement of this idea in her work is the idea that without otherness there can be no love, only narcissism. Her most concise study of this problem is the short story "Nine Lives."

5. Even the members of the ten-person clone in "Nine Lives," identical in all other ways, admit sexual division.

6. A "traitor" is not only one who loves the "other," he is also one who is not aggressive in his country's interest. Estraven is exiled for failing to prosecute the Sinoth Valley border dispute. The antithesis of a traitor is a patriot: Estraven defines patriotism as "fear of the other" (§1).

7. We should note that, just as the novel devalues public activity, the private bond between Orr and Heather Lelache is treated more ambivalently than are those between the heroic aliens in the "Hainish" novels. The private "way" that Orr seeks to follow is therefore significantly different from the kind of private love-bond that gives meaning to the lives of Ai and Rocannon.

8. I use this word on purpose. In her "Afterword" to the story in *Again, Dangerous*

Visions, Le Guin notes, somewhat apologetically, the conscious moralism of the tale.

9. The toughness of "The Word for World is Forest" is evident if we put it next to *Rocannon's World*. The central event of both works is a guerrilla attack against an imperialist occupation, and in terms of body count the two are very similar. But the enemy in RW is unseen and alien, and all friends are on the "good" side, while in "The Word for World is Forest" we, the human race, are the enemy, and Selver's close friend, Raj Lyubov, is a human. There are no easy answers in the later story.

David L. Porter

The Politics of Le Guin's Opus

To read Le Guin is to enter a sharply focused world of vivid political drama, from individual struggles to cosmic conflict. The following remarks (based on seven of her nine novels and five of her stories) first present the general framework of her political perception, then relate her insights, and her particular use of the future, to contemporary reality, and finally assess the relative effectiveness of her writings as a distinct medium of political communication.

1. Le Guin's perspective seems to have evolved from a more individualized existentialist orientation and anthropological concern in the mid-1960s to an emphatic embrace of Taoism. From there, by the mid-70s, she moved to a much richer social critique and explicit anarchist commitment. To speak of her evolution, however, is to describe only a shifting of emphases. In fact, Le Guin is amazingly consistent in her general preoccupation with the relationship of good and evil, the illusions of superior accomplishment, and the role of the individual in the face of catastrophic change. She shows a corresponding and equally constant disdain for the "ordinary politics" of exploitation, alienation, and egocentrism.

In Le Guin's view, the unity and equilibrium of good and evil in human nature reflects on the individual scale the larger universal balance and *interdependence of opposites* in the broader natural world. Her most emphatic early statement of dynamic equilibrium is in *A Wizard of Earthsea* (WE). The apprentice wizard, Ged, learns through an encounter with his own death-shadow nearly fatal to himself and to the world, the absolute need to acknowledge this balance: one cannot mock or evade death without endangering life itself. Le Guin's works abound with vivid examples of those who faill to comprehend themselves as the unification of opposites: e.g., the Fiia and Clayfolk in *Rocannon's World* (RW), the nations of Karhide and Orgoreyn on the planet Gethen in *The Left Hand of Darkness* (LHD), Dr. Haber in *The Lathe of Heaven* (LoH), the twin planets of Anarres and Urras in *The Dispossessed* (TD), Captain Davidson in the New Tahiti colony in "The Word for World is Forest" (WWF), and the "happy" citizens of Omelas in "The Ones Who Walk Away from Omelas" (OWO). By contrast, those who see the unity behind their own internal conflicts inevitably become Le Guin's leading protagonists: the wizard Ged in WE, Jakob Agat Alterra in *The Planet of Exile* (PE), Falk-Agad in *City of Illusions* (CI), Genly Ai in LHD, George Orr in LoH, Shevek in TD, Selver in WWF.

Self-deceiving illusions of superior accomplishment provide another favorite theme that takes a variety of forms. First and most spectacular is the *total* inability of one culture to comprehend another, thereby removing any reference points whatsoever. Three astronauts exposed to a mind-shattering total experience in the ruins of a Martian "city" lack any conceptual tools to communicate their findings back to Earth ("Field of Vision" [FV]). A second type of illusion of superiority is that form of cultural imperialism which sees the homeland's way of life as alone deserving recognition; appearing in virtually all of her writings, it is a dominant theme in WWF. Social self-deception also appears when competing societies (such as the Askatever and "farborns"—i.e., Terrans—of PE, and Karhide and Orgoreyn in LHD) complement each other's strengths and weaknesses. Another type of illusion appears when a highly "progressive" society depends for its very success on a fundamental moral failure; the ambiguously utopian Omelas community of OWO is her perfected model, though her most explicit imperialists—such as the Terran New Tahiti colony on Athshe in WWF and the Shing in CI—belong to the same family. A final self-deception derives from a society's inability to define progress in *broad* enough terms: thus Dr. Haber's attempt to end war on Earth in turn causes war with a non-Earth power (LoH), and even the anarchist utopia of Anarres develops its own brand of political tyranny by failing to protect that individual creativity essential to its own health.

Le Guin consistently concerns herself with individuals striving to preserve their integrity, and their resulting conflicts with society. In her earlier works, she focuses primarily on the individual. Social action, when it appears, comes in the form of defensive measures by key characters in a crisis (as in RW, PE, and CI). In this her tone is existentialist. In the middle transition phase she still emphasizes individual development, yet also reflects on the need for balance in the overall society as well. Here Taoist imagery predominates. Her most recent emphasis shifts to the broad nature and inevitability of constant social change itself and its effects on the individual (as in WWF, TD, and "The Day Before the Revolution" [DBR]). In this there is a much more definite political, specifically anarchist, tone. Each of these phases is closely related to the others. A continuity exists, but the different emphases within it seem to express Le Guin's own political maturation. In this evolution Le Guin represents a significant section of a whole generation of white radical American intellectuals, from the early 1960s to the present.[1]

Typical of her first phase are the chief characters of PE, Rolery and Jakob. These two, strangers from very different though neighboring races, make the existential leap into the absurd through a love affair that risks the very annihilation of both peoples. Despite the impending disaster, Le Guin implies that it is the integrity of the personal relationship, and the willingness to risk all for it, which really counts. Through the persistence of that integrity, the two previously irreconcilable groups eventually ally together in a successful defense and later (as we learn in CI) in a blending of their races.

Le Guin's Taoist tone appears most prominently in WE, LHD, and LoH, though it resonates in practically every one of her works. George Orr, Genly Ai, and Falk-Agat each literally confront the experience of chaos. Orr's world dissolves before his very eyes: "The buildings of downtown Portland, the Capital of the World...were melting. They were getting soggy and shaky, like jello left out in the sun.... It was an area, or perhaps a time-period, of a sort of emptiness" (LoH §10). With each heroic character, however—Le Guin says loud and clear—if the will is strong enough, if one is wholly committed to one's deepest understanding of the truth, and at the same time tolerant of ambiguities, it is possible to pass even through the realm of the void in confronting one's deadliest enemies, and still meet success.

Le Guin's third phase, that of anarchism, asserts that individuals must participate collectively in social change as a necessary precondition to maintaining and developing personal integrity. At the same time, self-development occurs only if social movements themselves are designed for individual growth instead of conformity. Both aspects appear prominently in the Odonian and Athshean revolutionary movements of TD, DBR, and WWF. Selver, for example,

realizes the incompleteness and ultimate impossibility of his people relying solely on spiritual, intuitional ("dream-time") fulfillment so long as material
("world-time") conditions were so destructive. Despite his previous pacifism,
he tells captured Terran colonists, "We had to kill you, before you drove us
mad" (WWF §6). On the other hand, while leading the growing resistance movement, Selver discovers that his political role in turn prevents "dream" consciousness. In addition, however necessary it may be for self-preservation, killing or violence changes the previously non-violent person: "it's himself whom
the murderer kills...over and over" (WWF §5).

According to Le Guin, to neglect the need for balance, for moderation, for
appreciation of the inherent contradictions in individuals and society, is to cause
individual and social egoism and all their disastrous consequences. The imbalance of egocentrism produces every type of human exploitation and disaster.
In her view, a conservatism which unabashedly glorifies egoistic fulfillment
through existing social structures and a liberalism which protects and encourages the same egoism behind labels of "social interest" are equally pernicious. Her detailed images of conservative logic in the character of Davidson
(WWF) and of liberal logic in Lyubov (WWF) and Dr. Haber (LoH) are powerful
indeed. So also is her denunciation of authoritarian collectivism, as symbolized
by the countries of Thu (TD) and Orgoreyn (LHD). For Le Guin, the *only* political
arrangement sensitive to the need for moderation, for non-egoistic social relations and identity of humans with nature is a classless society. This model
she offers consistently—despite its own significant problems—from the primitive
tribal groups in her earlier works to the planet-wide anarchist community of
TD.

2. Le Guin articulates her political dilemmas in credible and dramatic terms,
thus inviting the reader to think politically too. Her writing places believable
characters in easily recognizable political settings, and forces them to deal
with significant issues. The reader not only feels involved in the political drama,
but also receives data for independent agreement or disagreement with the
author—a rare quality indeed. Beyond her vividness and internal consistency,
her settings, issues, and solutions are similar enough to our own contemporary
world that the applicability of her thought and action to our own political
problems becomes practically self-evident.

Imperialist relations are clearly one of Le Guin's prime political insights,
a theme presented to greater or lesser degree in practically every one of her
writings. In WWF an ecologically sensitive, non-aggressive native population
is brutally tyrannized by a plundering colonist power all too familiar from the
history of European settlers in America, Africa, and Asia, and the recent U.S.
war in Vietnam. In the words of colonist Captain Davidson: "This world, New
Tahiti, was literally made for men.... Get enough humans here, build machines
and robots, make farms and cities, and nobody would need the creechies [the
native 'creatures'] any more"; "Cleaned up and cleaned out, it would be a
paradise, a real Eden"; "It's just how things happen to be. Primitive races
always have to give way to civilized ones. Or be assimilated. But we sure as
hell can't assimilate a lot of green monkeys" (§1). Typically, when the "creechie"
revolt begins, Davidson can't believe at first that the natives are involved;
it has to be a colonist or off-planet force. Once he is forced to believe that
there is a revolt, he responds by advocating genocide "to make the world safe
for the Terran way of life" (§4).

Beyond the particular issue of imperialism, Le Guin's works also explore
the other major contemporary foci of political crisis: racism, sexism, national-
ism, militarism, class society, authoritarianism, and ecocide. Sexism, like the
other common issues, usually appears as simply a given aspect of the status

quo. It becomes a dominant theme in LHD. Genly Ai, the male heterosexual envoy from the Ekumen, is forced to confront at the root of his psyche not only his own biases against women but a planet of *complete* bisexuals who regard him as sexually degenerate. Even after two years among them, "I was still.... seeing a Gethenian first as a man, then as a woman, forcing him into those categories so irrelevant to his nature and so essential to my own" (§1). By the end he finally sees in his friend Estraven what he "had always been afraid to see, and had pretended not to see in him: that he was a woman as well as a man. Any need to explain the sources of that fear vanished with the fear; what I was left with was, at last, acceptance of him as he was" (§18).

As with her statements of issues, Le Guin's particular political strategies are directly relevant to current American society. Overall, her solution is to develop awareness of exploitation, expose those structures producing it, and create alternative communities as open as possible to the fulfillment of all their members. She clearly favors anarchist and "counter-cultural" directions. But they must be followed consistently, with the open-endedness basic to their definition, to avoid the danger of new walls, new supposedly "liberating" forms of what might turn out to be the old exploitation. Sabul's quasi-politicking and Vea's supposed "sexual liberation" are emphatic examples of the latter in TD. Le Guin prefers Taoist non-action to Western assertiveness. At the same time, she realizes that some action is necessary (as with the Athshean revolt or Shevek's voyage to Urras) to arrive at the desired flexible equilibrium.[2] One must accept *no* walls, though coming home (to one's roots within the walls) is just as important, just as human, as going forth to adventure. Being *and* becoming is Le Guin's political stance, as it is the keystone to Shevek's revolutionary physics (TD §7).

Le Guin's alternative worlds in the future (from 1990 in FV to about 4800 in LHD) are primarily either a logical extension of present-day negative trends (such as militarism, ecocide, and egoism in general) or an analogic fantasy-context in which to present more selectively and thus more starkly certain of today's harshest contradictions. In the latter case, it hardly matters whether the society examined is 20 or 2000 years in the future. Her worlds are basically worlds of today. She subtracts or adds a small number of technologies, such as rapid space-flight and instantaneous galactic communication, but these are not essential to the inner dynamics of the particular planets involved.

The two main non-technological social innovations of Le Guin's stories are anarchism and parapsychological communication. Both have recognizable roots in contemporary practice and theory. Even so, Le Guin is ambiguous. Her anarchism seems a clearly superior political form when compared to hierarchical models (as in WWF, DBR, and TD). Yet to date she has placed her anarchist model either in an ecologically sensitive, economically undeveloped tribal-type setting (as in WWF), a limited emigrant enclave (as in PE), a situation of extreme economic scarcity (as in TD), or a vague cosmic setting with great spatial distances between constituent communities (as with the Ekumen in LHD). None of these has a clear direct connection to conditions in contemporary America; perhaps Le Guin will accept that challenge in writings to come. In the meantime, Le Guin clearly invites her US readers to seriously consider the *principle* of least contradictory, least egoistic politics for the society of which they are now a part.

Le Guin's parapsychology, like her anarchism, is both a critique of existing society and a positive alternative for the future. There is no more devastating critique of existing interpersonal relations, for example, than the deadly subconscious exchanges between shipmates in "Vaster than Empires and More Slow." The highly sensitive empath, Osden, when asked what he perceives with his talents, replies: "Muck. The psychic excreta of the animal kingdom. I wade through your feces." Le Guin's resolution to this story—a highly tuned-in "bliss-out" between sensitive and balanced beings—is perhaps one of her basic long-range social preferences.[3] Beyond the totally exceptional and fanciful experiences in LoH and FV, she does suggest that the development of telepathic talents might promote greater civilization and understanding. On the other hand, as the "mindlying" talents of the Shing in CI demonstrate, telepathy also has serious negative political potentials as well. Perhaps even greater beneficial potentials exist in the integration of waking and sleep. To dream (in the Athshean sense) is to get back in touch with the springs of reality" or subconscious roots (WWF §§ 2, 5). To dream is also, perhaps, to be more sensitive to parapsychological phenomena. In either case, the collective political effects of significant widespread personal growth in this area could be profound.

3. In conclusion, there is no doubt that Le Guin takes politics extremely seriously, both in her awareness of the destruction it currently produces and in her sense of better alternatives. Her images of contemporary existence are presented clearly and vividly *because* they are seen in a consistent though evolving political perspective. From this it follows that she herself must be taken seriously as a political writer-activist. Le Guin defends the SF *form* as a highly important and unique type of political communication:

At this point, realism is perhaps the least adequate means of understanding or por-traying the incredible realities of our existence. The fantasist...may be talking as serious-ly as any sociologist—and a good deal more directly—about human life as it is lived, and as it might be lived, and as it ought to be lived. For, after all, as great scientists have said and as all children know, it is above all by the imagination that we achieve perception, and compassion, and hope.[4]

At its best SF removes readers from the stale reference points of everyday political discourse and life.

It is true that SF is also inherently susceptible to becoming flippant fantasy, unrelated to the serious world of the present or at best useful merely as escapist relief. The right formula for positively changing political consciousness, especially in a mass audience, is amazingly elusive. Yet there is no doubt that Le Guin's skillful, sensitive, complex, adventurous, and vivid writing about *both* the micro- and macro-levels of society is one of the clearest proofs to date that SF can carry a general reader into a whole new realm of awareness—an awareness often rejected when presented by other activists with other manners of invitation. "Good artistry doesn't moralize; it seeks to engage one more"; a good SF writer may have "intense and intelligent" moral serious-ness, without moralizing and preaching: "He gambles; he tries to engage us. In other words, he works as an artist."[5] It is far easier for the average reader to dismiss a radical tract or a radical speaker than to set down a Le Guin writing, once begun. In her own manner, with her own special skills, Le Guin succeeds in taking us on that spiral journey of growth—adventuring outward, returning back home somewhat wiser—which is so central to her own political thought.

NOTES

1. By the 1950s a new generation of rebel intellectuals had emerged that were apparently not linked to the Old Left Marxist radicalism of the 1930s. Based on the existentialist concern with individual integrity, social protest concentrated on immediate issues of individual resistance to social immorality (such as the Chessman, anti-HUAC, Berkeley Free Speech, and original draft-card burning demonstrations). By the late 1960s this tendency had led, as in the case of SDS, to a fundamental alienation from

and confrontation with the entire political structure itself. Simultaneously the rise of drug use and alternative life-styles, combined with movement reaction against *macho* heaviness and Marxian dogmatism,then joined by massive government repression, drove many radicals into an ill-defined, ambiguously "apolitical" new stage. This was character-ized by inner-directed "counter-cultural" changes and a more contemplative and sporadically resisting political attitude toward the broader social structures. It was a time when the worth of assertive politics as a whole—radical as well as establishment—was subject to challenge. A new synthesis, the third stage increasingly adopted by the mid-70s, has attempted to integrate counter-cultural insights and radical politics into a consistent whole. Face-to-face and small-group politics are seen as just as essential as, yet also dependent on, the politics of the nation. Non-directive small affinity groups, less publicized local instead of spectacular national organizing, and an increasingly explicit anarchist focus characterize the behavior and orientation of large numbers of radicals in this current stage. Useful statements of this evolution, beyond the works of Le Guin, are found in several books by Michael Rossman and Theodore Roszak, as well as Julian Beck's *The Life of the Theatre* (City Lights Books, 1972). A 1949 philosophical pre-figuration of the same ideological evolution is found in Herbert Read's *Anarchy and Order* (reprinted 1971 by Beacon Press).

2. In her recognition of the necessary interdependence of the two traditions, Le Guin's politics are quite similar to those of Gary Snyder and Allen Ginsberg. See Snyder's essays, "Buddhism and the Coming Revolution" and "Why Tribe," in his *Earth House Hold* (New Directions, 1969), and Ginsberg's essay, "Consciousness and Practical Action," in *Counter-Culture*, ed. Joseph Berke (London: Owen, 1969). This position, as symbolized also in Le Guin's descriptions of Thu and Orgoreyn, seems clearly to set forth her attitude as well toward Marxist-Leninist models of organization.

3. Similar political potentials of paranormal behavior are implied in Roszak, in surrealist politics, and in research currently encouraged by the Soviet Union and Eastern Europe. See Theodore Roszak, *Where the Wasteland Ends* (Doubleday, 1972); "Sur-realism in the Service of the Revolution," a special issue of *Radical America*, January 1970; and Sheila Ostrander and Lynn Schroder, *Psychic Discoveries Behind the Iron Curtain* (Bantam Books, 1971). I differ here with Ian Watson in his apparent categorizing of paranormal behavior as *necessarily* "pararational," a romantic mystification unfit for serious political concern (see Watson's articles in SFS #5 and in the present issue).

4. Ursula K. Le Guin, "National Book Award Acceptance Speech," *Algol*, Nov 1973, p. 14.

5. Ursula K. Le Guin, "On Norman Spinrad's *The Iron Dream*," SFS 1(1973):43.

Douglas Barbour. Wholeness and Balance: An Addendum

The Dispossessed is not only an important addition to the small shelf of superior SF works, it is also a large and central piece in Ursula K. Le Guin's Hainish Universe mosaic. As I pointed out in "Wholeness and Balance in the Hainish Novels of Ursula K. Le Guin" (SFS 1:164-73), Ms. Le Guin uses a consistently paradoxical light/dark image pattern throughout the Hainish books plus a par-ticular image series in each novel to render the thematic concepts of wholeness and balance. In *The Dispossessed*, the most complex novel she has yet written, her continuing philosophical commitment to the theme of wholeness and balance is revealed once more in her imagery. Indeed, the concept of balance enters the very structure of the novel, as chapters are balanced between Urras and Anarres, with the first and last chapters linking the two worlds.

In a brief note I cannot hope to do more than point out that the paradoxical light/dark imagery is mixed in with a number of complementary local image systems. It would require a long article to explore the inter-relatedness of these image systems, and the complex philosophical and political explorations they invoke. Indeed, the number of local images and the ways in which they reinforce each other and the total conception of the novel is one sign of the novel's complexity. For example, much is made of Shevek's "light" eyes and

Takver's "dark" voice and eyes. Together, they are the yin/yang circle Ai points out to Estraven (LHD §19), the whole neither is separately. Thus even the sexual-love theme of this novel contributes to Le Guin's larger artistic statement.

One major local image—a brilliantly ambiguous one—is the wall, introduced on the first page of the novel. It is connected to the image/idea of the prison throughout; time after time the question of who is being locked out or in, which side of the wall one is on, is the focus of the narrative.

Perhaps it is wrong to call it an image series, but Shevek's obsession with number—which he images in his own mind—reflects his search for a balanced pattern (§2). This motif includes his passionate involvement with music (§6), and is connected to his search for a "General Temporal Theory." The concept of Time which this book presents, often in a charged imagistic manner, is the other major thematic presentation of balance, wholeness, the paradoxical reconciliation of the opposites of Sequence and Simultaneity (§3). This motif is often tied into the light/dark imagery which connects this novel to the whole Hainish series. Moreover, when Shevek finally arrives at the General Temporal Theory, the moment is presented in terms which recall the *Tao*: "There would be no trouble at all in going on. Indeed he has already gone on. He was there" (§9). Is he not on the Way?

The Dispossessed is politically more complex and mature than Ms Le Guin's earlier novels; its characterization is also, on the whole, denser than before. The use of particular image systems to render the single concept of wholeness and balance is but one thread of a carefully woven tapestry. Other image systems, such as the wrapping-paper/ornamentation one, contribute to other themes in the novel. Nevertheless, it is possible to state that Ursula K. Le Guin, while extending her art in all directions in *The Dispossessed*, has continued to explore the metaphysical paradoxes which light and dark have represented in her work from the beginning.

Judah Bierman. Ambiguity in Utopia: *The Dispossessed*

Ursula K. Le Guin's utopian tale *The Dispossessed* (TD) does not merely propose another blueprint for an anarchist commune in the SF skies—an escape from sour democracies or immanent fascist tyrannies on Earth, and so from all responsibility. Subtitled *An Ambiguous Utopia*, this spiritual autobiography and utopian quest of the brilliant physicist Shevek explores some dilemmas in the idea of an anarchist-socialist utopia. Further, like Plato and More, Le Guin also measures how the utopian vision presses a special responsibility and an alienation on the "knower." I propose to consider two senses in which the TD world of Anarres may be read: first, that the place is only ambiguously good, and second, that ambiguity is implicit in its organizing principle, that the dominant life style is not permanently set but permits, indeed demands, personal choices to meet inevitable social and environmental changes. Though obviously linked with Le Guin's earlier SF and wizard stories, TD is a moral allegory that should be read with other contemporary utopian tales. It is a prizeworthy contribution to the debate about the responsibility of knowledge, of the visionary and of the scientist, in a planned society.

Any working definition of utopia, beyond "imaginary, ideal place," begins with such criteria as physical isolation, political community, social beneficence, all generalizable characteristics that fit many particular formulae; but it must center on the modal fact that the institutions of that other country are always presented as obviously better, more desirable, than those of the author's own.

The improvement is seen to result from some special condition—lucky chance, an historical act, more usually the commitment to some organizing principle. In that obvious, non-ambiguous sense, Anarres, Shevek's Moon colony home, the country of the dispossessed, is a utopia. Anarres, the place beyond or without things (res), is the anarchist Moon colony founded some 200 years before the action begins by the followers of Odo. The inhabitants are all Odonians; none other may enter. It is her writings that provide the gospel principles for their practices. These include, most notably, on the personal level, an individual freedom based on absolute noncoercion, and on the social level, a non-profit, need-use economy. The people like it and believe it to be the best. Thus Anarres meets all the criteria for a traditional utopia. What is involved, then, in calling Anarres "an ambiguous utopia"?

What strikes the visitor to Anarres is not the familiar institutions but the setting. On Anarres the scene, continually discussed, continually described and referred to, determines the act. For this utopia is built on scarcity, almost deprivation. A moral choice for communion created and still sustains this holier community, but brute necessity enforces much of the functioning of the institutions. It is a necessity based on a desert landscape; nowhere in the geography of utopia is there an island apparently so fundamentally inhospitable to human flourishing. Thus, in simplest terms, Le Guin's allegory says that the more ideal place, contrary to the whole utopian record and all man's paradises, need not and should not be built on plenty. Perhaps she would not argue that scarcity is a sufficient or even a necessary condition. But to call a land without green leaf a utopia is surely to cast ambiguity over the term, over the whole idea. It is an ambiguity that, like all others, carries its own creative impulse. It forces the reader beyond the "soft primitivist" and other fantasy images to weigh the meaning of plenty.

The absence of plenty is reflected in one central detail worth special mention in a utopian fiction. The biography of Shevek takes him from birth through his childhood, parental conditioning, adolescent learning—all skillfully preparing us for the solitary bargainer who will try to convert the universe with the lever of his knowledge. The first critical hurdle in the quest comes in Shevek's formal training as a physicist: genius soon outgrows the limited facilities of this impoverished country. There is more here than an obvious plea for a world community of science to replace the super-patriotic, nationalistic institutes. It may be possible to contend that a beneficent social order does not require a beneficent natural scene. But the special case of Shevek makes clear that the nurture of genius—scientific progress—requires the materials and opportunity for intercourse that come only from a supported community of science, from the leisure of plenty. There is a very real ambiguity in calling a place where genius cannot flourish an utopia. It is an ambiguity that utopists have kept hidden till now. Utopias make good citizens, good soldiers, but when have they shown us flourishing geniuses other than founders?

Anarres may be considered an ambiguous utopia, then, because it shows us so many traditionally good institutions in a setting that imposes an absence of goods—traditional means to fulfillment. In his synoptic definitional survey, Darko Suvin pleads for the beginning of understanding that utopia is a verbal artefact: "Utopia is the verbal construction of a particular quasi-human community where sociopolitical institutions, norms, and individual relationships are organized according to a more perfect principle than in the author's community, this construction being based on estrangement arising out of an alternative historical hypothesis" (see his "Defining the Literary Genre of Utopia," *Studies in the Literary Imagination*, 6,ii[1973]:132). We have seen some ways in which the ideal community in TD meets the criteria of this useful definition, if ambiguously.

Structurally, most utopian tales contain a dialogue of criticism and a discourse of showing—the two parts are separated only in the two books of More's *Utopia*. More's specific criticisms of the penal institutions of England and his more general indictment of the capitalist and war-mongering society is a good example of utopian dialogue; Bacon's catalogue of scientific machines and activities in the second half of *New Atlantis* is a crude example of discourse: a kind of tour director's slide-show—"We have this, and we have this, and we have this." Calling TD "an ambiguous utopia" involves, minimally, a combination of dialogue and discourse that, in addition to discussing the defects and evil of contemporary society and showing the goodness of an alternative possibility, forces the reader to balance those present evils and possible alternative goods in a way that emphasizes the imperfect, tenuous balance. Le Guin has done at least that. If utopias are allegories of human vocation, the vehicles are more ideal social structures and the tenor is, always, a life in which the work and the play are the vocations to which humans should be called. Shevek's story embodies with formulaic clarity the central ambiguity necessary for all such fictions—a man whose soul rhythm does not vibrate quite synchronously with that of the ideal social structure, however convinced he is that the organizing principle of the society is the best. If a utopia is the tale one tells when one wishes to describe a more ideal place, then Le Guin has made the willingness to live in ambiguity, with continuing change and choice, both the existential condition of the place and the structural principle of the tale. It is one measure of the greatness of this utopian fiction that through her treatment of time and change, Le Guin establishes continuing choice as the human condition, burden and joy. Past, present and future may be distinguishable, but not separable. That instantaneous clear moment of unambiguous choice is only a necessary illusion; it is called the ansible.

The ansible in Le Guin's stories is the correlative for immediately felt, simultaneously held knowledge, the goal of communication—to feel and think together across the spaces and times that separate humans. Everywhere the sententiae that are her style prepare us for the brilliant insight to the utopian quest, so simply stated: Means are the ends men seek.

Ambiguity, in this essay, as in the sub-title, is not intended as a euphemism for legitimated confusion. Le Guin is rarely a simple, straightforward storyteller. TD is a complex utopian tale in which she violates the "unities." It opens with the quest journey, Shevek's mission to Urras. Shevek is born in Chapter two, on Anarres. Chapter Three goes back to the mission, Chapter Four to his biography, and so on. The book closes with Shevek returning to Anarres, with a visitor, Ketho the Hainishman, about to start anew. The structure of alternating chapters is more than a device to emphasize the continuity by which past and future are part of present. It is the mode for two journeys, combining romance and satire, quest and rejection. First, Shevek's spiritual biography on Anarres brings him through his own struggles to explore the anarchist paradise and to learn about the limitations of the dream in practice. At the moment of his crisis, Shevek meditates on his possible role in that society. "A healthy society" would let him exercise his "cellular function," "his individuality, the work he could do best" (§10). A good society finds its strengths and justification in the coordination of such diverse functions. If the Odonian society did not quite measure to that ideal, that only increased his responsibility:

With the myth of the State out of the way, the real mutuality and reciprocity of society and individual became clear. Sacrifice might be demanded of the individual, but never compromise: for though only the society could give security and stability, only the individual, the person had the power of moral choice—the power of change, the essential function of life. The Odonian society was conceived as a permanent revolution, and revolution begins in the thinking mind. (§10)

Life is not, therefore, merely a continuing search for pleasure, which always had an end, but outside that closed cycle "is the landscape of time. in which the spirit may, with luck and courage, construct the fragile, makeshift, improbable roads and cities of fidelity: a landscape inhabitable by human beings" (§10). One can often measure a utopian society by its dominant institution or norm. On Anarres the anarchist "syndicate" is the institution of the permanent revolution, given the individual's power of moral choice. But it is the syndicate of initiative that is the paradigm—it moves the action of this fiction. It is the structure of the choice-making that is the tale.

In the second journey—the alternate chapters on Urras—Shevek takes his quest out into the world. This part criticizes the evils of the capitalist, profit society. What is important for us here is how Le Guin forces Shevek to confront the balancing of good and evil. At this crisis in the quasi-drama, Shevek confronts the alternative side. When he calls Urras Hell, Keng, the Terran ambassador who has offered him asylum, responds by comparing Urras to the destroyed Earth:

"To me, and to all my fellow Terrans who have seen the planet, Urras is the kindliest, more various, most beautiful of all the inhabited worlds. It is the world that comes as close as any could to Paradise....

"I know it is full of evils, full of human injustice, greed, folly, waste. But it is also full of good, of beauty, vitality, achievement. It is what a world should be! It is *alive*, tremendously alive—alive, despite all its evils, with hope....

"My world, my Earth, is a ruin. A planet spoiled by the human species. We multiplied and gobbled and fought until there was nothing left, and then we died. We controlled neither appetite nor violence; we did not adapt. We destroyed ourselves. But we destroyed the world first. There are no forests left on my Earth.... This is a living world, a harmony. Mine is a discord. You Odonians chose a desert; we Terrans made a desert." (§11)

The burden of Keng's presentation is the lost opportunity—how humans forfeited their chance for such a society as that of Anarres. It is, of course, part of the allegorical warning. My immediate concern, however, is with Shevek—who is about to offer his simulsequentialist formulae which make possible the ansible, about to make the moral choice of giving his knowledge to humanity, not to his own society alone nor to the capitalist Urras, for peace, not war—and with his answer:

You don't understand what time is, he said. You say the past is gone, the future is not real, there is no change, no hope. You think Anarres is a future that cannot be reached, as your past cannot be changed. So there is nothing but the present, this Urras, the rich, real, stable present, the moment now. And you think that is something which can be possessed! But it is not real, you know. It is not stable, not solid—nothing is. Things change, change. You cannot have anything.... And least of all can you have the present, unless you accept with it the past and the future.... You will not achieve or even understand Urras unless you accept the reality, the enduring reality of Anarres. (§11)

And so out of his own balancing, he comes to the realization that his people were right and he is wrong. "We cannot come to you. You will not let us. You do not believe in change, in chance, in evolution. You would destroy us rather than admit our reality, rather than admit that there is hope! We cannot come to you. We can only wait for you to come to us" (§11). The immediate tenor of this allegory is surely that cleavage in our society which for some leaves only pleasure and the sight of the hopeless end, and for others the hope of a yet-to-be new beginning. But I feel this fiction embodies the ambiguity, the terror and the hope which we felt, if we had the strength, in Yeats' "The Second Coming."

I have tried to suggest here two ways Le Guin weds ambiguity and utopian speculation. They come together in her greatest insight, the knowledge and creed, the living principle of all Odonians: the means are and must be the ends. And is it not clear, Adeimantus, that once we have glimpsed that idea we can no longer, like aliens to each other, divide the world into mine and thine, or into knowledge and power? For Odonians, becoming is their being. You can go home again, but only if you know that home is where you have not yet been. The simulsequentialist physics and the ansible are—like the deprived landscape—fictional devices, part of the estrangement-setting that makes the ambiguity a life-force.

The greatest of her SF, TD is certainly no sport among Ursula Le Guin's creations. It is signed with the same moral sententiae, filled with the same compelling allegorical landscapes, uses the same estrangement setting. The common scene suggests a possible continuing purpose. Indeed, if we look back from TD to *Rocannon's World*, it seems clear that Le Guin is building her own space universe, exploring the crises of her times, preaching the spiritual evolution which alone can save us, as she constructs the history of that universe. Men are moral agents in Le Guin's universe, whether they realize it or not: their actions have consequences. Personal actions create the structure of moral possibility, they matter. Surely the importance of personal actions seem closer to the center in TD than in any of Le Guin's previous SF. What is involved in regarding TD as a *terminus ad quem*? Is the progression from Rocannon through Genly Ai and Ged to Shevek as real as it seems obvious?

Rocannon's task is to right a wrong, a misuse of knowledge that threatens a world. He is a scientist-spectator moved to action. As the current cover blurb puts it, "Rallying the primitive natives around him, Rocannon sets out to prove that technology was no match for courage and love of freedom." Evil is defined as superior technology without stronger moral purpose, as in our own world. Rocannon's problems are those of the sensitive observer of any imperialistic colonization, But however strongly he moves to redress the balance, Rocannon has no vision of positive alternative possibility—only nostalgic faint hope. He is, in terms of the crucial estrangement-setting, an alien who dies in exile, hero of the good fight.

The Left Hand of Darkness shares with *Rocannon's World* the excitement of human consciousness facing the dangers of a threatening environment. Beyond that, it shares also the emotional involvement of seeing human, social conflicts replicated in a strange environment. The importance of the terrifying geography may be lost in a book so filled with intrigue and exciting action. For example, if the context were utopian speculation one would expect that the kemmer phenomenon would have a significant effect on social relations. An androgynous society should be one free of "organized social aggression," especially war. The world of Winter-Gethen is free of war as we know it, but not necessarily for that reason:

Did the Ancient Hainish postulate that continuous sexual capacity and organized social aggression, neither of which are attributes of any mammal but man, are cause and effect? ...[The absence of war] may turn out to have nothing to do with their androgyne psychology.... The weather of Winter is so relentless, so near the limit of tolerability...that perhaps they use up their fighting spirit fighting the cold.... And in the end, the dominant factor in Gethenian life is not sex or any other human thing; it is their environment, their cold world. Here man has a crueler enemy than himself. (§7)

I draw attention to that small, almost hidden note, out of all the social and moral speculation in a complex book, because the physical environment becomes the critical factor in TD. One other note related to Le Guin's developing universe and reappearing in TD seems worth mention. Near the end of their terrifying and absorbing journey across the ice, Estraven wants to know, finally, why the Ekumen sent Ai alone, why the task of conversion is made so difficult. Genly Ai explains:

Alone I cannot change your world. But I can be changed by it. Alone, I must listen, as well as speak. Alone, the relationship I finally make, if I make one, is not impersonal and not only political. Not We and They, not I and It; but I and Thou. Not political, not pragmatic, but mystical. In a certain sense the Ekumen is not a body politic, but a body mystic. It considers beginnings to be extremely important. Beginnings and means. Its doctrine is just the reverse of the doctrine that the end justifies the means.... (§18)

This is the philosophy that makes Shevek run.

Yet like Rocannon, Genly Ai is essentially an outsider. He may be more knowingly involved in the making of a better world, but the story does not offer a compelling vision of a more desirable alternative possibility. Of course it need not. Nor are utopian fictions necessarily better than science fictions. But a moral allegorist must have a character who chooses and whose choices are central to the tale even if not necessarily decisive for the world. A spectator, a visitor, is not enough.

Moral choice does fill the center of the so-called "children's fantasy" world of Earthsea. That is also an estrangement-setting, and the working out of its moral allegory could well be seen as the proving ground in the development that brought Le Guin to Shevek, Urras, and Anarres. Seen in that limited and perhaps falsely colored light, Ged's spiritual quests are designed to teach the obligation of knowledge—Roke's magic is but science with another name—to power. He must learn to govern himself, to know the limits of application of his secret power, lest his learning remain still-born and he never come to exercise his art. And second, he must make the contribution he can—as Archmage or other—to preserve the social fabric, to close the hole in the wall of the world. In writing the Earthsea Trilogy, perhaps the most perfectly finished of all her works, Le Guin learned to focus the ponderables of moral choices in the acts of individuals who are at the center, not merely observers, of other social worlds in which the estrangement-setting provides the frame for moral allegory.

What distinguishes Shevek from the protagonists in her earlier stories is not his humanity, nor simply that he is an actor in his own environment rather than an observer with political intentions. What distinguishes him finally is the world he lives in. On Anarres we have no division of human capacities among differing species or even among contending nations. The qualities of men on Anarres and on Urras are much the same, in spite of the differing customs and costumes. But the means of expression and fulfillment are different, the social forms are different, political institutions are different. Shevek is the product of and embodies the principles of his utopian environment.

The acts of some men on Anarres are power-corrupted, even the acts of men of science. Yet, though power corrupts even in an anarchist society, though the same crippling conflicts arise in its incipient bureaucracy, still the acts themselves are part of the utopian truth of community. It is a community no longer so pure as in the founders' dreams. But Anarres is that special place where work is *not for something* in exchange, but a human vocation, the social task. Its slogan "to be whole is to be part," may seem no better than the slogan of Zamyatin's fascist United State in *We* "Nobody is one but one of."

But we can glimpse part of the difference if we rephrase Plato's original utopian question, "What is the best form of organization for a community and how can a person best arrange his life?" to read "What is the ideal social form for releasing human energy and capacity?" Is it not one which involves each person in the making of his own destiny—where the means are the end he seeks, and where the destiny is to find his place among other men and women?

Finally, it is Le Guin's fictional centering on the burden of moral choice that merits the judgement that in TD she "raises science fiction to major humanistic literature," as the quote on the cover-jacket says. Utopian fiction shares the estrangement-setting, its powers and limitations, with science fiction. But their real closeness, generic and sociological, is best seen in the common central theme, the social obligations of the "scientist"—him whose knowledge brings opportunities and dangers. Knowledge has a gift and a moral obligation to power, ambiguous but real, perhaps essential to its survival.

One must go back to Herbert Read's *The Green Child* or to Hermann Hesse's *The Glass Bead Game* to find a fiction that so vitally embodies the central paradox of utopian speculation. For "What is the ideal form of the ordered society?" demands more than a simple utilitarian answer. The question also asks "How can the ordered society produce and support 'creative' individuals, beyond the leader?" and it asks, even more profoundly, "What is the relation between beneficent order, freedom and creativity?" Of the more recent popular fictions that set out for utopia or skirt its shores, *Walden Two* and *Island* are primarily part of the perennial science-as-progress frontier of utopian speculation, whereas *We, 1984* and their spawn are primarily the "power-corrupts" anchor for such speculation. These all reflect a proper concern for the meaning of the means, but none measures how the vision of order presses on the creative and concerned citizen. Whether TD revives the tradition, perhaps never dead, never dying, it does like other great utopian fictions transport us through a country of the mind we detour round only at life's and society's peril. "To be whole is to be part—true voyage is return." Shevek breathes with the hope that a utopian vision need not be alienating.

If these speculations have any validity it should be possible to predict where Le Guin's voyage will take her next. I am struck by her need, the inner logic of the universe she is constructing, to return soon to "first causes." In TD Ambassador Keng suggests what I feel is the next, or a soon to be treated, part of that world. It is the oft mentioned world of the Hainish.

We are here now, dealing as equals with other human societies on other worlds, only because of the charity of the Hainish. They came; they brought us help. They built ships and gave them to us, so we could leave our ruined world. They treat us gently, charitably, as the strong man treats the sick one. They are a very strange people, the Hainish, older than any of us, infinitely generous. They are altruists. They are moved by a guilt we don't even understand, despite all our crimes. They are moved in all they do, I think, by the past, their endless past. (§11)

I feel Le Guin must go back to explore that Hainish guilt and past, and I hope she does. If she does, the book will surely begin with a lyric evocation of the theme, as in TD:

There was a wall. It did not look important. It was built of uncut rocks roughly mortared. An adult could look right over it, and even a child could climb it. Where it crossed the roadway, instead of having a gate it degenerated into mere geometry, a line, an idea of boundary. But the idea was real. It was important. For seven generations there had been nothing in the world more important than that wall.

Like all walls it was ambiguous, two-faced. What was inside it and what was outside it depended upon which side of it you were on. (§1)

Donald F. Theall

The Art of Social-Science Fiction:
The Ambiguous Utopian Dialectics of Ursula K. Le Guin

1. The Outside Observer in Utopia. The 20th century has seen the growth of the social sciences and the "humane sciences" as one of its more important developments in speculative thought, a fact increasingly reflected in the concepts of writers of SF, including utopian fiction. Although concern with social and cultural questions has always been a central feature of the utopian tradition within SF, a conscious use of concepts from the social sciences has been considerably slower to develop in SF than that of concepts from the natural sciences. In this development toward artistic self-consciousness the writings of Ursula K. Le Guin occupy a significant role; they are constantly concerned with questions of cultural interaction, cultural growth, communication, and the differences between fictional but always parabolic "highly intelligent life forms."

Le Guin's interest in humane sciences and cultural change appears to be linked to her concern with utopianism. Most of her imaginary societies are models critical of our present societies. Although her first major novel, *The Left Hand of Darkness* (LHD), did not, strictly speaking, provide a utopian model, both the nations of Karhide and Orgoreyn are meant as criticisms of the present social and cultural order: the former by contraries, in terms of its anarchistic directions, and the latter directly, in terms of its bureaucratization. Further, the broader background of the interplanetary organization of the Ekumen is an "ideal" model with implicit criticisms of contemporary intercommunication between nations. Thus, following the utopian tradition, Le Guin provides a tension between the here-and-now and her various fictional futures. But her fictional future worlds also differ sharply from each other, allowing her to further investigate the potential of various social and cultural developments. Such juxtapositions of fictional societies are a feature of all of her Hainish novels; her only non-Hainish SF novel, *The Lathe of Heaven*, is a psychological study of dreams which materialize, providing a variety of modes of life within the same culture. In her most recent novel, *The Dispossessed: An Ambiguous Utopia* (TD), Le Guin overtly juxtaposes the capitalist aggressive and competitive nations on the world of Urras and the anarchist satellite world of Anarres. These two worlds are juxtaposed within the broader framework of an interstellar community of planets containing a possible future world of Earth (Terra), and using the Terran ambassador as a choral commentator on the concluding action of the novel. This counterpoints the entire action of the novel with the here and now, so that Anarres and Urras assume a variety of complex relationships with societies of the present.

Such a strategy of utopian fiction begins with More's juxtaposition of Books I and II in *Utopia* as well as his counterpointing of Utopia as a whole with events in his own historical time. It continues through Swift, who developed it with greater compositional complexity (though not necessarily greater conceptual complexity) in *Gulliver's Travels*. This strategy involves a dialectical logic and an implicit critique of society as well as providing critical rather than futurological models of possible alternative ways of life. In order to achieve this end, Le Guin seems to have quite consciously developed some aspects of this utopian tradition (down to Thoreau and Morris), and in particular the role of the stranger visiting a new world. The actual sensory experience and subjective response of strangers or outsiders plays a central role in validating the carefully chosen and believable details which compose the thorough accounts Le Guin gives us of her fictional worlds. In *Rocannon's World* the hero is a museumologist who comes to the planet as a cultural investigator; in *Planet of Exile* both Jakob and Rolery are outsiders who cease to be total strangers in each other's culture; in *City of Illusions* the outsider is a total stranger to the world and unaware, for most of the novel, of his own identity. In each case the separateness of the outsider makes him an observer as well as a participant, and allows for the particularly descriptive approach. In LHD, interestingly enough, the stranger—who is also the main narrator—is a professional cultural analyst and cultural communicator, whose concern with a thorough account of the culture provides the novel with the characteristic features of an anthropological report. Yet even in this respect Le Guin employs the techniques of ambivalence, for her field-worker, her "mobile" from the Ekumen to the Gethenians, realizes that the "truth" of the humane sciences is founded in imagination as well as fact:

I'll make my report as if I told a story, for I was taught as a child on my homeworld that Truth is a matter of imagination. The soundest fact may fail or prevail in the style of its telling; like that singular organic jewel of our seas, which grows brighter as one woman wears it, and worn by another, dulls and goes to dust. (LHD §1)

Le Guin weaves into the utopian social-science-fiction the vigorous story-telling techniques used in adventure fantasy. This respect for an imaginative approach means among other things that Genly Ai's subjective emotions become part of his account, permitting others to judge it in the light of his subjective bias. In the telling, the subjective reactions of Ai (the name obviously involves a complex pun on "I," "eye," etc.) are illustrated: reactions to the coldness of the climate, to the sexual problems posed by a world where everyone is a neuter except during periods of *kemmer* when they can become either male or female, to the political anarchy created by a world where there are no worlds and the entire planet is, like Karhide, "a family quarrel" (LHD §1). Le Guin consequently can use Ai as an ambivalent focus, in the same way that Hythloday or Gulliver are used: Ai himself reveals some of the naivete which complicates the action of the novel and impedes the success of his mission. The subjective mode of telling is extended in TD to a technique where the third-person narrative reappears, but always with a sense that the action is being seen through the eyes and the feelings of Shevek. Like Ai, Shevek becomes an ambivalent narrator, although like Ai he grows in the process so that his insights by the end of the novel are more perceptive than those at the beginning. Even though Shevek is not the "professional" which Ai is, the work itself develops the fictional societies on Urras and Anarres with the same detail and thoroughness as was done in LHD. That is, we learn about the details of physical geography, sexual customs, cultural evolution, ideology, life-style, and the like on the two worlds. The relating of Shevek's learning process, while it includes a fairly thorough anthropoligical description of the societies in question, involves equally an account of the emotions of Shevek as he explains his experiences.

That Le Guin's overall conception is utopian is apparent in the history and nature of the Ekumen. In our world, where there has been a constant need and desire for a world federation of nations, Le Guin's Ekumen—the most utopian concept of LHD—acts as a critique of the everyday strivings in this direction. However, she manages to preserve a dialectical tension which also provides internal criticism of the Ekumen itself. The critique of the Ekumen that is part of the action of LHD is part of that idea itself, because the way in which the Ekumen encounters new worlds is to open up a communication or trade of idea in which processes of mutual change take place—just as the First Mobile, Ai, is changed through his contact with Estraven and with the Foretellers as the action unfolds. Thus, Le Guin has a very complex and sophisticated dialectical conception of utopia: the observing outsider is a visual and emotional "eye" that negates its "outside" character by the very process of observing. The tradition of Hythloday and Gulliver is reconstructed in a period highly self-conscious of the humane sciences. Therefore, Le Guin's works and the observers themselves show a high consciousness of these sciences.

2. Le Guin and the Humane Sciences: Communication, Education, and Social Critique.

To establish the degree of Le Guin's awareness of the humane sciences it is necessary to explore some of her main themes. These involve among other things: communications, intercultural interaction, social structure, role-playing, ideologies. The prime theme of her major novels and, in fact, the unifying theme of her Hainish novels, is *communication*, particularly communication between different kinds of highly intelligent life forms ("hilfs"). In many ways LHD provides a basic pattern for these concerns. Therefore, let us consider here the focus of communication in its action. First of all, Ai's particular mission, which gives rise to the action of the novel, is an attempt on the part of the association of planets, known as the Ekumen, to open communication with new areas where there are intelligent life forms. In performing his function, Ai is fully aware of the difficulties involved in the process of intercultural contact and the need for caution and prudence in the pursuit of intercultural exchange of knowledge. As he points out, the Ekumen send only one envoy (First Mobile) on the first contact with any new planet:

The first voice, one man present in the flesh, present and alone. He may be killed...or locked up with madmen...yet the practice is kept, because it works. One voice speaking truth is a greater force than fleets and armies, given time; plenty of time; but time is the thing that the Ekumen has plenty of.... (LHD §3)

He is preceded by a team of undercover investigators, some of whose reports are cited during the telling of his story; forty years after they leave, the First Mobile comes. He leaves his ship in space so that it is not observed, and comes only with his interstellar communication device (the ansible) and some pictures of his homeworld, so as not to intrude alien artifacts prematurely into the culture. The Stability of Ekumen has established a carefully rationalized method of inter-culture contact and communication. Exploring the deepest meaning of such communication becomes one of the central concerns of the novel.

The most relevant differences between Gethen and Ai's homeworld are the facts that each person can assume the role of either sex in sexual and parental relations, and that Gethen itself is at the very limit of coldness inhabitable by intelligent life. These facts pose two major problems for Ai, and provide the novel with some of its major metaphors. The communication between Ai and the hero of the action, Estraven—who saves Ai's life and opens Gethen up to the Ekumen—only comes about through a long and difficult process of understanding. Early on in his account, Ai suggests that sex or "biological shock" is perhaps the chief problem, in a world where he can say of the person he rents his quarters from: "He was so feminine in looks and manner that I once asked how many children he had. He looked glum. He had never borne any. He had, however, sired four" (HD §5). Eventually, after a long period of isolated companionship while fleeing across a great glacier, Ai comes to recognize how gender had been an impediment to communication with Estraven and how, sharing a constant threat of death, he has learned to overcome this and love Estraven. Speaking of his new awareness of Estraven gained while crossing the glacier, Ai says:

And I saw then again, and for good, what I had always been afraid to see, and had pretended not to see in him: that he was a woman as well as a man. Any need to explain the sources of that fear vanished with the fear; what I was left with was, at last, acceptance of him as he was. Until then I had rejected him, refused him his own reality.... I had not been willing to give my trust, my friendship, to a man who was a woman, a woman who was a man. (LHD §18)

The unrecognized biological shock has been an impediment to human communication; but once recognized, it provides Ai with a whole new relationship to the culture with which he must work. A symbolic support for the episode is provided by its setting on the glacier. The glacier is a world somewhat like Poe's world in the closing of *The Narrative of A. Gordon Pym*, for it is a world of which Estraven says, "There is nothing, the Ice says, but Ice" (LHD §16). The quality of whiteness on this ice world is reminiscent of the one in the writings of Poe and Melville, who would appear to be part of an American tradition of writing to which Le Guin's work is related.[1]

The incident on the ice illustrates Ai's coming to master the genuine art of communication with a Gethenian as a fellow human being, achieving mutual trust and understanding. This justifies the Ekumen's sending a single Mobile to first encounter a new society, as a means of having him learn to establish genuine relations with its inhabitants. Again and again Ai's perceptions, which shift from naivete to understanding as his account unfolds, focus on means of communicating with the society and of understanding the way of education and communication within the society itself. His investigation of the quasi-religious phenomenon of "foretelling," which is so central to Gethenian society, is just such a process, for he comes to realize that the Foretellers are using their understanding of the world in a peculiarly paradoxical way as a means of educating their fellow-Karhidians. The purpose of Foretelling is ultimately not to provide answers but to demonstrate that there is only one question that can be answered—"That we shall die." Therefore, as Faxe says, the basis of Foretelling is "The unknown,...the unforetold, the unproven, that is what life is based on. Ignorance is the ground of thought. Unproof is the ground of action" (LHD §5). Foretelling within the social structure of Karhide is a basic education in the values of the society. The Foretellers really teach that change cannot be brought about through the reading of prophecies or predictions; that uncertainty is of the essence of the social fabric. The process of Foretelling is a social dramatization of this fact, in that it provides correct answers which are not necessarily (in fact, not usually) helpful answers since they do not cover enough of the future contingencies.

The Ekumen has produced its own form of wisdom for learning the wisdom of others as well as communicating whatever wisdom it may also contain. As Ai attempts to tell the Commensals of Orgoreyn (the bureaucratic collectivist society of Tethen):

the Ekumen is not essentially a government at all. It is an attempt to reunify the mystical with the political, and as such is of course mostly a failure; but its failure has done more good for humanity so far than the successes of its predecessors. It is a society and it has, at least potentially, a culture. It is a form of education; in one aspect it's a sort of very large school—very large indeed. The motives of communication and cooperation are of its essence.... (LHD §10)

The Ekumen as an instrument of education is an instrument of communication, a way towards interplanetary wisdom. Such an approach, however—as Ai realizes and stresses—is essentially a dualistic approach, a fact dramatized in the structures that Le Guin chooses to create in her tales. In a section of Estraven's journal, the following exchange is recounted:

Ai brooded, and after some time he said, "You're isolated, and undivided. Perhaps you are as obsessed with wholeness as we are with dualism."

"We are dualists too. Duality is an essential, isn't it? So long as there is *myself* and *the other*."

"I and Thou," he said. "Yes, it does, after all, go even wider than sex...." (LHD §16)

This duality of "myself and the other" or "I and Thou" is naturally at heart of human communication, but it is also a duality which generates all of the other dualities in the processes of cognition and understanding. Such a sense of duality is common to all of Le Guin's writings, culminating in the duality of the opposed worlds of TD.

The very structure of her works is determined by this theme, for it is a structure of dualities—in LHD, of Gethen and the Ekumen, of Karhide and Orgoreyn, of Ai and Estraven. From the bringing together of the dualities and from the understanding that is generated by coming to terms with each of them, the process of discovery by which the meaning of the Ekumen is encompassed comes about. The process is dialectical and complexly critical, for each of the dual ingredients which will end up in creating a wholeness modifies and is modified by the other. Orgoreyn's bureaucracy displays both its greater rationality and its greater tendency towards totalitarianism when viewed against the anarchy and decentralized government of Karhide; Orgoreyn and Karhide show their provincialism in contrast to the Ekumen, but also some of the wisdom gained in having to come to terms more slowly—e.g. without an Industrial Revolution—on the world of Gethen. Finally, because of Le Guin's social-science consciousness, the presence of the contemporary world is to be found in the critical conceptions of LHD. The "simplicity" of Karhide becomes one mode of criticizing many contemporary phenomena; the centralization of Orgoreyn, another. Orgoreyn's prison camps, secret police forces, interminable politics, and incredible bureaucracy are modes of satirizing similar phenomena in our own culture. Karhide's Foretellers with their stress on ignorance become one mode of critical parable directed against the futurologists and the planners. All of Karhide with its different sexual arrangements and the relative peace which is maintained through them becomes a mode of critique of the over-use of sexual stimuli (see particularly §7 of LHD).

Le Guin, speaking of LHD, has suggested that she does use her novels to explore situations which have their parallel in the real world.[2] She designed the world of Gethen in part to explore the male-female problem in a context where it would be possible to examine the thoughts and feelings of individuals who could be both men and women. But LHD goes further, involving a large number of social and human issues, as all her novels do. They are utopian in the specific sense of creating some relative perfection as a contrast with the world of the reader.

3. Ambiguous Utopianism: Le Guin's Dialectics of Socialist Democratic Humanism. For this reason, it is not surprising that Le Guin's most recent, major novel, TD, was subtitled "An Ambiguous Utopia." The subtitle calls attention to ambivalence as an overt aspect of much of her work. In LHD, the nations of Gethen, in the act of intercultural contact with the Ekumen, also give rise to ambivalence; for example, many of the customs of Karhide, as Ai notes, have much to suggest by way of improvement to a Terran member of the Ekumen. But further, Le Guin uses the essential ambivalence of the utopian tradition. Beginning with More, many possible alternative fictional worlds were conceived as ambivalent, founded in the paradoxes generated by the juxtaposition of fictional models and real worlds. The fondness for paranomasia (puns) in More and Swift reflects this complex ambivalence by which they seduce the uncritical rationalist into double binds. An example which parallels Le Guin's treatment of Anarres occurs when "More" (the fictional character in *Utopia* who has listened to Hythloday's account, including the part about the use of gold and ornament in Utopia—an account paralleling the incident of the necklace in TD §10) remarks on the many values of Utopia but notes that among other qualities the virtue of magnificence—the ethical art of doing and making things well and in the grand manner—is absent from the commonweal. In the context of the narrative, More's (the author's) other works, and the values More saw in the play impulse, this creates precisely such an ambiguous tension; for the necessary critique which the Utopians have performed by suppressing such magnificence will eventually become a problem for them as their society evolves. Part of the tension of More's *Utopia* arises through a double historical vision: Hythloday's awareness—e.g. of the potential for change his own coming to Utopia represents—is more limited than that of "More" (the character) and, of course, More the author. Hythloday's Platonic Utopia is a static concept, though his intrusion into its society—like Ai's intrusion into Gethen—creates a process of historical change. The very nature of the collision between the processes of history and of utopianizing creates an ambiguity, which so many critics attempt to resolve in utopian novels in order to have a definite outcome.

Le Guin, though, is too aware of the tension in the tradition and the fact that it arises out of the process of estrangement which is bound to occur in intercultural communication; the Ekumen as a utopian conception is—as I argued in section 1—one way of taking this into account. The action of TD, therefore, begins before the utopian Ekumen has come into being, so that it explores the problem of utopia within a Pre-Ekumenian, relatively pre-utopian framework, so to speak. The parameters within which it does this, though, are the same parameters of "social-science fiction" which mark all of Le Guin's other SF novels.

In TD, therefore—as in LHD—communication is a central theme and motivation for producing the action of the novel. Intercultural contact again plays a major role and—though not as central to the novel as Ai—a Terran plays the role of chorus at its conclusion when Shevek is given sanctuary in the Terran embassy to Urras. The action of TD rises out of its central character's, Shevek's, growing realization that the presumably anarchistic utopian world of Anarres is seriously flawed in many ways, especially in terms of the freedom of communication in ideas. Metaphorically, the world of Anarres as a whole looms more and more like a prison (of which there are none on Anarres)—a metaphor the understanding of which goes back to a childhood experience of Shevek's when he and some of his schoolmates tried to recreate what prison was like on a world that does not have any. The metaphor of prison becomes even more closely linked to inhibition of communication when related to the dominant symbol of the novel—walls. The novel opens with a reference to walls:

There was a wall. It did not look important. It was built of uncut rocks roughly mortared. An adult could look right over it, and even a child could climb it. Where it crossed the roadway instead of having a gate it degenerated into mere geometry, a line, an idea of a boundary. But the idea was real. It was important. For seven generations there had been nothing in the world more important than the wall.

Like all walls it was ambiguous, two-faced. What was inside it and what was outside it depended on which side of it you were on. (TD §1)

The wall could be seen either as enclosing the universe and "leaving Anarres, outside, free" or it could be seen an enclosing Anarres and making it a "great prison camp, cut off from other worlds and other man, in quarantine" (TD §1).

One dimension of Anarres as an ambiguous utopia—and one that it shares with More's Utopia—is the necessity of cutting itself off from other men and other history. It can maintain its utopian purity only as long as it does not communicate with those outside itself, so that it becomes a total institution. This also means that within the individual groups of "syndicates" that form the anarchistic society there is a substantial control of ideas, a fact Shevek suffers from since his theories of time cannot be developed as he wishes, yet "it is of the nature of an idea to be communicated: written, spoken, done. The idea is like grass. It craves light, like crowds, thrives on cross-breeding, grows better for being stepped on" (TD §3). As Shevek grows and develops, he becomes dedicated to the liberation of ideas and of the mind; before leaving for Urras, he establishes a printing syndicate on Anarres to communicate ideas which were being inhibited. He finally decides to leave Urras in order "to go fulfill my proper function as a social organism. I'm going to unbuild walls" (TD §10).

TD begins with Shevek leaving Anarres for Urras, and his earlier life is presented through a series of flashbacks juxtaposed with his current life on Urras, a technique which has obvious affinities with his own Theory of Time. This strategy creates a constant tension between the values of the two worlds and their varying impacts on Shevek. It is one of the clearest devices for demonstrating the weaknesses (and hence ambiguities) in Anarres by exposing it to the one type of scrutiny which it forbids itself from doing. The tension is neither simple nor solely paradoxical, for in Shevek's intensely critical perspective on injustice, poverty, commercialism and other aspects of Urras, and in his final return to Anarres, the novel is achieving a sophisticated re-shaping of the world of Anarres within Shevek's vision of what it might be or ought to be. During their meeting, when Keng, the Terran, provides him with sanctuary, she takes exception to Shevek's view that "Hell is Urras." In comparison to the (future) Earth, ecologically destroyed and inhabitable only by means of "total centralization...total rationing, birth control, euthanasia, universal conscription into the labour force...," Urras seems

the kindliest, most various, most beautiful of all the inhabited worlds. It is the world that came as close an any could to paradise. I know it's full of evils, full of human injustice, greed, folly, waste. But it is also full of good, of beauty, of vitality, achievement. It is what a world should be! It is *alive*, tremendously alive—alive despite all its evils, with hope. (TD §11)

This newly introduced perspective performs a function similar to the removing of Karhide and Orgoreyn from the perspective of Gethen to that of the universe, though it is, again, not the final word on Urras, merely a testimony to the hope it still contains.

This complexity of perspectives which Le Guin develops is a characteristic of her works as a whole. *Rocannon's World*, *Planet of Exile*, and *City of Illusions* all strive for similar conceptual complexities by involving life on worlds with a variety of different peoples inhabiting them and the intrusion of outsiders into these worlds; the tendency in each is towards some ambiguity or ambivalance. In each case, too, the presence of history (a fictional world history) is an important ingredient of the works as well as a constantly implied comparison with the present. But only in TD is this overtly linked with a fully articulated theory of time and history which is an intrinsic part of the novel, since it is because of inhibitions to developing and disseminating this theory that Shevek travels from Anarres to Urras and back.

The theory of time propounded by Shevek dialectically interrelates a theory of sequence with a theory of simultaneity. As his social education matures throughout the novel, he comes to apply his theory to social and ethical questions. This suggests to him that—while he left Anarres for Urras because Anarres attempted to sever its communications with history and its past, with those who still lived in it on Urras—Urras as well as the Terran ambassador sever themselves from the future which Anarres presents to them. While Shevek's return to Anarres clearly indicates his preference for his home-world, he returns as a more critical and aware person to await the time when finally the Terrans or the Urrasti will seek out Anarres, ready to understnad its values. There's no attempt in the fictional situation to eliminate the am-bivalences in Anarres, for they are there partly as a result of a total socio-political situation—the Odonian flight from Urras. On the other hand, the story—just as Shevek's theory of history—does not eliminate the possibility of change or hope. In fact, contingency, chance, change are the factors which make Shevek's dream possible. He can begin to develop his unified field theory because he has finally accepted the fact that "In the region of the unprovable, or even the disprovable, lay the only chance for breaking out of the circle and going ahead" (TD §9). This, too, he discovers in history, the history of his subject—physics. There he learns that the ancient Terran physicist, "Ainsetain," in his unwillingness to accept the indeterminacy principle (in a way similar to the principles of the Karhidians and their Foretellers), had created flaws and inadequacies in his theory, but that the theory is still "as beautiful, as valid, and as useful as ever, after these centuries, and yet both depended upon a hypothesis that could not be proved true and that could be and had been proved false in certain circumstances" (TD §9).

This, though, demonstrates a greater affinity between art and science; Shevek had discovered that through the fate of his friend Turin, whose imagi-nation could not be contained within the world of Anarres. Le Guin, here, as in her other works, attracts the reader with an ambiguous kind of anarchist or—more generally—subservice dialectic, which has strong roots in the every-day situations of human living and in a sense of history. As in Ai's account, imagination becomes central to the Truth of this critique. The world of con-temporary Marxism, the world of contemporary capitalism, the Third World, and the variety of contemporary attitudes towards these, play through each of her novels—including Lathe of Heaven which breaks the normal pattern of his-torically-oriented works to investigate one founded in the world where dreams create possible future histories. Her dialectic uses the utopian ideas of social science and Marx as a counterpoint to imaginative speculations at every level of her works, from composition and setting to ideas and character. In TD, for example, the characters form a world of oppositions through whose communi-cation the mutual education of all develops. Shevek is a physicist, his wife Takver a biologist. Her awareness provides the critique of physical science necessary to come to terms with humanity. Tirin, as the artist, poses the challenge of creativity and of imagination to Shevek; Bedap, the propagandist-philosopher, shows the value of social awareness and social communication. While all of these characters are linked by the bonds of love and friendship, they differ enough so that they can interact, teach and learn from each other. Tirin, for example, "could never build walls.... He was a natural rebel. He was a natural Odonian—a real one" (§9). Yet Tirin was not a "strong person." The value of Tirin in the story is that he brings Shevek to see the necessity of unbuilding walls.

Le Guin's treatment of character by means of contrast and opposition parallels her way of dealing with ideas and structures in terms of both balance and imbalance. While balance is obviously a central feature of her writing, she also takes the concept of ambivalence very seriously, stressing history as perpetually upsetting the balance and creating new tensions. Le Guin sees balance as a dynamic principle mediating between oppositions. Hence her preoccupation with the paradox of communication: in order to communicate, it is necessary to recognize differences and to move toward an understanding of these differences. The stress on uncertainty and the recognition of "flaws"— becomes explicit in Shevek's theory—create a sharpened reinterpretation of the Taoist concept of balance in *LHD*, where she had expressed it by way of paradoxical epigram, e.g.: "Darkness is in the mortal eye that thinks it sees and sees not" (LHD §12). Le Guin is in some ways similar to a socialist humanist such as the Polish philosopher Leszek Kolakowski, who in the essay "In Praise of Inconsistency" pointed out that an acceptance of contradiction did not automatically result in a simple balance based on a reconciliation of opposites:

Inconsistency is simply a refusal once and for all to choose beforehand between any values whatever which mutually exclude each other. A clear awareness of the eternal and incurable antinomy in the world of values is nothing but conscious inconsistency, though inconsistency is more often practiced than proclaimed.[3]·

Kolakowski—who shares Shevek's fate of an exile from a "closed" society— suggests that inconsistency which is an "awareness of the contradictions in this world" is "a consciously sustained reserve of uncertainty."[4] With Le Guin as with Shevek, the uncertainty is an important aspect of the balance, for wholeness is only gained in a process of change and the process of change is only raised to consciousness through her ambiguous utopian dialectic.

NOTES

1. The rather striking parallel between the situation on the glacier and the conclusion of Poe's *The Narrative of A. Gordon Pym* is pointed out in David Ketterer, *New Worlds for Old* (New York: Anchor, 1974), p. 88. The ambivalent use of the situation and of the colour white suggests a wider range of American writing, all of which Le Guin seems conscious of. Melville's *Typee* and *Moby Dick* are immediate points of reference for aspects of the situation and the treatment of the colour white. Le Guin has a deep affinity with the American literary tradition, especially its New England aspects, and a fuller investigation of her work from this point of view would be of value. Much of her utopianism appears to echo traditions emanating from Thoreau, her interest in yin-yang and balance echoes Emerson, and her interest in black and white contrasts echoes Hawthorne, Melville, and Poe. Perhaps the most striking reminder of New England is the use of "walls" in *The Dispossessed*, with its obvious ironies directed towards a philosophy such as that examined in Robert Frost's "Mending Wall." There would appear to be a strong though again ambiguous connection between such a Puritan or Yankee tradition and Le Guin's sensibility, which manifests itself in descriptions such as those of the rigors of Karhide or the asceticism of Anarres.
2. Ursula K. Le Guin, "Is Gender Necessary?," in *Aurora: Beyond Equality*, ed. Susan J. Anderson and Vonda McIntyre (in press at New York: Fawcett, 1975).
3. Leszek Kolakowski, *Toward a Marxist Humanism* (New York: Grove, 1968), pp. 216-17.
4. Ibid., p. 214. The problem of inconsistency and uncertainty implicit in the "ambiguous" dialectics ought to be considered in relation to the role of *hope* in utopias, for both *The Left Hand of Darkness* and *The Dispossessed* end on a note of uncertainty but hope. See "On Hope the Principle," Ernst Bloch, *A Philosophy of the Future* (New York: Herder and Herder, 1970), *Man on His Own* (New York: Herder and Herder, 1970), and three essays of his in Maynard Solomon ed., *Marxism and Art* (New York: Random House, 1974); and about Bloch, for example, Jurgen Habermass, "Ernst Bloch— A Marxist Romantic," *Salmagundi* No. 10-11 (Fall 1969-Winter 1970), 311-25, and Fredric Jameson, *Marxism and Form* (Princeton: Princeton University Press, 1972).

Darko Suvin

Parables of De-Alienation: Le Guin's Widdershins Dance

1. The Dispossessing. My thesis is that *the main thrust and strength of Ursula K. Le Guin's writing lies in the quest for and sketching of a new, collectivist system of no longer alienated human relationships, which arise out of the absolute necessity for overcoming an intolerable ethical, cosmic, political and physical alienation.*[1] That this is the root experience present in the whole of Le Guin's opus could best be proved by an analysis of that whole. Here I shall have to content myself with a few—hopefully fundamental—indications, referring for the rest to such essays in this issue as Nudelman's, Porter's, and Jameson's.[2] However, it seems clear that such an analysis would, already in the sundered and dispersed races and communities of what could be called her "apprentice trilogy" (RW, PE and CI) no less than in its metaphorical system of coldness and depopulated landscapes, find an "objective correlative" of the alienation. Each of her novels is centered on a redeeming hero whose fierce loyalty to his companions and his task is an attempt to counteract the Fall of the symbolic territory—as is the development of mind-speech. In the apprentice trilogy, the hero is a stranger superior to the primitive territory. In LHD, the point of view of the stranger is for the first time shown as fallible, and the territory—though still cold and only artificially implanted with a human-yet-physiologically-inhuman population—has produced its own hero, the territorial traitor with a higher loyalty to humanity. This is exacerbated in WWF, where the well-meaning but sterile outsider can survive—both as character and narrative focus—only as part of the fertile indigenous liberation; and it is completely overcome in Le Guin's undoubted masterpiece TD where the hero and the territory are for the first time adequate to each other, since each (creative scientist-philosopher and classless society) is a dynamically evolving vanguard of humanity so that higher loyalty to humanity does not have to be treason to its exemplary territorial manifestation in this novel. Parallel to the evolution of the hero from outsider to characterological embodiment of the territory is the evolution of the social habitat. Except for LoH, which for reasons explained in my Introductory Note I shall here slight, it is a strictly non-capitalist habitat. It is first presented as a barbaric simplification within which direct human relations can still be shown as meaningful, using but already largely refunctioning SF and heroic fantasy clichés (in RW a mixture of Tolkien or even Dunsany with SF feudalism of the Poul Anderson type, in PE the abandoned colony and the savage onslaught, in CI the post-Catastrophe social reversion, the Vanvogtian two-minded hero unconscious of his superpower, the Tolkienian bad guys, and a decadently refined enemy city strongly reminiscent of Buck Rogers' place of captivity under the Han Air Lords). In LHD—the hinge and divide of Le Guin's opus, the novel within which she broke through the apprenticeship to mastery and which because of that groans under the richness of dazzling and not fully integrated or clarified concepts—the social habitat is not so much a regression to uncluttered earlier social formation, but rather a simplified alternative to the capitalist or commodity-economics model (see Jameson's article). All of Le Guin's opposed discords—foreignness and identity, loneliness and togetherness, fragmentation and connection, and a number of others all rooted in the split between I and Thou, Self and the Other—emerge in LHD in a thus far most concentrated and freeing form, materialized in the huge ice plateau of the novel's culmination. But at the same time, that culmination becomes a "place inside the blizzard" engendering its own values; the habitat has thrown up its own weavers of unification, personal and political—Estraven the Traitor and his appropriate successor, Faxe the Weaver.

Nonetheless, the fact that the ethical and the politico-religious strands of LHD still demand two (or three) bearers; or, that the Foretellers' religion and the other Gethenian myths with their metaphors of creation and still centre emerge as the main support unifying the novel's desparate thematic strands of geography, anthropology and political intrigue; or, in still other words, the richness yet fragmentation of the points of view, sundering narrator and hero—all these loose ends, though here turned to excellent formal account, admit of further conceptual and therefore also narrative stringency. In WWF a hero was found who could—at a price—unite action and reflection, world-time and dream-time, and show forth both vertical (relation of conscious-unconscious) and horizontal (relation of self and society) de-alienation. Very significantly, de-alienation is brought about by a liberating struggle against imperialist colonialism. Yet, though imperialist oppression is in our age the saber's edge of the crassest, crudest, and physically most murderous alienation (so that the characters of Ho Chi Minh or of doctors Ernesto Guevara and Frantz Fanon are quite relevant to that of Selver), unfortunately alienation within the all-pervading psychical eco-system of modern capitalism is not always so conveniently embodied in a malevolent Other. In everyday life *within* the imperial powers, the malignance of alienation lies largely in its insidious power to be internalized into the Self—and the defence of a balanced Self against death-bringing alienation of its own powers is the subject of Le Guin's *Earthsea Trilogy*. Seen from a purely formal viewpoint of internal consistency and stylistic clarity, that trilogy is her best work up to TD. But there is a price to pay for the pitiless simplification inherent in even the best heroic fantasy, and in particular when it is the parable of the Proper Namer, the artist-creator, whose lonley sin can only be irresponsible playing with a world whose sole arbiter he is. Beautiful, polished, and self-enclosed like a diamond necklace, *The Earthsea Trilogy* thus in the end deals with what a creator (say a writer) must do in order to live and create, and Ged's Dunsanian Taoism seems to me at a second—propaedeutic or therapeutic—remove from what Le Guin is trying to write about in her SF of collective practice. Therefore, the malevolent alienation, which comes from the outside but is mirrored inside the territory and the hero, was not disposed of in Earthsea. Even WWF only showed the emergence of the "translating" or mediating hero; the territory of WWF, the forest which is the word for the world in the language of Selver's people, is in a static balance, a closed circle of unhistorical time. Selver's horizontal, collective de-alienation is achieved at the price of a partial vertical, personal alienation into what Le Guin here still calls "the dead land of action" (§2).

Only Urras and Anarres in TD are a twin system, able to account for the threats and forms of both external and internal alienation; only TD reconciles linear and circular time—or cosmic, historical and personal sense—in Shevek's simulsequentialist physics, politics and ethics. And this is, if not caused by (one hesitates to say, just as in Shevek's physics, which is cause and which effect), certainly correlative to the ideologico-political breakthrough of Le Guin's identifying the privileged forms of alienation as propertarian possession. "The Dispossessed" is already in its title so much richer than the territorial titles of the "apprentice trilogy" or the Taoist mythopoetics (somewhat hollow in "The Lathe of Heaven," and beautifully pivoted in "The Left Hand of Darkness") of her middle-period book titles. The dispossessed are those who have no more possessions, the non-propertarians, but also those who are no more possessed (in the Dostoevskian sense of demon-ridden) or obsessed by the principle of Having instead of Being, no more ridden by profiteering possessiveness whether applied to things, other people, nature, knowledge (Sabul's and Urrasian physics) or to oneself (Urrasian—e.g. Veia's—sexuality). From a propertarian point of view, the Anarresians have voluntarily dispossessed themselves of life-sustaining property, of their very planet; from an anarchist or socialist/communist/utopian point of view, they have rid themselves of the demon possession. The Dispossessed means thus literally—in more beautiful, semantically richer, and thus more forceful English—The De-Alienated, those rid of alienation both as physical reification (by things and impersonal apparatuses) and as psychical obsession (by demons and what Marx calls fetishes). The things that are in saddle and ride the reified Possessed recur in the imagery of barriers between individuals as well as between people and things on Urras —its walls and wrappings. The fetishes or idols of the obsessed Possessed are ideological pseudo-categories such as freedom *from* rather than freedom *for* (§5) and linguistic idols such as the hierarchical "higher" or "superior" standing for excellent (§1). Of course, obsession and reification are only two faces of the same pale rider, in the sense suggested by the fundamental Marxist category of "commodity fetishism" which uses the most modern philosophical vocabulary to properly name the most ancient enslavement or alienation of humanity. Thus, the ideological pseudo-categories and idols in TD are themselves also walls and wrappings, and viceversa. Therefore Anarres is at least ideally committed to being the place of naked, open, not compartmentalized (e.g. professionally or sexually) and almost thingless human relationships. Its name testifies to its being not only the country of An-Archy (non-domination) and the negated (*an*) or reinvented (*ana*) Urras, but also (see Bierman) the Country Without Things (*res*); and Urras is not only a phonetically heightened shadow of Earth, but the primitive (*Ur*) and stunted (only disyllabic) opposite of Anarres; it is the place which has not yet got rid of *res*. The very real shortcomings and backslidings of Anarres do not ultimately detract from but instead reaffirm the exemplarity of its original, Odonian impulse.

2. The New Atlantis. To pursue and perhaps clinch this argument, let me analyze Le Guin's latest story, "The New Atlantis" (NA). In all evolutionary processes, in the Darwinian phylogenetic tree, in the spiral of social history, or in a writer's opus, the future—the latest point to which evolution has arrived, and the use of that point for a retrospective—is the justification and explanation of the past, and thus in a sense its cause. If this at first sight fairly abstruse story can be deciphered by using the theory that the centre of Le Guin's creation is the double star of identifying the neo-capitalist, individualist alienation and juxtaposing to it a sketch of a new, collectivist and harmonious, creation, then the theory will be shown to work.

NA is divided into two interlocking narrations, which gradually and parallel to each other define themselves and their mutual correspondences. As in TD, this is correlative to their presenting an old and a new world—here a declining or subsiding and an ascending or emerging one. Analogous to the parallelism of physics to ethics and politics in TD, the informing metaphor of NA is the substitution of geology for history. The old world, the old Atlantis of NA rushing headlong toward the chasm which engulfed the legendary Atlantis, is a somewhat extrapolated USA of advanced political and ecological breakdown, rather similar to one of Orr's alternative futures in the 2002 of LoH, and equally laid in Portland, Oregon, LoH's—and Le Guin's, who lives there— "centre of the world"). A "corporative State," a well-identified American variant of admass fascism, is conjured up simply by integrating into a seamless governmental totality all the already existing bureaucracies: stock-market and unions, health, education and welfare, credit-cards and mass-media, with interstices for regulated and parasitic "private enterprise." The system makes lavish use of the 20th-Century habits of false naming: the"Supersonic Superscenic Deluxe Longdistance bus" is a dilapidated coal-burner which breaks down when it tries to go over 30 mph; the "Longhorn Inch-Thick Steak House Dinerette" serves meatless hamburgers; the All-American Broadcasting Company confidently announces that the war in Liberia is going well for "the forces of freedom" and peace is at hand in Uruguay, interspersing this with weekly "all-American Olympic Games" and catchy commercials for "coo-ol, puu-uure U.S.G. [i.e. canned] water"; and so on. Also, a repressive bourgeois legality is only somewhat extended to cover Solzhenitsyn-like Rehabilitation Camps and Federal Hospitals for dissidents, compulsory full employment, reduction of universities to trade schools, etc. But within this fairly standard American radical nightmare, whose aspects can be found in a number of SF works from Orwell and Pohl to Spinrad, there are two new elements. First, in the sinking world there is a story of the narrator's scientist-husband Simon and a group of friends, not too dissimilar from Shevek's group (Simon publishes in Peking!) but in USA rather than Anarres and, correspondingly, incomparably more repressed. Working illegally, they invent direct energy conversion, which would in sane circumstances stop the ecological breakdown and thus obviate the economic necessity for the corporative—or any centralized—State and its way of life. But the circumstances are the opposite of sane, and, though the scientist-creators have found how to use physical power, they have no clue to how to find and use political power. This typical Leguinian ambiguity already makes the story superior to either the unfounded optimism by which technological inventions automatically save the world bringing about decentralization and similar (e.g. the same device in early Simak), or the gloom and doom arising from exclusive concentration—sometimes with an almost morbid satisfaction—on an ecologico-political breakdown (e.g. in Brunner's very similar environment of *The Sheep Look Up*).

However, the second specifically Leguinian element is embodied in the very composition and style of the story, and therefore much more important. It is the parallel picture of a new creation—alternating with the old as the Anarres chapters do with the Urras ones in TD—arriving at self-consciousness and self-definition, a bit as if Plato's or Butler's souls of the not-yet-born were being incarnated and were gradually defining their senses by defining their environment: an extraordinarily beautiful new Genesis of perception and cognition—of time, space, number and universe—by means of fitful lights. It is an (extremely un-Baconian) New Atlantis, an undersea creation which rises from a dark and cold pressure through mysterious tides to a final breakthrough into life. But the Genesis is, as always in Le Guin, an impure and ambiguous one. The light-bearing, Luciferic creatures announcing and inducing it are dwarfish and misshapen: "...all mouth. They ate one another whole. Light swallowed light all swallowed together in the vaster mouth of the darkness." Yet these cruel and poor "tiny monsters burning with bright hunger, who brought us back to life" define by their hungry lights the coordinates of collective space, the planes and towers of a city which had existed earlier but had fallen. The city is now being recreated through the act of beholding and remembering it, and raised by irresistible geological pressures. At the end, the dawn still arrives as a dark blue and cold, a submarine one—the awareness of light itself rather than of the objects lit—but the metamorphosis of light above the tops of the towers indicates that the city's emergence is at hand.

I have paraphrased the much more puzzling "submarine" strand of the narration as closely as I could in order to argue about its meaning in itself and within the whole story. Now, only second-rate writings in SF are rigid allegories with a one-to-one relationship of each item described to some dog-matic scheme. However, I would maintain that any significant writing in SF is necessarily analogical or parabolical—a parable being a verisimilar narration which has a determinable meaning or tenour outside of narration, but whose plausibility is not based upon such a transferred meaning but upon internal narrative consistency. Thus the classical (say New Testament) parable is ideologically closed or univocal, but stylistically always open-ended, waiting for the reader's application; its ultimate aim is the shock of estrangement re-orienting the reader's perception—in modern times, making him recognize the alienated world he lives in. It is not an allegory in that it does not substitute one thing for another (in the case of NA, alienation for the dark pressure which had so long prevented fallen Atlantis from rising again) but *sets one thing by the side of another*, the explicit by the side of the implicit. There-fore, in a parable the literal narrative and the meaning "do not coincide, as in an allegory; it is only parallels that exist between the two."³ And though the direction of the meaning is clear and univocal, there may be several levels of meaning; a parable is usually polysemous. All this seems particularly applic-able to Le Guin, whose Anti-Queen Utopa—Odo (in TD)—wrote two books, *Community* and *Analogy* (her analogies, if I understand the Anarresians well, have four "modes"—ethical, physico-technological, religious and philosophical—not unlike Dante's four modes of allegory), and who is one of the most con-sciously analogical or parabolic writers around. What, then, does the analogy of the New Atlantis stand for?

If the story NA is to have any unity, the emerging new City must be an analogy—here by contraries—to the dying American society, a new republic, community or life-form germinating up from the depths, symmetrically op-posed, as it were, to the perishing republic of the first strand. One key is supplied by the personal pronoun: the declining narration is in first person singular, the "I" being that of Belle, the disloyal but suppressed citizen of the corporate State and wife of the only momentarily freed concentration-camp prisoner Simon. The ascending narration is in first person plural, the "we" being a new community (shades of Odo!) which relates to that of the U.S.A. as collectiv-ism does to individualism and also—in view of the cognition and color imagery—as beauty and knowledge to pollution and ignorance of both self and universe. The Atlantis collective has been submerged and unconscious for ages, just as has the idea of a true and beautiful collective or classless society; the Fall of Atlantis, then, is here something like the fall from tribal into class society and the concomitant alienation of man into social institutions. A condition of pristine unity is presupposed in the whole of Le Guin's opus as a past Golden Age; it echoes through the present alienation from the unsplit Ancient One in RW, through the direct, unalienated communication he gives to Rocannon—mind-speech (whose development is the primary red thread of her writing up to LHD, rather than the Hainish chronology so ingeniously worked out by Watson in SFS #5), to Selver's integral forest in WWF and the other forest-minds and tree images in her opus. But by 1975, in NA, there is a New Atlantis rising: the forces of de-alienation are on the rise in Le Guin's writing, parallel to what she (one hopes rightly) senses as the deep historical currents in the world. Having achieved a balance with darkness in LHD, a partial victory in WWF and the first large-scale victory in TD, these forces of a new and better creation are now ready to rise in full stature to the surface of our Earth. We cannot tell exactly who they are and what they will be like: we can only tell that they are being raised up by tides stronger than even the ultimate class society of the corporate State, by the slow and inexor-able geological tides of history so to speak; that they have just begun to remember the past glories of their City; and that the Luciferic goads and precursors (the lantern-creatures, whom I would interpret as the revolutionary political and ideological movements of the last century or two, say since 1789 and 1917, swallowing each other up in fierce infighting and "all swallowed together" by the still stronger alienation), although themselves twisted and stunted, have awakened the new creation to self-awareness.

All this can be confirmed by the correspondences existing between adjoining sections of the two narrative strands. The American strand is divided into six segments, each of which precedes the corresponding segment of the New Atlantis strand; and each group of two segments from the juxtaposed strands has a correspondingly parallel or inverse motif. For example, the two No. 1 segments (pp. 61-64 and 64-66) are introductions to the world and theme of the segment—to American degradation vs. Atlantean creation; the two No. 4 segments (pp. 76-79 and 79-80) present the "cold sunrise"—the invention of direct conversion of solar power frustrated by the lack of political power vs. the deindividualized blue sunrise "the color of the cold, the color farthest from the sun"; the two No. 5 segments (pp. 80-83 and 83-85) balance the American dissidents' frustrated vision of a possible New (the solar cell and its implications) with the Atlantean collective's wondering memory of the wonderful Old (the jewel-like gracious city and its implications); and finally, the last two segments (pp. 85-86 and p. 86) present the end of the American narrator's private world-cell (the re-arrest of her husband) and the nearing end of the U.S.A. in earthquakes combated by atomic bombs, opposed to the breakthrough of the new Atlantis.

However, one final element reintroduces the realistic, bitter-sweet Leguinian ambiguity. For after all, it may be very well to know that the end of our creation means, at the same time, the beginning of a new and more colorful one; yet this is not a full consolation for our passing—for the passing of the courageous and well-meaning group of Simon's, and of the whole old continent with its future Schuberts (such as the Forrest whose compositions are also surreptitiously played by Simon's wife). And indeed it is the "yearning music from far away in the darkness, calling not to us [i.e. not to the Atlanteans but to the Americans—and to the reader] 'Where are you? I am here,'" which is echoed in the final segment spoken by the Atlanteans:

> Where are You?
> We are here. Where have you gone?

For the music of the "lonely ones, the voyagers" (like Schubert) called out for non-alienated man all along, through our whole history of fallen Atlantis. This music is not only the harmony of sounds—I would further interpret—but all harmony of art, science and philosophy, always harking back or looking forward to human unity: unity of man within himself, of men in society, of humanity in Earth, and of men with nature. By that same token, such music of sounds, concepts, shapes or formulas is a witness to the unborn potentialities and unfulfilled promises of the race that produced this music. That is why it calls to it, and not to the Atlanteans. But that is also why the Atlanteans' last question-segment—the end of their strand and of the whole NA, which is rendered all the weightier for consisting of only three sentences— must, subsuming as it does the voices of the old creation's music, be taken as a lament for lost potentialities, as an acknowledgement that the New will, paradoxically, be lonely without (and because of the failure of) the Old. In my interpretation, even the classless society, the more beautiful humanity, will always miss the lost potentialities of ours, all our mute, inglorious Miltons or unburned Brunos or 40-year-old Mozarts. In simpler and less elitist terms, it will always yearn for all the life-patterns lost in our unnecessary hungers, diseases and wars. Le Guin's future is lonely for the past, as ascetic Anarres is for the promises (the plant and animal creation as well as the people) of Urras.

I fail to see how else one can make full sense of NA.

3. The Price and the Hope. As the above analysis of NA and the elegiac tone (Nudelman) of Le Guin's whole opus indicate, the ambiguities never absent from it do not primarily flow from a static balancing of two yin-and-yang-type alternatives, two principles or opposites (light-darkness, male-female, etc.) between which a middle Way of wisdom leads. This may be an aspect or a "middle phase" (Porter) of Le Guin's, but I would think the attempts to subsume her under Taoism (which has undoubtedly had an influence) are in view of her development after LoH not only doomed to failure but also retrospectively revealed as inadequate even for her earlier works (LoH being, here again, an exception, but as Watson argued a purgative one). Rather, the Leguinian ambiguities are in principle dynamic, and have through her evolution become more clearly and indubitably such. That means that to every opposition or contradiction there is, as Mao Tse-tung[4] would say, a principal aspect which is dominant or ascendant and by means of which that contradiction renders asunder the old, transforming it into the new. That principal or dominant aspect is Selver's "godhood" translating new and terrible dreams into a new world-time, or Odonianism, the principle of classless and non-antagonistic community, analogically applied to man and the universe, transforming the old politics, ethics and physics. The synthesis of linear, sequential progress and cyclical, simultaneous fulness of being into spiral simulsequentialist dialectics is balanced only in the way a master skater or a hovering falcon is—in permanent revolution and evolution, which fails as soon as it is arrested. And it is always a left-hand skate or swoop, a counter-clock helix, a widdershins dance that goes against the dominant and alienated received ideas of our civilization.

Le Guin's heretic protagonists are culture heroes, in that each founds a major cultural concept, translating it from unnamed to named existence. The ingathering of races and recuperation of mind-speech which permits the naming of Rocannon's World, Estraven's "treason," Selver's liberation warfare, Shevek's unifying ansible, Simon's direct power conversion, are such concepts. In the long run, they assert themselves in the Hainish universe; but not necessarily in the short run. Realistically, the heroes pay a stiff price for their victories, though the price decreases through Le Guin's opus down to Shevek, the first Founding Father who is also a biological father and whose collective or *comitatus* is not destroyed at the end of the story—another way of saying he can live on to enjoy his victory. Almost everybody else, from Rocannon and Falk to Selver and Simon, is an ambiguous questing figure "lonely, isolated...out on the edge of things."[5]

Sometimes, especially in early Le Guin, this is almost an existentialist stance of envisaging the creator as necessarily lonely in the *a priori* alien world of practice, a stance which sociologically corresponds to a petty-bourgeois intellectualism. Thus, an elementary text of capitalist economics bores Shevek, and no doubt Le Guin, "past endurance" (§5), as can be gathered from the political economics—what and how people work, cook, buy or distribute, what share of social product they create and control—absent from LHD and LoH, even from TD and NA, and replaced at their centre by shifting counterpoints of ethics, politics, and "direct contact" with nature. Mythology and some forms of quasi-religious (though atheist) mysticism are a logical ground bass to these counterpoints. This is accompanied by a deep distrust of organized mass politics which (though historically understandable) even in TD leads to such half-truths as the "You cannot make the Revolution. You can only be the Revolution. It is in your spirit, or it is nowhere" (§9), explaining why the Urras revolt is the weakest link in that novel. Obversely, it also means a certain naive dissolution of politics into ethics, as in CI which is ideologically based on the conflict of the Shings' lie with Falk's truth. Indeed, mind-speech itself is (as in all SF) a kind of individualistic substitute for de-alienation or metaphor for a unifying collectivism, so that the Shings' possibility of mind-lying corresponds to a false collectivism (politically something like fascism, stalinism or—in its insistence on not taking life—Christianity)—which is why it is so horrifying. But this is a mystifying metaphor which translates the de-alienation into terms of the self rather than of the society. When the self is projected onto rather than taken as an analogy of the society or indeed the universe, narrative and ideological difficulties arise. A good example for projection vs. analogy are the two Portland tales, LoH and NA, the second of which seems to me to achieve what the first did not.

On the other hand, however, the insistence on personally meaningful ethics, on means commensurate to ends, is much more than petty-bourgeois sentimentality or liberalism. Though in actual practice things can never be as neat as in abstract planning, this is to my mind that demand of the old society, of radical and revolutionary middle-class (bourgeois and petty-bourgeois) traditions, for which the new society—or at least the movements toward socialism in the last 100 years—has to yearn as much as the New Atlanteans do for the old creation's Schubert-like music. In insisting upon it, Le Guin is taking up her characteristic dialectical position of being the devil's advocate not so much against the alienated old as against the insufficiently or ambiguously de-alienated new. Her political position can be thought of as a radical critic and ally of socialism defending its duty to inherit the heretic democratic, civic traditions, e.g. Jefferson's or indeed Tom Paine's. This would explain her great ideological affinity for the Romantics and the post-Romantic 19th Century democrats, especially for the left-wing "populists" culminating in Tolstoi, Hugo, and Thoreau (whose *Walden* is the "New Canon" of CI). That stance has some contradictions of its own (see Jameson's essay), but when taken as being itself an Old Canon flowing into the New Canon of libertarian socialism, it represents a precious antidote to socialism's contamination by the same alienating forces it has been fighting so bitterly in the last century—by power apparatuses and a pragmatic rationality that become ends instead of means. Le Guin's anarchism, then, can be malevolently thought of as the furthest radical limit at which a disaffected petty-bourgeois intellectual may arrive, a leftist Transcendentalism, or benevolently as a personal, variant name for and way to a truly new libertarian socialism. A choice between these two interpretations will be possible only in retrospect, a few years hence; and no doubt, judging from her own spiral development in the last six or seven years, both interpretations of sucn an anarchism are partly right. But to my mind, in spite of elements discussed in the preceding paragraph, the dominant or ascendant aspect of Le Guin's contradictory ideology is a useful one. It not only claims for socialism the self-governing tradition of the citizen (as opposed to that of the bourgeois),[6] e.g. the New England town-meeting tradition; it is not only a politically realistic warning; it also shapes accurate and therefore pleasurable *artistic analogies to the contemporary situation of the liberating New.* Just as her lonely heretics, the forces of the New are in truth—under the terrible pressures of the totalizing neo-capitalist commodity-economy (see Jameson) and of their own mistakes and dead ends (primarily the Russian example)—in an isolated minority within the North Atlantic if not the New Atlantean world. Their position and vicissitudes seem to me to explain not only the clear-eyed elegiac atmosphere of Le Guin's, but also the retrenchment she austerely—almost puritanically—operates in all of her work, culminating in TD. This "world-reduction" (Jameson) is not only a reaction to the polluted American abundance and a realistic diagnosis of a better model of life but also the sign of a situation where the bearers of the New, the Lucifers, are separated from the large majority of those for whom this New is intended. In this situation, the aridity—like that of Anarres—is a retrenchment from the "living flesh" (§4) of a natural community, a harsh but clean acceptance of asceticism. The beautiful passages of Shevek's recognition of animals (§5) no less than the end of NA seem to me to signify that gulf of unrequited brotherhood. (In a somewhat more melodramatic form, the power of the clone break-up in "Nine Lives," whose survivor, metamorphosed from being part to being alone, has to learn the lesson of alienation, surely also comes from this cluster of concepts.)

In an earlier article,[7] when faced with a group of 1969 novels including LHD, I noted that a clear group of "New left" SF writers (a term that, as used here, has to do more with sensibility and world view than political affiliation) had emerged. If I may be allowed to repeat myself, their common denominator is a radical disbelief in the individualist ideology—i.e., that a stable and humane system can be built upon a sum of individual, Robinson-Crusoe greeds as the measure of all values. They deal with a changed neo-capitalist society of mass disaffection, mass media and mass breakdowns in a perceptive form for which—as different from earlier SF—Joyce, Dos Passos, Malraux, Faulkner, Brecht and intermedia in art, or Marcuse and Mao in philosophy of history, are living presences though not sacred texts. Ursula Le Guin, with her unsentimental warm concern with collective humanism, is the clearest and most significant writer of this group, allowing us to recognize our central concerns through a detour of estrangement. Already, LHD spoke—to use the words of that novel—to our "strong though undeveloped sense of humanity, of human unity. I got quite excited thinking about this" (§8). Since then she has evolved through Lao Tzu to Kropotkin and Goodman. Le Guin is less flashy and abrasive than most other "New Left" writers—such as Brunner, Delany, Russ or Spinrad—and the major presences in her writing are rather poets from Marvell and Coleridge on, and social novelists from Dickens, Stendhal and Dostoevsky to Solzhenitsyn and Virginia Woolf. In a way, she is the most European and—in her sense of human relationships being determined by human institutions—most novelistic writer in present-day American SF, and the blend of 19th-Century Realism and a discreet Virginia-Woolf-type adoption of some techniques of lyric poetry with the ethical abstraction of American romances may account for much of her stylistic power and accessibility. Her clear and firm but richly and truthfully ambiguous Leftism situates her at the node of possibly the central contemporary contradiction, that between capitalist alienation and the emerging classless de-alienation. Because of that, Le Guin is today not only one of scarcely half a dozen most important SF writers in the world, but her SF parables from LHD on are to my mind among the most penetrating and entertaining explorations of the deep value shifts of our age. Like the basic image in her work, that of two different hands meeting the dark, her writings touch us gently and firmly, reminding us that across gulfs of otherness our brothers not only can but must be met. Her widdershins dance, denying alienation, figures forth a de-alienated humanity. That, I believe, is the basis for her wide popularity. Saying "no" to the old, she also says "yes" to the new—witness TD and NA. And if these tales were written less than a dozen years after she began publishing, what cannot we hope for, from her, in the future arising out of such a past?

NOTES

1. On alienation, see the two introductory anthologies, Eric Fromm, ed., *Socialist Humanism* (Doubleday Anchor, 1966), and Eric and Mary Josephson, eds., *Man Alone* (Dell, 1964); Istvan Meszaros, *Marx's Theory of Alienation* (London: Merlin, 1917); and a long further bibliography in Herbert Aptheker, ed., *Marxism and Alienation* (Humanities Press, 1965), especially the works listed by Fromm, Paul Goodman, Herbert Marcuse, Karl Marx, and C. Wright Mills.

2. For secondary literature on Le Guin's SF see Douglas Barbour, "*The Lathe of Heaven*—Taoist Dream," *Algol* #21(Nov 1973):22-24, and "Wholeness and Balance in the Hainish Novels of Ursula K. Le Guin," *SFS* 1(1974):164-73; David Ketterer, *New Worlds for Old* (Doubleday Anchor pb and Indiana Univ Press hb, 1974), §4, with Le Guin's rejoinder and Ketterer's reply in *SFS* 2(1975)137-45; Stanislaw Lem, "Lost Opportunities," *SF Commentary* #24(Nov 1971):22-24, with Le Guin's reply in #26(April 1972):90-92; Ian Watson, "Le Guin's *Lathe of Heaven* and the Role of Dick," *SFS* 2 (1975):67-75; Robert Scholes, *Structural Fabulation* (Notre Dame Univ Press, 1975), §4. My thanks are due to Ursula K. Le Guin and to Susan J. Anderson for supplying me with some of Le Guin's own essays, which are as relevant as any of the above for understanding her work.

3. Eta Linnemann, *Parables of Jesus* (London: SPCK, 1966), p 26; see also Bertolt Brecht, *Brecht on Theatre*, ed. John Willett (Hill and Wang, 1966); Rudolf Bultmann, *The History of the Synoptic Tradition* (Harper & Row, 1968); C.H. Dodd, *The Parables of the Kingdom* (Fontana, 1971); Geraint Jones, *The Art and Truth of the Parables* (London: SPCK, 1964); Abraham Kaplan, "Referential Meaning in the Arts," *Journal of Aesthetics and Art Criticism* 12(1964):457-74; Louis MacNeice, *Varieties of Parable* (Cambridge: Cambridge Univ Press, 1965); and Dan Via, *The Parables* (Fortress, 1967). On estrangement besides Brecht see Ernst Bloch's fundamental "Entfremdung, Verfremdung: Alienation, Estrangement," in Erika Munk, ed., *Brecht* (Bantam 1972). I have tried to apply their insights to SF in my theoretical essays in *College English* 34(1972):372-82, and *Genre* 6(1973):251-73. I cannot enter here into the ideologically very significant differences between various historical modes of parable, from the Greeks and Hebrews to our age, but I discuss a modern parable in my Afterword to the English-language editions of Stanislaw Lem's *Solaris*.

4. Mao Tse-tung, "On Contradiction," *Four Essays in Philosophy* (Peking: Foreign Languages Press, 1968), especially §4.

5. Le Guin's prefatory note to her story "The Masters," where such a figure first appears; see item C3 in Levin's bibliography in this issue of SFS.

6. See on this basic historical dualism Karl Marx, "On the Jewish Question," *Writings of the Young Marx on Philosophy and Society*, Lloyd D. Easton and Kurt H. Guddat, eds. (Doubleday Anchor, 1967).

7. D. Suvin, "The SF Novel in 1969," in James Blish, ed., *Nebula Award Stories Five* (1970).